OS X

THE LITTLE MAC OS X BOOK

version 10.1

ROBIN WILLIAMS

Peachpit Press
Berkeley · California

The Little Mac OS X Book

©2002 by Robin Williams

Cover art illustration: Terry Widener
Cover design and production: John Tollett
Interior divider pages: John Tollett
Interior design and production: Robin Williams
Index: Robin Williams
Editor: Nancy Davis
Production management: Kate Reber
Back cover photo of Robin: John Tollett
The illustrations of Url throughout the book are
from the mouse of the multi-talented John Tollett,
www.UrlsInternetCafe.com

Peachpit Press
1249 Eighth Street
Berkeley, California 94710
800.283.9444
510.524.2178
510.524.2221 fax

Find us on the World Wide Web at **www.peachpit.com**
To report errors, please send a note to errata@peachpit.com
Peachpit Press is a division of Pearson Education

ISBN 0-201-74866-5

10 9 8 7 6 5 4 3 2 1

Printed and bound in the United States of America

To my mother, Patricia Williams,

who made it possible,

and to my father, Gerald Williams,

who would have been proud.

Acknowledgments
Many, many thanks to
Nancy Davis for great editing;
Kate Reber for great
production control;
Barbara Sikora for
long-distance index editing;
Hope Ostheimer for the
bread-and-soup shipments
that helped keep us going;
Scarlett Williams for helping
with the table of contents,
cooking dinners, and running errands;
John Tollett for all of the fabulous
Url cartoons, the divider page
illustrations, the cover, for writing
a bunch of chapters, and for hanging
in there with me during this long haul.

Contents

THE BASICS

BEYOND THE BASICS

THE INTERNET

Introduction

Skip the intro. Read the book. New users, flip through the book and notice the gray "dots" in the upper corners of some pages, like this page. Those are the only pages you need to read. But do check out the Tutorial—I guarantee if you actually work through the tutorial you will have more control over your computer than many long-time Mac users.

Experienced Mac users, use the index and look up what you need. But I guarantee that if you actually read entire chapters, you'll be amazed at the tips and tricks you didn't know. I was.

I always write the introduction last, and now I'm really tired. It's been a long and winding book. I do hope you find it useful.

Mini-Glossary

These three pages contain a list of the terms you are most likely to run into when working on your Mac. If you don't find a word here, check the index because I probably explained the term in the main body of the book. For an incredibly extensive and up-to-date resource of definitions, check www.webopedia.com (unfortunately, though, I don't guarantee you will always understand the definition). Also check Sherlock (Chapter 24).

bits

bytes

kilobytes

megabytes

gigabytes

All of the terms listed to the left refer to **size.** It might refer to the size of a file, or how much space that file takes up on a disk. For instance, a small file like an icon might be 3K (kilobytes), and a large file like a high-quality photograph might be 15MB (megabytes). The layered Photoshop file for the cover of this book is 91MB.

Size might also refer to the size of your hard disk. For instance, you might have an 8GB (gigabtye) hard disk, or an 80GB hard disk. The bigger the disk, the more files it can hold.

- ▾ **bit:** The smallest unit of information on a computer. Each bit is one electronic pulse. These are the ones and ohs you hear about, 1 and 0.

- ▾ **byte:** 8 bits makes 1 byte. It takes one byte to produce one character, such as the letter A, on the monitor.

- ▾ **kilobyte:** 1024 bytes makes 1 kilobyte (capital K). A page in a word processor might take about 6 to 12K of disk space, depending on how much formatting was involved.

- ▾ **kilobit:** 1024 bits makes one kilobit (lowercase k). You'll see this in references to Internet connection speeds. It is not the same as a kilobyte (capital K in abbreviations)!

- ▾ **megabyte:** 1024 kilobytes makes 1 megabyte (MB). An 8-page newsletter with photographs and nice typography might take about 1.5 to 3MB of disk space, depending on how it was created. A software program like the one I am using to create this book (Adobe InDesign) takes about 60MB of disk space.

- ▾ **gigabyte:** 1024 megabytes makes 1 gigabyte. Most hard disks are measured in gigabytes. The Mac I am using at the moment has a 20GB hard disk.

Disk refers to the hardware pieces that hold data. Inside your Mac you have an internal hard disk. You might buy an external hard disk that connects to your Mac through a cable. Removable disks are those that go in and out of a disk drive, which is the mechanism that "reads" the removable disk. Removable disks include floppy disks, Zips, CDs, DVDs, etc.

disk

Download means to copy files from one computer directly to another (as opposed to putting the files on a disk and carrying them to the other computer). Typically, the other computer is "remote," or far away, and you download files from that computer to yours through the Internet. **Upload** means to copy files from your computer to a remote computer.

download, upload

Hardware is hard—you can drop it, break it, and throw it. If you can bump into it, it's hardware. Your computer is a piece of hardware, and so are external hard disks, scanners, modems, and printers. To send a piece of hardware to someone, you need a vehicle. Also see *software*.

hardware

Megahertz (MHz) refers to speed. In computers, the higher the megahertz, the faster the computer will process information. In 1993, a good computer had a speed of about 20MHz; today, even the cheapest computer is at least 400MHz, and more expensive machines reach a gigahertz. And every day they get faster and faster.

megahertz

Memory is the temporary storage place in your Mac, as opposed to the permanent storage space on a hard disk. There are various kinds of memory, but the one you're most concerned with is random access memory (RAM). The more RAM you have, the better everything on your Mac will work. A minimum amount of RAM is 128MB; a great amount is a gigabyte or two. See page 138 to find out how much RAM you have in your Mac. You can always buy more RAM and install it—it's easy.

memory, RAM

The **operating system** (OS) is what runs the computer. It's kind of like an engine in a car—you can have an entire car sitting in your front yard, but if it doesn't have an engine, it's not going to go anywhere. Operating systems get updated regularly so they can do more and more. You will probably get asked, "What OS are you running?" You'll sound like you know what you're talking about if you say, "Mac OS X version 10.1," which is actually pronounced, "Mac oh ess ten point one." Really.

operating system (OS)
OS X is pronounced
"oh ess ten"

Your monitor is composed of hundreds of thousands of tiny little spots; each one of these spots is a **pixel.** And each pixel is composed of three dots of light: red, green, and blue (RGB). The color in a pixel is a blend of varying amounts of those three colored lights. If all three colors are at 100 percent, the pixel is white. If no colors are sent to the pixel, it appears as black.

pixels

software   **Software** is invisible—it's the programming code written on the disks. You buy software—the applications, utilities, fonts, and games you use—and it comes to you on some sort of disk, or you download the software from another computer to yours (like over the Internet). The disk it came on or the disk you are storing it on contains the software. You can accidentally destroy the software while the disk it's on remains perfectly hard and whole. To send a piece of software to someone, you can use your modem and send it over the Internet.

Vaporware   **Vaporware** refers to software or hardware that has been promised for a while ("real soon now") but hasn't appeared on the market. You might also hear the terms wetware, liverware, or jellyware—that means us, the humans.

third party   Apple is the *first party:* they make the computer and the operating system. You are the *second party;* you use the computer and operating system. Other people who make things for you to use on your computer are the **third party.** This is a third-party book, as opposed to a manual straight from Apple.

volume   A **volume** refers to any sort of disk or part of a disk. A disk can be separated into different **partitions;** each partition is still considered a separate volume. See Chapter 39 on how to divide your large hard disk into separate partitions.

Your attitude is your life.
—*Robin*

Finding Your Way Around

1

If you just got your first Macintosh or if you just installed Mac OS X and don't know where to begin, start with this chapter. It'll give you a visual overview of what things are and tell you where to go for more details.

▼ **If you're new to the Mac,** after you skim through this chapter, go to the Tutorial in Chapter 2. If you run across any confusing terms in either chapter, check the index to find clarification.

Remember, as a new user, all you really need to read in this book are the pages with the "dots" at the tops. Come back to the rest later.

▼ **If you're an experienced Mac OS 9 user,** skip to Appendix A to find out where all of your favorite features have gone.

Mac OS X Map

The Desktop   The **Desktop** is what you see when you turn on your Mac. It's like home base; you'll get to know it well. For details about the Desktop, see Chapter 9.

*There will always be a **menu bar** across the top of your screen. The options in the menu bar are not always the same! You will see different menu items whenever you open another application or utility.*

> *For an overview of this menu bar and the various menus in it, see pages 8 and 9.*

> *For all the details about menus, see Chapter 5.*

*This is a window. This particular window is called a **Finder window.***

> *For an overview of windows, see pages 4 and 5.*

> *For all the details about windows, see Chapter 6.*

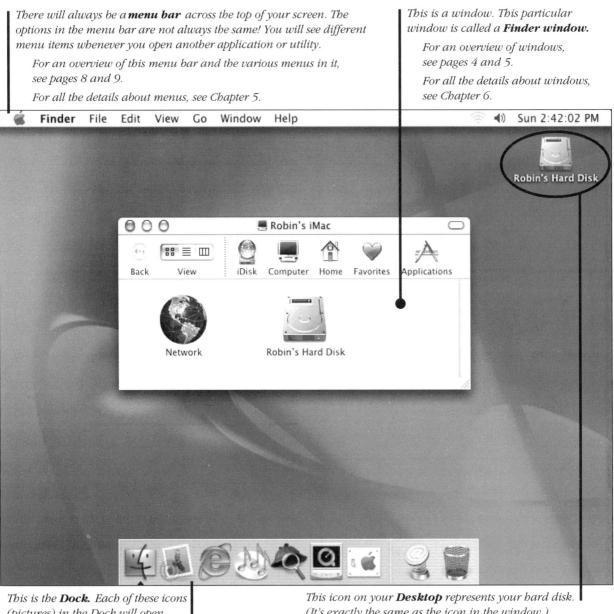

*This is the **Dock.** Each of these icons (pictures) in the Dock will open something when you click on it.*

> *For an overview of the Dock, see the opposite page.*

> *For all details about the Dock, see Chapter 8.*

*This icon on your **Desktop** represents your hard disk. (It's exactly the same as the icon in the window.)*

> *For an overview of the Desktop, see page 126.*
> *For all the details, see Chapter 9.*

> *For an overview of icons, see page 7.*
> *For all the details about icons, see Chapter 7.*

> *For an explanation of your hard disk (as opposed to memory), see page 220.*

> *For hard disks and "partitions," see Chapter 39.*

The **Dock** is that strip across the bottom of the screen. It will become your best friend. You might not see all the pictures in yours that you see in the examples below—things come and go from the Dock. You can add items and take items away. Most of the items in the Dock will "open" something when you click once on them: for instance, you might open an application to type in, or a web site on the Internet, or a window in which to find other files. Different things happen when you *click* once or when you *hold* the mouse button down (see Chapter 3 to learn to use the mouse). For a general idea of how the Dock works, see below. For details about using and customizing the Dock, including how to resize, hide, or move it, see Chapter 8.

The Dock

This is a generic Dock. You might see other icons (pictures) in yours, and some of the icons shown above might not be in yours at the moment. Don't worry—it will change constantly.

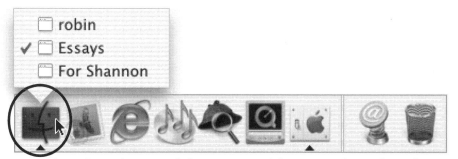

*This is the **Finder icon**. Click **once** on it and the main Finder window will open.*
Hold the mouse button down *on this icon and a menu pops up that tells you which other windows are currently open.*

*If something is in the **Trash**, **press-and-hold** the mouse button on the Trash basket to get this pop-up menu.*

The Finder Windows

The **Finder windows** display all the contents of your hard disk and other removable disks you might put in your computer. Learning how to "navigate" your way around the windows is one of the most important skills you can learn. There are three "views," or different ways you can see the contents of a window, as shown in the examples below. Choose the view you feel the most comfortable with. See Chapter 6 to learn all about finding your way around and controlling and customizing your windows.

Click one of the views in this View button to change the way the window displays the files.

Click the "Back" button to go back to the window you just looked at right before the current one.

This is the ***Icon View*** *for my "Home" folder.*

This is the ***List View*** *of the window above.*

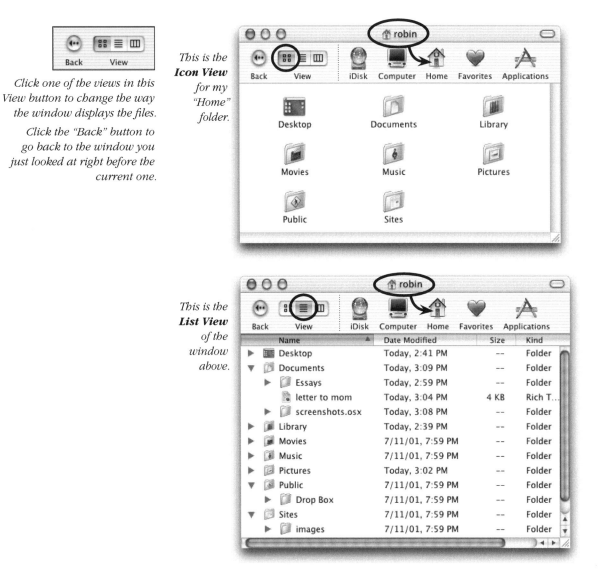

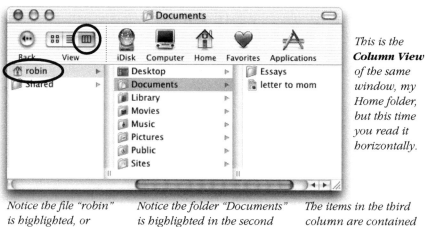

This is the **Column View** *of the same window, my Home folder, but this time you read it horizontally.*

Notice the file "robin" is highlighted, or selected, above. This indicates that the items in the column to its right are contained within "robin."

Notice the folder "Documents" is highlighted in the second column, above. That indicates that the items in the column to its right are contained within "Documents."

The items in the third column are contained in the folder called "Documents."

This is the **Hide/Show Toolbar** *button. You might see windows like this one that are missing the Toolbar.*

If you want the Toolbar visible, click the little, clear button in the upper-right of the window.

If you want to hide the Toolbar, click that same little button.

You won't see the tiny symbols inside the buttons until your mouse is positioned over a button.

Click the **red button** *(x) to put the window away.*

Click the **yellow button** *(-) to send the window down to the Dock, called minimizing; click once on its icon in the Dock to make it visible again.*

Click the **green button** *(+) to enlarge or reduce the size of the window (each click will do either one or the other, depending on the current size of the window).*

Home

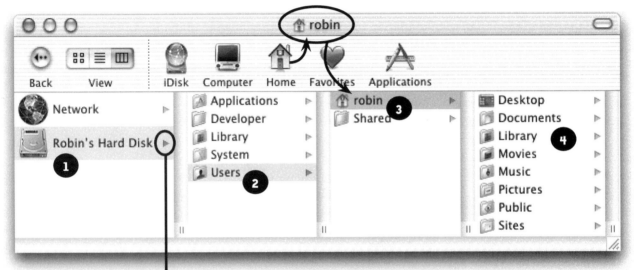

Home

Apple has created features that make it possible for a number of people to use the same computer, yet all users have their own private, protected space which includes a **Home,** your own Desktop, and your own, private Trash basket. Even if you are the only person using your Mac, you have a "Users" folder and a Home button.

Click the "Home" button icon in the Toolbar to go straight to your "home files." To learn all about Home and what it means to you, see Chapter 9. To learn to add or delete users, change a user's privileges, and share files between various users, see Chapter 20.

The right-pointing triangle in a column indicates the file is actually a folder or a disk (or a server) and you will see its contents in the next column to the right.

*You can see here in the Column View that the hard disk named "Robin's Hard Disk" is selected **(1)**, and on that hard disk is a selected folder called "Users" **(2)**, and in "Users" is a selected home folder called "robin" **(3)**, and in "robin" are folders **(4)** that are for that user's personal and private use (except the folder named "Public").*

Icons are the little pictures you see all over the Mac. Below are some of the ones you'll bump into right away and where you can find more information about them. Sometimes you click once on an icon to activate it, sometimes you double-click on it, sometimes you press on it. For all the details about icons, see Chapter 7.

The Icons

Window Toolbar icons

iDisk: *If you use a telephone modem,* **do not click this button** *until you know what it does. For details, see Chapter 33.*

Computer: *Click this button to see all the disks in the Mac that your computer recognizes. See Chapter 9.*

Home: *Click this to go straight to your own, personal home folder. See Chapter 20.*

Favorites: *Click this to see all of the folders, documents, web sites, and other files you have designated as favorites. See Chapter 23.*

Applications: *Click this to go directly to the window that stores all of your Mac OS X applications. See Chapter 28.*

Finder window icons

Robin's Hard Disk

Network

Hard disk icons: *This is what a hard disk case inside your computer looks like. Think of this as a filing cabinet— you look inside of it to find your files. See Chapter 9.*

Network: *A "network" is a system of wires and software that allows different people at different computers to share files and information. The Internet is a global network; you might also share files across the office. A click on this icon (in the "Computer" window) opens files that are available over a corporate network.* **(A click on this same icon in the Toolbar opens something completely different!)**

Dock icons

Finder: *When you click once on this icon, the main Finder window opens. All of the various files on your computer can be found in this window. Think of this as your office—you look inside of it to find your filing cabinets (hard disk) and documents (files). See Chapter 9.*

System Preferences: *This opens up a "pane" with lots of little utilities that let you customize your Mac. See Chapter 21.*

Trash: *This is where you throw away files you don't ever want to see again. Just drag them into this basket. See Chapter 17.*

The Menu Bar

Note: You might have several windows open on your Mac at the same time, but only one can be "active." Whichever one you click on instantly comes to the front and is active. See page 67 for more on active windows and why it's important to know.

As shown on page 2, you will always see a **menu bar** across the top of your computer screen. The items listed horizontally in the menu bar will change depending on what is "active" on your screen. For instance, if you have the general Finder window open because you clicked on the happy face icon in the Dock, you'll see the first menu bar shown below. You can tell the Finder is the active item because you see the word "Finder" in the menu bar.

This is the System Preferences icon you'll see in the Dock. You'll learn all about these preferences in Chapter 21.

If you click on the System Preferences icon (shown to the left) in the Dock to open the System Preferences pane, the menu bar will change. You can tell System Preferences is the active item because you see its name in the menu bar. Notice that some of the other items in this menu bar, as shown below, are different from the Finder's, above.

Every application you open will also have its own menu bar, as shown below. The application QuickTime Player is open, and you see its name in the menu bar. Notice this menu bar has different items from either of those above. Under the application menu, as shown below, the last item in the list of commands is always "Quit."

Tip: You might someday open a game or watch a DVD movie and discover that you have no menu bar. Even if the menu bar is not visible, you can always press Command Q to quit. See Chapter 5 for details on how to use a keyboard shortcut such as Command Q.

Shown below is every **menu** you'll see while you're at the Desktop and the **Finder** is "active" (see the note on the opposite page). The pages or chapters listed are where you will find information about each menu command.

The Finder Menus

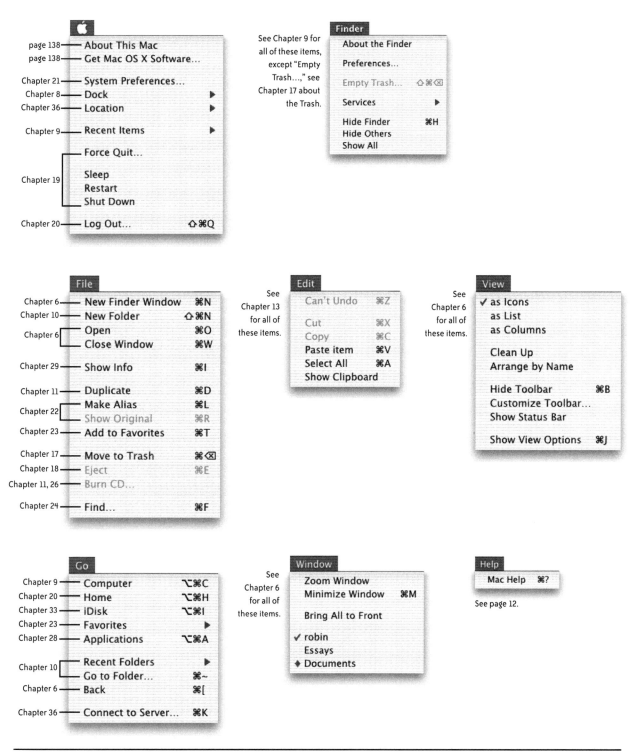

page 138—— About This Mac
page 138—— Get Mac OS X Software...

Chapter 21—— System Preferences...
Chapter 8—— Dock ▶
Chapter 36—— Location ▶

Chapter 9—— Recent Items ▶

Force Quit...

Chapter 19 ⎰ Sleep
⎱ Restart
⎱ Shut Down

Chapter 20—— Log Out... ⇧⌘Q

See Chapter 9 for all of these items, except "Empty Trash...," see Chapter 17 about the Trash.

Finder
About the Finder
Preferences...
Empty Trash... ⇧⌘⌫
Services ▶
Hide Finder ⌘H
Hide Others
Show All

File
Chapter 6—— New Finder Window ⌘N
Chapter 10—— New Folder ⇧⌘N
Chapter 6 ⎰ Open ⌘O
⎱ Close Window ⌘W
Chapter 29—— Show Info ⌘I
Chapter 11—— Duplicate ⌘D
Chapter 22 ⎰ Make Alias ⌘L
⎱ Show Original ⌘R
Chapter 23—— Add to Favorites ⌘T
Chapter 17—— Move to Trash ⌘⌫
Chapter 18—— Eject ⌘E
Chapter 11, 26—— Burn CD...
Chapter 24—— Find... ⌘F

See Chapter 13 for all of these items.

Edit
Can't Undo ⌘Z
Cut ⌘X
Copy ⌘C
Paste item ⌘V
Select All ⌘A
Show Clipboard

See Chapter 6 for all of these items.

View
✓ as Icons
as List
as Columns
Clean Up
Arrange by Name
Hide Toolbar ⌘B
Customize Toolbar...
Show Status Bar
Show View Options ⌘J

Go
Chapter 9—— Computer ⌥⌘C
Chapter 20—— Home ⌥⌘H
Chapter 33—— iDisk ⌥⌘I
Chapter 23—— Favorites ▶
Chapter 28—— Applications ⌥⌘A
Chapter 10 ⎰ Recent Folders ▶
⎱ Go to Folder... ⌘~
Chapter 6—— Back ⌘[
Chapter 36—— Connect to Server... ⌘K

See Chapter 6 for all of these items.

Window
Zoom Window
Minimize Window ⌘M
Bring All to Front
✓ robin
Essays
◆ Documents

Help
Mac Help ⌘?

See page 12.

Sherlock

If you click the Sherlock Holmes hat you see in the Dock, you'll get the application shown below, called **Sherlock.** Sherlock is the tool you use to find any file on your hard disk, or to find things on the Internet like old friends, shopping bargains, definitions of strange words, research articles, entertainment, and more. See Chapter 24 for all the details.

Click any of the other "channels" to log on to the Internet (providing your connection is set up first) and find various sorts of information.

First *click on this "channel."*

Second, *type in the name of a file to find its location on your hard disk.*

Third, *click this button to have Sherlock search your hard disk for the desired file.*

The Mac lets you customize a great number of the features of your computer to accommodate your personal working habits. In the Dock, click the **System Preferences** icon (shown to the right) to get the "pane" shown below (or you can go to the Apple menu and choose "System Preferences..."). You can click on any icon to get a new pane in which you can customize features. You'll be using this a great deal. See Chapter 21 for all the details.

System Preferences

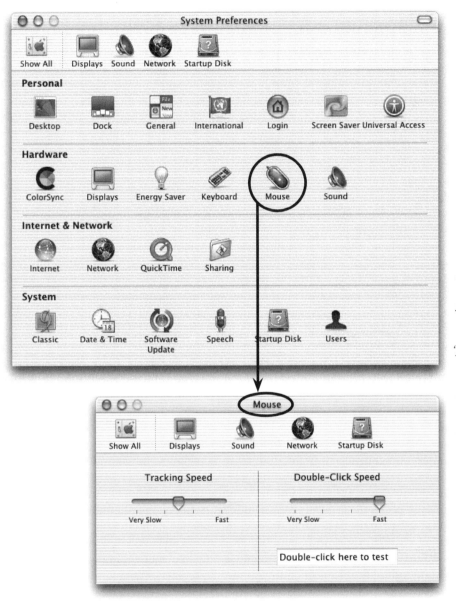

Single-click on one of the icons in the System Preferences and you'll get choices for customizing that particular feature, as shown below. This new "pane," below, will replace the original one, above.

To go back to the entire pane of all System Preferences, single-click the icon in the upper-left corner, "Show All."

Getting Help

Note: A number of Apple's Help files are kept on the web where they can be updated regularly. If you have a permanent Internet connection, such as cable or DSL, you won't even notice. But if your modem has to dial a phone number to get to the Internet, then you must connect first, then go to the Help page you need. Don't worry, you'll know when it happens.

You will always have a **Help menu** in the menu bar, no matter which application you are using. Below are several examples of what the Help menu might display, depending on what is "active" on your screen. When you choose one of these items, you will get Apple's Help files, as shown further below. This is a great place to check for immediate information about almost every feature on your Mac.

When you're at the Desktop, this is what you'll see in the Help menu.

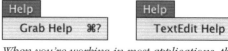

When you're working in most applications, the Help menu will offer you help for that application.

Non-Apple applications will have different sorts of Help files, not the ones shown below. But you can usually access any application's Help file from this menu.

When you choose "Mac Help," you'll get Apple's help files. Click on a question or type in a word or words at the top, then click the "Ask" button.

If Apple has answers for you, you'll get a window like this. Click on any phrase to go to that answer.

This is a typical answer. Unfortunately, the answer is rarely as thorough as you'd like, but it's a start and it's often useful.

Click this button to go back to the previous screen.

An Easy Tutorial 2

If you're new to your Mac, I suggest you start here. This tutorial follows a logical pattern that I have found to be successful in my classes (but it's not meant to be completed in one day!). These steps skip all over the book—I apologize for the hopping around you'll have to do, but you really shouldn't read *everything* about windows or the mouse or whatever at once. You need to know just enough to feel comfortable, then come back later for more. If you get overloaded, turn off the computer and have a cup of tea with me.

After you've finished the brief tutorial, spend a few weeks working on your Mac. Then come back to the book and read other parts that now interest you. Not only will the tips and tricks make more sense, but you'll find you can actually absorb the rest of the information.

Don't Limit Yourself!

You might think, in your eagerness to get right into a program and start creating something or sending email or browsing the web, that you want to skip all these dumb little exercises at the Desktop like making windows smaller and larger or trashing blank folders. But trust me—it's too easy to turn on the computer, find the button for your program, and go right into it. But then you're limited. You won't have complete control over your computer. Some things will always confuse you. You'll never be a Power User (your Goal in Life, right?).

Quick Start

But for the person who wants to instantly create, save, print, and quit, the steps are quite easy, as long as you know what all the terms are, like "icon" and "Dock" and "double-click."

▼ **Open** your word processing program (or other program of your choice):
It the application icon is in a window, double-click it.
If the application icon is in the Dock, single-click it.

▼ **Save** the new document:
From the File menu, choose "Save As...."
Name the file and click "Save."

▼ **Create** something: start typing, drawing, painting, or whatever.
Save regularly as you work (from the File menu, choose "Save").

▼ **Print** the document:
From the File menu, choose "Print...."
Click the "Print" button.

▼ **Quit** the application:
From the File menu, choose "Quit."

This is the same basic process you will go through in any application—it's really that easy. But to be truly powerful—ahh, that takes a little more time.

So here are my recommendations on what you should spend time doing if you are impatient or your time is very limited. Actually, this is a good way to start even if you have lots of time; there is so much information to be absorbed that it works best to absorb a little now, then come back for more later. It also helps to run into a few problems because then when you discover the solution, the solution actually makes sense.

Start Using the Tutorial Here

First of all, you don't have to read very many pages of this book to become proficient on your Mac. Flip through the book and you'll see **half-dots** on the edges of the pages—those are the only pages you really need to read. The rest of the book will answer your questions as you bump into things you want to know more about. But to get started, just follow the dots!

Follow the dots

On many pages, including some without dots, there are gray boxes that contain short **practice exercises.** This tutorial will direct you to the practice exercises you really need right away, and then you can do the others whenever you feel like it.

Follow these dots.   *These are the practice exercises.*

Turning it On

This is the Power symbol.

Some Power symbols look like this.

You've probably already done this, but just in case you haven't, learn how to **turn on** your computer. On most Macs these days you'll find a flat button with the "Power" symbol on it, as shown to the left. The button might be on the keyboard, the monitor (as on iMacs), or the tower (the big box that holds the actual computer parts). (The Power On button is not always the Power Off button—see Chapter 19 when you're ready to shut down your Mac.)

Older Macs have a large button on the keyboard with a triangle on it. This Power On button *does* turn your Mac off, as well as on.

If you work in a large office or a computer lab at school, you might run across other Macs that turn on in different ways, or ones that have been set up to turn on differently—they might have buttons on the back, on a power strip, or somewhere else. But don't let it confuse you—even if you forget half the other stuff in this book, once you figure out how to turn on your computer you probably won't forget it.

The Desktop, Finder, and Home

What you see when you turn on the Macintosh is called the **Desktop.** It is also called the **Finder** because the software program that runs the Desktop is the Finder. You might have seen the map of your Desktop on page 2. Get a general idea of the Desktop features by reading pages 125–127, then learn about your **Home** area on pages 132–133.

Using the Mouse

Read pages 23, 25, and 26. Follow the practice exercises for using your **mouse.** You'll be using the mouse every time you use your Mac, so it's good to practice enough to feel comfortable with it. If you go through the rest of the exercises, you'll quickly become a pro.

Getting Familiar with the Keyboard

Skim through the first part of the **keyboard** chapter, Chapter 4, pages 33 to 41, plus the top half of 42. There are no practice exercises in this section, but try to become familiar with all those odd keys on your keyboard. Don't worry about memorizing what they do—when you need to know, you'll know where to find the information. Just pick out the keys you've been wondering about, or skim through the information and find the keys that you think sound useful for the future.

Using the Dock

You will gradually come to use the Dock more and more as you become familiar with your Mac. At the moment, just read the first three pages of Chapter 8, pages 119–121. This will familiarize you with the Dock enough so you can work effectively. When you want to know more, read the rest of the chapter.

Read pages 53–58 in Chapter 5 about **menus** and **how to choose commands** (you can read the rest of that chapter some other time). Follow the practice exercises. You will be using the menus and commands constantly every time you use your Mac, so make sure you understand them. By now you're probably pretty good with that mouse, huh?

Using Menus and Menu Commands

Chapter 6 about **windows** is pretty long, but windows are *very important*. Almost everything you do at the Desktop/Finder involves a window, and every application you use will display itself in a window, so you need to know how to control them. This is where you should commit to spending a bit of time (won't take more than an hour or two) to go through the chapter carefully, do all of the practice exercises, and make sure you feel comfortable. Believe me, if you don't feel comfortable using the windows, you will never be quite at home on your Mac.

Controlling the Windows

Read pages 105–112 about icons in Chapter 7, and do the practice exercises. Skip the rest for now! Even if you don't see too many icons at the moment, remember that icons tell you a lot; they are rich in visual clues that help you understand your computer.

Don't double-click on anything except folder icons at the moment.

Recognizing Icons

Use the **keyboard commands** to do some of the tasks you've already been doing with the mouse and menus. Read page 59, "Keyboard Shortcuts." Using the keyboard shortcuts is a sign of becoming a Power User.

Taking Advantage of Keyboard Commands

The trick to making a keyboard shortcut work is that you must *first* select the item you want to affect. For instance, if you want to open a folder, *first* click once on the folder to select it, *then* press Command O to open it (as explained on page 59).

Do each of these things using a keyboard shortcut:

❏ Open a window.

❏ Close a window.

❏ Select every item in a window.
   (To deselect the items, click in any white space in the folder.)

Word Processing (typing)

Next to using the windows proficiently, the other main skill you need on a computer is **word processing,** or **typing.** Whether you type a novel or a note, it's important to know how the computer works with text. Learning how to word process will also teach you other important techniques, such as how to open an application, start a new document, cut, copy, and paste. Read and do the practice exercises on pages 195–214. Then recreate the sample shown on page 216. If you spend the time to do this (maybe an hour or two), you'll know more than most people who have been using a Mac for a long time.

Saving your Documents

If you want to keep a document you are working on, you must **save** it and give it a name. Read the first four pages of Chapter 14, pages 219–222, to learn how important it is and why to save your documents, and to learn how to do a quick and easy save. This is very important!

Printing

Now you need **to print your document.** If you are connected to a color inkjet printer like an Epson Stylus or an HP DeskWriter, all you have to do is go to the File menu, choose "Print...," and click the blue Print button. (Of course, first make sure your printer is plugged into your Mac, plugged into a power supply, and is turned on and warmed up.)

If printing doesn't work automatically, you probably need to tell the Mac where your printer is. Read pages 236–240. It's also a good idea to install the software that came with your printer—it's on a CD that arrived in your printer box. Many times you don't have to install the software, but if you do you might discover you have extra printing options.

Quit

You need to **quit** the application if you are done for the day. Save the document again before you quit: just use the keyboard shortcut Command S. Then from the File menu, choose "Quit." The Quit command is always the very last item, and the keyboard shortcut is always Command Q. You really should read pages 247–251 in Chapter 16 so you understand the difference between closing and quitting.

This is a list of **several other basic Desktop tasks** you need to learn because you will be doing them everyday:

Basic Desktop Tasks

▾ Read pages 145–151 about **folders.** Make a new folder. (What is the keyboard shortcut?!) Name your new folder.

▾ Make a **duplicate** of this new folder: click once on the folder to select it, then find the command for duplicating. Which menu is it in, and what is the keyboard shortcut (see page 171)? Change the name of this duplicate folder.

▾ Use the **Trash** basket (read pages 265–269). Throw away the duplicate folder you just made. Empty the trash.

▾ **Backup** your work! You should do this to every file you want to keep, especially your documents. If you have a Zip drive, copy a folder or document onto a Zip disk, as explained on page 173. If you have a built-in CD or DVD burner in your Mac, read pages 176–177. In case the file on your hard disk gets lost or trashed or your hard disk dies, you will have this extra copy.

If you have a Zip drive, you'll use **Zip disks** to store extra files or copies of files. The Zip disk goes in the drive with the label-side facing up (or toward the top of the drive, if you have an external drive sitting sideways), the round thing on the bottom. The metal end slides in first. **CDs** go in the tray or in the slot with the label-side up. See Chapter 18 about ejecting disks.

Inserting Disks

There are several **very important features** on your Mac you can learn that will make you the life of any party. Here are suggestions for specific things you need to be in control of:

Other Very Important Features

▾ Learn how to use **Sherlock.** Read pages 363–367 and experiment. Later, another day, read the rest of the chapter and learn how to do more complex searches (when you know what you're searching for) and search for things on the Internet.

Sherlock

▾ Learn how to use some of your **System Preferences:** skim Chapter 21. Check out only the preference panes that interest you (ignore the others). An easy one to experiment with is the Mouse preferences (see pages 28–29).

System Preferences

▾ Learn how to use **aliases.** Read pages 343–347. I guarantee you will find aliases to be one of the greatest features of organization and convenience on the Mac.

Aliases

▾ Read the book called *The Mac is not a typewriter.* It's little.

p.s.

User Groups!   One of the best things you can do for yourself is join your **local user group!** Macintosh users have a history of joyfully sharing information, and a user group is an incredible source of help and support. To find the user group in your area, check the Apple website: **www.apple.com/usergroups.** You can find the user group nearest where you live or where you will be traveling to, based on the zip code or even by the cross streets.

If you're ever in Santa Fe on the first Wednesday of the month, visit the Santa Fe Mac User Group! I teach the beginners' session before the main meeting. Check our award-winning web site at **www.santafemug.org.**

The Mouse 3

The **mouse,** of course, is that handy little piece of hardware that controls the movement of the pointer on the screen. As you move the mouse across the desk, a pointer, sometimes called a cursor, moves across the screen in the same direction. In most Macintosh applications, you cannot fully utilize the program without the mouse. A few programs give you the option of doing absolutely everything from the keyboard if you choose; but who wants to learn 450 keyboard commands?

This short chapter helps you get familiar with the various ways of using and taking care of your mouse.

Connecting the Mouse

[**If your mouse is already connected,** you can skip this page!] The mouse plugs into a port (a socket). Most Macs (including all iMacs, G4s, Cubes, iBooks) have what are called "USB ports" into which you plug "USB devices," including your mouse. You have two USB ports on the top sides of your keyboard; you can plug your mouse into either one. USB ports are rectangular, so of course the mouse cable has a rectangular connector on the other end of the cable. (If your mouse cable has a round connector, see the information below about ADB ports.)

 This is an illustration of two USB ports.

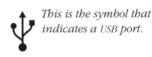 *This is the symbol that indicates a USB port.*

Some stand-alone monitors (as opposed to iMac monitors) also have USB ports around their bases, making it even easier to connect keyboards and mice. Check your monitor.

You can plug and unplug your USB mouse while the computer is up and running, although Apple recommends that you first quit any open applications. Plugging and unplugging while the computer is running is called "hot swapping." For more information about USB, see Chapter 38.

Older Macs and ADB ports

Older Macintoshes don't use USB ports; they have something called ADB ports instead. ADB ports are round and have a different symbol identifying them, as shown below. Of course, you must have an ADB mouse to plug into an ADB port. If you have ADB ports, always shut down first before plugging and unplugging anything from your computer, including the mouse or the keyboard. You cannot hot swap from ADB ports!

This is an illustration of an ADB port.

This is the symbol that indicates an ADB port.

Left-Handed Mousing

If you are left-handed, all you need to do is plug the mouse into the port on the left side of the keyboard. Unless you have bought a special mouse that curves to fit the right hand, your mouse will fit just as well into the left hand as the right.

Older keyboards with ADB ports often have a port in the middle of the keyboard so you can just move the mouse to the left side.

The Pointer

As you move the mouse, a **pointer** moves around the screen. The only part of the pointer that does the trick is the *very* tip, called the "hot spot." When you need the pointer to activate something, be sure that the extreme point of the arrow is positioned in the area you want to affect. For instance, to click in the little red button in the top-left corner of a window to close it, position the pointer like so:

This is the hot spot . . . .

*The **tip** of the pointer (the hot spot) does the trick.*

Using the Mouse

You'll use the mouse in several different ways. Always, the mouse sits on a flat surface and you roll it around with your hand on top of it, your index finger resting on the front end of the mouse (the part that clicks). We often call the front part of the mouse the "button," even though there's not really a button. Do not hold the mouse in the palm of your hand, and do not pick it up and point it at the screen.

Single-click

A **single click** is a quick, light touch on the front end of the mouse, with the "cursor"—a pointer, an I-beam (page 196) or other shape—located at the spot of your choice on the screen.

> Single-click with the I-beam to set down an insertion point for typing.
>
> Single-click with the pointer on an icon on your Desktop or in a Finder window to *select* that icon.
>
> Single-click an application or document icon in the Dock to *open* that application or document.

Practice: Single-click on the icon of your hard disk, in the upper-right corner of your screen. A single click will "select" the hard disk.

Double-click

A **double-click** is a quick click-click on the front end of the mouse, again with the pointer located at the appropriate spot on the screen. A double-click has to be quick and the mouse must be still or the Mac will interpret it as two single clicks.

> Double-click on an application or document icon to *open* that application or document (as long as the icon is not in the Dock— single-click items in the Dock).
>
> Double-click on a folder icon (not in the Dock) to *open* the window for that folder.
>
> Double-click on a word to *select* that word for editing.

Practice: Double-click on the icon of your hard disk, in the upper-right corner of your screen. A double-click will "open" the hard disk and show you its window.

Press

To **press** means to point to something and *hold the mouse button down.*

Press on the arrows in a scroll bar of a window to scroll through that window.

Press on items in the Dock to get their menus.

Often directions tell you to "click" on things when they really mean "press." If clicking doesn't work, try pressing.

Press-and-drag

Press-and-drag means to point to the object or the area of your choice, *hold/ press the mouse button down, keep it down,* and *drag* somewhere, then *let go* when you reach your goal. (This is sometimes called click-and-drag.)

Press-and-drag to move icons across the screen.

Press-and-drag to select a range of text.

Shift-click
Command-click
Option-click
Control-click

You'll see the terms **Shift-click, Command-click, Option-click,** and **Control-click.** This means to *hold down* that key (Shift, Command, Option, or Control) and then *click* the mouse button once. Different things happen with this action.

Shift-click individual icons (when a window is in Icon view) to *select* more than one icon, or to *deselect* from a group of selected icons (see pages 160–165 for details about selecting).

Shift-click file names (when a window is in Column or List view) to *select* all of the files between the two clicks.

Command-click individual file names (when a window is in Column or List view) to *select* more than one file, or to *deselect* from a group of selected icons.

Control-click on various items on the Desktop to get "contextual menus," which are menus that offer different choices depending on what you Control-click (see page 56).

Option-click on application icons in the Dock to give you a menu choice to force that application to quit.

Option-drag
Command-Option-drag

You'll see terms like **Option-drag** or **Command-Option-drag,** which mean you must *hold down* the Option and/or Command keys and *drag* the mouse.

Option-drag a file from one window to another to make a copy of that file.

Command-Option-drag a file to another folder or to the Desktop to make an alias of it (alias information is in Chapter 22).

Mouse Pad

You've surely seen or have a **mouse pad,** a small pad to put on your desk to roll the mouse across. The pad has nothing to do with the operation of the mouse, really—the mouse will work just fine without a pad. The purpose of a mouse pad is simply to provide better traction and a clear spot on your desk for the mouse. You can use a book, illustration board, a coaster, paper, or even just the deskop.

Moving the Mouse
when you've run out of
space

Sometimes you may be **moving the mouse** across the mouse pad or the desk and **run out of space** before the pointer or the I-beam gets where you want it to go. Just do this: Keep your finger on the mouse button, pressing it down. Pick up the mouse, keeping the button down, and move the mouse over to where you have more room. Then just continue on your path. Try it.

Adjust the Tension
on an Optical Mouse

If you have an **optical** mouse, one with a little red glow on the underside, you can adjust the tension in the click. More tension makes the mouse button feel a little stiffer; less tension makes the clicking easier.

1. Turn the mouse over.

2. There is a plastic ring around the center of the mouse with a small dot at the top. Press on that ring with your thumbs and move it to the right for more tension, to the left for less tension. You can barely see a tiny plus or minus sign in the little round dots as you move it to the right or left.

Mouse Preferences

This is the System Preferences icon in the Dock. Click it once.

This is the icon that opens the Mouse preferences pane. Click it once.

One of the first sets of preferences you might want to customize are the Mouse preferences (if you have a laptop with a trackpad instead of a mouse, see the following page). You'll read about all the preference panes in Chapter 21, but this one is simple to use and shows you how easy it is to customize many of the features on your Mac, so take a look at it as soon as you feel comfortable using the mouse and pulling down menus. If you are brand-new to your Mac, come back to this page in a couple of days.

1. Click on the "System Preferences" icon in the Dock, as shown to the left, to open the Preferences window. Click the "Mouse" icon, also shown to the left, to open the Mouse preferences panel.

Show All	Displays	Sound	Network	Startup Disk

Tracking Speed

Very Slow — Fast

Double-Click Speed

Very Slow — Fast

Double-click here to test

2. When the **Tracking Speed** is set on or near "Very Slow," you have to move the mouse a long way on your desk to move the pointer across the screen. If you choose "Fast," you only need to move the mouse a short distance to move the pointer across the screen. Try it—position the pointer on the colored button and drag it from one end to the other. Let go, then drag your mouse across the screen *without* pressing the button down. You'll notice the effects immediately. Most people find they prefer the faster setting.

When you work in a drawing, painting, or image editing program, you may want to come back to this preference pane and set the speed to "Slow" so you have finer control over tiny details in your drawing.

If you use a tablet with a stylus for drawing, drag the button all the way to "Very Slow."

3. The **Double-Click Speed** adjusts how fast you have to click twice so the computer knows you want a double-click, instead of two single clicks. If you find that you don't double-click quite fast enough to make the computer happy, lower the double-click speed.

If you set the speed to the fastest setting, you run the risk that the computer will interpret a single click as a double click if you have the slightest bit of shakiness in your click. A good choice is right in the middle.

To test the double-click speed you chose, position the pointer over one of the words in that sentence you see in the pane, "Double-click here to test." Double-click as you normally would. If the word becomes highlighted (is surrounded by a darker color), that speed is good for you. If the word doesn't become highlighted, set a lower speed and test it again.

4. After you adjust the tracking and double-click speeds, click the close button (the red one in the upper-left corner) to put this preference panel away.

5. To put the entire window of System Preferences away, position the pointer on the bold heading in the menu across the top of your screen, "System Prefs."

Click once on that heading.

Click once on the command at the very bottom of that menu, the one that says "Quit System Prefs."

System Prefs	
About System Prefs	
Services	▶
Hide System Prefs	⌘H
Hide Others	
Show All	
Quit System Prefs	⌘Q

Trackpads and Trackballs

Some people prefer to use a different "pointing device," such as a joystick or a trackball. The Macintosh laptops use trackballs or trackpads.

A **trackball** is like an upside-down version of the roller-ball mouse—instead of moving the little mouse box around to make the ball roll underneath, you use your fingers to roll the little ball on top as it sits in the box. Trackballs have buttons to press that act like the button on the mouse. Depending on what kind of trackball you have, you may click the button with a finger or, as seems to be easier on some laptops, with your thumb.

The **trackpad** is a flat space and you use your finger to drag the pointer around the screen. It takes a little time to get used to it.

Trackballs and trackpads are particularly convenient for those people who have to use the mouse backwards. Yes, I have met several people who have to turn the mouse with the tail facing themselves. When they push the mouse to the right, the pointer on the screen moves to the left. If more than one person uses the same computer, each person has to turn the mouse around. With a trackball or pad, individual idiosyncrasies don't matter.

▼ Generally, move your finger around the trackpad. When you want to click on an item, tap the bar under the trackpad.

▼ A checkmark in the "Clicking" checkbox tells the Mac you want to tap your finger on the trackpad (instead of the bar) to click on items. This is a great feature—just roll your finger around and tap to select files (or open Dock icons), tap-tap to open files.

▼ If you check "Clicking," then the checkbox for "Dragging" becomes available. A checkmark in the "Dragging" checkbox lets you click-and-a-half with your finger to drag items: On a regular double-click, you click twice, then let go. In a click-and-a-half, you keep the mouse button down after the second click. Try it. Then you can drag selected files.

▼ Once you check "Dragging," then "Drag Lock" becomes available. This feature will grab the selected item and drag it after the first click. Be careful—this feature can make you crazy if you aren't perfectly aware of what's going on. Experiment.

If your mouse has a little red glow in the middle, it's an **optical** mouse and uses light to communicate with the monitor. Check the bottom of it regularly—grunge builds up on the white plastic edge and can affect the way the mouse moves around on the pad.

If you have an **older mouse with a ball** on the bottom, it's important to keep the ball and pocket clean—cat hairs and dustballs get inside. Take it apart regularly and clean it, following these steps:

1. Take the mouse in your right hand and turn it upside-down.

2. With your thumbs, slide the round wheel to the left to open the lid.

3. Flip the mouse back over into your left hand so the lid and the ball fall out into your palm.

4. Clean the ball with a soft, dry cloth; clean the rollers inside with a cotton swab dipped in rubbing alcohol.

5. When clean, put the ball in your left hand; with your right hand place the mouse on top of the ball and flop your hands over. This places the ball safely into its little pocket.

6. Put the lid back on and twist it to the right, lining up the marker with the "L" for Lock (if you see one). That's it!

Cleaning the Mouse

Quiz

Would you single-click (**S**), double-click (**D**), press (**P**), or press-and-drag (**P&D**) to accomplish each of the following tasks? Circle the appropriate abbreviation in the margin for each task.

S   D   P   P&D   Zozobra   Zozobra

1. Select an icon (always **select** an item before you do something to it).

S   D   P   P&D   Robin 2001   Robin 2001

2. Open a file, such as your financial record so you can enter your new information.

S   D   P   P&D   Cancel   Save

3. Activate a button.

S   D   P   P&D   Heresy rheumatic starry offer former's dodder.

4. Select a whole word for editing (to change it).

S   D   P   P&D   Robin's Stuff   Robin's Stuff

5. Open a folder to see what's in it.

S   D   P   P&D

Window
Minimize Window   ⌘M
Bring All To Front
Robin's Stuff

6. Choose something from a menu.

S   D   P   P&D

7. Open an application or document that is in the Dock.

Shift-click

Command-click

Option-click

Control-click

ratz.c

Help

Open
Move To Trash

Duplicate
Make Alias

Choose one of the actions in the far-left column for the next three questions.

8. Get a contextual menu on an item.

marysidney.jpg
MS quill.tif
prince.tiff   *or*

am.jpg   bc.jpg

cw.jpg   df.jpg

9. Select a group of items.

Blue Mermaid 100 rgb
marys home.tif
marysidneysmall.jpg
MS quill.tif
prince.tiff
Url w/clouds cmyk.tif   *or*

am.jpg   bc.jpg

cw.jpg   df.jpg

10. Deselect items from a selected group.

Answers on page 750.

Keys and the Keyboard 4

There are several important **keys** on your keyboard that are particularly useful. They come in handy for shortcuts, manipulating images, accessing alternate characters, and any number of things in specific applications.

There are a variety of keyboards for the Mac. If you have a Mac that is using OS X, you have an **extended keyboard** that includes all the "function keys" (the keys with the Fs on them) and other little groups of keys, including a numeric keypad.

Many of the **Macintosh laptops** have smaller keyboards where several keys do double-duty; that is, you might see tiny letters or symbols in another color on a standard key. See pages 45–46 for directions on how to use those specialized keys.

There are a number of fancy keyboards you can buy separately that bend in the middle or have special ergonomic features. All keyboards have certain standard characters, although they may appear in different places on different models. No matter where they are placed, though, all the keys perform the same function (although the function of some keys varies from program to program).

Don't forget to look at the **underside of your keyboard** and pull out that little lever that puts your keyboard at a slight tilt; the tilt is a better position for your hands.

What are All These Keys?

On these two pages are photographs of the two main sorts of **keyboards** you'll find attached to your Mac, with callouts telling you where to go for more information about particular keys. For a laptop keyboard and its special features, please see pages 45–46.

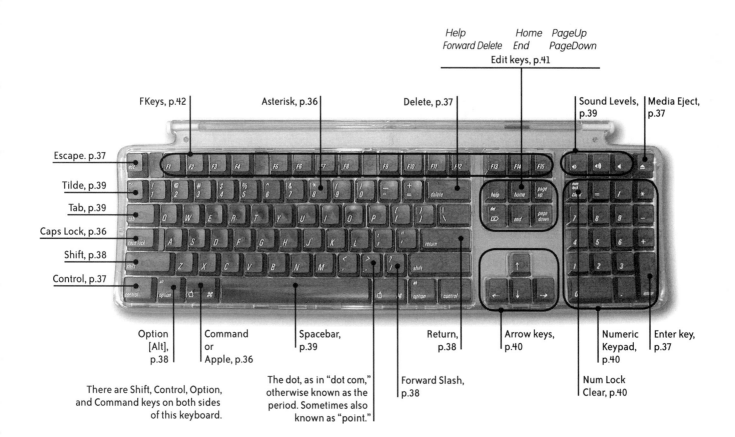

Help
Forward Delete
Home
End
PageUp
PageDown
Edit keys, p.41

FKeys, p.42
Asterisk, p.36
Delete, p.37
Sound Levels, p.39
Media Eject, p.37

Escape. p.37
Tilde, p.39
Tab, p.39
Caps Lock, p.36
Shift, p.38
Control, p.37

Option [Alt], p.38
Command or Apple, p.36
Spacebar, p.39
Return, p.38
Arrow keys, p.40
Numeric Keypad, p.40
Enter key, p.37

There are Shift, Control, Option, and Command keys on both sides of this keyboard.

The dot, as in "dot com," otherwise known as the period. Sometimes also known as "point."

Forward Slash, p.38

Num Lock Clear, p.40

The keyboard shown below is the one that typically comes with **iMacs,** as well as with many other Macs. The Fkeys are smaller, there is no Forward Delete key, and the Edit keys are across the top of the numeric keypad. If you find you don't feel comfortable with this smaller keyboard, you can always buy the larger one (as shown on the opposite page), or any number of other brands of keyboards.

The smaller keyboard

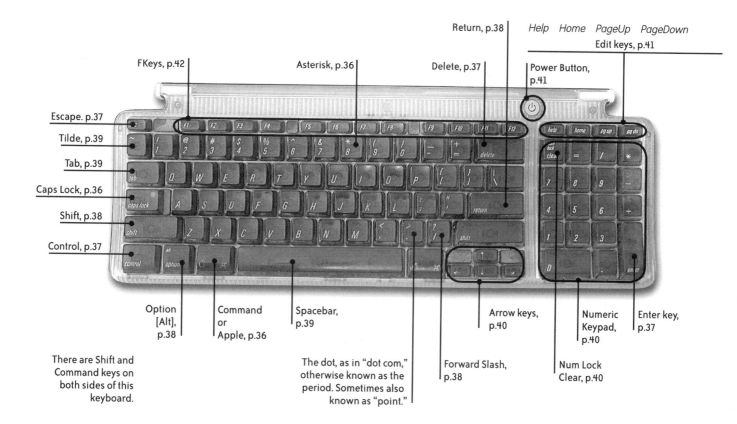

Return, p.38

Help   Home   PageUp   PageDown
Edit keys, p.41

FKeys, p.42

Asterisk, p.36

Delete, p.37

Power Button, p.41

Escape. p.37

Tilde, p.39

Tab, p.39

Caps Lock, p.36

Shift, p.38

Control, p.37

Option [Alt], p.38

Command or Apple, p.36

Spacebar, p.39

Arrow keys, p.40

Numeric Keypad, p.40

Enter key, p.37

There are Shift and Command keys on both sides of this keyboard.

The dot, as in "dot com," otherwise known as the period. Sometimes also known as "point."

Forward Slash, p.38

Num Lock Clear, p.40

Modifier Keys

The symbols shown in the outer column under each of the following headings are the symbols that will appear in menus to indicate those keys.

Some of the keys on the keyboard are called **modifier keys** because they don't do anything by themselves, but are used in combination with regular keys to make something happen, like keyboard shortcuts (see "Keyboard Shortcuts" on page 59). The Shift key, for instance, is a modifier key you are already familiar with: the Shift key doesn't do anything when you press it by itself, but if you hold it down while you type an alphabetic character, you get the capital letter instead of the lowercase letter.

Modifier keys: Shift, Option, Command (also called Apple), Control.

Sometimes a keyboard shortcut uses more than one modifier. Always *hold down all the modifier keys together* (Command, Shift, Option, etc.) while you give *one quick tap on the associated letter key*. For instance, to *paste* an item, the shortcut is ⌘ **V**: hold down the Command key and type a quick V. If you *hold* the character key down (such as the V key) instead of *tapping* it once, you will usually end up repeating the command many times.

Any Key

There is no **Any key.** When a direction tells you to "PRESS ANY KEY," it means to press any key you want on the whole keyboard.

Asterisk

*

The **asterisk** (*, Greek for "little star") is used as a multiplication symbol in calculators, spreadsheets, databases, etc. You can use the asterisk on the numeric keypad, or you can press Shift 8 to get the asterisk you see above the number 8 on the keyboard. Thank goodness this key is also known as the Star key because so few people can spell or pronounce "asterisk."

Caps Lock Key

When you press the **Caps Lock key** down, everything you type is in capital letters. If you've ever used a typewriter, you'll find that Caps Lock is different from the Shift Lock on a typewriter: Caps Lock does *not* type the characters above the numbers or above the punctuation, such as the *, $, @, or < >, nor even the ?. If you want to type these Shift-characters you must press the Shift key, even if Caps Lock is down.

Some keyboard shortcuts will not work if the Caps Lock key is down, so check its position if you're having problems.

Command Key
Apple Key

⌘

The **Command key** is on the bottom row, the key with the California freeway cloverleaf symbol on it: ⌘. On most keyboards this key also has an apple symbol on it, and you may hear it referred to as the **Apple key** or **Open Apple.** For over fifteen years, the proper term has been the "Command" key; in the Mac OS X Help files, however, you'll see references to the "Apple" key, even though the symbol in the menus is still the Command symbol.

Most keyboard shortcuts use the Command key. Do not confuse it with the Control key!

The **Control key** is standard on Macintosh keyboards—it's usually on the bottom, far-left, and often on the far-right as well. Contextual menus on the Mac (page 56) usually use the Control key, as do a number of other keyboard shortcuts. Also, this key makes it easier for those who are running DOS or Windows software on the Macintosh. Be sure to read directions carefully and make sure you use the *Control* key when the directions call for *Control* and the Command key when they call for Command.

Control Key
ctrl or control

The **Delete key** is located on the upper-right of the main body of keys. You might hear people refer to it as the Backspace key because it used to be called such. The name was changed to "Delete" long ago because that's really what it does—whatever character is to the *left* of the "insertion point" will be deleted as you "backspace" over it. In applications, whatever item is *selected* will be removed when you hit the Delete key.

There is another delete key located in the little group of Edit keys, called the Forward Delete, that deletes the character to the *right* as you type. See page 41.

Delete Key
(Backspace Key)

The **Eject Media Disk key** is not on every keyboard. If you have it, it's on the numeric keypad (the set of number keys on the right side of your keyboard), the very right-uppermost key. Use the Eject Media Disk key to eject CDs and DVDs: *you don't even have to select the disk,* just hit this key. As its name implies, this key only works on CDs and DVDs (media disks, as opposed to data disks); that is, this key will not ject a Zip or Jaz cartridge.

If you don't have an Eject Media Disk key, try the F12 key.

Also use this key in combination with the Control key to shut down your computer: Hold down the Control key, press the Eject Media Disk key, and you'll get a message asking if you want to shut down your computer now, along with options to restart, sleep, and cancel.

Eject Media Disk Key

Keyboard shutdown

The **Enter key** on the *numeric keypad* (the set of number keys on the right side of your keyboard) will also activate buttons with the double border, just the same as the Return key (following page), and Enter will usually start a new paragraph as well. Different programs use the Enter key in different ways.

Enter Key

The **Escape key** (labeled **esc**) on the upper-left of the keyboard is used in a few applications.

> **Tip:** Press Command Option Esc to bring up the dialog box to force quit an application. (See pages 262–263 about force quitting.)

Escape Key
esc

Forward Slash
/

The **forward slash** (/) is used as a division symbol in calculators, spreadsheets, databases, etc. It's also used in World Wide Web addresses. You can use the slash on the regular keyboard (the same key as the question mark) or the one on the numeric keypad. Don't use the straight slash (|) or the backward slash (\, backslash), which are both situated above the Return key, when you want to divide or when you type a web address.

The forward slash is an "illegal" character in file names in Mac OS X, which means you are not allowed to use it (it means something important to the Mac operating system). You can't use a colon (:) either.

Option Key
(Alt Key)
⌥

Next to the Command Key is the **Option key.** The Option key is often used in combination with the Command key and/or the Shift key. With the Option key, you can type the special characters such as ¢ and ®, as well as accent marks, as in résumé and piñata (see page 215).

This key sometimes has the word "alt" on it as well because the Option key is often comparable to the **Alt key** when using Windows programs on the Mac (if the Alt key doesn't work in a Windows program, try the Shift key).

Return Key
¶

The **Return key** is used for many things other than simply beginning a new paragraph. For instance, any button that is "pulsing" can be activated with the Return key instead of the mouse. Different programs use the Return key in different ways. Most things you do with the Return key you can also do with the Enter key, which is found in the numeric keypad.

Whenever you see a button pulsing, like the "Save," "Open," or "Create" buttons shown above, you can always press the Return key (or the Enter key) to activate that button instead of clicking on the button with the mouse.

Shift Key
⇧

The **Shift key** is one of the most commonly used modifier keys in keyboard shortcuts, as well as regular typing. Its symbol is an upward arrow, as shown to the left. You have a Shift key on both sides of your keyboard.

Some keyboards have **Sound Level keys** just above the numeric keypad. Use the two keys that have vibration symbols to lower or raise the volume. The key with no vibrations in the symbol is the **Mute** key; press it and your computer will not make any sounds, not even alert sounds. Instead, when it wants to beep at you, your menu bar will flash.

Sound Level Keys

The **Spacebar** is represented in menus by the symbol shown to the right, or sometimes *as a blank space*. That blank space can really throw you. How long does it take to figure out that "⇧⌘ " means to press the Shift key, the Command key, and the Spacebar?

Spacebar

The Tilde (~, pronounced *till′duh*) is located on the upper-left of the main set of keys on most keyboards and next to the Spacebar on older keyboards. This Tilde was never used much in English until the World Wide Web was invented—now we see it all the time in web addresses so you had better know how to type it (hold down the Shift key, then tap the Tilde key).

Tilde
~

The **Tab key** in the upper-left acts like the Tab key on a typewriter (if you've ever used a typewriter) in that after you press the Tab key you'll start typing at the next tab stop that's set. In most **word processing** programs, there is a default tab set every one-half inch; to make others, simply click in the ruler you see across the top of the screen to create a tab stop in the selected paragraph (to remove tabs, press-and-drag the tab markers down off the ruler).

Tab Key
» →

You won't see a symbol for the Tab key in menus, but you might see it on your word processing page; the symbol varies from program to program.

In **spreadsheet** and **database** programs, the Tab key will move the selection to the next cell or field *to the right,* just as it would move your typing to the right (the Return key will move the selection to the next cell or field *down*). Hold the Shift key down as you press Tab to move the selection backwards to the left (or Shift Return to move up).

When you are in **dialog boxes,** press the Tab key to select *edit boxes* (the small spaces where you can type something new, as shown circled to the right). Just try it: Open a dialog box, then press the Tab key to cycle you through the edit boxes. If there is something in an edit box already, the box will highlight; *anything you type will replace what is highlighted*

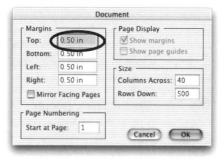

Do you see the seven edit boxes in this small dialog window? The first one, "Top," is highlighted and ready for you to enter a new value. Hit the Tab key to select the next edit box.

(which means you don't have to hit the Delete key first—just type). If the edit box is empty, the insertion point will flash to indicate you can now type in it. Using the Tab key to select the next field also works on most forms on **web pages.**

Arrow Keys

--→ ←-- ↑ ↓

Document

First Page	⇧⌘↕
Previous Page	←--
Next Page	--→
Last Page	⇧⌘↕
Go To Page...	⌘N
Go To Previous View	⌘←-
Go To Next View	⌘-→
Go To Next Document	⇧⌘-→

These are examples of menu commands that use the arrow keys for shortcuts.

Depending on your keyboard, you may have **arrow keys** (keys with nothing but an arrow on each of them) tucked in with your letter keys, or you may have a separate little set of four arrow keys, or on laptops your arrow keys are added onto existing character keys. Arrow keys are used for different things in different programs.

In **word processing** programs you can use the arrow keys to move the insertion point (the insertion point is that thin, flashing, vertical bar that moves along with the text as you type).

> **Tip:** In most programs, hold down the Shift key as you press the arrow keys, and the text will be *selected* as the insertion point moves along. Try it.

In some programs, such as **page layout** or **graphics** programs, you can use the arrow keys to nudge objects around on the screen. In **spreadsheets** and **databases,** the arrow keys might be used to move the insertion point or to select other cells or fields. In **dialog boxes,** the arrow keys will move the insertion point within the selected edit box.

RightArrow
LeftArrow
UpArrow
DownArrow

You'll notice when I write about commands that use **arrow keys** I write them out like this: RightArrow, LeftArrow, UpArrow, and DownArrow. For instance, I might tell you to press Shift LeftArrow. I do this because I have seen beginners follow a command such as "Press Command + left arrow" by pressing the Command key and then looking for the key that says "left," plus an arrow key. (And many new users also try to press the + key.) So even though it may seem odd at first, combining the two words that describe the arrow keys makes it clearer that there is just one key.

Numeric Keypad
Clear Key
Num Lock

On the far-right of the keyboard is a **numeric keypad** that looks like calculator keys. If you have a laptop, don't think you are missing a numeric keypad—see pages 45–46. In some applications, these numeric keys will type numbers, and in other applications they will move the insertion point (see page 196 for a description of the insertion point).

In some applications these keys can do both—they can type numbers *or* they can move the insertion point, depending on whether the **Num Lock** key is down; when down, it locks the keypad into typing numbers instead of moving the insertion point.

When you use the Calculator utility (see Chapter 29) or work in a spreadsheet or financial program, use the numeric keypad to enter data into the Calculator and perform functions. The asterisk (*) is the multiplication key, and the forward slash (/) is the division key. The **Clear key,** of course, acts like the clear key on a calculator.

The **Power key** might be an actual key on the keyboard, or it might be a round or oblong **Power button** embossed or printed with a left-pointing arrow or the standard power symbol (both shown to the right). It you have one on your keyboard, it's at the top-center of some keyboards and at the upper-right in others. Various models of iMacs also have a Power button on the monitor. Some of the newest keyboards do not have either a Power key or button on the keyboard itself—you have to use the button on the case or the monitor. A Power key on the keyboard makes it very easy for your cat or your small child to turn on your Mac when you least expect it.

The Power button or key will also **shut down** your Mac, or on some models you can set the Power button to put the Mac to **sleep** (check your Energy Saver preferences, Chapter 21). If you have a Mac tower with the Power button on the tower, you might have to hold the button in to the count of five to turn off the machine (or use "Shut Down" from the Apple menu).

If you have cats and kids swarming around your house, you might find your computer turning on or off at odd times. Fortunately, you do get a warning beep asking if you really want to shut down, and even if the cat steps on the Return key (which chooses "Okay" to shut down), the Mac will save any files that were left open before it turns itself off. See Chapter 19 for more details about shutting down your computer.

Power Key
Power Button

If you have an extended keyboard, you have an extra little set of keys between the alphabet keyboard and the numeric keypad called the **edit keys.** These keys help make the Macintosh compatible with PC programs, as well as provide you with extra little features. Not all Mac programs use these keys, although if you read your manual you may be surprised. Try them in your word processor. Or open a Desktop window and try the **PageUp** and **PageDown** keys, as well as Home and End. Try them in Save As and Open dialog boxes. At the Desktop, the **Help** key will open the Apple Help file. In some applications, hitting the Help key gives you a question mark—you can then click on any menu item in your application and you will get the Help file about that menu item.

In most browsers on the World Wide Web, you can hit **End** to take you to the bottom of the web page, and **Home** to take you to the top of the web page. PageUp and PageDown might take you up or down a window's length. Experiment.

Edit Keys

⑦ **?** Help

I← Home

→I End

↕ PageUp

↕ PageDown

⊠ Del

(In AppleWorks, the ↕ symbol refers to the Enter key, not the PageUp key.)

The **Forward Delete key (del),** one of the edit keys mentioned above, is a particularly handy key: it deletes the character to its *right* (forward) as you type. This is just the opposite of the Delete key we usually use, which deletes the character to its *left* (backward). Unfortunately, some keyboards (like the ones that comes with iMacs) don't have this useful key. On your **laptop,** press the **fn** key (lower-left, see page 45) and tap **F8** to forward delete.

Forward Delete Key
(del)

Fkeys
F1–F12 or F1–F15

The **Fkeys** run along the top of your keyboard, that row of keys labeled F1, F2, F3, etc. Fkeys are used in many shortcuts, as you can see in the menu to the left.

If you're using an application in Classic (see Chapter 40), you can press F1 to undo your last action; press F2 to cut an item, F3 to copy, and F4 to paste (see pages 210–212 for explanations of undo, cut, copy, and paste). In Classic you can also program the extra keys yourself: use the Keyboard control panel and click the button "Function Keys...." But in Mac OS X, you cannot program the Fkeys.

Keyboard
Repeat Rate

In the Dock, click once on this icon to open System Preferences.

In the System Preferences pane, click once on this icon.

You can control a couple of features on your keyboard through the **Keyboard** system preferences. To get the "pane" shown below, click once on the System Preferences icon (shown to the left) that you'll find in the Dock. Then click once on the Keyboard icon (also shown to the left).

Every key on the Macintosh keyboard will *repeat,* meaning if you hold the key down it will continue typing that character across the page. In the Keyboard pane, shown below, the **Key Repeat Rate** lets you control just how fast that key repeats across the page—drag the marker left or right.

The **Delay Until Repeat** options, either "Off" or between "Long" and "Short," give you control over how long you can hold your finger on a key before it starts to repeat. This is wonderful if you're heavy on the keys—set it for a long delay so even if your fingers plod along on the keys, you won't end up with extra characters all over the page. If you drag over to "Off," the keys will not repeat at all, no matter how long you hold them down.

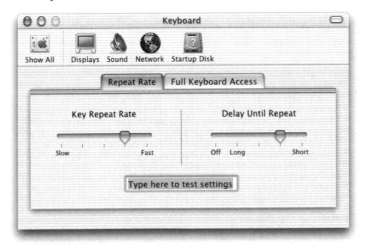

*Use this pane to see how your settings affect your typing—
just type and it will replace the text in "Type here to test settings."*

Full Keyboard Access lets you do a lot of actions with your keyboard so you don't have to pick up the mouse to click buttons, use menus, open applications and menus in the Dock, jump from tab to tab in dialog boxes, and more. This might be a convenience for you, or you might have trouble using a mouse and so it might be a great and necessary tool.

Full Keyboard Access only works in applications that have been created specifically for Mac OS X—it does not work in Classic, nor does it work in applications that open in both OS 9 and OS X.

Open the Keyboard preferences, as explained to the right, and click the "Full Keyboard Access" tab, as shown below.

Full Keyboard Access

In the Dock, click once on this icon to open System Preferences.

In the System Preferences pane, click once on this icon.

Check the box to **turn on full keyboard access.** As it says, you can press Control F1 at any time, whether this pane is open or not, to turn keyboard access on and off.

Once it is turned on, press the Control key plus one of the function keys noted above to focus on a certain part of your screen. **For instance:**

To use the menu bar with the keyboard instead of the mouse, press Control F2. The Apple menu will instantly drop down.

Once the menu bar is thus selected, **use the RightArrow and LeftArrow keys to select menus;** each menu will drop down as you get to it.

When a menu is visible, **use the Up and DownArrow keys to highlight items,** and the **RightArrow** to open a submenu.

When the menu command you want is highlighted, press the **Spacebar.**

To choose nothing, press the **Escape key.**

You can also use Tab to move to the right across the menu bar, and Shift Tab to the left, but who cares since the Arrow keys work just fine.

—continued

The Return or Enter key also works to choose highlighted items, but if there is a throbbing blue button, the Return or Enter key will activate the blue button instead of your selected item. So it's a good idea to get in the habit of using the Spacebar.

You can use the same technique to access the **Dock** and use the arrow keys to select each item in the Dock. **To open an application,** press the Spacebar. **To pop up a Dock menu,** press the UpArrow. **To select an item in the Dock menu,** press the Spacebar.

If an application has a Toolbar, as in Mail or Address Book, you can select the Toolbar and its items. You can select palettes that a program might use.

If you choose to highlight "Any control," you can select every button and edit box in the entire dialog box from the keyboard. That is, as you press the Tab key, each button, edit box, checkbox, or radio button is highlighted in turn, and then you can use the keyboard (as listed below) to act on the selected item.

If you use Keyboard Access regularly, you might discover that it is difficult to type some of the key combinations. For instance, Control F6 really takes two hands. So you can choose to use letter keys instead, such as "Control d" to focus on the Dock. Or choose the "Custom keys" option and select your own keys to use as shortcuts.

This particular access key is not functioning yet, at the time I write this. It's coming soon.

Frankly, I didn't find that this keyboard access feature works consistently and effectively yet, so don't worry if it doesn't seem to work as expected—it's not you. I'm sure it will get better.

Once you focus on the item of your choice, use these keys listed below to highlight and select.

To highlight items:

Highlight the next item in a list, set of tabs, or in a menu: **Arrow keys**

Highlight the next control: **Tab**

Highlight the next control if an edit box is currently selected: **Control Tab**

Highlight the next window in the active application: **Command ~**   (Tilde key, upper-left)

Move sliders and spin buttons*: **Arrow keys**

Highlight a control attached to an edit box**:
Control Arrow keys

Reverse the order of selection: Add the **Shift key** to the Tab or arrow keys you were using

To choose highlighted items:

Select the highlighted item: **Spacebar**

Click the default button (throbbing blue) or perform the default action: **Return** or **Enter**

Cancel a dialog box or close a menu without choosing an item: **Escape**

*Spin buttons are the ones that cycle around, like when moving the hours, minutes, and seconds up and down in the Time pane.

**As in an edit box where you can type in a font size, and next to it is a menu with font size choices.

On most Mac **laptops,** there is a key with the tiny symbol **fn** on the bottom-left, in a different color. You see other keys with tiny symbols or characters also in that color, such as *num lock, clear, home, end, pg up, pg dn* (page up or down), as well as numbers. Also check the Fkeys. If you press the **fn key,** then the keys change their standard function to the symbols or characters in that matching color (the color that matches the **fn**), as described below.

fn Key on Laptops (Function Key)

F5 Num Lock
F7 Insert (used in some applications)
F8 Forward Delete

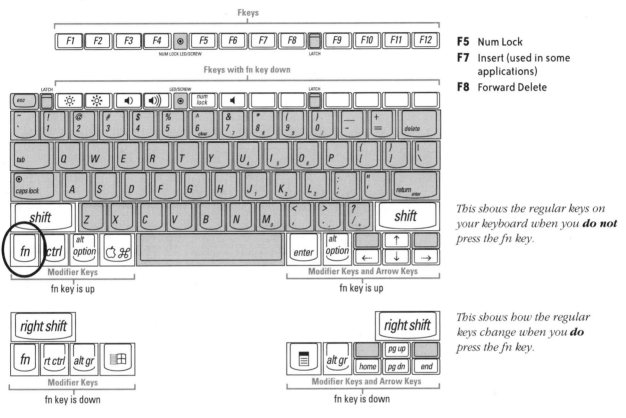

*This shows the regular keys on your keyboard when you do **not** press the fn key.*

*This shows how the regular keys change when you **do** press the fn key.*

Hold down the **fn** key and tap F8 to **forward delete.**

The **arrow keys** on the bottom-right turn into Home, PageUp (pg up), Page-Down (pg dn), and End (see page 41) when you hold down the **fn** key.

The **Control key** becomes the Right Control key (rt ctrl), and the **Shift keys** become Right Shift keys, which are necessary in some games where the right-side keys can have different features from the left-side keys. The **Option keys** become Alt GR keys, and I haven't found anyone who knows what these are.

The **Option, Command,** and **Enter keys** take on the functions of a PC keyboard when you hold down the **fn** key. This is useful if you're running Windows emulation software, such as Insignia SoftWindows or Connectix Virtual PC, that lets your Mac run Windows: The Command key becomes the **Windows key** that brings up the Windows Start menu. The Enter key becomes the **Windows Menu key** that accesses the right-button menus (like the Mac's contextual menus). And the Option key becomes an official **Windows Alt key.**

This icon represents the Windows key.

This icon represents the Windows Menu key.

Numeric Keypad on Laptops

If you look carefully at your laptop keyboard, you'll see tiny numbers and mathematical symbols in a different color on the keys under your right hand (u, i, o, p, etc., as shown below).

If you hold down the **fn** key, this embedded **numeric keypad** becomes active. Use these numbers as you would in any application on any Mac, such as a spreadsheet or the calculator. *You have to keep the fn key down to use the numbers.*

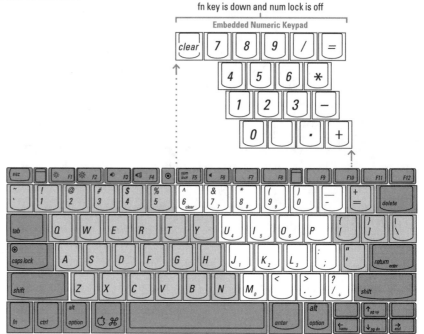

Lock in the numbers

As shown above, you have to hold down the **fn** key as you type numbers. However, you can disable all other keys *except* for the numeric keypad so you won't have to hold down the **fn** key as you type numbers: press **fn** and the **num lock key** (F5), then you can let go of **fn**. To type the alphabetic characters again, press the **fn** key once more to release it.

*Some applications, such as Microsoft Word and Adobe PageMaker, have always utilized the numeric keypad for moving the cursor, and you have to **turn on** num lock if you want to type numbers. On a laptop, these keys can't do both (move the cursor **and** type numbers), so in Word and PageMaker, when the fn key is down and num lock is on, the cursor moves—you don't get the numeric keypad.*

If you need to type with the characters of another language, you can—see the following page. You can also choose a language in which to see the menus, dialog boxes, and even the Apple Help files. Use the International preferences pane, as described below.

To change the language shown in menus and dialog boxes:

1. Click once on the System Preferences icon in the Dock.

2. Click the "International" icon. You'll get the pane shown below.

3. Click the tab "Language," if it's not already visible.

4. In the "Languages" list, drag the language you want to the top of the list—press and drag the name. You'll see a black bar appear as you drag; when that black bar is all the way to the top, let go. The language you want should be the first one in the list.

5. In the lower-left portion of this pane, select the appropriate "script" for your chosen language. On the lower-right, choose the "text behavior" for the chosen language. Quit the System Preferences (press Command Q or use the File menu).

6. If any applications were open, **quit** them (don't just *close* their open windows), then reopen the application to see the new language in that application. To change your entire Mac to the new language, log out (go to the Apple menu, choose "Log Out..."), then log in again.

International Keyboard Layouts

 This is the System Preferences icon in the Dock.

 This is the International icon in the System Preferences.

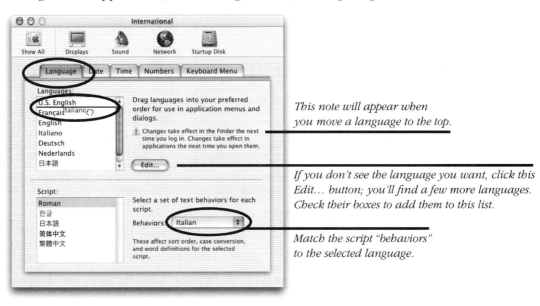

This note will appear when you move a language to the top.

If you don't see the language you want, click this Edit... button; you'll find a few more languages. Check their boxes to add them to this list.

Match the script "behaviors" to the selected language.

—continued

After you log out and log back in again, or after you shut down and/or restart, your Finder menus and dialog boxes will appear in the chosen language. It's amazing.

If you plan to switch your entire computer to another language, also click each of the other tabs in this International preferences pane and choose the same language so your text inputs correctly (see the following two pages).

Notice the new menu item next to "Help," which is called the "Keyboard" menu. For information about this menu and how to input text with the special characters of another language, see the opposite page.

When you log in again, everything will be in the new language. Notice the new Keyboard menu (circled).

As explained on the previous pages, you can enable your Mac to display menus, dialog boxes, and even Help files in another language. But you might also want to *type* using the special characters of another language, whether or not your menus display English.

To change the keyboard layout and the input language:

1. Click once on the System Preferences icon in the Dock, then click the "International" icon. You'll get the pane shown below.

2. Click the tab "Keyboard Menu."

3. Put a checkmark next to each language that you would like to have accessible in the Keyboard menu in the Finder.

*Click the "Options..." button to learn the keyboard shortcuts that will switch you back and forth between different "scripts" (Roman and the other) that you might have chosen in the Language pane, **or** between different languages in the "active" (currently selected) script.*

Also choose whether you want the Mac to automatically switch (synchronize) to another script that's already in text on the page when you start typing in that text.

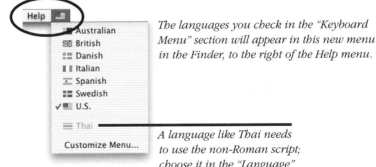

The languages you check in the "Keyboard Menu" section will appear in this new menu in the Finder, to the right of the Help menu.

A language like Thai needs to use the non-Roman script; choose it in the "Language" pane, as shown on page 47.

International Date, Time, and Numbers

There are a number of applications and features on your Mac that automatically format dates, times, and numbers—from the date in your menu bar to your spreadsheet or financial application—according to the language of choice. For instance, in the United States we write the date with the month first, then the day, then the year; but in most other parts of the world, the date is written with the day first, then the month. If you want the date, time, and/or number formatting to use the style of a particular region, use the International preferences pane.

To choose a regional format for dates, times, and/or numbers:

This is the System Preferences icon in the Dock.

This is the International icon in the System Preferences.

1. Click once on the System Preferences icon in the Dock.

2. Click the "International" icon. You'll get the pane shown below.

3. One at a time, click the tabs "Date," Time," and "Numbers." In each pane, choose the "Region" that creates the formatting you want. An example of the formatting is displayed at the bottom of the pane.

   You can also enter your own formatting: just select any existing text in an edit box and type to replace it with the formatting of your choice.

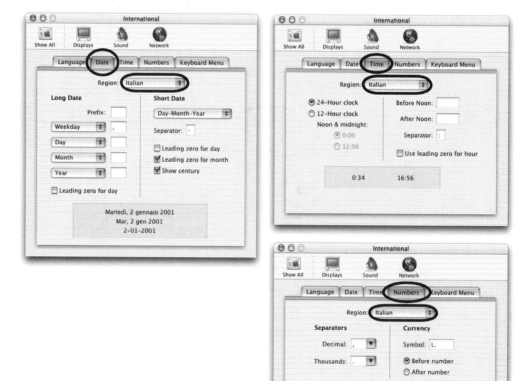

In Mac OS X, the character encoding technology has changed. In all previous versions, the Macintosh operating system used ASCII, an international standard for Roman characters, that allows a maximum of 256 characters. Mac OS X uses something called Unicode, which allows over 65,000 characters, which means the Mac can now set type in alphabets such as Japanese, Arabic, or Chinese. But in Mac OS X applications that use Unicode, such as TextEdit, fonts like **Zapf Dingbats** and **Webdings** do not appear correctly. In fact, they don't appear at all. If you want to type with a dingbat font, you'll have to go through the steps described below.

To type with a dingbat font or symbol font:

1. Click once on the System Preferences icon in the Dock.

2. Click the "International" icon. You'll get the pane shown below.

3. Click the tab "Keyboard Menu," as circled below.

4. Put a checkmark next to "Dingbats" and "Symbol" (scroll down to find "Symbol"). Close the pane.

5. In your menu at the Finder, you now have a new item, a little flag, to the right of the Help menu. This is the Keyboard menu. Press on it and you'll see options for Dingbats and Symbol.

6. When you want to type in one of these fonts, Webdings, for instance, go to the Keyboard menu and choose "Dingbats" (for the Symbol font, of course, choose "Symbol"). Then go back to your application and type the characters you need.

7. When you are finished typing the special characters in the dingbat or symbol font, go back to the Keyboard menu and choose the language you need (usually "U.S.").

Using Zapf Dingbats, Webdings, or Symbol

Only read this if you've discovered a problem typing with these fonts!

Zapf Dingbats:

Webdings:

Symbol:

$$\int 6 \sum \Theta \eta \xi \mu \rho \delta \Omega \approx$$
$$\sqrt{} \ \textcircled{} \in \cap \cup \Xi \Psi \zeta \theta \ni$$
$$\cong \aleph \vartheta \wp \Im \in \gamma \infty \cup \tau$$

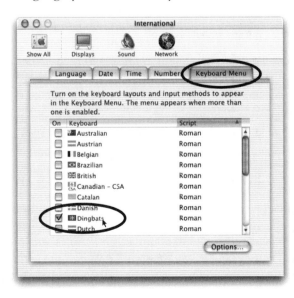

This is the Keyboard menu.

✱✝✰✿ ✰✝ ✿...▼ ✱✰✰✿✿.rtf

Don't forget to switch back to U.S. (English) before you save the file or its name will appear in dingbats!

Choose the Dingbats and Symbol keyboards in this dialog box. Even if you use them rarely, it won't hurt anything to have them available at all times.

1. If you want to select another edit box in this dialog box, ("Find:" is currently selected), which key would move the selection from box to box?

○ ○ ○	Find
Find:	John
Replace with:	

Replace All Scope   Find Options
◉ Entire File   ○ Selection   ☑ Ignore Case

[Replace All]   [Replace]   [Replace & Find]   [Previous]   [Next]

2. If you want to activate the "Next" button in the dialog box above, but don't want to pick up the mouse, which key would you press?

3. Which keys would you press to:

Window	
Cascade	⇧⌘J
Tile	▶
Close All	⌥⌘W
Toolbars	▶
Hide Menu Bar	**F9**
Articles	
✓ Bookmarks	**F5**
Thumbnails	**F4**
✓ ReadMe.pdf	

Tile ▶   Horizontally ⇧⌘K   Vertically ⇧⌘L

Document	
First Page	⇧⌘↕
Previous Page	←
Next Page	→
Last Page	⇧⌘↕
Go To Page...	⌘N
Go To Previous View	⌘←
Go To Next View	⌘→
Go To Next Document	⇧⌘→

Hide the menu bar? _____

View the bookmarks folder? _____

Close all the open windows? _____

_____

Tile the open windows vertically? _____

Go to the first page in the file? _____

Go to a previous view of this window? _____

4. Write the letter identifying the key with its symbol:

Escape key _____	a) ⭥	PageUp key _____	l) ⌥
Option key _____	b) ⭡	PageDown key _____	m) ⇧
Control key _____	c) esc	LeftArrow key _____	n) ⌫
Command (Apple) key _____	d) ~	RightArrow key _____	o) ⭣
Tilde key _____	e) →	UpArrow key _____	p) /
Asterisk, or Star _____	f) ⌘	DownArrow key _____	q) ∧
Shift key _____	g) ⊢	Home key _____	r) →⊣
Forward slash _____	h) ⭥	End key _____	s) ⋯→
Backslash _____	i) ⌫	Forward Delete key _____	t) *
Tab key _____	j) \	Enter key _____	u) ←⋯
Delete key _____	k) ⇱	Spacebar key _____	v) ↵

Answers are on page 750.

Menus and Shortcuts 5

Whenever you are at the Finder level of your Macintosh or whenever you're in any program on the Mac, you'll see a **menu bar** across the top of the screen, as shown below. Also shown below is a **drop-down menu:** when you click on a word in the menu bar, a list of menu commands drops down. In addition to these drop-down menus, on the Mac you'll also find pop-up menus, contextual menus, and others. This chapter discusses all the various sorts of menus, the commands, and how to use them.

You'll see a lot of typical "dialog boxes" in this chapter from a variety of applications. Don't worry that you haven't seen that same dialog box yet— the Mac is amazingly consistent and if you don't see that exact dialog box, you will run into something similar.

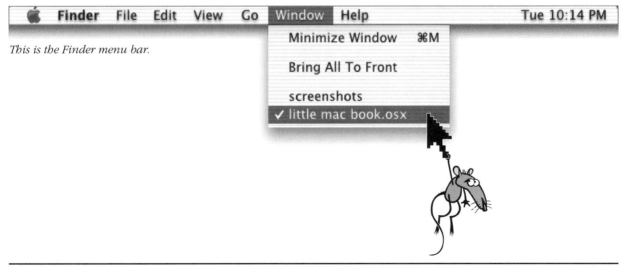

🍎 **Finder** File Edit View Go Window Help	Tue 10:14 PM

This is the Finder menu bar.

> Minimize Window ⌘M
>
> Bring All To Front
>
> screenshots
>
> ✓ little mac book.osx

Choosing a Menu Command

To choose a command from a menu, click once on any of the choices along the menu bar. The menu will pop open for you. As you move your mouse down the list of commands, the different choices *highlight,* or become *selected,* as you pass over them. When the one you want is highlighted, click on it.

The command "Clean Up" is highlighted—click on it to activate it.

Changing your mind

If you change your mind halfway through the menu list and don't want to choose anything, just move the pointer off of the list, then click. If you were dragging the pointer down the list with the mouse button down, simply move off of the menu and let go of the mouse button. The menu will disappear and nothing will be chosen.

Practice: Position the pointer over any word in the menu bar, then click on that word. Run the pointer down the list and watch the various commands highlight.

Don't click anything yet unless you know what it will do!

In some programs the menu itself contains a **pop-out menu** where you not only slide *down,* but also *out to the side,* usually in the direction of the arrow. These are also known as **hierarchical menus,** or **h-menus.**

Pop-Out and Pop-Up menus

This is an example of a hierarchical menu.

You will also find **pop-up menus** where you press on an item toward the bottom of the screen and the list pops upward.

This is an example of a pop-up menu. The Dock uses pop-up menus.

Practice: Go to the Apple menu, as shown above, and position the pointer over any menu item that has an arrow to its left. Practive moving your mouse over to the right and sliding down the hierarchical list — it can be tricky!

Don't click on any command yet unless it has an ellipsis in the menu (see page 58), which means you will get a dialog box that you can cancel out of.

Contextual Menus

The Finder has **contextual menus:** hold down the *Control* key (not the Command/Apple key), click anywhere, and a menu pops up. These are called "contextual" menus because the context of the menu varies depending on what you click upon: an application icon, a folder icon, a document icon, a disk icon, a blank spot inside a window, a blank spot on the Desktop, etc. What you see in these menus might also change as time goes by and more features are added.

Contextual menus in applications

Many applications use contextual menus. Try this in your favorite program: hold down the Control key and click on the window in your program, or on an object, the text, any buttons in the toolbar, etc., and see what happens.

In some programs, such as Netscape Communicator or OmniWeb (web browsers), you don't even need to hold down the Control key—just press. **Try it:** In a blank area on a web page in Netscape, press and *hold* the mouse button down and you'll get a contextual menu to go back and forward. Press on a graphic and you'll get choices to save or copy the graphic. Press (don't click) on a link and you can open that link in a new window (and you'll still have the current page visible on your Desktop).

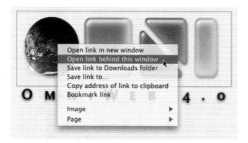

This graphic on a web page is both an image and a web page link, so the contextual menu has many options, including h-menus.

| Back |
| Forward |
| Stop Loading |
| Send Page... |
| Page Source |
| Page Info |

Press on any blank spot on any web page while in Netscape and you'll get this useful contextual menu.

It was a
barbarous destiny
ahead

| Cut |
| Copy |
| Paste |
| Font ▶ |
| Size ▶ |
| Find/Change... |
| Check Spelling... |
| Text Frame Options... |
| Insert Special Character ▶ |
| Insert White Space ▶ |
| Insert Break Character ▶ |
| Fill with Placeholder Text |
| Change Case ▶ UPPERCASE |
| Show Hidden Characters lowercase |
| Title Case |
| Sentence case. |

This is an example of a contextual menu within an application (Adobe InDesign), using Control-click. These are the options I have for the selected text.

Two-button mouse

If you have a **two-button mouse,** you can use the right-hand button to open contextual menus, without holding down the Control key!

In a list of menu commands, some **commands** are in **black** letters and some commands are in **gray.** When a command is gray, it means *that particular command is not available at that moment.*

The most common reason a command is unavailable is that you did not *select* something before you went to the menu. For instance, you cannot choose "Open" from the File menu until you select a disk or file as the item to be opened. You cannot "Copy" text unless you first select the text you want to copy. (To select *text,* press-and-drag over it; to select an *object,* click *once* on it.)

Gray vs. Black Commands

Edit	
Undo Typing	⌘Z
Redo	⇧⌘Z
Cut	⌘X
Copy	⌘C
Paste	⌘V
Delete	
Select All	⌘A
Find	▶
Spelling	▶

Some commands are gray; some are black. In this example, "Cut" and "Copy" are gray because there is no text selected to cut or copy. If nothing is selected, the Mac has no idea what you want to cut or copy, and the computer certainly can't make that decision on its own.

One important rule on the Mac is this: Select first, then do it to it.

Practice: Click on a blank area on the Desktop so nothing is selected, not even a folder or window; then click on the View menu and notice how many items are gray. Now click on an open window and take another look at the View menu.

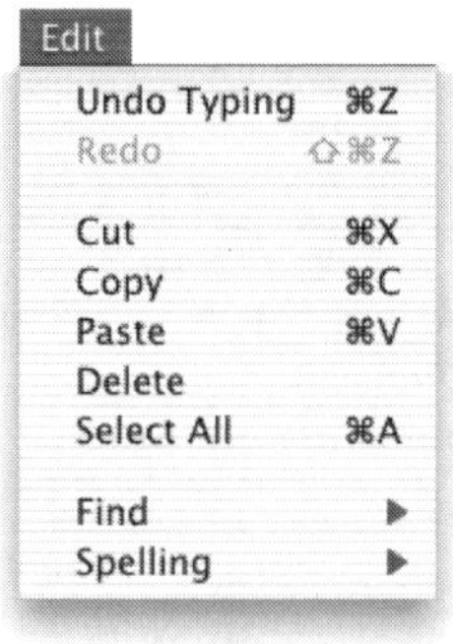

Edit	
Undo Typing	⌘Z
Redo	⇧⌘Z
Cut	⌘X
Copy	⌘C
Paste	⌘V
Delete	
Select All	⌘A
Find	▶
Spelling	▶

*This is the same menu as shown above, but this time I selected some text on the word processing page before I went to the menu. Now I am able to cut or copy the **selected** text.*

Practice: Hold down the Control key and click on a folder, a blank spot in a window, a disk icon, a document, or an application.

To put away a contextual menu, just click anywhere outside the menu.

Ellipses in the Menus

Often you will see an **ellipsis** (the three dots, **...**) after a menu command such as "Open**...**" or "Save As**...**." The ellipsis indicates that you will get a **dialog box,** as shown below, when you choose that command. If there is no ellipsis, that command will activate as soon as you select it.

There are different varieties of dialog boxes, such as alert boxes, message boxes, or edit boxes, plus dialog "sheets" that drop down from the title bar, but basically they all are meant to communicate with you before they activate a command.

Dialog boxes almost always give you an option to **Cancel,** so it is quite safe to explore menu commands that have ellipses: Just choose a command that is followed by an ellipsis, check out the dialog box, then click Cancel. Even if you click around on buttons or type in the dialog box, clicking the Cancel button will make sure none of your changes are put into effect.

Practice: Find several menu items that are followed by ellipses and select them. Go ahead and click buttons in the dialog box, pull down menus, type values, etc., but make sure to click the Cancel button to close the box.

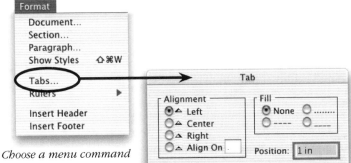

Choose a menu command with an ellipsis and take a look at the dialog box.

There is almost always a Cancel button which will cancel all of your actions and put the dialog box away.

You can use the keyboard shortcut (as explained on the opposite page) ***Command Period*** *to cancel most dialog boxes instead of clicking on the Cancel button, even if there is no Cancel button.*

To the right of the commands in the menus you often see a little code, such as ⌘ **N** (pronounced "Command N" or sometimes "Apple N"). This is a **keyboard shortcut** you can use *instead* of using the menu. You memorize the shortcut, then the next time you need that command you use the shortcut *instead* of picking up your mouse and pulling down the menu.

File	
New Finder Window	⌘N
New Folder	⇧⌘N
Open	⌘O
Close Window	⌘W
Duplicate	⌘D
Make Alias	⌘L
Show Original	⌘R
Add To Favorites	⌘T
Move To Trash	⌘⌫
Eject	⌘E
Find...	⌘F

Often the keyboard shortcut will include other symbols representing other keys; **see Chapter 4 for explanations of every symbol and special key on your keyboard.**

A **modifier key** is a key that doesn't do anything when you press it all by itself. For instance, when you press Shift, nothing happens; when you press the Command key, nothing happens. A modifier key makes *other* keys perform special functions. For instance, when you hold down the Shift key then type the number "8," you get an asterisk (∗).

So to use a keyboard shortcut *instead* of the menu command, hold down the **modifier key** or **keys** you saw in the menu. While you hold down this key or keys, type the **letter key** you also saw in the menu—just *tap* the letter, *don't hold it down!* The computer reacts just as if you had chosen that command from the menu. For instance, if you click once on a file to select it and then press ⌘**O,** the selected file will open just as if you had chosen that command from the File menu with the mouse. Thoughtfully, many of the keyboard shortcuts are alliterative: ⌘ **O** **o**pens files; ⌘ **P** **p**rints; ⌘ **D** **d**uplicates a selected file; ⌘ **W** closes **w**indows; etc.

You'll often see keyboard shortcuts spelled out with a hyphen, a plus sign, or perhaps a comma between the keys. *Don't type the hyphen, plus sign, or comma!* Just press the keys! For instance, if you see a shortcut written as "Command + Shift + B," ignore the plus signs—just hold down the Command and Shift keys, then tap the letter B.

How to use a keyboard shortcut

Practice: In the File menu in the Finder, you notice that Command W is the shortcut to close windows. So make sure there is a window open on your Desktop, then hold down the Command key and tap the letter W. The window will close. You're on your way to becoming a Power User.

Other Menus and their Visual Clues

You'll find other menus in all kinds of odd places. Well, they won't seem so odd once you become accustomed to the **visual clues** that indicate a menu is hiding. In the dialog box below, can you see the menus?

Double arrows

Double arrows are one visual clue that a dialog box contains a menu. Whenever you see that double arrow, as shown below, you can click anywhere in that horizontal bar and a menu will pop up or down.

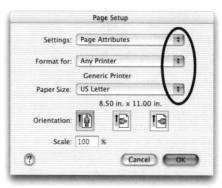

Do you see the three menus in this dialog box? You recognize them by the double arrows. Click on any one of these and a menu will pop up or down.

Watch for shadows

In the example below, the box next to "Field Type" has a little **shadow** behind it, as well as an arrow. Even without the arrow, that little shadow is your **visual clue** that if you press or click on the word, you will get a pop-up menu, as shown in another example further below. Look for that shadow!

See this little shadow behind the box? That indicates a menu.

Also, what do you think will happen if you click the "Options…" button?

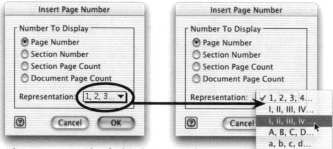

This is an example of what happens when you press on a menu in a dialog box.

A **single** downward-pointing **arrow** or **triangle** does *not* indicate a menu. A triangle typically expands a dialog box to present more information, as shown below. The fact that this information is hidden indicates that it is not necessarily critical at all times—you only pop open that information when you need it. As you are learning to use your Mac, click that arrow or triangle whenever you see it so you become familiar with the options, whether you use them or not.

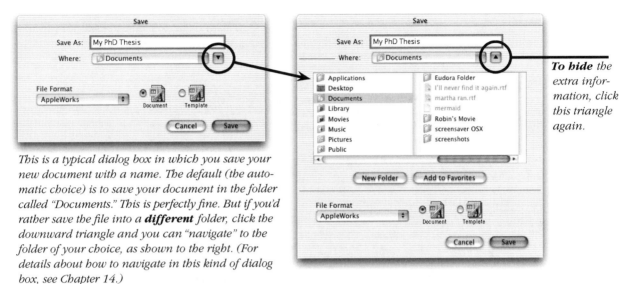

*This is a typical dialog box in which you save your new document with a name. The default (the automatic choice) is to save your document in the folder called "Documents." This is perfectly fine. But if you'd rather save the file into a **different** folder, click the downward triangle and you can "navigate" to the folder of your choice, as shown to the right. (For details about how to navigate in this kind of dialog box, see Chapter 14.)*

To hide *the extra information, click this triangle again.*

Edit boxes

The boxes that do *not* have shadows behind them (as shown in the dialog box below) are called **edit boxes.** You can type into these edit boxes to change the specifications.

*These are called **edit boxes.** Type in them to change the values. There is no shadow behind them, which means they are not menus. How many edit boxes do you see here? How many menus?*

File

New	▶
Open...	⌘O
Close	⌘W
Save	⌘S
Save As...	⇧⌘S
Revert	
Properties...	
Insert...	
Show Clippings	⌘2
Macros	▶
Mail Merge...	
Page Setup...	
Print...	⌘P
Open Recent	▶
Quit	⌘Q

Watch for those visual clues!

1. Which menu command is selected?

2. How many of these commands have h-menus (hierarchical menus that pop-out to the side)?

3. How many of these commands will give you a dialog box when you choose them?

4. How many of these commands are not available at the moment?

5. How many of these commands have keyboard shortcuts?

6. What is the keyboard shortcut you could use to activate the selected command instead of choosing it from the menu?

7. If you were to press Command P, what would happen?

8. How many menus are there inside the dialog box shown to the left?

More Search Options

Custom ▢

Find items whose:

☑ file name   contains ▢ [   ]
☑ content includes [   ]
☑ date created   is ▢   8/26/01 ▢
☑ date modified   is ▢   8/26/01 ▢
☑ size   is less than ▢ [   ] KB
☑ kind   is ▢   alias ▢

▼ Advanced Options

(Delete...) (Save As...)   (Cancel) (OK)

9. How many edit boxes are there inside this dialog box?

10. What keyboard shortcut could you press to Cancel this dialog box?

Answers on page 750.

How to Use the Windows

A **window** is a basic, fundamental element of the Macintosh.

> When you open any **folder** or **disk,** including your hard disk, the Mac displays the contents of the folder in a **Finder** window.

> When you open any **application,** such as your word processor, database, or spreadsheet, the Mac gives you a window in which to type your **document,** work with your database, or create your spreadsheet.

Although they are very similar, on the following page is a visual explanation of the main differences between these two types of windows. The major part of this chapter is devoted to the features you will find in the windows on the **Desktop,** the **Finder** windows that open to display the contents of **folders** and **disks** (not document windows). Once you know how to maneuver your way through the Finder windows, the document windows will make perfect sense to you. And that's most of what you need to know on the Mac.

Finder Windows vs. Document Windows

Below you see two different windows. On the top is a **Finder** window, sometimes called a Desktop window, the kind you'll see when you open a folder or disk on the Desktop. A **document** window is the kind you'll see when you are using most applications, or programs, in which you create your work. You'll notice both sorts of windows have a number of similar features, but the Finder windows are more complex and confusing. I'll first explain the details of the Finder window, and later in this chapter you'll see how those features are also built into document windows.

*When a Finder window is open and **active** (in **front** of any other windows), this menu item is always "Finder."*

*You can tell this is a **Finder window** because in the menu bar across the top of the monitor, just to the right of the apple, is the word "Finder." The Finder is the software that runs the Desktop, so all of the windows on the Desktop are considered **Finder windows.** Don't let that confuse you—just think of the Desktop and the Finder as the same thing, for all practical purposes.*

The items inside a Finder window might be shown as icons, as a list, or in columns.

*This is the name, or **title,** of the Finder window that is open. This particular window is called "robin" because it is my "Home" folder that contains my personal files.*

Under the title of the window is the Toolbar, which I explain at length on the following pages.

This area at the top of the window is the Toolbar.

This is the name of the application.

*You can tell this is a **document window** because in the menu bar across the top of the monitor, just to the right of the apple, is the name of the application in which this document is being created. TextEdit is a word processing application on your Mac (see Chapter 13 for tips on how to use it).*

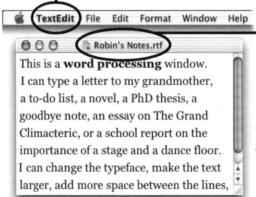

*This is the name, or **title,** of the document I have created in this application. Every document you create will be in its own window.*

You can see that the biggest difference between this window and the one above is that there is no "Toolbar" across the top of this window.

Finder windows are those windows that open to display the contents of folders or disks, including your hard disk.

The Macintosh allows you a great deal of control over the look and the feel of your computer and the options available so you can arrange your work and your working environment in a way that is most effective for *you*. The **Finder windows** are a good example of the control you have on the Mac—you can choose to display what's in your window in a variety of ways, all appropriate for different purposes or styles; you can organize the windows any way you like; and you can customize the window Toolbar for your convenience. You can even change the color or add a picture to the background of a window, which might help you organize certain projects or recognize important folders.

Finder Windows

There are so many options in OS X that it can be very confusing, so you might want to read through this entire section to get an overview of how things work, spend some time with the windows, then go back through it again and decide how to customize your windows so they work best for you.

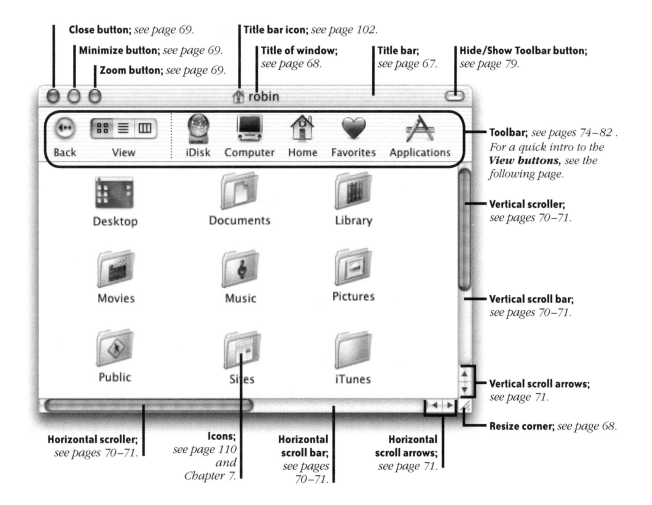

Close button; *see page 69.*

Minimize button; *see page 69.*

Zoom button; *see page 69.*

Title bar icon; *see page 102.*

Title of window; *see page 68.*

Title bar; *see page 67.*

Hide/Show Toolbar button; *see page 79.*

Back　View　iDisk　Computer　Home　Favorites　Applications

Desktop　Documents　Library

Movies　Music　Pictures

Public　Sites　iTunes

Toolbar; *see pages 74–82. For a quick intro to the* **View buttons,** *see the following page.*

Vertical scroller; *see pages 70–71.*

Vertical scroll bar; *see pages 70–71.*

Vertical scroll arrows; *see page 71.*

Resize corner; *see page 68.*

Horizontal scroller; *see pages 70–71.*

Icons; *see page 110 and Chapter 7.*

Horizontal scroll bar; *see pages 70–71.*

Horizontal scroll arrows; *see page 71.*

Three Views of the Same Contents

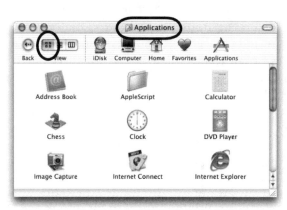

These are the View buttons you see in the Toolbar—click one to change the view of the active window.

You can also change the view of the active window by using the "View" menu at the Desktop.

You can change how you **view the contents** of a Finder window. Some people like to see their window's contents as icons, some prefer to view a list of names, while others prefer columns showing the contents of multiple folders at once. Below you see the same window contents in three different views. We're going to look at each of these views in detail later; for now, I just want you to know what they are and how to change them if you like.

*This is the contents of the Applications folder, shown in **Icon View.***

*Double-click any folder icon to see the contents of that folder (the new contents will **replace** what you see in this window now).*

See pages 83–87 for details of Icon View.

Practice: In the Dock, single-click the "Finder" icon (shown below) to open a Finder window. In the window, click the View buttons one at a time to see how the contents appear in each of the different views.

Finder icon

*This is the contents of the Applications folder, shown in **List View.***

Single-click on the triangle pointing to a folder to display a sub-list of what is contained in that folder.

Or double-click a folder icon to display its contents in this window.

See pages 88–91 for details of List View.

Choose the **Icon View** and do the short Practice exercises on the following five pages.

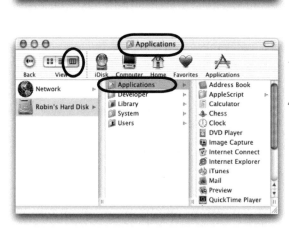

*This is the contents of the Applications folder, shown in **Column View.***

*Can you see that "Applications" has the darkest highlight? That's a **visual clue** that the contents in the column to the right belong to the highlighted Applications folder. The title in the title bar tells us the same thing.*

See pages 92–94 for details of Column View.

The **title bar** is the striped bar across the top of a window in which, logically, the title appears. This title is the name of the disk, folder, or document you have opened. The title bar also holds the little colored buttons.

Title Bar

Every window has a title bar.

To move any window around the screen, position the pointer in the title bar of the window, then press-and-drag. Just let go of the mouse button when you have the window placed where you want.

Moving the window

If you have more than one window open, only one will have the little round buttons *in color* in its title bar. The colored buttons are a **visual clue** that this window is the **active window.** If windows are overlapping, the active window is the one that is in front.

The **active window** is the only window that the commands from the keyboard or the menu will affect. For instance, if you go to the File menu and choose "New Folder," the new folder will appear in the *active* window. If you go to the File menu and choose "Close," it will close the *active* window. It's very important to be conscious of which window is active!

To make a window active, simply click on any visible part of it; this will also bring that window to the front of any others. If you know a window is open somewhere but you can see it, go to the Window menu and choose its name (see page 95).

The active window

Practice: Try **moving** any window around the screen — just press in the title bar and drag.

The next time you find more than one window open on the screen, notice which one is **active.** Click on a window that is not active and watch its title bar change.

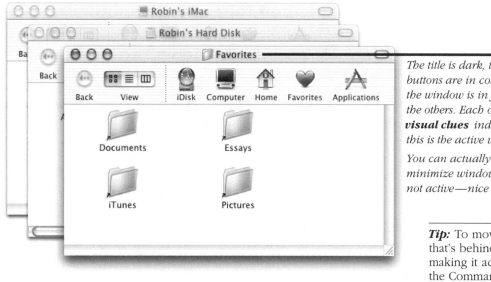

*The title is dark, the buttons are in color, and the window is in front of the others. Each of these **visual clues** indicates that this is the active window.*

You can actually close or minimize windows that are not active—nice trick.

Tip: To move a window that's behind others *without* making it active, hold down the Command key while you press-and-drag the title bar. Try it.

The path in the title bar

The title bar can always tell you where a particular folder is stored. The list that you see dropping down from the title bar below is called the **path** to the document.

To see the "path" to where a folder is stored, hold the Command key down and click on the title bar; a menu will appear. You can slide the mouse down the menu and choose any item to open that item's Finder window. (Don't worry if you don't quite understand what a path is and what it's telling you—you might never need to know this information!)

Practice: This technique works in document windows and Finder windows. So try it on any window that is open: Hold down the Command key (not the Control key), and while the key is down, click on the name in the title bar.

You'll learn more about paths, if you care to, in Chapter 14.

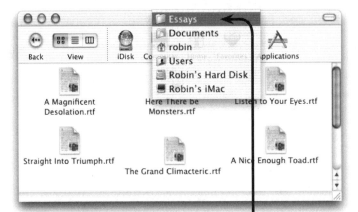

So this path tells me this folder named "Essays" is stored in a folder called "Documents," which is in the Home for "robin," which is in the folder called "Users," which is on the hard disk named "Robin's Hard Disk," which is on the computer named "Robin's iMac."

*Notice the tiny icons to the left of the path names are **visual clues**.*

Resize Corner

The bottom-right corner is the **Resize corner.** Press-and-drag in that box to manually make the window larger or smaller (as opposed to clicking the green zoom button, as described on the following page). This is useful when you have several windows open and you want to resize and rearrange them so they all fit on your screen without overlapping. Or you might want to resize a window smaller or larger than the zoom button will automatically make it.

Practice: Open any window. Press in the lower-right corner and drag in any direction.

This is the Resize corner to manually resize any window.

Window Buttons

In the upper-left corner of each window are **three little buttons: red, yellow, and green.** These are in color in the *active* window and gray in all other windows behind that one (although when your mouse brushes over the buttons in any other window, they burst into color and you can click them without making that window active).

From left to right, the buttons are red, yellow, and green.

When the pointer is positioned near the buttons, tiny symbols appear.

▾ Click in the **red** button to **close** the window. This puts it away, back into the folder or disk it came from.

Or press Command W.

▾ Click the **yellow** button to **minimize** the window, which sends the window down into the Dock, as shown below.

Or double-click in the title bar.

Or press Command M.

This is the minimize button.

When a window is minimized, it floats down into the Dock as an icon, out of the way until you need it again. When you want it back, simply click once on its icon. See Chapter 8 for details about using the Dock.

If you have several windows in the Dock, position your mouse over one (don't click) and that window's name will appear above the Dock.

▾ Click the **green** button to **zoom** the window large enough to see everything, or to zoom it smaller. How large or small the window becomes depends on what is in the window and how large or small it was before you clicked the button.

Practice: If you don't have a window open, click once on the Finder icon in the Dock to open one. Use the **red** button to **close** the window.

Open a window, then use the **yellow** button to **minimize** it. To open the minimized window again, click once on its icon in the Dock.

Open a window, then use the **green** button to **resize** it.

Useless Tip: To minimize an open window in **slow motion,** hold down the Shift key when you click on the yellow button.

Tips: To **close all** open windows in the active application, hold down the Option key and click the red button. You will be asked to save any unsaved documents.

To **minimize all** open windows in the active application, hold down the Option key and click the yellow button.

Scroll Bars and Scrollers

Along the right and bottom edges of the window are the **scroll bars.** The scroll bars allow you to view everything in the document, even if everything cannot all fit on the screen at once or if the window is sized too small.

Scroll bars are huge **visual clues.** When a **blue scroller** appears **in the scroll bar,** *that's a visual clue that there is more information in the window that you can't see.* In fact, how big the scroller is and how much space is above and below the scroller tells you exactly how much you can't see.

You see a scroller in the vertical scroll bar on the right side of the window, which tells you there are more items in this window that you can't see at the moment.

In this example, there is no horizontal scroll bar at all, which tells you there is nothing more in the folder in the horizontal direction than what you can already see.

If there is **no scroll bar** at all or if there are no "scrollers" or "arrows" in the scroll bar area (as you can see, above, on the bottom edge), that tells you there is nothing more in that direction—you are viewing everything there is.

In the example below, however, you see scroll bars and scrollers on *both* edges, so you know there are items or information that you can't see in both directions. You can also tell, in the example below, by the proportions of the scrollers in the lengths of the bars, that you're not missing much.

*These scrollers **almost** fill each of the scroll bars, which is your **visual clue** that **almost** everything is visible in the window.*

Use the scrollers to make the other items in the window visible. **Press-and-drag a scroller** to move it to any position on the scroll bar, let go, and the window will immediately *jump* to that particular place rather than slide past everything. This is very handy inside a window with hundreds of items where scrolling with the arrows (described below) would take a while. Instead of holding the mouse button down on an arrow, just drag the scroller all the way to the bottom.

Press-and-drag the scroller

There's yet another way to use the scroll bars: simply **click** the pointer in any *gray* area of the bar, and the window will move up, down, or across. It will jump you right to that position in the window (say, in the middle of the window, vertically) if you click in the middle of the vertical scroll bar.

Click in the scroll bar

If you want to jump from one section of the window to the next, you can use the PageUp or PageDown keys. Depending on your keyboard, these keys might be in the small section of "edit keys" to the left of the numeric keypad, or they might be tiny little keys directly above the numeric keypad (see Chapter 4 if you can't find them). Experiment with these keys. Also try them on web pages or in page layout applications.

Use PageUp and PageDown

("pg up" and "pg dn" on some keyboards)

When a scroll bar has a scroller, it also has two **scroll arrows.** These arrows might be at either end of the scroll bars, or they might both be at one end, depending on what is chosen in the General preferences (shown on the following page). When you see scroll arrows, *press* on one arrrow to make the contents of the window glide past, like the scenery outside a train window. If you've never used scroll arrows before, it might seem like things are gliding past in the opposite direction you expect, but you'll soon get accustomed to it and you'll instinctively learn which arrow to press to slide the contents in the direction you want.

Scroll Arrows

This window has no scrollers or arrows at all. What does that tell you? That you are seeing everything there is to see in this window.

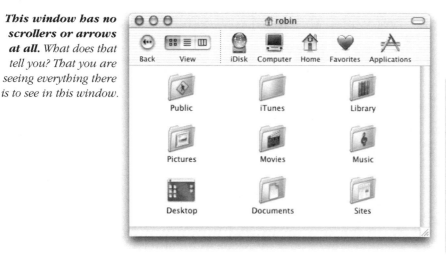

Practice: Open a window. Click once on the Applications icon in the Toolbar. Use the techniques on these two pages to see all of the contents in the window.

If there are no blue scrollers in a window that you want to practice on, use the Resize corner (as explained on page 68) to make the window smaller so the scrollers show up.

Window Scroll Preferences

System Preferences   *General*

As mentioned on the previous page, you can choose to have one scroll arrow at either end of the scroll bars, or set them together at one end of the scroll bar (which allows you to scroll through a window in either direction without having to move your mouse to the other end of the scroll bar).

You can also choose what you want to happen when you click in the gray area of a scroll bar, as shown below.

To change the scroll arrow and scroll click options:

1. In the Dock, click on the "System Preferences" icon (as shown above-left).

2. When the System Preferences window opens, find the icon named "General" (also shown above-left), and single-click on it. You'll get the "preferences pane" shown below.

3. Find the options circled below. Click to make your choices.

4. Quit the System Preferences: press Command Q.

Tip: Once you become accustomed to what will happen when you click in the scroll bar, you can try this trick. Hold down the Option key and click in the scroll bar—it will do the opposite of what you have selected in these preferences.

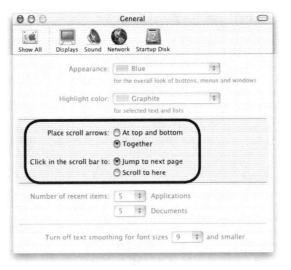

If you like, you can add a **status bar** to all your windows that tells you how **Status Bar**
many items are in an open window. The bar also tells you how much disk
space is available, how your icons are arranged, as well as the sharing status
(for more information on sharing, see Chapter 35).

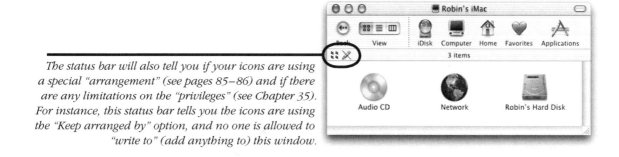

*This is the **status bar**. As you can
see, it says there are nine items in this
window. Since you can see six of them,
you instantly know exactly how many
are not visible at the moment.*

*It also tells you how much empty space
you have left on this hard disk.*

*The status bar will also tell you if your icons are using
a special "arrangement" (see pages 85–86) and if there
are any limitations on the "privileges" (see Chapter 35).
For instance, this status bar tells you the icons are using
the "Keep arranged by" option, and no one is allowed to
"write to" (add anything to) this window.*

To add the status bar to all windows in all views:

1. Open any Finder window.

2. From the "View" menu, choose "Show Status Bar."

   When you want **to get rid of the status bar,** open any Finder window,
   go to the View menu, then choose "Hide Status Bar."

The Toolbar The Toolbar is an important and useful feature of Finder windows. Below and on the following pages you see what each Toolbar icon represents (each icon is a button; click *once*). On pages 80–81, learn how to customize the Toolbar to help you work more efficiently.

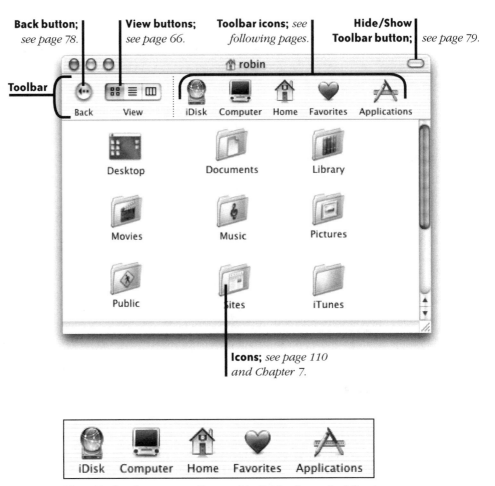

These Toolbar buttons are discussed individually on the following pages.

iDisk: If you have signed up for an iTools account (see Chapter 33), you will see an iDisk icon in your Toolbar. Don't worry if you don't see it—if you want an iTools account after reading about it, you can always sign up later. iDisk provides you with hard disk space on a special computer at Apple called a "server." You can put digital photographs, documents, movies, and more into this hard disk space (you'll "upload" the files), then tell your family and friends your iDisk password and they can go get the photos or movies or whatever and copy them ("download" them) to their own computer. This is often easier and faster than trying to send the same files as email attachments. See **Chapter 33** for all the details about iDisk.

The iDisk icon in the Toolbar

*This is the web page on Apple's site where **other iTools members** can go to your Public folder on your iDisk; see Chapter 37.*

*You can also share files, using Apple's HomePage, with people **who are not iTools members** or who do not use a Macintosh; see Chapter 37.*

Practice: If you have a broadband connection (always on) and you click the iDisk icon, your Mac will open your browser and take you to Apple's web site and your iDisk.

If you use a telephone modem to dial up to the Internet, understand that when you click on this icon, your Mac will try to connect to the Internet and take you to the iDisk web site.

If you like, go there and poke around, or read Chapter 33 first.

The Computer icon in the Toolbar

Computer

Computer: This window displays the icons of your hard disk and any other disks that are in your computer, as shown below. Any disk icons in this window will also appear on your Desktop.

Every time you click the Finder icon in the Dock, the window will open or change to display this Computer level. If you would rather it always open to your Home folder, see page 96.

This is what you named your computer when you first started it up. To change this name, see page 658.

Robin's iMac

| Back | View | iDisk | Computer | Home | Favorites | Applications |

Network

Robin's Hard Disk

Robin's Computer

| Back | View | Computer | Home | Favorites | Applications |

Mac OS X   Robin's Stuff   Robin's Hard Disk

Network   robin

Audio CD   Book Projects

Your "Computer" window will always show at least these two icons.

The "Network" icon gives you access to any files or applications that are available over a corporate network, if you're on one.

The hard disk icon is labeled with whatever you named your hard disk (see page 115 if you want to rename it).

To see what is stored on your hard disk, double-click the hard disk icon (not the "Computer" icon).

This is the same window, but on a different computer. You see three hard disk icons here because I have "partitioned" my main hard disk into three separate sections, and the computer sees each section as an individual hard disk (see Chapter 39 about partitions and how to set them up).

The network icon called "robin" represents another computer that I am sharing files with over the network in my home office (see Chapter 36).

The icon that looks like a CD is a music CD that I'm listening to (see Chapter 26).

The icon called "Book Projects" represents a removable Zip disk that is in the Zip drive (if you have a floppy disk drive, its icon looks just like the Zip drive icon).

To see the files that each of these disks contains, double-click each icon. When you double-click, the contents of that disk you double-clicked will replace the contents you currently see in the window. If you want to come back to the "Computer" window, either single-click on the Computer icon again, or single-click the "Back" button on the left side of the Toolbar.

Practice: Click once on the **Computer** icon to see the disks that are "mounted." Notice that every disk icon in this window is also sitting right on your Desktop.

Home: When you first turned on your Mac with OS X, you had to create a name and a password for yourself; this is your "user" account. If more than one person uses the computer, each person can have his or her own user account. All users can customize the Mac to their own particular likings, and all persons' files are protected from everyone else. You need a password to enter your own Home, and don't ever lose that password! Write it down!!

Each user has their own "Home" space, with their own Home folders, as shown below. When you single-click the "Home" button icon in the Toolbar, your Home files are displayed in the window. To learn all about your Home and how to take advantage of it, see Chapter 9.

The Home icon in the Toolbar

Practice: Click once on the **Home** icon to see the folders that Apple has already set up for you. You can open each folder (double-click the icons) to see what is inside each one, but there is probaby nothing there yet. It's up to you to put files inside.

This is my Home.

Favorites: On the Mac, "Favorites" are folders, documents, web site addresses, or any other files that you want easy access to. Once you create a Favorite, you can access it a number of ways. If it's a web address, you might want to go to the site; if the Favorite is a folder, you might want to save items into it; if the Favorite is a "server" (another computer that you are connected to), you might want to copy files from the server or store files onto it. All of the Favorites you create will be stored in this Favorites folder. For all the details, see Chapter 23.

The Favorites icon in the Toolbar

Practice: Click once on the **Favorites** icon to see any Favorites you might have created. Don't worry if this folder is empty at the moment; when you learn why and how to create Favorites (Chapter 23), they will automatically be stored in this folder.

The Applications icon in the Toolbar

Applications: Apple has supplied a number of applications for your education and entertainment and has stored them in this special Applications folder. You'll notice, as you poke around your Mac, that there is more than one folder called Applications. The one that appears when you click the button in the Toolbar is the "system-wide" folder; that is, anything in this folder is available to all users. If you want to install a new software application just for your own use, you'll install it into the Applications folder that you find in your Home window. For details about how to use some of the applications provided by Apple, see Chapter 28. For details about users and Homes and how to install new applications into this folder, see Chapter 20.

Practice: Click once on the **Applications** icon to see the applications Apple has provided. Use the scroll arrows or scrollers to see the applications stored toward the bottom of the window.

The Back button in the Toolbar

Back button: Your Mac is automatically set up so that when you click a new Toolbar icon to view its contents, the new contents **replace** what was already in the window. This prevents having a screen full of individual windows all displaying their contents.

If you want to go back to the contents you previously viewed *in this particular window,* use the Back button. If you've used a web browser, you'll find it's much the same.

It's possible to individually open *new* windows instead of *replacing* the contents of the current window. See page 91 for details.

You'll find that sometimes the Back button is gray, which means you cannot go back. This happens when you get all the way back to the window you started with. If you open a *new* window, the button is gray since the window is new and there is nowhere to go back to.

Practice: Single-click the **Computer** icon in the Toolbar, then the **Home** icon, then the **Favorites** icon, then the **Applications** icon.

Now click the **Back** button once and you'll go back to the contents of the Favorites window. Click the Back button once more and you'll see the Home window, etc. Try it.

Hide/Show Toolbar button: As its name implies, click this button to hide the Toolbar; when it's hidden, click this button to show the Toolbar. When the Toolbar is hidden, a very important change takes place.

> **When the Toolbar is visible,** double-clicking on a folder icon displays the new folder's contents in the *existing* window, replacing what was there.
>
> **When the Toolbar is hidden,** double-clicking on a folder icon opens *another* window to display the contents of that folder.
>
> Once you hide the Toolbar, all new windows that open from this one will automatically have a hidden Toolbar.

If you *always* want folders to open to new and separate windows, whether or not Toolbars are hiding, see page 96.

The Hide/Show Toolbar button in the Toolbar

	Name	Size	Kind	Date Modified
►	Desktop	--	Folder	Today, 7:01 PM
►	Documents	--	Folder	Today, 3:12 PM
►	iTunes	--	Folder	Today, 4:57 AM
►	Library	--	Folder	Today, 5:13 AM
►	Movies	--	Folder	Today, 9:20 PM
►	Music	--	Folder	Today, 9:20 PM
►	Pictures	--	Folder	Today, 7:16 PM
►	Public	--	Folder	Today, 6:53 PM
►	Sites	--	Folder	Today, 7:59 PM

This is the window with the Toolbar showing.

	Name	Size	Kind	Date Modified
►	Desktop	--	Folder	Today, 7:01 PM
►	Documents	--	Folder	Today, 5:10 PM
►	iTunes	--	Folder	Today, 4:57 AM
►	Library	--	Folder	Today, 5:13 AM
►	Movies	--	Folder	Today, 9:20 PM
►	Music	--	Folder	Today, 9:20 PM
►	Pictures	--	Folder	Today, 7:16 PM
►	Public	--	Folder	Today, 6:53 PM
►	Sites	--	Folder	Today, 7:59 PM

This is the same window as above, with the Toolbar hiding.

Practice: While the Toolbar is visible, double-click any folder. The contents of the new folder **replaces** the previous contents.

Click the **Back** button to go back to the previous folder.

Click the **Toolbar Hide/Show** button to hide the Toolbar.

Double-click a folder icon and you will see it open into a **new window,** and the previous window will still be on your screen. The new window has no Toolbar (click the button to bring the Toolbar back).

Remember, to **close** a window, click in the red button in the upper-left of the window.

Customize the Toolbar

You can **customize the Toolbar** to suit your working habits. You can *rearrange* items, *remove* any of the existing button icons, and *add* icons of folders, applications, files, servers, and more. Once you rearrange or add new items to a Toolbar, they appear in the Toolbar of every Finder window.

To rearrange items in the Toolbar:

Just drag them (for some items you have to hold down the Command key and drag). As you drag sideways, other icons move over to make room. When you have an item positioned where you want it, let go.

To customize the Toolbar using the "Customize Toolbar" pane:

1. Open any Finder window.

2. Hold the Shift key down and click the Hide/Show Toolbar button. **Or** from the View menu, choose "Customize Toolbar…."

3. From the pane that appears, press-and-drag any icon you like into the Toolbar and drop it there (if you change your mind, just drag the icon off the Toolbar and drop it on the Desktop; it will disappear).

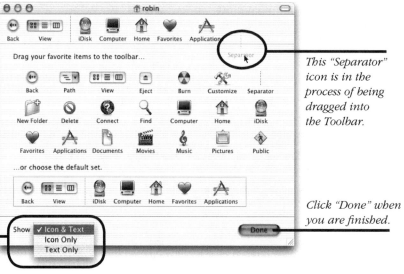

This "Separator" icon is in the process of being dragged into the Toolbar.

This little menu changes how the icons are displayed in the Toolbar. Choose each one to see how it looks. The last one you choose is the one that will apply to the Toolbar when you close this pane.

Click "Done" when you are finished.

4. If you add more icons than will fit, a tiny double-arrow icon will appear at the end of the Toolbar, indicating there are more items in the Toolbar. Click on that double-arrow and a tiny menu will appear with the other items listed; you can select from that menu.

5. Click the "Done" button in the bottom-right corner when you are finished and want to apply the changes you made.

Some of the **icons in the Customize pane** represent items you already have in your Toolbar. They exist because it's possible to remove every single item from the Toolbar, even the Back button or the Views button, and you might one day want something back that you previously removed. Below is a list of the items we haven't already talked about that you can put in the Toolbar and what they do:

Icons in the Customize pane

Path: An open window represents the contents of a disk or a folder. Click on this Path button to see where the current disk or folder is located on the computer; you'll get a menu showing the folders inside of folders, etc., of where the item is stored. You can choose any location from this menu to open *that* window. Clicking this button is exactly the same as Command-clicking on the title bar, as explained on page 68.

Eject: If you click the "Computer" icon in the Toolbar and *select* a removable disk in that window (click once on its icon), you can then click this Eject button to eject the *selected* disk. This button doesn't work if you select the disk icon on the Desktop—you have to select it in the Computer window. This can be more trouble than dragging a disk to the Trash/eject (see Chapter 18).

Burn: If you have a writable CD or DVD drive, you can click this button to begin the burn process. First *select* the CD or DVD icon in the Computer window.

Customize: Click this button to open the Customize pane (the one shown on the opposite page).

Separator: Drag this into position on the Toolbar to create a dividing line between groups of icons.

New Folder: Click this to put a new folder in the *active* window (which would be the one whose Toolbar you're clicking in).

Delete: Click this to delete any *selected* item(s) in the window. This button will be gray until you select something. The item you delete will go into the Trash basket (see Chapter 17).

Connect: Click this to connect to any other computers in your office that are already networked (see Chapter 36 about networking).

Find: Click this to open Sherlock, which you can use to find files on your computer or information on the Internet (see Chapter 24).

Documents, Movies, Music, Pictures, Public: Each of these represents one of the folders in your Home. Put its icon in your Toolbar, then you can just click to access that folder. Or you can drop files onto the icon in the Toolbar and the files will actually go into the folder.

Default set: Drag this entire block up to the Toolbar and it will replace everything you have customized and make the Toolbar exactly how it was when you first started.

Add folders or files to the Toolbar

You can **add any folder** to the Toolbar. When you put a folder in the Toolbar, you are actually placing a *copy* of the folder icon in the Toolbar; the real folder stays right where it is. But you can drop files onto the Toolbar folder and the files will go straight into the real folder. You can click the folder icon in the Toolbar and its window will instantly appear, as shown below.

You can **add any document** file to the Toolbar. When you click a document icon in the Toolbar, the application you created that document in will open and your file will appear.

You can **add any application** to the Toolbar. When you click an application icon in the Toolbar, it will open that application.

To add folders, files, or applications to the Toolbar:

Just find the file icon in a window, then drag it to the Toolbar and let go. Remember, you can always rearrange icons by just dragging them left or right.

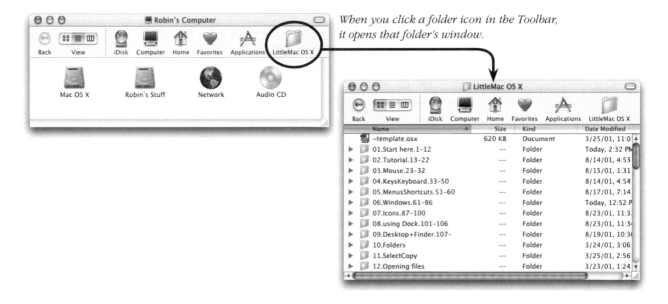

When you click a folder icon in the Toolbar, it opens that folder's window.

Remove items from the Toolbar

To remove items from the Toolbar: When the Customize pane is open, you can just drag any icon off of the Toolbar and drop it on the Desktop.

You can also remove any icon anytime you like, *without* having to open the Customize pane: Some icons you can just drag off and drop on the Desktop. If that doesn't work, hold down the Command key and drag it off.

If you have a lot of items in the Toolbar, the item you want to remove might not be visible. You'll have to open the window wide enough to see the icon (drag the Resize corner, see page 68), then drag it off.

As I mentioned on page 66, you can **view the contents** of a Finder window in three different ways, one of them as **icons.** Icons are the pictures that represent the various types of files on your computer. The biggest advantage to viewing windows in icons is that you can quickly and easily tell what is a folder, an application, a document, etc. (see Chapter 7 about icons).

Using Icon View

To view a window as icons: Click the Icon View button in the Toolbar (shown circled, below). Or go to the View menu and choose "As Icons."

Icon View obviously shows icons.

To select an item that you know is in this folder but you can't see it: Type the first couple of letters of its name. For instance, in the example above, you can't see the application called Stickies. So type "st" and the window will instantly scroll itself down and Stickies will be selected.

Tricks in Icon View

To "launch" (open) an application: Double-click its icon.

To open a folder and display its contents, double-click a folder icon. This will open the new folder *in this same window;* the contents of the new folder will *replace* the contents of the current window.

To open a folder in a new window: Hold down the Command key and double-click the folder. You will get a new window, plus the previous window will *remain* on the Desktop. The Toolbar is automatically hidden in the new window.

As I mentioned on page 79, whenever the **Toolbar is hidden** (click the little button in the top-right of the window), a folder will open into a *new* window when you double-click on it. The new window automatically has the Toolbar hidden; once the Toolbar is hidden, you can double-click on any folder in that window and it will automatically open into a new window (you don't have to hold the Command key down).

Always open a folder into a new window: If it makes you crazy to have only one window for all your folders, use the Finder preferences (see page 96), to make sure every time you double-click a folder icon (or single-click a folder icon in the Toolbar), you get a new and separate window.

Clean up the arrangement of the icons

There are two items in the View menu that pertain only to windows in Icon View: "Clean Up" and "Arrange by Name." If your window is in any other view, these items are gray, which is a **visual clue** that you can't use them.

There is an invisible underlying grid in every window, and when you choose to **Clean Up** the window, the Mac moves each icon into the nearest little square on that grid, the nearest square that the icon is already next to. When you choose **Arrange by Name,** the Mac moves each icon into *alphabetical* order in neat rows and fills every invisible square in order.

The arrangement of the icons is also affected by the options you can choose in the "View Options," as discussed below and on the opposite page.

To clean up the icons in a window:

Practice: Open a window and view it by icon. Using the mouse, drag the icons around in the window so they are a mess. (If the icons won't move into new positions, see the information about "Icon Arrangement" on the opposite page.)

From the View menu, choose **Clean Up** and see what happens.

Now from the View menu, choose **Arrange by Name** and see what happens.

1. Make sure the window you want to clean up is active: click once on it.

2. From the View menu, choose "Clean Up" or "Arrange by Name."

There are several features you can change in the Icon View, using the **View Options** dialog box, as shown below. To get this dialog box, go to the View menu and choose "Show View Options," or press Command J.

Once this dialog box is open (as shown below-right), you'll notice that its title bar changes its name depending on which window is *active.* That is, once you open it, you can open a whole bunch of other windows and whichever window is in *front,* the one that has the three buttons in color, is the one that this View Options box will apply to. Even if you have only one window open, if you switch to another folder in that same window, this View Options box will switch to displaying the options for the new contents.

What you see in the View Options depends on which view the active window is displaying. For instance, if you have a window in Icon View and you click its button to change the window to List View, the View Options box will change. (There are no options for Column View.)

Here are explanations for each of the Icon View options. First of all, you have two choices that determine where you will see any options you apply.

> **This window only:** This option means just what it says. Any changes you make in View Options will apply only to the *active* window whose name appears in the title bar of the View Options box.
>
> If you make individual changes to a window, then at some point decide you don't like those individual changes, at any time you can open the View Options, click the "Global" button, and the active window will revert to your Global options.
>
> **Global:** If you click the "Global" button, any changes you make in this View Options box will apply to every window on your entire computer (when viewed in Icon View).

View Options in Icon View

*The View Options title bar shows the name of the **active** window. The changes you make in this box will apply to the window whose name is in this title bar.*

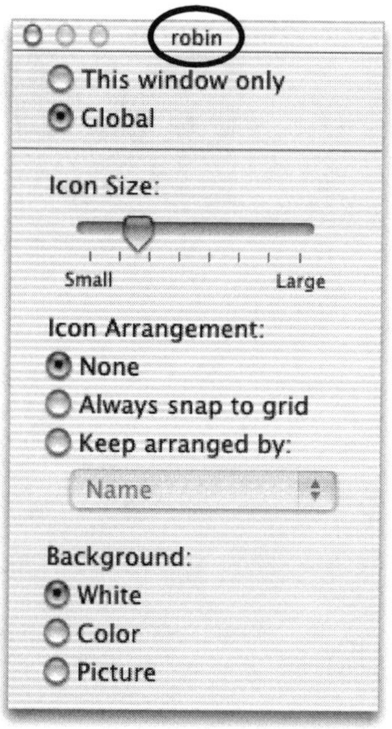

View Options in Icon View

(Icon Size and Icon Arrangment)

Below the dividing line in **View Options** are the actual options you can choose.

Icon Size: Simply slide the blue slider back and forth to choose a size for your icons. As you slide, you'll see the changes take place immediately in the active window.

Icon Arrangement

None: With this button checked, you can move the icons around wherever you please.

Always snap to grid: With this button checked, when you move icons around in the window, they will always snap into the nearest open square in the underlying invisible grid that I mentioned on page 84. This keeps the window looking nice and neat. The size of the grid depends on the icon size you chose in the scroller (described above).

Keep arranged by: If you check this button, not only will your icons stay in the nice, neat grid, but they will automatically arrange themselves by whatever you choose from the pop-up menu (shown to the left). That is, if you drop a new folder or document or application into a window that is arranged by *name*, then that item will automatically put itself in alphabetical order and all the other icons will shift places to accommodate it. (You won't get the pop-up menu until you click the "Keep arranged by" button.)

Name: In alphabetical order.

Date Modified: The date you last opened and saved changes to this file.

Date Created: The date the document, folder, application, or other file was originally created.

Size: How large the file size is, which means how much space it takes up on your disk in kilobytes or megabytes.

Kind: Whether this file is a document, application, folder, etc.

Label: There are no labels in Mac OS X, but if you applied labels to files in previous versions of the Mac operating system, you can choose to organize them by those labels. If you don't know what labels are, don't worry because you can't make them anymore anyway.

If you choose to organize your icons by "Always snap to grid" or "Keep arranged by," you will see a little icon in your status bar (if you choose to show your status bar, as described on page 73).

This icon indicates the window is organized in "Always snap to grid."

This icon indicates the window is organized as "Keep arranged by."

Background: You can leave the background of your windows white, or you can apply a color or a photo. As with the other options, you can choose the background for all windows (global) or just the active window. Or both: You might have a global color, but choose to put a photo in one or two windows.

> **White:** Removes any existing color or photo.

> **Color:** Click this button and a little box appears. Click on the box and you'll get Apple's "Color Picker," as shown below. Choose a color "model" along the left side of the Color Picker (the model called "Crayon" is fun and easy), then on the right side, choose or create a color. The color in the "New" box when you click OK is the color that will appear as the background of the active window.

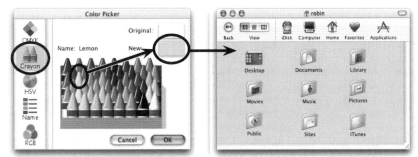

In the "Crayon" model, just click on a crayon color.

> **Picture:** Click this button and a "Select..." button appears. Click that button and you'll get the standard "Open" dialog box that will automatically open to "Desktop Pictures," as shown below. If you know how to use this dialog box, you can "navigate" (see Chapter 12) to any folder on your computer and select a photo of your choice instead of the ones that are already in the Desktop Pictures folder.

The folder "Desktop Pictures" is probably selected for you. Click once on a picture name in the right column.

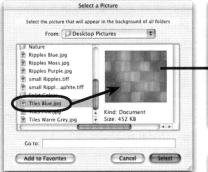

When you click on a picture name, you'll see it on the right. Click "Select" and it will appear in the window.

Depending on which photo you choose, it might fill the entire space or just a corner.

Using List View

View

The **List View** is another way of looking at the items in a window. Below you see a typical list. Notice there are several columns; you can resize these columns, rearrange them, get rid of them, or choose different ones. You can organize each column in order backwards or forwards. The List View lets you "expand" several folders in the same window (you can see the folder "Documents" expanded in the example below) rather than opening a new window for each one as with Icon View.

This is the List View button.

Name	Size	Kind	Date Modified
▶ Desktop	--	Folder	Today, 6:16 PM
▼ Documents	--	Folder	Today, 6:21 PM
Budget with graphs	--	RTF with ... document	Today, 6:18 PM
▶ Essays	--	Folder	Today, 5:56 PM
Letter to John.rtf	4 KB	Rich Text ... document	Today, 6:17 PM
Letter to Mom.rtf	4 KB	Rich Text ... document	Today, 12:25 AM
Letter to Ryan.rtf	4 KB	Rich Text ... document	Today, 12:25 AM
Robin's Notes.rtf	4 KB	Rich Text ... document	Today, 4:30 AM
▶ Ryan's Writing	--	Folder	Today, 7:23 PM
▶ Screenshots	--	Folder	Today, 6:14 PM
▶ iTunes	--	Folder	Today, 6:13 PM
▶ Library	--	Folder	Today, 5:13 AM

Window title: robin. Toolbar: Back, View, iDisk, Computer, Home, Favorites, Applications, Documents.

Second window (robin), resized narrower. Toolbar: Back, View, iDisk, »

Name column: Desktop, Documents (expanded: Budget with graphs, Essays, Letter to John.rtf, Letter to Mom.rtf, Letter to Ryan.rtf, Robin's Notes.rtf, Ryan's Writing, Screenshots), iTunes, Library.

*This is the **Expand** triangle. Click it to display the contents of that folder in a List View. See below.*

*This is the **Sort Order** button. Click it to sort (arrange in order) in the opposite direction that it is at the moment. See below.*

This is the same window as shown to the left, just resized narrower.

Expand triangles: Click on an **expand** triangle to open and display the contents of that folder in this same window. This triangle allows you to see the contents of a number of windows in the same folder. This makes it easier to move files from one folder to another, to compare folders, and even to select items from several different folders at the same time. As you can see in the example above, you can expand folders inside of folders (as with the "Essays" folder inside the "Documents" folder). Click the triangle again to **collapse** the folder. See Chapter 10 for details on this feature.

Sort Order triangle: When a column heading is selected (click on it to select it; it will turn blue), a tiny upward- or downward-pointing triangle appears. This indicates the order in which the contents in that column are **organized,** or **sorted.** For instance, in the example above, the "Name" column is organized alphabetically in order from A to Z (the pointy tip of the triangle indicates the lower end of the sort order). If you want this column organized from Z to A, click that triangle; the triangle will point downward and the items will be sorted alphabetically backwards. Try it.

You can **resize and rearrange the columns** of information that are displayed in your window when you view items in the List View.

> **To rearrange the columns,** press directly on any column heading (except Name) and drag to the left or right. As soon as you start to drag, the pointer tool turns into the grabber hand, which is your **visual clue** that you are about to rearrange the columns. The only column you cannot move out of position is "Name."

> **To resize the columns,** position the pointer on the line right between two column headings. The pointer will turn into a two-headed arrow, as shown below, which is your **visual clue** that you can resize the columns—just press that two-headed arrow and drag to the left or right.

Resize and rearrange the list columns

Practice: Just follow the directions to the left.

If you see a one-headed arrow, that's a visual clue that you can only resize that particular column in the direction the arrow is pointing.

How can you tell by looking at this window that the files are arranged by name? (The obvious visual clue is in the column heading.)

You can **choose which columns** will appear in a List View, as well as how **dates** will appear (if you choose to show dates), and the **size** of icons.

1. Open any window and click the List View button.
2. Go to the View menu and choose "Show View Options," or press Command J. The "View Options" dialog box will appear, as shown to the right.
3. As explained more fully on page 85, click **This window only** if you want to make changes just to the active window. Click **Global** if you want changes to apply to *every* window when shown in List View.
4. The column headings you check under **Show Columns** will appear in the *active* window as headings. See the following page for explanations of each column.
5. **Use relative dates** will display "Today" and "Yesterday" where appropriate (as shown above), and regular dates for older files.
6. If you check **Calculate all sizes,** your window will display the size of folders and various other files that it doesn't normally show, but it can be kind of slow to do this sometimes.
7. Experiment with the **Icon Size** options to see which you prefer.

Options for List View

Choices in "Show Columns"

Below are explanations of the columns that can appear in your List View.

Date Modified lists files in chronological order according to the last time you opened a file or folder and changed something in it. Arranging folders by either Date Modified or Date Created can come in handy when, for instance, you have several budget documents and you want to see the most recent edition.

Date Created lists the files in chronological order according to when they were first made. The Mac looks at the creation date as determined by the date and time you've set in the Date & Time preferences (details for Date & Time are on page 334–335).

Size lists the files in order of how much space they take up on your computer. When you are in List View, you may notice that folders and certain other files show no size. If you want to see their sizes, you have to check "Calculate all sizes" which is towards the bottom of the "View Options" dialog box (shown to the left).

Kind lists the files in groups: applications, various sorts of documents, and folders. This is handy if you want to see a list of all the photographs in your family folder or all the documents you've stored in your budget folder.

> **Tip:** "Arrange by Kind" is particularly useful for a folder that holds an application (or a game) plus all of its accessories—the dictionaries, tutorials, technical files, samples, etc. The view by "Kind" will always put the application (or game) at the top of the list so it's easy to find.

Version displays the version number of each application. The version number tells you how current the software is; every time it is updated, it gets a new version number. For instance, your Mac is now using the tenth major version of the operating system.

Comments will display the first several characters and the last characters of any text that was typed into the Comments box in the Show Info window (see page 520), as shown below.

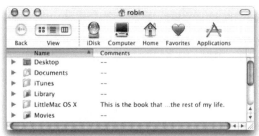

This is what the Comments might look like in the window.

If you hold the pointer over the Comments (don't click!), in a couple of seconds the entire message will appear.

To make the entire comment appear instantly, *press the Option key (don't click).*

You can **open folders,** as shown on page 88, by clicking the expand triangle and the contents of the folder will drop down in the list. **Or** you can double-click any folder and the contents of that new folder will replace the contents of the current window, as shown below.

Opening folders in List View

I single-clicked this triangle to display the contents of this folder right in this window, in a list.

*I could **single-click** this **triangle** to display the contents of this folder (which is inside the Documents folder) in this list.*

*Instead, I **double-clicked** the **folder icon** and it replaced the contents of this window with the new folder's contents, as shown to the right.*

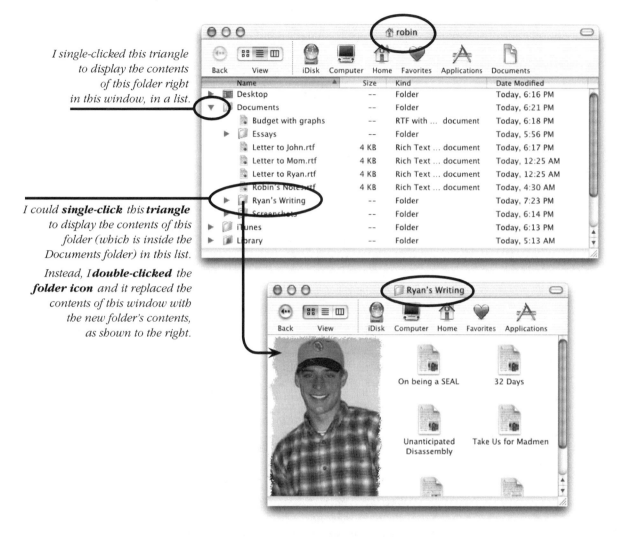

Notice the new window displays the contents **in the same view that I last used in this folder,** *not* in the view of the window I just came from. You might love this feature or hate it. You can use the Finder Preferences to make all new windows open in the same view, and even make all new folders open in a new, separate window; see page 96.

Using Column View

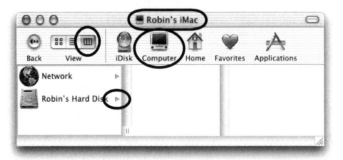

View

The **Column View** is a new thing on Macintoshes. At first, it can be quite confusing and frustrating to work with, so walk yourself through these two pages to get the gist of how it works, and then you'll simply have to use it enough until it begins to make sense. It's important to understand the Column View concept because every time you save a document or have to "navigate" or "browse" through your computer to open a file, you'll bump into this Column View.

*This is the Computer level of your Mac, shown in Column View. Notice each of the icons on the far left, on the Computer level, show a triangle pointing to the right. This is a **visual clue** that you can single-click on that name (the "Hard Disk" or the "Network" icon) and you will see, in the next column, what is stored on that level (shown below).*

If you don't see the tiny triangles or the thick borders between columns, you are not using Mac OS X, version 10.1, but the previous version (10.0, although it's not really called that). The Column View still acts the same, though. When you upgrade, your system will look like this, complete with resizable columns.

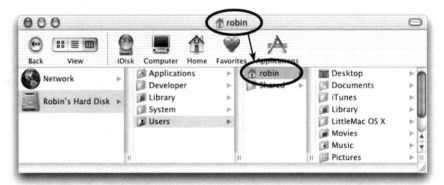

*Following the example above, in this window you can see by the highlight (the darker area) that I single-clicked on **Robin's Hard Disk** to see what was stored on the hard disk. Its contents are displayed in the second column.*

*In the second column, I clicked on **Users,** which I can tell is a folder, to see what is stored in that folder. Its contents opened in the third column.*

*In the third column, I clicked on my own Home folder, **robin** (I can tell it's actually a folder because of the tiny triangle pointing to the right), to display what is stored in my Home folder. There I see the folders I know and love.*

(These columns can be handy, but you can already understand that it would be much easier to see your Home folders if you just click on the Home icon button in the Toolbar.)

Continue following the progression on the next page.

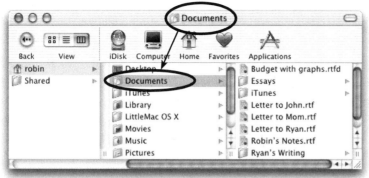

The title bar displays the name of the folder that is selected, or highlighted.

*You can still see the **robin** Home folder on the far left, highlighted, but it is a lighter highlight than in the next column, where **Documents** has a darker shade. This indicates that it is actually "Documents" that is the **active** item here (because I clicked once on it).*

The column on the far right shows the contents of the Documents folder.

*How many **scrollers** do you see? The one across the bottom indicates that you could scroll back to the left, back to the Computer level. The two vertical scroll bars indicate there is more in each of those columns.*

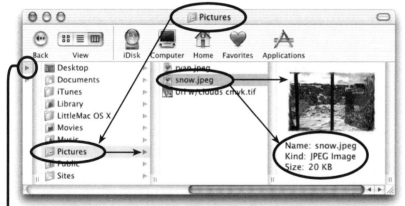

*This final column will display either an icon or the actual image of the **selected** document.*

If you select a movie, you can actually play the movie right here in Column View.

In the example at the top of the page, I clicked on the Pictures folder, then I clicked on one of the pictures inside that folder. This made the Home column (with "robin" and "Shared") scoot to the left, where you can barely see it; you can just see the tiny triangles, and "robin" is still highlighted, although you can only see the triangle.

*The **Pictures** folder is highlighted, which is our clue (along with the name in the title bar) that the files in the next column are stored in the Pictures folder.*

*Now we are finally looking at documents (notice the documents have no tiny triangles pointing to the right). The file **snow.jpeg** is highlighted, and it's the darkest highlight so we know this is actually what is **active** at the moment, and this is what is shown in the very last column.*

Once you find a file in a column, you can double-click it to open it within its application.

Navigating in in Column View

Navigating refers to finding your way around the Desktop on your Mac, or in a dialog box or window. You have to navigate to the document you want so you can open it, or to a disk icon so you can eject it. In the Column View, you can use the arrow keys to select items left and right, as well as up and down. For instance, in the example below, "robin" is currently selected (its highlight is the darkest; the lighter highlights to the left show where it came from). If I press the RightArrow key, I will select the first item in the next column. Once in that column, I can press the UpArrow or DownArrow keys to select a folder.

When you get to the Open and Save As dialog boxes, you'll find the Column View there as well, where you can still use the arrow keys to navigate.

The Tab key will also move the selection to the right, and Shift-Tab to the left, but the arrow keys are easier and more consistent throughout the Mac.

Resizing columns in Column View

You can **resize the columns** in Column View. You've probably noticed the little "thumbs" at the bottoms of the scroll bar column dividers (circled below). **To resize,** just press and drag on any thumb. This actually resizes all of the columns at once.

To resize one individual column at a time, hold down the Option key and drag the thumb.

If you don't see the little "thumbs" on the bottoms of the column dividers, you're not using Mac OS X version 10.1. You can't resize the columns in versions prior to 10.1.

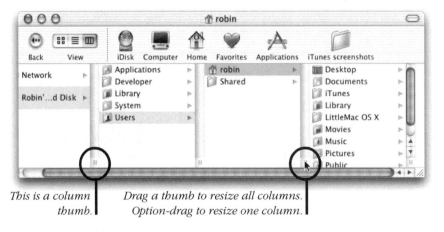

This is a column thumb.

Drag a thumb to resize all columns.
Option-drag to resize one column.

At the Desktop, you have a menu called **Window.** In it you will find a list of the titles of every window that is currently open on your Desktop. (When you are in an application, this menu will list the open documents in that application.)

▼ A checkmark next to a window title indicates the active window.

▼ A diamond indicates that window is minimized (in the Dock).

▼ Select any title in the menu to bring that window to the front.

You might have a number of windows open—some from applications, several Finder windows, and a couple from a utility you're using. These windows might all be visible on the screen at once, layered over and under each other. Click on one Finder window, then choose "Bring All to Front" from the Window menu, and all of the windows of that type will come forward (although only one can actually be *active* and on top of the others).

The Window Menu

There are a number of ways to close or minimize all windows at once.

▼ To simultaneously **close every window** that is open on your Desktop, hold down the Option key while you click in any window's Close button (the red one); all the windows will go away one after another!

▼ In the File menu there is a command to "Close Window." If you hold down the Option key, that command changes to "Close All."

▼ The keyboard shortcut to close a window is Command W. **To close all the windows at once,** press Command Option W.

▼ **To minimize all the windows at once,** hold down the Option key and click the Minimize button (the yellow one) in the upper-left corner of any window. This also works in applications when you have more than one window open.

▼ You might have the feature turned on that always opens folders in new windows (see the following page), but often the folder you want to open is buried within several folders. To prevent having too many windows open that you don't need, hold the Option key down while you double-click to open those folders to get to your file. **The windows will close up behind you** as you go along.

▼ When you turn off the computer, the Macintosh remembers which windows were open when you left. When you turn the computer back on, those windows will re-open in the same position in which you left them. You can take advantage of this fact and arrange your windows before you Shut Down.

Close or minimize all of the Windows

...and other window tricks

Finder Preferences

There are a couple of items in the **Finder Preferences** that refer to using Finder windows. These options are global, meaning they will apply to all windows on the Desktop until you go back and change them.

To open the Finder Preferences:

1. Make sure you are at the Finder/Desktop. Look at the menu bar: If the menu item next to the apple is not "Finder," then click once on an empty spot on the Desktop, or click on a Finder window.

2. When you see "Finder" in the menu bar, click on it and choose "Preferences…" from the menu. You'll get the box shown below.

▼ Whenever you open a new Finder window, it automatically opens to the "Computer" level. You probably don't need to use much on the Computer level; everything you need is in your "Home." In the Finder Preferences you can choose to have **new Finder windows open to your Home level** instead.

▼ If you are an experienced Mac user, you're probably accustomed to a new window opening every time you double-click a folder icon, instead of the contents of the new folder *replacing* what was already in the window. In the Finder Preferences you can choose to **have a new window open every time you double-click a folder.**

▼ If you prefer one window view over another, it might make you crazy that you never know what view the next folder will appear in. You can choose that all view*s in the window you're working in* will stay the same as the view you have currently selected. That is, if you set a window to Icon View, all the folders that open *within that window* will be in Icon View.

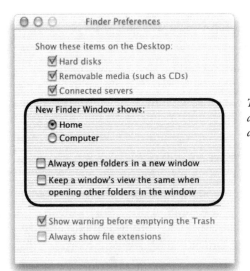

These are the options that apply to Finder windows, as explained above.

All the information in the previous pages has pertained to Finder windows, the ones you will use at the Desktop. But the Mac also uses windows in every application; when you open an application and create something, you create it in a **document window.** A document window has most of the same features as Finder windows, with a few differences. Below is a typical document window (although every application is slightly different). You can see that it has the same features as the Finder windows, without the Toolbar.

Document Windows

Important note: *If you open an application in Classic (Mac OS 9), your windows will not look quite like this. If you don't know how to use Classic windows, please see Chapter 40.*

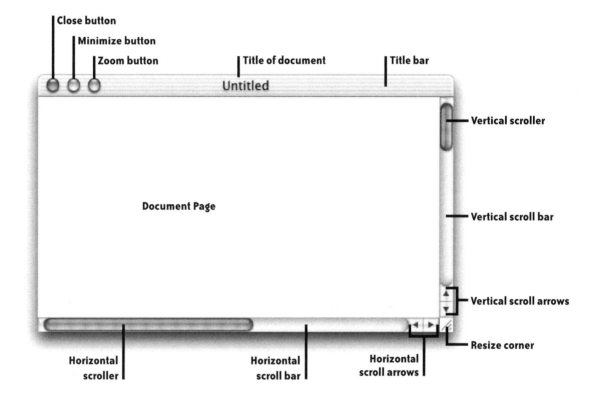

On the following page are examples of document windows.

Examples of document windows

This is an example of a **document window** in a page layout application. Notice there are differences between this window and the one on the previous page; every application applies its own details. But all of the items in the example on the previous page are also present in this window.

You'll find the buttons and scrollers and title bars and resize corners in just about every application on the Mac, no matter what the "document" looks like. Below is the iTunes application for listening to music on your Mac (see Chapter 26 for iTunes details). Notice this window has the same features as every window we've talked about so far, you should feel comfortable with it as soon as you open it—you already know how to close it, minimize it, move it around the screen, resize it, etc.

Buttons   *Title*   *Title bar*

Scroll bar, scroller, and arrows

Resize corner

The **scroll bars and scrollers** are particulary important in document windows because they tell you how much of your document is not visible, or even where it is. Many times I have been called to students' desks who were panic stricken because the papers they were writing "disappeared." I would point out that the scroller was all the way to the bottom of the document window, and that if they dragged it back up, their papers would reappear. In a page layout application, the scrollers might be all the way to the left or right, hiding the page that is in the middle.

Document scroll bar clues

The Creature.rtf

An Entertaining Creature

Yes, that's what she called him. "An entertaining creature." As if he had been born and raised to provide her amusement. How droll, she had said. She acts like she's some long-lost countess who has just been released from a time warp. Well, he would show her. He would just turn himself into a real creature and

In this example, there is no horizontal scroll bar at all, which tells us there is nothing more in the document in the horizontal direction than what we can already see.

There is no scroller in the vertical scroll bar on the right, which tells us this story ends right where we see it—there is nothing more to see in the vertical direction.

The Creature.rtf

creature. As if he had been born and raised to provide her amusement. How droll, she had said. She acts like she's some long-lost countess who has just been released from a time warp. Well, he would show her. He would just turn himself into a real creature and . . . and what? He didn't know how to turn himself into a creature. He wasn't some gall-darned warlock or anything. Oh, he could cast simple spells like the kind to make acne go away or to find enough money to take himself to a movie, but not the kind to make babes like Eliza fall in love with him. Or to turn

The size of the scroller in the scroll bar is proportionate to how much of the entire window is visible to you.

The amount of space above and below the scroller is proportionate to how much of the window you cannot see at the moment.

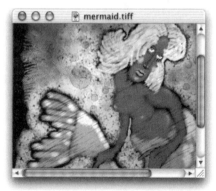

mermaid.tiff

This example has scroll bar scrollers along both the right and bottom edges, indicating there is a lot more of this image than is visible in the window at the moment.

***To open the window** enough to see the entire image (if it will fit on your monitor), click the green button.*

***Tip:** **To go to the very end** of the document (in most applications), hit the "End" key.*

To go to the very beginning of the document, hit the "Home" key.

Title bar in a document

Document windows also have **title bars,** the striped bar across the top of a window in which, logically, the title appears. This title is the name of the document you have created. *You* are responsible for the title; when you *save* the file, its name will appear here (see Chapter 14 about saving).

Remember, you can also double-click in the title bar to **minimize** a window.

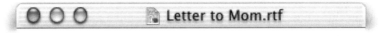

Every window has a title bar.

The document path in the title bar

The title bar can always tell you *where* a particular document is stored, once you have actually saved the document and given it a name. The list that you see dropping down from the title bar below is called the **path** to the document.

> **Practice:** This technique works in document windows and Finder windows. So try it on any window that is open. You'll learn more about paths, if you want, in Chapter 14.

To see the "path" to where a *saved* document is stored, hold the Command key down and click on the title bar; a menu will appear. You can slide the mouse down the menu and choose any item to open that item's Finder window.

> Robin's Notes.rtf
> Documents
> robin
> Users
> Robin's Hard Disk

This is a w... ...dow.
I can type... ...ther,
a to-do lis... ...a
goodbye note, an essay on The Grand
Climacteric, or a school report on the
importance of a stage and a dance floor.
I can change the typeface, make the text
larger, add more space between the lines,

So this menu tells me that this document named "Robin's Notes.rtf" has been saved into a folder called "Documents," which is in the Home for "robin," which is in the folder called "Users," which is on the hard disk named "Robin's Hard Disk."

Notice the tiny icons to the left of the path names are also visual clues.

Moving the document window

To move any document window around the screen, position the pointer in the title bar of the window, then press-and-drag. Just let go of the mouse button when you have the window placed where you want.

If you have more than one document window open, only one will have the little round buttons *in color* in its title bar. The colored buttons are a **visual clue** that this window is the **active window.** If windows are overlapping, the active window is the one that is in front.

The **active window** is the only window that the commands from the keyboard or the menu will affect. For instance, if you go to the File menu and choose "Close," it will close the *active* window. If you choose "Save," it will save the *active* window. It's very important to be conscious of which window is active!

To make a window active, simply click on any visible part of it; this will also bring that window to the front of any others.

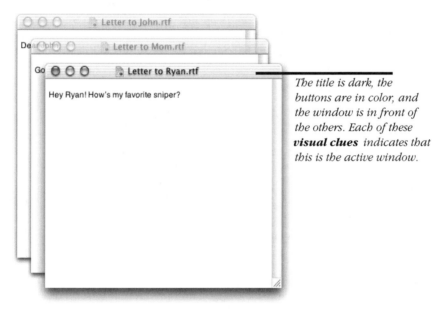

The active document window

*The title is dark, the buttons are in color, and the window is in front of the others. Each of these **visual clues** indicates that this is the active window.*

Tip: To move a window that's behind others *without* making it active, hold down the Command key while you press-and-drag the title bar. Try it.

Dot in the red button of a document window

Sometimes you may see a round dot inside the red button, as shown in the example below. This dot is a **visual clue** that you have made changes to the document but haven't "saved" them yet. That is, a new document is "untitled" and unsaved until you go to the File menu, choose "Save As...," and give the document a name. This process puts a new, permanent file in your Documents folder. But whenever you make any changes to that document, such as adding more text, those changes are *not* included in the permanent file until you "Save" once again (either press Command S to save, or go to the File menu and choose "Save"). See Chapter 14 for all the details about saving.

In this example, you can see the red dot that indicates there have been changes made to this file and they are not saved yet. Also notice that the small document icon in the title bar is gray.

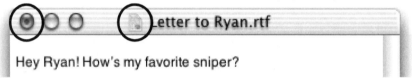

I saved the changes to the file, and now the red button has no dot, plus the document icon in the title bar is now darker.

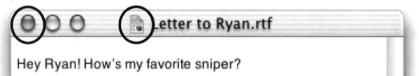

Dot in the Window menu

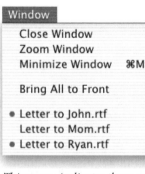

This menu indicates there are three open documents in this application, and two of them have unsaved changes.

Most applications have a "Window" menu that lists all the open documents in that application, as shown to the left. Notice in that list of document windows, two files have dots to the left of their names; these dots are **visual clues** that changes have been made to those documents but haven't been "saved" yet (as explained above). You can select one of the names in the menu to bring that document forward, and then save it. (Remember, to do something to a file, the document must be the *active* window, as explained on the previous page).

Because windows are so incredibly important and because there are so many details about them to know, this quiz is two pages long!

1. Label the window below with the following parts:

a. Close button	**f. Scroll arrows (2)**
b. Scroll bar	**g. Resize corner**
c. Title bar	**h. Scroller**
d. Minimize button	**i. Zoom button**
e. Title	

2. Describe three ways to **minimize** a window.

3. How can you instantly tell **how much you can't see** in a document?

4. How can you **move a window** without making it active?

5. What is the **visual clue** that tells you a document has not been saved recently?

—continued on next page!

continued from previous page!

6. Do you single-click or double-click on anything in the Toolbar?

7. How would you arrange a Finder window to see how large your files are?

8. Name two ways to open a folder into a new, separate window (without changing the Finder Preferences).

9. In List View, what is the quickest way to organize files by another column heading?

10. How would you resize a single column in Column View?

11. How can you alphabetically organize a window in Icon View?

12. How can you close all the Finder windows at once without touching the mouse?

13. How can you see a list (the path) of all the folders in which a folder or document is nested?

14. What would you do if you want to change the positions of your scroll arrows?

15. How can you add a status bar to your windows?

Answers are on page 750.

All About Icons

Icons—the little pictures you see on the screen—are an intrinsic part of the look and feel of the Macintosh. Instead of having to type a code to open an application or document (which you had to do before the Mac was invented), you simply double-click on an icon.

An icon can represent any kind of **file**—a file is any form of information you see on your computer. The term "file" might refer to an application, document, clipart, photograph, folder, email letter, web page, or anything else.

The icons offer rich **visual clues.** At first they may look like an odd collection of stuff, but once you really look at them you'll see how much information icons instantly provide. This information is valuable to you, and that's the purpose of this chapter—to help you take advantage of these clues.

Most of the techniques in this chapter, such as moving an icon or changing its name, apply whether your files are represented by icons or shown as names in a list.

Highlighted, or Selected, Icons

Favorites

When an **icon is dark,** like the one shown to the left, it is **highlighted,** or **selected**—it got selected because you clicked once on it, or perhaps you typed the first letter or two of its name. Selecting is important because you must select an icon before you can do anything with it. For instance, menu commands, such as "Open" or "Duplicate," only affect highlighted (selected) icons. Selecting is so important I wrote an entire chapter on it (Chapter 11).

Icons: Single-Click or Double-Click?

Icons represent files on your Mac. You need a basic understanding of what the various icons are telling you about themselves, which is the main point of this chapter. But you also need to know that you must treat icons differently *depending on where they are on your computer.* For instance, to **open** an application from the Dock, you **single-click** on the icon; to **open** an application from the Applications folder, you **double-click** on the icon. This can be confusing, so let's look at it visually right now.

In any Toolbar

Practice: Single-click each item (except iDisk, if you have it). The window contents will change to show you what is contained in each item.

Single-click icons in the Toolbar. The icons on the left side of this Toolbar are buttons; on the right side, they actually represent folders that contain other files (except for the iDisk icon; if you have or want iDisk, you can learn all about it in Chapter 33).

In the Dock

Practice: Single-click the "Finder" icon (circled, to the right) to open the Finder window.

If you clicked on any other icon and don't know what to do now, do this: hold down the Command key (⌘) and tap the letter Q to quit.

Single-click to activate any icon in the Dock. However, what each one does when you activate it is different—some of the icons represent applications which will open, others represent system tools that provide information, and several connect you to the Internet. See Chapter 8 for details.

On the Desktop

Practice: Select your hard disk icon: Single-click on it.

Open your hard disk window: Double-click the hard disk icon.

To close the window: Single-click on the tiny red button in the top-left of the window.

Robin's Hard Disk

Robin's Hard Disk

To select an icon on the Desktop, **single-click.**

To open a folder, document, or application icon (as described in the following pages), **double-click.**

This window is showing the Icon View.

To select *an icon in a window in Icon View,* **single-click.**

To open *a folder, document, or application icon (as described in the following pages),* **double-click.**

In the Icon View of a window

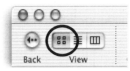

To change any window into the Icon View, click the button circled above. (If you don't see this "toolbar" above your window, click the tiny oval in the upper-right of the window.)

This window is showing the List View.

To select *an icon in a window in List View,* **single-click** *the icon itself,* **not** *the tiny triangle to its left.*

To open *a folder, document, or application icon (as described in the following pages),* **double-click** *the icon itself,* **not** *the tiny triangle to its left.*

In the List View of a window

See Chapter 6 for details about the List View, and see Chapter 10 to learn how to use folders within the List View.

This window is showing the Column View.

To select *an icon in a window in Column View,* **single-click.**

To open *a folder, document, or application icon (as described in the following pages) in its own window,* **double-click.**

In the Column View of a window

See Chapter 6 for details about how to work in the Column View, and see Chapter 10 to learn how to use folders within the Column View.

Types of Icons

Now let's look at individual **types of icons.** Having a general idea of what the icons represent is helpful while working on your Mac.

Disk Icons

When your Desktop is visible (the Desktop is shown and described on page 2), you'll always see icons of any **disks** that are in your Mac. When a disk icon appears on the Desktop, we say that disk is "mounted."

▼ You will always see the hard disk icon, as shown below, that holds all of the files on your computer.

▼ When you insert a CD or a DVD, an icon of the CD or DVD will appear.

▼ If you have bought something called a "Zip drive" in which you insert a small, removable hard disk called a "Zip disk," you'll see its icon on the Desktop as well.

You might, at some point, "partition" your main hard disk into several separate compartments; the Mac considers each of these partitions a separate hard disk and so you would see individual icons for each one. You might buy another hard disk and install it inside your computer or plug it in to the back of your Mac so the "external" hard disk sits on your desk; its icon will also appear on your Desktop.

▼ Single-click on a disk icon to *select* it.

▼ Double-click on a disk icon to *open* it; you will see a window displaying all the files on that disk.

Practice: To select the hard disk, single-click the icon on the Desktop or in the Finder window.

To open its window and display its contents, double-click the hard disk icon.

To close the hard disk window, click the tiny red button in the upper-left of the window.

Mac OS X

*Hard disk icon
(your icon is
probably named
something else)*

FontDisc

CD icon

CASABLANCA

DVD icon

Little Mac Book

Zip disk icon

Whenever you have a Finder window open, most likely you'll see **folder icons.** They act just like folders in your filing cabinet in that you store items in them for organization, and you can open them to see what's inside. Be sure to read Chapter 10 on folders since they are an incredibly important tool that you will be using constantly.

Folder Icons

*To **select** a folder in a window in Icon View, **single-click.***

*To **open** a folder in Icon View, **double-click.***

*To **select** a folder in List View, **single-click** the icon itself.*

*To **"expand"** a folder so you can see its contents in this window, **single-click** the tiny triangle.*

*To **open** a folder in a new window, **double-click** the folder icon or name.*

*To **select** a folder in Column View, **single-click.***

*To **open** a folder into its own window, as shown on the far-right, **double-click.***

Which view your window displays, or if you get a window at all, depends on your Finder preferences as described on page 96 in Chapter 6.

Fancy Folders

Many of the folders you see are identified with special icons. These **fancy folders** are created by the Macintosh operating system and they have special functions. Below you see the folders that are in your Home window. If more than one person uses the computer, each person can have his or her own Home window and their own set of these folders. Anything a user puts in these folders is accessible only to that user, with the exception of the Public folder; whatever is put in the Public folder is accessible to anyone using the machine. Please see Chapter 9 for details about each of these folders, and Chapter 20 for details about how to add more users to your Mac.

The Desktop and Home icons are actually folders, but their icons have been totally changed.

Don't change the names of any of these folders! Many of them have very specific purposes that depend on their names.

Desktop   Documents   Library

Movies   Music   Pictures

Public   Sites

robin   Drop Box   Pictures

Home is actually a folder with a special icon.

A blue arrow indicates a folder with write-only privileges. See page 134.

A red "Do not enter" sign indicates a folder with no privileges. See page 135.

Trash, or Wastebasket Icon

The **Trash,** or **waste basket,** icon in the Dock is an important icon that you will use regularly. Its icon represents exactly what it does: items that you don't want anymore, you drag down to the Trash and throw them away. Please see Chapter 17 for all the details.

Application (or **program**) **icons** are typically rather fancy ones. These belong to the actual applications (the software programs that you work in). Each application has its own design so they all look different, but what they have in common is that many try to give some sort of **visual clue** as to what they do. For instance, below you can see that the TextEdit icon represents a word processing program; the iMovie icon represents a movie-making program. When you create your own *document* in an application, the document usually has some visual clue that it belongs to that particular application, as you can see below and on the following page.

Application Icons

TextEdit   martha ran.rtf   iMovie   summer.mov

Each of these application icons (TextEdit and iMovie) gives you a visual clue of what it does. Each of their documents also gives you a visual clue that it was created in that particular application.

Practice: Single-click the Application icon in the Toolbar (shown circled, to the left).

Find the **Chess** icon.

To open the Chess application, double-click the Chess icon.

To play, drag a white piece into the square of your choice. The Mac will make the next move. To get a hint of where to move next, go to the Move menu and choose "Show a hint."

To quit the application, go to the "Chess" menu and choose "Quit."

Document Icons

Document icons represent documents, or files, that **you** (or someone like you) have created in any particular application. Whenever you are working in an application and you save your document with a name, a document icon is created for you somewhere on your Mac.

Document icons almost always look like a piece of paper with the top-right corner folded down, as you can see in the examples below. Typically document icons have some resemblance to the application they were created in, as shown below and on the previous page.

Notice most document icons have an "extension," which is a two- to four-letter code at the end of the name. These extensions are very important in Mac OS X; see Chapter 14 to learn about extensions.

▾ Single-click a document icon to **select** it.

▾ Double-click a document icon to open the application **in which the document was created,** which will also place that particular document on the screen. This means the application will open first, and then the document will open inside that application. *A document cannot open on the screen without some sort of application opening first.*

Now, just because you have a document icon doesn't guarantee that you also have the application that created it! For instance, your friend might send you a file in a word processing application that you don't have. There are a number of things to do in this situation; see the information on the opposite page, as well as page 520.

template.id   summer.mov   Travel Stories.rtf   xmascard.pdf   sonnets.idd

This document icon has the ***bottom-right corner*** *turned up. This indicates that the file is a* ***template,*** *or* ***stationery.*** *When you open it, you get a new, untitled copy of the original document. See Chapter 12 for more information about templates and stationery*

You can see the top-right corner turned down in all of these document icons.

Quicken   Robin 2002   Acrobat   xmascard.pdf

Each document icon matches its application icon.

jane.jpg   jane.jpeg   family photo.tiff   santafe.gif   BookaCook logo.eps

These document icons actually represent graphics (you can tell by the extensions; see Chapter 14). Graphic documents can be opened in a number of different applications, and they can also be placed on the pages of other documents; for instance, you can insert a photo of Jane in your letter to the dog pound.

Occasionally you will see a **blank document icon.** This usually means one of two things:

1. A blank document icon often means that the application in which this document was created is not on your computer. For instance, the blank document shown below, left, is the same file as the InDesign document (Adobe InDesign is a page layout program) on the right. When this file is in a computer that has InDesign installed, it looks like it belongs to InDesign. But if I copy the same file to a computer that does **not** have the application InDesign installed, the icon is blank.

Hondo ad.idd   Hondo ad.idd   *Sometimes, just to confuse you, your document does appear with an icon, even if the application is not in your Mac.*

2. Many of the files that help operate Mac OS X look like blank document icons. To protect you from messing up your computer, you're generally not allowed to open these. If you try, you get the message shown below. You'll only find these blank system icons if you go poking around where you shouldn't be (anywhere except your own Home folders).

CaslonPro.otf   PkgInfo   *Almost all the files in the system folders are blank. Just leave them alone.*

If you double-click a blank document icon, you will usually see this message:

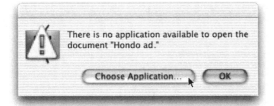

You can click "Choose Application…" to get an "Open" dialog box where you can choose from your list of applications; select one that you think might open this document.

Or instead, try dragging the **document** icon on top of various **application** icons, as illustrated in Chapter 12. If an application can open a file of this type (AppleWorks, for instance, can open almost any text file), the application icon will become highlighted. This is your clue that this application can open this file; let go of the document and it will try to open in that program (it doesn't always work).

Blank Document Icons

Tip: Sometimes if you rebuild the Classic Desktop, as explained in Chapter 40, blank icons will get their icons back, depending on why it was blank in the first place.

dreamland.hqx

You might also see this "generic" icon, which indicates that Mac OS X recognizes it as a file but is not sure which application it belongs to.

System Icons   If you click the Computer icon in the Toolbar and view it in Column View, as shown below, you'll see several "system" folders, or folders that the system uses to run your Macintosh. Inside most of these folders are **system icons** that represent programming that performs essential operations. You'll see a variety of types of icons, most with some sort of "extension," or additional file abbreviation after a period.

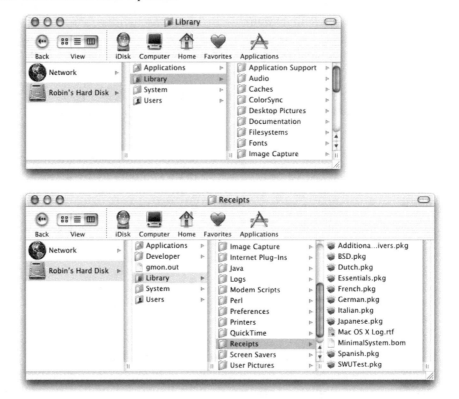

▼ Double-clicking on most system icons (the ones that aren't blank, as discussed on the previous page) will give you the message shown below. This is because most system icons are just visual representations of the data on your disk that makes them work—there's really nothing to look at besides the cute little icon.

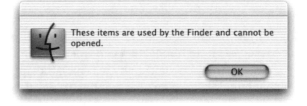

To rename any icon—a folder, a document, a program, a disk—just click once on the icon's *name* (not on the icon's *graphic*); wait a second or two until a box appears around the name so you know you're changing it, then simply type the new name. **Or** instead of clicking directly on the name, click anywhere on the icon to select it, then press Return to get that box around it (this is actually faster than clicking on the name).

Renaming Icons

Don't rename any of the folders in your Home folder!

Click once on the name to select it . . . *you'll see a box around the name . . .* *then just type to replace the selected name.*

In changing the name, you can use standard word processing techniques, as detailed in Chapter 13, to set an "insertion point" (the flashing vertical bar, your **visual clue** that you are in typing mode). Or double-click a *word* to select the whole word, backspace to delete characters, etc. You can use your arrow keys to move the insertion point. In fact, press the UpArrow or DownArrow to move the insertion point to the very beginning or the very end of the name. As soon as you click somewhere else, or hit the Return or Enter keys, the name is set.

Tip: You can also use the Show Info box to change the names of icons. Open Show Info for a selected icon (press Command I), then retype the name at the top of the box.

If you do **accidentally change the name** of an icon (which is very easy to do—files have been known to mysteriously change their names to \\\\\\ \\\\\\ or `````` while you weren't doing anything but leaning on the keyboard), you do have one chance to restore the name to its original form: **Undo.** As soon as you see the mistake has been made, from the Edit menu choose "Undo." *If you haven't done anything* since this minor catastrophe (and things could be worse), Undo will restore the original name, even if you forgot it. In fact, you can undo the name on one file until you change another name—check the Edit menu; if you can still Undo the change, the first thing in the Edit menu will be "Undo Rename"; choose it. If you are too late to catch Undo, you'll just have to rename it yourself (if you know what it was). Remember, the keyboard shortcut for Undo is Command Z.

Undoing a Name Change

You **cannot change the name** of a folder, disk, application, or any other icon that is **locked,** as described on the following page.

If You Can't Change the Name

Locking a File

You can see information about every file icon in a **Show Info** window (details about Show Info are in Chapter 29). One of the things you can do in a Show Info window is **lock** a file so no one can make changes to it.

To get the Show Info window: In the Finder, click once on an icon, then press Command I *or* go the the File menu and choose "Show Info."

There is a "Locked" checkbox in the lower-left corner of the Show Info window. If you check this box (click once on it), this file cannot be renamed or inadvertently thrown away—as soon as it hits the Trash, a dialog box comes up telling you a locked file cannot be thrown away. It also becomes a **read-only** file: anyone can open and read the file, but no one can save any changes to it. You can't even change the Show Info comments. This is handy for sending around copies of a document and ensuring no one accidentally changes anything.

To lock the file, click in the checkbox.

To unlock the file, click in the checkbox again. If there is no ✔, the file is unlocked.

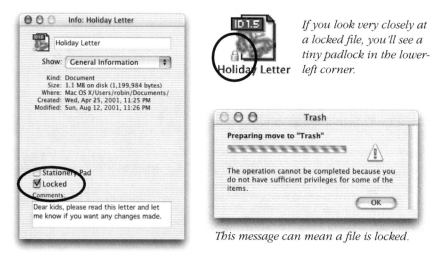

If you look very closely at a locked file, you'll see a tiny padlock in the lower-left corner.

This message can mean a file is locked.

As you can see, this isn't a very secure way to safeguard a file—all anyone has to do is Show Info and unlock it. It's just a way to prevent things from happening to the file accidentally.

You'll find there are a number of files you cannot lock, including all of your Home folders. Apple is trying to protect you from yourself.

Tip: If Mac OS X yells at you because a file is locked, but the "Locked" button is not checked in Show Info, it may have been checked in OS 9 in Get Info. Restart your Mac in OS 9, unlock the file, then go back to OS X.

Moving Icons

To move icons, simply press-and-drag them. You can put any icon into or drag any icon out of any *folder* icon.

> When you drag an icon (or any file, no matter what it looks like) from one place to another **on the same disk,** the computer **moves** it to the other place.

> When you drag a file **from one disk to another disk,** the computer **copies** it to the other disk. For details about copying, see Chapter 11.

Creating Your Own Icons

You can **create your own icons** and apply them to any existing icons, and you can copy icons from one file and apply them to another.

▼ Open an OS X graphic program like AppleWorks (paint or draw). Or use any clipart or photo image instead.

▼ In the graphic program, create the little picture that you want as your icon. No matter what size you make the art, the Mac will reduce it to an appropriate size as it becomes the new icon. But if you make it too large, it will be unrecognizable when reduced.

▼ Select the image you created or found; copy it (from the Edit menu).

▼ Go back to a Finder window.

▼ Click once on the icon whose picture you want to replace. From the File menu, choose "Show Info" (**or** press Command I).

▼ Click once on the icon that appears in the upper-left of the Show Info window (see below, circled).

▼ From the Edit menu, choose "Paste" (**or** press Command V).

▼ Close the Show Info window (press Command W).

Although this can be a wonderful trick, I don't like to encourage beginners to change all their icons because that original icon tells you so much information. If you start changing icons, how do you know what will happen when you double-click? Is this object a folder that will open to a window, or is it an application, a document, a system icon, or what? Just be sensible.

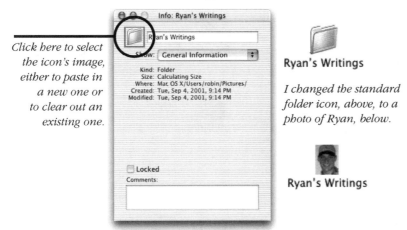

Click here to select the icon's image, either to paste in a new one or to clear out an existing one.

Ryan's Writings

I changed the standard folder icon, above, to a photo of Ryan, below.

Ryan's Writings

To change an icon back to the original, select its tiny icon in the Show Info window; from the Edit menu, choose "Cut." The original icon will appear.

Draw lines to match the description with the icon. Carefully read through the list first—although there are several similar icons, each has a different visual clue.

application

hard disk

CD

folder

document

Zip disk

unknown document

selected icon

locked icon

Trash can

DVD

ready to rename

stationery/template

Little Mac Book

Ryan's Writings

FontDisc

sonnets.idd

CASABLANCA

Favorites

PkgInfo

great words

To Do List

Mac OS X

Holiday Letter

TextEdit

Answers on page 750.

All About Using The Dock

The **Dock** is that strip across the bottom of your screen that contains a number of icons. Apple has put those icons in the Dock for your use, but you can customize it endlessly, as explained on the following pages. You can add folders, applications, web sites, documents, windows, or just about anything else to the Dock—once an item is in the Dock, you just single-click to open it. You can delete items, rearrange items, move the Dock to the left or right of your screen, enlarge it, reduce it, hide it, and more.

This is the Dock. If you're a Mac user from way back, you'll discover that the Dock takes the place of the traditional Apple menu, the Application menu, and the Application Switcher.

The Basic Dock

Below is a typical Dock with brief explanations of what each item does and where you can find more information about it. Items marked with an asterisk (*) will *automatically* connect you to the Internet (if your connection has been set up and is ready to go; if not, see Chapter 32).

The Finder; click to open the main Finder window. See Chapter 9.

This is the Internet Explorer browser for viewing web pages.* See Chapter 32.

Use Sherlock to find files on your disk or information on the Internet; see Chapter 24.

Dividing line: *applications to the left, everything else to the right.*

Throw files away in the Trash basket. See Chapter 17.

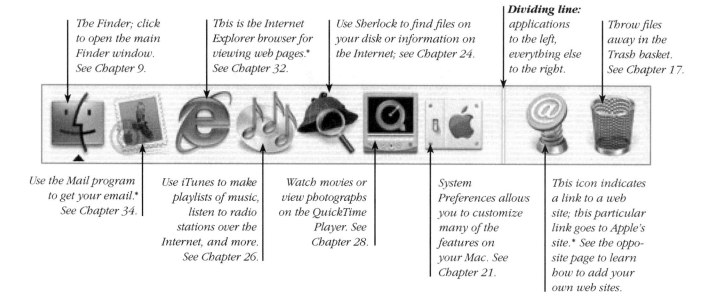

Use the Mail program to get your email.* See Chapter 34.

Use iTunes to make playlists of music, listen to radio stations over the Internet, and more. See Chapter 26.

Watch movies or view photographs on the QuickTime Player. See Chapter 28.

System Preferences allows you to customize many of the features on your Mac. See Chapter 21.

This icon indicates a link to a web site; this particular link goes to Apple's site.* See the opposite page to learn how to add your own web sites.

Every now and then one of your Dock icons might turn into a questions mark or the generic OS X icon.

Drag the question mark out of the Dock and replace it with another, as explained on the opposite page.

The generic icon is okay. It still works just the same, and when you restart your Mac, your real icon will probably come back.

Position your mouse over a Dock item (don't click or press), and a "tool tip" appears to tell you what that item is.

To find the window that stores a particular icon, press (don't click!) to get a pop-up menu; choose "Show in Finder" and the window that holds the icon will open.

Or *Command-click on the icon and the folder that holds the icon will instantly open.*

Add Items to the Dock

You can **add** anything you want to the Dock. Typically, you'll add files and folders that you want easy access to. You'll notice when you add *application icons,* they go on the *left* side of the dividing line. All other icons must stay to the *right* of the dividing line.

To add a file: Find its icon (folder, application icon, document icon, etc.), then simply drag that icon down to the Dock and let go. You are not actually *moving* the file—you are simply adding an "alias" of it to the Dock (an alias goes and gets the real file; see Chapter 22 about aliases).

To add an open application: While the application is open and active, you will see its icon in the Dock. Press on that icon and you'll get a pop-up menu; choose "Keep in Dock" (shown to the right).

To add a web site: Using Internet Explorer, go to the web site you like. In the Address bar, drag the little @ symbol (circled, right) down to the Dock. If you are using Netscape, drag the Bookmark icon (next to the Location box) to the Desktop, then drag that icon into the Dock.

When you add a folder, you can *click* its icon in the Dock to open the folder window, or *press* to pop up a menu listing every item in the folder (shown to the right). Slide up to choose an item in the list and that particular file will open. If you have folders inside this folder, you will get a submenu showing the items in that subfolder. Notice, however, that the folder icon in the Dock gives you no visual clue as to *which* folder it is. You can customize its icon, if you like (see page 117), so you can identify individual folders without having to mouse over each one.

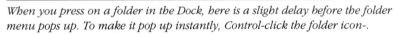

When you press on a folder in the Dock, here is a slight delay before the folder menu pops up. To make it pop up instantly, Control-click the folder icon-.

Rearrange Items in the Dock

To move the positions of items in the Dock, simply press-and-drag them. Only application items are allowed to the left of the dividing line, however; everything else must stay to the right.

Remove Items from the Dock

To remove items from the Dock, simply press-and-drag them off the Dock and drop them anywhere on the Desktop. A cute little "poof" will appear. Don't worry—you won't destroy the original files. All you remove is an icon from the Dock—you won't hurt the original application, folder, file, web site, or anything else. (You cannot remove the Trash basket or the Finder icon, though.)

This is the "poof" that appears when you remove something from the Dock.

Dock Preferences

System Preferences icon

Dock icon

You have control over several aspects of the Dock. To get the Dock preferences pane shown below, click the System Preferences icon (as shown to the left) in the Dock, and then click the "Dock" icon (also shown to the left).

Or from the Apple menu, choose "Dock...." From there you can either change several settings using that menu, or choose "Dock Preferences..." to get the preferences pane shown below.

The effects of "Magnification" are shown below.

Check here and the Dock will automatically hide after you click on it. When you slide your mouse into the side of the screen where it's hiding, it will automatically reappear.

If you don't like the way windows slither into and out of the Dock, like a genie in a bottle, you can switch to the "Scale" effect.

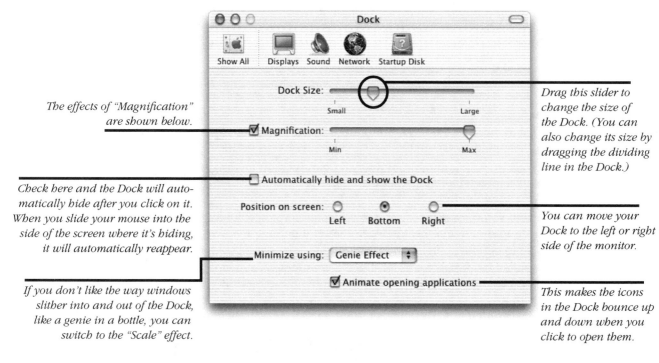

Drag this slider to change the size of the Dock. (You can also change its size by dragging the dividing line in the Dock.)

You can move your Dock to the left or right side of the monitor.

This makes the icons in the Dock bounce up and down when you click to open them.

When "Magnification" is checked, the Dock icons grow as you run your mouse over them. How large they grow depends on where you set the Magnification slider.

*There is a **shortcut** to get the Dock preferences: Control-click on the divider line in the Dock and change your preferences from the pop-up menu.*

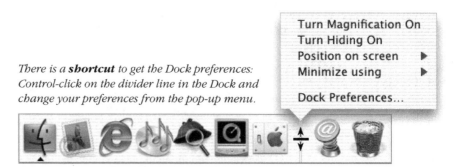

The **triangles** you see under certain icons in the Dock are very important **visual clues.** A triangle means that particular application is open at the moment. Because you can see the Dock at all times (unless you choose to hide it), you are constantly aware of which and how many applications are open at any given moment.

Triangles in the Dock

If you need to **quit an application,** you don't even need to bring the application forward: just press on its icon in the Dock, and in the pop-up menu, choose Quit.

Quit an Application from the Dock

Show In Finder
Quit

The triangle indicates the application is open.
Press on the icon to get the pop-up menu to Quit.

Here are a few extra tips and tricks for using the Dock.

Dock Tips and Tricks

To enlarge or reduce the Dock, simply grab the dividing line (shown at the bottom of the opposite page), press, and drag. The Dock will enlarge or reduce as you drag. Let go and it will stay that size until you change it again.

To hide the window that's currently in the foreground when you open or go to another application: Hold down the Option key when you click an application icon in the Dock, or when you click any visible area of the Desktop.

To hide all the windows of all other open applications, hold down the Command and the Option keys when you click an application icon in the Dock.

To find where a docked item is located on your hard disk: Hold down the Command key and click on its icon in the Dock—the folder in which the item is stored will open on your Desktop. As mentioned and shown on page 120, you can also press on the icon to get a pop-up menu, then choose "Show in Finder."

To switch between open applications: Hold down the Command key and tap the Tab key. Each time you tap the Tab key, the next open application icon in the Dock (moving towards the right) will highlight. Just keep pressing Tab until you select the icon you want—then let go of the Command (and Tab) key and the selected application will come forward. (The Finder window is considered an application.) Try it.

To cycle through the open applications in the other direction (going left in the Dock), hold down Command and Shift, then tap the Tab key.

To send windows to the Dock in slow motion: Hold down the Option key when you close a window. Useless trick, but pretty. Try it.

Practice: Position your mouse over the dividing line in the Dock, press, and drag upward to **enlarge** the Dock. Drag downward to **reduce** it.

Hide and show the Dock:

1. Hold down the Control key and click on the dividing line to get the pop-up menu; choose "Turn Hiding On."

2. Now move your mouse away from the Dock and watch the Dock slide away.

3. Then move your mouse down to the bottom of your screen (don't press the mouse button down) and the Dock will slide up; when you move your mouse away, the Dock disappears.

4. If you want the Dock visible all the time, slide your mouse down so the Dock appears. Hold down the Control key and click on the dividing line to get the pop-up menu; choose "Turn Hiding Off."

1. Describe two ways to move the Dock from the bottom of the screen to either side.

   _____

2. How do you remove an item from the Dock?

   _____

3. How do you rearrange items in the Dock?

   _____

4. Which items in the Dock cannot be moved nor rearranged?

   _____

5. What sort of files can you add to the Dock?

   _____

6. If you add a folder to the Dock, what happens when you **click** on the folder icon?

   _____

7. If you add a folder to the Dock, what happens when you **press** on the folder icon?

   _____

8. How can you resize the Dock itself?

   _____

9. Describe three ways to get the Dock preferences.

   a._____

   b._____

   c._____

10. How can you hide the Dock?

   _____

Answers on page 750.

The Desktop, Finder, and Home

The **Desktop** is what you see on your computer monitor when you start up your Mac. It's the background that the windows and the Dock sit on, and you probably have disk icons also sitting on the Desktop. The Desktop is a *place*. (In your Home area you'll see an icon called "Desktop" which is actually a folder that holds the same things you see on the Desktop itself.)

The **Finder** is actually a *software application* that displays and controls the windows, menus, icons, etc, that you see on the Desktop. **Finder windows** are those windows on the Desktop that show you what is stored inside of your computer.

Home is a collection of folders that are for *your* use, as opposed to the collection of folders that the *Mac* uses to run itself with. You'll keep all of your work and personal files, fonts, and applications in your Home folders. You can create multiple users for one computer, and every user has his or her own Home. When more than one person uses the machine, or on a "network" of connected Macs, as in a school or office, everyone's Home folders are protected from every other user.

The Desktop Below you see a **Desktop,** which probably looks very similar to the one on your Mac. You can store items directly on the Desktop, as shown below—you don't have to put everything in the Dock that you want to keep handy. The big difference between storing things in the Dock vs. on the Desktop is that the Dock is always available and accessible, no matter which application you are using, whereas the Desktop might be covered up by the window of an application. Keeping that in mind, feel free to store some of your most-used folders, documents, or applications right on the Desktop. It's best to use **aliases** for most things you want to keep on the Desktop—see Chapter 22 for alias details.

This is my Home window. Click once on the Home icon in any Toolbar, like you see here, to open your Home area.

This is actually a folder. It contains the same things you see sitting directly on the Desktop.

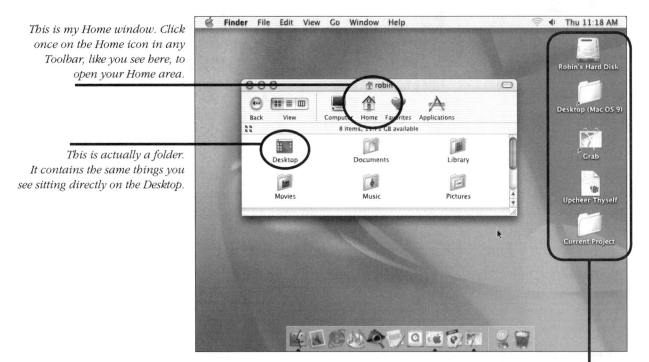

You can see here that I'm storing several files right on the Desktop. If I were to double-click the "Desktop" icon in the window you see above, it would show me these same four items.

*The folder named **Desktop (Mac OS 9)** is an "alias," or an empty icon that goes to get the real thing. If you were using Mac OS 9 and had stored items on the Desktop, you'll now find those items in this folder.*

Every Mac will display this folder, but it actually only works if you have Mac OS 9 installed on the same hard disk or "partition" as Mac OS X. If you have multiple partitions, each volume will have its own "Desktop Folder" with all of the items that you had left on the Desktop.

*If you double-click this file and you get a message that the **original item could not be found**—don't worry. Just throw this icon in the Trash basket (see Chapter 17).*

You can **change the background of your Desktop.** Apple provides several collections of images for you, from solid colors to nature scenes to wild abstract graphics. Or you can use any graphic you have on your computer as a background. You might want to use your favorite holiday photo, a family portrait, or your daughter's kindergarten handprint.

If you have images outside of your computer and don't know yet how to get them inside, have a friend help you. Once an image is "digitized," or turned into a digital image so the computer can handle it, put the image in your Pictures folder, which is in your Home. Then follow the directions below to use it as a background.

To change the background of the Desktop:

1. From the Apple menu, choose "System Preferences...."

2. In the System Preferences pane, click on the button "Desktop," shown to the right. (If you don't have this button, you're not using Mac OS X v.1; instead, go to the Finder menu and choose "Preferences....") You'll get the Desktop pane, as shown below.

3. Now you can do one of several things:

   ▼ You see a row of images along the bottom. Click once on any one of those images and it will appear in the "well" above.

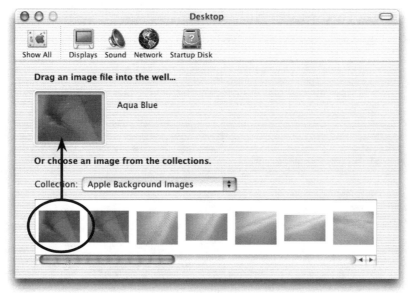

Click one of these to apply it as the new background. Notice you can scroll over to see more.

The images that are narrower are for monitors with "cinema display."

Desktop Colors, Patterns, or Pictures

▼ **Or** click on the "Collection" menu and choose from other collections Apple has provided. The example shown below is from the "Nature" collection.

Tip: If an image is very large, it will fill the screen (all of the images provided by Apple fill the screen). But if you choose a small photo, perhaps one you created yourself, that photo will be repeated across the entire background (which can be rather obnoxious). Experiment with your own photos: in an image-editing application, perhaps create a solid, large background and position your photo within that background. Then use that large file as your background image.

▼ **Or** drag an image from anywhere on your computer and drop it right into the well. You'll have to find the file you want to drop in and position it on your screen so when you open the Desktop pane, you can still see the file. Then just drag it from your Desktop to the well.

▼ **Or** store images you want to use in your Pictures folder in your Home. Then here in the Desktop pane, click the "Collection" menu and choose "Pictures Folder." All of the images you have in your folder will appear in the slot along the bottom. Click one of them to change the background.

Adorable as my oldest son is, his face repeated across the screen a hundred times is rather annoying and makes it difficult to see what's on the Deskop.

If you like to keep icons on your Desktop, you have a few **options** for how they are arranged and how large they appear. You can also use the "Clean Up" and "Arrange by Name" choices in the View menu (see Chapter 6). Just make sure you first click on the Desktop so the *Desktop* is active, not a window, before you go to the View menu and make a choice.

To change the size of icons on the Desktop:

1. Make sure the Desktop is active: click once on it.

2. From the View menu, choose "Show View Options," or press Command J.

3. In the View Options dialog box, as shown to the right, you should see the word "Desktop" in the title bar. If you see anything else, just click right now on an empty spot on the Desktop and the name in this title bar will change to "Desktop."

4. To change the size of icons, just drag the "Icon Size" slider bar (circled, left). You'll see the icons currently on your Desktop change shape. When you like their size, just close this box.

Desktop View Options

You can tell when the Desktop is properly selected because all other options in this menu will be gray, except the ones shown above.

There is an invisible, underlying grid on the Desktop. The size of the grid depends on the size of your icons. You can choose to force all of the icons on the Desktop to snap into the cells of this invisible grid by choosing **Always snap to grid,** as shown to the right.

As you add and delete icons from the Desktop, you can force them to stay in a pre-arranged order by choosing **Keep arranged by,** then click on the menu that appears and choose the order in which you want them arranged. Now when you add or delete an icon from the Desktop, you will see all of the icons rearrange themselves instantly according to your choice.

Computer Level

The **Computer level** in a Finder window shows you all the possible "storage devices," or "volumes," you have available. Storage devices include your own hard disk, including any "partitions" you might have separated it into (see Chapter 40 about partitions). If you are in an office or school facility that uses "servers," or big computers that store files and send them out to other computers for others to use, you will see icons for the servers in the Computer level. You will also see any computers that you are connected to over any kind of network, such as in a small home office (the Mac considers all computers that you are connected to in any way to be "servers").

If you have an extra hard disk attached to your Mac, such as a FireWire hard disk, its icon will appear here. Any removable disks you have "mounted" (inserted into your Mac and are now available to use) will show their icons here. So this level basically shows you every possible media that is connected to your computer at the moment, media that you can take files from or store files onto.

Click this icon to see the Computer level of your Mac. Notice the title bar tells you whose computer you are looking at.

*This **Computer level** shows three hard disks, which are the three partitions my main hard disk is divided into (see Chapter 40 about partitions).*

You see three network icons (robin, john, and scarlett), which are three of the other computers in my home office that I can share files with.

You see two removable disks: one is a Zip disk, the other is a floppy, even though their icons are the same. You see one CD, which is a music CD.

The big world icon named "Network" is actually a folder that provides access to I STILL CAN'T FIND OUT WHAT THIS IS!!!!

In the **Finder Preferences,** you have control over several Desktop features.

To open the Finder Preferences:

At the Desktop, go to the Finder menu and choose "Preferences...."

You can decide which icons automatically appear on the **Desktop.** As shown below, you can uncheck the "Hard disks" box so hard disk icons do not appear on the Desktop. You can also uncheck "Removable media," which means you won't see any CD, DVD, Jaz, Zip, floppy, or any other kind of icons that represent disks you have inserted into drives. If you are on a network and can connect to other computers, an icon appears on your Desktop that represents the other computer, or server; you can turn off that icon as well. The reason it's not important to have these appear on your Desktop is that every one of these icons appears in your Computer level window, as described on the opposite page. So you can uncheck these boxes and clear off your Desktop.

When you first click on the Finder icon (the smiling face) in the Dock, and whenever you press Command N to get a new window, the Mac automatically opens a **Finder window** that displays the **Computer** level, as shown on the opposite page. It might be more useful to you if the window always opened to display your **Home** folders instead; if so, click in the "Home" button. Home is explained on the following pages.

Finder Preferences

"Show these items on the Desktop"

"New Finder Window shows"

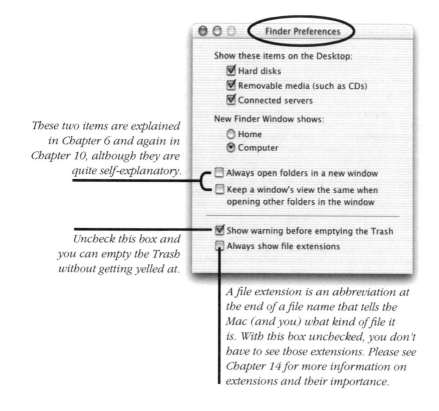

These two items are explained in Chapter 6 and again in Chapter 10, although they are quite self-explanatory.

Uncheck this box and you can empty the Trash without getting yelled at.

A file extension is an abbreviation at the end of a file name that tells the Mac (and you) what kind of file it is. With this box unchecked, you don't have to see those extensions. Please see Chapter 14 for more information on extensions and their importance.

Your Home

Home is an area of your Mac that Apple has set up for you to work in. It has a number of folders already created in which you can store your work, and a Public folder in which you can put files you want to share with others who might use the machine. If you are the only person who ever uses the computer, you are still considered one of the "users" and you have a password—remember that password you choose the first time you turned on the machine? You had better remember that password.

Do not move or rename any of the folders in your Home area!

They have important jobs to do and Mac OS X depends on being able to find their names and locations.

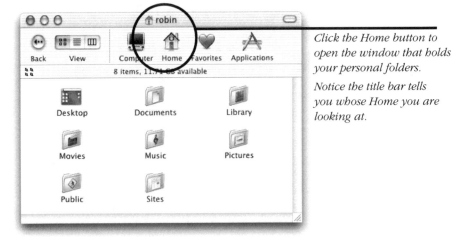

Click the Home button to open the window that holds your personal folders.

Notice the title bar tells you whose Home you are looking at.

The folders you see above each have specific purposes.

Desktop: Although its icon is different, this is actually a folder. It contains any folders or documents that are sitting on your Desktop, as described on page 126. Anything you put on the Desktop (except disks and servers) will appear in this folder, and anything you put in this folder will appear on the Desktop. (Disk and server icons appear in the Computer level window, as explained on page 130.)

Documents: When you are creating your own documents, such as letters, brochures, flyers, etc., and choose to "Save" the file, the Mac automatically opens your Documents folder so you can save it in there. This way you always know where to go to find what you created. It's certainly possible to save your documents into any other folder you want, including new folders you make; see Chapter 14.

If you've opened iTunes yet, you'll find a folder inside Documents called "iTunes." When you import songs from audio CDs, they are automatically stored in this folder. You can change the location of this folder through the iTunes preferences; see Chapter 26.

Library: The Library folder stores a lot of other folders that hold information the Mac needs to run your Home. This is where you will put new fonts, where your new applications will store their own preferences, and more. Don't be putting things in the Library unless you know for certain they belong there (if you know what belongs in the Library, I doubt if you're reading this book).

Movies: If you use iMovie to create a movie from your video camera, the Mac will automatically save your movie into this folder. If you have a still digital camera that records short clips, the Mac will automatically offload them from your camera to this folder. You can choose to save it elsewhere, but if a movie is stored in this folder, you can easily post it to the web for others to see (see Chapters 33 and 37).

Music: Put music files in this folder if you want to share them with someone through the Internet (see Chapters 33 and 37).

Pictures: When you import photographs from your digital camera, they are automatically saved into this folder. You can put the photos anywhere else you like, but if they are in this folder they are easily accessible when you want to change your Desktop background (see pages 127–128), make a customized screensaver (Chapter 29), upload them to your iDisk (Chapter 33 or 37), or send as iCards (Chapter 33).

Public: Files you put in the Public folder are accessible to other users of the computer, while the rest of your Home folders will be locked to anyone else. No one can *remove* the file from your Public folder—it will always be automatically *copied* to another user.

Other users can put files *for you* into your "Drop Box" folder, which is inside your Public folder (see the following page). But no one can take anything *out* of your Drop Box, so if you want to give someone a file, be sure put it in the Public folder.

Sites: If you turn on "Web Sharing" in the Sharing preferences pane, any web pages you store in this folder can be seen on the Internet, once you are connected and tell someone the address. See Chapter 37.

The **Shared folder** is not in your Home area, but one level back, in the "Users" level (as shown on the following page). Anything you put in this folder can be used by all other users, and they won't have to open your Home area to get to it. If you want to share a file with every other user on this computer, like a teacher might in a school lab, you can put the file in this Shared folder and everyone can copy it to their own Home Documents folder. This is an easier way to share among multiple users than to copy the file into every one of their Drop Box folders.

A file from the Shared folder cannot be *removed*—it will be always be *copied* to another user's folder.

Every user uses the same Shared folder. But only the user who put the file inside the Shared folder in the first place will be allowed to move it, rename it, trash it, etc. Everyone else can only copy it.

The Shared folder

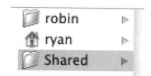

In the Users folder, you will see icons for every user. Only the person who is logged in will have the Home icon next to their name.

The Shared folder is accessible to everyone.

Safe and protected An important feature about the Home area is that it is automatically **protected** from anyone else who uses the same computer. And there are several extra ways you can protect your personal files, fonts, and applications.

- ▼ You can make the Mac ask for a login password when the machine is turned on, even if you are the only user.

- ▼ You can set up the screensaver to turn on when you are away from the computer, and then make it pasword protected—someone must type in a password before the screensaver turns off.

- ▼ You can set up two users for yourself: Create one that has administrative privileges so you can add and delete applications, fonts, etc. Set up another user for yourself that does not have administrative privileges, then log on as that user. Even if someone did use your machine, they could not add or delete any files in critical folders (although they would have access to your personal folders).

See Chapter 20 for details on how to make all of these things happen.

Sharing files with another user When others log in as **different users,** they each get their own Home areas. They can load their own fonts; safely store their own documents; set the Desktop preferences, Finder preferences, and window view preferences to accommodate themselves; add new folders; and organize their files however they like. Even the Trash basket belongs to each alone—every user has their own Trash and can choose to empty it when they feel like it.

This computer has two users, me and Ryan. You can tell I am the user logged in at the moment because the Home icon is next to "robin."

*But I have selected the user folder "ryan" and I can see his Home folders. Notice every folder except "Public" and "Sites" has a "Do not enter" symbol on it. This is a **visual clue** that I cannot open or put anything into his other folders.*

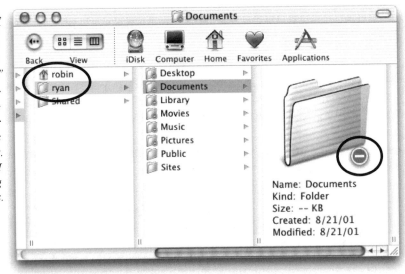

Although you are locked out of most of the other users' folders, you can **give a copy of a file** to someone else by dropping it in their **Drop Box,** which is located in their Public folder, as shown below. (For more information about moving or copying files from one folder to another, see Chapter 11.)

The Drop Box

This is Ryan's Home folder.

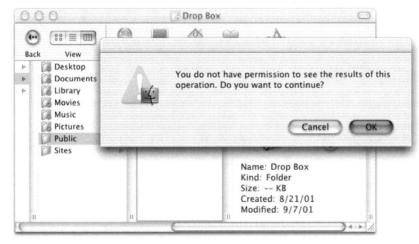

This symbol indicates you can put things inside this folder.

I am logged on as the user "robin." Here, I selected Ryan's Home folder, then his Public folder, then the Drop Box.

*I dragged a document file from the Desktop and dropped it in Ryan's Drop Box (**not** in the Public folder—you are not allowed to put things in someone else's Public folder). This message appears, which is okay— you just have to trust that the file gets copied into the folder. It will.*

For details about how to create new users, delete others, share files, add applications and fonts to your Home, and more, see Chapter 20.

General Preferences

The **General** preferences give you several options that apply to different parts of your computer. To open this, go to the Apple menu, choose "System Preferences…," then click on the "General" icon.

Appearance: Choose between the Blue or the Graphite look for all of your buttons, scroll bar sliders, the selection bar in menus, etc.

Highlight color: Click this menu to get a list of color choices, or choose "Other…" and build your own color. The one you choose will be the color of the selection when you select text in a word processor, a file in a window, or an entry in an "edit box" in any dialog box.

Place scroll arrows and **Click in the scroll bar to:** I explained these in Chapter 6, page 72. They're fairly self-explanatory.

Number of recent items: Click these menus to choose how many applications and documents the Mac will keep track of and list in the "Recent Items" command in the Apple menu. See page 139 for details.

Turn off text smoothing: Text smoothing is a feature that blurs the edges of text so it appears smoother on the screen (not in print). Sometimes, however, in very small type (say, 8 or 10 point) the blurring effect makes the type more difficult to read; hence you have this option to turn it off for smaller sizes. You can't turn it off altogether, though. Experiment with the size options and see what you prefer.

If you've worked with image-editing programs, you are probably accustomed to the "aliasing" and "anti-aliasing" technique; well, "text smoothing" is "anti-aliasing."

Once you know how to do one thing,
move on to the next.
—James Baldwin

Once you know how to do one thing,
move on to the next.
—James Baldwin

These two examples are the same text, same size, same typeface, in the same application. The top example has text smoothing applied; the bottom one doesn't.

Each of the items on the *left* side of the **Finder menu bar** are explained either in the following pages or in other chapters, as noted below. The items on the far-*right* of the menu bar appear not just in the Finder, but in every application. That is, you will always have access to whatever is on the right side. They are explained on this page.

You can remove these items, if you like, and there are others you can add. If you *can* add or remove something, you'll find a checkbox in its preferences (found in the System Preferences pane) that says something like, "Show the clock in the menu bar."

The Finder Menu Bar

If you have an AirPort card installed in your Mac, you'll see this icon. See Chapter 32 about AirPort.

See pages 138–139. *See page 142.* *See Chapter 6.* *See page 95.*

See pages 140–141. *See Chapter 13.* *See page 143.* *See page 12.*

Tip: To **remove** items from the right side of the menu bar, hold down the Command key and drag their icons to the Desktop, then let go. Poof. To **rearrange** items, Command-drag an icon left or right.

At any time you can change the volume on your Mac using this Sound menu.

Click once on the time and you'll get this menu where you can see the full date, choose to view a simple clock icon instead of the time, and open the "Date & Time" preferences pane, as shown below.

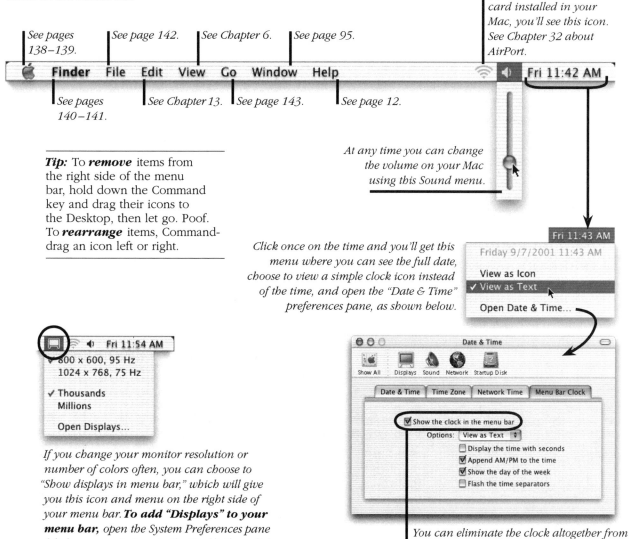

*If you change your monitor resolution or number of colors often, you can choose to "Show displays in menu bar," which will give you this icon and menu on the right side of your menu bar. **To add "Displays" to your menu bar,** open the System Preferences pane (click once on its icon in the Dock), then click the "displays" icon, and you'll see the checkbox.*

You can eliminate the clock altogether from the menu bar if you uncheck this box.

The Apple Menu

This is the Apple menu, something you will become very familiar with.

___

Tip: Click on the version number in the "About" box and you will see the "build" number of the version of Mac OS X you're running. Click again and you'll see the serial number of this Macintosh.

___

The **Apple menu** is the only menu on the left side of the menu bar that stays the same no matter which application you are using or where you are in your computer, so everything you see in this menu you can use at any time. Some of these items are discussed elsewhere in this book, but the others are explained below.

About This Mac: Choose this item to check on which version of the operating system you are using, as well as how much RAM (random access memory) you have installed in the machine. It also tells you, in case you didn't know, which "processor," or chip, is running your machine. As you can see by the dialog box to the right, this machine is "running" the operating system Mac OS X, version 10.1.1. It has 1.2 gigabytes of memory installed, and the Mac is using a PowerPC G4 processor.

Get Mac OS X Software: When you select this item, your web browser software will open, your Mac will try to connect to the Internet and if it is successful, you will be taken to Apple's web site where you can download software that you can use in OS X. You'll find free software ("freeware"); free updates for software you might already have ("updates"); software you can download to see if you like it ("demo") and if you do, you can buy it; and more. Also see the "Software Update" preferences in Chapter 21.

If you want to use this command and you have a "dial-up" Internet account (your modem dials a phone number and you're not permanently connected), *first* open your connection, *then* choose this command.

System Preferences: This opens the System Preferences pane, where you can customize a number of the features on your Mac, as well as set up your networking, choose to share files, and more. Choosing this item from the Apple menu is exactly the same as clicking on the System Preferences button in the Dock. Some of these preferences are explained individually in the chapters where they are pertinent, and the rest are in Chapter 21.

Dock: This provides a menu where you can change some of the Dock preferences, as you might have learned in Chapter 8, instead of having to open the Dock preferences pane. Choosing this is the same as Command-clicking on the Dock dividing line.

Location: A "location" is a set of networking preferences for connecting to the Internet or to other computers. Depending on your situation, you might only have one set that connects you to everything and so you never need to worry about this item. Or, like me, you might have one set of networking preferences to dial up through your modem to get connected to the Internet, and a different set that uses an "Ethernet" connection to share files with other computers. Or you might use a laptop and need different locations to get your laptop connected in different places. If so, use the Apple menu to quickly switch to a different location. For details about why and how to make locations, see Chapter 36.

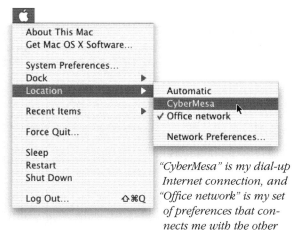

"CyberMesa" is my dial-up Internet connection, and "Office network" is my set of preferences that connects me with the other computers in my office.

Recent Items: Your Mac keeps track of a certain number of applications that you have recently used, as well as a certain number of documents that you have recently opened. Sometimes it is faster to go to the Apple menu and choose an application or document from Recent Items than it is to go digging around in your folders for them. You can determine how many items (if any) the Mac keeps track of in the General preferences, as shown on page 136. If you want to get rid of everything in the list and start over, choose "Clear Menu" from the list.

*You have a list of **"Recent Folders"** in the Go menu; see page 143.*

Recent items also appear in "Save As" and "Open" dialog boxes.

Force Quit: Sometimes applications get hung up and act stupid and you have to force them to quit. If you choose this item, you'll get a dialog box asking which program you want to force to quit. This is the same dialog box you get when you press Command Option Escape. Details about force quitting are in Chapter 16.

Sleep: When you put your computer to sleep, the Mac goes into a low-power mode that saves energy. The screen fades to black and your Mac sounds like it turned itself off, but it didn't. Depending on your computer, your power button might "pulse" yellow when it's asleep. Use the Energy Saver preferences (Chapter 21) to make your Mac go to sleep automatically after a certain period of inactivity.

Restart and **Shut Down:** Restart will power down your machine and bring it back up again without actually turning off the power to it. Shut Down will close everything up neatly and turn off the power. See Chapter 19.

Log Out: If there are multiple users on a machine, one logs out so the other can log in and access her own Home files. See Chapter 19.

Finder Menu   Most of the items you see in the **Finder menu** also appear in every program's **application menu,** which is what this actually is—it's the Finder's application menu. For instance, when you open the application Grab, there is a "Grab" menu that has these same menu items. When you open Internet Connect, there is an "Internet Connect" menu that has these same items. So below are explanations of these items that you will see in every program.

About the Finder: This gives you a small commercial about whatever application you're in. It might tell you who created it and when, and usually provides the "version number" of the software (every time software is improved and updated, it gets a new version number).

Preferences: Every application has preferences that you can change to customize the program for yourself. The **Finder Preferences** are explained on page 131.

Empty Trash: This is a feature specific to the Finder (that is, you won't find it in the application menu of other programs). Notice in this example there is an ellipsis (three dots) in the menu command. The ellipsis, remember from Chapter 5, is a **visual clue** that you will get a dialog box when you choose this item. In this case, the dialog box asks if you really want to throw away the stuff in the trash. Now, if you go to the Finder Preferences as shown on page 131 (choose "Preferences..." from this menu) and uncheck the box to warn you about emptying the trash, the ellipsis will disappear from this menu. This indicates, of course, that you *won't* get the warning dialog box.

Services: This is an interesting feature that you'll find in most applications that were created specifically for Mac OS X. It integrates the capabilities of a number of other possible applications into the one you're using. For instance, let's say you're viewing a web page that has an interesting article. You can select the text in the article (click at the beginning, hold down the Shift key, and click at the end to select everything between the two clicks), then go to Services and choose "Summarize"; the Mac will take the first couple of sentences of each paragraph and put them into a TextEdit document for you. Or you might want to email a quote from the article: select the text you want to quote, from Services choose "Mail," then choose "Mail Text," and the Mac will open your email program, create a new message, and paste this quote into it. Or you might want to save a piece of text as a note to yourself: select the text, choose "Make Sticky," and the Mac will make a sticky note with your text in it.

(See Chapter 29 to learn how to work with Stickies and TextEdit, and Chapter 34 for email.)

Hide Finder: Every application will change this command so it lets you "hide" the current application you are using; that is, if you're using AppleWorks, this item will be "Hide AppleWorks." When you hide something, it just temporarily disappears from the screen. It doesn't close or quit or really go away—it just becomes invisible. You will always know an application, document, folder, or window is still open because its icon will be in the Dock with a triangle under it. You can always go to any application menu (this menu, in any application or at the Desktop) and choose "Show All" to make everything that was hiding reappear (everything in every open application).

In the Finder (at the Desktop), when you choose this item, all of the open windows will disappear without getting sucked into the Dock; just click once on the Desktop and they will all reappear.

Hide Others: This will hide (as explained above) everything else on the screen *except* the windows in the current application. You will still see any icons you have sitting on the Desktop.

Show All: As explained above, this command will make everything reappear that had been previously hidden. "All" really means everything—every application and window that is open on your Mac—not just the windows in the active application.

Tip: To automatically hide the application you are currently working in when you go to the Desktop, hold down the Option key and click on any visible part of the Desktop. Your application will hide so you have a clear view of the Desktop.

File Menu

File	
New Finder Window	⌘N
New Folder	⇧⌘N
Open	⌘O
Close Window	⌘W
Show Info	⌘I
Duplicate	⌘D
Make Alias	⌘L
Show Original	⌘R
Add to Favorites	⌘T
Move to Trash	⌘⌫
Eject	⌘E
Burn Disc...	
Find...	⌘F

The **File menu** in the Finder has a collection of commands that only apply to certain things that are *active* or *selected* in the Finder. Be sure to make the desired window *active* first (click once in it) or *select* the icon first (click once on it) before you choose one of these commands.

New Finder Window: Opens a new window (you don't need to activate or select anything first). Actually, it opens another window of the *same* window that's on your screen. This is useful when you want to open, say, the Applications window, but you don't want to close the current window on your screen. Just open a new Finder window and click on its Application icon.

New Folder: This creates a new, untitled folder in the *active* window.

Open: This opens the *selected* icon, whether it's a folder, document, application, or anything else.

Close Window: This closes the *active* window.

Show Info: This brings up the Show Info dialog box that tells you information about the *selected* icon. See Chapter 29 for details.

Duplicate: This makes a copy of the *selected* icon. The copy will appear in the same folder and its name will be the same as the original, with the word "copy" at the end.

Make Alias: This makes an alias, or a pointer, to the *selected* file. See Chapter 22 about how to use aliases.

Show Original: *Select* an alias icon, then choose this command to open the folder that stores the original item. The original item will be selected.

Add to Favorites: This makes an *alias* of (a pointer to) a selected item and puts that alias in the Favorites folder. Once an item is in that folder, you can open it from the Favorites submenu in the Go menu (see the opposite page), or you can open the Favorites folder and double-click the item in there. You can save into or open Favorites right from the Save As or Open dialog boxes. See Chapter 23 about Favorites.

Move to Trash: This moves the *selected* item or items to the Trash basket.

Eject: This ejects the *selected* removable disk. It will also disconnect you from a *selected* server.

Burn Disc: If you have a Mac with a drive that allows you to burn (copy or record onto) CDs and/or DVDs, use this menu command to start the process. Notice there is an ellipsis (three dots) in the command, which means you will get a dialog box before the process actually begins. See Chapter 14 for details.

Find: This command brings up Sherlock. With Sherlock you can search for files on your computer, or find information, go shopping, look up old lovers, and more on the Internet. See Chapter 24.

The first five commands in the **Go menu** provide you with menu access or keyboard shortcuts to open the various windows of the icons you see in your Finder window Toolbar. For instance, even if there is no window open at all, you can choose "Applications" from this menu, or press Option Command A, and the Applications folder will open. You could close up your Toolbar, if you like, and use these keyboard shortcuts instead.

From the "Favorites" submenu, you can open the Favorites folder, or directly open any of the individual Favorites you have saved (see Chapter 23 about Favorites).

Recent Folders: Gives you a list of the ten folders you last opened. The list is in alphabetical order, not the order in which you opened the folders.

Go to Folder: In the box that appears when you choose this item, you can type the "path" to a folder name, hit Return, and that folder will open. The trick is you have to *know* the path, or the folders within folders where this particular folder is stored. Heck, if you know the path, it will take longer to type it in than to just open the folders and find the dang thing yourself.

The forward slash (/) indicates folders; type a slash between each folder name. The tilde (~) indicates Home folders; type ~ryan to open Ryan's (or whichever user you named) Home folder.

Go Menu

Go

Computer	⌥⌘C
Home	⌥⌘H
iDisk	⌥⌘I
Favorites	▶
Applications	⌥⌘A
Recent Folders	▶
Go to Folder...	⌘~
Back	⌘[
Connect to Server...	⌘K

Go To Folder

Go to the folder:

~robin/documents/robin's docs/

[Cancel] (Go)

If there are no windows open on the Desktop when you choose "Go to Folder...," you get this dialog box.

You do not have to worry about capital letters when typing the path in this box.

Go to the folder:

~robin/Documents/Robin's docs/

(Cancel) (Go)

If a window is open, this "sheet" drops down out of the title bar.

If the folder you want is in this window, you don't have to type the path. (But if the folder you want is in this window, all you have to do is type the first couple letters of its name to select it anyway.)

Back: This is the same as clicking the Back button in the Toolbar. Notice there is a keyboard shortcut you can use instead (Command LeftBracket). This is the same keyboard shortcut that will take you back a page in the web browsers Netscape or Internet Explorer.

Connect to Server: If you are on a network and want to connect to another computer to share files, use this command. See Chapter 36 for details.

1. Every disk and server icon that you see on the Desktop is also displayed in which window?

2. Every document and application icon you might see on the Desktop is also displayed in which window?

3. How would you make the "New Finder Window" command (Command N) open to the Home level instead of the Computer level?

4. Can you stores files directly on the Desktop, instead of keeping all of them in the Finder?

5. Describe how to arrange the files on your Desktop alphabetically.

6. How do you change the color or picture of the Desktop?

7. How can you change the size of the icons on the Desktop?

8. How can you temporarily get rid of (hide) the windows of all applications you're not using at the moment?

9. What is the Power User tip to go to the Desktop and make the windows of the active application disappear at the same time?

10. If you want to share a file with everyone who uses the computer, where would you put it?

Answers on page 750.

How to Use Folders

Folders are essential to organizing your work on the Mac. Folders are, of course, visual representations of our office and home environments, and they function in much the same way.

You can consider your computer to be a big filing cabinet. When you store items in a filing cabinet, you don't just toss them in the drawer, do you? Can you imagine what a mess your filing cabinet would be without folders? A Macintosh can become just as messy and just as difficult to find work in if you don't have some sort of organizational system. It's very important to learn to take advantage of the folders.

Organizing Your Disk Using Folders

Folders keep your computer **well-organized.** Your Mac is basically arranged like a filing cabinet. You have several "drawers" already set up for you: Computer, Home, Favorites, and Applications. You can set up new storage drawers by placing your own folders in the Toolbar (see page 153). Within each drawer/folder (except Computer) you can add other folders, and folders inside of folders.

If you're a new user, you'll probably end up keeping most of your files in the Documents folder. That's fine until you start amassing a large collection of work—then you'll want to start organizing.

This is what your Documents folder can look like if you don't take advantage of organizing your files with folders.

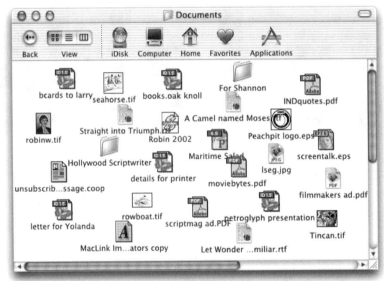

Make new folders inside the Documents folder (or almost anywhere, actually) to organize all of your files.

The title bar menu shows that this folder "MacBook OS X" is stored on the hard disk called "Robin's Projects," which is on the Mac named "Robin's Computer."

MacBook OS X	
Robin's Projects	
Robin's Computer	

Back   View   iDisk   Computer   Home
55 items, 5.2 GB available

Name	Size
▶ 01.Start here.1-12	--
▶ 02.Tutorial.13-22	--
▶ 03.Mouse.23-32	--
▶ 04.KeysKeyboard.33-52	--
▶ 05.MenusShortcuts.53-62	--
▶ 06.Windows.63-104	--
▶ 07.Icons.105-118	--
▶ 08.using Dock.119-124	--
▶ 09.Desktop+Finder.125-144	--
▶ 10.Folders.145-	--
▶ 11.SelectCopy	--
▶ 12.Opening files	--
▶ 13.Typing	--
▶ 14.Saving docs	--
▶ 15.Printing	--
▶ 16.Close&Quit	--
▶ 17.Trash	--
▶ 18.Ejecting disks	--
▶ 19.ShutdownRestart	--
▶ 20.Home & Multiple Users	--
▶ 21.SystemPrefs	--
▶ 22.Aliases	--

MacBook OS X

Back   View   iDisk   Computer   Home
82 items, 5.2 GB available

Name	Size
▶ 01.Start here.1-12	--
▶ 02.Tutorial.13-22	--
▶ 03.Mouse.23-32	--
▶ 04.KeysKeyboard.33-52	--
▼ 05.MenusShortcuts.53-62	--
05.menusShortcuts	1.2 MB
05.urlmenus.eps	180 KB
menus.arrow clues.tif	44 KB
menus.button w ellipse.tif	44 KB
menus.cleanup.tif	40 KB
menus.context image.tif	40 KB
menus.context in app.tif	24 KB
menus.context page.tif	24 KB
menus.contextual1.tif	24 KB
menus.contextual2.tif	20 KB
menus.contextual3.tif	28 KB
menus.edit boxes.tif	40 KB
menus.ellipses dialog.tif	32 KB
menus.ellipses menu.tif	28 KB
menus.finder menubar.tif	28 KB
menus.gray commands.tif	28 KB
menus.hmenu.tif	48 KB

To store all of the files for this book, I made one folder named "MacBook OS X." Inside of that folder I made a separate folder for each chapter.

Each chapter folder contains the page layout file for the chapter, plus every illustration or screenshot (picture of something on the screen) that belongs in that chapter.

I named the folders according to their chapters. The numbers at the ends of the folder names are the current page numbers for that chapter so I can easily find what I'm looking for either by chapter number, title, or page number.

Understanding Folders
and how they display their
contents in the different views

The contents of folders are always displayed in windows. As explained in Chapter 6, you can choose to see the contents of any window in three different views: Icon View, List View, and Column View. How you **open and display the folder** is a little different in each of these views.

Icon View

Icon View: In Icon View, **double-click** a folder to see its contents. Typically, the contents of this newly opened folder will *replace* what was just there. You can, as explained in Chapter 6, arrange to have a *new* window open every time you double-click a folder; see pages 79 and 96.

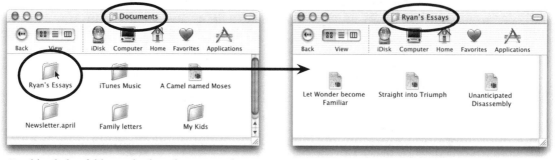

Double-click a folder to display what is stored inside. Notice the title bar will tell you which window is open.

Here you see the contents of the folder "Ryan's Essays," as you can tell by the title bar. Click the Back button to go back to the previous folder window.

Column View

Column View: In Column View, **single-click** a folder to see its contents in the column to its right, as shown below. You can also **double-click** a folder in Column View and its contents will open to *replace* this entire window instead of appearing in the next column. There are two exceptions to this:

▾ *If* you checked the box in the Finder Preferences (page 96) to make sure every window opens in the same view as the one before it, then nothing will happen when you double-click a folder.

▾ *Or if* you checked the box in Finder Preferences to always open folders into new windows, then a double-click opens a new window.

If you checked *both* boxes, the folder will open in a new window *and* it will be in Column View. But that's too much to think about—just work with the Column View and it will slowly start to make sense. As you grow accustomed to columns, experiment with the Finder Preferences; see page 96.

Single-click on a folder icon to display its contents in the column to the right.

The title bar tells you which folder the contents on the far right are contained in.

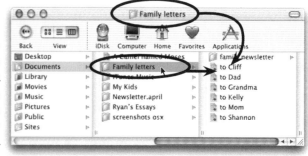

The **List View** is sometimes known as the **outline mode.** There's a tiny triangle next to each folder's name, and if you **single-click on that triangle** you can see what's in that folder without opening another window—as in the folder "Family letters" shown below. The items contained within a folder are indented just a little from the left, which is your **visual clue** that the items are *inside* the folder.

List View

In the outline mode, you can keep opening folders within folders until you are all the way to the bottom level of your filing system, *with everything displayed in the same window.*

One benefit to this view is that you can see at a glance exactly how your files are organized and what's in them. You can move items from one folder to another, even if the folders are several levels apart. You can Command-click (page 163) to select items from any number of different folders, which is impossible to do if the folders are opened as individual windows. (See Chapter 11 about selecting files.)

▼ **To expand,** or *open* a folder, single-click on the little sideways-pointing triangle (or click on the folder icon and press Command RightArrow).

Expanding a folder

▼ **To compress,** or *close* a folder, single-click on the downward-pointing triangle (or click on the folder icon and press Command LeftArrow).

Compressing a folder

▼ To simultaneously **expand all the folders,** press Command A to select everything in the window. Then press Command RightArrow.

Expanding all folders

▼ To simultaneously **compress all the folders** that are expanded, press Command A to select everything in the window. Then press Command LeftArrow.

Compressing all folders

▼ **To open a folder in its own window,** *double-click* the folder icon, not the triangle. The contents of the new window will replace the current contents.

Opening a folder in its own window

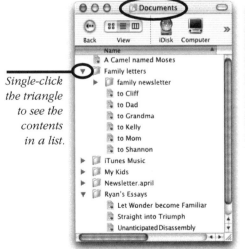

Single-click the triangle to see the contents in a list.

Double-click the folder (not the triangle) to open the folder in its own window.

Creating a New Folder

It's easy **to create your own** new, empty folder.

1. If you want the new folder to sit directly on the **Desktop** (not in another window), first click on the Desktop.

   In **Icon View** or **List View,** make sure the window in which you want a new folder is *active* (click on it).

   In **Column View,** it's a little tricky to select the proper column; see the illustrations and captions below.

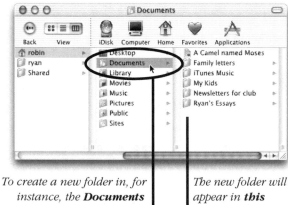

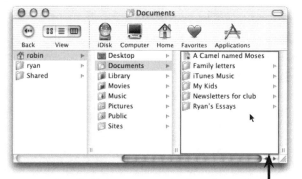

*To create a new folder in, for instance, the **Documents** folder above, click directly on the Documents folder.*

*The new folder will appear in **this** column, which shows the **contents** of the Documents folder.*

*Or click an empty spot in the column that shows the **contents** of the Documents folder. The column will get a dark border around it, which is your **visual clue** that this column is selected and the new folder will appear in here.*

2. Once the proper location is selected, from the File menu, choose "New Folder," or use the keyboard shortcut, Command Shift N. A new, "untitled folder" will appear in the active window, as shown below. See the opposite page on how to name it.

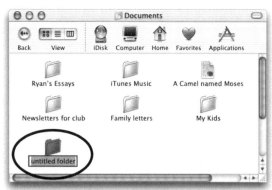
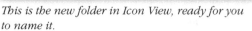

This is the new folder in Icon View, ready for you to name it.

This is the new folder in Column View, ready for you to name it.

You can also create a new folder when you save a document, as described in Chapter 14.

When the new folder appears in the active window, it's already *highlighted*, or *selected* (the **visual clue** is that it's dark), it has the name "untitled folder," and there is a border around the name, as shown below, because the Mac assumes you want to **change the name.** So while the folder is highlighted and has a border, **just type the name you want it to have and the new name will appear.** Yes, really, all you do is type. If you type an error, just backspace over the error (use the Delete key in the upper-right of the main keys) and continue typing. (See the following page if you blew it already.)

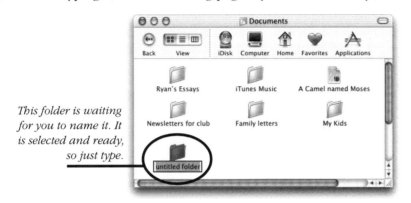

This folder is waiting for you to name it. It is selected and ready, so just type.

Tip: Don't start a folder name with a period (.), and don't use a colon (:) or a slash (/) in the file name. Those characters are reserved for special items within the Mac.

You can type up to 256 characters in a folder name, but you can't type a colon. If you *try* to type a colon, the Mac will substitute a hyphen. And don't ever start a folder name (or any file name) with a period.

After you name the new folder, the border disappears as soon as you click anywhere else, or when you hit the Return or Enter key. When the border disappears, you are no longer in the naming mode.

A **file extension** is a short abbreviation after a file name, always starting with a period, such as "Letter to Mom**.rtf**" or "Family Photo**.jpg**." In Mac OS X, extensions are very important; they often tell the Mac which program to open a document in. Many users add extensions to their files so they will know what kind of file it is themselves; for instance, I always put extensions on different graphic formats so I know what they are, and I add extensions to documents to tell myself which versions I'm working on. But Mac OS X will yell at you if you try to add certain extensions, as shown in the experiment below. Depending on the extension, this can be a problem—the icon can actually turn into something else if you put the wrong extension on it. See page 227 in Chapter 14 for more information about extensions.

Names with file extensions

chapter8

chapter8.dock

The folder above was just fine until I added the extension ".dock." Then the Mac thought it was an entirely different file! It will no longer open as a folder. (If I take the extension off, it turns back into a folder.)

The Mac assumes that anything after a dot (period) is an extension.

The folder "now jido" may no longer appear as a folder if you rename it "now.jido". Are you sure you want to add a file extension?

Cancel   OK

Changing the Name of a Folder

If you accidentally un-highlight the new folder before you change its name, or if you want to **change the name** of any other folder (or any icon of any sort), it is still very easy to do: simply click once on the *name* and the icon will change color, the name will highlight, and a border will appear around the name. The border and highlight are **visual clues** that whatever you type will *replace* the current title. So go ahead and type the new name while you see the border.

Tip: Once you click on the name, it seems to take a "long time" (like a whole second or two) for the border to appear. If you want faster service, click on the icon or the name, then hit the Return key to get the border.

Use standard word processing procedures (Chapter 13) to type the new name: press-and-drag to select text; click to insert an insertion point; backspace to delete characters, etc. Hit the UpArrow to move the insertion point to the beginning of the name, and hit the DownArrow to move it to the end of the name.

Whether your window is in Icon View, List View, or Column View, when you click once on a folder its name will highlight and you'll see the border around the name so you can change it.

Where Did Your New (or renamed) Folder Go?

How your window is arranged or sorted, such as by name or by size, will affect where your new, *untitled* folder will appear. For instance, if you view your window as a list which you have sorted by "Name," the untitled folder will appear near the bottom of the list, alphabetized as "untitled." If you sort by "Date Modified," the untitled folder will appear first in the list because it is the most recent.

After you name the untitled folder and click anywhere or hit the Enter key, *the new folder gets arranged in the list according to the view you have chosen.* That is, if the list is sorted by "Name," the folder instantly gets alphabetized into the existing list, *which means it may disappear from your sight.* You can use the scrollers to go find it, or just type the first letter or two of its name and it will pop up again right in front of your face.

To put something inside a folder, press-and-drag any file icon (except a disk) over to the folder; when the folder changes color (highlights), let go and the file will drop inside. This **moves** the file from one place to another. Remember, it is the *very tip* of the pointer that selects the folder, *not* the shadow of the icon that goes inside.

You can have folders inside of folders inside of folders, which is technically called the *Hierarchical File System* (HFS). You can drag an item from one window and put it into a folder in another window.

A folder does not have to be closed to place an item inside of it. The folder window can be displaying icons, a list, or columns.

The only trick to putting something inside a folder is that you have to be able to see both the *item* you want to drop in and the *folder* you want to drop it into. Since the contents of new folders replaces the previous contents, this can be kind of tricky; sometimes it requires opening multiple windows and moving your windows around the screen so you can see both items at once. Following are several techniques that make it easier to access folders without having to have lots of open windows: putting folders in the Toolbar, putting folders in the Dock, and storing folders on the Desktop.

Putting Something inside a Folder

You'll find that you use some folders more often than others. And you might use one folder for a while and then you're done with that project and need to use two or three other folders for a while. It can be annoying and sometimes tricky to keep digging up the folder you want, either to put stuff in or take stuff out, but here is a great trick: **Drag the folder into the Toolbar.** This actually creates an "alias" in the Toolbar, a *copy* of the folder's icon, but it acts just like the real thing. You can drag files into it, single-click to open it, and it's always available right in front of your face.

Storing a Folder in the Toolbar

When you no longer need such easy access to your favorite folder, **just drag it off the Toolbar**—the folder alias will disappear in a poof. *Only the alias icon disappears*—the real folder stays safe and secure right where it was.

Of course, you can drag files directly into the Home, Favorites, and Applications windows by dropping the files directly on top of the Toolbar icons.

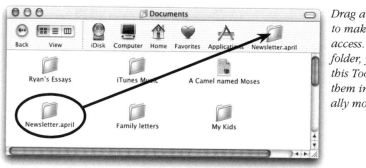

Drag a folder into the Toolbar to make the folder easy to access. To put things in this folder, you can drag them to this Toolbar folder and drop them in—the items will actually move to the real folder.

Storing a Folder in the Dock

You can also store a "copy" of a folder in the Dock: just drag the folder down to the *right* side of the Dock and drop it. The other items will move over to make room. This does not *move* your folder—it automatically places an "alias" in the Dock. Your original folder stays right where it is. But now you can open the folder from the Dock: you can open a full window, or you can pop up a menu that displays all of the items stored inside this folder.

To see the name of the folder in the Dock: Position the pointer over the folder icon in the Dock and just "hover" (don't click). The name of the folder will appear just above the Dock.

To open a folder in the Dock to a new window: Click once on the folder icon in the Dock.

To pop up a menu that displays the contents of the folder: Press (don't click) on the folder icon in the Dock.

To put a file inside a folder in the Dock: Drag it to the folder and drop it in.

To take a file out of a folder in the Dock: Click once on the icon to open its window, then drag the desired file out.

Press on the folder icon and in about two seconds a menu will pop up. Slide up the menu and select an item to open it.

Single-click the folder in the Dock to open its window. Above you see a folder that contains aliases of my favorite applications. Instead of having to dig through folders to find their icons, I put aliases of my favorite applications in this one folder, then put the folder in my Dock for easy access. (See Chapter 22 for information about aliases.)

If your folder in the Dock has folders inside of folders, you will get the hierarchical menus, as shown here, when you press on the icon.

Tip: Once you've opened a window whose folder is stored in the Dock, try to remember not to **minimize** that window—**close** it instead. If you minimize the window, you'll end up with two icons in the Dock for the same thing: the folder icon *plus* the minimized window icon.

You can always make a **new folder** directly on the Desktop: click on the Desktop to select it, then press Command Shift N.

Or you can **drag any folder** from a window to the Desktop. This doesn't make a copy or an "alias" of the folder—it literally *moves* the original folder onto the Desktop (unless you are dragging it from another disk, in which case it does make a copy).

Or make an **alias of a folder** on the Desktop. The alias, as explained in Chapter 22, looks just like the original, but it's actually kind of like a spirit image—it's not *really* the folder. But you can put files into the alias and they will actually go straight into the real folder. **To make an alias,** hold down the Command and Option keys and drag the folder to the Desktop. When you get to the Desktop, let go, and the alias will appear on the Desktop. You'll know it's an alias by the tiny arrow in the lower-left corner.

Storing a Folder on the Desktop

john

An alias has a tiny pointer in the lower-left corner.

Opening a Folder in a New Window

To move items from one folder to another, you can also **open the folders in two different windows.** As explained in Chapter 6, hold down the Command key and double-click a folder icon to open that folder into a new, separate window. Then you can arrange the two windows side by side so you can **move** items from one folder to another.

Or click the Hide/Show Toolbar button in the upper-right of the window, then when you double-click a folder icon it will open in a new, separate window.

Now, this can get sort of frustrating because you have to open one folder into a new window, then go back to the first window and navigate around to find the file you wanted to move into the second folder. So here is yet another option:

New Finder Window

Open the window that contains the file you want to move. Press Command Shift N to get a **new Finder window** (the new window is probably a duplicate of the one that's already open). Position the two windows side by side. In the new window, find the folder icon that you want to move the file into. Then just drag the file from one window and drop it onto the folder icon in the other window.

Drag a File to the Desktop

Sometimes it's easiest to **drag a file to the Desktop,** then find the folder icon you want to move the file into, then drag the file from the Desktop into the folder icon (or its open window).

As I mentioned earlier, if you use certain folders often, just drag them to the Toolbar so you can move files in without having to find the folder in a window. Plus you'll always have that folder accessible so you can single-click to open it.

To **move or remove** something from a folder, you have to *open* the folder first so you can see the files inside. Open a folder in the various views as explained on pages 148–149. Then simply press-and-drag a file out of the folder; drag it either to the Desktop or to another folder or window, then drop it. The important thing to remember is this:

Moving vs. Copying Files

If you drag the file to someplace else **on the same disk,** the file will just pop out of that first folder/window and **move** into the other folder.

I dragged this file into the folder to its left.

*The file **moved** into the folder and is gone from this window.*

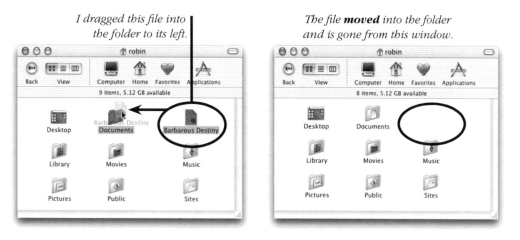

BUT if you drag the file **to a different disk or to a server,** the original file will stay put in the original folder and the Mac will put a **copy** of the file on the other disk.

*I dragged the file onto the Zip disk. Notice the tiny plus symbol next to the arrow—a **visual clue** that the file will be copied, not moved.*

*The file was **copied** onto the Zip disk and the original stayed right where it was.*

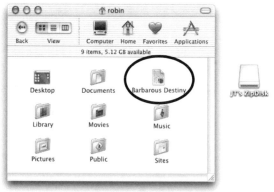

See Chapter 11 for tips on selecting more than one file at a time, as well as for moving and copying files.

157

1. What is the purpose of a folder?

2. At the Desktop, when you go to the File menu and choose "New Folder," how do you know where that new folder will appear?

3. What is the keyboard shortcut to create a new folder?

4. How do you rename a folder, and what is the **visual clue** that tells you a folder is ready to be renamed?

5. How do you open a folder in each of the three views?

6. What happens when you open a folder, and what do you see?

7. What are the keyboard shortcuts for expanding and compressing folders in the List View?

8. How can you close all of the expanded folders at once?

9. What are two big advantages to the List View?

10. Name four ways to make it easier to move files from one folder to another.

Answers on page 751.

Selecting, Moving, and Copying Files

You'll often need to **move** files around to rearrange them. And **copying** files is an everyday task. You may need to copy a small utility from its original disk onto your hard disk; copy a report to give to a coworker; copy a document and its graphics to take to a service bureau for high-resolution printing; create the ever-necessary backup copy; etc., etc., etc.

Copying files usually involves moving them, and before you can move or copy any file, you must first **select** it.

Apple has made it as easy as possible to copy files on the Mac (which is why *pirating,* or copying software without paying for it, has always been such a problem). Copying files has no effect on the *original file,* nor is there any loss of quality in the new version—there is absolutely no difference from the original to the copy.

Selecting Individual Files

Before you can move or copy files, you have to know how to select them. **Selecting one file** is easy—as long as it's not in the Dock or a window Toolbar, click once on it. (If you click once on an icon in the Dock or Toolbar, it *opens* that item instead of selecting it.)

Type the first letter

To select any single file, even if you can't see it in the window, **type the first letter** of the name of the file and it will be instantly selected. If there are several files with the same first letter, quickly type the first two or three letters. This technique makes it a lot easier to find your folder named "Waldo" in an alphabetized list, for instance, or a file that starts with Z, or any icon in a crowded folder.

Arrow keys

You can also use the **arrow keys** to select files. *Once you have a file selected,* either by clicking on it or typing its first letter, the arrow keys will select the next icon or file name in the window. In List View and Column View, the UpArrow and the DownArrow select, of course, the next file in the list. In Icon View, the four arrows select the icon to the left, right, up, or down, unless there is nothing else in that direction. Take a minute and try it.

Select the next file alphabetically

No matter how you select a file, you can select the next file alphabetically. For instance, perhaps you typed the letter S because you wanted to select the folder named Scarlett, but instead it selected Sally. *Except in Column View,* you can do this:

- ▾ To select the icon that would be alphabetically *after* the currently selected icon, tap the **Tab key.** You can continue to tap the Tab key to keep selecting files in alphabetical order.

- ▾ To select the icon that would be alphabetically *before* the currently selected icon, hold down the **Shift key** and tap the **Tab** key. Continue to tap the Tab key to select files in backwards alphabetical order.

Selecting more than one file at a time

You've probably noticed that once a file is selected, it gets *de*selected the instant you click somewhere else. So an important trick is knowing how to **select more than one file** at a time. Once you select multiple files, you can drag them *all together,* either to the Trash, into another folder, onto another disk, or simply to clean up the joint.

How you select multiple files depends on which view you are in. In Icon View and Column View, you can only select items from inside **one folder.** In List View, you can select multiple items from **different folders.** We'll look at how you can select files in each view.

Practice: Open a window, like your Home folder. Select a file by clicking once on it (not on a Dock icon!). Then try each of the techniques listed on the page.

You may have noticed in **Icon View** or on the **Desktop** that when you *press in an empty space and drag the pointer,* a colored rectangle comes out of the tip—this is the **selection marquee** found in many Mac programs. Any file that is even partially enclosed in this marquee will be selected. You can tell which files are selected because they are highlighted, as shown below.

Selecting Multiple Files in Icon View and on the Desktop

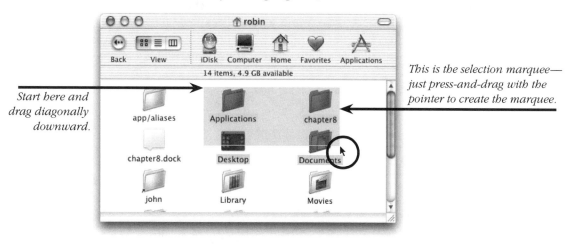

Start here and drag diagonally downward.

This is the selection marquee— just press-and-drag with the pointer to create the marquee.

Selecting icons this way will highlight all of the icons that were touched by the marquee. Now:

- ▼ When you press-and-drag on the *highlighted* area of one of the selected items, they will all drag together.

- ▼ Click in any *white* space, on any unselected icon, or on the Desktop to *deselect* all the files.

Using the above method, you can only select files that are *next to each other.* But often you might want to **add** another icon to this collection, or you might want to **pick and choose** individual files that are not next to each other. Or you might want to **deselect** just one of the selected files in a group. Here's how to do it:

Add or delete individual icons from the selection

To SELECT individual files to add to a group of selected icons, hold down the Shift key *or* the Command key (not the Control key), and single-click on individual files.

To DESELECT individual files that are in a collection of selected icons, hold down the Shift key *or* the Command key (not the Control key), and single-click on individual files.

> **Practice:** This is a technique you will use daily, so follow the directions above to select multiple files, then deselect individuals files from the group.

Selecting Multiple Files in List View

If you view your window as icons or columns, you can select items *from only one window or column at a time.* But in List View, you can **expand** the folders and **select** *any number of files from any number of expanded folders within that one window,* as shown in the examples below.

Drag the selection marquee

Just as in Icon View, you can **drag to select files that are next to each other:** Press in a white space in the window next to a file name and start to drag. The colored **selection marquee** will appear when you drag, and any item that is even partially enclosed within the marquee will be added to the selection.

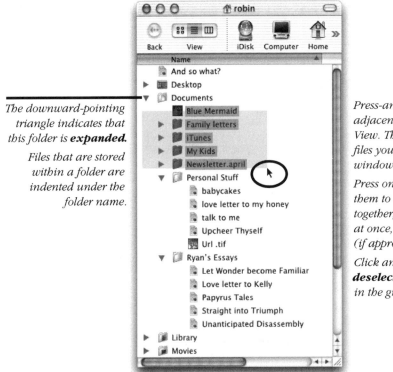

*The downward-pointing triangle indicates that this folder is **expanded**.*

Files that are stored within a folder are indented under the folder name.

*Press-and-drag to select adjacent items in a List View. The five highlighted files you see in this window are **selected**.*

Press on any one of them to drag them all together, to open them all at once, to print them all (if appropriate), etc.

*Click anywhere else to **deselect all** of the items in the group.*

To SELECT INDIVIDUAL files to ADD to the collection, hold down the Command key (not the Control key, nor the Shift key) and single-click on individual files that are not already in the collection. Each file you click on will be *added* to the group.

To DESELECT INDIVIDUAL files FROM the collection, hold down the Command key (not the Control key, nor the Shift key) and single-click on individual files that are in the collection. Each file you click on will be *deselected* from the group

To ADD CONTIGUOUS files to the top or bottom of the collection, hold down the Shift key and tap the UpArrow or DownArrow key.

To DESELECT all files, click in any white space.

Practice: If you don't learn the difference between the Shift key and Command key while selecting, it can make you crazy! Try these techniques.

To select individual files from different folders in List View, first expand the folders whose contents you need to see: click once on the tiny triangles pointing to the folders (see Chapter 6 for tips on expanding and compressing all folders at once). Then **Command-click** on the files you want to select (hold down the Command key while you single-click on icons).

Command-click

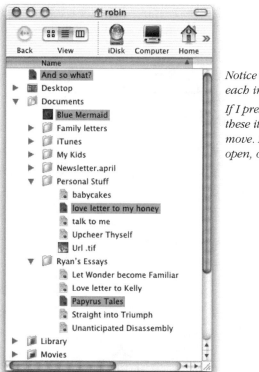

Notice the four selected files are each in a different folder.

If I press-and-drag any one of these items, all four of them will move. I can copy, trash, print, open, or move them, all at once.

To DESELECT individual files FROM the collection, hold down the Command key (not the Control key, nor the Shift key) and single-click on individual files.

To DESELECT all files, click in any white space.

Practice: This is the selection technique you will probably use most often. Try it.

Shift-click   Another method of selecting more than one item in List View is to **click–Shift-click.** This method only selects items that are *contiguous,* or next to each other, although you can always use the method on the previous page to add individual files to the collection.

1. **Click once** on the first file in the list you want to select.

2. Hold down the **Shift key and click** on the last file in the list you want to select. Everything between the first click and the Shift-click will be selected.

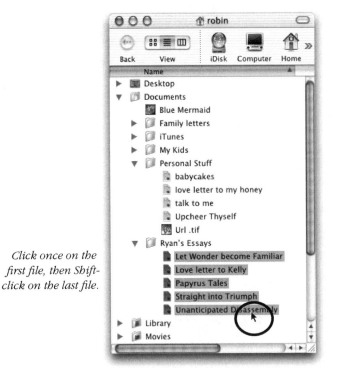

Click once on the first file, then Shift-click on the last file.

To ADD CONTIGUOUS files to the collection, hold down the Shift key and click a file higher or lower than the selected collection, or tap the UpArrow or DownArrow keys (with the Shift key down).

To DESELECT CONTIGUOUS files from the collection, hold down the Shift key and click a file inside the selected collection; all files between the beginning or the end of the collection (whichever your pointer is closest to) will deselect.

To ADD INDIVIDUAL files to the collection, hold down the Command key (not the Control key, nor the Shift key) and single-click individual files.

To DESELECT INDIVIDUAL files from the collection, hold down the Command key (not the Control key, nor the Shift key) and single-click individual files.

To DESELECT all files, click in any white space.

Practice: This technique also works when you select text: Click, then Shift-click and everything in-between (text or files in a list) will be selected. Try it.

The **Column View** gives you the impression you can select files from different columns, but you can't. Column View is a cross between Icon View and List View, as far as selecting items goes.

To select multiple individual files in one column, hold down the Command key and click on each one.

To select contiguous files in one column, press-and-drag to draw the selection marquee around the files. Any file even partially enclosed by the marquee will be selected.
OR click on the first item in the list, then hold down the Shift key and click on the last item in the list. All files between the first click and the Shift-click will be selected.

All of the tips listed on the bottom part of the opposite page also work in one column of Column View.

Selecting Multiple Files in Column View

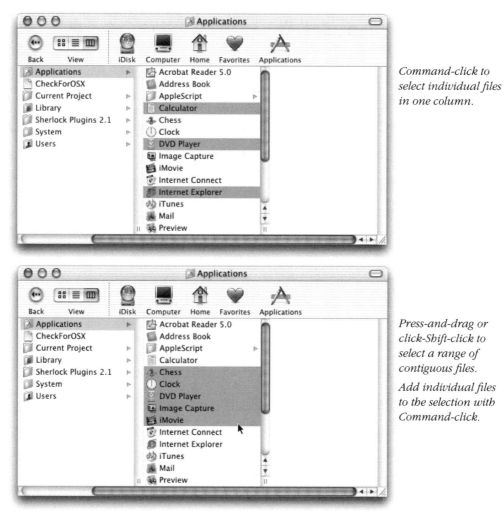

Command-click to select individual files in one column.

Press-and-drag or click-Shift-click to select a range of contiguous files.

Add individual files to the selection with Command-click.

Using Sherlock to Select Files

You can also **use Sherlock to select files** from all over your hard disk (see Chapter 24 on *Sherlock* for all the intimate details).

All of the found files will be shown in one window, and you can select their icons from that "found" window and drag them to the Trash, open them, move them, etc. (Remember, press on *one* selected item and *all* selected items will follow.) Make it a point to learn to use Sherlock—you'll discover it comes in handy in a number of ways.

I often use Sherlock to select a file even when I know where it is because it's so much faster than digging through levels of folders. If I need a document, I hit Command F, type in a few letters, hit the Return key, then lo and behold, there is my file in front of my face. I double-click the file name to open it, and off I go.

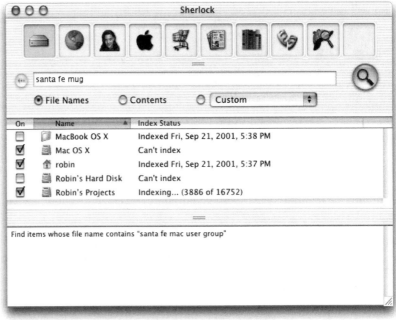

It's quick and easy to find a file with Sherlock. See Chapter 24.

You can use the **edit keys** on an extended keyboard to **scroll** through a window. This doesn't *select* anything, but it makes it easier for you to find and click on files. The edit keys are that little set between the alphabet keys and the numeric keypad on most keyboards, or above the numeric keypad on smaller keyboards, like the ones that usually come with iMacs.

Moving Around in a Window

Although the edit keys don't select anything, they come in handy when you want to get to the top or the bottom of a window instantly or if you want to scroll through the window in a hurry.

Home scrolls the window straight to the top.

End scrolls the window straight to the bottom.

Page Up (pg up) and **Page Down (pg dn)** scroll the window one window-sized section up or down.

Moving Files

Once you have selected a file or two or more, you can **move** them to another place on your Mac. When you move a file, it's just like moving something in your kitchen—the thing is no longer in the position you took it from. That is, moving does exactly what it says—it does not leave a copy behind.

To MOVE a file or files from one place to another:

1. First make sure you can see the files you want to move **and** the folder or window you want to move them into.

   There are detailed explanations on pages 153–156 on how to make folders easier to access. Briefly, you can open a folder into a new, separate window (Command–double-click on it); store a folder in the Dock; store a folder in the Toolbar; or keep an alias or the original folder right on the Desktop.

2. **Select** the files as explained on the previous pages.

3. Then, *making sure you have no keys pressed,* grab one of the selected files and **drag** it to its new position. Dragging one selected file will drag *all* of them, as shown below.

4. As usual, the **tip of the pointer** is the critical factor—wherever the tip of the pointer is when you **let go** of the mouse button, that is where the files will move to.

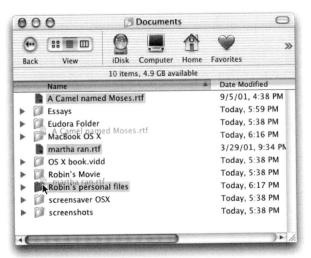

If the folder you want to move files into is in the same window as the files you want to move, then just select the files and drag them.

Above, I Command-clicked on the two document files," A Camel named Moses.rtf" and "martha ran.rtf."

*Then I let go of the Command key, **pressed** on "martha ran.rtf," and dragged both selected files to the folder.*

*Notice the **tip** of the pointer is directly on the folder "Robin's personal files," selecting it, and the shadows of the selected files are following along.*

If the folder you want to move files into is not visible, first make it visible (as explained on the opposite page) before you select the files.

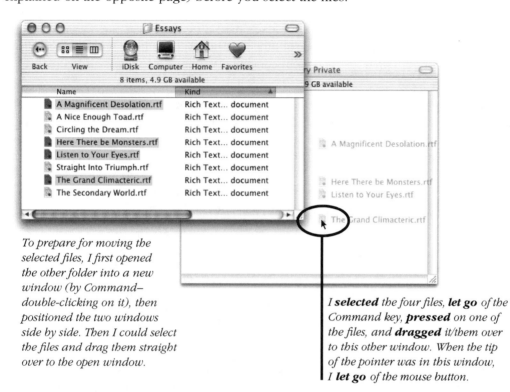

To prepare for moving the selected files, I first opened the other folder into a new window (by Command–double-clicking on it), then positioned the two windows side by side. Then I could select the files and drag them straight over to the open window.

*I **selected** the four files, **let go** of the Command key, **pressed** on one of the files, and **dragged** it/them over to this other window. When the tip of the pointer was in this window, I **let go** of the mouse button.*

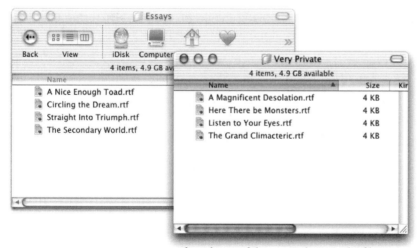

After I let go of the mouse button, the files moved right into the new folder. Notice they are no longer in their original folder.

Copying Files

Copying files is an everyday task. You'll copy files from one folder to another so you can have multiple versions; you'll copy files onto removable disks to give to someone else or as backup for yourself; you'll copy files from removable disks onto your Mac's hard disk so you can use them; and you'll probably find a number of other reasons to copy files. When you duplicate or copy *folders,* every item contained within that folder is also copied.

Go back to work while the computer is copying

If you have a large file to copy, you can **go back to work** on something else while the computer is going through its copying process. You can go back to your application, browse through your windows, empty the Trash, connect to the Internet, or do other Finder tasks. Most machines today are so fast, though, you will rarely have time to get back to work before they're finished copying! Also, you don't have to wait for one file or collection of files to finish copying before you start another.

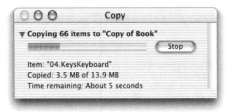

*This message will appear when you copy. The lines in the title bar are a **visual clue** that you can drag this box around on the screen. For instance, you might want to move it out of the way so you can do something else while the item is copying.*

Your visual clue of the copying process

Sometimes you might think you are just *moving* a file, but the Mac actually *copies* it. This is because when you "move" a file from one *disk* to another *disk* (rather than from one *folder* to another *folder*), the Mac automatically makes a copy instead of moving the original. Your **visual clue** that you are actually copying a file is in the arrow—you'll see a small plus sign (+).

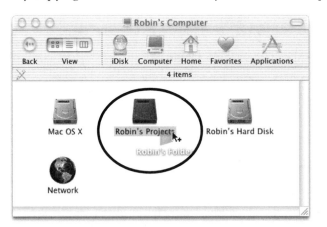

You can see the shadow of the file I dragged to the hard disk icon. Because this file was originally on another one of these partitions (which the computer sees as a separate hard disk), when I drag the file to another partition, the Mac automatically copies it. I realize this when I see the arrow sprout a plus sign.

Sometimes you want to make another **copy of a file on the same disk.** The Mac *automatically* copies a file when you drag it to another *disk,* but to make a copy on the same disk you have to do it yourself. There are three ways to do this.

1. To make a COPY (DUPLICATE) of the file in the same folder:

1. First click *once* on the file icon to select it, or select several files as described on pages 162–165.

2. From the File menu, choose "Duplicate" (*or* press Command D). This creates a second version in the same folder named "_____ copy." If you make more copies of the same file, they will be named "_____ copy 1," "_____ copy 2," etc.

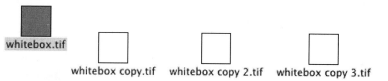

whitebox.tif
whitebox copy 3.tif

This looks odd because I held down the Command key and tapped the D key three times. This made three duplicates in the folder, stacked one on top of the other.

whitebox.tif   whitebox copy.tif   whitebox copy 2.tif   whitebox copy 3.tif

I just dragged the duplicates off to the right so I could see their individual icons and names.

When you use the Duplicate command, the new file appears with the word "copy" at the end of its name. If you want to avoid this, just Option-drag a file to make a copy, as detailed below.

2. To drag a copy of a file into another folder on the same disk or onto the Desktop:

▼ Hold down the **Option key and drag** the file to the other folder or to the Desktop. This puts a copy of the file into the other folder or on the Desktop, but does not rename the file "_____ copy."

You'll know it's making a copy instead of moving the file because you'll see the plus sign appear next to the arrow as soon as you hold down the Option key.

(Actually, you can also Option-drag a file in the *same* folder to make a copy, but because you cannot have two files in the same folder with the same name, you will still get the word "copy" at the end of the file name.)

3. Contextual menu

There is a great little technique to copy a file into another folder without first having to arrange both folders on the screen, like you do when *moving* a file from one folder to the other. (I wish this technique worked for moving, as well as copying.) This only works in Icon or Column Views.

Tip: Use this technique or the one on the opposite page to **back up** your files—make a copy on another disk. If you have very important files, makes copies on two different disks, then store one of the disks off-site. This way if your office is plundered or caught in a fire or flood, you still have copies of your important files.

3. To put a copy of a file (or multiple files) into another folder on the same disk or onto the Desktop (or on any other disk, actually):

1. First click *once* on the file icon to select it, or select a number of files, as explained on pages 162–165.

2. Hold down the Control key (not the Command key) and click on one of the selected files to get the contextual menu, as shown below. Choose the "Copy items" command. (If *one* item is selected, the copy command will name the item.)

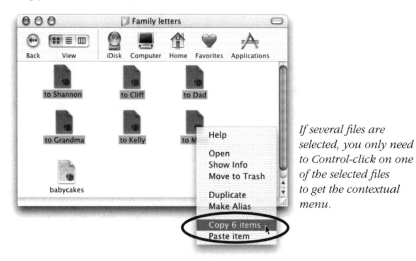

If several files are selected, you only need to Control-click on one of the selected files to get the contextual menu.

3. Open the window or the column where you want to put the file(s).

4. In an empty space in that window or column, hold down the Control key and click; you'll get a contextual menu, shown below.

5. Choose the "Paste items" command and the file(s) you copied will be pasted into this window or column.

You can't select a folder icon to have the items pasted inside that folder—you must open its window first.

You can also use the Paste command from the Edit menu, as shown on page 175.

You can copy from your hard disk onto a removable disk, from a removable disk onto your hard disk, or directly into a specific folder on any other disk. In every case, make sure the icon of the disk or folder you are copying *into* becomes *highlighted* (highlighting is darker or colored), which is your **visual clue** that the disk or folder is *selected* as the place to copy to. When the icon is highlighted, that means it's ready to accept the file(s). If the icon is not highlighted, you'll end up just placing the file *next* to the disk or folder, not *inside* of it. The *tip of the pointer* is what highlights any icon, as you can see in the example below.

Make sure the disk or folder you are copying to is selected!

When you drag a file to another *disk* or partition, the Mac automatically copies the file. This is how to back up your files onto Zip or Jaz disks.

To COPY a file from one disk to another disk (such as from your hard disk to a Zip disk):

1. At the Desktop, click once on the file you want to copy.

2. Press-and-drag that selected file to the icon of the disk that you want to copy it onto. This icon might be right on the Desktop or in the Computer window—you can drag to either one.

   You will see a small plus sign appear next to the arrow, and a little message comes up telling you the file is being copied.

Copying files from the Mac to a removable disk
(not onto a CD; for that, see pages 176–177)

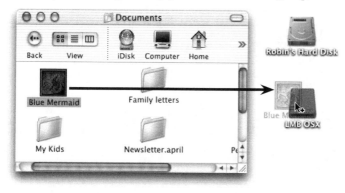

You can see three things here:

1) *The shadow of the icon I am dragging over to the Zip disk.*

2) *The tip of the pointer is positioned directly on the disk icon to select it— that's what highlights the disk.*

3) *The pointer sprouted a small plus sign as soon as it reached the disk, which tells you the file will be copied, not moved.*

You could also drag a file to the disk icon that appears in the Computer window, but that is not as easy as dragging it to the Desktop, generally.

Copying from a removable disk to the Mac

There are a couple of ways to copy files from your **removable disk** (such as a Zip disk, a CD, or a floppy) to your hard disk, depending on whether you want to copy selected files or the entire removable disk. Although these methods specifically detail copying from your "removable disk" to your "internal hard disk," you can use these same methods to copy from one disk to any other disk or volume, as long as there is room on the other volume.

To COPY SELECTED FILES from a removable disk to your internal hard disk:

1. Insert the removable disk.

2. Double-click the removable disk icon to open its window.

3. Take a look at the files on the removable disk, *then selectively* choose the ones you need to copy. Press-and-drag the chosen files to the hard disk icon, or drag them directly into a folder on the hard disk. As usual, you need to be able to see the folder, window, or column you want to drag the files into.

To COPY THE ENTIRE DISK to your internal hard disk:

This method copies *every single item* from the removable disk to your internal hard disk. Make sure that's what you really want to do.

1. Insert the removable disk into its drive.

2. If you try to *drag* the removable disk icon onto your hard disk icon, you'll notice a tiny curved arrow will appear next to the pointer, as shown below. This indicates that dragging the item will create an *alias*—it will not *move* the disk, nor will it make a *copy*. (See Chapter 22 about aliases.)

Note: Don't ever copy another operating system onto your hard disk (unless you really know what you are doing and why).

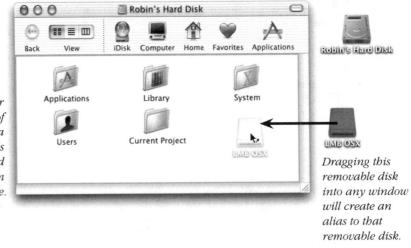

*Notice the border around the inside of the window. This is a **visual clue** that this window is selected as the destination for the file.*

Dragging this removable disk into any window will create an alias to that removable disk.

3. Instead of dragging the disk, hold down the Control key and click on the removable disk icon to get the contextual menu, as shown below.

4. From the contextual menu, choose the "Copy item" command.

5. Open the window you want to copy the entire removable disk contents into. The contents will copy into the *active* window.

6. From the Edit menu, choose the "Paste item" command (or use the contextual menu as shown on page 172).

When you choose the Paste command, the contents of the removable disk you copied will be pasted into the active window. You'll get the Copy message, as shown above.

7. After the copy/paste process is finished, you'll have an icon of the removable disk in the window. Don't get confused and think that this represents the actual removable disk! It doesn't—it is a *copy* of the entire contents on that disk. The icon is actually a folder with a customized image.

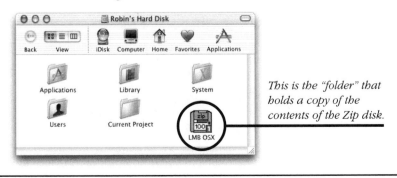

This is the "folder" that holds a copy of the contents of the Zip disk.

Copying Files onto a CD

When you **copy files onto a CD**, it's called **burning a CD**. A CD burner uses a laser beam to burn digital information into the surface of a CD. You can't just burn any ol' CD, though—you need to understand the differences between CD-ROM, CD-R, and CD-RW.

CD-ROM (Compact Disc–Read Only Memory): You cannot erase information from or copy information to a CD-ROM, such as an old application installation disc that you don't need any more. If you've been saving that stack of AOL CDs to use for backups, forget it. They're CD-ROMs.

CD-R (Compact Disc–Recordable): CD-Rs are the most common type of disc for burning data and music files. Using Apple's CD burning software, you can "write" once (a single burn session) to a CD-R. You can't erase a CD-R. Some other CD burning software, such as Roxio's Toast, enables multiple CD burn sessions of data files, but not if you're burning a music CD. CD-Rs hold between 650 and 700 megabytes of data and are very affordable, usually in the range of one dollar per disc or lower. However, the disc quality and dependability drop along with the price.

CD-RW (Compact Disc–ReWritable): CD-RWs can be rewritten and erased many times, making it a media that's ideal for backing up files that change over time. If you use Apple's CD burning software, you can write to a CD-RW more than once, but only if you erase its current content. Some CD burning software, such as Toast, allows you to selectively erase or rewrite files repeatedly on a single CD-RW, or you can choose to rewrite only files that have been changed since the last backup to the disc. Depending upon the quality of the CD-RW and the quantity you buy, the price per disc may be similar to CD-Rs, or maybe two to three times more.

Do not use CD-RWs for creating music CDs—they only work in computers, not CD audio players.

To burn a CD:

1. Insert a blank CD.

2. This disc needs to be prepared. Name the disc, and choose a format based on the information on the next page.

Tip: To avoid potential problems, before you burn a CD, make sure your Mac will not go to sleep during the process. To do this, go to the System Preferences, and choose Energy Saver. Set the top slider (System Sleep) to "Never," and uncheck the bottom two options (Display Sleep and Hard Disk Sleep).

This is the CD icon before burning. The letters "CDR" indicate this is a CD-Recordable disc that has not been burned.

Is "compact disc" spelled with a "c" or a "k"? Well, as you can see in this dialog box, even Apple can't keep it straight.

> This disk needs to be prepared for burning. Do you want to prepare this disc?
>
> Name: Mac OS X book
>
> Format: ✓ Standard (HFS+/ISO 9660) 666.8 MB
> MP3 CD (ISO 9660) 666.8 MB
> iTunes (Audio) 79 Min.
>
> Ignore

Choose the **Standard** format to copy data and multimedia files to a CD that can be read by a Mac or a PC. These data files can be recognized by a computer, but not by a CD player or MP3 player.

Choose **MP3 CD** to create a *data* CD in which music files are stored in MP3 format. MP3 compression enables you to put the maximum number of songs possible on a CD. Music in this format can be played on computers using software such as iTunes, or loaded onto MP3 players such as Apple's iPod. *You cannot play an MP3-formatted CD on a standard CD player.*

Use the **iTunes** format to create *music* CDs that you can play on standard CD players or on your computer. If you select this format when preparing to burn a CD, iTunes opens so you can select a Playlist (or selections from a Playlist) to burn.

3. Drag folders and files to the CD icon, according to the choice you made in Step 2:

If you chose the **Standard** or **MP3 CD** format, drag the folders and files you want to copy and drop them on top of the CD icon on your Desktop. A "copy" window opens to show the progress.

If you chose the **iTunes** format to create a music CD, select a Playlist (or songs in a Playlist) from the iTunes window that opens, then click the "Burn CD" button in the top-right corner of the iTunes window.

4. It sounds strange, but drag the CD icon to the Trash. As soon as the CD icon moves, the Trash icon changes to the "Burn CD" icon.

5. As your files are prepared, burned, and verified, the "Burn Disc" window shows your progress.

6. The letters "CDR" are gone from the icon, indicating that this disc has been burned. Eject the disc—select it and press Command E.

Circle the correct choice in the following multiple choice and true/false questions.

1. **When you drag a file from your hard disk to a removable disk, you are:**
   a. Making a copy of the file onto the removable disk.
   b. Making a copy of the file onto the hard disk.
   c. Simply moving the file from one place to another.

2. **When you drag a file from one window on your hard disk to another window on your hard disk, you are:**
   a. Making a copy of the file onto a removable disk.
   b. Making a copy of the file onto the hard disk.
   c. Simply moving the file from one place to another.

3. **When you drag a file from a removable disk to your hard disk, you are:**
   a. Making a copy of the file onto the removable disk.
   b. Making a copy of the file onto the hard disk.
   c. Simply moving the file from one place to another.

4. **If you want to make a copy of a file on the same disk, the fastest and most efficient way is to:**
   a. Make a copy onto a removable disk, then drag that copy back onto the hard disk.
   b. Select the file, then from the File menu, choose "Duplicate." Or select the file and press Command D.
   c. Hold down the Option key as you drag the file into another folder or window.

5. **In the List View, you can select multiple files:**
   a. By dragging around them with the pointer tool.
   b. That are in different folders.
   c. Both a and b.

T F 6. It's always okay to drag the icon of the removable disk onto the icon of the hard disk when you want to copy something onto your hard disk.

T F 7. To select more than one file at a time, hold down the Option key as you click each one.

T F 8. You can press-and-drag the pointer around any number of files to select them all.

T F 9. The quickest (and coolest) way to select a file is to type the first letter or couple of letters of its name.

T F 10. Once a file is selected, the Tab key will select the next largest file.

Answers on page 751.

Opening Apps & Docs

12

(applications and documents)

A **file** is a generic term referring to just about any icon on your computer. A file might be an **application,** which is the program you use to create things, or a **document,** which is the thing you created in your application, or a "font," which is a typeface, or a number of other sorts of digitized pieces of information. The files you will work with the most are applications and documents. This chapter gives you some basic guidelines so you can understand and work with them.

What is an Application?

AppleWorks 6

*This is **not** an application icon—it is the folder that stores the application. Open this folder to find the application icon.*

The terms **applications** and **programs** are often used synonymously (although an *application* is only one form of programming). *Application* refers to the software package you use to create your documents, such as AppleWorks, PageMaker, FreeHand, Quicken, Photoshop, Internet Explorer, Mail, etc. They all do something different; they each have a particular function. For instance, you can keep track of your finances in Quicken, but you can't open photographs in Quicken. You can open and edit photographs in Photoshop, but Photoshop will not help you with your finances. Sometimes it takes a little research to discover which software applications meet your specific needs.

Application versions

Every application has a **version number** that tells you how up-to-date it is. For instance, you might have AppleWorks 6 and your friend has AppleWorks 5. Version 6 is newer and has more features (does more stuff) than version 5.

Sometimes the company adds just a few new features and fixes a few old problems instead of revising the entire program. In that case, they usually don't jump to a whole new number, like from 6 to 7; instead, they might say this is version 7.2 (minor updates) or 7.5 (fairly serious update when it's a half number), or 7.5.2 (*very* minor fixes when it's the third number).

The period in these version numbers is pronounced "point." So version 7.5 is pronounced "seven point five." And 7.5.2 is "seven point five point two." Sometimes, of course, we shorten it to say, "Oh, this is version seven five."

AppleWorks 6   **Chess**   **Internet Connect**

These are application icons. They are stored in various folders on the Mac, but the same application will always have the same icon, although the icon might be larger or smaller, depending on where you see it.

To open an application, or software program, you need to find its icon or file name on your hard disk. Application icons, as noted in Chapter 7, typically look "fancier" than most other kinds of files.

Opening an Application

These examples use AppleWorks, which might or might not be on your Mac. You can following along with TextEdit, found in the Applications folder.

▼ If an application's icon is in the Dock, *single*-click on it.

▼ If an application's name, icon, or alias is in a Finder window or sitting on the Desktop, *double*-click on it.

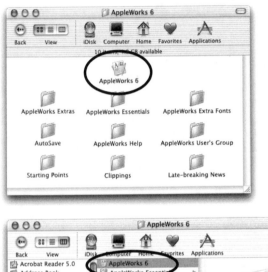

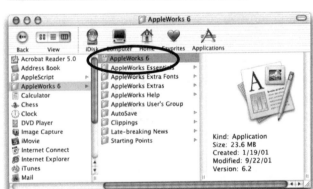

Find the Application Some applications have very busy folders and it can be difficult to **find the actual application icon** to double-click. If you use the List View, you can sort your window by "Kind," as shown below, which forces the *applications* towards the top of the list. Simply click on the heading "Kind" to change the organization of the columns.

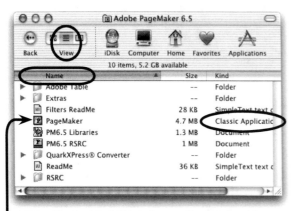

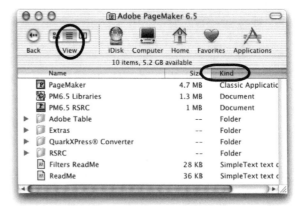

All the files in this folder belong to PageMaker. The window is organized by "Name," as you can see by the colored column header, circled above. You really have to look to find the actual PageMaker application. Do you see it?

This is the same folder, but now the items are organized by "Kind." (Just click in a column header to organize by that column.) Do you see that the application is now listed first?

Practice: Find and **open the application TextEdit:**

Open any Finder window.

Click the "Applications" icon.

Type the letter "T" to select the TextEdit icon (or scroll to find it).

Double-click the TextEdit application icon to open it.

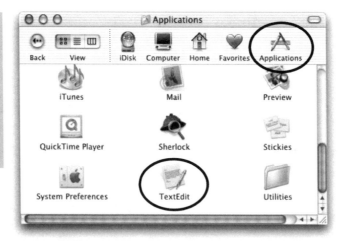

When your application opens, *one* of the following things will happen:

A. A blank page will open for you, as shown to the left, ready for you to create a new document. Go ahead and start working.

B. You will get a dialog box asking what sort of document you want, as shown below, or how you want your pages set up.

Your application opens

Many applications will automatically open to a blank page, waiting for you to create something. Shown above is a new page in TextEdit.

Because AppleWorks has several different modules, when you first open the application it asks you which module you want to create a new document in. Click the icon of your choice.

C. You'll get a commercial that will go away when you click on it. Then, see the following note.

D. It appears that nothing happened. It did—look carefully at your menu bar and you'll see the name of your application on the left, next to the Apple. You need to go to the File menu and choose **"New"** to create a **new,** blank page, or **"Open"** to find a document you previously created that you want to **open** again.

There are times when you might open Internet Connect and nothing will appear on your screen. But Internet Connect is actually open, as you can see by the menu bar.

Practice: TextEdit automatically opens a clean, blank page for you to type on.

Read as much as you can take of the rest of this chapter, **or skip right now to the next chapter** and learn word processing techniques. Just leave this new window open and use it for the practice

**Application icons
in the Dock**

You'll notice, after you open an application, that **its icon then appears in the Dock** and has a triangle beneath it, which indicates it is open, as shown below. If you are opening an application in Classic (see Chapter 40), it may take a few minutes; be patient. You can tell an application is trying to open because the icon bobbles up and down (depending on how you have set your Dock preferences).

You can see that AppleWorks is open.

Tip: See Chapter 8 if you want to add icons to the Dock, and see Chapter 22 if you want to know how to use aliases to access your applications without having them clutter up the Dock.

**Tip on switching
applications**

Advanced tip: When there are several applications open, you can **switch** between them with this keyboard shortcut: Command Tab. For instance, let's say you're using your word processor to work on a report and you want to pop over to your web browser to check some information on the Internet (assuming you have a full-time connection). The web browser is already open because you used it this morning. Just hold down the Command key and tap the Tab key—you'll see the application icons in the Dock highlight with each Tab tap. When you have selected the application you want to switch to, let go of the Command key and it will appear in front of you.

The Tab order moves from left to right and then back to the beginning again. If you want to go in the reverse order, hold down the Shift key along with the Command key, then tap the Tab key. Try it.

Once an application is up and running, in the File menu you see two choices: **New** and **Open.** This confused me at first because I thought, "Well, I want to *open* a *new* one." The difference is this:

New vs. Open

- ▾ **New** creates a clean, blank page on which you can begin a *new* document from scratch.

- ▾ **Open** takes you to a dialog box (shown and explained on pages 190–193) where you can choose to *open* a document that was previously created and saved.

A **document** is a file that you or someone else created in an application. For instance, if you open an application like AppleWorks and type a letter, that letter is a document. If you open a page-layout application such as PageMaker and create a newsletter, that newsletter is a document. If you open an image-editing applicatin such as Photoshop and edit a photo, that photograph is a document.

You can't create a document without an application, and **you can't open a document unless it has an application to open into.** When you double-click a document icon to open it, it will try to find the application that created it, then *both* the application and the document will open. If the Mac cannot find the application that created the document, it will try to find some other application to open the document in. If the computer can't find anything, it will ask you what to do; see pages 186–188 if you have trouble opening documents.

What is a Document?

letter to mom

This is a document icon. As explained in Chapter 7, all documents have the upper-right corner turned down.

Opening a Document

Tip: To open a number of documents at once, select all the files (see Chapter 11 about selecting multiple files), then press Command O. Every document (and every necessary application) will open.

To open a document that has already been created and saved in an application, find its icon. Then:

▼ If a document's name, icon, or alias is in a Finder window or sitting on the Desktop, *double*-click on it.

letter to mom

Double-click any icon except when it's in the Dock or in a window Toolbar.

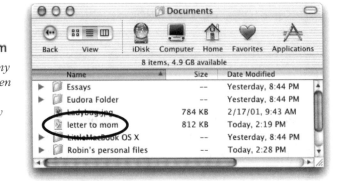

▼ If a document's icon is in the Dock, *single*-click on it.

Important reminder: When you open a document, *you actually open the application also!* That's because a document cannot put itself on the screen—only an application can put a document on the screen. If you get a message complaining that "There is no application available…," all is not necessarily lost. See the next two pages, as well as page 520.

You can also open a document by **dragging the document icon** and **dropping it** on top of its application icon. The application icon might be in the Dock, in an Applications folder, anywhere in your Home area, or even an alias on the Desktop.

Opening a Document with Drag-and-Drop

You'll notice that the application icon will highlight (turn dark), which is the **visual clue** that if you let go your document will open. (Usually.)

*I dragged this AppleWorks **document** icon and dropped it onto the AppleWorks **application** icon. If the application is not open, this will open it.*

Now, the great thing about this trick is that you can often **open a document in an application other than the one it was created in.** For instance, the application AppleWorks is able to open documents created in many other programs. If you have a word processing document someone gave you but you don't have the program they wrote it in, you can drag the foreign document on top of the AppleWorks application icon. If AppleWorks highlights, let go of the document and the program will (probably) open the file. (If not, try the technique on the following page.)

So if you ever get a blank document icon with no clue where it came from or even whether it's a photograph, a letter, or a spreadsheet, drag the icon over every application program you own. Whichever application icon highlights will (usually) open the document.

Drag a file onto application icons to see if an application can open that file. (Sometimes the application attempts to open the file, but then decides it can't.)

In this example, I dragged a graphic I found on the Mac and dropped it on top of the Photoshop application icon. The application icon highlighted, as you can see, and it opened the file.

Check Chapter 22 on **aliases** for directions on creating an alias of each application you own. You can keep these aliases in your Dock or on your Desktop, either individually or in a folder. This makes them easily accessible for opening files with the drag-and-drop method.

Aliases for application icons

Opening a Document in a Different Application

Now, just because you have an icon representing a document you or someone else created in a certain software application doesn't mean you can open up that document on any computer. Clicking on a document icon will only open it **IF** the application itself is also in the computer, either on the hard disk, on another disk that is inserted into one of the drives, or if it's accessible on a network. If the application can't be found, then the document doesn't have anywhere to put itself! Generally, you must have the same version of the application (see page 180) as the one in which it was created.

Sometimes, however, certain applications can open certain documents that were created in other applications. And sometimes you *want* to open a document in a different application; for instance, perhaps you want to open a photograph in Photoshop instead of QuickTime Preview, but when you double-click the photograph icon, it automatically opens in QuickTime Preview. And sometimes the document is from an earlier version of the application, and the new version really can open it. In any of these situations, first try the drag-and-drop technique explained on the previous page. If that doesn't work, then try the suggestion below. For a more permanent solution, see page 520.

1. First open the application that you are pretty sure will open the document.

For details on how to use the Open dialog box, see pages 190–193.

2. From the application's File menu, choose "Open." This will display the "Open" dialog box, as shown below.

3. In the Open dialog box, find the name of the file you want to open. If the name is visible and is black (as opposed to gray), the application can probably open it. Double-click the file name.

   If the name doesn't appear at all, the application can't "naturally" open it, **BUT** the Open dialog box in your application might have a little menu or two, like the ones circled below, that give you more options for what sorts of files this application can open. If it does, choose something like "All Types" or try to find the specific "extension" (abbreviation at the end of the name) and see if that makes your document name appear in the list. If the document's name does appear in black, it will probably open when you double-click its name.

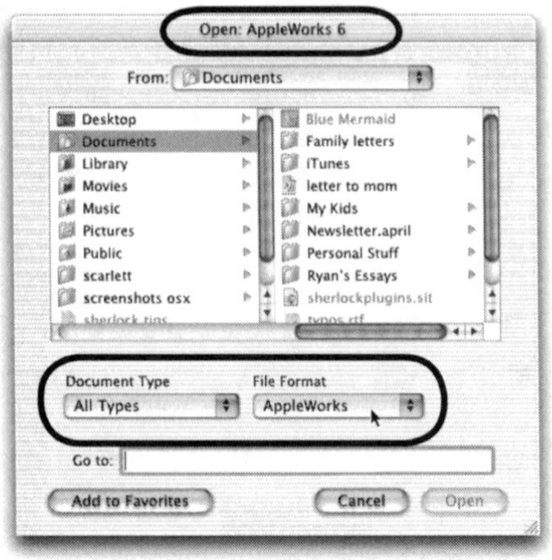

Check the "File Format" menu to see what other sorts of files can be opened.

Some documents don't really need to be *opened* before you can use them. For instance, you don't have to "open" photographs or clipart if you want to put them on a page of a text document such as a letter, newsletter, or email. Instead, you need to "insert" or "place" the image into the document.

Opening Clipart or Photos

To place clipart into a document:

1. Click the insertion point at the position where you want the clipart or photograph to be in the document.

2. Find the command in that application to "Insert," "Place," "Get picture," or something similar.

3. Use the dialog box that comes up to find the photo or clipart you want to place on the page. (This assumes you know how to "navigate" in an Open dialog box; if not, see the following pages.) When you find the name of the graphic you want, double-click it.

4. The image will land in your text right where the insertion point was flashing. In most programs you can resize the image: click once on the image, hold the Shift key down, then drag the bottom-right corner diagonally upward.

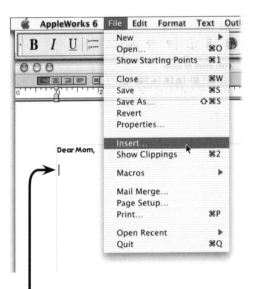

The insertion point is flashing above, just below "Dear Mom." That's where the graphic will drop in, as shown to the right.

An "Open" Dialog Box

Finding your way around an **"Open" dialog box** is called "navigating." It's one of the most important skills you can learn, and you'll need this skill in other dialog boxes, like when you save documents or when you import or export text. Try to take the time to understand and absorb what each part of the dialog box is telling you.

*The name in the **From menu** is the specific folder or disk that contains the files you see in the directory (lists) below*

*In this example, the "From" menu **(A)** says you can open a file from the Documents folder. The Documents folder is selected in the left column **(B)**, and the contents of the Documents folder are listed in the right column **(C)**. At the moment, then, you can open any document stored in that Documents folder— just double-click on the file name in the right column.*

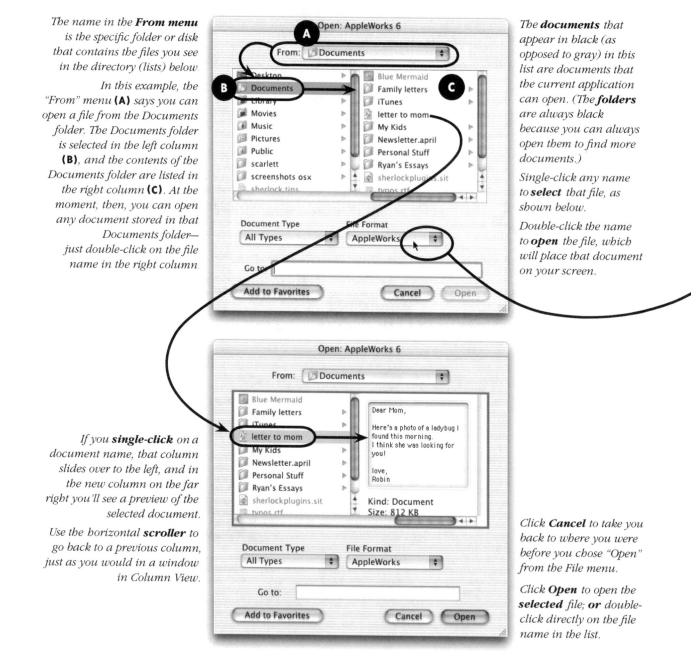

*The **documents** that appear in black (as opposed to gray) in this list are documents that the current application can open. (The **folders** are always black because you can always open them to find more documents.)*

*Single-click any name to **select** that file, as shown below.*

*Double-click the name to **open** the file, which will place that document on your screen.*

*If you **single-click** on a document name, that column slides over to the left, and in the new column on the far right you'll see a preview of the selected document.*

*Use the horizontal **scroller** to go back to a previous column, just as you would in a window in Column View.*

*Click **Cancel** to take you back to where you were before you chose "Open" from the File menu.*

*Click **Open** to open the **selected** file; or double-click directly on the file name in the list.*

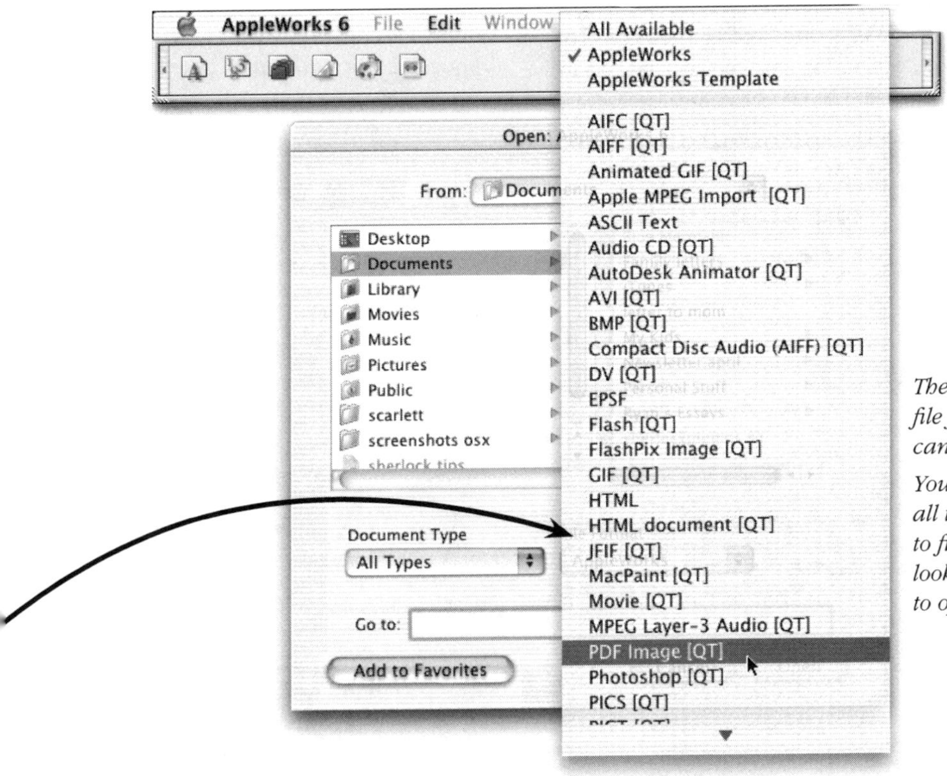

AppleWorks 6	File	Edit	Window	All Available

✓ AppleWorks
AppleWorks Template

AIFC [QT]
AIFF [QT]
Animated GIF [QT]
Apple MPEG Import [QT]
ASCII Text
Audio CD [QT]
AutoDesk Animator [QT]
AVI [QT]
BMP [QT]
Compact Disc Audio (AIFF) [QT]
DV [QT]
EPSF
Flash [QT]
FlashPix Image [QT]
GIF [QT]
HTML
HTML document [QT]
JFIF [QT]
MacPaint [QT]
Movie [QT]
MPEG Layer-3 Audio [QT]
PDF Image [QT]
Photoshop [QT]
PICS [QT]

Open:

From: Documents

Desktop
Documents
Library
Movies
Music
Pictures
Public
scarlett
screenshots osx
sherlock tips

Document Type
All Types

Go to:

Add to Favorites

These are some of the different file formats that AppleWorks can "read," or open.

You don't have to know what all these are—I don't. Just try to find one that sounds or looks like the file you're trying to open.

File won't open?

If the name of the file you want to open is shown in the list in gray (instead of black), that doesn't necessarily mean it's impossible for the current application to open it. Most applications have a number of other "file formats" they can "read," or open. Click on the "File Format" menu (circled on the opposite page), if your application has one, to get the list of formats it can open. As you can see above, AppleWorks can open an incredible range of file formats.

If your application has a menu like the one shown above, called something like "Document Type" or anything similar, make sure it is set to try to open "All Types" of documents.

—continued

Open another folder   If you've been saving all of your documents in the Documents folder, then you won't have to navigate anywhere else to find your documents. But at some point you will start making new folders in which to store your work, and you need to know how to find these in the Open dialog box.

If you learned how to work with the Finder windows in Column View (Chapter 6), you'll find the Open dialog box very familiar—you can enlarge the dialog box and go find other folders, as shown on the opposite page.

There is also a list of menu options that will take you to **certain folders or disks** on your Mac, as shown below. This menu can be a shortcut to help you find the document you want to open.

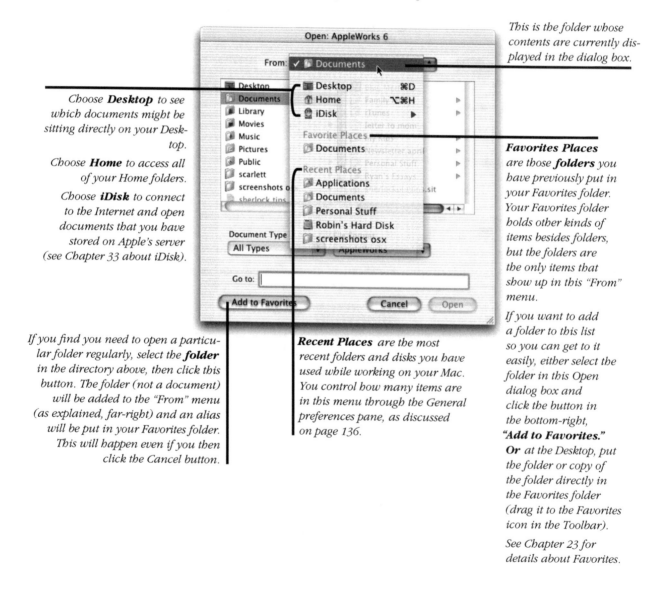

This is the folder whose contents are currently displayed in the dialog box.

*Choose **Desktop** to see which documents might be sitting directly on your Desktop.*

*Choose **Home** to access all of your Home folders.*

*Choose **iDisk** to connect to the Internet and open documents that you have stored on Apple's server (see Chapter 33 about iDisk).*

*If you find you need to open a particular folder regularly, select the **folder** in the directory above, then click this button. The folder (not a document) will be added to the "From" menu (as explained, far-right) and an alias will be put in your Favorites folder. This will happen even if you then click the Cancel button.*

Recent Places are the most recent folders and disks you have used while working on your Mac. You control how many items are in this menu through the General preferences pane, as discussed on page 136.

*Favorites Places are those **folders** you have previously put in your Favorites folder. Your Favorites folder holds other kinds of items besides folders, but the folders are the only items that show up in this "From" menu.*

*If you want to add a folder to this list so you can get to it easily, either select the folder in this Open dialog box and click the button in the bottom-right, **"Add to Favorites." Or** at the Desktop, put the folder or copy of the folder directly in the Favorites folder (drag it to the Favorites icon in the Toolbar).*

See Chapter 23 for details about Favorites.

You can open the dialog box wider and **navigate** through it just like you navigate through the Column View windows on the Desktop. Press the Tab key to select the From menu or the columns below. Use the arrow keys to move left or right from column to column, or up or down in one column.

Drag the bottom-right corner to widen the window.

Column views in the Open dialog box

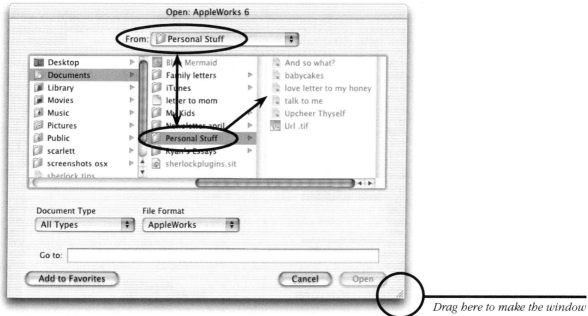

Single-click a folder or a disk to see a list of the files inside that folder or on that disk, and the title of that new folder or disk will be displayed in the "From" menu above the list.

Drag here to make the window larger or smaller.

Use the slider bar to scroll to the left and get to the Home level of your Mac, or even to the Computer level, so you can locate the folder and document you want to open.

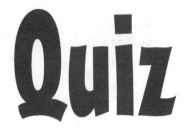

Splash.mov

1. Is this file an application or a document?

_____

2. What will happen when you double-click on the icon in #1?

_____

Internet Explorer

3. Is this file an application or a document?

_____

4. What will happen when you double-click on the icon in #3?

_____

5. What would be the fastest way to view a window by "Kind" so you can tell which file is the application?

_____

6. In the File menu in an application, what is the difference between "New" and "Open"?

_____

7. Label these parts of the Open dialog box to the left:

    a. the directory, or list of files and folders you can open.

    b. a document that can be opened.

    c. the name of the folder that contains the files you see in the list.

    d. the menu that will display favorite and recent folders.

Answers on page 751.

Word Processing

(also known as "typing")

You may have grown up **typing** on a typewriter or you may have grown up **word processing** on a computer of some sort. Typing and word processing are very similar, of course, in that they use a similar keyboard. The difference is that word processing is much more fun. You can delete text with the click of a button; rearrange single words, paragraphs, or entire pages of text; automatically number all the pages; resize the text so it fills out the requirement for your project; use italic, bold, and different typefaces for emphasis; add headers and footers (information at the tops and/or bottoms of every page, such as the date, time, page number, title, etc.) and much more.

You're going to be typing in some manner everywhere on your Mac. In some applications typing is the main point, as in word processing, page layout, and email. In others, it is the way to input the data (information) you need to manipulate, as in databases or spreadsheets. In others, typing is a sideline that is occasionally necessary, as in paint programs. And all over your Mac you'll find dialog boxes where you type some answer or other, and even on your Desktop you type the names of files and folders. Fortunately, in the consistent Mac environment, typing follows the same patterns and features everywhere, so you should read this chapter no matter what you plan to use your computer for.

Practice: To do the practice exercises in this chapter, either open your favorite word processor **or** use TextEdit, which is on your Macintosh.

To open TextEdit: In any Finder window, click on the Applications icon to open the Applications window. In that window, find the TextEdit icon and double-click it.

If you want TextEdit to be more easily accessible, do this: When TextEdit is open, go to the Dock, press on the TextEdit icon, and choose "Keep In Dock."

I-Beam

You may already be familiar with the Macintosh word processing **I-beam** (pronounced eye-beam). It looks like this (or very similar): ⌶ The tiny cross-bar just below the center of the I-beam indicates the "baseline" of type, that invisible line that type sits upon.

On the Mac, the I-beam is a **visual clue** that you are now in a typing mode, as opposed to seeing an arrow or a cross-hair or any number of other "cursors" that appear in various applications.

> *The I-beam is simply another pointer.* And just like the pointer,
> it doesn't do anything until you *click it* or *press-and-drag it.*

Insertion Point

When you move the I-beam pointer to a spot within text and *click,* it sets down a flashing **insertion point** that looks like this: | (but it flashes).

This insertion point is extremely important! After you click the mouse to set the insertion point, then you can move the I-beam out of the way (using the mouse)—**the insertion point is what you need to begin typing,** *not the I-beam!!* The I-beam just positions the insertion point.

With the insertion point flashing, anything you type will start at that point and move out to the right. This is true whether the insertion point is at the beginning or the end of a paragraph, in the middle of a word, in a field of a dialog box, in the name of an icon at your Desktop, or anywhere else. (The only time the words will not move to the right in a word processor is if the text is centered or flush right, or if you've set a tab other than left-aligned.)

At any time you can use the mouse to move the I-beam pointer somewhere else, click, and start typing from the new insertion point.

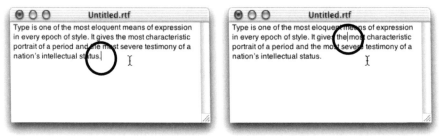

Do you see the insertion point at the end of the paragraph? If I start to type again in this story, it will begin at that insertion point. The I-beam (do you see it?) is just hanging around waiting to be useful.

Do you see where I moved the insertion point to? If I start to type again in this story, it will begin at that insertion point.

Also from that insertion point, press the **Delete** key (found in the upper right, called the **Backspace** key on older keyboards or typewriters) to backspace *to the left* of the insertion point and remove any text along the way.

So you can backspace/delete to **correct typos** as you type, *or* you can click to set the insertion point down anywhere else in your text and backspace from that new position.

When you want to continue typing at the end of your story, use the I-beam to position the insertion point at the end of the story.

Delete (or Backspace)

Type is one of the most eloquent means of expression in every epok of style. It gives the most characteristic portrait of a period and the most ere testimony of a nation's intellectual status. |

This paragraph has a typo. Do you see it? I need to go back and fix it.

Type is one of the most eloquent means of expression in every epok of style. It gives the most characteristic portrait of a period and the most ere testimony of a nation's intellectual status.

*I used the I-beam to move the insertion point just to the **right** of the typo. Now I can hit the Delete key to erase that wrong letter and type the correct one in its place.*

Practice: In the paragraph you typed earlier, take note of where the insertion point is, then hit the **Delete** key several times. Watch as it deletes the characters **to the left** of the insertion point.

If you have a **Forward Delete** key (del), experiment with that one as well.

If you have a full-sized keyboard with the little pad of edit keys in the middle, as shown on page 34, you have a **Forward Delete** key. It's marked with "del." This is a fabulous key—it deletes characters *to the right* of the insertion point (the regular Delete key deletes to the left, or backwards as you type).

Forward Delete key

What?! One space after a period? If you grew up on a typewriter, this is a difficult habit to change, I know. Or if you were taught keyboarding skills by someone who grew up on a typewriter, they taught you typewriter rules. But characters on a Macintosh are not *monospaced* as they are on a typewriter (except for a few typefaces such as Monaco, Courier, and Andale Mono), so there is no need to use two spaces to separate two sentences. Check any book or magazine on your shelf; you will never find two spaces after periods (except publications produced on a computer typed by someone still using typewriter rules). If you find this hard to accept, read *The Mac is not a typewriter*. If you're interested in creating fine typography, read *The Non-Designer's Type Book*. Yes, I wrote them.

One Space After Periods

For the ultimate authority on the question, check the question-and-answer page on the web site for the *Chicago Manual of Style:* www.press.uchicago.edu/ Misc/Chicago/cmosfaq.html

Selecting (Highlighting) Text

When you **select text,** it becomes **highlighted.** Once it is selected, you can do things to it, such as change its size, the typeface, delete it, etc.

If you take the I-beam and double-click on a word anywhere on the Mac, the entire word is selected, indicated by the highlighting.

This word is highlighted. I double-clicked on the word to select it.

To select more than one word, press-and-drag over the entire area you wish to highlight. The entire sentence is highlighted.

To select all of the text in an entire document, use the keyboard shortcut Command A.

To un-highlight (deselect) text, click once anywhere, even in the highlighted space.

Practice: In the paragraph you typed earlier, use the I-beam to **double-click** on a word to select it.

Select a range of text: Position the I-beam somewhere toward the top of the paragraph, press the mouse button down and hold it down, then drag the mouse downward. You can move backward as well, as long as you keep the mouse button down. When you have a range of text selected, let go of the mouse button.

Replacing highlighted text

Once a word is selected (highlighted), anything you type will **entirely replace the selected text.** That is, you don't have to hit the Delete key first to get rid of the text—just type. This is true everywhere on the Mac.

While the text is selected you can now change the font (typeface) or style or size of the text using your menu commands. Or you can copy or cut or delete that text. Or you can paste something in to replace it. In fact, you *cannot* do any of these things *unless* the text is first highlighted. (Each of these procedures is explained in this chapter.)

Practice: In the paragraph you typed earlier, use the I-beam to double-click on a word to select it. Without hitting the Delete key to delete the selected text, just type a new word and watch it replace the selected word.

Try selecting a range of text, as above, and while it is highlighted, type a new sentence.

Try these shortcuts for **selecting text** anywhere on the Mac:

▾ Double-click in the middle of a word to select the whole word.

▾ Triple-click in the middle of a sentence to select either the whole line or the entire paragraph (depending on the application).

▾ The arrow keys move the insertion point backward and forward, up and down. Hold down the Shift key as you use the arrow keys, and the text will be *selected* along the way.

▾ If you have a lot of text to select, try this:

1. **Click** (don't press and drag) at the *beginning* of the text you want to select.

2. Scroll, if necessary, to the *end* of the text you want to select, even if it's on another page.

3. Hold down the **Shift** key and **click.** Everything between **click and Shift-click** will be selected. You gotta try it.

This also works in spreadsheets and database lists. In page layout applications, it only works within one linked story.

▾ In many applications, the numeric keypad will either type numbers (when the Num Lock key is down) or it will move the insertion point (when Num Lock is not down). Experiment with it. For instance, in Microsoft Word or Adobe PageMaker, the number 1 will bounce the insertion point to the beginning of a line, and the number 7 will bounce it to the end. Other keys move the insertion point up or down a paragraph, a page, a word, etc. And if you hold the Shift key down, the text will be selected as the insertion point moves.

Several selection tips

Very few applications* let you select "discontiguous" text— that is, it's generally not possible to select one line from the first paragraph, plus a line from the third paragraph. The selected text must all be contiguous, or connected together.

*One notable exception is the great word processor called Nisus Writer from Nisus Software, www.nisus.com.

Practice: You can skip these techniques if you are new to word processing—come back later when you feel more comfortable.

If you've been word processing for a while, experiment with each of these techniques. They are incredibly handy.

When to Use the Return Key

A word wrap is sometimes called a soft Return (although technically it isn't).

For typewriter users: The Return key is the equivalent of the carriage return on a typewriter.

Word wrap: In a word processor, you should *never* hit the Return key at the end of your line *unless* it is the end of the paragraph or unless you *really do* want the line to end there, as in an address. This is because word processors *word wrap*—when the words get close to the right margin, they just wrap themselves around onto the next line. Why is that? Well...

Hard Return: When you press the Return key you insert what is called a *hard Return* that tells the computer to always stop the line at that point. So if you change your margins, your line *always* breaks at that hard Return, as shown below. Just keep those nimble fingers moving along and only hit the Return key when you really want a new paragraph.

Practice: In Text Edit, type a paragraph, but this time hit a Return at the end of each line as you approach the right margin.

Then take your mouse and position the pointer (notice it's not an I-beam once you are out of the word processing space), and drag the bottom-right corner to resize the window. Notice how your lines always break at those Returns you typed, no matter how you change the margins.

(If your margins don't change in TextEdit, go to the Format menu and choose "Wrap to Window.")

As you make the margins narrower, you will get other line breaks where the text automatically adjusts itself to the new margins, as they should.

Tip: To the computer, a **paragraph** is created every time you hit the Return key. So the computer thinks a return address of three lines is really three paragraphs.

Although you can't see it, I typed a hard Return at the end of each of these lines. It looks fine at the moment.

Type is one of the most eloquent means of expression in every epoch of style. It gives the most characteristic portrait of a period and the most severe testimony of a nation's intellectual status.
Peter Behrens

When I widened the margins by enlarging the size of the window in TextEdit, the lines still broke at the hard Returns. This can be okay sometimes.

Type is one of the most eloquent means of expression in every epoch of style. It gives the most characteristic portrait of a period and the most severe testimony of a nation's intellectual status.
Peter Behrens

But when I made the window narrower, which in TextEdit makes the margins narrower, you can see the problem that results from those hard Returns.*

Type is one of the most eloquent means of
expression in every epoch of style. It gives
the most characteristic portrait of a period
and the most severe testimony of a nation's
intellectual status.
Peter Behrens

*In TextEdit, if your margins don't change when you make the window narower, go to the Format menu and choose "Wrap to Window."

Double-Return: Hitting the Return key twice creates a double space between the lines. This is for extra space between individual paragraphs (although in any good word processor you can ask for an automatic increase of space between paragraphs instead of a double-Return).

If you want the entire document, or even just a piece of it, double-spaced—that's different: there is always an instant way to change your spacing to double-spaced, usually just a button to click *after you select all the text.* Check your manual for the method for your particular application.

Removing a Return: The computer sees a Return as just another character, which means to remove a Return you simply *backspace over it* with the Delete key, just as you would to remove an unwanted character. The problem is that in most programs you can't *see* the Return character. So you must set the insertion point just to the left of the first character on the line and backspace/delete, like so:

Tip: Most word processing programs (but not TextEdit) have a command for showing invisible characters such as Returns and spaces, which makes it easier to get rid of unnecessary ones. The command might be something like "Show invisibles," "Show ¶" or "Display ¶." Check your menus.

> Let's say I'm typing away and my dog shoves his big head under my arm
> and suddenly
>
> my text starts typing on the wrong line, like this. What to do?

Set the insertion point directly to the left of the text that's on the wrong line (as shown below).

> Let's say I'm typing away and my dog shoves his big head under my arm
> and suddenly
>
> my text starts typing on the wrong line, like this. What to do?

Hit the Delete key to remove the empty line above that new, unwanted paragraph (**you** don't think it's a paragraph, but the computer does). Now it will look like this:

> Let's say I'm typing away and my dog shoves his big head under my arm
> and suddenly
> my text starts typing on the wrong line, like this. What to do?

Delete again to wrap the sentence back up to the one above.

> Let's say I'm typing away and my dog shoves his big head under my arm
> and suddenly my text starts typing on the wrong line, like this. What to do?
> Oh, it's all fixed!

Changing Fonts (typefaces) and Rule No. 2

Or as my friend Don Nissen, a design instructor at Ivy Tech State College, explains more elegantly: "Select, then affect." "This seems to clarify to students that, if something isn't selected, it ain't gonna be affected."

Throughout the entire Mac environment, to make any changes to anything you must follow this rule, Rule No. 2:

Select First, Then Do It To It.

For instance, **to change to a different font,** or typeface:

1. First *select* the characters you want to change (press-and-drag over the text). If you want to change all of the text, press Command A to select all.

2. Then *choose* the font name you want to change it into.

    The font list is found in your menu under various labels, depending on your application. It might be under Fonts, Type, Format, or something similar.

    In TextEdit, go to the Format menu, choose "Font," then "Font Panel…." Select a font from the list that appears.

Formatting the insertion point

Notice that the insertion point picks up whatever font, style, size, and alignment *is directly to its left*. No matter where you set the insertion point, you will type in the font, etc., of the character to its left, even if that character is an empty space. **But you can format the insertion point.**

Now, let's say you want the next few words you're going to type to be in a different font. Do you need to type the text first and then select those characters and change the font? No!

1. Make sure your insertion point is positioned where you are going to type with the new font.

2. *With no text selected,* choose the font (and style and size, if you like).

    When there is no text selected, all the formatting gets poured into the insertion point—whatever you type next will be in the font you just chose.

    As soon as you place the insertion point elsewhere, though, it will again pick up all the formatting of the character to its left.

Practice: Use the paragraph you typed earlier and **change some text to a different typeface,** like this:

Double-click a word to select it, or drag over a range of text.

Then go to the Font menu in your application and choose a new font.

Or change the typeface before you type:

Position your insertion point at the end of your existing text.

Hit a Return.

Now, while the insertion point is flashing, choose a different font.

Start typing.

Style refers to whether the type is plain, **bold,** *italic,* condensed, etc. To change the style of the type, you need to follow Rule #2: *select first, then do it to it.* **Select** the type you want to change (highlight it), then **choose** the style you want from the menu. Depending on the application, you can choose more than one of these; for instance, you can have a face that is ***bold italic condensed.***

Not all typefaces have all of the options, as shown below. Many applications limit you to just the designed faces; that is, in some programs you can force a typeface to fake an italic, but in most you can't do that anymore.

If you're using an application that lets you apply pretend italic or shadow or outline to a typeface, you can remove all of the style choices at once: *select* the text and *choose* Plain or Normal from the font style menu.

Changing Style

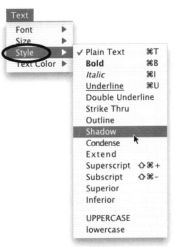

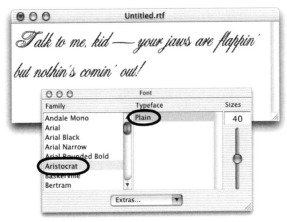

In the Font panel in TextEdit, you see a list of fonts on the left. On the right are the individual style choices that are available for the selected typeface. Notice this typeface, Aristocrat, has only one option, Plain. That's because you can't have an italic version of a script like this, and the designer apparently did not create a bold face for this font (well, she might have, but it's not loaded on this Mac).

In AppleWorks, this is the list of styles you can apply, whether they are designed into the font or not. To remove all applied styles, choose "Plain Text."

(In TextEdit, however, "Plain Text" is something completely different! Don't choose it—see the following page for information about what "Plain Text" is in TextEdit.)

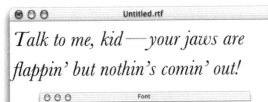

This selected font family, Baskerville, has a broader range of styles from which to choose.

Practice: Follow the practice exercise on the opposite page, but this time choose a different

Changing Styles Mid-Sentence —
without using the menu

As explained on page 202 about changing *fonts*, you can just as easily choose the style you want from the menu *before* you type the text (as long as you don't move the insertion point after choosing). But even that's a pain if you just want to italicize the next word and then return to normal text. This is an easier method:

Notice the keyboard shortcuts in the menu shown below? In most applications they are the same: Command **B** for Bold, Command **I** for Italic, etc. (Some programs may use Command Shift B and Command Shift I, etc.)

Learn these keyboard shortcuts!

▾ As you're typing along, simply press Command **B** and the next word you type will be **bold.**

▾ When you want the next word to be *not* bold, press Command **B** again and it will take *off* the bold (that's called a *toggle switch*— when choosing the same command turns that command off).

▾ Logically, you can press Command **B I** to create a word that is (guess!) ***bold italic.***

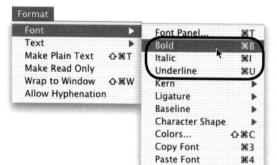

These are the typical keyboard shortcuts to make selected text bold, italic, or underline.

Remember, though, you should only choose italic or bold if you know that typeface has a real italic or bold designed in the family.

If you don't know how to find out (see Chapter 25 if you care), just look carefully at the text on the screen. If it looks like regular text that has been fattened or slanted instead of designed, it's fake.

Practice: In your word processor, go to the Style menu and see exactly which keyborrd command it uses to apply the bold or italic style (it's most likely Command B for bold and Command I for italic).

Type a few words.

Press the keyboard command for **bold,** then type a few more words. They should be in bold.

Now type the keyboard command for **bold** again, which will remove it.

Type a few more words and they should be in the regular style, not bold.

Try it again, this time press Command B I to change to both bold and italic at once.

▾ If you want to take all the extra formatting off at once (for instance, you want to remove the shadow, the outline, and the bold), select the text and apply the shortcut for Plain, Normal, or Regular style—whatever your application calls it.

(This trick doesn't work in TextEdit. "Plain Text" in TextEdit actually refers to ASCII text, which is type stripped down to nothing but standard characters—no italic, no bold, no underline, no indents, only one font, etc. Choose "Plain Text" in TextEdit when you want to send this document to someone using a PC so their machine doesn't get confused by the character formatting.)

Size in type is measured in *points*. There are 72 points in one inch, but you don't have to remember that. In your menu you see different numbers (points) referring to the size of type; logically, the bigger the number, the bigger the type.

As usual, **to change the size of characters:** *select first, then do it to it.*

1. Select the text.

2. Go to the Size menu and choose a point size.

   In TextEdit, there is no "Size" menu. Go to the Format menu, choose "Font," then "Font Panel…." You'll see the size slider on the far right, as shown below.

Or set your insertion point and choose the size from the menu *before* you type (see the previous two sections on changing fonts and styles).

Changing Type Size

8 point type

48 pt.

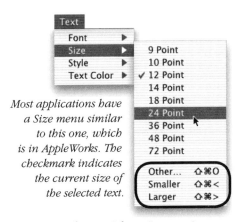

Most applications have a Size menu similar to this one, which is in AppleWorks. The checkmark indicates the current size of the selected text.

Choose "Other…" to type in a number that isn't on the list.

Use the other two keyboard shortcuts to make the selected type smaller or larger right in front of your eyes: Hold down the Shift and Command keys, then tap the LessThan (<) or GreaterThan (>) symbols over and over; each tap reduces or enlarges the selected type by one point.

This is TextEdit. Notice the text in the window is selected. Once your text is selected, you can either type in a new number in the box on the right side of the Font panel, or click to select one of the sizes in the scrolling list.

Practice: Follow the two steps above to change the point size of selected type.

If you're using AppleWorks, try

Alignment

Alignment refers to where the text is lined up.

▾ *Align left:* text is lined up on the left side, and the right is ragged, as shown in these sentences. Also known as *flush left*.

▾ *Align right:* text is lined up on the right, and the left edge is ragged. Also known as *flush right*.

▾ *Align center:* text is centered on a vertical axis *between your margins*. If you change your margins, your centered text will shift.

▾ *Justified:* text is lined up on both the left *and* right margins, as seen in the paragraphs below.

To change your alignment, you know what to do! That's right: *select first, then do it to it*—highlight the text, *then* choose the alignment from the menu or the buttons, as shown below.

Alignment is **paragraph-specific** formatting; that is, whichever alignment you choose will apply to the *entire paragraph*—it's not possible to apply it to only one line in the paragraph. (Remember, to the computer, every time you hit a Return you create a new paragraph.)

The important thing about this concept is that you don't have to select every character in a paragraph to change the alignment—selecting a few characters or even just clicking your insertion point anywhere in the paragraph *selects the entire paragraph*.

This is different from **character-specific** formatting such as font, size, and style, where the commands only apply to the *individual, selected characters*.

Rulers

Every word processor has a **ruler** that appears at the top of a document, as shown below. If you don't see it, you'll find a menu command that says something like "Show Ruler." Generally, all the buttons you see in the ruler are also listed as menu commands, but the ruler makes it so convenient.

If you're practicing in TextEdit right now and you don't see the ruler, go to the Format menu, choose "Text," then choose "Show Ruler." Or just press Command R.

Alignment buttons: left, center, right, and justified.

This changes the spacing between lines.

This typical ruler is the one in AppleWorks.

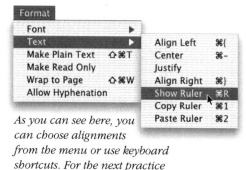

As you can see here, you can choose alignments from the menu or use keyboard shortcuts. For the next practice exercise, show the ruler.

Below are two examples of text that is **selected** to change the alignment. If you want to apply an alignment to more than one paragraph, you must select every one that you want to change. The paragraphs must be contiguous, or next to each other; that is, is most applications you cannot select the first paragraph and the third paragraph at the same time.

Here is an important thing to remember about rulers: ***every paragraph has its own ruler.*** Alignments, margins, tabs, line spacing—everything applies to the *entire* paragraph and *only* to the selected paragraph(s)!

These are the alignment buttons in TextEdit's ruler. Just select the text and click a button.

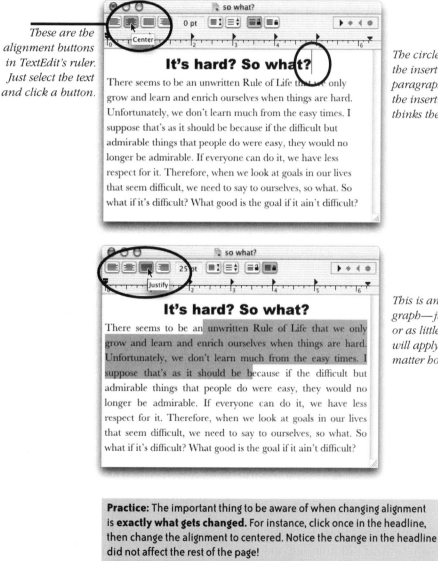

The circle in the headline is around the insertion point—to select a paragraph, all you need to do is click the insertion point in it (the computer thinks the headline is a paragraph).

This is another way to select a paragraph—just grab a piece of it, as much or as little as you want. The alignment will apply to the entire paragraph no matter how little of it you select.

Practice: The important thing to be aware of when changing alignment is **exactly what gets changed.** For instance, click once in the headline, then change the alignment to centered. Notice the change in the headline did not affect the rest of the page!

Now click once in the body copy, and take a look at the alignment buttons—the flush left button is still selected, **not** the centered button. That 's because **the ruler affects only the selected paragraphs.** If you click once again on the headline, you'll see the centered alignment button selected.

Blank Spaces

The computer thinks a **blank space** is just the same as any other character—it has no idea that you can't see that character. Every Tab, Return, Spacebar space, etc., that appears invisible to us is an actual thing to the Mac. This means you can select blank spaces, blank lines, blank tabbed spaces, or Returns to delete them. Select and delete them just as you would any other character.

The space between these█words is highlighted.

█████This tabbed space is highlighted.

If you hit double Returns, you can also select the blank space between the lines, as shown below, and delete it.

██

The bar above is the blank space indicating an empty line.

Also, since these blank spaces are characters, you can actually change the size of them (font size, that is, as explained on page 205), as well as the *leading* (space between the lines), the paragraph spacing, etc., all of which would affect the size of the empty space.

But the most important thing to understand about blank spaces is that the Mac takes them into consideration when you center lines or paragraphs, when you try to align columns, and during other word processing techniques. So you must be conscious of where those blank spaces are!

Practice: Type a couple of paragraphs. Use several double-Returns and a couple of tabs (just hit the Tab key, then type).

Now using the selection techniques you practiced on page 198, select not the words, but the blank spaces.

Centering Text

As explained on the opposite page, when you center a word or line, the Mac takes all those blank spaces into consideration, so any Spacebar spaces or any indents or any tabs you've inserted will be used to calculate the center of the line, making the line appear to be uncentered!

If you want to center a headline or a paragraph of text, *do not* use a centered tab to do so! Instead, find the button in the toolbar (shown on pages 206 and 207) to center the text. Centered tabs are only for centering columns of text.

This line is centered.

This line is also centered◄————— *I hit the Tab key before I typed the first word*
but the line includes an invisible tab. *in this centered line. Thus the line appears,*
to our eyes, to be uncentered. (The Mac,
however, believes it to be centered.)

The invisible tab character
that is disrupting the alignment
must be highlighted
and removed, like so:

This line is also centered.◄————— *I selected the tab space and deleted it.*

Then it will center just fine:

This line is also centered. ◄————— *After I deleted the invisible space,*
the line centered just fine.

Cut, Copy, and the Clipboard

Almost anywhere you can type, you can cut or copy text. When you **cut** text (or graphics), it is *removed* from your document and placed on the "Clipboard." When you **copy** text (or graphics), the original text *is left in your document* and a *copy* of it is placed on the Clipboard. Well, what the heck is a Clipboard?

The **Clipboard** is an invisible "container" somewhere in the depths of the Mac. It holds whatever you have *cut or copied,* be it text, spreadsheet data, graphics, an entire folder, etc. Once something is on the Clipboard, it waits there until you paste it in somewhere (we'll get to that in a minute).

The most important thing to remember about the Clipboard is that it holds *only one thing at a time;* that is, as soon as you cut or copy something else, whatever was in the Clipboard to begin with is *replaced* with the new selection.

In some programs, including the Finder, you'll find a menu command called *Show Clipboard,* in which case it appears as a window with its contents displayed, as shown below. In most programs, though, you never see the actual Clipboard—simply trust that it's there.

The Clipboard appears as a window (if it's available for looking at in your program). No matter where you copied or cut an item from, you can always go to the Finder's Edit menu and show the Clipboard to see what you've got.

If your application lets you see the Clipboard, it will be a command in the Edit menu.

Items will stay on the Clipboard even when you change applications: you can put a paint image on the Clipboard in a paint program, then open a word processing document and paste the paint image into a letter.

Items will disappear from the Clipboard when the computer is turned off or if there is a power failure—the contents are stored in RAM (memory), so anytime RAM gets wiped out, so do the contents of the Clipboard. (There's an explanation of memory on page 220.)

Practice: The practice exercise for cut, copy, and paste is on page 212.

How to Copy: Simply select, then do it to it. For instance, select the text **Copy** you wish to copy (press-and-drag over it), then from the Edit menu choose "Copy." The text will *remain* in your document and a *copy* will be placed on the Clipboard.

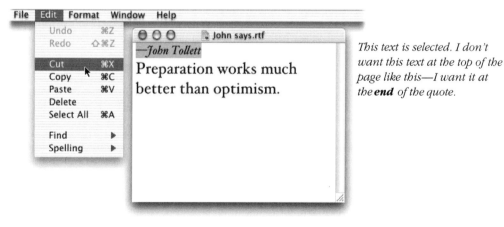

This text is selected and the Copy command is chosen.
You can see it on the Clipboard on the opposite page.

OK, it's on the Clipboard. Now what? Well, the Clipboard holds objects for *pasting*. You can take text or a graphic out of one place and paste it into your document somewhere else, just as if you had a little glue pot. We'll get to that in just a moment (next page).

How to Cut: Simply select, then do it to it. For instance, select the text you **Cut** wish to remove from the document (press-and-drag over it). Then from the Edit menu choose "Cut." The text will be *eliminated* from your document and placed on the Clipboard. (Be sure to read about "Delete" further on in this chapter.) Now you can paste it somewhere; see the following page.

*This text is selected. I don't want this text at the top of the page like this—I want it at the **end** of the quote.*

Paste

How to Paste: All you do is go to the Edit menu and choose "Paste," but it's important to know *where* it will paste into.

▼ Whatever was on the Clipboard will be inserted in your document *beginning at the flashing insertion point.* So if you want the pasted item to appear at a certain place in your document, **first** click the I-beam to position the insertion point.

▼ If you have a *range of text selected,* the pasted item will *replace* what was selected.

Say you have a paragraph in Letter A that you want to use to replace a paragraph in Letter B. Copy the paragraph in Letter A, open Letter B, select the paragraph you don't want in Letter B, paste, and the paragraph from Letter A will *replace* the selected paragraph in Letter B.

▼ Spreadsheet data, graphics, etc., can be pasted in as well. In some programs, especially graphic programs, the pasted object will just land in the middle of the page.

As long as something is on the Clipboard, you can paste it in a million times in many different applications.

Practice: First type a headline, a paragraph or two of body copy, and a byline ("by you").

Cut the byline from the bottom of the page and **paste** it in just after the headline, like this:

Cut the byline from the bottom of the page: Select it, then press Command X. The byline disappears.

Click at the end of the headline to set the insertion point.

Hit Return to give the byline its own line.

Paste (press Command V). The byline appears in this place.

Now **copy a paragraph** and paste it somewhere else, like this:

Triple-click anywhere in a paragraph to select the entire paragraph.

Press Command C. It will look like nothing happened.

Set the insertion point at the end of your text and hit two Returns.

Press Command V to **paste** the paragraph in, starting at the insertion point.

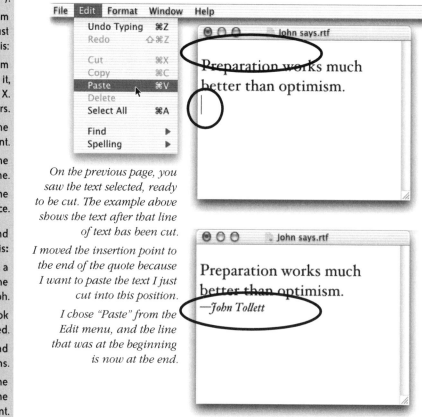

On the previous page, you saw the text selected, ready to be cut. The example above shows the text after that line of text has been cut.

I moved the insertion point to the end of the quote because I want to paste the text I just cut into this position.

I chose "Paste" from the Edit menu, and the line that was at the beginning is now at the end.

Cut, copy, and paste are not limited to text. You will use these features in every program you have, as well as the Desktop. Below is an example of copying a graphic image from a drawing program and pasting it into the text in a word processing document. The application I used is AppleWorks, which includes not only drawing and word processing, but paint, database, spreadsheet, and slideshow modules.

Cut and paste graphics, also

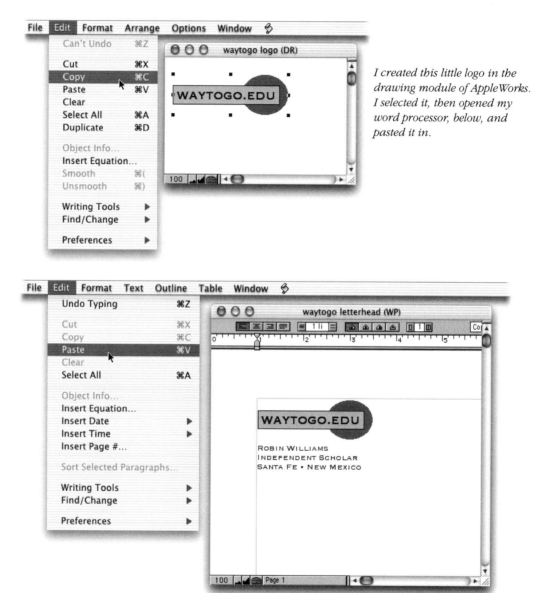

I created this little logo in the drawing module of AppleWorks. I selected it, then opened my word processor, below, and pasted it in.

Delete or Clear and the Clipboard

Now, the **Delete** key (found on the upper-right of the main group of keys, called **Backspace** on older keyboards and typewriters) works a little differently from Cut: if you hit this key while something is selected, whatever is selected is *deleted* but is *not* placed on the Clipboard. This means if you are holding something in the Clipboard to paste in again, whatever you *delete* from your document will not replace what is currently being held in the Clipboard. But it also means that you don't have that deleted item anymore—whatever you delete is really gone. **Clear,** in the Edit menu, does the same thing as the Delete key.

Undo

Undo can sometimes save your boompah (no, that's not computer jargon —it's Grandma's euphemism). When you do something that makes you scream, "Aack! Oh no!" then try Undo. It's always the first command in the Edit menu (or press Command Z).

> **Note:** What Undo can undo is *only the last action that occurred.* For instance, if you selected two paragraphs of brilliantly witty text that you spent three hours composing and then the cat walked across your keyboard and obliterated the entire work, Undo could give it back to you **IF** you Undo before you touch *anything*. If you start fiddling around with the keys and the mouse, then what you will undo is that fiddling around. So if something goes wrong, don't scream—**UNDO.** Then scream.

> (Some applications, such as illustration programs and page layout applications, can Undo multiple times. Check your manual.)

Commands Z, X, C, V

Thoughtfully, the keyboard shortcuts for the undo/cut/copy/paste commands are very handy. Notice on your keyboard the letters **Z, X, C,** and **V,** all lined up in a row right above the Command key. Remember, select first (*except to Undo*); then hold down the Command key and lightly tap the letter.

Command **Z** will Undo (Z is very close to the Command key).

Command **X** will Cut (X like eXiting or Xing it out).

Command **C** will Copy (C for Copy).

Command **V** will Paste (V because it is next to C; it's sort of like the caret symbol ^ for inserting).

Special characters are the symbols you have access to on the Macintosh that weren't available on typewriters, such as upside-down question marks for Spanish (¿), the pound symbol for English money (£), the cents sign (¢), the registration or trademark symbols (® ™), etc. You can view all these with your **Key Caps** utility; see pages 506–507.

Accessing Special Characters

Below is a short list of special characters you can experiment with. For each character, hold down the modifier key (Option, Shift, etc.) and tap the character key noted. For instance, to type a bullet, hold down the Option key and tap the number 8 on the top of your keyboard (not the number 8 on the keypad). It's no different from typing an asterisk, where you hold down the Shift key and tap the 8. A complete list is in Appendix B.

•	bullet	Option 8
©	copyright	Option G
™	trademark	Option 2
®	registration	Option R
¢	cents	Option $
°	degree	Option Shift 8
…	ellipsis	Option ;
–	en dash	Option Hyphen
—	em dash	Option Shift Hyphen

You can type **accent marks** on the Mac, as in résumé and piñata. There is a complete chart in Appendix B, but it's easy to remember that you use the Option key, and the accents are hiding beneath the keyboard characters that would usually be under them. For example, the acute accent over the **é** is **Option e;** the tilde over the **ñ** is **Option n.**

Using Real Accent Marks

Here is a list of common accent marks:

´	Option e
`	Option ~
¨	Option u
~	Option n
^	Option i

To type accent marks, follow these steps (using the word Résumé):

1. Type the word until you come to the letter that will be *under* the accent mark; e.g., **R**

2. *Before* you type that next letter (the letter **e** in this case), type the Option combination (**Option e** in this case, which means hold down the Option key and tap the **e** once)—*it will look like nothing happened.* That's okay.

3. Now type the character that is to be *under* the accent mark, and both the mark and the letter will appear together; e.g., **R é s u m é**

Practice: Type the word **résumé** as explained here.

Now type **piñata.**

How about **Voilà!** You'll find that accent mark in the far upper-left of the keyboard, on the same key as the tilde (~).

Practice What You Learned

In TextEdit or your favorite word processor, type the text below, or make up your own. Just type it in as you see it, with double Returns after each paragraph, then format it as you see on the opposite page.

▼ **To type the bullet (•),** hold down the Option key and type the number 8 on the keyboard (not the number 8 in the numeric keypad).

▼ Remember, when formatting on the opposite page, that *every paragraph has its own ruler settings.* That is, you can select the first paragraph, click the centered alignment button, and it doesn't affect any other text on the page.

My Summer Vacation

Type two Returns to create this extra space. If you plan to do a lot of word processing, find out how to add extra paragraph spacing automatically (read the manual for your word processor). This will do two things: You won't have to hit two Returns, only one; and you won't have this huge gap between paragraphs because you can choose a smaller amount of space.

Well, my summer vacation was too boring to tell you about because all I did was work every day, all day, sometimes all night. But if I could do whatever I wanted, this is what I would do:

• I'd take a long hike across the desert every morning at sunrise.

• I'd carve massive pieces of stone into vibrant sculptures.

• I'd mosaic landscapes and ravens and dancing people onto my walls, and a mermaid in the bathroom.

• I'd read and study a Shakespeare play every week.

• I'd cook hot and spicy soups and hearty bread.

• I'd go back to school, some big, fancy school, and study something really important and write brilliant papers about it and become the world's expert in my field.

I'd make this list much, much longer but it's probably boring you already. Instead of my list, type in your own list of what you still want to accomplish today, this week, and in this life. Risk looking like a fool!

These three "paragraphs" have only one Return between them.

Robin Williams
Santa Fe
New Mexico

Yes, type this letter "t."   t

Format the text with bold and italic words; align the text as shown. This example uses **TextEdit,** but the process is similar in any word processor.

Format the text

> **To see the page outline,** as shown below, go to the Format menu and choose "Wrap to Page." *Or* press Command Shift W.

> **To show the ruler,** go to the Format menu, choose "Text," then choose "Show Ruler." *Or* just press Command R. ***Anything you choose in the ruler applies to the entire paragraph that is selected.***

> **To show the Font panel,** as you see below, go to the Format menu, choose "Font," and then choose "Font Panel...." *Or* press Command T.

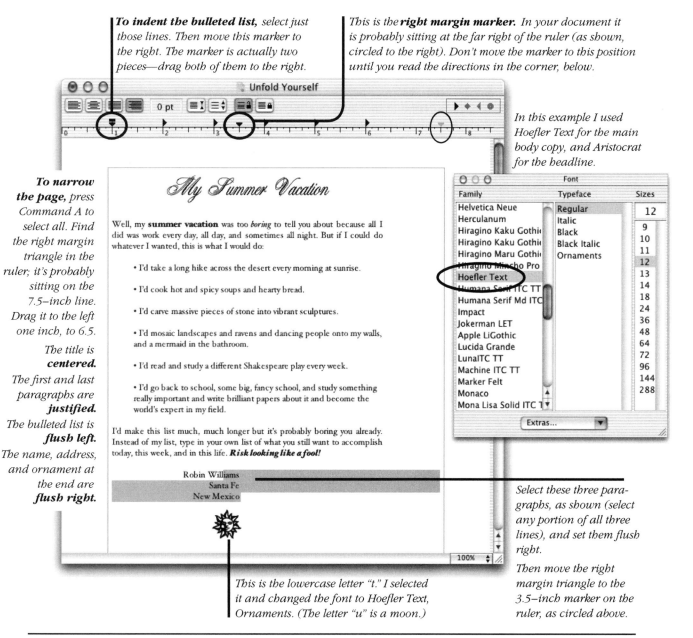

To indent the bulleted list, select just those lines. Then move this marker to the right. The marker is actually two pieces—drag both of them to the right.

*This is the **right margin marker.** In your document it is probably sitting at the far right of the ruler (as shown, circled to the right). Don't move the marker to this position until you read the directions in the corner, below.*

In this example I used Hoefler Text for the main body copy, and Aristocrat for the headline.

*To **narrow the page,** press Command A to select all. Find the right margin triangle in the ruler; it's probably sitting on the 7.5-inch line. Drag it to the left one inch, to 6.5.*

*The title is **centered.***

*The first and last paragraphs are **justified.***

*The bulleted list is **flush left.***

*The name, address, and ornament at the end are **flush right.***

Select these three paragraphs, as shown (select any portion of all three lines), and set them flush right.

Then move the right margin triangle to the 3.5–inch marker on the ruler, as circled above.

This is the lowercase letter "t." I selected it and changed the font to Hoefler Text, Ornaments. (The letter "u" is a moon.)

1. What is Rule No. 2 on the Mac?

2. Draw an I-beam, an insertion point, and a pointer.

3. Which of the three items mentioned above do you use to select text?

4. When you press the Delete key, which of the three items above backs up?

5. Name the two ways that an insertion point knows which typeface, size, and style to type in.

6. What is the keyboard shortcut to make selected text bold? Italic? Underlined?

7. How can you make the next word you type appear in bold, without going to the menu? After you type it in bold, how do you make the next word you type appear in plain text?

8. If you decide you want the last paragraph in your document to be the first paragraph, what are the four steps you must take to make that happen?

9. What are the keyboard shortcuts for cut, copy, and paste?

Extra Credit (50 points):
How many spaces should you type after a period?

10. What is the difference between "cut" and "clear"?

Answers on page 751.

Saving Your Documents

While you are in the process of creating a document of any sort within any program, the information you put into that document is floating around in the computer's *memory,* which is only a temporary storage place. If you were to turn off the computer, that document would disappear. In fact, if there was a power flicker, the document would disappear. If your computer crashed, the document would disappear. You probably want to keep a permanent copy of it, right? So you need to **save the document** onto your hard disk. Later you can save a backup copy onto a removable disk such as a Zip or Jaz cartridge or a CD or DVD.

14

RAM: Random Access Memory

Until you actually go through the process of naming a document and saving it, the document hangs around in **RAM,** which stands for **Random Access Memory.** RAM is sort of like the top of the desk in your office, where you spread your stuff out as you work. Your *hard disk* acts more like a filing cabinet where you store all your folders of information.

Your oak desk is very much like your computer's RAM— a temporary working space.

The metal filing cabinets in your office are very much like the computer's hard disk—a permanent storage space.

When you are working on a project, you don't keep running to the filing cabinet every time you need a little piece of information, do you? No, you take all the applicable info out of the filing cabinet and put it on your desk, then when you're finished you put it all away again and take out something else. RAM is sort of like that: when you open an application the computer puts a copy of that application into RAM, also called *memory.* This way the computer doesn't have to keep going into the filing cabinet (the hard disk) to do its work and it can operate much more efficiently.

When you quit that first application and open another one, the Mac puts the first one back where it came from and puts the new application into RAM. If you have lots of RAM, you can open lots of applications and leave them open, as discussed on page 258.

When you create a document, it sits in RAM, too, until you put it in the filing cabinet—your disk. You put the document on your disk by **saving** it. Once it's on a disk, it will stay there until you trash it yourself.

All that time your document is in RAM, it is in **danger.** At any moment, if there is a power failure, even for a split second, or you accidentally hit the wrong button, have a system crash, the screen freezes, your child pulls out the power cord, or any other catastrophe of considerable dimension happens to befall, then everything in RAM *(memory)* is gone. Just plain gone. No way on earth for a mortal person to get it back. Not even the software that can get files out of the Trash after you've emptied the Trash basket can bring back information that only existed in memory.

Danger!

The prevention? **SOS:** Save Often, Sweetie. Save Save Save. Every few minutes, when you're just sitting there thinking about your next marvelous move, Save. In every application it's this easy: just press Command S. Then if there *is* a catastrophe, you will have lost only the last few minutes of your work. Of course you won't listen to me until you have experienced a catastrophe of your very own.

**Rule #1:
Save Often!**

To save a document for the first time, it must be given a name. Under the File menu are the commands **Save As...** and **Save.** At first the subtle difference can be confusing.

**Save As...
vs. Save**

> **Save As...** is the command you use *first* to give the document a name (every file must have a name). "Save As..." gives you a dialog box such as the ones shown on the following pages (they're slightly different from program to program).

Save As...

> **Save** is the command to use *after* you have named the document and you want to save the new changes onto that same document. *Save* just goes ahead and does it—you won't get a dialog box, but you will see the Edit menu flash for a quick second. Get in the habit of typing Command S (the keyboard shortcut to save) regularly.

Save

Note: If you have not yet given the document a name, choosing "Save" (or using Command S) will usually give you the "Save As..." dialog box.

The Quick-and-Easy Save

If you are new to computers, all you need to do is this **quick-and-easy save.** This will store your document in the Documents folder, which is in your Home area. When you are ready to learn more about saving and how to save into different folders, then come back and read the rest of this section.

To save your document:

1. From the File menu, choose "Save As…" to open the "Save As" dialog box, shown below.

2. Type the name of your file.

3. Click the Save button (or hit the Return or Enter key).

Tip: Give your document a name you will remember! A name like "Photo 1" is going to confuse you when you have a folder of thirty photos.

Practice: If you've been following along in the practice exercises and have a document open, **save it now** (if you haven't already).

Just go to the File menu and choose "Save As…."

Type the name of the document.

Hit the Enter key or click the Save button.

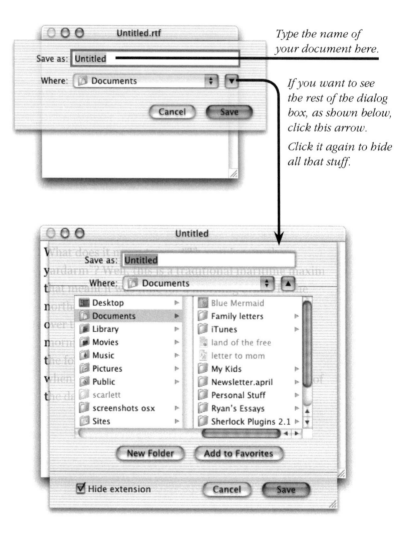

Type the name of your document here.

If you want to see the rest of the dialog box, as shown below, click this arrow.

Click it again to hide all that stuff.

If you want to know all about the Save As dialog box and how to use it, read on. It will give you more control over where you are saving files. It's not as scary as it looks. Drag the bottom-right corner of the dialog box to enlarge it so you can see more of the directory at once.

The Entire "Save As" Dialog Box

*Type here to **name** the document (**1**). The highlight is a **visual clue** telling you that this current name, "Untitled," is **selected**—just type, and this highlighted text will be replaced (that is, you don't have to delete the existing text first).*

If you don't see the directory below, as shown here, click this button.

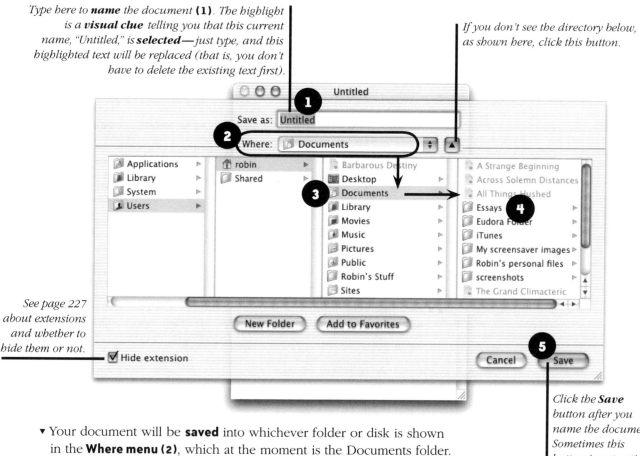

See page 227 about extensions and whether to hide them or not.

*Click the **Save** button after you name the document. Sometimes this button is not active until you have given the document a name.*

- ▼ Your document will be **saved** into whichever folder or disk is shown in the **Where menu (2)**, which at the moment is the Documents folder.

- ▼ You see the Documents folder is selected (**3**), and the ***contents*** of the Documents folder (**4**) are in the far-right column.

- ▼ This tells you that, as it is right now, your saved file will go ***inside*** the Documents folder along with the rest of the Documents folder contents.

- ▼ **To save into a different folder,** single-click any folder name in any column to ***select that folder.*** That folder name will appear in the "Where" menu and its contents in the next-right column. If you then click the Save button (**5**), your file will be saved into *that* folder.

See the following page for an explanation of the "Where" menu, how to make and save into new folders, and how to add a folder to your Favorites so you can easily save into it.

Advanced Tip: Drag any folder from the Desktop or from a Finder window and drop it anywhere inside the Save As dialog box. This will automatically choose that folder as the destination for your saved file. Try it!

Using the Where Menu Take advantage of the **Where menu** to save into folders that you use often.

▼ **The very first item** in the "Where" menu is the currently selected folder; if you hit the Save button, you will save the document into the folder that is at the top of this list. In the example below, that would be the Documents folder.

▼ Choose **Desktop** to save the document directly to your Desktop.

▼ Choose **Home** to save the document into your Home folder, or to open any of your Home folders.

▼ Choose **iDisk** to connect to the Internet and save documents directly onto Apple's server (see Chapter 33 for details about iDisk).

▼ **Favorite Places** are those *folders* you have previously put in your Favorites folder. Your Favorites folder holds other kinds of items besides folders, but the folders are the only items that show up in this "Where" menu so you can save into them.

To add a folder to the Favorites list so you can get to it easily, find the folder in the directory of the dialog box, select the folder, and click the button in the bottom-right, **"Add to Favorites." *Or*** at the Desktop, put the folder or copy of the folder directly in the Favorites folder (drag it to the Favorites icon in the Toolbar), and then it will appear in this menu. See Chapter 23 for details about Favorites.

▼ **Recent Places** are the most recent folders and disks you have used while working on your Mac. You control how many items are in this menu through the General preferences pane (see page 136).

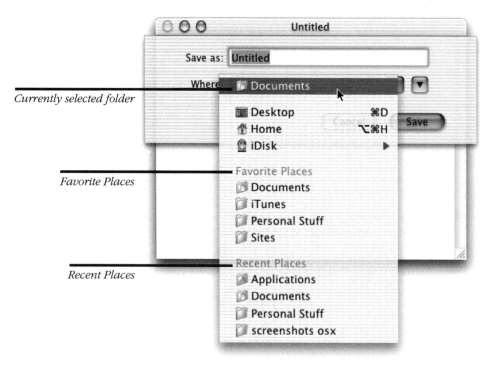

Currently selected folder

Favorite Places

Recent Places

One of the best ways to keep your work organized is to **create a specific new folder** for a new project *before* you create the documents for the project, and then save the documents right into their own folder. For instance, if you are about to create a newsletter in which there will be ten to twelve separate stories, it's best to store all these files in one folder with a recognizable name. If you didn't create a new folder before you started a document, you can always create it here in the Save As dialog box.

Creating a New Folder to Save Into

To create a new folder in the Save As dialog box:

1. Decide where you want to store the new folder and make sure that location is what you see in the "Where" menu. For instance, in the example on the opposite page, "Documents" is the location; if you click the "New Folder" button in that dialog box, the new folder will be placed inside the Documents folder. If you want the new folder on the Desktop, choose "Desktop" from the "Where" menu.

2. Click the button "New Folder." If you don't see that button, click the single, blue, downward-pointing arrow at the end of the "Where" menu.

3. In the little window that appears, as shown below, type the name of your new folder, then click the "Create" button.

No matter where you store the folder at the moment, you can always move it later.

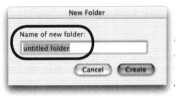

You don't have to delete this text first (on the left)—just type the new name and it will replace whatever is selected (shown to the right).

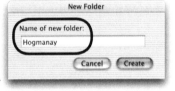

4. Your new folder will appear in the directory, as shown below, already selected and waiting for you to name your document and save it directly into this folder.

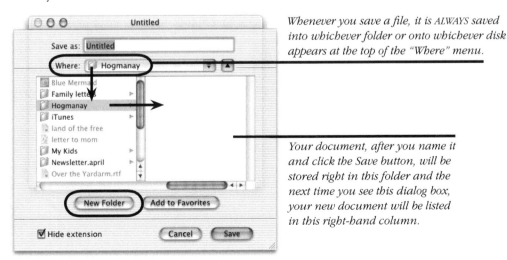

Whenever you save a file, it is ALWAYS saved into whichever folder or onto whichever disk appears at the top of the "Where" menu.

Your document, after you name it and click the Save button, will be stored right in this folder and the next time you see this dialog box, your new document will be listed in this right-hand column.

Visual Clues and Navigating in the Dialog Box

As is typical on the Mac, the dialog box has many **visual clues** that tell you what to do or what to expect, as well as clues to navigating (moving around and selecting files in the dialog box).

Look carefully at the two dialog boxes below. The most important visual clue, one that you should become accustomed to noticing, is the **selection** in each box.

- ▼ On the left, the edit box is selected, where it says "Untitled," waiting for you to type the name. Notice the border around the edit box.

- ▼ On the right, the folder "Documents" is selected. Notice the border is around the directory now, instead of around the edit box.

This is important to notice because when you start to type, your typing will **either** change "Untitled" **or** it will select a folder. That is, if the edit box is selected, what you type will be the name of your new document. But if the directory is selected, what you type will select a folder.

To select the edit box or the directory, hit the Tab key. Whichever one is selected at the moment, the Tab key will select the other. Try it.

To navigate through the directory, hit the Tab key to select the directory, if it isn't already. Then use the arrow keys to move left and right from column to column, and up and down within one column.

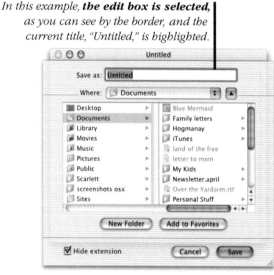

*In this example, **the edit box is selected,** as you can see by the border, and the current title, "Untitled," is highlighted.*

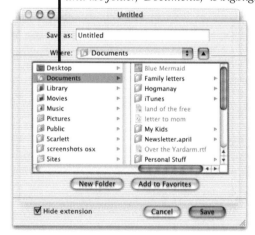

*In this example, **the directory is selected,** as you can see by the border, and the folder, "Documents," is highlighted.*

*When a file name is gray, it is a **visual clue** that the file itself is in the folder, but you can't do anything with it because this is the Save As dialog box. But you can see what other files are already stored in a particular folder.*

*Folder names are black, which is a **visual clue** that you can select them (single-click) to store documents inside.*

*As everywhere else on the Mac, there are all the standard **visual clues** such as scroll arrows and scrollers (or lack of), menu arrows, a disclosure triangle, a pulsing button, and the insertion point (when you are typing the file name).*

In Mac OS X, every file name has an **extension** (whether you see it or not), which is a short abbreviation at the end of a file name, preceded by a period, such as *.jpg*. This extension tells the Mac what to do with the file.

You can add your own extension to the end of a file name, if you know the exact characters for your document, or you can just let the Mac add the correct one for you; what you *don't* want to do is add an extension without knowing that the *Mac* has added an extension to your extension. To make sure that doesn't happen, or to make sure you get the extension you want, you can choose to see the extensions on a file-by-file basis, or you can choose a global setting to *always* see the file extension or *never* see it.

robin's story   robin's story.rtf

The extension is so important to some files that if you take it off, the Mac doesn't know what to do with the file when you try to open in. In the example above, the Mac cannot open the file on the left, even though it is exactly the same as the file on the right, minus the .rtf extension.

chapter8   chapter8.dock

Adding an extension of .dock to this folder in which I stored files for the Dock chapter turned the folder into a "dockling." Unfortunately, Apple does not provide a list of extensions that you should avoid.

To make the extensions visible or invisible on an individual basis, use the Info window: Click once on an icon to select it, then go to the File menu and choose "Show Info, or press Command I. From the pop-up menu, choose "Name & Extension." Check or uncheck the box to "Hide extension."

Notice when you hide the extension, it is hidden from the file name you see on the Desktop (shown at the top of the Info window), but the "File system name" that the Mac uses retains the extension.

To hide or show extensions globally, from the Finder menu, choose "Preferences...." Check or uncheck the box to "Always show file extensions." If you choose to always show them, you won't inadvertently add your own extension as well.

Illegal characters in file names: Do not start file names with a hyphen or period. Do not use a colon (:) or a slash (/).

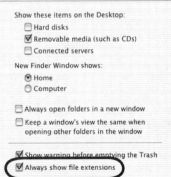

Naming Your Files and Extensions

Below is a list of some (not all) common file extensions you might run across.

Document extensions

.doc	Word document
.txt	Plain Text
.rtf	Rich Text Format
.rtfd	Rich Text Format Directory
.pdf	Portable Document Format
.psd	Photoshop file
.qxp	QuarkXPress document
.pps	PowerPoint Show
.xls	Excel spreadsheet
.mov	QuickTime movie

Graphic file format extensions

.gif	Graphic Interchange Format, ideal for web graphics
.jpg, jpeg	Joint Photographic Experts Group, photos, ideal for web
.tif, tiff	Tagged Image File Format, graphic for printing
.eps	Encapsulated PostScript, sillustration graphic

Compression extensions

.sit	StuffIt Deluxe
.sea	self-extracting archive
.zip	stuffed file from a Windows machine; your Mac can open it with StuffIt Deluxe
.exe	executable file, which is typically a Windows application that you can't use on your Mac

Reverting to a Previously Saved Version

Sometimes you might make a bunch of changes to a document and then decide you don't like the changes. In that case, check the File menu to see if your application has a command called **Revert**. If so, choose it and the document will revert *to exactly how it was the last time you **saved** it*. So if you haven't saved it yet, you can't revert. (I recommend saving a file even before you begin typing, although some applications won't let you save until you have at least typed one character.)

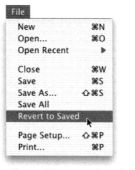

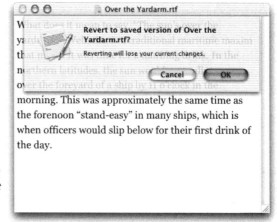

Choose "Revert to Saved," then click OK in the dialog box to revert the document back to the last time you saved it.

If there is no Revert command, then *close* the document. When you see the box that asks if you want to save the changes (shown below), click the button that says "Don't Save" or "No." Reopen the document and everything will be exactly the way it was *the last time you saved it*. This means, of course, that anything you did since you last saved it, *the good stuff as well as the bad,* will be gone.

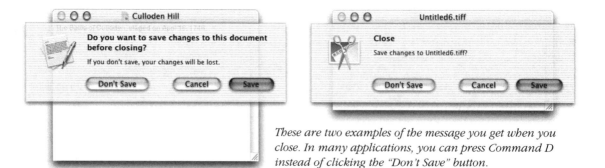

These are two examples of the message you get when you close. In many applications, you can press Command D instead of clicking the "Don't Save" button.

Sometimes you might want to create changes in a document, but you still want to keep a **copy of the original without the changes.** For instance, let's say you write a witty letter to Uncle Jeff, then decide you also want to write to Uncle Cliff. You have a few things to tell Cliff that Jeff isn't interested in, but you don't want to retype the entire letter. That's when you'll use *Save As...* a *second* time to give the document a *new* name, which actually creates a new, separate file and leaves the original file intact.

Making Several Versions

To make a version separate from an original:

1. Save the original document. Let's say you've named it "Witty letter to Uncle Jeff." Don't close the document.

2. While that document is still open on the screen, from the File menu, choose "Save As...."

3. Change the name, say from "Witty letter to Uncle Jeff" to "Witty letter to Uncle Cliff."

This automatically puts the original document (to Uncle Jeff) safely away on your disk and opens a new one (the copy to Uncle Cliff) right on the screen. You'll notice the name in the title bar of your document changes to what you renamed it. Any changes you make to *this* document (Uncle Cliff's) will not affect the original (Uncle Jeff's).

Witty letter to Uncle Jeff   Witty letter to Uncle Cliff

Witty letter to Uncle
Lloyd

Witty letter to Uncle
Merwyn

All of these letters are based on the original letter to Uncle Jeff. I just kept choosing "Save As" and giving the new ones new names. The information, layout, type choices, etc., all stayed the same, but now each letter is separate and I can add or delete details in each.

Templates and Stationery

Another way to make several versions of the same letter, or to keep a master copy of your newsletter or budget report, etc., is to make a **template** or **stationery pad** of the document. Once you turn a document into a template, the original file doesn't open anymore—when you open the template you get a brand new, untitled *copy* of the original. (Well, you *can* open the original file if you need to; see the note on the opposite page.)

Depending on your project, you might want to make a *copy* of the original, then turn the *copy* into a template.

Take a look in the "Save As" dialog box in your application—some applications have a button or a menu choice to create a template, as shown below. If your application can't make a template (or even if it can), you can always use the Show Info window, as explained on the opposite page.

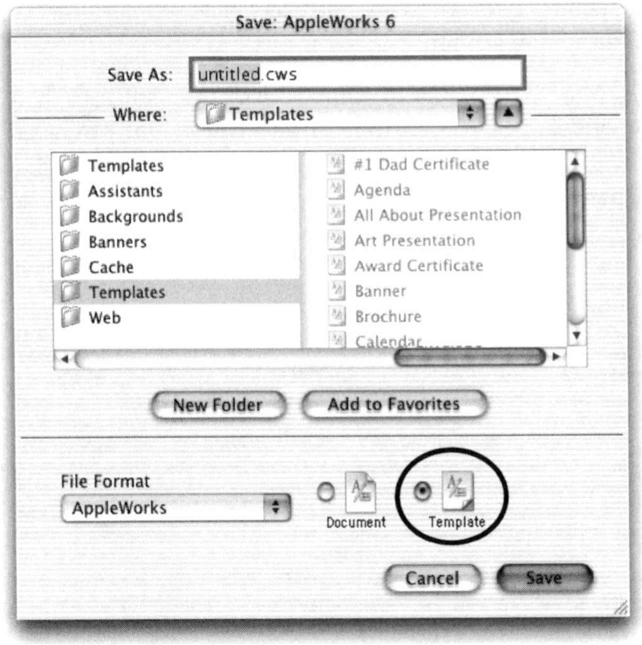

In AppleWorks, as soon as you click the "Template" button, the Templates folder is selected (on the left and in the "Where" menu), waiting for you to save your new template into the folder. (You can choose to save the template anywhere you like.)

To make a template (stationery pad) of a document using Show Info:

1. Select the document on the Desktop or in a Finder window (click once on the document icon to select it).

2. From the File menu, choose "Show Info," or press Command I.

3. Click the checkbox at the bottom for "Stationery Pad" (circled, below). Now the selected document is what the Mac calls a "stationery pad," also known as a template. It contains all the fonts, formatting, information, etc., that was in the original document.

When you double-click a stationery pad, the original does not open—a **copy** of the original opens. You can tell the document is a copy because in the title bar it says "Untitled." The original stays on your Mac, intact, so any changes you make to the copy do not affect the original.

To Do List

*This is the original document. Notice it has the **upper-right** corner turned down. Click once on it to select it, then choose "Show Info" from the File menu.*

To Do List

*The document is now a stationery pad, also known as a template. Notice it has the **lower-right** corner turned up.*

Double-click this file and it will open as an untitled document, waiting for you to make changes.

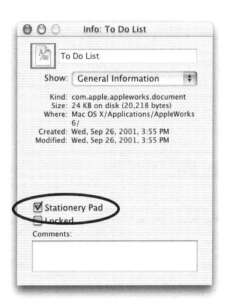

In the Show Info box, click this checkbox.

To open the original document again, instead of the template, select the document icon, press Command I to Show Info, and uncheck the "Stationery Pad" box. Then you can double-click the document icon and it will open the original file.

Use the dialog boxes shown below (A or B) to answer the first five questions.

1. Which dialog box has the directory, or list, selected?

_____

2. Which dialog box is ready for you to name the document?

_____

3. If you were in dialog box **A** and typed the letter "P," what would happen?

_____

4. In dialog box **A,** what would happen if you were to click on the folder named "Hogmanay"?

_____

5. If you were in dialog box **A** and you wanted to name the document, which key would you press to select the edit box?

_____

6. What would you press to get the menu, **C,** shown to the left?

_____

7. What would happen if you were to choose "Home" from this menu, **C**?

_____

8. Briefly describe two ways to avoid saving your changes.

_____

9. Where is the document before you save it?

_____

10. Which command would you use to save another copy of a document, but with a new name?

_____

Answers on page 751.

Printing Documents

Printing is usually the point, right? It's well and good to create all these great things on the computer, but most of the time we need to actually *print* our creations to make them useful. In this chapter I'll walk you through the printing process, but keep in mind that each of the hundreds of printers for the Macintosh has its own software, so details might look different from what I show here. Please read the documentation that came with your printer!

Also, different applications often create their own Page Setup and Print dialog boxes, so the ones you use might not exactly match the ones I show in this chapter—but they're all similar.

Printers

First of all, it's a good idea to know whether you have a **PostScript printer** or a **non-PostScript printer.** Here's an easy way to tell: If your printer cost less than $1,000, it's non-PostScript.

It's also good to know whether your printer is **USB** or **serial.** You can tell by the connector on the end of the printer cable, the end that plugs into the computer. If it's small and rectangular, it's USB. If it's round, it's serial. Most people at home or in a small office today have USB printers, especially if it's plugged directly into your computer rather than on a network.

See Chapter 38 if you care to know about "USB" and "serial" in reference to printers.

You don't need to read the rest of this page—it's here if you want to come back to it later. If ever.

Non-PostScript printers

Most printers with the word "inkjet" in their names are examples of **non-PostScript printers,** with "resolutions" ranging from about 75 to 600 dots per inch (the higher the resolution, the smoother the printed image). Inkjet cartridges typically are small (they fit easily in your hand) and you have one small cartridge for black and another one for the colors (cyan/blue, magenta/red, and yellow). The ink tends to smear easily on the page. Printed images can look vastly different depending on the paper used. Inkjets usually have only one paper tray.

PostScript printers

PostScript is a "page description language," a programming language, that a **PostScript printer** can interpret. Black-and-white desktop PostScript printers are laser printers, not inkjet (though not all laser printers are PostScript). They create high-quality, very clean type and images. Personal PostScript printers are rather expensive, typically around $1,000 to $3,000 for black-and-white (color printers often run above $4,000). They're expensive because they have a powerful computer inside, complete with memory and a specialized CPU (central processing unit, the tiny chip that runs the entire process). They're relatively large printers, and a typical black toner cartridge is about the size of a bread loaf that costs around $100. Although they're expensive, they are workhorses and will print many thousands of pages for years and years and years. You can highlight text on the page and it won't smear.

Imagesetters

There are also *very* expensive (like $100,000), very high-end PostScript printers with resolutions of around 1270 or 2540 dots per inch, such as the Linotronic. These machines, called **imagesetters,** output (print) onto resin-coated film, not plain paper, and the hard copy looks virtually like traditional phototypesetting, limited only by the professional expertise of the person who input (typed in) the text.

Service bureaus

Since the high-resolution machines are so expensive, you only find them in **service bureaus** — shops where they offer the "output" (the hard copy, the printed pages) as a service. You take the disk containing your document to them, leave it there, and they print it up for you. It usually costs from $4 to $10 a page, but it's beautiful. Then you take those pages to a print shop for reproductions.

Quick Start

Here are the briefest of directions for **printing your pages.** If it works, *then you can skip the rest of this chapter,* unless you want to understand what all the options are. For this very quick start, I have to assume you have the printer plugged in to both the wall and the computer with the appropriate cables, there is paper in the printer, and the printer is turned on and warmed up. If so:

1. Open the document that you want to print.
2. From the File menu, choose "Print...."
3. Click the "Print" button (or hit the Return key).

That's all. **If it worked,** skip to page 241 to learn about the various printing options.

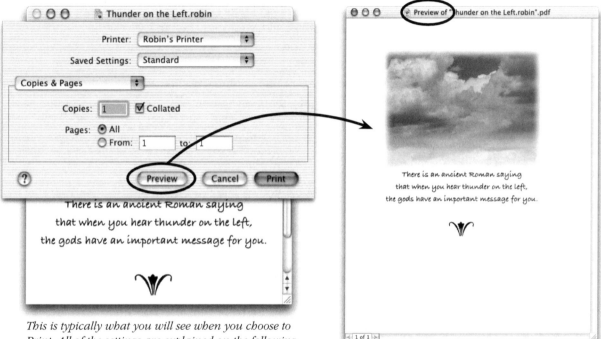

This is typically what you will see when you choose to Print. All of the settings are explained on the following pages, but if you just want to print the page or pages in your document to make sure printing works, you can safely hit the "Print" button without bothering about anything else.

Click the "Preview" button in the Print dialog box to see what your document will look like when printed on the page. The Preview button actually creates a PDF file, which then opens in the application Preview. check out your menu options in Previe, and see page 479.

IF THE STEPS ABOVE DIDN'T WORK, the only thing you probably need to do is add your printer to the list so the Mac knows it's there, or maybe you need to turn on AppleTalk. Both are explained on the following pages.

Making Sure Your Printer is Connected and Turned On

If your printing didn't work automatically, **check** the following:

▼ I'm assuming that if you bought a printer, you made sure it was **compatible** with your Macintosh; for instance, if your computer uses USB ports (which it does if it was built since late 1998), you must get a USB-compatible printer and a USB cable.

Even though there is a USB port in your keyboard, don't plug your printer into that port—your printer will usually work more reliably if you plug it directly into your computer, or at least into a "hub" with a power source. (See Chapter 38 for some information on ports and hubs and the things that plug into them.)

▼ You also need the correct **cable** to connect your printer to your Mac. Many printers don't come with a cable to connect it to the Mac (you have to buy it separately), so if you brought your printer home without one you will have to go back to the computer store or catalog and get one before you can print. This cable connects the printer to the Mac.

▼ Make sure your printer is plugged into a **power** socket in the wall or into a "surge suppressor" (an outlet strip that you can buy at any office supply store; it protects your printer and your computer from daily power spikes). You must **wait** several minutes after you turn on the printer before you try to print; wait until all printer noises have stopped.

▼ When you bought your printer you got a disk with **software** on it. If you went through the steps on the previous page and your printer didn't work automatically, follow the directions in the printer's manual to install the software. Besides helping your Mac connect to the printer, the software will often provide more options in the print dialog boxes.

If these things are all okay, you probably need to add your printer to the printer list, as described on the following pages.

Your Mac needs to put your computer in its **Printer List** so you can choose to print to it and so the computer knows what that particular printer is capable of doing. For instance, if you choose to print to a color inkjet, the Print dialog box will provide color options, but not paper tray options. If you choose to print to a black-and-white PostScript laser printer, you won't have any color options, but you will have paper tray options.

To add a printer to the List, you can either go back to the Print dialog box in your document, or you can open the Print Center directly. Either way is exactly the same, as follows:

1. Turn on the printer(s) you want to add to the List. Wait until it is fully warmed up.

2. **Either:** While your document is open, go to the File menu and choose "Print." In the Print dialog box, click on the "Printer" menu and choose "Edit Printer List...," as shown below. Go to Step 3 on the following page.

Adding a Printer to the List

> Thunder on the Left.robin
>
> Printer: ✓ Robin's Printer
> West of the Pecos
>
> Saved Settings:
>
> Edit Printer List...
>
> Copies & Pages
>
> Copies: 1 ☑ Collated
>
> Pages: ⦿ All
> ○ From: 1 to: 1
>
> ⑦   (Preview) (Cancel) (Print)

Or: At the Desktop, open any Finder window.
Click on the Applications icon in the Toolbar.
From inside that window, open the Utilities folder.
Inside the Utilities folder, find the **Print Center** icon, as shown to the right.

Print Center

Double-click on the Print Center icon.
Go to Step 3 on the following page.

3. Both of the methods described on the previous page will open the Printer List, as shown below. This List shows you the printers the Mac knows about already. The printer with the gray dot to the left of its name is the default printer.

To add another printer to the list, click "Add Printer...."

To change the default printer,
select one of the printers in this List.
Go up to the Printers menu in the menu
bar (it appeared when this dialog box
appeared) and choose "Make Default."

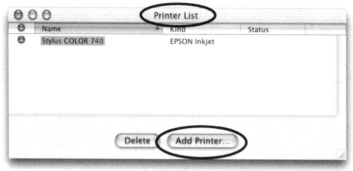

4. A dialog "sheet" will slip down from the title bar, as shown below. Click on the menu circled below to see your options.

To add a USB printer to the list, choose "USB" from the menu.

To add an AppleTalk printer, which is probably on a local network, to the List, choose "AppleTalk." If your printer is a PostScript laser printer, it is probably on an AppleTalk network whether you realize it or not.

If you have the DNS name or IP address of a **line printer** you can connect to through the Internet, choose "LPR Printers using IP." If that doesn't make sense to you, you're probably not using a line printer; if you think you may be, talk to your network administrator.

If your computer is at home or
in a small office, you won't use
Directory Services. *If you are*
in a large corporation or school
with a large network, talk
to your network administrator
about Directory Services.

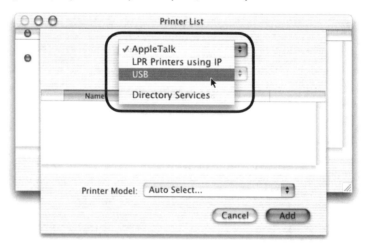

5. If you chose "AppleTalk," you might get a message that you have to turn AppleTalk on—*if you don't get this message, skip this step.* If the message shown below appears, go ahead and click the button, "Open Network Preferences."

The Network preferences pane will appear. ***If you don't see the AppleTalk tab,*** as circled below, check the "Show" menu to make sure "Built-In Ethernet" is selected, not "Internal Modem."

Click the checkbox to "Make AppleTalk active," click the "Apply Now" button at the bottom, and close the Network preferences. Go back to the Printer List dialog box.

Go to Step 6.

Note: If the entire pane is gray, you are not the administrator of this machine and you cannot make these kinds of changes. Find the administrator and ask for help.

If the Mac still yells at you about AppleTalk, perhaps you have the wrong "Location" chosen. Check to see if there are any other Locations in the menu, and try changing the AppleTalk checkbox in the other Locations. For more information about Locations, see Chapter 36.

6. After you choose the type of printer, you will get a list of those printers that are turned on and available for you to use.

If you don't see your printer in the list, click on the "Printer Model" menu and choose the model you know is attached and turned on. This should make it appear.

7. Click on the printer name in the list, then click the "Add" button.

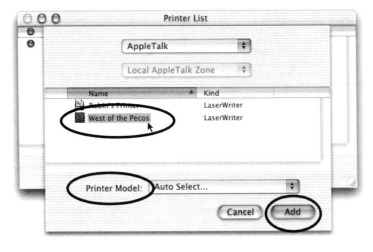

8. You will automatically go back to the Printer List, which can be confusing because it makes you think you should click the "Add Printer…" button again—*don't*. (Well, you can if you want, but it will just take you back to the dialog box above.)

Just click the red close button in the upper-left corner of the window. That printer is now added to the list and you will be able to choose it in the main Print dialog box.

Close this box with this button.

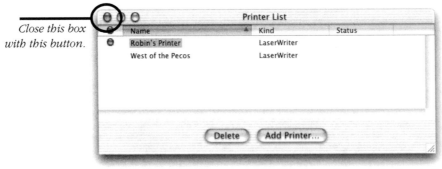

*The default printer (the automatic choice) has the **gray button** to its left. If you have more than one printer in this list and you want a different printer to be the default, do this: Click once on the printer name, go to the Printers menu, and choose "Make Default."*

You should get in the habit of checking the **Page Setup** command in the File menu. Page Setup opens a dialog box where you can set specifications for printing the document—use these in conjunction with the individual Print dialog box specifications, as shown on the following pages. Below are sample Page Setup boxes, but your particular application may have added other features of its own.

Page Setup

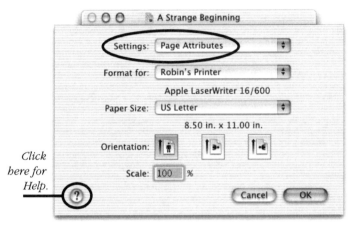

Click here for Help.

See below for the "Summary" option that is also available in this menu.

If you have different printers in your list, use the "Format for" pop-up menu to choose the one you plan to print to so the Mac will find the specific details about it, like how many paper trays it has, what kinds of color options, etc.

▼ **Paper Size:** This refers to the size of the paper that the document will be printed on, not the size of the page you are typing on. For instance, you might be creating a business card, but you can't put paper sized 2 x 3.5 through your printer—usually, the cards will be printed on regular letter-sized paper. If you have other-sized paper to use, choose it from this menu.

▼ **Orientation:** The Mac wants to know if the document should print upside right or sideways (8.5 x 11 or 11 x 8.5); also known as Tall or Wide, Portrait or Landscape.

▼ **Scale:** Enter a number here to enlarge or reduce the printed page. For instance, enter 50% to print your work at half size. Remember, half of an 8.5 x 11 is 4.25 x 5.5—you must halve both directions. On paper, this looks like the image is ¼ the original size; it isn't—it's half of both the horizontal and the vertical.

Reducing an image reduces it in both directions, not just one.

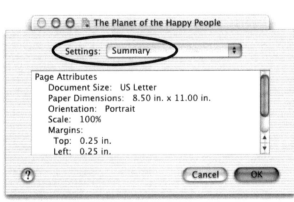

*This is a **Summary** of the specifications chosen in this dialog box, as well as those chosen in the document itself, such as the margins.*

Adobe InDesign is the page layout application I designed and produced this book with.

The more sophisticated an application is, the more it might change the Page Setup to suit itself. For instance, below is Adobe InDesign's version of Apple's Page Setup; InDesign calls it the Document Setup. It actually reflects specifications set within the document, such as the number of pages and the size of the created document, rather than the paper size.

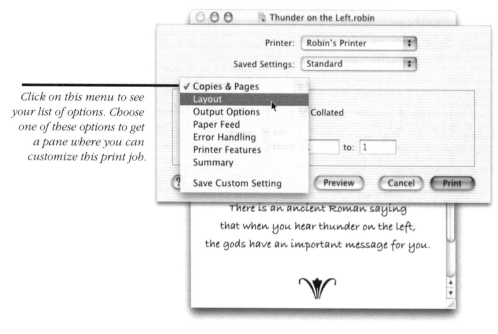

Extra features shown here are specific to the application, and "missing" features (as compared to the example on the previous page) are actually included in InDesign's own Print dialog boxes.

Print Specifications

One you have successfully added your printer to the list, you can print merrily away. On these next few pages are explanations of the various printing options you have. You may see different print dialog boxes depending on which printer you are connected to, and the dialog boxes within different applications may look slightly different from what you see here, but basically all you need to do is answer the questions they ask.

Click on this menu to see your list of options. Choose one of these options to get a pane where you can customize this print job.

Very often you will not need to go beyond this first dialog box, where you can choose the **pages** to print and **how many.**

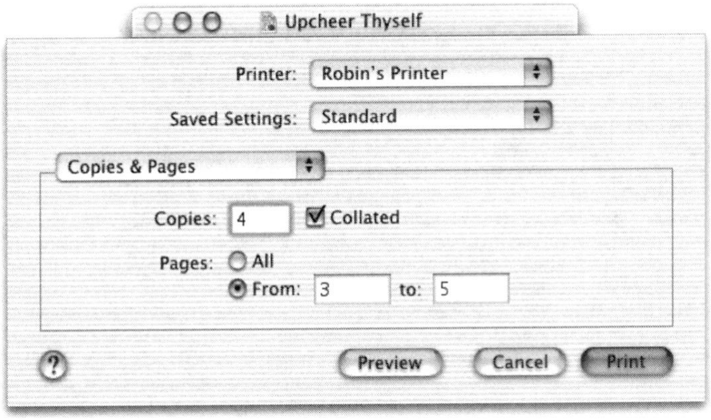

Copies & Pages

```
○ ○ ○        Upcheer Thyself

         Printer:  Robin's Printer        ▲▼

   Saved Settings:  Standard              ▲▼

  Copies & Pages               ▲▼

        Copies:  4      ☑ Collated

        Pages:  ○ All
                ● From:  3     to:  5

  ?                    Preview   Cancel   Print
```

▾ **Copies:** Type in the number of copies you want to print.

▾ **Collated:** If you're printing more than one copy of a multi-page document, you can make the printer collate the copies—it will print all the pages of one set, then print the next set. If you *don't* click collate, you will get, for instance, 5 copies of page 1, 5 copies of page 2, 5 copies of page 3, etc. But keep in mind that it takes longer for the printer to collate than to print multiple copies of one page at a time.

▾ **Pages: All** or **From __ to __:** You can choose to print *all* of the pages contained in your document, or just pages 3 through 12 (or whatever your choice is, of course). If you don't know the number of the last page, enter something like "999" and the printer will print to the end.

Choose **All** to override any numbers in the **From/To** boxes.

In this dialog box, you cannot print non-consecutive pages, such as pages 3, 7, and 11. If you use a page layout or other sophisticated application, you will have the option to print non-consecutive pages.

Layout   Choose **Layout** when you want to print multiple pages on one sheet of paper. This is handy when you have, for instance, a presentation to give and you want to create handouts for your audience or students so they can follow along. Or it can help you see your overall project at a glance so you can get a better idea of how things are working together (or not).

In this example, I have chosen six pages per sheet, a layout direction of left to right, and a single hairline border around each individual miniature page.

- ▼ **Pages per Sheet:** Choose how many pages of your document you want to see on each printed sheet of paper. Every page will be reduced to fit, of course.

- ▼ **Layout Direction:** Click on a layout to determine how the pages are arranged on the sheet. As you click each button, the display on the left will show you how your pages will be arranged. In the example above, the first button is clicked.

- ▼ **Border:** Choose a border so each page will be clearly defined on the printed sheet. The display to the left will give you an idea of what to expect with each border option as you choose it.

In the **Output Options** pane you are not *printing* the file—notice the "Print" button has changed to a "Save..." button. In this pane you can choose to **save** your document as a **PDF file.** PDF stands for "portable document format" and is especially designed to save your document in a format that you can send to anyone on any kind of computer and they will see it exactly as you do. For instance, maybe you created a nice invitation to your sister's birthday party and you want to send her a copy to make sure she likes it. You can save it as a PDF, then email the PDF to her for approval, knowing she will see it exactly as you do even if she doesn't have the fonts, the graphics, or the application you created it in.

If the person receiving the file is using Mac OS X, she already has the software application Preview that will open and display PDF files—she just needs to double-click on the PDF file icon.

If the person receiving the file is using an older Mac or a PC, she needs the free software "Acrobat Reader," which is probably already installed on her computer. If not, send her to **www.adobe.com** to download and *install* the Reader.

Output Options

Once you click in the "Save as File" checkbox, all of your Print dialog boxes will have a "Save" button instead of a "Print" button. If you want to print instead of save the file as a PDF, uncheck the box!

Thunder.pdf

If you are connected to a PostScript printer (as explained on page 234), you can make a **PostScript file.** You see, when you make a *PDF* file through this Print dialog box, you don't have any options to adjust the PDF for its intended use. But if you have the full (not free) Adobe Acrobat application with the "Distiller," you can drop a *PostScript file* on the Distiller and have options to make the file low-resolution so it looks good on the screen, but still emails quickly. Or you can make it a high-resolution file so it can be printed on a high-quality press, or a mid-resolution file for desktop printers.

Thunder.ps

Tip: If you don't have a PostScript printer but need to make a PostScript file, make a "virtual PostScript printer." See page 255.

Print Settings

*Your Print Settings might
not look exactly like the
ones shown. Read the
manual for your particular
printer to learn all the
details about every option.*

The dialog boxes on these two pages only appear in color printers. In color inkjet printers, the type of paper that you specify and put in the printer makes a remarkable difference in the finished image. A low-quality mode with cheap paper makes an image look worse than in the newspaper comic strip. Photo-quality paper with a high-quality mode can make the same image look like a photograph you had enlarged at a photo studio. Use the **Print Settings** to specify the paper ("Media Type") you have ready in the printer, plus the "Quality" of your finished product.

*Click the "Custom" radio button
to get the "Custom Settings" menu
where you can make minor adjustments for different sorts of projects.*

Advanced Settings

The **Advanced Settings** includes several of the options you set in the dialog box shown above. Changing the options here will automatically change them in the "Print Settings."

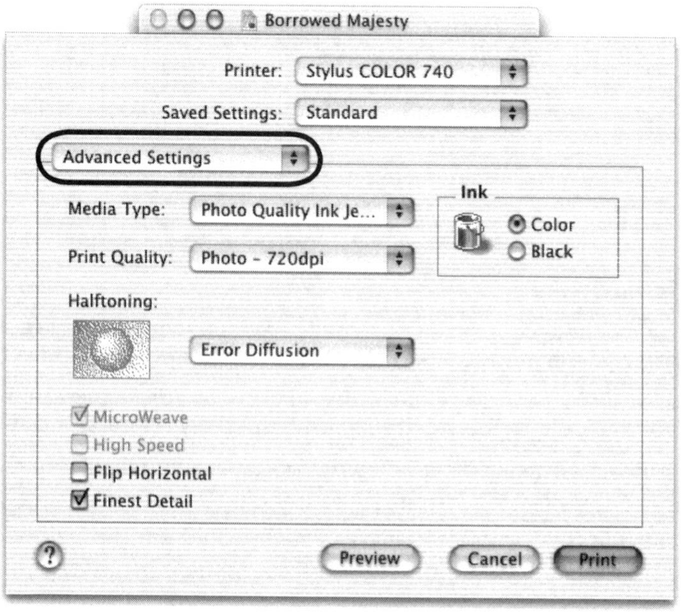

*"Halftoning" is for photographs;
choose "Error Diffusion" or
"Fine Dithering." The image to
the left of the menu will give you
an example of what to expect.
Dithering usually works best on
photos, but experiment.*

If you are experienced with printed color, you can make some adjustments in the **Color Management** dialog box—if your printer displays this one. Even if you're not experienced, you can adjust the brightness and contrast of the printed page, and maybe take out some of the magenta if your brother's face looks too red in the photo, etc.

Color Management

Paper Feed

The **Paper Feed** pane only appears if you have a big printer with several paper trays (the Mac discovers this from the software you installed for your printer). Generally you'll just print from the main paper tray, but there might be times when you want to do something special, like print the cover of a report on heavier red stock, and the rest of the report from a tray that holds nicer paper than the regular cheap stuff. So you can set up the dialog box as shown below: You'll manually feed in the heavier red stock for the cover, then let it take the rest of the pages from the tray you specify.

Error Handling

Error Handling will print you a special report telling you what the problem is (as long as the problem doesn't involve the actual printing or how could it print you a report?). Chances are you won't understand what the report is talking about anyway, but you can click this button when you get desperate and hope to find some kind of clue about why things aren't working properly. Good luck.

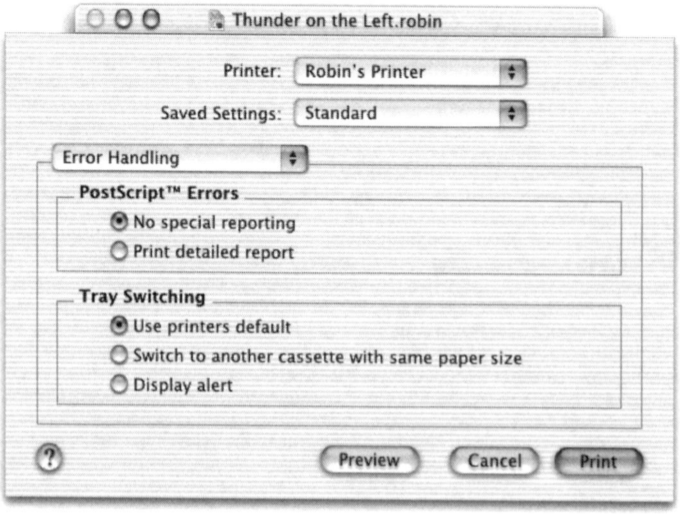

The **Printer Features** menu may change and might not even be there for you, depending on your chosen printer. You can see below that the same dialog boxes for two different PostScript Apple laser printers are different.

"FinePrint™" and "PhotoGrade™" are technologies built into certain Apple laser printers that are designed to improve the printing of type and line art (FinePrint) as well as photographs and paintings (PhotoGrade).

Application-specific features Most applications will have a menu with features **specific to the application,** as shown below. Always check these out.

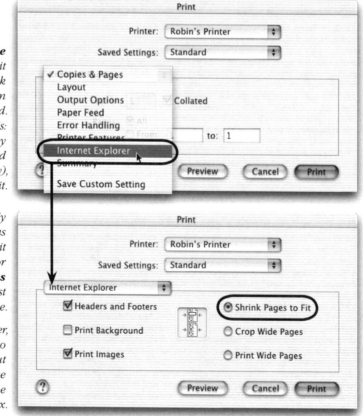

The web browser **Internet Explorer** has features that will put "headers" and "footers" on each printed page. A header is a line of information at the top of the page, and a footer is a line of information at the bottom on the page. Typically this information tells you the web address, the date, the time, etc. To see exactly what will print, click the "Preview" button. If you use the browser **Netscape,** you have even more control over what prints; check its Page Setup to control exactly what is displayed in the headers and footers.

*Rarely do you want to **print the background** of a web page because it will use up your entire (expensive) ink cartridge. The one exception is when the text is white on a dark background. But rather than do that, try this: select the text you want to print, copy it, paste it into TextEdit, select and change the text to black (if necessary), and print from TextEdit.*

*Have you ever printed a poorly designed web page that prints twice as many pages as you need because it is about half an inch too wide for the paper? If so, click **Shrink Pages to Fit** to force pages to shrink just enough to fit on the page.*

In some versions of Netscape, however, the default is checked on to "Fit to page," which prints web pages about an inch big. To fix this, go to Page Setup, choose "Netscape" from the pop-up menu, and uncheck that box.

The **Summary** pane displays a list of the options you have selected for printing this particular document. It's a good idea to skim through this list and make sure there are no leftover options chosen in dialog boxes that don't apply to this document.

Check this out before you print.

If you are working on a document and every time you go to the Print dialog box you choose "2 to 7 pages" and you print it in a layout with six miniature pages on a printed sheet with a thin line around each page, you can choose to save these options so you don't have to make the same choices every time you go to print. In fact, you can use these same options on other documents. Just make all of your selections, then from the menu, choose **Save Custom Setting.** Now in the "Saved Settings" menu, you'll be able to choose "Custom." You can only make one custom setting; if you make a new one, it *replaces* the existing one.

Using the Print Center

The **Print Center** just works away without you having to do anything about it until you have a problem. Or until you decide you want to do something like get a bunch of documents ready to print so you can go to lunch and have them all print while you're gone. Generally, when you are in your application and choose to print, the Mac opens the Print Center (you'll see it appear in the Dock) and it does its business; when it's done, the Print Center disappears from the Dock and you never have to worry about it. But there are a number of things you can do in the Print Center, should you find the need. If the Print Center is not in the Dock and you need it, follow the steps below to open it directly.

To open the Print Center directly:

1. In any Finder window, click on the Applications icon to open the Applications window.

2. Inside the Applications window, find the Utilities folder (type the letter U to select it and put it in front of you) and open it (press Command O or double-click the folder).

3. Inside the Utilities window, find the Print Center (type the letter P to select it and put it in front of you) and open it (press Command O or double-click the icon).

Print Center

This is the Print Center icon in the Utilities folder.

This is the Print Center icon in the Dock. The little number tells you how many pages in the document are left to print.

Keep the Print Center in the Dock

While you're printing, the Print Center icon will appear in the Dock, as shown above, then disappear when the job is finished. If you print regularly, though, it comes in handy to have the Print Center more easily accessible—I like to keep mine permanently in the Dock. To do this, drag the icon from the Utilities folder and just drop it in the Dock. *Or* when you open the Print Center and its icon is already in the Dock, click once on that icon and you'll get the menu shown below, left. Choose "Keep in Dock," and it will stay there even after the printing is done.

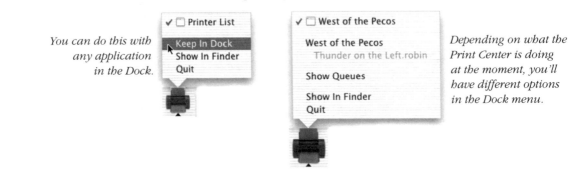

You can do this with any application in the Dock.

Depending on what the Print Center is doing at the moment, you'll have different options in the Dock menu.

When you open the Print Center directly, you'll probably see the Printer List, as shown below. This is exactly the same Printer List that appeared when you added a printer on pages 237–238. When the Printer List or the Queue window (also shown below) is visible, you have new menu items. These are things you can do using the menus and the windows.

Control printing

Tip: If you close both of these windows, the Print Center will quit!

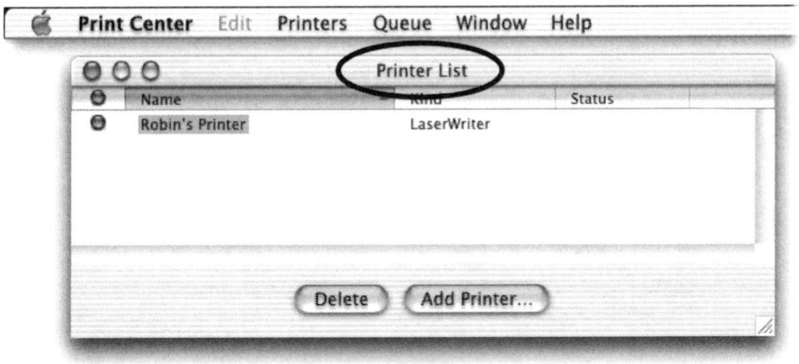

This is the **Printer List** where you can add or delete printers, or make any printer the default printer so it is automatically chosen when you print a document. Notice the menu bar across the top of the screen.

Double-click on a printer's name to bring up its Queue window, as shown below.

This is the **Queue** window where you can stop all printing, stop the printing of individual jobs, delete printing jobs altogether, and more.

The **name in the title bar** of the Queue window is the name of the printer that is printing these jobs.

To control printing of individual documents and also of the entire printer:

▼ **Show Queue:** A "queue" is a line. In this case, it is a line of documents ("jobs") that are waiting to print. Choose "Show Queue" from the "Printers" menu to see which documents are lined up waiting to print (shown directly above and on the following page). You can also click on the Print Center icon in the Dock and choose "Show Queues" from the pop-up menu. Each printer has its own Queue window.

If you tell a job to print and it doesn't print and you keep telling it to print over and over again, you'll come to this queue and see all of those documents waiting in line to print, just like you told them. Just select their names and delete them (click the "Delete") button.

▼ **STOP ONE JOB from printing:** In the Queue window, click once on the name of the document in the list, then either click the "Hold" button or go to the Queue menu and choose "Hold Job." This does not *delete* the job from the Queue—it just puts it on hold.

▼ **RESUME printing one job:** If a job has been put on hold, select its name in the Queue window. Then click the "Resume" button, or

```
⊗ ⊖ ⊖                    West of the Pecos

         ┌──┐      Go Singing through the World
         │&│      Page 1 of 10
         │& │
         └──┘
                   Preparing data
                   ▬▬

  Status      Name                       Priority          ▲
  Printing    Go Singing through the World   Normal
  –           Across Solemn Distances        Normal
  Hold        Not for the Slow-Headed        Normal
  –           All Things Hushed              Normal


         (  Delete  ) (  Hold  ) (  Resume  )
```

The selected file is already on hold, so the Resume button is now available. If you select a file that is not on hold, the Hold button will become available.

go to the Queue menu and choose "Resume Job."

▼ **STOP ALL THE DOCUMENTS from printing:** If the jobs are in the process of printing, the first item under the Queue menu is "Stop Queue" (shown on the previous page). This stops the entire line-up of documents waiting to print. While it is stopped, you can delete jobs, print an individual job, go to lunch, etc.

If you try to print several times and nothing goes through, check to make sure the "Stop Queue" item has not been selected! You'll know the queue has been stopped because the first menu item in the Queue menu will be "Start Queue."

▼ **START ALL THE DOCUMENTS to print:** If the queue has been stopped, the first item under the Queue menu is "Start Queue." This will start the printing process for the entire line-up of documents.

▼ **CANCEL a print job:** In the Queue window, click once on a document name to select it, then hit the Delete button, or go to the Queue menu and choose "Delete Job."

You can select more than one job to delete: hold down the Command key and click on each document name you want to delete.

It's possible to put a bunch of documents in a queue, then **print that queue later,** like right before lunch. Just open the Print Center, go to the Queue menu, and choose "Stop Queue." Yes, you are stopping the queue before you even begin to print. Open each of your documents and tell them to print; they will all line up in the queue. Later when you turn on your printer, choose "Start Queue" and the files will print in the order you sent them.

Collect Files to Print Later

If you need to make a PostScript file but you don't have a PostScript printer, you can make a "virtual" (pretend) PostScript printer that will work.

Create a Virtual PostScript Printer

To make a virtual PostScript printer:

1. Open Print Center (as explained on page 252). If you don't see the Printer List, go to the Printers menu and choose "View Printer List."
2. Click the "Add Printers…" button.
3. In the menu at the top of the Printer List dialog box, choose "LPR Printers using IP."
4. In the new dialog box you get, enter the information shown below, then click the "Add" button.

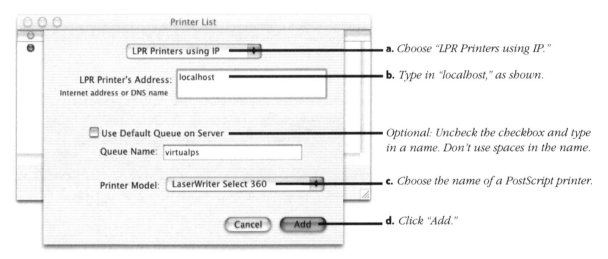

Printer List

a. *Choose "LPR Printers using IP."*

LPR Printer's Address: localhost
Internet address or DNS name

b. *Type in "localhost," as shown.*

☐ Use Default Queue on Server

Optional: Uncheck the checkbox and type in a name. Don't use spaces in the name.

Queue Name: virtualps

Printer Model: LaserWriter Select 360

c. *Choose the name of a PostScript printer.*

Cancel   Add

d. *Click "Add."*

5. In your document, press Command P to Print. Choose the virtual printer, go to the "Output Options" menu, check "Save as File," and choose the "PostScript" format, as shown below. Click "Save…."

Across Solem

Printer: virtualps

Saved Settings: Standard

Output Options

☑ Save as File   Format: PostScript

?   Preview   Cancel   Save…

1. Is the printer that you print to PostScript or not?

2. Is your printer USB or serial?

3. Explain how to make a printer the default printer.

4. Where would you (generally speaking) tell the printer to print your job "sideways"?

5. How could you tell the printer to print a number of miniature pages on one sheet of paper?

6. How do you open the Print Center to monitor a print job in progress?

7. What's the difference between putting a job on "Hold" and choosing to "Stop Queue"?

8. If you have a report of eight pages and you need to pass this report out to five people, how could you make the printer collate the report for you?

9. Describe two ways to put the Print Center in the Dock so it stays there.

10. To save a PDF file from your document so you could send it to your boss who uses a PC, which Print pane would you choose?

Answers on page 751.

Closing and Quitting 16

There is a big and important difference between **closing** and **quitting.** You **close** *a document,* but you **quit** *an application.* This is a vital concept to understand, so don't skip this short chapter.

Quit vs. Close

At first it seems a bit confusing—what's the big deal, **quitting** or **closing.** Either way, you're finished, right? Wrong.

Essentially, this is what happens: Say you open an ***application*** like your word processer—that is comparable to putting a typewriter on your desk. Then you start a new ***document***—that is comparable to putting a piece of paper in the typewriter.

When you choose "Close" from the File menu, that is comparable to taking the piece of paper (the *document*) out of the typewriter. The typewriter, though (the *application*), is still on the desk! On a computer, both the desk and the "typewriter" are rather invisible so you might *think* the typewriter (the application) is gone.

But the typewriter—the word processor—stays on the desk (in the computer's *memory,* called *RAM*) until you physically put the word processor away. When you choose "Quit" from the File menu, that is comparable to putting the typewriter away.

If you leave too many applications open without quitting or too many large documents open without saving, the memory on your Mac gets full and you'll get errors, you might not be able to print or copy files, and you might hear your hard disk "thrashing," or clicking continuously. If you have a huge amount of memory, you can get away with leaving applications and documents open and not worry.

How much memory is a "huge" amount, and how do you know how much you have? Go to the Apple menu and choose "About This Mac." The little window that appears tells you how much memory is installed. Apple recommends a *minimum* amount of 128 megabytes. A good-sized amount is at least three or four times that, and if you can afford a gigabyte or two, that's excellent.

Note: A gigabyte is over 1000 megabytes, and a megabyte is over 1000 kilobytes, and a kilobyte is over 1000 bytes, and it takes 1 byte to make a standard character on the screen, like the letter "A." And because I know you're dyin' to know, 1 byte is made of 8 bits. And that's as small as it gets.

This says I have 1.2 gigabytes of memory (RAM) in my big Mac. That's a nice big chunk, but my friend Bob Levitus has over 2 gigabytes.

Closing
a Document Window

When you are finished working on a document, you can **close that document window** in a number of ways:

- ▾ **Either** click the red button in the upper-left of the window.
- ▾ **Or** choose "Close" from the File menu.
- ▾ **Or** in most applications, the keyboard shortcut to close a document is usually **Command W,** just like closing a Finder window.

Whichever method you use, you are simply *closing the document window* (putting away the paper) and *the application (the software program) is still open and taking up memory.* You still see the menu belonging to the application, even though the rest of your screen may look just like your Desktop, and even if you see windows that belong to other applications or to the Desktop!

Close a window when you are finished with a document and perhaps want to start another. If know you are going to come back to this application later, you don't really need to quit (if you have enough memory).

Unsaved changes

If a document window has a dot in the middle of the red button, that means it has **unsaved changes,** meaning you made changes to the document since last time you saved it (if ever). Perhaps you wrote more, fixed a typo, or changed the typeface. If you don't save those changes before you close, you'll get a message warning you, as shown on the following page.

When the red close button has a dot in it, you need to save the file.

To Tipperary

It was a long way to Tipperary. It was an especially long way to Celia because she had no idea where Tipperary was. She couldn't even positively state that it was in America. It could be in Timbuktu for all she knew. And if it was in Timbuktu, well, how on earth was she going to get there? She certainly didn't have a boat. My goodness, Celia barely had shoes.

Quitting an Application

The item "Quit" is always the last command in the File menu. If you don't see Quit in the File menu, you are probably at the Desktop/Finder.

To quit an application, you must choose the Quit command. This command is always in the File menu, and "Quit" is always the very last item. In every application you can use the keyboard shortcut instead: **Command Q.**

If you haven't saved all of your changes in any of the open documents, the Mac will politely ask if you want to save them at this point (it also asks when you *close* an unsaved document). Thank goodness.

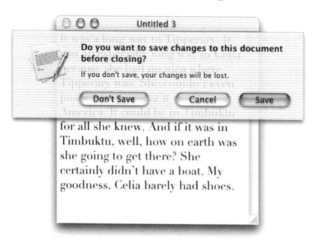

▼ Click the **Don't Save** button if you decide at this point you don't want the changes (or the document, if you've never named it). Often you can use the keyboard shortcut Command D instead of actually clicking the "Don't Save" button. In some applications, you can just hit the letter D.

▼ Click **Cancel** to return to your document without saving any changes or quitting. You can always press Command Period to cancel.

▼ If you click **Save** and you haven't yet even saved the document with a name, you'll get the "Save As…" dialog box (page 222) to name the document before quitting because nothing can be saved without a name. You can hit the Return or Enter key instead of clicking the Save button, and in some applications you can press S.

Quit when you are finished working in the application for the day (or if you are having memory problems—see page 258). Once you quit, the application is removed from the computer's memory.

Shortcut

***Press** on an application icon to get this menu.*

There is a sweet little **shortcut to quit.** You don't even have to open the application to do this. Just press (don't click) on the application's icon in the Dock. In the pop-up menu that appears, choose "Quit."

If you're not sure if you have quit your application or not, check the Dock. Any application icon that appears in the Dock with a **triangle** beneath it is still open and taking up memory. If you want to quit that application, click once on its icon, then press Command Q to quit, even if you don't see the application anywhere! Trust me. (You can't quit the Finder, however.)

Remember, applications are only on the *left* side of the Dock, to the left of the dividing line. That's why you never see triangles on the right side, even if a folder in the Dock is open.

Check to see if applications are open

The Finder is always open because it runs the Desktop.

You can see that four other applications are still open. If you have lots of memory, you can leave lots of applications open.

When you choose to Log Out, Restart, or Shut Down, the Mac will **automatically quit** all open applications for you. If you have documents still open that need changes saved, you'll get a message for each one, giving you the opportunity to save them. This is a great option for anyone who tends to leave lots of applications open—at the end of the day, instead of taking the time to make each application active one at a time and quit it (as described above), just Shut Down and they will all quit anyway.

Quit applications upon Log Out, Restart, and Shut Down

Are you sure you want to quit all applications and log out now?

Cancel   Log Out

This is the message you'll get if you choose to Log Out (from the Apple menu) while applications are still open.

Tip: If you have a lot of applications open, don't choose "Shut Down" and then walk away from your computer! Wait until you see the blue screen because if there is an unsaved document anywhere on your Mac, a message will pop up asking you to save it. If you aren't there to deal with it, the Shut Down process (or Logout or Restart) times out and your computer just sits there, patiently waiting for you to come back.

Force Quit Sometimes an application gets a little screwy and you have to force it to quit. You might not be able to get to the application's File menu to choose "Quit," but there are several other things you can do. You can also use these techniques to **force quit** applications that you're not using at the moment.

In Mac OS X when one application goes down, it doesn't take the rest of the computer down with it, as happened in previous operating systems. And if you're a Mac user from way back, you'll be happy to learn that force quit in OS X actually works.

To force quit an application, either:

1. From the **Apple menu,** choose "Force Quit...."

2. In the dialog box that appears, click once on the name of the application you want to quit.

3. Hit the Return or Enter key, or click the "Force Quit" button.

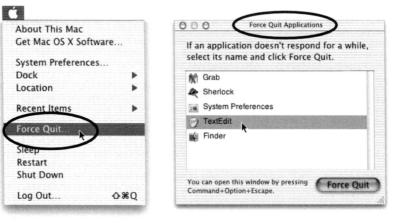

Choose "Force Quit..." from the Apple menu to get the dialog box.

Choose the application you want to force quit, then click the button.

Or:

▼ Instead of going to the Apple menu, you can press **Command Option Escape** to get the "Force Quit Applications" dialog box. (Remember, *hold down* Command and Option, then *tap* the Escape key. The Escape key is in the upper-left corner of your keyboard, and it has "esc" on it.)

Or:

▼ Hold down the **Option key and press** on the application's icon in the Dock (don't click—*hold* the button down). The menu that pops up typically says "Quit," but with the Option key down it changes to "Force Quit." Choose that item and it will force quit the selected application.

The Dock menu for TextEdit (the selected application) shows a window that is open in that application, the command to "Show In Finder," which will open the window that this application is stored in, and "Quit," which will quit just this one application.

With the Option key down (either before or after you choose this menu), "Quit" changes to "Force Quit."

Relaunch the Finder

If you have trouble in the **Finder** (at the Desktop), you can't *quit* the Finder. But you can **relaunch** it which might clear up any weird little problems you may be having. Relaunching the Finder does not affect your other applications or open windows.

To relaunch the Finder:

1. From the **Apple menu,** choose "Force Quit...," or press Command Option Escape.

2. In the dialog box, click once on "Finder."

3. Click the Relaunch button.

> ○ ○ ○   Force Quit Applications
>
> If an application doesn't respond for a while, select its name and click Force Quit.
>
> 𝕄 Grab
> 🖼 System Preferences
> 📝 TextEdit
> **💻 Finder**
>
> You can open this window by pressing Command+Option+Escape.   (**Relaunch**)

Quiz

Circle the correct answer to these questions:

close   *quit*   **1.** To put away a document.

close   *quit*   **2.** To put away an application.

close   *quit*   **3.** Press Command W.

close   *quit*   **4.** Press Command Q.

close   *quit*   **5.** Take the "paper" out of the "typewriter."

close   *quit*   **6.** Put the "typewriter" away.

Use this illustration of the Dock to answer the rest of the questions:

7. How many applications (besides the Finder) are open at the moment?

_____

8. Describe how to quit Sherlock (the icon with the Sherlock Holmes hat).

_____

9. If you have a dozen applications open and you're ready to leave your Mac for the day, what is the fastest way to quit all of the applications?

_____

10. Describe three ways to force quit an application.

_____

_____

Answers on page 751.

Using the Trash

The **Trash basket** on the Mac works just like the trash can in your yard—you put things in it you don't want anymore and the garbage collector comes and takes it away and you never see it again. The Trash basket is kept in the Dock, as shown below. Since the Trash is such an important part of working on the Mac, it gets its own chapter with tips about using it.

If your machine has **multiple users,** each user has their own personal Trash basket: no one but that user can empty that basket, and no user can see what any other user has in their Trash.

This is the Trash, the waste basket.
Right now it's empty.

Putting Something in the Trash

*The paper in the basket is an obvious **visual clue** that there is something in the garbage.*

To put something in the Trash, press-and-drag an icon over to the Trash can (actually, it looks like a wastebasket). *When the basket turns black,* let go and the file will drop inside. Don't let go of the file before the basket turns black! If you find a bunch of garbage hanging around outside the Trash or sitting in the Dock, *it's because you didn't wait for it to turn black*—you just set the trash down *next* to the basket.

The trick is that the **tip of the pointer** must touch the Trash basket! Whether you are putting one file in the Trash or whether you have selected several icons and are dragging them all together to the Trash, **the tip of the pointer** is the thing that selects the wastebasket. The shadows of the objects have nothing to do with it—forget those shadows trailing along behind—just make sure the tip of the pointer touches the basket and turns it black. Then let go.

*You can see the original file (the top one), plus the shadow that is pulled by the pointer (over the Trash basket). When the **pointer** touches the basket, the basket turns dark. That means you can let go.*

Here you can see I selected three files (I held down the Command key and clicked on each one.)

*Then I **let go** of the Command key, dragged **one** of those selected files to the Trash, and the rest followed.*

*You can see all three shadows of the files, but notice where the pointer is. It's that **tip** of the pointer, not the shadows of the icons, that selects the Trash so the files can drop in.*

You might have chosen to **hide your Dock** (as explained on page 123). If so, you can't see the Trash basket. But don't worry—as you drag a file down toward the Dock, it will pop up, you can drop the file in the Trash, and then the Dock will hide again. Or you can use any of the methods below to throw away a file without ever having to see the basket.

**Trashing Files
when Dock is Hidden**

There are several other ways to **move an item to the Trash** besides physically dragging a file and dropping it in the basket.

**More Ways
to Trash Files**

▾ Select the item (click once on it). From the File menu,
   choose "Move to Trash."

▾ **Or** select the item (click once on it). Press Command Delete.

▾ **Or** hold down the Control key (not the Command key) and
   click on a file you want to throw away. A little menu (called a
   "contextual menu," shown below) pops up and gives you, among
   other things, the option to move that item to the Trash. Choose it.

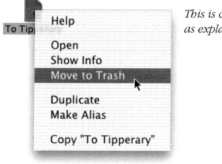

*This is called a contextual menu,
as explained in Chapter 5.*

Taking Something out of the Trash

To remove something from the Trash, click once on the basket and you'll find that it opens up to a window, just like any other window. So if you decide you want that item you just threw away, you can go get it. But don't forget—you can only get items back from the Trash if you have *not* emptied the Trash!

▼ If you change your mind directly after you throw something away, press Command Z (the "Undo" command) and the item(s) you just put in the Trash will be instantly put back where it came from.

Keep in mind that Command Z only undoes *the very last action you did;* that is, if you put a second file in the Trash, it is the second file that will be put back, not the first one. Or if you threw away a file and then you made a copy of a different file, Undo (Command Z) will undo the copying, not the trashing.

▼ You can always open the Trash window and drag the file out of the window and put it back where it belongs, as long as you have not emptied the Trash yet.

The Trash opens to a window. Drag any file out and put it wherever you want.

Anything you put in the Trash basket will stay there, even if you turn off the computer, *until you consciously empty the Trash*. Once you do that, everything in the basket is gone forever. No amount of crying or pleading will bring it back. Believe me.

Sometimes you throw away files because you want to make space on a disk. Keep in mind that the Trash must be emptied before the space will open up; that is, until you actually empty the Trash, the files continue to take up space on your hard disk or any other disk.

To empty the Trash (you don't have to select the basket first):

▼ If "Finder" is not in the menu bar, click once on the Desktop. Then from the Finder menu, choose "Empty Trash…." The ellipsis (three dots …) after this command indicates you will get a dialog box. **You will get a warning** asking if you really want to throw those files away. Click OK.

To avoid this warning, hold down the Option key when you choose "Empty Trash…," *or* turn off the warning altogether; see the following page.

▼ **Or** instead of going to the Finder menu, press (don't click) the mouse button directly on the wastebasket and hold it for a second or two; a little menu will pop up. Choose "Empty Trash," then let go of the mouse button. **You will NOT get the warning message.**

▼ **Or** instead of going to any menu, use the keyboard shortcut Command Shift Delete. **You WILL get the warning message** unless you have turned it off; see the following page.

Emptying the Trash

Well, if you empty the Trash and tragically realize that you threw away your only copy of something very important, there is software and there are technicians who can often bring back your information, so if you lose something important call your local guru, power user, or user group. In the meantime, don't turn off your computer or create new files.

In general, to be safe, when you toss something in the Trash, consider it gone.

Stop the Trash Warning

Some people appreciate having a **warning** that items in the Trash will be forever deleted if they empty it, but it makes others crazy to have to click the button every time they want to empty the Trash. As mentioned on the previous page, there are a couple of ways to avoid the Trash warning temporarily, but you can also turn it off permanently (until you want to turn it back on again).

To turn off the Trash warning:

1. At the Desktop, go to the Finder menu and choose "Preferences...."
2. Uncheck the box, "Show warning before emptying the Trash."
3. Close the Finder Preferences.

When there is a checkmark, you will get a warning.

Uncheck the box (click once in it) to disable the warning.

Note: When the warning is disabled, you'll see a subtle **visual clue** in the Finder menu. The command "Empty Trash" will no longer have the ellipses (three dots), which means you won't get a dialog box—the command will be carried out instantly.

If a file is **locked,** you cannot **throw it away;** if you try, you'll get a message telling you that you don't have "sufficient privileges" to trash the item. This warning, "sufficient privileges," covers a lot of ground—it might mean the file is simply locked in the Show Info box and you can go unlock it (explained below), or perhaps it belongs to some other user, or perhaps only the administrator of the computer can throw it away because the file is some sort of important system file.

Throwing Away Locked Files

Upcheer Thyself

This is a locked file—you can see the tiny lock on the bottom-left corner of the icon. You can unlock most files in the Show Info box.

You'll probably see this message more often than you care to.

If the file is yours and you created it and it doesn't have anything to do with operating the Macintosh, you can usually unlock it using Show Info.

To unlock a locked file:

1. Click once on the file that you think may be locked.

2. From the File menu, choose "Show Info," *or* press Command I.

3. If there is a checkmark in the "Locked" checkbox, click once in the checkbox to remove the mark. Close the Show Info window.

Uncheck this box to unlock the file.

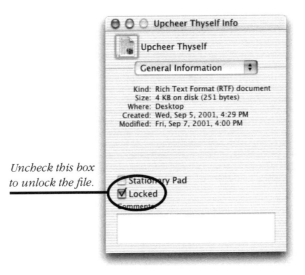

If the file is not locked and you still can't throw it away, perhaps you locked this particular file when you were working in Mac OS 9. If you think that might be so, you'll need to restart using OS 9 and unlock the file from there. If that does not solve the problem and you know the file is yours and you are the administrator of the Mac, see Chapter 20.

1. What does it indicate when the Trash basket icon appears to have wadded paper in it?

2. When do the files in the Trash disappear?

3. Describe four ways to move an item to the Trash.

4. What happens if you click on the Trash basket?

5. If you decide a file should not be in the Trash after all, how do you get it out?

6. What is the keyboard shortcut that can put a Trashed file back where it belongs, if you think fast enough?

7. If you have emptied the Trash, can you get your file back?

8. How can you avoid the Trash warning temporarily, and how can you avoid it permanently?

9. How can you throw away a locked item?

10. How can you drag a file into the Trash if the Dock is hidden?

Answers on page 751.

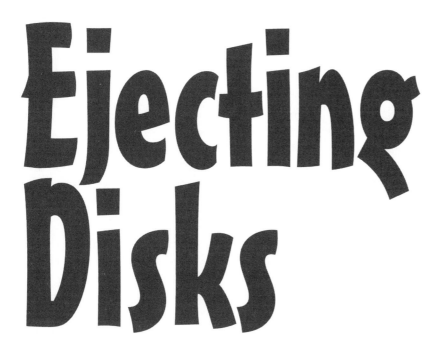

Ejecting Disks

Disks go in and disks come out. Sometimes they don't come out. Sometimes they get stuck. Sometimes they won't "mount," which means their icon doesn't show up on the Desktop. This short section covers all the tricks to getting removable hard disks, CDs, DVDs, and even floppy disks in and out of your Macintosh.

Mounting and Unmounting

You may hear talk of **mounting** and **unmounting** disks, rather than inserting and ejecting them. The terms *mount* and *unmount* refer to hard disks (internal or external), removable hard disks such as Zips and Jaz, CDs and DVDs, as well as floppies, if you have a floppy drive.

It is possible and very common to have more than one hard disk attached to your computer. You probably have removable hard disks that you insert into a cartridge drive sort of like inserting a video tape into a VCR (Zip or Jaz). But even though that hard disk is attached to the computer or you have inserted a disk into a drive, that does not guarantee that its icon will show up on the screen. If the icon does not appear (which means the computer cannot "read" the disk), we say that the disk did not *mount*.

Someone might ask you to *unmount* a disk, which is to remove it from the computer's grasp. If you have a CD/DVD tray, you'll find that you cannot open the tray by pushing its button until you first *unmount* the CD or DVD; that is, you have to drag the disk icon to the Trash basket or press Command E (for eject) before the button will open the CD tray. Or press F12 to open and close the tray, even if a CD or DVD is still mounted. Make sure you quit everything you were using on the CD/DVD before you eject the disk.

Ejecting a Removable Disk

You may sometimes need to eject a floppy disk or removable hard disk to trade it with another, or simply to take your disk and go away. There are actually several ways to **eject a removable disk.** These techniques work for any removable disks you might use, such as Zip, Jaz, CDs, DVDs, or floppies. Except for using the Media Eject key, as explained on page 276, all of these techniques require that you be at the Desktop.

Always make sure before you eject a disk that you have closed any documents and quit any applications you used from that disk. If you don't, you'll get this message when you try to eject:

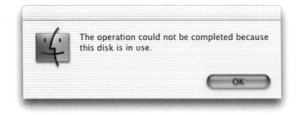

If you get this message, check to see if you opened a ReadMe file or some other document from that disk and maybe it's still open. Check the Dock to see which applications are still open; select any application you might have used from the disk, then quit that application. Or did you load fonts directly from the disk? If you loaded fonts, close them. (If you don't know how to open or load fonts, you didn't.)

One easy and obvious method to eject a disk is to use the command in the File menu.

1. Select the disk (click once on it).

2. From the File menu, choose "Eject." (If "Eject" is gray, it means you did not select a removable disk.)

   Or use the shortcut **Command E.**

Another simple and effective method is to eject the disk through the Trash. Aack, you say! Yes, that's a frightening thought, but calm down; it's quite all right. *The Trash doesn't erase anything off your disk.*

Ejecting a disk through the Trash

The Trash icon changes to the Media Eject icon when you select a disk.

1. Simply **press on the disk icon, and drag it down toward the Trash.**

2. As soon as you press on the disk, take a look at the Trash basket— it has turned into an "Media Eject" icon, as shown to the right. Drag the disk down to this new icon **and drop it directly on top.** The disk will pop out safely.

Yet another easy method to eject a disk is with a contextual menu.

Ejecting a disk using a contextual menu

1. Hold down the **Control key and click** on the disk.

2. A contextual menu pops up—choose "Eject."

Help

Open
Show Info
Eject

Duplicate
Make Alias

Copy "LMB OSX"

This contextual menu pops up when you Control-click on a disk.

Tip: If your hard disk is partitioned into separate volumes, it's possible to eject an individual partition using any of these methods. If you want that partition mounted again, you must restart the computer. Go to the Apple menu and choose "Restart."

Ejecting multi-session CDs   If you have a **CD** on which there are **several sessions,** which the Mac thinks are individual *volumes,* you can eject all of the volumes at once using any of the methods explained on the previous page. You do *not* need to select every volume on the disk—you only need to select one. Also read about the Media Eject key, below.

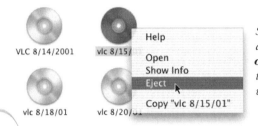

*Select one of the volumes on a CD, then press Command E, **or** drag it to the Trash, **or** use the contextual menu, and all volumes will unmount and eject.*

Media Eject Key

▲

This is the symbol for the Media Eject key, if you have one on your keyboard.

Some keyboards have a **Media Eject key.** If you have it, it's in the upper-right of the keyboard, the most upper-right key there is at the top of the numeric keypad. It has the symbol shown to the left. The great thing about this key is that you don't have to select the disk—just hit the key and the CD or DVD will eject. In fact, you don't even have to be at the Desktop—you can hit the Media Eject key while you're working in another OS X application and the disk will eject. Just make sure you first close any documents and quit any applications that opened documents from that CD before you eject the disk.

F12 Key

If you don't have an Media Eject key, use the **F12 key** (it's just above the Delete key). This will not only eject a mounted CD or DVD, but if you have a CD tray, it will open or close the tray. Try it.

Eject on Shut Down or Restart

When you restart your Mac or when you are done for the day and **shut down** the whole computer (from the Apple menu choose "Shut Down"), most of your disks will automatically eject, except CDs and DVDs. If you're having trouble getting rid of CDs or DVDs, see the tips on the opposite page.

For details about shutting down, restarting, and logging out, please see Chapter 19.

If for some reason, perhaps because of a power outage or a system error or a bug on the disk, your CD or DVD is stuck in the computer, try the good ol' **mouse trick:**

> Hold down the mouse button. *Keep holding it down* and turn the computer back on; your disk(s) should pop out like toast.

If you have a **Media Eject key** on your keyboard, in the upper-right, you can use a similar trick as described above. Restart your Mac, and right after you hear the start-up sound, hold down the Media Eject key until the CD ejects.

If all else fails, notice that tiny hole next to the CD slot, internal Zip drive, or floppy drive? That hole is **paperclip** size. Unbend a paperclip and push it in. It's very safe as all you're doing is releasing the mechanism that holds the disk in place—push firmly. You can even do this if the computer is turned off or unplugged and stored in a closet.

If you have an internal Zip drive, you might discover that the paperclip hole in the outer plastic casing does not exactly line up with the release mechanism on the drive inside. If you have trouble, pop the front off of the Mac (if that's possible on your machine) and stick your paperclip directly into the hole on the front of the drive.

The Mouse Trick

The Media Eject key Trick

The Paperclip Trick

New machines might not have a paperclip hole!

1. What are four easy ways to eject a disk?

   _____

2. Say you inserted a CD and opened the ReadMe file that was on the CD.
   Now when you eject the disk you get a message telling you that operation
   could not be completed because something is still in use. What do you do?

   _____

3. What does it mean to say a disk didn't "mount"?

   _____

4. If a CD or Zip is stuck in an internal drive and won't come out, describe two
   emergency measures to get it unstuck.

   _____

   _____

Answers on page 751.

Restart, Shut Down, or Log Out

If you've been working your way through the practice exercises in this book, you're probably ready to **Shut Down.** Shutting down is the computer's process of tying up all the loose ends inside of itself and "parking" the hard disk before it's turned off. It is certainly possible to turn the computer off without going through the Shut Down process, but you run the risk of losing data and possibly damaging mysterious but important elements. At the very least, turning off your Mac without choosing Shut Down leaves your computer in an unstable state. So follow this simple ritual when you are finished for the day!

Sometimes you don't want to completely shut down, but **Restart** or **Log Out.** This chapter covers all those bases.

The Options

In the Apple menu the last four options are **Sleep, Restart, Shut Down,** and **Log Out.** Here is a brief description of when you might use each of these options.

All four of these commands are in the Apple menu, but you can also accomplish any of these tasks without opening the Apple menu.

▼ **Sleep** does two things: 1) It turns off the monitor display so your screen goes black, and 2) it stops the hard disk from spinning. Both of these features save energy. You can control when your Mac goes to sleep; for instance, you might want it to automatically sleep whenever you haven't used it for twenty minutes. You can tell the monitor and the hard disk to go to sleep at two different times, since it takes longer for the hard disk to wake up than the display (some people get annoyed waiting for the hard disk to start spinning again, so you can have the display sleep but not the hard disk, if you like). For all the details, see page 325.

▼ **Restart** shuts your Mac down and starts it up again without ever turning off the power. This is easier on the computer than turning off the power and rebooting (turning it back on). You often have to restart after installing new software or anytime things just start acting weird. See the opposite page for details.

▼ On **Shut Down,** the Mac takes care of internal business, cleans up everything, and turns itself off (it actually turns off the power). Shut Down when you are done for the day or longer. Actually, you don't have to ever Shut Down in Mac OS X—you can leave your machine on for weeks at a time, setting it to sleep automatically after a certain number of idle minutes. My partner John leaves his computer on for days on end; I shut mine down most nights. Do what feels best to you. See pages 282–283 for details.

▼ Use **Log Out** to switch between multiple users. If you are the only user, you can use it as a safety precaution. See page 283 for details.

Restart does exactly that: it restarts your Mac, but without turning the power off. It's sort of like turning your Mac off and then turning it back on again, but without the stress of powering completely down and up. You usually have to restart after installing most software. Sometimes when things are just acting goofy, Restart can clear up the problem.

You can choose "Restart" from the Apple menu, obviously, but occasionally your Mac is acting so weird you can't get to the Apple menu. So there are several other ways to Restart, depending on what kind of Mac you have.

Restart

▼ If you turn on your **Mac with a big Power Key** on the keyboard, the one with a triangle outline on it (not the flat, round button with the circle on it), you can usually Restart with this trick: Hold down the Command and Control keys, then press that Power Key.

▼ If you have an **iMac,** press the Power button on the keyboard (not the one on the monitor) and you should get the message shown below where you can choose to Restart.

Instead of the Shut Down option, you can choose to Restart.

▼ Also on an **iMac,** look in the little panel on the right side of the computer. You'll see two tiny buttons, one with a tiny, solid triangle. That's the Restart button; push it to Restart. Don't push the other button—that's a programmer's switch (it's actually indented a little to make it difficult to hit accidentally). But if you do accidentally push the programmer's switch and you get weird stuff on your screen, go back and push the Restart button this time.

On **older iMacs,** it's not a button, but a solid triangle above a tiny hole—unfold a paperclip and push it in the hole to Restart. Don't stick the paperclip in the programmer's switch!

▼ On most **G3 and G4 towers,** there is a tiny Restart button (and programmer's switch) right below the Power button on the front of the tower. The Restart button has a solid black triangle on it.

▼ When you **install software** that needs your computer to Restart, they'll provide you with a Restart button in a dialog box.

▼ You can choose to **Restart Classic** separately from OS X using the Classic preferences pane; see Chapter 40.

First, Good Housekeeping

When you're done with the Macintosh, it's good housekeeping to close up all your windows on the Desktop because any window you leave open will reappear in front of your face when you turn your computer back on. It's kind of like walking into the kitchen in the morning and finding last night's dinner dishes still on the counter. Press **Command Option W** (or Option-click on a red close button) and every open Finder window will tuck itself away where it belongs. Wish the dishes did that.

However, you can take advantage of these windows staying where you left them and perhaps leave open your nice, neatly organized Home window and perhaps your favorite project folder so when you return to the Mac they are ready and waiting for you.

Then Shut Down

From the Apple menu, choose **Shut Down.** All open applications will quit, any extra hard disks will unmount, you will be disconnected from any servers you were connected to, and the Mac will automatically turn its own power off.

There are several ways to Shut Down, depending on the Mac you have.

▼ If you turn on your **Mac with a big Power Key** on the keyboard, the one with a triangle on it (not the flat, round button with the circle on it), you can usually push that key again to turn the Mac off. Fortunately for those with cats or small children, the Mac will ask if you want to save any unsaved documents before it turns everything off. Click "Cancel" if hitting this button was a mistake.

When you press the Power key to shut down, this message usually pops up, depending on which Mac you have. You can hit the Return or the Enter key instead of clicking the "Shut Down" button.

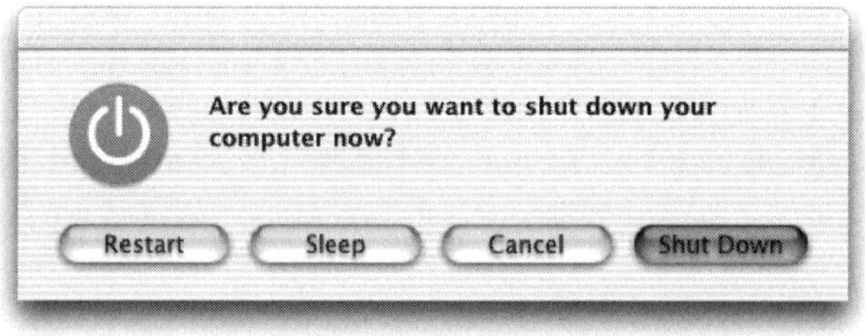

Are you sure you want to shut down your computer now?

Restart   Sleep   Cancel   Shut Down

▼ If you have a **G3 or G4 tower,** you can usually push the Power button in and hold it to the count of 5 to Shut Down. You won't get any warning message unless you have unsaved documents still open. (Sometimes this button puts the Mac to Sleep instead of Shut Down.)

▼ If you have a keyboard with a **flat, round, green-glowing Power button on the keyboard,** you can push that to Shut Down and you will get the message shown above.

▼ If you have a **laptop,** this combination usually works to Shut Down: hold down Control Shift fn, then press the Power key.

▼ This works on Macs that have an **Eject Media key** in the upper-right of the keyboard: Hold the Control key and press the Eject Media key.

▼ If you have an **iMac** with a Power button on the keyboard *and* a Power button on the monitor, push the button on the ***keyboard*** to get the message shown on the opposite page.

The Power button on the ***monitor*** will do one of two things: it will either put your Mac to sleep, as described on page 280, ***or*** it will instantly quit all open applications, Shut Down, and turn off your Mac without any warning UNLESS you have unsaved documents.

Log Out

Choose to **log out,** even if you're the only user on the whole machine, when you are going to be away from your Mac for a while. Once you are logged out, no one else can get to your personal documents, fonts, applications, or even your Trash basket. For extra protection, you can use the "Login" preferences pane to disable the Restart and Shut Down buttons that appear on the log in screen (although I'm not clear on what good that does because anyone can just restart with the Restart button). Log Out does not turn off the power to the computer, as Shut Down does, although it does go into a low-power mode. See Chapter 20 for details about multiple users.

Tip: As another safety feature, you could create a password for your screensaver so if you are away from your desk and the screensaver turns on, the only way to get back to your computer is to type in a password. See page 318.

Unsaved Documents

Several times in this chapter I've mentioned **unsaved documents.** If you try to Restart, Shut Down, or Log Out and the Mac finds documents that you haven't saved yet, or that have had changes made that you didn't save, a message will appear asking if you want to save them, as shown below.

Now, if you hit the button to Log Out, for instance, and then you walk away from your computer and the Mac finds an unsaved document, it will wait several minutes for you to respond. **If you don't respond** because you've done something like left the building, then the Log Out (or Restart or Shut Down) process times out and your computer goes back to normal without logging out, restarting, or shutting down. **If you click the Cancel button,** you don't just cancel the saving of the document, you cancel the entire Log Out, Restart, or Shut Down process.

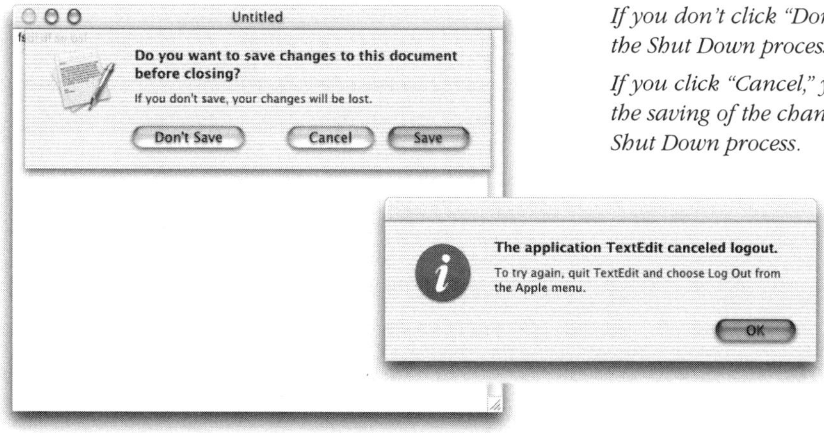

If you don't click "Don't Save" or "Save," the Shut Down process will time out.

If you click "Cancel," you cancel not just the saving of the changes, but the entire Shut Down process.

1. Of the four options in the Apple menu (Sleep, Restart, Shut Down, and Log Out), which is the only one that turns off the power?

2. Of these four options, which is the only one that helps protect your Mac from snoops?

3. What symbol does a Restart button have on it?

4. What will happen to open applications if you choose "Shut Down" before you have quit each application?

5. What is the keyboard shortcut to close all of your Finder windows at once?

Answers on page 751.

Multiple Users & their Homes

Mac OS X is specifically built for what's called a **multiple user environment;** that is, Apple expects that more than one person is probably using the same machine, whether it's in a school, office, or home.

If you are the only user who ever has or ever will use this computer, skip this chapter altogether. But are you really the only user? Perhaps your grandkids come over and want to use your Mac. Or maybe your husband uses your machine from time to time. Or sometimes you have relatives staying for a week who just want to use your Mac to get their email. In all of these cases, you can set up another user so no one else can access your personal letters, change the sound level, poke around in your financial files, put up a dorky picture as the Desktop background, or change any of your settings at all.

Advantages of Having Multiple Users

First, let me explain the **concept and advantages of having multiple users** set up on your Mac so you can decide if you need or want to create other users. You already have one user, you, which was automatically created when you first turned on your Mac and went through the setup process.

You might not have noticed that you are a "user" because Apple sets a default so when you turn on your Mac, you are automatically "logged in" without having to type in a password. Once you have other users set up, you can change this default so everyone must log in with a password. If others use your Mac only occasionally, like your grandkids, you can set it to automatically let you in daily; then when the kids come over, all you have to do is log *out,* which means they must then log *in* with their own settings and yours will be protected. I'll explain how to do that—it's so easy.

One user, the first (which was you, if it's your own Mac), is automatically created as the original, main **Administrator (Admin)** of the computer (if you are the *only* user, you are still the Administrator). All other people are "users" and are limited in certain ways:

▼ Applications can be made available to everyone, or limited to specific users. This means you could install a game in your child's Home folder and it won't clutter up your own Applications folder. If the game has to change the resolution of the monitor and the number of colors and your child cranks the volume way up, it won't affect what you see and hear when you log back in.

Also for kids and grandkids, you can customize their Dock so they have easy access to their own programs, and you can eliminate from the Dock the icons they don't need.

It also means you can install your financial program in your own Home folder so others cannot use it nor access your files.

▼ Even if an application is available to everyone who uses the machine, individual users can set their own preferences because the preferences are stored in the user's personal Library folder.

▼ Every user can customize the Mail program, and all of the email is privately stored in each user's personal Library folder.

▼ Every user can set up her own screen saver. Favorites, Internet search sites (see Sherlock, Chapter 24), fonts, window and Desktop backgrounds, and Dock placement and preferences are individually customizable. Preferences are also individual for the keyboard, mouse, Internet, web browser bookmarks or favorites, international keyboard settings, Classic, applications that startup on login, and QuickTime.

▼ The features that make the Mac easier to use for people with challenges can be customized by user. This includes the Universal Access settings, full keyboard access, Speech preferences (talking to your Mac to make it do things), etc.

▼ Users who need international settings, such as for date, time, numbers, or for typing other languages, etc., can customize the Mac without bothering other users. If you have a laptop that you travel with, you can set yourself up as another user, such as "Carmen in Belize," and customize those settings for that country without affecting all your settings for home.

▼ Users *cannot* change the date or time (except for the menu bar settings), nor can they change the preferences for energy saving, file sharing, networking, or the startup disk. They cannot add new users nor change certain parts of the login process.

As the Administrator, you can **assign Admin status to any other user** (see page 292). When that user logs in, he can make system-wide changes that regular users cannot, he can create and delete other users, and do all the things you can do. But your personal Home files are still protected from everyone else, including other Admins.

Can be more than one Admin

Automatic login allows *one* selected user to use the Mac without having to enter a password. If automatic login is enabled (page 295), then to switch to another user you must make sure to **Log Out** instead of shutting down or restarting (because when the machine starts up again, it will automatically log in the selected user).

If automatic login is *not* enabled, then it doesn't matter how you turn off the Mac—it will always display a **Log In** screen where every user, even Admins, will have to enter a password.

Logging Out and Logging In

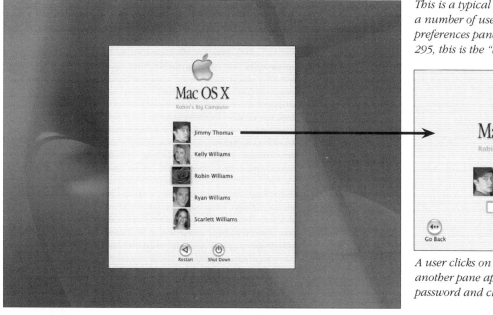

This is a typical login screen with a number of users. In the Login preferences pane, shown on page 295, this is the "list" option.

A user clicks on his name, left, and another pane appears where he enters his password and clicks the Log In button.

Creating New Users

Users

Login

If you are the Admin (as explained on the previous pages), you can create new users. There are two preference panes you'll work with, **Users** and **Login.** In the Users pane, you'll create the new user, plus assign them a login picture and password. In the Login pane, you can make adjustments to the login window and provide the password hint.

Individual users (as well as the Admin) can use part of the Login pane to make certain applications open on startup, as explained on page 294.

To create a new user:

1. Open the System Preferences: either click on the icon in the Dock, or go to the Apple menu and choose "System Preferences...."

2. In the System Preferences pane, click once on "Users." You'll get the dialog box shown below, except it probably has only one user listed, you. The one user is also the Admin.

The first Admin in the list is the original, main Administrator.

Click to lock the padlock icon and even an Administrator will have to enter an Admin name and password to change items here.

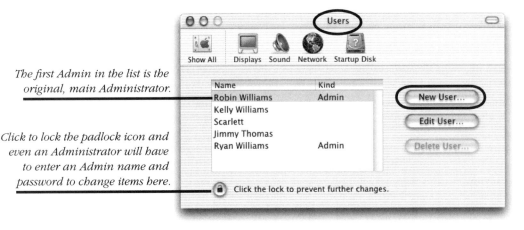

3. Click "New User..." to get the dialog box shown on the next page.

Type in the full **name** (or anything else you prefer) in the "Name" edit box. A **short name** will be automatically created for you, but you can edit it. The short name can be no longer than eight characters, you can't use capital letters or spaces, and it's best to avoid any non-alphabet characters (like *, !, ? or /).

Mac OS X can use either the short name or long name. But the short name is necessary if you ever use FTP, Telnet, or other applications that let you log in to your Mac from some other location.

You will never be able to change the short name after you click Save! The only way to "change" it is to delete the entire user and make a new one! (To do this, first create a new user with the correct short name, transfer all necessary files/folders, such as Documents, into the new user's account [through their Drop Box], *then* delete the first user whose name you didn't like.)

4. Choose a login picture. There are three ways to do this.

a. Either click once on any picture in the sliding pane shown at the bottom of the dialog box.

b. Or click the "Choose…" button, which will open the standard Open dialog box where you can select any photo or graphic image on your Mac.

c. Or open a folder that contains the photo or image you want. Position the folder window to the right of your screen. Drag a photo from that window and drop it onto the picture "well" in the Identity pane, as illustrated below.

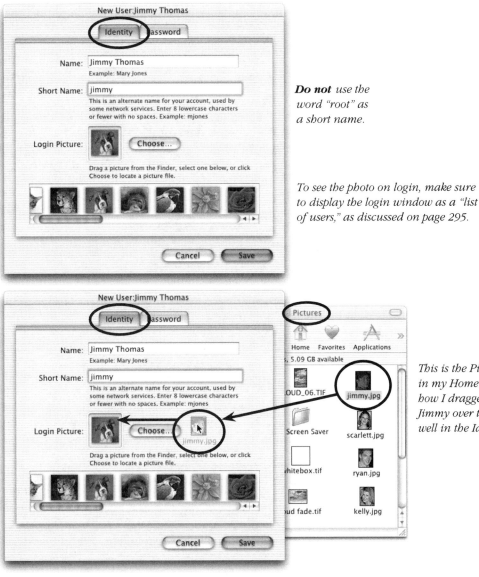

Do not use the word "root" as a short name.

To see the photo on login, make sure to display the login window as a "list of users," as discussed on page 295.

This is the Pictures folder in my Home. You can see how I dragged the image of Jimmy over to the picture well in the Identity pane.

—continued

5. Click on the **Password** tab. As you've probably seen before, you need to type in the password twice to make sure you've spelled it right, since you can't see it.

Passwords are "case sensitive." That means capital or lowercase letters **change the password:** "ChoCo" is *not* the same password as "choco." So be dang sure when you write your password down somewhere that you make note of any capital letters.

Use up to eight characters or numbers, no spaces, no apostrophes or quotation marks or other non-alphanumeric characters, and don't use a word that can be found in the dictionary. (You can type in more than eight characters, but the Mac only checks the first eight).

It is possible to leave the password blank, but that makes that user's Home easier to break into.

The password you provide here is the same one that will be used with the **screen saver** to protect your Mac when you walk away—you leave the computer, the screen saver starts, and the password must be entered to get back to the Desktop. See pages 316–319 for details.

You can, if you like, enter a **password hint.** On login, if a user enters the wrong password three times, a message appears with this hint. But make sure the checkbox is checked in the Login preferences pane to tell this message to appear! (See page 295.)

Tip: *If you have a very young user or two, you can set them up as a user with no password so all they have to do is click on their picture to log in. Or make the password something like "xxx" so it's really easy for them.*

When you see the bullets that are hiding your password, you'll often notice there are more bullets than the characters in your password. This is a protective device to help prevent snoops from trying to guess your password. Don't worry that maybe it's a different password from what you remember!

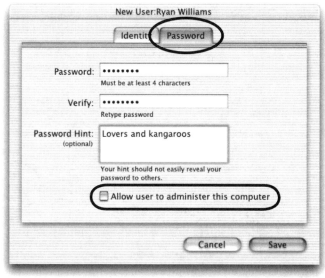

6. This pane is also the place where you can **change a user's status to Admin:** Check the box to "Allow user to administer this computer." You can have as many Admin users as you like, but that means your Mac would not be very well protected.

7. When you click the **Save** button to save the new user, this sheet will drop down in front of you, asking about **automatic login:**

I just made the new user "Ryan Williams," but this message reminds me that my Mac is set to automatically start up with "robin," meaning I (as "robin") do not have to go through the login screen and enter a password whenever the Mac starts or restarts. Because the Mac will automatically log me in, the only way Ryan can get to his Home folder is if I go to the Apple menu and choose "Log Out...," or if I turn off the automatic login for myself. Which one you choose depends on how often the other user will need your machine; if it's infrequent, you can let yourself automatically log in daily, then log out when the other user arrives to log in.

Only one user can be assigned the automatic login.

To change the automatic login without going through the new user process, use the Login pane, as shown on page 295.

This is Ryan's new Home. He has exactly the same folders as you have in your Home. Everything in his Home is private except for the files he has added to his Public folder—any other user can read and copy those files.

Setting up a User's Login

Login

Once users are set up and logged in, they can go to the Login preferences. There are two panes in Login: a regular user has access to the first one, Login Items, but only Administrators have access to the second one, Login Window.

In **Login Items,** a user can choose to have certain items automatically open during the login process (this window applies only to the user who is currently logged in). You can have your favorite applications open, or utilities, documents, even movies or music. If you choose to have a document open, the application it was created in will have to open, as well, even if you don't have it in the list.

For instance, below you see a number of items set to **open on startup,** or login. Mail and Chess are applications. The text document will open, but it will force the application TextEdit to open as well. The photo will open, but it will force the application Preview or QuickTime to open as well. The music file, .mp3, will force iTunes to open and the song will automatically start playing.

In my experience, it doesn't work very well to add Classic applications to the Login Items.

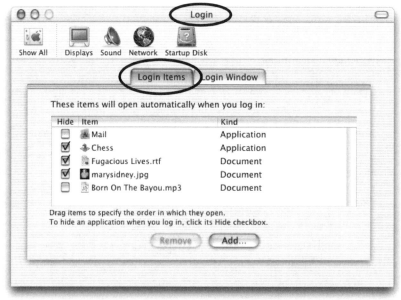

The files will **open in the order they are listed.** Drag any file in the list up or down to change the order.

If you don't want to see a certain application right away, click in the box to **hide** it. It will still open, but its windows won't be visible on the screen. The application icon in the Dock will have the triangle, though, so you know it's open and you can access it at any time.

The other pane in the Login preferences, the **Login Window,** is accessible only to Administrators. Here the Admin can do a number of things:

▼ Turn off the **automatic login** altogether, or change the user who gets automatically logged in. To change the user, just replace the name in the "Name" edit box, and type in that user's password.

See the note below and on the following page about disabling Restart and Shut Down and automatic log in.

▼ If you **"Display Login Window as"** the "Name and password entry fields," then on login you'll see a small window with two edit boxes: one for the user name and one for the password.

If you display the "List of users with accounts on this computer," on login a window appears with the list of all accounts on this machine. The pictures that were chosen in the User Identity pane (page 291) appear next to the names of the users. It's really cute.

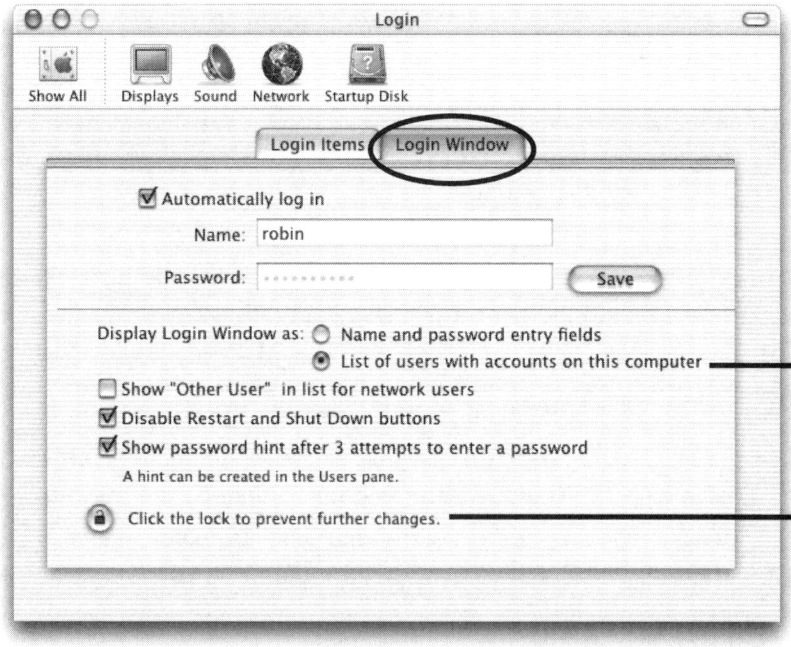

Choose this option to see the user photos that were selected in the Identity pane, page 291.

An example of this list is on page 289.

Click the padlock icon and even an Administrator will have to enter an Admin name and password to change items here.

▼ You can choose to show an extra, unnamed user as **Other User** for those who log into this Mac through a network. Talk to your system administrator about how to take advantage of this. If your network is a small, local network in an office with cables connecting the Macs, you won't need to use this, except perhaps to allow the root user to log in (see pages 298–299).

▼ If you **"Disable Restart and Shut Down buttons,"** it adds a wee bit more security for your Mac. See, when you log out, your computer does not turn off. It sits there with a little window where you can log back in again, and there are two buttons, one to "Restart" and one to "Shut Down." If your Mac is set to automatically log you in on startup, then an unauthorized user can walk by after you have logged out, click the Restart button, and your Mac will restart and automatically log you in. Even if you're not set up to automatically log in, someone could restart, hold down the Option key (on some Macs), and boot your Mac with OS 9, thus accessing your computer. Or someone could shut down your Mac, insert an OS X CD, and boot up the Mac and get access to your whole computer. By disabling the Restart and Shut Down buttons, an unauthorized user cannot click them, which would make your Mac one step closer to being protected.

However, there is nothing to prevent anyone from pushing the Restart button on the Mac, so if you really don't want people getting into your Mac, do not enable automatic log in, and don't leave your OS X CD laying around accessible.

▼ If a user has provided a password, you can check the button to **show password hint** if the user types in the wrong one three times. The hint provided is the phrase that was entered in the User preferences pane, as shown on page 292. The login window is kind of cute when you enter the wrong password—it shakes back and forth, like shaking its head no.

Folders for Sharing Files with Others

Once a user is set up, the default is to allow **access** only to the Public folder, the Sites folder, and the Drop Box. The Shared folder belongs to everyone who uses the Mac. If you plan to share files between users on this one computer, please see Chapter 35, which explains all this in detail (the Sites folder is explained in Chapter 37). Here are very brief explanations:

▼ Put files in your **Public** folder that you want others to be able to read, copy, or print. They have to open your Public folder to do so.

▼ Other users can put files for you into your **Drop Box,** which is located inside of your Public folder. They cannot open your Drop Box, not even to see if their file successfully transferred.

▼ Put files in the **Shared** folder that you want everyone who uses the Mac to have access to. This is a good way to distribute something to everyone on the Mac without having to copy it to each individual user's Drop Box.

▼ The **Sites** folder is where you can store a web site that you want people to access through the Internet. See Chapter 37.

You can also change the sharing "privileges" for any folder in your Home. That is, you can turn *off* the sharing privileges for the Public folder and the Drop Box so no one can access them, and you can also choose to share *any* or all of your other folders, with varying levels of access. Please see Chapter 35 for details.

Any Admin can **delete a user.** When a *user* is deleted, their *files* are not really deleted, but are moved to an Admin's Home folder—you have a choice of which Administrator's Home to move them to. This gives you an escape in case you decide it was a drastic mistake to remove a user—at least you have the important files.

Deleting Users

To delete a user:

1. Open System Preferences and single-click "Users."

2. Click once on the name of the user you want to delete.

3. Click the button, "Delete User...."

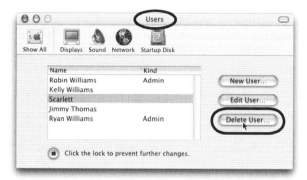

4. You will be asked if you really want to delete this user, and where to reassign (move) the user's folders. The folders can only be reassigned to an Administrator's account. Click "Cancel" if you change your mind, and click "Delete" if that's what you really want to do.

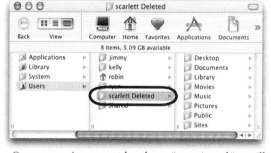

This shows two choices because there are two Admin users on this Mac.

Once a user's account has been "reassigned," you'll see it in the Users folder with the word "Deleted" appended to its name. All of the folders are accessible to the Administrator of this account.

5. Now you are stuck forever with the "Deleted" folder in your Home folder. You can throw away all the files inside the "Deleted" folder, but you can't throw away the actual folder itself. To get rid of it, you have to log in as the "root" user. See the directions on the following pages if you want to do that.

Log in as Root User

There is another user on the Mac, called the **root user,** or superuser. By logging into this account, you can change any file on the entire Mac, even system files that you as the Admin are not allowed to touch. By default, the root account is disabled in Mac OS X because it is phenomenally easy to destroy your entire system with the click of a mouse. But sometimes you try to throw away items you created or you might try to install software into the Applications folder and the Mac yells at you that it's not possible, usually because you don't have sufficient privileges. And you wonder, "Well, I'm the only person who has ever used this machine—if I don't have privileges, *who on earth does!?*" This is when you might have to log in as the **root user.** It's not something you want or need to do often, and you don't want to leave your computer sitting around with the root user available because as the root user, you (or anyone using your machine) has access to read, write, and destroy any file on the Mac, including all other user files.

But if you need to do it, log in as the root user, do what you need to do, then log out and disable the root user when you're done. You must know the Administrator's short name and password to do this.

To enable the root user and log in:

NetInfo Manager

This is the NetInfo Manager icon in the Utilities folder.

1. Click on the Applications icon in any Finder window, or go to the Go menu and choose "Applications."

2. In the Applications window, open the Utilities folder.

3. In the Utilities window, find and double-click "NetInfo Manager."

4. In the NetInfo Manager window, click the padlock icon in the bottom-left corner.

> local @ localhost.cybermesa.com – /
>
> Directory Browser
>
> / ▶ afpuser_aliases ▶
> aliases ▶
> config ▶
> groups ▶
>
> Directory: /
>
> | Property | Value(s) |
> | --- | --- |
> | master | localhost/local |
> | trusted_networks | <no value> |
>
> Click the lock to make changes.

5. In the dialog box that appears, type in the *short* name of the main Admin of the Mac, plus that Admin's password. It must be the name of the main, original Administrator—not a user who has been granted administrative status. Click OK.

6. From the Domain menu, slide down to "Security," and then choose "Enable Root User," as shown to the right.

(If the root user has already been enabled, this item says "Disable Root User"; skip to Step 9.)

7. If there is not a root password already, you will be asked to create one. Use the standard password guidelines: difficult to figure out, a combination of letters and number, no non-alphanumeric characters, no spaces, etc. Capital letters and lowercase letters are different characters in a password. *Write this password down somewhere!!*

After you type the password the first time, you'll be asked to type it again to verify it. Click the Verify button.

8. You have now enabled the root user. The padlock in the NetInfo window will automatically shut—you'll get a message that you must "re-authenticate" to make any more changes. Quit NetInfo.

9. Next you need to **log out** so you can **log in** as the root user. But before you log out, go to the Login preferences pane (in the System Preferences). Click the "Login Window" tab.

10. Check the "Display Login Window as" radio button to display "Name and password entry fields." *Or,* if you want to keep the list of user accounts that displays the photos the users have chosen, then check the box to "Show 'Other User' in list for network users." Either choice will give you an edit box where you can log in as the root user.

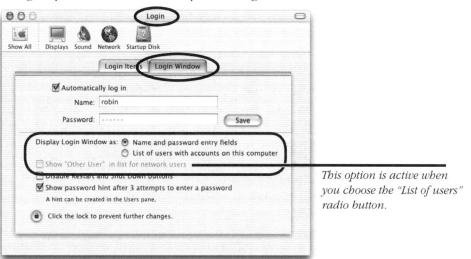

This option is active when you choose the "List of users" radio button.

11. From the Apple menu, choose "Log Out...." In the Login window that appears, type "root" as the user name, and type the root password you assigned earlier. Voilà. You can now delete files that you weren't allowed to delete earlier. Be careful.

12. When you're finished doing your root business, log out, log back in as yourself, and disable root access in the NetInfo Manager.

Installing Applications

On a corporate network, applications can also be installed on the main network server so all users can access them.

If you've never installed anything before, I'll explain how to do it in just a moment. But first you need to make a decision about *where* to install.

To install applications so **all users** have access to them, install them into the main Applications folder, as circled below, left. Only users with Administrative privileges are allowed to install applications into this folder.

If you want to be the **only one** who can use an application, create a new folder in your Home folder, as circled below, right, and call it something like "My Applications" or "Applications for Lew." Install the application inside this folder. Any user can install an application into their own Home folders.

Install into this folder so all users of this Mac can open and use the application.

Create your own personal applications folder and install into it so only you can use the application.

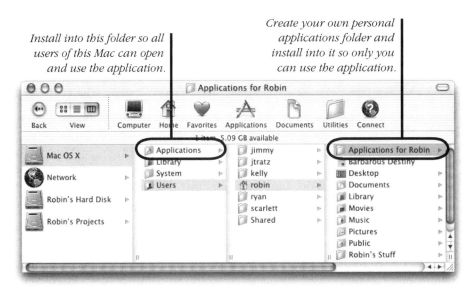

What form is your application in?

There are a **number of ways** you might install an application, depending on what form it's in at the moment. For instance, do you have an original CD with an "installer" file? Or did you download a "compressed" file from the Internet? Or do you have a disk with the uncompressed application that is already in a folder? Or perhaps you just want to drag an application that's already installed on your Mac from one folder to another, or from one computer on the local network to another. We'll walk through each instance one at a time.

One of the most common ways you'll get new software is on a **CD.** This kind of CD almost always has an "installer" file that will do the installation with very little help from you. It's great. Generally you should quit all other applications while you install new software.

To install an application from a CD:

1. Insert the CD into the drive, label-side upwards. It takes a few seconds for the CD icon to appear on your Desktop. (If you changed the Finder preferences so "removable media" does not show up on your Desktop, click the Computer icon in a Finder window to see the CD icon.)

   The install window often pops open automatically, as shown below. If it doesn't, double-click the CD icon.

Adobe® InDesign®
*This is the CD
I used to install
Adobe InDesign.*

An install CD typically has an "installer" icon at the top of the window. There are lots of other files on the CD, but you can ignore them all except the installer.

After you install, you might want to see if there is documentation on this CD that you can print, or other useful tools that need to be installed.

2. Double-click the installer icon. You will be asked to agree with the license agreement, and you have to tell the installer where to put the application (choose where to put it based on the restrictions mentioned on the opposite page).

*If the location
described here is not
where you want to
store the application,
click the menu button
and navigate to the
folder you want.*

3. You will usually have to enter your registration number. Once you do that, the installer will whiz merrily along. Often you must restart after installing new software.

Tip: You'll find the registration number with the documentation that came with the CD. The number is typically a combination of numbers and capital letters. Press the Caps Lock key down, and then you can type both letters and numbers without having to hold the Shift key down.

What is a disk image?

Often you won't know what type of file you're downloading until you see its name in the Download Manager, as shown on the next page.

*A **.sit** file is not a disk image, although it might unstuff into a .dmg. See page 306 for installing from a .sit.*

Tip: If your only copy of the software application is the downloaded version, make a backup of the .dmg or .img file before you throw it away. See pages 170–177 about making backups.

A **disk image** is a file that has been compressed, or made smaller for faster transmission across the Internet or to fit onto a removable disk. It is a special file that temporarily looks and acts like a removable hard disk. When you open the uncompressed disk image into its disk window, you'll find the installer for installing the application (or other large file).

The file extensions **.img, .dmg,** and **.dmg.gz** indicate files that will uncompress to disk images. In your Utilities folder you have a small application called Disk Copy that opens these files. Most of the time you can just double-click the disk image file and it will automatically open Disk Copy, uncompress, and quit Disk Copy.

The **.dmg** files are specifically for use with Mac OS X—don't try to open them in Classic or Mac OS 9.

The file extension **.smi** stands for self-mounting image, which means you do not have to use an application such as Disk Copy—the files will automatically uncompress themselves into the disk image.

After the software is successfully installed, you can **throw away** the .dmg or .smi files, as well as the disk image in the Computer window. To throw away the disk image, press Command E as if ejecting the disk, or drag it to the Trash basket.

OmniWeb-4.0.5.dmg   OmniWeb-4.0.5.dmg.gz   AppleWorks 6.2.1.smi

These are examples of disk image files. After you have successfully installed the application, you can throw these away.

*The icon circled above looks like a typical removable disk, such as a Zip disk or Jaz disk. But it is actually a **disk image.** After the software has been installed, you can throw this away. Press Command E as if to eject the disk, and it will disappear.*

When you download a large software file from the Internet, you will typically download a compressed **disk image.** This might seem confusing at first, but if you just follow the simple steps it all works itself out. Below and on the following pages are examples of downloading and installing two different types of disk images.

To download and install software from the Internet:

1. In this example, I'll download the free (and very sexy) web browser called OmniWeb, and then install it. The process is basically the same no matter where you download software, even if you buy it at an online store. Follow the links on the web site of your choice until you find a link called something like "Download Now."

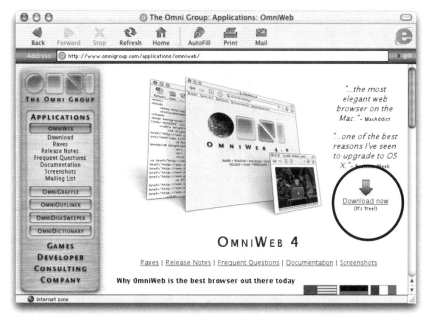

On OmniWeb's site (www.omnigroup.com), this is what the page looks like today, as I write this. It will undoubtedly change.

2. The Download Manager might or might not appear in front of you. If it doesn't and you're using Internet Explorer, go to the Window menu and choose "Download Manager." You don't have to do this, but it's comforting to be able to see the progress of your download. If what you're downloading is a "disk image," the file will have an extension of .dmg or .smi.

File	Status	Time	Transferred
✓ downloadSingle	Complete	21 Minutes	15.9 MB
OmniWeb.dmg.gz		4 Minutes	347 KB of 4.1 MB, 14 KB/sec

Notice the extension on the file name that tells you what sort of file you are downloading! (A .gz file indicates a file that is compressed with a certain type of compression by GZIP.)

OmniWeb-4.0.5.dmg.gz

Disk Copy

OmniWeb-4.0.5.dmg

3. When the file has finished downloading, you'll see an image like the one shown to the left, **A.** (If you downloaded an .smi file, see the following page; for .sit files, see page 306.)

Double-click the .dmg (or .img) file and it will automatically open the utility called Disk Copy, **B,** and uncompress; Disk Copy will automatically quit when finished.

4. The .dmg.gz uncompressed into the typical disk image file icon, **C.** Double-click it.

5. In your Computer window you will now see the image of a removable hard disk, **D**—this is the actual disk image.

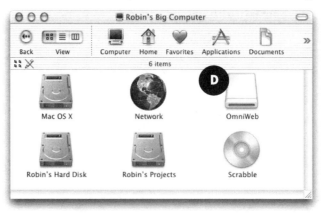

6. Keep going—we're almost there. Double-click on the disk image and it opens to a window, just like any other disk. Below you see the window for the OmniWeb disk image. Just do as it says— in this case, drag the icon and drop it into your Applications folder.

OmniWeb

After the installation is complete, you will have a folder or an icon in the designated Applications folder.

You could drag this installer icon and just drop it directly on the Applications icon in the Toolbar.

7. Now in your Applications folder you have the installed application, as indicated by a folder or icon for the application.

Some disk image files you will download will be in the **.smi** format, which means they are self-extracting and don't need a separate application, such as Disk Copy, to open them.

To download and install an .smi file:

1. Click the download link on the web page. As mentioned on page 303, you might or might not see the Download Manager.

2. A file with an extension of .smi will appear on your Desktop. It will automatically open Disk Copy and unstuff itself. (If it doesn't work automatically, double-click the .smi file.)

AppleWorks 6.2.1.smi

This file will automatically open Disk Copy.

3. You will see the disk image on your Desktop and/or in your Computer window, as shown below. Double-click the disk image.

4. The disk image opens to a window with an installer (sometimes called an "updater") in it. Double-click the installer and it will install (or in the example below, update) the application.

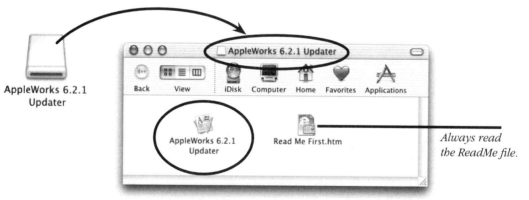

AppleWorks 6.2.1 Updater

Always read the ReadMe file.

Remember, you can throw away the disk image and the .smi file after the software has successfully been installed.

If this is your only copy of the software, you should probably make a backup of the .smi file (not the disk image itself).

Install from a .sit file   You don't always know what kind of file you will end up with when you download stuff off the Internet. A **.sit file** is created using the compression utility named StuffIt Deluxe. You have StuffIt Expander on your Mac so you can automatically download any .sit file.

To download and install a .sit file:

1. Find the software you need on the web and click its download link. As mentioned on page 303, you might or might not see the Download Manager.

This tells me I can find the file in my Home folder (indicated by the tilde ~), inside the folder named Desktop, and the downloaded file is called ar500enu.sit.

I love this Download Manager in OmniWeb because it tells me where the file is being downloaded to so I can find it, what its name is, and as a shortcut, I can click the button "Reveal in Finder" and the file I just downloaded will appear in front of me. This is really important because, as you can see, the downloaded file name is so weird I would never find it if I went looking for it. The file I am downloading is Acrobat Reader!

2. Your Mac and most browsers cooperate when you download a .sit file to make the file unstuff itself automatically. The .sit files don't use Disk Copy, like the disk images do —.sit files use StuffIt. In your Utilities folder is a copy of StuffIt Expander; if a .sit doesn't unstuff automatically, drag the file and drop it on top of StuffIt Expander and it will unstuff.

When I downloaded the file for Acrobat Reader, these two files appeared on my Desktop. "They" automatically unstuffed to give me the installer you see below.

Tip: If your only copy of the software application is the downloaded version, make a backup of the installer file before you throw it away.

3. Below is the installer that automatically appeared on my Desktop. I can double-click it to install the free application Acrobat Reader. When software is free, you don't need a registration number. You will be asked where you want to install the file.

Acrobat Reader Installer

When the software is successfully installed, you can throw away the installer and any .sit files that are still sitting on your Mac.

I sometimes keep the installers (not the .sit files) in a special folder just in case I ever need them again.

If you have software already installed on a Mac running OS X, it is sometimes possible to **drag** that software folder to another Mac through your file sharing connection, or drag it from a Zip disk onto another Mac. This isn't the best way to install most software because many applications put files in various Library folders as they go through the installation process, but it will usually work. Remember, though, that when you buy software, you don't really buy the *software*—you buy the *right* to use that software on *one* computer, so you can't be dragging your $600 version of Photoshop onto all your friends' computers. You can, however, give all your friends a copy of **freeware** (such as Acrobat Reader) or **shareware** programs, provided your friends know where to send their small shareware fee.

There is one important thing to know about dragging software files or folders from one Mac to another. Every file or folder, when dragged to another computer, comes along with its **access privileges.** These access privileges can limit who uses the software. If it's an extremely useful freeware product such as Acrobat Reader and you plan to install it into the general Applications folder so everyone can use it, you want to make sure it is acessible to everyone who uses that Mac. You must be the Admin user to change the privileges.

To make sure all users have privileges to use an application:

1. Click once on the folder that stores the application. If the application does not come in its own folder, click once on the application itself.

Click on the application folder to check the privileges.

AppleWorks 6

2. Press Command I to get the Show Info box. In the menu in that box, choose "Privileges," as shown to the right.

3. Make sure the privileges are set so "Everyone" can "Read & Write."

4. Click the button to "Apply" these privileges to all enclosed folders so the application has no trouble accessing its dictionary, templates, and other folders as it works.

For details about privileges and what they all mean, see Chapter 35.

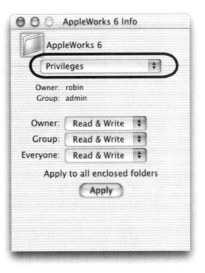

Install by dragging

Shareware *is software that is distributed freely. If you install it, use it, like it, and decide to keep it, you have a moral obligation to check the ReadMe file that came with the software and send its author their small fee, usually something like $5 to $20.*

If You Forgot a Password

After you **forget your password** for this or for that a few times, you get in the habit of writing it down. By the time you read this page, it's probably too late and you've totally and utterly forgotten your password, or one of the users on your Mac forgot his.

Change a user's password

The main Administrator of the computer (the first Admin, the one who first turned on the machine and set it up) can change the password of a user or of a secondary Administrator.

To change a user's password:

1. You must be the main Admin of this computer, or have the name and password of the Admin so you can log in as Administrator.

2. Open the Users preferences (from the Apple menu, choose "System Preferences…," then click "Users").

3. Click once on the user's name, then click the "Edit User…" button.

4. Click the "Password" tab.

5. Delete the existing password, then type in the new password in both edit boxes ("Password" and "Verify").

6. Click the "Save" button.

After you click the "Save" button, you may get the message shown below:

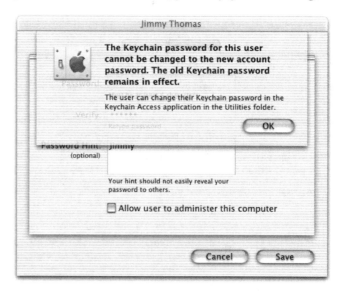

If you have never used and never plan to use Keychain Access, this doesn't matter anyway. If you have no idea what Keychain Access is, you're not using it. See pages 508–516 if you want to know and need to change the password.

It's not quite so easy to **change the main Administrator's password.** You need the original Mac OS X installer CD, not the 10.1 update CD. You don't need to be the Admin to do this, which means anyone with the original CD can change the Admin password, so protect your copy of the CD from unauthorized hands.

Change the main Admin password

To change the original Administrator's password:

1. Start up the Mac with the original installer CD for Mac OS X (put the disk in, restart, hold the C key down).

2. When the first install window finally appears, ignore it. Notice in the upper-left corner, next to the Apple, there is a menu item called "Installer." From that Installer menu, choose "Reset Password...."

3. In the dialog box that appears, click once on the hard disk icon that stores your OS X system.

4. Below the icons of the hard disks, there is a menu that lists all the users of your Mac. Choose "System Administrator (root)" from that menu.

5. Enter the new password in both of the edit boxes.

6. Click the Save button.

7. Go back to the Installer menu and choose "Quit Installer," or press Command Q. You will be given an option to Restart your Mac. Go ahead and restart, and this time, *write down your password!*

1. Can there be more than one Administrator on one Mac?

_____

2. Can regular users create more users?

_____

3. Why is it important to make sure the short name is the one you really want before you click Save?

_____

4. How do you know which Administrator is the main, original one?

_____

5. Why is "dog food" not a good password?

_____

6. If the password is "2002mtxlpk," would "2002MtxlpK" get you in?

_____

7. Which preferences pane do you use to assign Admin status?

_____

8. If you delete a user, do you delete all of their files?

_____

9. If you want all users of this Mac to be able to use an application, where should you install it?

_____

10. If you want only a specific user to have access to a certain application, where should you install it?

_____

Answers on page 752.

Customizing Your Mac with System Preferences

The **System Preferences** allow you to change the settings of a number of features on your computer. This will become a familiar process to you as you work with your Mac. You might want to skim through this chapter to learn what each of the various preferences offer, then come back when you decide you want to change something.

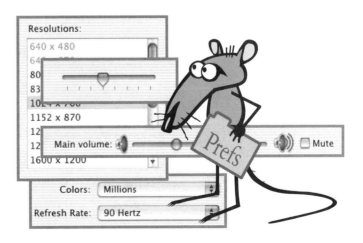

System Preferences

The **System Preferences** pane holds all of the individual preferences. If you are an experienced Mac OS 9 user, you'll recognize these as the replacements to the control panels.

To open System Preferences:

This is the System Preferences icon that is probably in the Dock.

▼ The icon shown to the left should be in your Dock. Click once on it.

▼ You can always go to the Apple menu and choose "System Preferences...."

The "favorites toolbar" across the top can be **customized:**

▼ **To add** a preference to the toolbar for easier access, drag any icon from the pane up into the toolbar.

▼ **To remove** a preference from the toolbar, drag any icon off of the toolbar and drop it on the Desktop.

▼ **To hide the Toolbar** altogether, go to the View menu and choose "Hide Toolbar," or click the Hide/Show Toolbar button in the upper-right of the window.

This is the favorites toolbar. Many Mac OS X applications have their own favorites toolbar like this, and they can always be customized.

*Single-click any icon to open its preference pane. The new pane will **replace** this one you see. **To come back to this pane,** single-click the "Show All" button in the upper-left of the window, or press Command L.*

Once System Preferences is open, you can use the "View" menu to choose different preference panes, even if the main pane is closed.

The **Personal** set of System Preferences are those that change the look of your screen and its various parts, which include the **Desktop, Dock, General,** and **Screen Saver** panes. This is also where you access the **Login** preferences for multiple users. The **International** preferences can change the language that appears in all the menus, dialog boxes, and even on the keyboard. **Universal Access** provides features that make it easier for people who have trouble using the keyboard with two hands or find using the mouse to be difficult. These are either explained below, or there is a note telling you where else in the book you will find detailed information.

Personal

Use the **Desktop** preferences to change the color of your background on the monitor. Instead of a color, you can choose a photograph or an abstract image. You can also use any photo or graphic image of your choice. Just put that photo or image in your Pictures folder, then choose "Pictures Folder" from the Collection menu (circled, below) to add the photo. For details on how to use these Desktop preferences, see pages 127–128.

Desktop

Desktop

Drag a photo or graphic from anywhere on your Mac and drop it into this spot, called a "well," to turn it into your monitor's background. The original image will not be removed from its storage place.

Choose "Pictures Folder" from this menu to choose a photo or graphic image of your own.

Single-click on any image to turn it into the background image on your monitor.

The narrow images are designed for a cinema display. If you don't know what that is, you don't have one.

Dock

Dock

The **Dock** preferences pane lets you control several features of the Dock, including its size, whether it enlarges as your mouse rolls over it, where the Dock appears on your screen, and more. For explanations and illustrations of each feature, please see Chapter 8.

You can also access the Dock preferences two other ways:

▼ **Either** from the Apple menu, choose "Dock."

▼ **Or** hold down the Control key and click on the dividing line in the Dock.

Both of the techniques mentioned above give you a menu where you can choose several of the options you see in the preferences pane. Also in those menus you can call up this entire pane.

The "Magnification" setting, for example, adjusts how large these icons become as your mouse moves across them. If you leave the box unchecked, they do not enlarge at all.

The **General** preferences pane offers a variety of options, all of which have been discussed at other places in this book. If something in the pane doesn't make sense to you, please check the reference page for that item.

General

See page 136.

See page 72.

See page 136.

See page 136.

The **International** preferences pane actually allows you to change the menu bars, menus, and dialog boxes into other languages, as well as change the keyboard layout so you can type appropriately. You can also choose options to display the time, date, and numbers in the particular style of other languages. See pages 47–50 for full details.

International

The **Login** preferences pane is where you can set up other people to use the computer. All users get their own Home folders that no one else can access. All users can customize the Mac using any of these preference panes, and they even get their own Trash baskets that no one else can get into. There is a Shared folder that all users can access, and private Drop Boxes for sharing files. See Chapter 20 for all the details.

Login

Screen Saver

Screen Saver

The **Screen Saver** preferences let you set up a series of images that will automatically appear on your screen. The basic function of a screen saver is to prolong the life of your monitor and to prevent static images from being "burned" into the screen. But if you have a monitor that's newer than five years old (which you most probably do because monitors rarely live longer than five years), an image is not going to get burned into your screen even if you left it on for a month. To prolong the life of your monitor, especially flat screen displays, you should probably use the Energy Saver monitor option (see page 325).

Although the screen saver is not necessary to protect the *monitor,* you can use it to protect the *data* on your computer by **requiring a password:** After the screen saver automatically activates, a person would have to enter a password before the screen saver would go away.

And even though it's not necessary, this screen saver is really quite lovely and makes for a nice look in an office with all the monitors dissolving into various photos of beaches and forest and the universe. If you are a web designer, make screen shots of your web sites (see page 518) and use them as the screen saver to impress your clients. If you're an illustrator or photographer, user your own images as the screen saver.

If you want your Mac to go to sleep to save energy after a certain amount of time, use the Energy Saver, described on page 325. It will go to sleep even if the screen saver is active.

To turn off the screen saver so you can work again, click anywhere, tap a key, or wiggle the mouse.

See page 325 for information about the Energy Saver preferences pane.

Below are explanations of the screen savers that are prepared for you.

▼ **Basic:** This displays a dark gray screen with an Apple logo and the computer's "name." For instance, mine says "Robin's Friend." If you want to change the name that is displayed, go to the Sharing preferences pane and change the "Computer Name."

▼ **Aqua Icons:** This makes a screen saver out of the icons on your Mac. Click the "Configure" button to get a little dialog box with several self-explanatory options.

▼ **Abstract, Beach, Cosmos, Forest:** These are photos supplied by Apple for your enjoyment. You cannot configure anything with these sets.

▼ **Slide Show:** This automatically uses any images you have stored in the Pictures folder in your Home area. If you want to use a select few of your images as your screen saver, do this:

1. Go to the Desktop and make a new folder inside the Pictures folder: Open the Pictures folder and press Command Shift N.

2. Name the new folder something like "My Screen Saver."

3. Put the images (or copies of the images) you want to appear in the screen saver inside this new folder.

4. Go back to the Screen Saver preferences pane and click once on "Slide Show."

5. Click the "Configure" button. It automatically opens to the Pictures folder, as shown below. Find your new folder to the right of Pictures and single-click it, then click "Open."

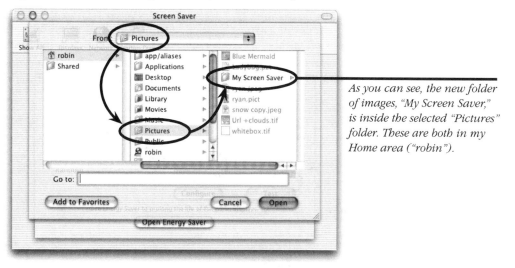

As you can see, the new folder of images, "My Screen Saver," is inside the selected "Pictures" folder. These are both in my Home area ("robin").

▼ **Random:** Choose Random and the Mac will randomly select from one of the various screen savers in the list. Every time the screen saver turns on, you'll get a different one.

—continued

Screen Saver Activation

You can determine **when** you want the screen saver to automatically appear, and whether or not to require a **password.** The password that will wake the screen saver is the password for the current user.

If you are the only user, you were asked to provide a password and a hint when you first set up your Mac. If you've *forgotten* your password and need a hint, see page 292. If you *don't know* the password even if someone gave you a hint, see pages 308 and 309.

Drag the slider bar to one of these time slots. When you don't use your Mac for that period of time, the screen saver will automatically start.

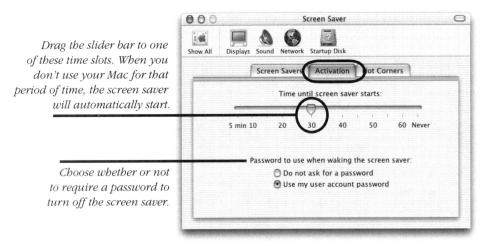

Choose whether or not to require a password to turn off the screen saver.

Screen Saver Hot Corners

The **Hot Corners** pane lets you select a corner that will **turn on** your screen saver when you shove the mouse into it. For instance, in the example below there is a checkmark in the upper-right corner of the screen image. If you push your mouse into that corner (*without* pressing the mouse button down), the screen saver instantly activates without waiting for the pre-scribed period of time, as chosen above. If you set a hot corner with a minus sign, you can shove your mouse into that corner and the screen saver **will not activate** as long as the mouse stays in that corner, even if the time's up.

To check the boxes:

If a checkbox corner is empty, click once to put a check in it.

Click once again to change the check to a minus.

Click once again to clear the checkbox.

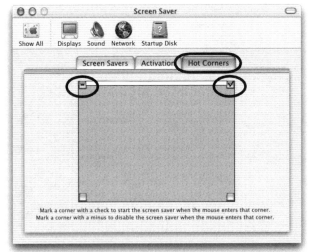

The **Universal Access** preferences pane makes using keyboard shortcuts and the mouse easier for people who find it difficult. For instance, keyboard shortcuts often require that two or three keys be held down at once, and then tap yet another key. This can be impossible for many users. Also, some people cannot use the mouse for one reason or another. In the Mouse pane of Universal Access, you can switch to using the numeric keypad to move the cursor up, down, left, or right. If you or anyone you know needs to have their Mac adjusted for these issues, use these preferences.

Universal Access

Universal
Access

Keyboard: "Sticky Keys" has been on the Mac for almost forever. This is what it does: You press the Shift key five times in a row. It doesn't matter how fast or slow you press it. After five times, you'll hear a little beepy musical that tells you Sticky Keys is now activated. Then, let's say you want to make a new folder in a Finder window; the keyboard shortcut is Command Shift N. Just tap the Command key, then tap the Shift key, then tap the N key.

Universal Access Keyboard

Tap the Shift key five more times when you want to turn off Sticky Keys.

If you have the two checkboxes shown below checked, to **beep** and to **show pressed keys,** then you will hear a small beep when the modifier key has been tapped, and you will see an image of the key(s) appear in the upper-right corner of the monitor (shown to the right).

You'll see images of the modifier keys as you type them.

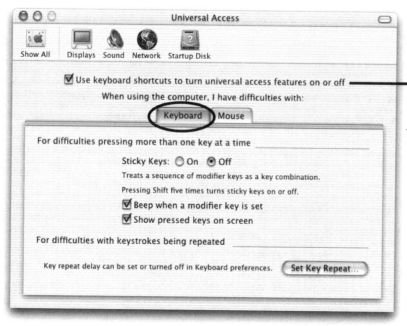

This box is checked by default. It means you can press the Shift key five times to turn Sticky Keys on. If this box is unchecked, you will have to open this preferences pane to turn Sticky Keys on.

If keys are repeating across the page and you don't want them to, click the "Set Key Repeat..." button, which opens the Keyboard preferences. On the right side of that pane, slide the "Delay Until Repeat" bar over to the left, all the way to "None," as shown on page 42.

—continued

Universal Access Mouse   If you or someone you know has trouble using a mouse, you can turn on the Universal Access features and use the numeric keypad to guide the mouse pointer. You can even select items and drag things around.

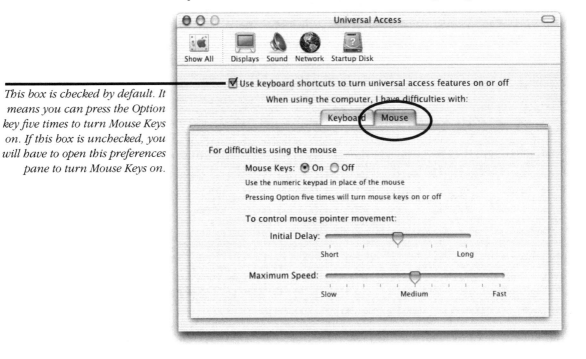

This box is checked by default. It means you can press the Option key five times to turn Mouse Keys on. If this box is unchecked, you will have to open this preferences pane to turn Mouse Keys on.

Mouse Keys: Tap the Option key five times to turn "Mouse Keys" on. Now tapping on the numeric keypad will move the pointer around the screen. If you think of the number 5 as the center of a wheel with spokes radiating out, that is how the numbers around the 5 in the keypad will move the pointer. See below.

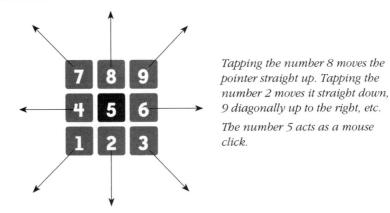

Tapping the number 8 moves the pointer straight up. Tapping the number 2 moves it straight down, 9 diagonally up to the right, etc.

The number 5 acts as a mouse click.

To click the mouse: Tap the number 5.

To select an item to drag it: Position the pointer on the item you want to drag. Then tap the 0 (zero) key. Use the number keys to drag the item. This works to drag windows around, to move the scroll slider bars, to access and select from menus, and even to select text, as explained below.

To let go of an item you're dragging: Tap the decimal point (.).

To select a command in a menu:

1. Use the number keys to position the pointer on the menu name.
2. Tap the 5 key to select the menu, which pops it open.
3. Use the number keys to slide the pointer to the command you want.
4. Tap the 5 key to activate the command.

To select text:

1. Use the number keys to position the pointer in the text.
2. Tap the 5 to set the insertion point down.
3. Tap the 0 (zero) so you can start dragging/selecting.
4. Use the number keys to move the insertion point over the text; you'll notice the text highlights as the insertion point moves.
5. When you have selected the text you want, tap the decimal point (.). Now you can use the pointer to change the font, the size, delete or replace the text, etc.
6. To deselect the text, tap 5.

The other two options in the Mouse pane of Universal Access let you control the **initial delay,** or how long it takes after you tap the number key to actually make the pointer move. If your hands are quick, make it a short delay so as soon as you tap the key, the pointer takes off. If you have trouble tapping the numbers very quickly, then give it a longer delay so the pointer doesn't run away before you know where it's going.

Set the **maximum speed** that you want the pointer to whiz across the screen. Again, if your hands are quick and confident, let it speed along at a fast pace. If you want it to move more slowly so you have more time to react, set a lower speed.

Hardware
The **Hardware** preferences include *ColorSync, Displays,* and *Energy Saver,* which all have to do with your monitor. You can also customize the *Keyboard* and *Mouse,* as well as the *Sound.*

ColorSync

ColorSync is an industry-standard color management technology that creates "profiles" embedded in color files. The profiles contain information used by scanners, monitors, presses, high-end copiers, and other hardware. In the process of creating catalogs, web pages, magazines, books, videos, Quick-Time movies, transparencies, and other creative media, this standard helps to ensure that the color you or anyone in the entire workgroup sees on all machines and output on all projects is as similar as possible.

Exactly how to use ColorSync is beyond the scope of this book. If you are a professional who needs to take advantage of this technology, you'll find lots of information at **www.apple.com/colorsync.**

Displays

The **Displays** preferences give you various controls, depending on the type of monitor you have. If you don't see some of what's shown here, like the "Geometry" section, you probably have those controls built into your monitor somewhere else—check your monitor manual.

You will certainly have the options to change the colors and the resolutions of your monitor display. Here are explanations of typical settings you might find in your preferences pane.

Resolutions: You may be accustomed to working with the resolution of a printer or output device, where more dots per inch make an image look better. But the term resolution as applied to a monitor is something completely different. The measurements here are pixels per inch; a pixel is a tiny unit on your monitor, like a tiny square. The more pixels you display on the screen, the *smaller* everything looks, so if you want to fit more stuff on the screen, choose a higher resolution (1024 x 768). If you want everything to look *larger,* choose a lower resolution (800 x 600).

Colors: Switch between thousands and millions of colors. The more colors, the more "resolved," or better-looking, photographs and other digital images will appear. If you don't have much RAM (memory), use thousands because it takes more memory to create millions of colors. Using thousands of colors instead of millions can also make everything in the Finder work a little faster, especially if you have a larger monitor.

Refresh Rate: Your monitor redraws the entire screen many times per second; this is called the "refresh rate." If your refresh rate is too slow, it makes the screen appear to vibrate (and gives me a big headache).

Show modes recommended by display: It's possible to have a long list of resolution options, but that doesn't necessarily mean your monitor can actually display all of those various options. To see only the resolutions that your particular monitor can display, check this box.

Show displays in menu bar: Check this box to put a small icon on the right side of your menu bar that gives you a menu with the choices of colors and resolutions. You can also open the Displays preferences from this menu.

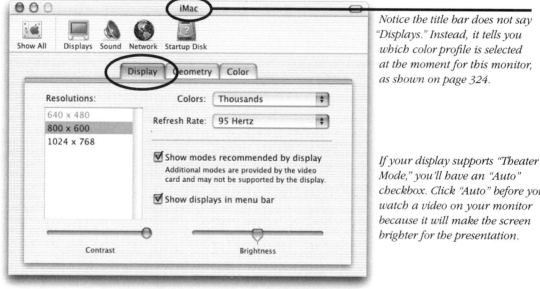

Notice the title bar does not say "Displays." Instead, it tells you which color profile is selected at the moment for this monitor, as shown on page 324.

If your display supports "Theater Mode," you'll have an "Auto" checkbox. Click "Auto" before you watch a video on your monitor because it will make the screen brighter for the presentation.

With these Contrast and Brightness controls, you can obviously adjust the contrast and brightness. If your Displays pane doesn't have these, your monitor has its own controls (read the manual for your monitor).

—Displays continues

If you have a **Geometry** tab, experiment with the buttons and arrows—if you mess things up, just press the "Factory Defaults" button to take the monitor back to its original state. You can move the monitor image up or down or left or right, expand or contract it, rotate it, fix a keystone (where the image appears wider or narrower at the top than at the bottom), and more. If you find that the black edges are slowly encroaching upon your image area, use the "Height/Width" button and arrows to fix it.

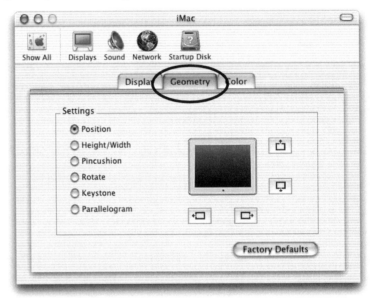

The **Color** tab lets you choose a ColorSync profile, if you know what that is and why you might need to do it sometimes. Only rare graphics professionals need to change the profile. If you're one of those, you know what to do here. If you don't have a clue what color profiles are, never mind. If you want to know more, go to **www.apple.com/colorsync**.

The color profile selected here is the one that all of these settings will affect, as shown by its name in the title bar.

Click "Calibrate" to adjust the color settings. Most of it is self-explanatory.

The **Energy Saver** preferences let you determine when or if your Mac goes to sleep to save energy. When it goes to sleep, the screen turns completely black. **To wake it up,** hit any key or click the mouse.

There are actually two different pieces of your Mac that go to sleep: the monitor (display) and the hard disk. The monitor wakes up pretty fast, but if the hard disk goes to sleep, it can be mildy irritating waiting for it to spin back up again (gosh, it could take a whole minute). You might want your monitor to go to sleep after ten minutes of inactivity, which would kick in when you go for a short break. But you might want the hard disk to keep spinning until at least twenty minutes has gone by just to make sure it doesn't go to sleep every time you run down the hall.

Many people prefer to let their machine go to sleep at night instead of shutting it down. You might want to set it to sleep after one hour of inactivity so after you leave work, you can rest assured that your Mac will sleep even if you forgot to tell it to.

Energy Saver

You can always choose to put the Mac to sleep instantly: from the Apple menu, choose "Sleep," or press Command Shift 0 (zero).

Note: Sleep will kick in even if the screen saver is active.

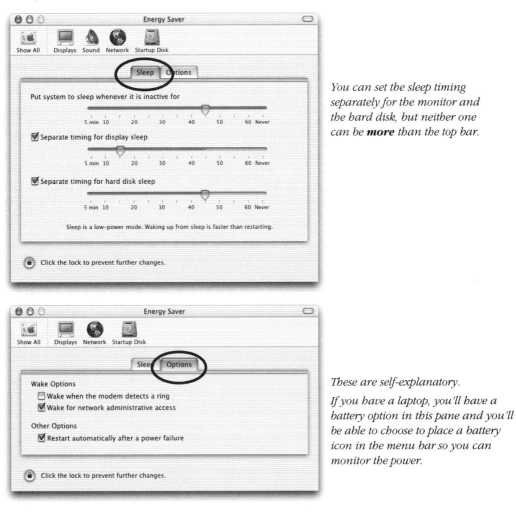

*You can set the sleep timing separately for the monitor and the hard disk, but neither one can be **more** than the top bar.*

These are self-explanatory.

If you have a laptop, you'll have a battery option in this pane and you'll be able to choose to place a battery icon in the menu bar so you can monitor the power.

Keyboard

The **Keyboard** preferences let you decide how fast keys will repeat when you hold them down, and how long it takes before they start to repeat. This is useful if you tend to be heavy on the keys—if you find you often type more than one of the same character in a row, or too many spaces between words, go to the Keyboard preferences. You can also choose to turn on Full Keyboard Access, which lets you select and activat items using the keyboard, without having to pick up the mouse. Details of all these features are explained on pages 42–44.

Mouse or Trackpad

The **Mouse** preferences are explained in detail on pages 28 and 29, along with the **Trackpad** preferences on page 30, if you're using a laptop. You can make the mouse move "faster" along the screen as you move the mouse across a mouse pad—when it moves "faster," you don't have to move your hand so far to make the mouse move across the screen.

If you find you have trouble making the mouse double-click because your hands are a little slow, slow down the double-click speed. See Chapter 3 if you need more details.

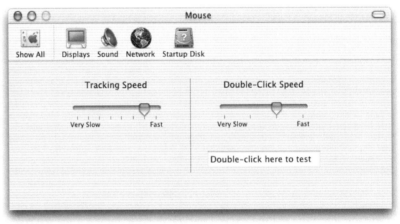

If you're doing precise work in a photo-editing application, for instance, you might want to make the mouse move slower. If you use a drawing tablet, you'll probably find that a slower mouse speed works better because it is in more direct proportion to your hand movements.

The **Sound** preferences let you choose an alert sound (the sound you hear when the Mac wants to yell at you about something), how loud that alert is, and how loud the general sounds on your Macintosh are, like music and video. You can also choose to put a sound volume icon in the menu bar so you don't have to open this preferences pane to change the volume.

Sound

Sound

Notice you have **two volume settings!** One is for the alert sounds, and the other is the main volume control on your computer.

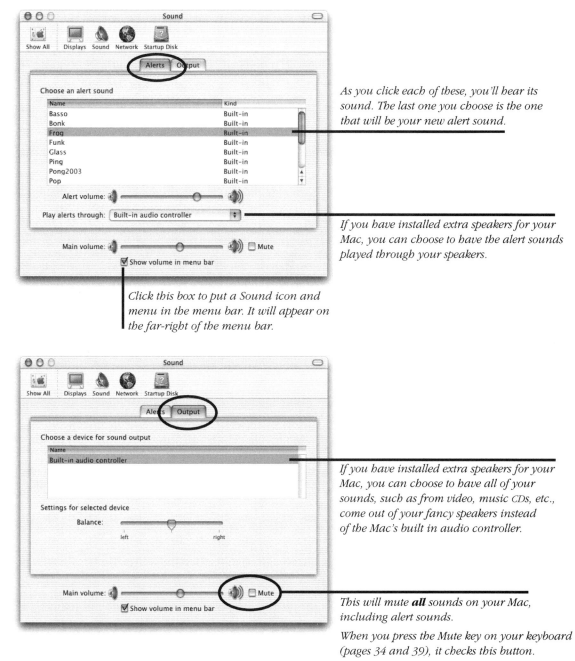

As you click each of these, you'll hear its sound. The last one you choose is the one that will be your new alert sound.

If you have installed extra speakers for your Mac, you can choose to have the alert sounds played through your speakers.

Click this box to put a Sound icon and menu in the menu bar. It will appear on the far-right of the menu bar.

If you have installed extra speakers for your Mac, you can choose to have all of your sounds, such as from video, music CDs, etc., come out of your fancy speakers instead of the Mac's built in audio controller.

*This will mute **all** sounds on your Mac, including alert sounds.*

When you press the Mute key on your keyboard (pages 34 and 39), it checks this button.

Internet & Network

The **Internet & Network** preferences cover the settings for connecting you to the *Internet,* for connecting *(networking)* the computers in your office, for *sharing* files between local computers once they're connected, and for using *QuickTime.*

Internet

The **Internet** preferences are explained in Chapters 31 through 37 (check the index for a particular feature). Here is where you can sign up for an iTools account, if you haven't already, which gives you access to Apple's great email greeting cards, storage space on their server so you can share files with other Mac users, and more. This is also where you'll set up your email specifics, your web preferences, plus the setting for newsgroups if you want to take advantage of them. All of these things and more are explained in the Internet chapters.

Having an iTools account is free, so why not?

The **Network** preferences apply to both your Internet connection (some-times) and to your local area network (LAN) that you might have in your small office or home office. If you are on a big network, you'll probably want to talk with your network administrator before changing anything in these panes.

Network

Network

Everything in this preferences pane has been explained elsewhere in the book, in context to networking and connecting. Please see Chapter 36 about networking several computers together in a small office to share files, and Chapter 31 about connecting to the Internet.

```
┌─────────────────────────────────────────────────────────────────┐
│ ⊖ ⊙ ○                        Network                         ⊂⊃  │
│  ┌──┐  ┌──┐  ⊙  ⊙  ┌──┐                                          │
│  Show All  Displays  Sound  Network  Startup Disk               │
│                                                                   │
│              Location: │ Office network        ▼│                │
│                                                                   │
│     Show: │ Built-in Ethernet              ▼│                    │
│                                                                   │
│          ┌ TCP/IP ┐ PPPoE ┐ AppleTalk ┐ Proxies ┐               │
│                                                                   │
│       Configure: │ Manually              ▼│                      │
│                                                                   │
│                          Domain Name Servers (Optional)          │
│       IP Address: │ 192.168.0.18 │    ┌──────────────────┐      │
│                                       │                  │      │
│      Subnet Mask: │ 255.255.255.0 │   └──────────────────┘      │
│                                                                   │
│          Router: │ 192.168.0.1 │     Search Domains  (Optional)  │
│                                       ┌──────────────────┐      │
│                                       │                  │      │
│                                       └──────────────────┘      │
│                                                                   │
│   Ethernet Address: 00:0a:27:96:a5:00   Example: apple.com, earthlink.net │
│                                                                   │
│  🔒 Click the lock to prevent further changes.     ( Apply Now )  │
└─────────────────────────────────────────────────────────────────┘
```

QuickTime

QuickTime, briefly, is software that plays audio and video files on your computer. QuickTime is also a technology standard for delivering "streaming" audio and video. Ordinarily, an audio/video file has to completely download to your hard drive before it will play. If the media file is streaming, data is displayed as it arrives, but does not remain on your hard disk.

QuickTime Plug-In

The **Plug-In** settings affect the behavior of QuickTime in your web browser.

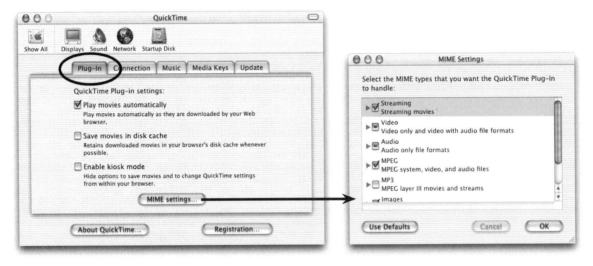

The **QuickTime Player** *application can play slide shows, audio and video files, live streaming content, virtual reality files, and 3D media (see Chapter 29). The "Pro" version of QuickTime is an authoring environment for creating and editing multimedia content.*

Play movies automatically: This is checked for you.

Save movies in disk cache: As explained, this option will keep downloaded movies in your browser's disk cache "whenever possible," making instant replay of downloaded movies possible instead of having to reload them. If you want to use this feature, you may need to find your browser's preferences and assign more space to your browser's cache.

Enable kiosk mode: When you're viewing a movie in a browser, you get a pop-up menu with various settings you can adjust. This checkbox disables that pop-up menu and hides options to save movies (including drag-and-drop copying of movies). This is useful in a classroom setting or when your grandkids are over so they don't fill your hard disk with big files.

MIME settings: MIMEs (Multi-purpose Internet Mail Extensions) identify different types of data so they can be handled appropriately by a server or by your own computer. The "MIME settings" pane lists general data type categories that you can choose to have QuickTime handle. Click the triangle to the left of the checkboxes for submenus of various file types that are included in each general category, plus each file's possible MIME types. Below each file type are extensions that are common to that kind of file. You can customize which file types you want handled by QuickTime by selectively clicking the main category checkboxes or the submenu boxes. To return to the default settings, click "Use Defaults."

The **Connection** settings affect the download speed and quality of QuickTime media playing in your web browser.

QuickTime Connection

Connection Speed helps QuickTime optimize the delivery of media to you, based on the limitations of your hardware and the speed of your connection to the Internet. From the menu, select the option that best describes your Internet connection.

Allow multiple simultaneous streams: This option is only available when the Connection Speed is set on one of the two modem (slowest) options. Unless you're really getting 56K from your modem connection (unlikely), you'll probably want to leave this option unchecked.

Transport Setup: This opens the "Streaming Transport Setup" window. These settings tell QuickTime which *protocol,* or set of rules, to use for getting data from one computer to another. UDP (User Datagram Protocol) and HTTP (HyperText Transfer Protocol) are communication protocols.

> *Auto Configure* will check your system and automatically make this, and the next two selections, for you.
>
> *RTSP* (Real-Time Streaming Protocol) insures the best performance of streaming data.
>
> *Port ID* is an identification number attached to the header of a streaming file, identifying the file type and enabling its identification and handling.

If your Internet connection is protected by a firewall, RTSP may not work. If not, select HTTP from the Transport Protocol options, then click "Auto Configure." If your computer cannot configure itself to your firewall, you may be able to use proxy server software to work around this problem. Apple provides proxy servers for most popular firewalls. Contact your network administrator for assistance.

QuickTime Music   If you have installed third-party **music** synthesizer software, it will appear in this list. To have music files handled by your favorite synthesizer, select its name in the list, then click "Make Default." Most people will have only the QuickTime Music Synthesizer that appears here.

QuickTime Media Key   QuickTime files are sometimes encoded by their creators with a password, or **media key,** that locks the file. To play secured media files such as this, you need to obtain the media key and file category information from the creator of the file and enter that information into the Media Keys pane. This will authorize your access to the file, allowing it to play.

To add media key information, click the "Add…" button. **To edit** existing media keys, click one in the list, then click "Edit…."

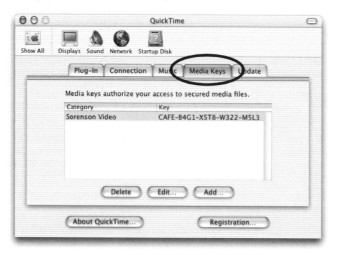

The **Update** pane makes it easy to check online for QuickTime software updates and to install QuickTime or third-party software.

QuickTime Update

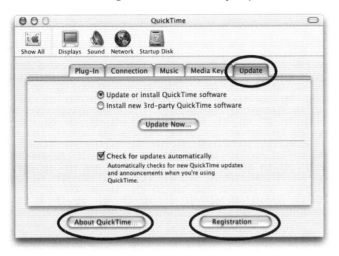

Click the **Update Now...** button and your computer will connect to the QuickTime web site to check for updates or to install new software from third parties (if you don't have a permanent connection, QuickTime will ask if you want to connect through your phone line). You can also choose to update anytime the QuickTime Player is open—use the application menu (the one that says "QuickTime Player").

Check for updates automatically checks for new or updated software anytime you're connected to the Internet and using QuickTime.

About QuickTime is simply a slide show of QuickTime developer logos and their web site address information.

The **Registration** button opens a window where you can enter your name and registration number, if you already have one. If you haven't registered your copy of QuickTime, click the "Register Online" button to go to the QuickTime web site where you can register and choose to upgrade to the Pro version for a small fee. When you register online and pay the Pro upgrade fee, you'll receive an email with a "key." The key is a number that you enter into the Registration pane to unlock the Pro features of QuickTime. If you just want to use the Player and don't think you'll need the content creation and editing features of the Pro version, don't register and pay for the upgrade. You can always do it later if you change your mind.

The **Sharing** preferences pane is where you set up your computer to connect to other computers in your home or office, and to set up your Web Sharing. You can rename your computer here, and find out your current IP address. See Chapters 35 through 37 for all the details about sharing files.

Sharing

Sharing

System   The **System** section includes preferences that control a number of software features on your Mac, including *Classic, Date & Time, Software Update, Speech, Startup Disk,* and *Users.*

Classic

Classic is the Mac OS 9 operating system that you'll need for the next few years until all of the software you use has been updated for OS X. When you open an OS 9 application, it will automatically open in Classic. Essentially, you will be switching between two different operating systems. If you have no OS 9 applications, you will never need to use Classic and you don't even need to install it.

If you do use Classic, I recommend you go to the preferences pane and tell it to automatically start up when you log in to your Mac. For all the details about working in the Classic environment, see Chapter 40.

Date & Time

The **Date & Time** preferences obviously allow you to set the date and time. This is important even if you personally don't care what the date is because your Mac uses these settings to do things like time-stamp all of your documents, make decisions about when to show you alerts you might have programmed in various applications (like when to pay bills), and when to time-out software you have downloaded.

Tip: You can also use the Clock feature to make an actual clock appear, either analog or digital as shown below. It can sit in the Dock or float around the Desktop. See page 470 for details.

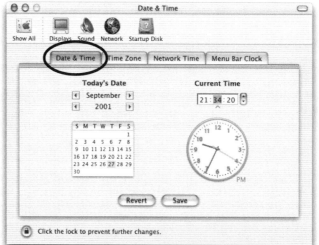

To change the date, *click the month and year arrows up or down, then click on a date in the month.*

To change the time, *click on the hour, minutes, or seconds, then either type the new number or use the arrow buttons. Or you can drag the hour and minute hands around the clock.*

When everything is correct, click the "Save" button.

If you cannot change the date or time *(and you want to), go to the "Network Time" pane, and uncheck the box, "Use a network time server."*

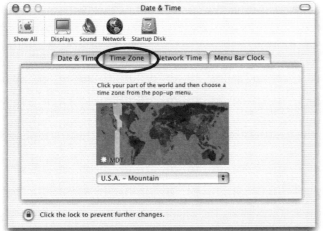

I guarantee you'll learn some interesting things about the world as you click on different areas. Do you know which small country has its own time zone? (IRT)

If you are in a time zone that switches between daylight savings time and not, your Mac will automatically make the switch for you.

If you have a full-time connection, such as DSL, cable, satellite, ISDN, T1, or similar, you can choose to connect to a network time server that will always make sure your computer displays exactly the correct time. Once you check this box, you will not be able to change the time in the "Date & Time" pane.

If you have a dial-up connection, don't check this box.

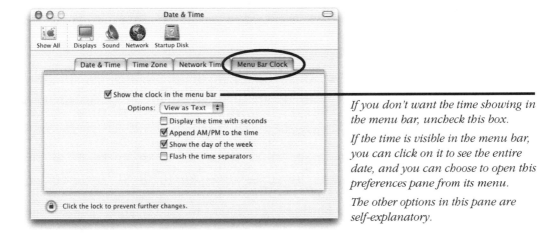

If you don't want the time showing in the menu bar, uncheck this box.

If the time is visible in the menu bar, you can click on it to see the entire date, and you can choose to open this preferences pane from its menu.

The other options in this pane are self-explanatory.

Software Update

The **Software Update** preferences let you determine when your computer will go to the Internet and check to see if any of your **Apple software** has downloadable versions of free updates. If you have a permanent connection, such as ISDN, DSL, T1 , cable, etc., then it is safe to tell your Mac to automatically check for updates.

If you have to dial-up to connect to the Internet, you should probably check the "Manually" option, then when you have time to let the computer go do its updating, log on through your dial-up and click the "Update Now" button.

This will show you a list of which files were updated and when.

From the Apple menu, you can choose "Get Mac OS X Software…." This command automatically opens Internet Explorer and takes you to an Apple web site where they keep track of software that is available for Mac OS X. You can choose to download these files. Most are free. See page 138 for details.

In the **Speech** preferences you can arrange to talk to your computer. Using your voice, you can open and close applications and windows, copy and paste, get your mail, ask the date or time, and more. You can make other applications listen to you, and if you know how to write AppleScripts, you can write new commands for applications. You can add spoken commands for any keyboard shortcut you see in the menu. The Mac will even tell you jokes. To teach you how to use Speech effectively would take a small book, so I'm afraid I'll just be able to give you a few tips here. You can find a lot of information in the Help files.

Speech

Speech

▼ The **voice** the computer uses is the one you choose in the Text-to-Speech pane, shown on page 339.

▼ Once you turn on "Apple Speakable Items," the round **feedback window** appears, as shown to the right.

To send this window down to the Dock, double-click it.

To get a list of commands that are ready for you to speak, click on the tiny arrow at the bottom of the feedback window and choose "Open Speech Commands window" (shown to the right).

—continued

Above is the feedback window, and below that is the list of commands already built in and ready for you to speak.

Unlike other voice recognition packages, you don't have to train Apple Speakable Items to learn your voice.

Listening You can choose that your Mac listens and responds to you only when you activate it with the "listening key," or you can make it stay on all the time so you can speak commands without having to hold down a key. The default listening key is the Escape key (esc).

When you choose the "Listening Method" to **Listen only while key is pressed,** that means you need to hold down the Escape key for about half a second to let the Mac know you are about to give a command (you don't have to hold it down the whole time). You hold Esc, let go, speak your command, and the computer will either activate your command or speak back to you.

If you plan to play the Chess game included in your Applications folder or you have other speakable applications you use throughout the day, you might want to change the "Listening Method" to **Key toggles listening on and off.** In this case you hold down the Escape key for about a second, which turns listening on *until* you hold down that key again. While listening is on, you must call the computer by name so it knows you are about to tell it something. The default name is "Computer." For instance, you would say, "Computer. Tell me a joke." Try it.

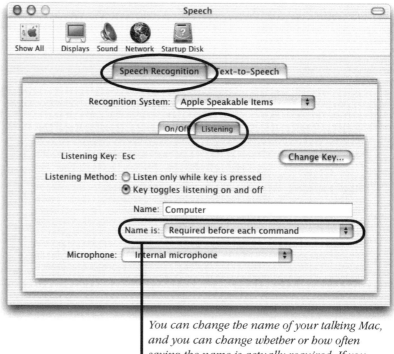

You can change the name of your talking Mac, and you can change whether or how often saying the name is actually required. If you work all by yourself and never speak out loud, you can choose not to say "Computer" at all.

In the **Text-to-Speech** pane, choose a voice for the computer to use. As you choose each one, it will say something out loud. You can adjust the speed at which most of them talk. You'll hear this voice whenever an application can speak to you, including the built-in voice recognition explained on the previous pages. Try this experiment:

Text-to-Speech

1. Open TextEdit.

2. Type something (it's really fun to type something naughty).

3. From the Edit menu, slide down to "Speech," then out to "Start speaking." If no text was selected, the speaker will read the entire page to you. If text was selected, just the selected text will be read.

Click on a voice and it will automatically speak something. The last one you choose is the one that will be the voice used for all speaking applications.

Startup Disk

The **Startup Disk** preferences pane lets you choose which disk you want your computer to start up from next time you restart or turn it on. If you have a CD inserted that holds an operating system, that CD will also appear in this pane. You might need to restart from a different operating system so you can update the system, fix problems, use Mac OS 9 instead of OS X, or other reasons.

Click once on an icon to select it as the startup disk. Next time you start up the computer, that will be the operating system.

Click the "Restart" button if you want to restart from the selected disk immediately.

The **Users** preferences pane is where you can create the special Home areas for multiple users of your computer. All users have their own Homes, their own Trash baskets, and can set their own preferences. You can even create login buttons with their photos. See Chapter 20 for all the details about using these preferences.

Users

Users

This shows there are two users of this computer at the moment. You can edit the preferences for each user at any time, and add new ones. You can delete any user except the Administrator.

Which preference pane would you use to accomplish each task below?

1. Make the mouse move more quickly over the screen without your hand having to move much at all.

2. Change the pattern of your Desktop.

3. Start file sharing between several computers.

4. Change the rate of how fast a keyboard character will repeat across the page when you hold the key down.

5. Enlarge or reduce everything you see on the screen.

6. Change the time that shows up in your menu bar.

7. Create a separate and private area on your Mac for someone else who will be using the computer.

8. Set up a new iTools account.

9. Change the settings for your Internet connection.

10. Choose special preferences to make the mouse and keyboard easier to use for people with challenges.

Answers on page 752.

Using Aliases

Aliases are one of the greatest features of the Mac. An alias is an icon that represents the real thing—you double-click the alias and it goes and gets the real thing and opens it. This can make your life so much easier because you can put the aliases in easy-to-access places and so get to your most-used files very quickly without having to dig down into folders.

For instance, let's say you're working on a newsletter for your greenhouse enterprise and you have an "April Newsletter" folder. Inside this folder is a PageMaker file for the newsletter itself, plus all of the word processing stories and all of the photographs that will be dropped into the newsletter file. This "April Newsletter" folder is stored in your Home area, inside the Documents folder, inside the "Greenhouse" folder. Instead of having to dig down into all of those folders to get to the PageMaker file, make an alias of the PageMaker file and put the alias right on your Desktop. Then you'll just double-click the alias to open the newsletter and get right to work.

Aliases are very easy to create and work with, so take advantage of them!

What is an Alias?

An **alias** is an "empty" icon that represents the real thing. Aliases are especially useful for applications. You see, most applications must stay in the folder they were installed into because when the application opens, it calls upon resources within its folder. If you store the application icon itself (without all of its resource files) in a different folder or on your Desktop, you run the risk that the application won't be able to function properly. That's where the alias comes in: You make an alias, which *represents* the application, and you can put that alias anywhere. In fact, you can make a dozen aliases of the same application and store them in all sorts of handy places. When you double-click an application alias, it goes into the original folder and tells the real application to open.

Let's say you have an application you use frequently—your word processing program, for instance. You can make an alias of AppleWorks or Quicken or whatever you use and put it just about anywhere. You might want to put it right on your Desktop, in a folder full of application aliases, or in your Home folder. Since you can have many aliases of the same file, you can put aliases to the same item in several places!

Aliases only take up about 2 or 3K of disk space (which is a really tiny bit), so you can make lots and store them all over the place, wherever they come in handy.

You can make aliases of applications, documents, partitions, folders, utilities, games, etc. Aliases are wonderful tools for organizing your work—anything you want to use is only one double-click away from wherever you are. Remember, an alias is just a picture that goes and gets the real file.

Before I tell you *how* to make them, here are ideas for **using aliases** so you will *want* to make them (how to make an alias is on the following page).

▼ Store aliases of documents in two or three places at once, including right on your Desktop. For instance, you may want to keep budget reports in folders organized by months, as well as in folders organized by projects. When you update the real document, every alias will open the updated document.

▼ Leave aliases of applications neatly organized directly on your Desktop. This makes your applications available to you for the **drag-and-drop trick of opening files,** including files from other applications. (As explained in Chapter 12, you can drag any document onto the icon of the application to open the document. Many applications can open files created in other programs, so if you come across a file from a program you don't have or perhaps you don't know where it came from, you can drag the unknown file over the top of all these aliases that are sitting on your Desktop. Any icon that changes color when you drag the document on top of it will try to open that document.)

▼ You might find you use a particular utility regularly. If so, put an alias of that utility right on your Desktop. (Utilities are stored in the Utilities folder, which is in the Applications folder.)

▼ Put aliases of all your applications in a folder, then put that folder in the Dock. When you want to open an application, no matter where you are (meaning you don't have to go back to the Finder), just press on that folder icon in the Dock to get the pop-up menu and choose your application from there (shown to the right).

Using Aliases

This is my folder of the applications I use most often. Putting all of these in the Dock would make the Dock too small and crowded.

Automatic Aliases

There are a several places on your computer where the Mac **automatically creates an alias** for you: When you drag an item into the **Dock,** the original item doesn't actually *move* to the Dock—the Mac puts an alias in the Dock. That's why you can delete the icon from the Dock in a puff of dust and you still have the original file in your folder. The same thing happens when you drag an item into any Finder window **Toolbar**—the Mac puts an alias in the Toolbar. The **Recent Places** menu that appears in "Save As" and "Open" dialog boxes, as well as the Apple menu, uses aliases that are automatically created for you.

When you drop a file on the Favorites icon in the Toolbar, *or* when you select a file and use the Favorites command in the File menu ("Add to Favorites," or press Command T), the Mac automatically puts an *alias* of the file in the **Favorites folder.** (See Chapter 23 about Favorites.)

Making an Alias

jimmy.jpeg

*An alias looks just like the original icon, but there's a tiny arrow in the bottom-left corner. Unfortunately, the arrow is too dang tiny to be a very good **visual clue.***

Making an alias is so easy:

1. Select the item you want to make an alias of (click once on it).

2. Then choose one of these four easy ways to make an alias:

   a. **Either** from the File menu, choose "Make Alias."

   b. **Or** press Command L instead of going to the File menu.

   c. **Or** hold down the Control key and click on the item you want to make an alias of. A contextual menu will pop up, as shown below; choose "Make Alias."

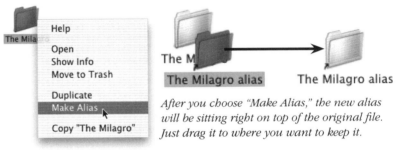

After you choose "Make Alias," the new alias will be sitting right on top of the original file. Just drag it to where you want to keep it.

   d. **Or** hold down Command Option and drag the file—if you drag it to a *different* folder or to the Desktop, when you let go you'll have an alias with the word "alias" removed from its name; if you drag to somewhere else in the *same* folder, you'll have an alias with the word "alias" at the end of it.

You can also **make an alias of any open document:**

1. Save the open document.

2. Drag the tiny picture in the title bar and drop it on the Desktop or in any folder. You'll notice the pointer has a tiny arrow attached to it, which is a ***visual clue*** that you are in the process of making an alias.

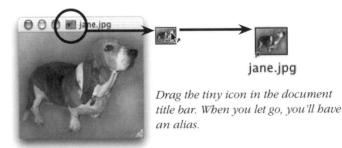

jane.jpg

Drag the tiny icon in the document title bar. When you let go, you'll have an alias.

The **new alias icon** will look the same and will be named the same, with the word *alias* added (unless you used the Command-Option–drag trick). If you want to remove the word "alias" (I do because it makes the name too long) first move the alias out of the folder the original file is in because you cannot have two files with the same name in one folder.

Drag the icon to wherever you want to keep it. Rename it if you like. The new file does not have to have the word "alias" in its name. *And it doesn't matter if you move the original file*—the alias can always find it.

Important note: An alias is not a copy of a file—it is just a pointer. Although you can throw away any alias, do not throw away the original file!

Details of Aliases

Making aliases is easy, but here are some **details** you should understand.

▼ An alias isn't a *duplicate* of anything; it's just a **pointer** to the real thing. If you double-click an *alias* of Quicken, you'll open your *original* Quicken application, even if the original Quicken is stored in a completely different folder.

▼ If you **delete** an alias, you don't delete the original—the original is still stored on your hard disk. So you can keep revising your filing system as your needs change. Don't want that alias of Budget Charts cluttering up your Project Plans folder any more? Fine; throw it away. The original Budget Charts is still where you stored it.

▼ If you put an item into an *alias* of a **folder,** the item actually gets put into the *original* folder.

▼ You can **move** an alias and even **rename** an alias. The Mac will still be able to find the original and open it whenever you double-click on the alias.

▼ Even if you move or rename the **original** file, the alias can still find it.

▼ If you **delete** the *original* file, the Mac does *not* automatically delete any of the aliases you created for that file. When you double-click on an alias whose original has been trashed, you will get a message telling you the original could not be located. See the following page.

Finding the Original File

Sometimes you want to find the original file that the alias is linked to. For instance, maybe you need to get something from an application's folder, but you don't want to dig down through all the other folders to get there.

To find the original file belonging to an alias, follow these simple steps:

1. Click once on the alias to select it.

2. From the File menu, choose "Show Original," **or** press Command R.

   The original file will appear in front of you, selected.

Linking an Alias to a New Original

If necessary, you can **link an alias to a different original.** It doesn't even have to be the same sort of file; that is, if the alias is a folder icon and you now link it to a document, the alias icon will change to a document icon. The *name* of the alias, however, will not change to the name of the file you now link it to—you'll have to change the alias name yourself.

1. Click once on the alias to select it.

2. Press Command I to get the Show Info box.

3. Click the button, "Select New Original…."

4. You'll get the same "Fix Alias" dialog box that you see on the opposite page. Find the file you want to link to this alias, and click OK.

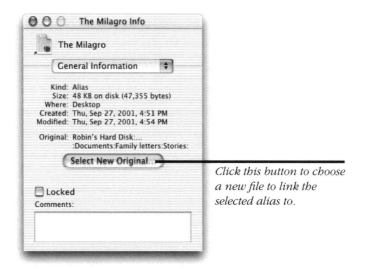

Click this button to choose a new file to link the selected alias to.

If something happened to the **original file,** like it got thrown in the Trash and the Trash was emptied, or maybe the original is on a removable disk, you'll get the message shown below.

**Original File
Could Not Be Opened**

If you think the file is just lost on your Mac, you can try the "Fix Alias…" button. This takes you to a dialog box exactly like an "Open" dialog box, and you can choose a file to link to the alias. But if the computer couldn't find the original, don't count on finding it yourself. Unfortunately, the original is probably gone and all that "Fix Alias" will do is let you link this alias to a different file.

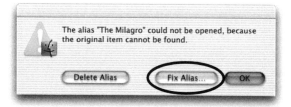

*If you click the "Fix Alias…" button, you'll get a dialog box, as
shown below, where you can navigate to the original item or
to a new item. If you don't know how to navigate yet, just click
"Delete Alias" and then make a new alias from the original item.*

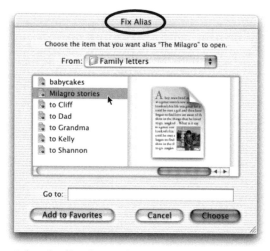

Select the file of your choice to link to the alias.

1. What is an alias, anyway?

_____

2. How large, in file size, is a typical alias?

_____

3. Name at least four ways to create an alias.

_____

_____

4. What is the quickest way to put an alias into the Apple menu?

_____

5. If you throw away an alias, what happens to the real item?

_____

6. If you throw away the real item, what happens to all of its aliases?

_____

7. What is the easiest way to find the original of an alias?

_____

8. If you use the Calculator utility several times a day, where would be a good place to keep an alias of it?

_____

9. If you put a file into an alias of a folder, what happens to that file?

_____

10. What happens if you make an alias, then rename the original?

_____

Answers on page 752.

Making & Using Favorites

Favorites are files that you have chosen to have easy access to. For instance, maybe you have a folder you save your research papers into, and it's stored inside several other folders which are inside the Documents folder. If you make the research folder a Favorite, you can save files into it, open it on the Desktop, and even open the folder inside of Open dialog boxes in applications—all with just one or two clicks, instead of having to dig down through the directory. This chapter explains how to use and create Favorites.

The term "favorites" on the Mac also refers to the icons that appear in toolbars across the tops of application panes, such as System Preferences or Mail. (I hate it when they give the same name to two completely different things!) Internet Explorer uses the term "Favorites" to describe their bookmarks. America Online lets you select "Favorite" places, also designated with a little red heart. All of these "favorites" are similar in that they make it easy for you to open and use files and settings that you need often. *But this chapter is only concerned with Favorites as it applies to the Favorites window in the Macintosh Finder.*

What are Favorites?

*Briefly, to make an alias: Click on a regular file icon and press Command L. This makes a **copy** of the **icon** (not of the file itself), and you can put that copy, that alias, anywhere on your computer. When you double-click the alias, it will go find and open the original file.*

You've most likely opened the **Favorites** window by now—click once on the red heart in any Finder window Toolbar. If you haven't put anything in this folder yet, it probably has only one icon in it, an "alias" of the Documents folder. Favorites use the alias concept quite a bit, so if you don't know what aliases are, please skim Chapter 22 before you work with Favorites.

Most files in the Favorites folder will be aliases, although you can certainly store original files in here as well.

In the example below, you see the sorts of files that can become favorites: folders, applications, documents, servers, partitions, and even web sites. (Do you see the one file in this collection that is *not* an alias?)

Anything that you want to be able to get to easily, either to open it or to save into it, you can turn into a Favorite. Because most Favorites are aliases, you can safely delete them (the aliases) when you don't need them anymore.

Favorite folders will be available in the Open and Save As dialog boxes. The last folder in this row, "Robin's favorite sites," is not an alias.

These Favorites are applications.

These Favorites are documents.

These two Favorites are servers. They act as shortcuts to connect.

These Favorites are web locations.

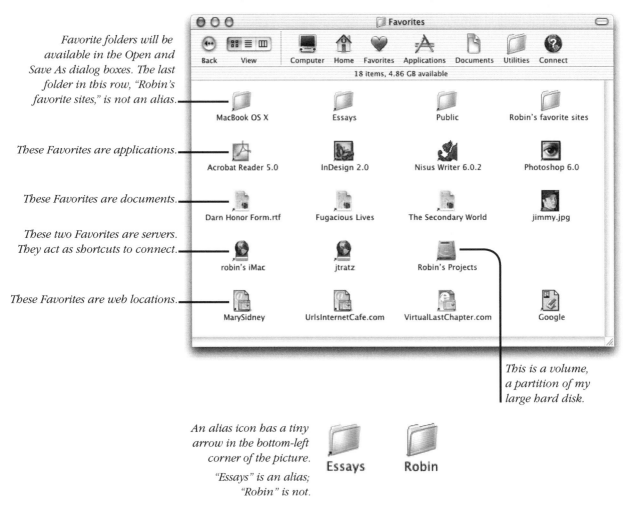

This is a volume, a partition of my large hard disk.

An alias icon has a tiny arrow in the bottom-left corner of the picture. "Essays" is an alias; "Robin" is not.

Favorites can make it much easier to access your favorite folders, documents, web pages, etc. Here are some ways to **take advantage of Favorites.**

Taking Advantage of Favorites

▼ Rather than go hunting for **the folder you are using most often this week,** make it a Favorite. Then you can go to the Favorites submenu or Favorites folder to open it quickly, rather than having to dig through the Finder windows. For instance, at the moment I need to get to my folder that stores all of the chapters for this book. It resides in a "partition" (a separate section of my hard disk), which means to get to it I have to open that disk partition from the Computer window and open another window or two to get to my book folder. Instead, I made the folder a Favorite. Now from the Go menu I can open the folder directly, or open my Favorites folder with a click on the icon, then open my book folder.

Go	
Computer	⌥⌘C
Home	⌥⌘H
iDisk	⌥⌘I
Favorites	▶
Applications	⌥⌘A
Recent Folders	▶
Go to Folder...	⌘~
Back	⌘[
Connect to Server...	⌘K

Go To Favorites	⌥⌘F
Acrobat Reader 5.0	
Darn Honor Form.rtf	
Essays	
Fugacious Lives	
Google	
InDesign 2.0	
jimmy.jpg	
jtratz	
MacBook OS X	
MarySidney	
Nisus Writer 6.0.2	
Photoshop 6.0	
Public	
Robin's favorite web sites	
robin's iMac	
Robin's Projects	
The Secondary World	
UrlsInternetCafe.com	
VirtualLastChapter.com	

*A problem with the Favorites submenu is that there are **no visual clues** as to whether a file listed is a folder, application, document, web site, server, etc. You have to be very familiar with the files you put in here.*

Notice that Favorite folders have no submenus—you can't go straight to a document in a folder, but you can open the folder.

Notice also that if you have a large number of Favorites (as shown here), it sort of defeats the purpose of making things easy to find and open. There are other ways to make files accessible, so use Favorites as a rotating collection of the files you need the most at this particular moment.

▼ Another advantage to putting my book folder in Favorites is that when I need to **open** another book chapter, the folder is listed in my menu in the **Open dialog box,** as shown below. I don't have to hunt around the directory to find it. I love this feature.

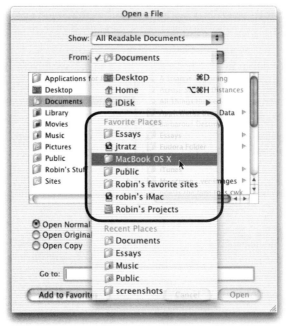

In some applications' Open dialog boxes, only the folders, partitions, and servers in the Favorites folder appear in this "From" menu.

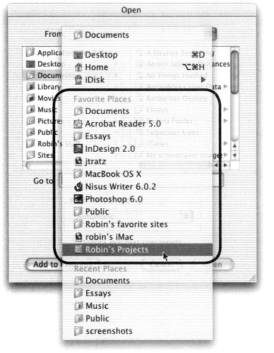

*In other Open dialog boxes, the Favorite applications also appear in this list. However, if you select a Favorite application, the dialog box opens the **folder** that the application is stored within, not the application itself.*

▼ Yet another advantage to putting my book folder in Favorites is that when I need to **save** a new chapter, the folder is listed in the "Where" menu in the **Save As dialog box,** as shown below. I don't have to hunt around the directory to find it. I love this feature, too.

▼ If you are on a network, either a small one in your home office or a larger corporate network, you can **make a Favorite of a server icon** (directions are on page 360). Then when you need to connect, you can just double-click the server Favorite.

If you originally logged on to that server as "Guest," you won't see any dialog boxes when you connect with the alias—the server will just appear almost instantly. If you originally signed on with a name and a password, you will have to type the password.

robin's iMac   jtratz

Server Favorite icons are automatically named with the volume they are connected to, but you can change their names to anything that helps you remember which ones are which.

Making Favorites

There are several ways to create Favorites. Which one you choose depends on what you are selecting as a Favorite and where you are. Below is a list of techniques.

To make a Favorite using the menu command:

1. Select a file in a Finder window or on the Desktop (click once on it).
2. From the File menu, choose "Add to Favorites."

To make a Favorite using the keyboard shortcut:

1. Select a file in a Finder window or on the Desktop (click once on it).
2. Press Command T.

To make a Favorite of a file using drag-and-drop:

1. Open any Finder window and make sure the Toolbar is visible, with the Favorites icon showing.
2. Drag a file from any Finder window or the Desktop and drop it on the Favorites icon in any window Toolbar, as shown below.

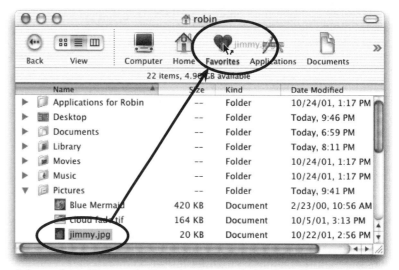

*I dragged this file up to the Favorites icon in the Toolbar. If you look carefully, you can see the shadow of the file name in the Toolbar, and you can see the pointer has a tiny arrow attached. That is my **visual clue** that the file I am dragging is about to become an alias. The original file will stay right where it is.*

Important Note: If you drag a file to the Favorites icon in the Toolbar, the Mac will always make an **alias** for the file. But if you drag a file icon directly into the open Favorites window, that will simply **move** most original files into that window, *not* make an alias. Be aware! (Servers and disks will always appear in the Favorites folder as aliases, no matter how you drag them in.)

To make a Favorite of an open document using drag-and-drop:

This only works in applications that were written specifically for Mac OS X; that is, this technique won't work from Classic applications, or even those programs that are written to be used in both Mac OS 9 and OS X.

1. Open a document. If it hasn't been saved recently, save it now. There are two visual clues that tell you the changes have not been saved: There is a dot inside the red button, and the tiny document icon in the title bar is a shadow.

The red close button has a dot in it.   *The document icon in the title bar is a shadow.*

2. After you've saved the file, drag the tiny document icon and drop it onto the Favorites icon in the Toolbar, as shown below.

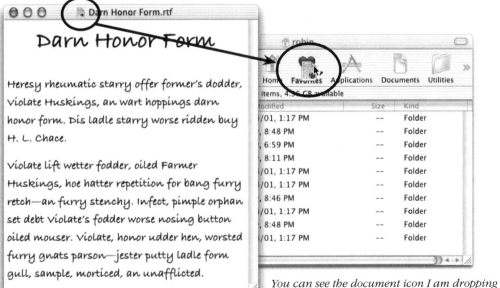

*You can see the document icon I am dropping onto the Favorites icon in the Toolbar. You can also see the tiny arrow next to the pointer, my **visual clue** that an alias is being made.*

To make a Favorite of any folder while in Save As or Open dialog boxes:

You've probably noticed the button "Add to Favorites" in the Save As and Open dialog boxes. Once you have fumbled around the directory and found the folder you need, you can add it to your Favorites instantly so it will appear in the "From" and "Where" menus, as shown on pages 354 and 355. You can only add *folders* and disks, including partitions, this way (not documents or applications or anything else).

1. In your application, Save As (Command S) or Open (Command O).

2. If you don't see the full directory and "Add to Favorites" button, click the triangle button circled below.

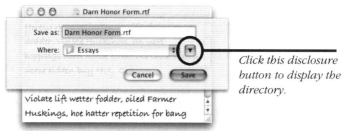

Click this disclosure button to display the directory.

3. Click once on a folder name to select it, then click the "Add to Favorites" button. The folder will instantly appear as the selected folder at the top of the "Where" or "From" menus, as well as in the Favorites section of the menu list.

Select a folder in the directory list, then click the "Add to Favorites" button. If you don't know how to find your way around the directory, see pages 223–226.

*Notice a document is selected here, not a folder. This gives you the impression you can add a document to Favorites, but when you click the button, it actually adds the **folder** that this document is stored within.*

To make a Favorite of a web page:

You can't directly make Favorites of web page addresses, but you can make "Web Internet Location" files of web pages and add those to your Favorites folder. Then when you choose that Favorite, it will open your default web browser and display that page. You can also drag any location file, whether it's a Favorite or not, and drop it right in the middle of any web page (not in the address bar)—the browser will go to that page.

*The web browser Internet Explorer (IE) has something called "Favorites" which are not the same as the Favorites we're talking about here. Internet Explorer Favorites are essentially bookmarks to web pages you want to find again easily. Anything you save as a Favorite in IE will **not** appear in the Favorites folder on your Desktop. Nor will anything in the Favorites folder on your Desktop appear in IE.*

1. Open your web browser and go to a page you like.

2. In the address bar, where you type in a web address, you see a little icon (shown below). Grab that icon and drag it to the Desktop or directly into any folder. You cannot drag this icon onto the Favorites icon in the Toolbar—you'll have to drag it directly into the folder.

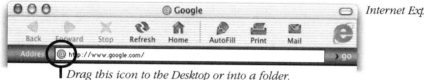
Internet Explorer

Drag this icon to the Desktop or into a folder.

OmniWeb

Drag this icon to the Desktop or into a folder.

3. When you drag the little icon to the Desktop or a folder and let go, you'll get a new file, as shown below. Each of these shown is an Internet Web Location.

www.ratz.com/
From OmniWeb.

The Virtual Last Chapter of.url
From Internet Explorer.

Google
From Netscape.

Tip: In web browsers developed for Mac OS X, you can drag that tiny location icon and drop it directly in the Dock, on the right-hand side. It becomes a little spring icon with an @ symbol; click once on this Dock icon and it will open the web page it came from. Unlike most other items in the Dock, however, if you remove this web address from the Dock, it is really gone because you have no other file for it.

4. You'll notice if you drag the browser icon directly into the Favorites folder, it does not make an alias—it is still an original location file. This is perfectly fine, as long as you remember that if you ever want to throw this file away, you are throwing away the original.

If you want only aliases in your Favorites folder, make another folder in which to store all of your Internet Web Location files, then drop just the locations you want to use as Favorites onto the Favorites icon in the Finder window Toolbar.

To make a Favorite of a server connection:

Information about connecting to servers is in Chapter 36.

Once you have a Favorite of a server connection, you need only select the Favorite from the Go menu or double-click its icon in the Favorites window, and you will be connected automatically.

If you originally logged on to that server as "Guest," you won't see any dialog boxes when you connect with the alias—the server will just appear almost instantly.

If you originally signed on with a name and a password, you will have to type the password. If you originally chose a volume when you connected, you won't have to select the volume when you use the Favorite because the volume choice is part of the server Favorite.

1. Connect to the server as usual. You'll see your server icon in the Computer window and/or on the Desktop, as usual.

2. Drag the server icon either directly into the Favorites open window, or drop it on the Favorites icon in any Finder window Toolbar. Either way will make an alias in the Favorites folder.

   You could also click once on the server icon to select it, then press Command T.

Even after you disconnect from the server, log out, shut down, or restart, your server Favorite will stay in the Favorites folder and you'll have a shortcut for connecting.

To make a Favorite of a partition or other volume:

1. Open the Computer window.

2. Click once on the volume you would like as a Favorite.

3. Drag it up to the Toolbar and drop it on the Favorites icon, *or* press Command T.

If you make a Favorite of a removable hard disk, CD, or DVD, the disk will appear in the Save As and Open dialog boxes as long as the disk is in the computer. When you take the disk out of the computer, the alias link will be broken; when you reinsert the disk, the link will connect once again.

Deleting Favorites is easy. Just remove them from the Favorites folder.

Most Favorites, *but not all,* are aliases, so it's important to check before you throw away a file from the Favorites folder. For instance, if you dragged a folder, document, application, or web location directly into the open Favorites window, the Mac did not make an alias—the original file was *moved* into the folder. (When you drop a file on the Favorites icon in the Toolbar, it always makes an alias.)

So you can *remove* files from the Favorites folder to delete them as Favorites, but check the icon before you actually *delete* files!

*Do you see the two files in this folder that are **not** aliases?*

1. Are Favorites always aliases?

2. Name at least six sorts of files that you can make Favorites of.

3. If you want an easy way to access all of your applications on the Mac, is making Favorites of all of them the best solution?

4. Can you change the name of a Favorite?

5. If you drag a file into the open Favorites window, what happens?

6. If you drop a file onto the Favorites icon in the Toolbar, what happens?

7. Describe how to make a Favorite of an open document.

8. In the Open and Save As dialog boxes, what sort of files can be selected and made into Favorites?

9. Can you make a Favorite of a removable disk? Is that useful?

10. Can you safely delete every Favorite in the window?

Answers on page 752.

Finding Things with Sherlock

24

Sherlock is a wonderful time-saving and frustration-reducing feature that helps you search for any file on your computer or attached disks, and it can even **search the contents** of any file.

If you are connected to the Internet, Sherlock can also find shopping bargains on the web, old friends and lovers, the latest news, research items, products and support from Apple, and more. It's not a complete replacement for the search tools you find on the web itself, but it can provide a quick and easy way to locate many things.

Note: If America Online is your only email/Internet service, you must first open and log on to AOL before you can use Sherlock to search the Internet!

 This is the icon in the Dock that opens Sherlock. Click once on it.

Channels

When you position the pointer over a channel, a help tag appears that tells you what that channel is for.

The buttons across the top of Sherlock represent what Apple calls **channels,** or customizable sources of information. Position your mouse over any of the buttons and pause a few seconds—a hint, called a "help tag," appears that tells you what that channel can help you find, as shown to the left. Try it.

Across the row in the example below, the channels are Files, Internet, People, Apple, Shopping, News, References, Entertainment, and a channel called My Channel that you can customize. Plus there are empty slots where you can add other customized channels and your own icons (see page 382). **All of the channels except Files search for information on the Internet.**

Click on a channel to select it; the contents in the middle panel will change with each channel. Try it.

This is the Search button. After you have typed in a request, click this button to have Sherlock find it.

*This **channel** is selected (notice the slightly darker shade).*

*In this **edit box,** type in what you want to find (details on opposite page).*

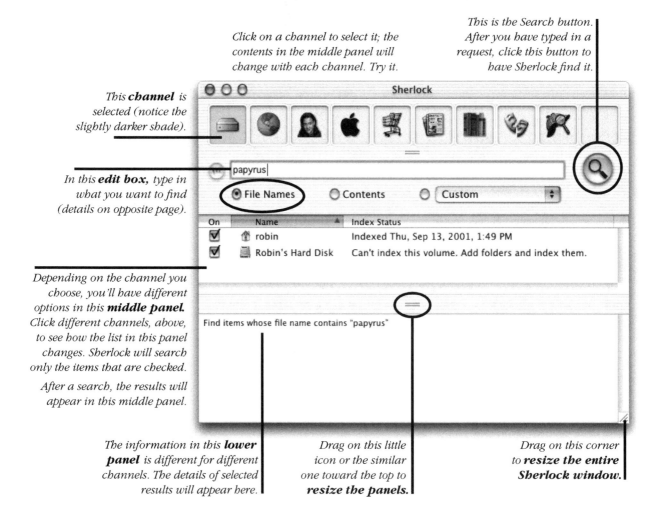

*Depending on the channel you choose, you'll have different options in this **middle panel.** Click different channels, above, to see how the list in this panel changes. Sherlock will search only the items that are checked.*

After a search, the results will appear in this middle panel.

*The information in this **lower panel** is different for different channels. The details of selected results will appear here.*

*Drag on this little icon or the similar one toward the top to **resize the panels.***

*Drag on this corner to **resize the entire Sherlock window.***

A *file* is anything on your hard disk. Documents, folders, applications, fonts —everything is considered a file. Every file on your Mac is represented by an icon and has a **name.** Sherlock can find files by their names.

To search for a file on your hard disk:

1. From the Dock, click the Sherlock icon (shown to the right). **Or** go to the Desktop and press Command F.

2. Click the first channel button, the one with the picture of a computer (circled, below; it's probably already selected).

3. In the middle panel of the window you'll see the name of your hard disk and Home, as shown below. Depending on how your computer is set up, you might see other items in that panel, such as any "partitions" you might have, or any disks that are mounted (CDs, Zips, etc.). Make sure there is a checkbox in any disk you want to search.

4. In the edit box (see below), type a word that is in some of the file names on your computer. For instance, type "letter" or "setup."

5. Make sure the round radio button for "File Names" is checked (shown below).

6. You'll notice in the lower panel that Sherlock reiterates what you are looking for.

7. Click the Search button (the round, green one with the magnifying glass). Then turn this page and continue.

Find a File on Your Hard Disk

This is the Sherlock icon in the Dock.

Tips: It doesn't matter whether you type capital or lowercase letters—Sherlock will find "Love Letter" even if you search for "love letter."

Spaces, however, *do* matter. That is, "love letter" will not find "loveletter."

If you don't know the exact name of the file, just type any part of it that you think is in the file name, such as "love."

*Choose the **Files channel** to search for files on your hard disk.*

*Type your request in this **edit box.***

Make sure this button is selected so Sherlock will search for your request in a file's name (as opposed to its contents).

Click this button to search.

Right now this panel reminds you of what you are looking for.

Opening a found file

Sherlock will take several seconds to search your entire hard disk. The results will look something like those shown below. In the **middle panel** of the window is a list of all the files that have your request in the file name; **click once** on any one of those files, and in the **lower panel,** Sherlock will tell you where that file is stored.

When necessary, click this Back button to return to the list of volumes you just left. There is no "Forward" button to return to this window—you'll just have to click the Search button again.

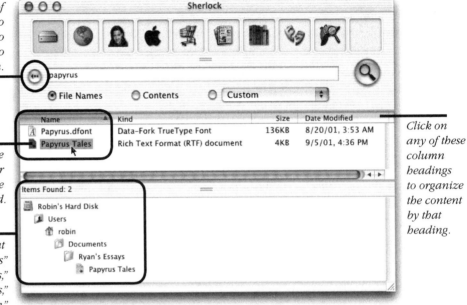

Click on any of these column headings to organize the content by that heading.

Click once on the file you were looking for, and in the lower panel you'll see exactly where that file is stored.

This example shows that the selected file "Papyrus Tales" is in a folder called "Ryan's Essays," which is in the folder "Documents," which is in the home of "robin," which is stored in the "Users" folder, which is on the hard disk named "Robin's Hard Disk."

Quick search tip: If you're looking for a file you created or worked on today or yesterday, try the "Custom…" menu.

Once you have located the file you want, there are several things you can do. First, click once on the file name in either the middle or the lower panel of Sherlock to select that file. Then do one of the following:

- ▾ **To open the file,** double-click the file name, or single-click the file name to select it and press Command O. This will, of course, also open the application that the file was created in.

- ▾ **To open the folder** in which the file is stored, press Command E.

- ▾ **To print the item** (if it's a document), press Command P.

- ▾ **To move the item,** drag it to wherever you want, outside of Sherlock.

- ▾ **To copy the item,** hold down the Option key and drag the file somewhere outside of Sherlock.

- ▾ **To delete the item,** drag the file from the window to the trash basket, *or* select the file and press Command Delete.

- ▾ **To find the original of an alias,** select its icon and press Command R.

For the following technique, you must select the file in the *middle* panel—it won't work if you select the file in the lower panel.

- ▾ **To make an alias of the file,** hold down the Command and Option keys and drag the file to the Desktop or into a folder; let go and an alias will appear (see Chapter 22 for information about aliases).

File	
New Window	⌘N
Open Item	⌘O
Open Enclosing Folder	⌘E
Open in New Browser Window	⌘B
Print Item	⌘P
Move to Trash	⌘⌫
Close Window	⌘W
Show Original	⌘R
Save Search Criteria...	⌘S
Open Search Criteria...	

Tip: Click on a file name to select it, then go to the File menu to see what your options are for that particular type of file.

New Search without Losing Previous Search

After you've done one search, you can **start another** without eliminating the search criteria or the results from the first search. Just go to the File menu in Sherlock and choose "New Window," or press Command N. You can have any number of search windows open at the same time.

How to Quit Sherlock

When you want to put the Sherlock *window* away, click in the little red button in the upper-left corner of the window.

When you want to put the Sherlock *application* away (that is, you want to quit), press Command Q or choose "Quit Sherlock" from the Sherlock menu.

Search a Specific Folder

Sometimes you want to **search one particular folder** or several folders instead of every mounted disk. That's easy to do. (Sherlock calls all folders or disks "volumes.")

To search a particular folder:

1. First:

   ▼ **Either** find the icon for that folder on your Desktop or in a Finder window. Drag the folder icon and drop it in the middle panel of the Sherlock window.

   ▼ **Or** from the Find menu in the menu bar across the top of the screen, choose "Add Folder…." Then use the dialog box to navigate to the folder of your choice. Select the folder and click "Add."

2. Back at the Sherlock window, make sure there is a check in the box next to each folder you want to search.

3. Continue with the search as you did on the previous pages.

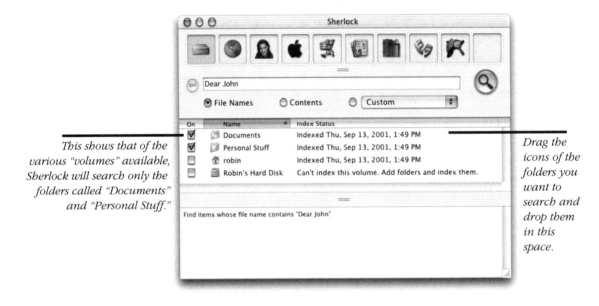

This shows that of the various "volumes" available, Sherlock will search only the folders called "Documents" and "Personal Stuff."

Drag the icons of the folders you want to search and drop them in this space.

To remove a folder from Sherlock:

1. Select the folder you want to remove. You must select the *name* of the folder. That is, clicking in the checkbox does not select the folder to remove it.

2. From the Find menu, choose "Remove Folder."

If the quick-and-easy search gave you too many results, you can **narrow the search** to more specific attributes. For instance, you might want to find only the files named "love letter" that were created between certain dates. (This is only available in the Files channel, not in the Internet searches.)

To narrow a search:

1. Open Sherlock and click the "Files" channel button (the computer icon).

2. Click the buttons to select the volumes you want to search, or limit the search to specific folders (as described on the opposite page).

3. Click the "Custom" menu and choose "Edit…"; you'll see the dialog box shown below.

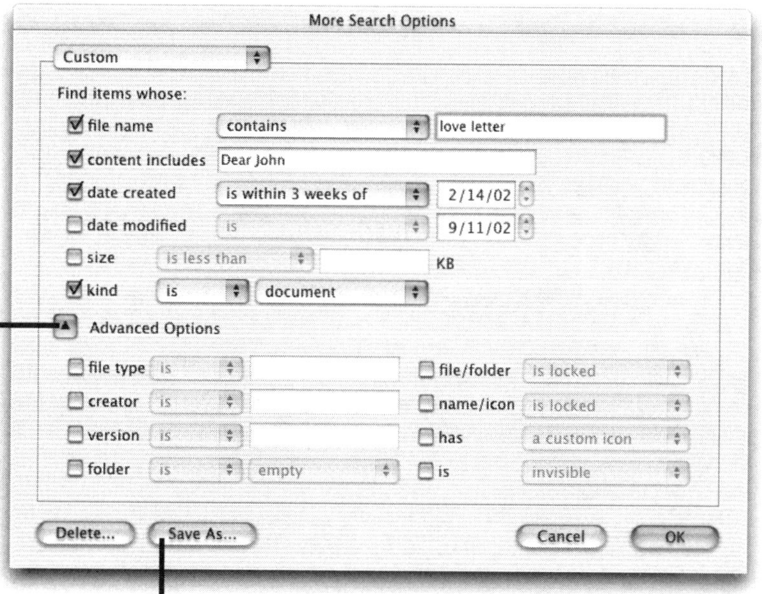

More Search Options

Custom

Find items whose:

☑ file name   contains   love letter
☑ content includes   Dear John
☑ date created   is within 3 weeks of   2/14/02
☐ date modified   is   9/11/02
☐ size   is less than   KB
☑ kind   is   document

Click this box to see these Advanced Options.

☑ **Advanced Options**

☐ file type   is   ☐ file/folder   is locked
☐ creator   is   ☐ name/icon   is locked
☐ version   is   ☐ has   a custom icon
☐ folder   is   empty   ☐ is   invisible

Delete…   Save As…   Cancel   OK

See page 371 about saving your search criteria so you can use it again.

These particular parameters, or search criteria, will force Sherlock to find just the files that have "love letter" in the file name, that also have the words "Dear" and "John" in the body of the document, that were created within three weeks of February 14 (three weeks on either side of that date, before or after), and that are documents (as opposed to applications or aliases, etc.).

4. Take a few moments to see what your options are here. *Once you click a checkbox, the various options will become available to you.* For instance, you can see above that the "date created" choice is checked, so the menu next to it is now available. Whereas "date modified" is *not* checked, so its menu is *not* available yet.

Check the boxes, then click on their menus to see what you can do. Be sure to *uncheck* any options you don't want to apply before you click the OK button!

Tip: To uncheck every option at once, press Command T, *or* go to the Edit menu and choose "Turn Off All."

5. After you set up the parameters and click the OK button, you'll end up back at the main search window and Sherlock will summarize your search options in the lower panel, as shown below. Then click the Search button.

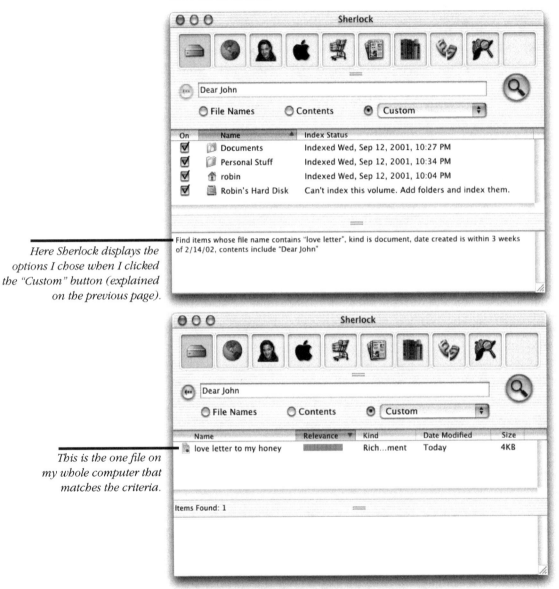

Here Sherlock displays the options I chose when I clicked the "Custom" button (explained on the previous page).

This is the one file on my whole computer that matches the criteria.

You can choose to **save the search criteria.** Sometimes you create a great, narrow search that takes you to exactly the files you're looking for on a disk or on the Internet. If you save this criteria, Sherlock will make a file for the saved criteria, and when you want to find that same information, open the saved file, as described below and on the following page. Sherlock will run the search and display the results.

There are two ways to do this, with two different results. The first method is only available for **searches on your hard disk;** the saved criteria will appear in the "Custom" menu, as shown below. The second method can be used for searches on your hard disk and **also for Internet searches,** and the saved criteria file will be stored in your Documents folder. It will not be available through the "Custom" menu.

To save the criteria from a search on your hard disk:

1. Open Sherlock. Click the "Custom" menu, and choose "Edit…." Set up the criteria you like.

2. Click the "Save As…" button at the bottom of the window.

3. You'll get the "Save Custom Settings" dialog box, as shown. Name and save your criteria.

Saving a Search for Files on Disks

4. Now from the "Custom" menu, you can select that search.

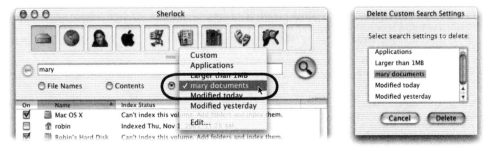

To delete the search, go back to the Custom search window and click "Delete…." You'll get this little dialog box where you can select and delete the search criteria.

To save the criteria from a search on your hard disk or the Internet:

1. Open Sherlock.

   Either click the Files channel, then click the "Custom" menu, choose "Edit...," and set up the criteria you like.

   Or click one of the Internet channels (explained on pages 376–379) and enter your search criteria.

2. From the File menu, choose "Save Search Criteria...," or press Command S.

3. The typical "Save As" dialog box will appear, as shown below, and the default is to save the search criteria into your Documents folder. You can rename the file—it will not affect the search.

file name ends with ".png", kind...ter 9-1-01

If you don't choose to change the file name, it will end up being really long.

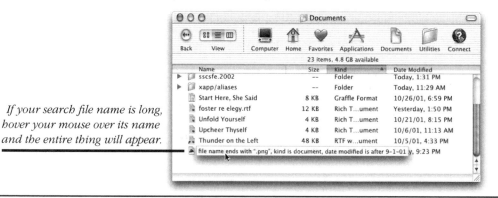

4. When you want to run that search again, do the following:

   Either open your Documents folder and double-click the file you saved in there. Even if Sherlock is not open, it will open now, the correct channel will be chosen, your selected search sites will be chosen, and Sherlock will run the search.

   Or open Sherlock, go to the File menu, and choose "Open Search Criteria...." You will get the standard Open dialog box, from which you can choose your saved search.

If your search file name is long, hover your mouse over its name and the entire thing will appear.

Sherlock will **search through the contents** of most text files. For instance, maybe you're working on a research project and you've created dozens of files on the topic of chess. You want to find all the papers in your collection that mention "en passant." That's when you click the "Contents" button; instead of searching for just the *name* of a file, Sherlock will actually read the *contents* of files. For instance, you might have written an article that you named "Special Moves in Chess," and in the article itself you wrote about the en passant move, but you also mention en passant in three other articles with different names—Sherlock will find every file that includes the phrase "en passant" in the text.

BUT Sherlock cannot search the contents of your files *until* it has first **indexed** every file. That is, Sherlock has to read every file on your computer and then organize every word into a database that it can search when you request it. Logically, if you write more articles after Sherlock has indexed the files on your hard disk, Sherlock has to index things again to update and add those new files to its database.

The "Contents" Button and Indexing

*Sherlock cannot search the text in **every** file. It can search files saved in the Rich Text Format, in Plain Text, most PDF documents, and some word processing documents. If you have lots of files you want to search and Sherlock can't do it, buy Adobe Acrobat and learn to use it. It's amazing.*

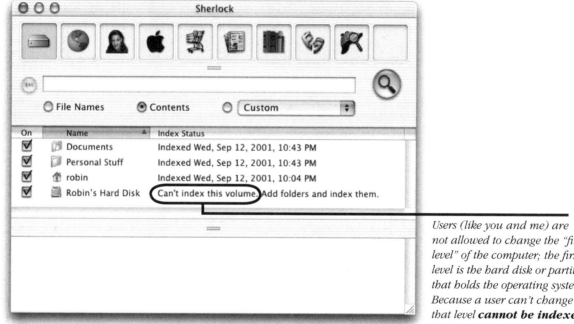

*Users (like you and me) are not allowed to change the "first level" of the computer; the first level is the hard disk or partition that holds the operating system. Because a user can't change it, that level **cannot be indexed.** As the note says, you can add individual folders from that disk into Sherlock (as explained on page 368) and index the individual folders. (This message does not mean to add folders to that disk.)*

Indexing schedule Sherlock **automatically indexes** your hard disk(s) every day, which is an option you can change if you like. Depending on how many files you have and how fast your Mac is, indexing can take a while. If you find it annoying that Sherlock starts to index every time you open it, you might want to uncheck the boxes shown below. Then when you want Sherlock to index, open Sherlock, go to the Find menu, and choose "Index Now."

To open Preferences, go to the Sherlock menu and choose "Preferences...."

When you choose to search for something on the Internet, your Mac will make a number of simultaneous connections to a number of sites. You might be in an office or school where your computer has to go through a "proxy server" that limits the number of connections that can be made simultaneously. If so, find out from your network administration what the number is and limit the number from this menu.

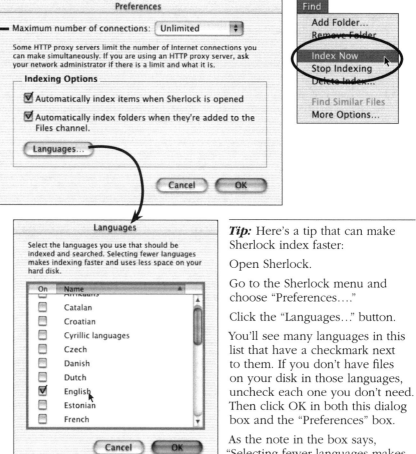

Tip: Here's a tip that can make Sherlock index faster:

Open Sherlock.

Go to the Sherlock menu and choose "Preferences...."

Click the "Languages..." button.

You'll see many languages in this list that have a checkmark next to them. If you don't have files on your disk in those languages, uncheck each one you don't need. Then click OK in both this dialog box and the "Preferences" box.

As the note in the box says, "Selecting fewer languages makes indexing faster and uses less space on your hard disk."

As you create and install more and more files that get added to the index, the index database can become huge, which means it uses a large chunk of your hard disk to store the index. You can't throw this file away because it's invisible (which means you can't even find it), but you can use Sherlock to **delete** it. (If you have a huge hard disk and are not worried about space, don't worry about eliminating the index file. If you eliminate it, of course, Sherlock cannot search by content.)

Delete the Index

1. When Sherlock is open, click once on the *name* of the volume whose index you want to delete. You must click on the *name—* as shown below. Clicking the checkbox will not select the volume for this procedure.

2. Go to the Find menu and choose "Delete Index...." (If the message is gray, you didn't select the volume properly. Go back and click once on the *name,* as shown above, not the checkbox.) You'll get the message shown below.

> **Do you really want to delete the index for "Documents"?**
>
> Deleting the index will disable content searches for this item.
>
> Cancel   OK

3. If this is what you want to do (you can always create a new index), click OK.

Find Something on the Internet

Besides searching your disk, Sherlock will also search the Internet and the web. Each of the buttons across the top of Sherlock is called a "channel." Each channel is set up to search specific areas of the web (except the very first channel, which finds files on your computer). When you click on a channel to select it, you'll see the middle panel of Sherlock change to fit the channel's specifications. Try it.

To search the Internet, Sherlock has to *go* to the Internet, which means you must have your Internet connection already set up and working before you use this feature of Sherlock. **If America Online is your only email/Internet/web service, you must first open and log on to AOL before you can use Sherlock to search the Internet!**

To search the Internet:

Internet

People

Apple

Shopping

News

Reference

Entertainment

When you choose any of the Internet channels and go to the web, you'll get advertisements in the very bottom portion of Sherlock.

1. Open Sherlock (click the Sherlock Holmes hat in the Dock or press Command F when you are at the Desktop).

2. Click once on the "Internet" channel (the globe).

   If you are looking for a person, click the "People" channel button instead of the "Internet" channel. If you're looking for news, reference material, or Apple support information, click the appropriate channel. If you want to go shopping, take a look at pages 378–379.

3. Type in the item you wish to look for. If it is a phrase, put quotation marks around the phrase; for instance, if you are looking for a recipe for chocolate pecan pie, type "chocolate pecan pie" in quotes.

   If you don't use the quotes, Sherlock will find every web page with the word "chocolate" on it, plus every page with the word "pecan" on it, plus every page with the word "pie" on it. But with the phrase enclosed with quotes, you should only get pages that contain the entire phrase "chocolate pecan pie."

4. Click the Search button (the big one with the magnifying glass).

   If you have a full-time connection, Sherlock will jump on it and do the search.

   If you have a dial-up account, Sherlock will log on to the Internet through your ISP (Internet Service Provider). If it doesn't connect automatically, see page 551 in Chapter 31.

   If you use AOL you must first open and log on to AOL before you click the Search button.

5. You will get a list of "results," as shown on the opposite page. Click once on a result and details of that web page will be displayed in the lower panel (also shown). To go to that web page, either double-click the title in the middle panel of Sherlock, or single-click the underlined link in the lower details panel. Read the captions on the opposite page.

1. *Click the appropriate channel that you want to search.*

2. *Type in what you're looking for.*

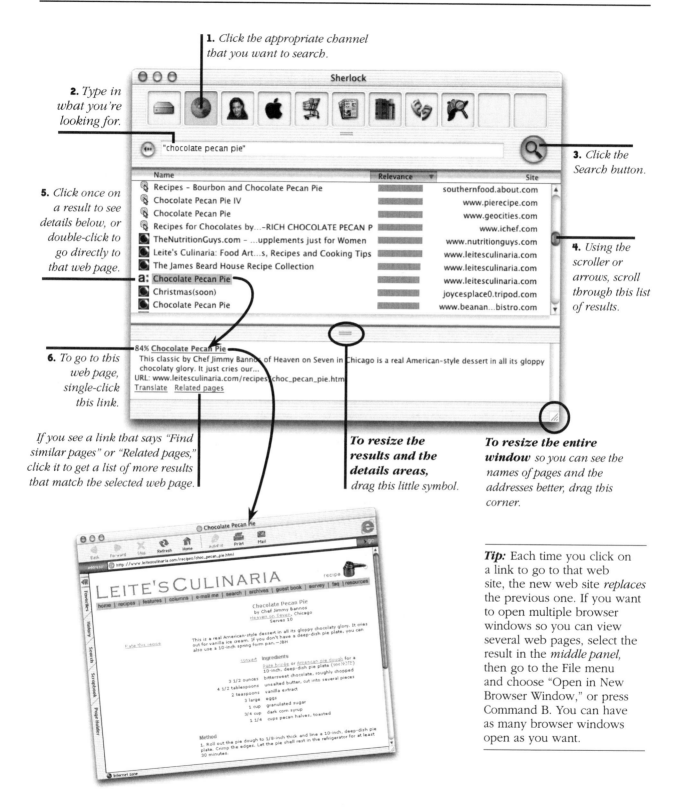

3. *Click the Search button.*

5. *Click once on a result to see details below, or double-click to go directly to that web page.*

4. *Using the scroller or arrows, scroll through this list of results.*

6. *To go to this web page, single-click this link.*

If you see a link that says "Find similar pages" or "Related pages," click it to get a list of more results that match the selected web page.

To resize the results and the details areas, *drag this little symbol.*

To resize the entire window *so you can see the names of pages and the addresses better, drag this corner.*

Tip: Each time you click on a link to go to that web site, the new web site *replaces* the previous one. If you want to open multiple browser windows so you can view several web pages, select the result in the *middle panel,* then go to the File menu and choose "Open in New Browser Window," or press Command B. You can have as many browser windows open as you want.

Shop on the Internet

Sherlock doesn't just *find* items for sale on the Internet—it actually provides you with their prices and availability. Amazing.

Keep in mind that what Sherlock finds is dependent on what is offered for sale *through the selected search sites;* in the case of the Shopping channel, you can see below that Sherlock is only looking through selected sources. That is, if you want to compare prices of a down jacket from Lands End, L.L. Bean, and Orvis, Sherlock is not the right tool to use. But considering there are literally millions of items for sale in the search sites listed in Sherlock, it's not a bad place to look for many things.

Search using the Shopping channel just as explained on the previous pages:

1. Click the Shopping channel button.

2. Type in your request (use quotation marks for phrases).

3. Click the Search button; wait for the results.

4. Double-click the result of your choice to go to that web site, **or:**

5. Single-click your choice to see more details appear in the lower panel, then if you still want to go to that site, click the link in the lower panel.

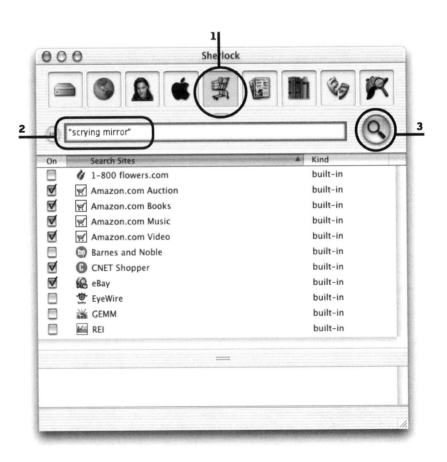

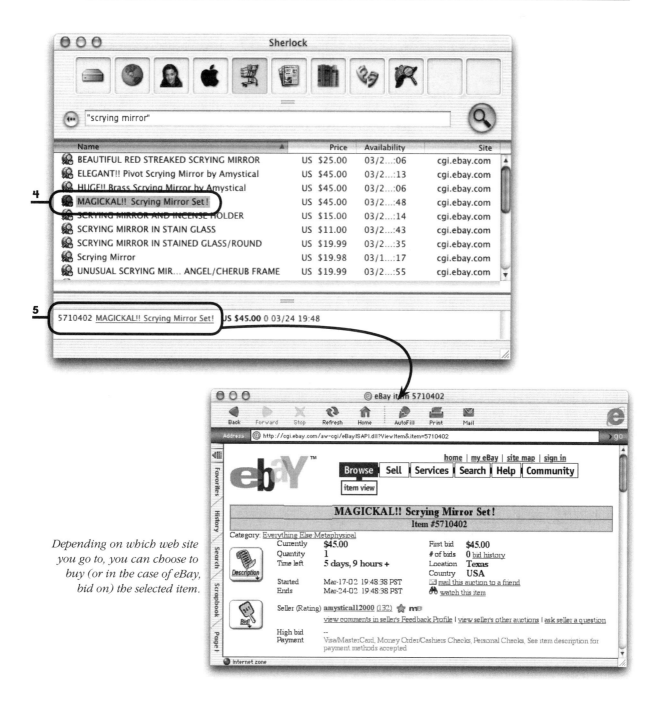

Depending on which web site you go to, you can choose to buy (or in the case of eBay, bid on) the selected item.

Boolean Operators

Most of the search engines on the web use Boolean operators. For more information, go to just about any search engine site and click the "Help" button or the "Advanced Search" button, and look for information about Boolean.

The intimidating term "Boolean operators" (good name for a rock band) simply refers to using words like AND, NOT, and OR in your search. For instance, in the example below, I was able to find only research information that had the words "Mary Sidney" *plus* the word "Countess" on the page. If I did a search for just "Mary Sidney," I would have gotten a huge number of genealogy sites in the results.

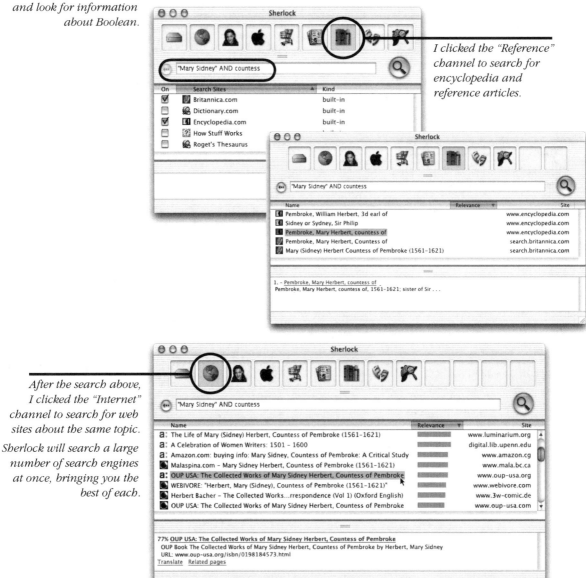

I clicked the "Reference" channel to search for encyclopedia and reference articles.

After the search above, I clicked the "Internet" channel to search for web sites about the same topic.

Sherlock will search a large number of search engines at once, bringing you the best of each.

Tip: To find information about computer jargon, use the Reference channel and type in the term you want to understand.

You can grab any result you find in Sherlock and make a "Web Internet Location" of it. Once you make this "location," you can do several things with it. You can store the location icon in your Favorites folder, which means the location will appear in the Go menu, under Favorites; you can select the location from the menu and your Mac will connect to the Internet, open your browser, and take you to that site. Or you can drag the location file to the Dock so it's always available. Or you can leave the location icon on your Desktop, then just double-click it when you want to go to that site (remember, if you use AOL, you must log on to AOL first).

Adding a Site to Your Favorites

To make a Web Internet Location:

▼ Drag one of the results in the Sherlock panel to the Desktop (just press on the link and drag it, let go when you reach the Desktop). You'll get an icon as shown below.

Drag the result to the Desktop to create the location.

To make a Web Internet Location a Favorite:

▼ Drag the Web Internet Location icon and drop it onto the Favorites icon in any window Toolbar. It will automatically appear in the Go menu under "Favorites." If you have a lot of these, create a new folder in the Favorites folder in which to store them; the folder will appear in the Go menu under "Favorites."

Make New Channels and Customize Existing Channels

You can make your own **new** channels and **customize** existing channels by adding search sites to them or changing their icons.

To make a new channel:

1. Open Sherlock, if it isn't already.

2. From the Channels menu, choose "New Channel...."

3. In the "New Channel" dialog box (shown below), type the name and, if you like, a description of this new channel.

> **New Channel**
>
> **Name the Channel:**
> Robin's Research
>
> **Channel type:** Searching
>
> **Description (optional):**
> Sites for my specialized research
>
> **Icon:**
>
> Cancel OK

Click here to cycle through the channel icons. You can use the same icon as many times as you want.

4. Press on the menu for "Channel type" and choose the sort of channel you want this to be.

5. On the top-right, click the scroll arrows to cycle through a selection of icons to represent your channel.

   Or drag any graphic file from your hard drive and drop it into that little "well," as shown below.

Drag a graphic from anywhere on your hard disk and drop it in this icon well. That graphic will become the icon for your new channel.

6. Click OK. Now in the Sherlock window you will see your new channel.

You can **rearrange the channels.** This might be more useful once you have added a number of new channels to Sherlock. Unfortunately, it's not as easy as rearranging the Dock—the channels cannot slide over to make room for a new one.

If you drag one channel directly on top of another, it will *replace* the existing one. If this is not what you want to do, it means you must first rearrange the other channels so you have an empty spot to move your desired channel into. To rearrange channels, drag them one by one to empty spots.

You *cannot replace* any of the default channels even if you want to—you'll have to move them out of the way first, then move your own into position. In the example below, I moved each channel one by one over to the right so I had an empty space in the second spot. Then I was able to move my customized channel into that second spot.

Rearrange the Channels

To move a channel, drag and drop it into an empty spot.

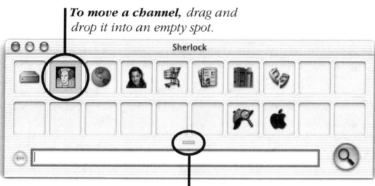

Drag this little marker to make more or fewer channels visible. If you can't display all the channels and slots, first enlarge the entire Sherlock window by dragging the size box in the very bottom-right corner.

Internet Search Sites

Sherlock does what it does by using special "plug-ins" for various search sites on the Internet. In your Home's Library folder is a folder called "Internet Search Sites" (which is different from the "Internet Plug-Ins" folder). The "Internet Search Sites" folder contains all the plug-ins for all the search sites that Sherlock looks through. If the plug-in for your favorite search tool is not in this folder, Sherlock can't search it.

Whenever you open Sherlock at the same time your Internet connection is open, Sherlock will automatically go to Apple's web site at **www.apple.com/sherlock/plugins.html,** get the latest updates for the plug-ins that Apple provides, and install them for you.

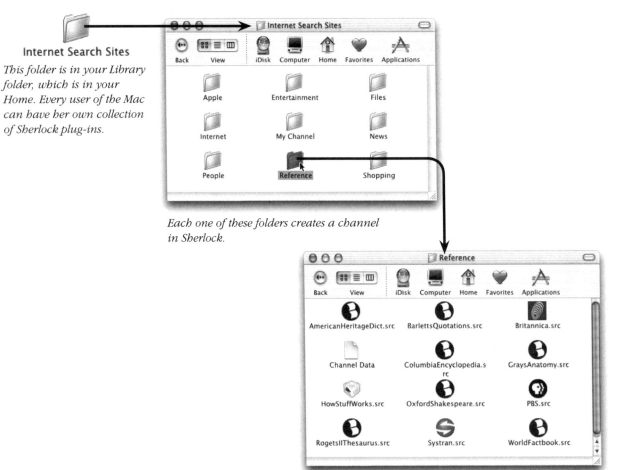

Internet Search Sites

This folder is in your Library folder, which is in your Home. Every user of the Mac can have her own collection of Sherlock plug-ins.

Each one of these folders creates a channel in Sherlock.

This is what the .src files look like in the various folders in the Internet Search Sites folder. If you don't have an .src file for a site, Sherlock can't search it.

There is a great web site that offers a fabulous **collection of Sherlock plug-ins.** You can download the entire collection, then pick and choose which ones you want to use.

To find and add new search sites:

1. **Quit Sherlock** if it's open (be sure to quit, not just close!), connect to the Internet if you're not already, and open your browser.

2. Go to **www.searchstandard.com.** Click the link called "Download Sherlock Plugins." (Keep in mind that web sites change—if that exact link isn't there, poke around to find the current link.)

3. A folder will be downloaded (copied) to your Mac. You'll see the Download Manager appear on your screen, telling you how much time it will take (just a couple of minutes on a phone line).

   When the download is finished, you'll be asked if you want to send a return receipt; you should because then you'll be notified of updates, which happen regularly because these .src files go out of date quickly. The receipt is free and optional.

   When all is said and done, you'll find these two files on your Desktop:

sherlockplugins.sit

Sherlock Plugins

a) *This .sit is a compressed file. It will automatically uncompress and create the actual folder full of plug-ins, shown to the right. After you find the folder, throw this .sit away.*

b) *When the .sit file uncompresses, you'll see this folder, which contains folders of .src files.*

4. In the folder "Sherlock Plugins" you'll find a "ReadMe" file. Read it. Just double-click on it and it will open.

   There is an "Install Plugins" application inside of this same folder, but at the time of this writing, the installer did not work for Mac OS X, although the plug-ins work. Read the ReadMe file to find out if the installer will now work for you, then follow its directions to install the plug-ins.

   If the installer doesn't work yet, or even if it does, you can use the steps on the following pages to add these new plug-ins to Sherlock.

5. The folder "Sherlock Plugins" contains quite a few individual folders. Each of these folders, when installed, will appear in Sherlock as a new channel, as shown on the opposite page, with a variety of .src files. You'll be able to pick and choose which channels you want to install.

Position the "Sherlock Plugins" folder to the right on your Desktop, as shown below.

6. Double-click the "Sherlock Plugins" folder to open it, then change the view to List View. Narrow the open window and position it to the right on your Desktop (you can cover up the folder icon).

7. Open your Home window, then change the view to Column View.

8. In your Home, single-click on the "Library" folder.

9. In the "Library" folder, single-click on the "Internet Search Sites" folder. The column to the right will display the contents of the "Internet Search Sites" folder.

10. Position the two windows as shown below, the plug-ins folder on top.

11. Click on a folder in the "Sherlock Plugins" window that you want to add as a channel. To select more than one folder at a time, hold down the Command key and click on several folders.

12. Let go of the Command key (if you used it), then drag *one* of the selected folders to the left (they will all come along together) and drop it directly into the column that displays the contents of "Internet Search Sites."

13. Open Sherlock, then read the opposite page.

You could also use any of the techniques described in Chapter 10 for moving files from one folder to another, or any other technique you have discovered.

Also check out the method described on the bottom half of the opposite page.

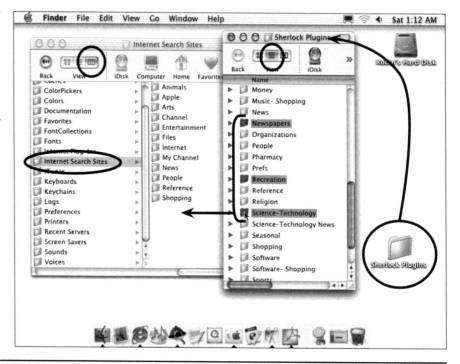

After you have installed these new channels, you'll see their icons in Sherlock, as shown below. Click on each one to see what they offer.

These are the new channels. You can customize and rearrange their icons, as explained on pages 382 and 383.

You might want to **add only a few** of these new search sites. You can always do this: Open any folder inside of the "Sherlock Plugins" folder, then drag individual .src files and drop them on the channel "well," where the icon sits. The channel called "My Channel," with the Sherlock Holmes hat, is empty and waiting for you to do just this. Or you can add new .src files to almost any channel.

You might go to a search site and find a little icon that represents a Sherlock .src file. Download it, then add it to any channel either by the method described on the previous pages, or by dropping it directly on the channel icon, as shown below.

Add individual .src files

You can always open the "Internet Search Sites" folder or the "Sherlock Plugins" folder and put .src files directly into the channel of your choice. Drag them from the folder and drop them right on a channel icon.

1. In Sherlock, do you have to type in the exact and entire name of the file you're looking for?

2. Do you have to type capital and lowercase letters exactly as in the file name?

3. Do you have to type spaces in exactly the right place?

4. How do you tell Sherlock whether to search **a)** by file name, **b)** by content, or **c)** the Internet?

5. How would you find a file you wrote sometime in March '02 that you know had the word "budget" in the file name? You have hundreds of reports with the word "budget" in the names.

6. Once Sherlock has found a web site you want, what is the easiest way to display that site?

7. How can you save a web site address so you can go to it whenever you like?

8. What keyboard shortcut can you press to open the folder that contains a file found on your Mac?

9. How can you trash a file that's displayed in the Sherlock results list?

10. Sherlock found lots of files for you on your hard disk (not web sites). How can you organize them in the results window so they're grouped according to what kind of file they are?

Answers on page 752.

Fonts on Your Mac 25

If you don't know much about fonts, or typefaces, you probably get frustrated looking at the font list in Mac OS X because you have no idea what all those names represent. So the first half of this chapter shows you what all of your fonts like. Even if you're a new user you might like to then customize the Font Panel in TextEdit.

For experienced font users, the last part of the chapter provides the basic technical information about the font changes in Mac OS X and what to do about your font management utilities.

What Your Fonts Look Like

You have quite a few **fonts (typefaces)** available in Mac OS X. On these next several pages are examples of what is installed at the moment I write this (Apple always seems to add and remove a few fonts with every system upgrade). I've divided them into categories so it's easier to find the sort of font you need.

This list includes the Mac OS X fonts, as well as the OS 9 fonts that are automatically installed along with Mac OS 9 (and are somehow available in Mac OS X). If you installed Mac OS X without installing OS 9 at all, you won't have a number of these typefaces. Many applications automatically install their own fonts in a separate place so they are only accessible when that application is open, so you may find fonts in your font list that you don't see here.

You'll see there are a number of typefaces that you will probably never use, so to clean up your font list, you should probably sort them into collections, as explained on pages 406–409. It will only take a couple of minutes.

If you are a font collector, you really need a font management program, which you probably already have. See pages 414–415 for current information about font management programs for Mac OS X.

Print up your own list

Apple has provided you with a "script" that will open TextEdit, type dozens of sentences (the same sentence over and over), and change each sentence into a font sample, labeled with that font name. Then you can print that up and have it next to you.

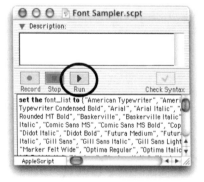

This is the Script Editor that will open. Just click "Run" and it will do what it's supposed to do.

To open and run the Font Sampler script, do this:

1. Press Command Option A to open the Applications folder, or click on the Applications icon in any Finder window.

2. Double-click the "AppleScript" folder.

3. Inside that folder, double-click the "Example Scripts" folder.

4. Inside that folder, double-click the "Info Scripts" folder.

5. Inside that folder, double-click on the file named "Font Sampler.scpt." The Script Editor will open, as shown to the left.

6. Click the "Run" button.

   The script will do as I explained above, then you can print those pages. Quit the Script Editor when you're done.

A **serif typeface** (pronounced *sair ′ if,* not *sa reef ′*) has small bits on the ends of the strokes, called serifs. This kind of typeface works better than most others when you need to set lots of text in print. This is the kind of type you are most likely to see in a book, such as this one, or any novel. The more distinctive the typeface, like Humana Serif, the more difficult it is to read in long blocks of text, although Humana Serif's distinctive look is perfect for something like a brochure.

Serif faces

Several of the serifs are circled above.

Baskerville Regular, *Italic*
SemiBold, *SemiBold Italic*
Bold, *Bold Italic*

Georgia, *Italic,* **Bold,** *Bold Italic*

Hoefler Text Regular, *Italic*
Black, *Black Italic*

Hoefler also has a set of ornaments, shown on page 403.

Humana Serif Light, *LightItalic*
Humana Serif Medium, **Medium Italic**

Palatino, *Italic,* **Bold,** *Bold Italic*

Times, *Italic,* **Bold,** *Bold Italic*
Times New Roman, *Italic,* **Bold,** *Bold Italic*

*These two versions of **Times** are basically the same typeface. The reason you have both is because Windows uses Times New Roman instead of Times, so if you are creating a document that will be used on or sent to a Windows machine, use Times New Roman.*

All caps Several fonts are **all caps** (capital letters) and so their use is limited. Words in all caps are much more difficult to read. But these are great for short bursts of text or a distinctive touch here and there.

BLAIRMDITC

CAPITALS

COPPERPLATE LIGHT, REGULAR, **BOLD**

Specialty serif faces The typefaces shown below are **serif faces** that have special uses. All of these are particularly elegant at large sizes of type, but difficult to read at small sizes.

Didot is what's considered a classic Modern typeface, with strong contrasts between the thick and thin parts of the letters. Use it nice and large where you want a classy look.

Didot Regular, *Italic,* **Bold**

Bodoni SvtyTwo Book 1234567890, *Book Italic,* **Bold**

Bodoni SeventyTwo and Big Caslon are both specially designed to be used at very large point sizes, as you can see in the examples on the opposite page. Compare the numerals in the two Bodonis.

Bodoni SvtyTwo OS Book 1234567890, *Book Italic,* **Bold**

Big Caslon

The "OS" you see in some typefaces stands for OldStyle. These faces give you the beautiful numerals shown in the example to the far right.

The 58 Times of Day
1564 Noon Square
Beloxi, MI 98765
505.438.9762

This is Bodoni SeventyTwo with the regular (called "lining") numerals. They appear too large.

The 58 Times of Day
1564 Noon Square
Beloxi, MI 98765
505.438.9762

This is Bodoni SeventyTwo OS with the oldstyle numerals. So pretty!

This is Bodoni SeventyTwo os set in 72 point.

These two examples, above and below, compare a typeface that is specifically designed for large print with a regular typeface that is designed to be used in body copy. Notice how the Palatino face looks so heavy and horsey because the thicker lines that make it readable in smaller sizes are too large for this size of text.

The typeface above looks great in the large size, but those thin strokes that look so good when set large will disintegrate when printed at small sizes.

This is Palatino set in 72-point type.

Sans serif faces   The word "sans" is French for "without," so **sans serif faces** are those without the serifs. Sans serifs are best for headlines, signage, and emphasis, as you see throughout this book. Many of them are also good for faxing, copying, and printing on cheap paper because they hold up very well.

Arial Regular, *Italic,* **Bold,** ***Bold Italic***
Arial Black
Arial Narrow, *Italic,* **Bold,** *Bold Italic*
Arial Rounded Bold

Futura Medium, *Medium Italic,* Condensed Medium, **Condensed ExtraBold**

Gadget

Helvetica Regular, *Oblique (Italic),* **Bold,** *Bold Oblique (Italic)*

Helvetica Neue Regular, *Italic,* ***Bold, Bold Italic***
Helvetica Neue Light, *Light Italic*
Helvetica Neue UltraLight, *UltraLight Italic*
Helvetica Neue Condensed Bold, Condensed Black

Lucida Grande Regular, **Bold**

Optima Regular, *Italic,* **Bold,** *Bold Italic,* **Extra Black**

Skia Regular

Stone Sans Semibold, *Semibold Italic 12345*
Stone Sans Bold 12345
Stone Sans Semibold Italic OS 12345
Stone Sans Semibold OS 12345
Stone Sans OS Bold 12345
Stone Sans Semibold SC (small caps) 12345

Here are three more fonts with oldstyle numerals, as well as a SMALL CAPS face (SC).

Trebuchet Regular, *Italic,* **Bold,** *Bold Italic*

Verdana, *Italic,* **Bold,** ***Bold Italic***

On the chance that you need text that lines up in columns, emulates a typewriter look, or is necessary in some techy terminal stuff, you have several **monospaced fonts.** Monospaced, also called fixed-width, means every character takes up the same amount of space, as on typewriters. As shown below, a comma takes up the same amount of space as a capital M.

Typefaces that are not monospaced are called **proportional,** or sometimes variable width.

The typeface American Typewriter, shown on page 398, emulates the look of a typewriter, but with the professional typesetting features in regard to letterspacing, character shape, and other features. But American Typewriter is not monospaced like a real typewriter.

Monospaced faces

Andale Mono

Courier, *Oblique,* **Bold,**

Bold Oblique

Courier New, *Italic,* **Bold,**

Bold Italic

Monaco

VT100 Roman, **Bold**

Script faces   **Scripts** are wonderful for that elegant, casual, party, or personal accent.

Apple Chancery

Aristrocrat—oh yes, we are!

Brush Script

Bickley Script—a casual affair

Party.—Let's Whoop it Up!

For directions on which keys to press to type all of the great little drawings built into the Party font, see page 402

Zapfino is a very elegant face.

Same with **handlettered** fonts.

Handlettered fonts

Bradley Hand

Comic Sans Regular, **Bold**

Marker Felt Thin, Wide

Sand

Papyrus

Textile Regular

Decorative fonts

Decorative faces are the most fun to use. They're just irresistible. Use them big and bold—don't be a wimp!

American Typewriter Light, Regular, **Bold**
Condensed Light, Condensed Regular, **Condensed Bold**

BERTRAM—WHAT A CLOWN

Bordeaux Roman Bold

HERCULANUM

Impact—boy does it have one

Jokerman—you are one

Luna—as in Lunatics of the Moon

MACHINE —MADE IN USA

Mona Lisa Solid

PORTAGO —EXPEDITE

Techno Regular

Tremor —hey, it looks like California

Wanted —Alive and Well

One of the big deals about Mac OS X is that it uses **Unicode.** See, most computers and fonts use ASCII, an international standard of character encoding. ASCII uses one electronic "byte" of information per character. One byte of information is eight bits. Each of these eight bits is either a one or a zero, an on or an off signal. If there are two options (on or off) for each of the eight bits, that's 2^8, which is a total of 256 different characters that can be created. This is okay for English, but is totally inadequate for many **non-Roman languages** such as Japanese, Chinese, Korean, etc.

Well, Unicode uses *two* bytes (16 bits), so that's a possibility of 2^{16}, or over 65,000 different characters in a font. Unicode, combined with the International and Keyboard preferences built into the Mac, makes your computer truly international. To that end, Apple has supplied several OpenType fonts that will type various languages, once you have activated those languages as explained on pages 47–51. The OpenType format is the only font format that can take advantage of Unicode.

Type for non-Roman languages

Apple Gothic
Apple LiGothic Medium

Hei Regular

Hiragino Kaku Gothic Pro W3
Hiragino Kaku Gothic Pro W6
Hiragino Kaku Gothic Std W8
Hiragino Maru Gothic Pro W4

Hiragino Mincho Pro W3
Hiragino Mincho Pro W6

Osaka Regular, Regular-Mono

WebDings   These are just a few of the characters available in **WebDings.** Also try typing any character with the Option key held down, then with both the Option and the Shift keys down. Each time you'll get different characters.

a	b	c	d	e	f	g
✔	🚲	☐	◆	🎁	🚒	■

h	i	j	k	l	m	n
🚑	ⓘ	✈	🐝	✦	❗	●

o	p	q	r	s	t	u
⛴	🚓	()	✗	?	🚇	🚉

v	w	x	y	z
🚌	⛳	🚫	⊖	🚭

A	B	C	D	E	F	G
🏗	🏘	🏙	🏚	🌵	🏭	🏛

H	I	J	K	L	M	N
🏠	🚩	🏝	🛣	🔍	⛰	👁

O	P	Q	R	S	T	U
👂	🌲	⛺	⛰	🏟	🚢	📢

V	W	X	Y	Z
📢	▶	◀	♥	💐

Bodoni Ornaments

Below are the available ornaments in the font **Bodoni Ornaments** which you might or might not have on your Mac. Either select the Bodoni Ornaments font and then type the character shown below to get the ornament you want, or type the character first and then change the character's font to Bodoni Ornaments.

a b c d e f g h i j k l m

n o p q r s t u v w x y z

A B C D E F G H I J K L M

N O P Q R S T U V W X Y Z

1 2 3 4 5 6 7 8 9 0 - =

, . / [ ] \ { } |

Hold down the Option key and press:

` 2 3 4 5 6 7 8 w e r

t y u s g b m .

Party Ornaments

Follow the directions as explained on the previous page.

=

hold down the Shift key and press:

`   1   2   3   6   +   ,   .

hold down the Option key and press:

1   2   6   7   r   t   g   /

5   9   0   =   w   d   b   .   h   j   Shift Option p

hold down the Shift and the Option keys and press:

7   8   =   g

Hoefler Ornaments

Follow the directions as explained on page 401.

a b c d e f g h i j k l m

n o p q r s t u v w x y z

A B C D E F G H I J K L M

N O P Q R S

1 2 3 4 5 6 7 8 9 0 - =

, . / [ ] \ { } |

This is the character }
typed over and over.

Using the Font Panel

Many applications that are built specifically for Mac OS X, including TextEdit and Mail, use the **Font Panel.** Professional design applications will use their own version of the Font Panel, but there is a lot you can do with this built-in version. The most useful task is to organize your font list so you don't have to scroll through so many fonts you don't need.

To open the Font Panel in TextEdit:

▼ Press Command T.

You can also go to the Format menu, choose "Font," then slide out to the right and choose "Font Panel...."

In applications other than TextEdit, you might find the Font Panel in another menu, but its command is usually always Command T.

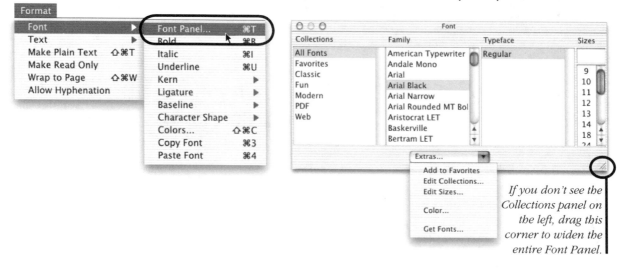

If you don't see the Collections panel on the left, drag this corner to widen the entire Font Panel.

Switch to a Size slider

This is not terribly important, but a nice feature: you can change the **Sizes** control so you can drag a slider to resize your seleted text. As you drag, the text grows bigger or smaller. This is nice if you don't know exactly what point size of type you want, but you'll know it when you see it.

The Font Panel shown above uses the "Fixed List." You can add specific fonts to that list in this little dialog box.

Click the "Adjustable Slider" button to change that fixed list to an adjustable slider, as shown here.

Not all typefaces have the same number or types of **styles** available. For instance, in the Font Panel shown below, on the left, you see the "Family" name Arial chosen, and in the column next to it, you see four "Typeface" (or style) choices: Regular, Italic, Bold, and Bold Italic. This means the designer created four typeface variations of Arial, and if you choose the keyboard shortcut or click the button or menu command to make the selected Arial text italic or bold, you will get the designed style.

But you will only get the designed style *if* the designer built it into the font in the first place, and *if* that style variation is installed in your Mac. For instance, in the Font Panel shown on the right, you see "Arial Black" is chosen, and the "Typeface" column only lists "Regular." This means there is no italic or bold italic of this font installed in your Mac (it might not have ever been designed). If you try to make the Arial Black font into an italic or bold version, you will either hear a beep, which tells you it's impossible, or the application will apply a fake italic or bold, which is a bad thing—not only does it look bad, but it can cause printing problems.

Choosing the right style

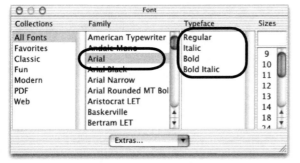

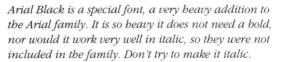

Arial has the same four standard variations as most of the basic fonts.

Arial Black is a special font, a very heavy addition to the Arial family. It is so heavy it does not need a bold, nor would it work very well in italic, so they were not included in the family. Don't try to make it italic.

Font Panel collections

The Font Panel allows you to create **collections,** or subsets of the list of fonts. Several collections are made for you, and you can make as many others as you like. You might make a collection of the four fonts you want to use in a particular report, or the six fonts you use in your monthly newsletter. You can add the same font to any number of collections. When you click a collection name, all of the other fonts in the list disappear temporarily, which makes it much easier to choose the fonts you need. The fonts are not gone, disabled, or removed—they just don't appear in the collection's list. Below you see the Font Panel with a collection in use.

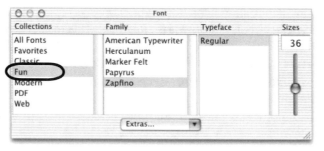

Whoever made up the names of these collections certainly didn't know anything about type. Don't be fooled into thinking these "Fun" fonts are the most "fun" ones you have on your Mac, or that the "Classic" fonts or "Modern" fonts are actually classic or modern.

With a collection chosen (in the left panel), the list of fonts in the "Family" column is limited to just those in the selected collection. This is much easier to work with than scrolling through the long list in "All Fonts."

To see the entire list of fonts again, *choose the collection "All Fonts."*

Add or delete fonts from the Favorites collection

In the **Favorites collection,** you can add not just a font family, but a specific style ("Typeface") and point size.

To add fons to or delete fonts from the Favorites collection:

▾ **To add a font:** In the Font Panel, click once on any font "Family" name, plus any "Typeface" style you want, plus a point size.

From the "Extras…" menu at the bottom of the Font Panel, choose "Add to Favorites."

▾ **To delete a font,** select it, then from the "Extras…" menu, choose "Remove from Favorites."

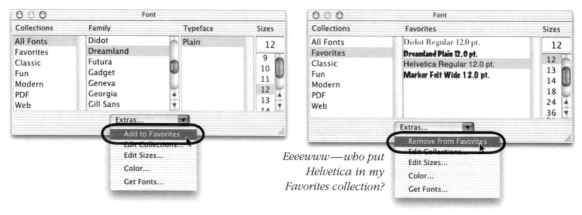

Eeeewww—who put Helvetica in my Favorites collection?

You can **create new collections** for yourself. These might be project-specific collections, or category specific. For instance, you might want a collection that displays all of the available script faces so when you want a script, you don't have to scroll through the entire list. You might want a collection that eliminates all of the fonts you don't need at the moment, like the ones designed for non-Roman characters, math and science characters, and the terminal application fonts. Remember, it is impossible for you to remove fonts from your Mac in this way—you are merely removing them from the list subset.

Any new collections you make in the Font Panel will appear in all other applications that use the Font Panel the next time you open the application.

To create a new collection:

1. From the "Extras…" menu at the bottom of the Font Panel, choose "Edit Collections…."

2. Click the **+** symbol in the bottom-left of the window.

3. A new collection name appears in the left column, named "New-1."

4. Click the "Rename" button, then select the text "New-1" and replace it with your own word or words.

5. Now add (or delete) fonts to your new collection as described on the following page.

   Note: *In the current version of Font Panel, once you quit the application, you cannot edit your own collection! You cannot add or delete fonts from it. This must be just a bug and will surely be fixed in a future version.*

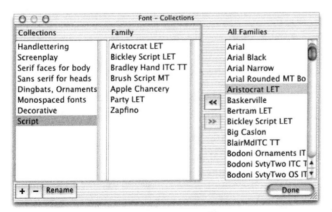

I created more reasonable and typographically correct collections for myself.

To delete an entire collection (which does not delete any fonts), select the collection in the left column, then click the **–** button.

Add a font to an existing collection

You can **add** fonts to your new collections. In fact, you can add the same font to as many collections as you like. (To add to the Favorites collection, see the previous page.)

To add fonts to a collection:

*Note: At the moment, you cannot add or delete fonts from the collections that came with Font Panel—you can only add or delete from a **new** collection, and after you quit this application, you can no longer add or delete even from your own collection. This will surely change. You can always add or delete entire collections.*

1. From the "Extras…" menu at the bottom of the Font Panel, choose "Edit Collections…."

2. Click once on a collection name.

3. In the column on the far-right labeled "All Families," click on the name of the font that you want to **add** to the collection.

4. The double-arrow button that points to the left will appear. Click it to move a copy of the selected font over to the list of fonts in the collection.

Delete a font from an existing collection

You can **delete** fonts from your new collections, or delete a collection altogether. Deleting fonts from a collection does not delete them from your Mac, or even from the "All Fonts" or "Family" list.

To delete fonts from a collection:

1. From the "Extras…" menu at the bottom of the Font Panel, choose "Edit Collections…."

2. Click once on a collection name in the far-left column.

3. Click on the name of the font in the middle column, labeled "Family," that you want to **delete** from the collection.

4. The double-arrow button that points to the right will appear. Click it to delete the font name from the collection.

Share your collection

If you love using type and learning about type or maybe you teach typography and so you've created a lovely **assortment of collections** to keep your fonts organized, you can spread your affection to those who care less. That is, if you've taken the time to organize your fonts into collections, you can give those collection files to others (like students) so their Font Panels are as neat as yours.

In the illustration below, you see where the collections files, called **.fcache,** are stored. Just copy them from your folder, give them to another user, and he should put them into his own personal FontCollections folder.

If the other user has never made a collection, he won't have a FontCollections folder. In this case, go ahead and copy your entire FontCollections folder into his Library folder.

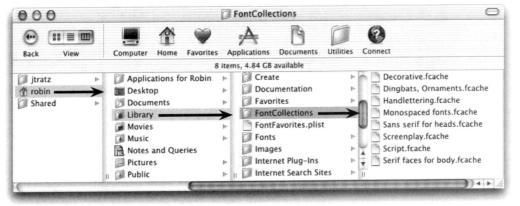

*The **.fcache** files are stored in each user's personal Library folder, in the FontCollections folder.*

The "Get Fonts…" menu option

You've probably noticed the menu option in the "Extras…" menu called **"Get Fonts…."** If you haven't clicked it already, here's what it does *not* do: it does *not* take you to a place on your Mac where there are extra fonts just waiting for you to install. It does *not* take you to a place online where someone is giving away free fonts to add to your system.

This menu option *does* take you to an Apple web site where you can choose to *buy* more fonts (the menu choice should be "Buy Fonts…," not "Get Fonts…"). If you have a broadband connection (a very fast connection that is "on" all the time), this automatic connection might be nothing more than an inconvenience. But if you have a dial-up account (you have a telephone modem that dials the phone to connect to the Internet), this can be a pain in the wazoo because you have to wait for either the connection to be made, or a message telling you the connection couldn't be made for one reason or another (maybe because someone else is already using that line). If you have a dial-up Internet account and want to check out this web page, I suggest you connect to the Internet first, *then* choose this command.

Installing New Fonts

If you are the system administrator for a corporate network, you can install fonts in the Network Fonts folder as well.

Installing new fonts that you have bought or acquired is quite simple. Fonts are stored in several places on the Mac, but as a regular user, you are really only concerned about two of these places, as described below.

1 If you want the newly installed fonts to be **available to everyone** who uses the Mac, install them in the System's Library Fonts folder, as shown in **1,** below. You must be logged in as the Administrator or have the Administrator name and password to install into this folder.

2 Fonts can also be installed into the Fonts folders in individual users' Homes, as shown in **2,** below. The fonts will only be **available to that one user.**

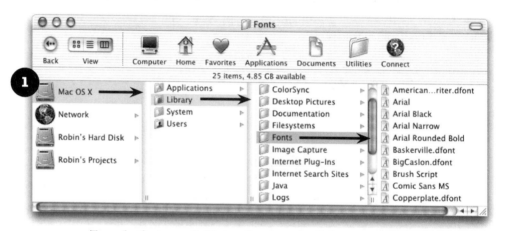

To make fonts available to all users, install them into the folder shown above: On your main hard disk, the one that has Mac OS X on it, open the Library folder, then open the Fonts folder.

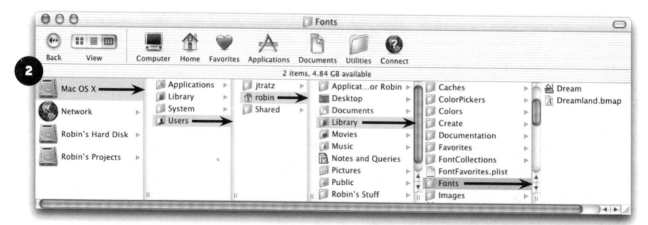

*So fonts will be **available to a single user** (you must be logged in as that user), install them into the folder shown above: On the main hard disk, the one* *that has Mac OS X on it, open the Users folder, then open that user's Home folder, then open her Library folder, then open her Fonts folder.*

DO NOT put fonts in the **main System** Library Fonts folder. Actually, it's impossible for you to put fonts in there, to remove fonts, or to rename anything in that folder, so don't worry. If you are trying to install fonts and you get the message shown below, you're putting them in the wrong place. Check the screen shot **#1,** on the opposite page, to make sure you've got the correct folder.

DO NOT try to install fonts in the System itself

If you're trying to install fonts for everyone and you get this message, you've got the wrong folder. Go through the first "Library" folder, as shown on the opposite page, not the "System" folder shown above.

There is **one more place** where any user can **install fonts,** and that's in Mac OS 9. If you use a lot of Classic applications (applications that have not been rewritten yet to work in Mac OS X), you can install fonts as usual into the Fonts folder inside the System Folder.

There's one more place . . .

Classic applications cannot access the Mac OS X fonts—the applications call on the fonts that are installed in the Mac OS 9 System Folder or from your font manager, if you use one.

If you're a Type Hog, like me, and have so many fonts that you use a font manager such as ATM Deluxe, Extensis Suitcase, Alsoft MasterJuggler Pro, or DiamondSoft's Font Reserve, you can still use those managers just fine with your Classic applications. For instance, I wrote this entire book in Adobe InDesign 1.5 in the Classic environment, using ATM Deluxe as my font manager with fonts installed in Mac OS 9, while running Mac OS X.

Technical Font Stuff

The **technical font stuff** is changing once again. Mac OS X uses a new font technology, actually a couple of new font technologies, but hasn't abandoned the ones we've been using for years. Because I've written entire books and chapters in other books (including a chapter in all of the previous editions of *The Little Mac Book*) about font technology, I'm not going to explain all the details here. Most people don't care anyway. I'll just tell you the important stuff. If you don't know what these font formats mean and you care, please see any previous edition of *The Little Mac Book,* or *How to Boss Your Fonts Around (second edition),* or *The Non-Designer's Scan and Print Book.*

These are the sorts of fonts you can install in Mac OS X:

▾ **PostScript Type 1:** You must install both the printer fonts and their matching screen fonts, as usual. They don't always have extensions.

▾ **Mac TrueType:** The font name usually has a **TT** in it, but not always.

▾ **Mac .dfonts:** The extension is **.dfont**. These are basically TrueType fonts with all of the information contained in the data fork, instead of in the separate resource fork. They are binary files that can be used on other platforms.

▾ **Mac OpenType fonts:** The extension is **.otf**. OpenType fonts can contain over 65,000 different glyphs (characters), as explained on page 399, which allows type to be set in non-Roman languages such as Japanese and Korean. It also allows lots of extra characters in Roman fonts for truly professional typesetting. Applications must be specially written to use OpenType and Unicode; TextEdit and Adobe InDesign are both ready.

▾ **Windows TrueType fonts:** The extension is **.TTF**. This is true—you can install and use Windows TrueType fonts, as shown on the opposite page. This is great for cross-platform work because you can use the exact same font on both platforms. But be careful—not every font works perfectly. For instance, in the example on the opposite page there are three Windows TrueType fonts installed in my Fonts folder. One file, ITCEdscr.TTF (love those Windows filenames), is an elegant Edwardian script that shows up on the screen, but would not print nor convert to outlines. So before you create an entire project using a Windows font on your Mac, make sure it really does work on both platforms, looks exactly the same (same line breaks, etc.), and will print to your final output device.

▾ **Windows OpenType fonts:** The extension is **.OTF**. Same as above.

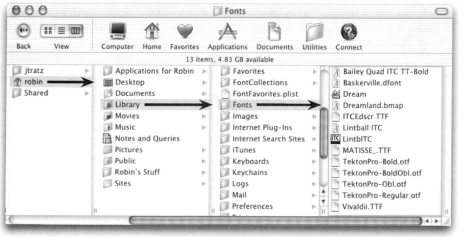

This is my user Fonts folder.
In it you see these font formats
in order:

Mac TrueType

Mac .dfont

Mac PostScript Type 1
(printer font and screen font)

Windows TrueType

Mac PostScript Type 1
(screen font and printer font)

Windows TrueType

Mac OpenType family
(four members)

Windows TrueType

THIS IS MATISSE. THIS PARTICULAR VERSION IS A WINDOWS FONT.

Vivaldi has always been a favorite.

These two examples are fonts I borrowed from my PC and installed in Mac OS X, as you can see above. They appeared in the font list, rendered nicely on the screen, and printed just fine. Amazing.

ATM and Mac OS X

Many of us are accustomed to using **Adobe Type Manager (ATM)** to make PostScript fonts look clean and smooth on the screen. In Mac OS X, the font rendering on the screen and to the PostScript printer is taken care of by the system so you don't need to install ATM. In fact, Adobe is abandoning both ATM and ATM Deluxe, the font manager.

Font Management

Making collections of typefaces in the Font Panel (if the application has one) is fine for a small number of fonts. But I happen to have over 150 megabytes of them, which is probably over 3,000 fonts, and those are just the ones I have installed. There's no way I can drop all of those into my Fonts folder—my font list would be 12 feet long and my computer would probably drop dead. So I use a **font management** utility, which you probably do too if you're reading this paragraph.

If you haven't used a font management program yet, this is what it does: Instead of installing all of your fonts into the Fonts folder, which makes every font open all the time, you can store your fonts in a separate folder anywhere in your Home area that you like. For instance, you could have a folder called "My Fonts" in your Home folder. Then your font management utility lets you create **sets of fonts** from this folder so you can open just the ones you want when you want them. Sets are sort of like the font collections in the Font Panel, except all of the fonts that you're not using at the moment are actually "disabled" and *do not* take up memory or processing power at all. The unused fonts are just sitting in their folder doing nothing, like all other files that are not open. In your application's font list, you see only the fonts you need for that particular project.

Current status of font managers

If you currently use **Adobe Type Manager Deluxe,** you're going to have to switch to another font manager because Adobe is abandoning this product. It still works fine in the Classic environment, so until you switch over your main application to an OS X version, ATM Deluxe will continue to work for you. If you plan to use OpenType fonts, you might want to upgrade to ATM Deluxe version 4.6.

Judging from their web site, it looks like it will be a while before Alsoft's **MasterJuggler** makes it to Mac OS X. **www.alsoft.com**

DiamondSoft **Font Reserve** will have a Mac OS X version out soon, if it isn't already here by the time you read this. Font Reserve is a fabulous font management program, very powerful. If you already use it, hang in there and wait for the upgrade. **www.fontreserve.com**

Extensis **Suitcase** is already available for Mac OS X. The latest version actually works in both OS 9 and OS X. As shown below, it's lovely, powerful, and easy to use. As with Font Reserve, you can activate or deactivate entire sets or individual fonts with the click of a button, view individual fonts or entire sets, get information about what type of font and who the vendor is, collect fonts for output, and many more features. Suitcase is dedicated to supporting the new font formats. **www.extensis.com**

Extensis Suitcase

You can turn sets on and off right from the Dock. Fabulous.

1. What sort of type family is best for lots of body copy, like in a book?

2. When would you use a typeface like Big Caslon?

3. What does it mean when a typeface name has the abbreviation "OS" in it?

4. If you want to install fonts for your own personal use, where would you put them?

5. If you want to install fonts for every user of the Mac to use, where would you put them?

6. What is a monospaced font?

7. If a font is not monospaced, what is it?

8. From the fonts automatically installed on your Mac, can you type Comic Sans in italic or Brush Script in bold? If not, why not?

9. Can your Mac use Windows fonts?

10. Are you a Font Hog?

Answers are on page 751.

iTunes

With the **iTunes** application, you can create music CDs that will work in just about any regular CD player (and on your Mac), or create digital music files to play while you're working on your Mac. iTunes can convert music files from one format to another (known as encoding). iTunes can organize your music files into Playlists. It can create CDs of your customized music playlists. iTunes can connect to the Internet's CD Database and retrieve information about your CDs, including artist, song titles, album name, and music genre. iTunes can connect to dozens of Internet radio stations offering a wide variety of music and talk radio. And it can put on a dazzling, live, visual effects show that's synchronized to the current music selection. What more could you ask? How about this—if you have an iPod (Apple's MP3 player with a 5 gigabyte hard disk), iTunes will upload and synchronize the iPod with your iTunes Playlist (up to 1,000 songs) using a lightning-fast FireWire connection.

For even more detailed information about iTunes, compression, sound quality, custom bit rates, sample rates, and more, get The Little iTunes Book, *by Bob Levitus, available from Peachpit Press.*

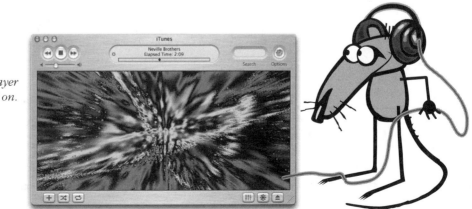

This is the iTunes player with visuals turned on.

Playing CDs

You can play any music CD you stick in your Mac. Make sure your sound is on and turned up (if it isn't, see page 327).

This is the iTunes icon in the Dock.

These are iTunes icons in the Applications folder. The one on the left is the original iTunes, and on the right is iTunes 2, which you should download if you don't have it already.

Choose which columns to display in a CD's detail window: From the Edit menu, choose "View Options..."

To play a music CD:

1. Insert a CD into the drive, label side up.

2. Open iTunes, if it isn't already open:
   If the iTunes icon is in your Dock, click once on it.
   If there is no icon in the Dock, open the Applications folder, find the iTunes icon, then double-click it.

3. The CD icon appears in the Source pane, as shown below. Click the CD icon to see the song list and other information in the Song column.

   If you're connected to the Internet, iTunes will automatically go to the CDDB (CD Database) web site, retrieve the song titles, and place them in the Song column and other displayed columns.

   If you're not connected to the Internet when you insert a CD, song titles will appear as track numbers.

This is the Source pane. You'll see an icon for the CD that is in your Mac.

This is the Song column that lists all the songs on the selected CD.

To see the actual song titles, if they have not appeared:

1. Connect to the Internet (if you're not already).

2. From the Advanced menu, choose "Get CD Track Names."

If you want iTunes to do this automatically every time you put in a CD, see the information about iTunes preferences on page 433.

When you import (rip, encode) a music file from a CD, it is automatically encoded as an MP3 file and placed in the **iTunes Library.** Once a song is in the Library's Song list, you can add it to a customized Playlist for your personal enjoyment, as explained on the following page. Simply playing songs from a CD does not add them to the Library.

The iTunes Library

To add songs to the Library:

1. Insert a music CD into the drive, label-side up.

2. In the CD list that appears, check each song in the list that you want to add to the Library.

3. Click the "Import" button in the upper-right of the window.

To view all the songs in the Library, click the Library icon in the Source pane, circled below. When you drag a song file from the Library to a Playlist collection, as you'll do on the next page, the song remains in the Library. You're not actually moving the digital file—you're creating a directory that tells iTunes which songs are attached to different collections. You can put the same song in as many Playlist collections as you want without bloating your computer with copies of large music files.

You may already have music files somewhere on your computer that you want to add to the iTunes Library. There are two ways to do this:

▼ **Either** go to the File menu and choose "Add to Library…," then find and select your music files.

▼ **Or** drag a file from any location on your hard disk to the Library icon in the iTunes Source pane.

Tip: Each song takes up from 3 to 5 megabytes, at least, of hard disk space, so make sure you have plenty of space before you go crazy with your music files!

This is the Source pane, and you can see that the Library icon is selected. This indicates that the Song list you see to the right are all songs in the Library.

Choose which columns to display in the Library window: From the Edit menu, choose "View Options…."

This is how much of my hard disk is filled with music files in the Library.

Creating a Playlist

A **Playlist** is your customized collection of audio files. You can create as many Playlists as you like, and you can arrange the songs in any order you prefer by dragging selections up or down in the list. You create Playlists so you can play them on your computer, download them to a portable MP3 player, or burn them onto CDs.

To create a new Playlist:

1. Type Command N, or click the "New Playlist" button at the bottom-left of the iTunes window. A new Playlist icon will appear in the Source pane with a generic name of "untitled playlist."

2. Change the name of the new Playlist to something appropriate by typing in the highlighted field.

    You can change a Playlist name at any time: click once on the title, then type a new name in the highlighted field.

When you create a new Playlist, the Mac knows you want to change its name so it highlights the field for you. Just type to replace the existing name.

To add selections to the Playlist from a CD:

1. Insert the CD whose songs you want to add to a customized Playlist.

2. Click the CD icon in the Source pane to open its song list.

3. Drag desired selections from the Song column and drop them on your new Playlist name in the Source pane, as shown below.

    When you drag a song directly from a CD to a Playlist, the song is automatically encoded (imported) to an "MP3" format, placed in the iTunes Library, and added to the Playlist.

Choose which columns to display in a CD's Playlist window: From the Edit menu, choose "View Options...."

New Playlist button

"Songbird" is the name of the CD that is in the Mac and whose songs are showing in the window. "Robin's Favorites" is the name of the new Playlist. You can see song #10 being dragged over to the Playlist name.

To add a song to a Playlist from the Library:

1. In the Source pane, select the Library icon to display your Library collection in the Song column.

2. Drag a selection from the Song column to a Playlist icon in the Source pane.

There's another method for **creating a new Playlist** that's even easier:

1. In the Source pane, select the Library icon to display your Library collection in the Song column.

2. Select the desired songs in the Song column (hold down the Command key and click each song).

   Note: The checkmarks do not indicate whether a file is selected. They indicate two things: songs that will play when you click the Play button, and songs on a CD that will be imported when you click the Import button.

3. From the File menu, select "New Playlist From Selection." iTunes will automatically create the Playlist and add the selected items to it. You can change its name.

You can drag **multiple selections** all at once to the Playlist:

▼ To make *contiguous* multiple selections (of songs that are next to each other in the list), Shift-click the song names. Or click on one song, then Shift-click on another song, and all songs between the click and the Shift-click will be selected.

▼ To make *non-contiguous* multiple selections (of songs that are *not* next to each other in the list), Command-click selections.

This is an example of a Playlist called "Joshua's choice." Now with your Playlist, you can listen to this collection on your compuer, download the collection to a portable MP3 player, or burn a CD of this particular collection of songs.

Play the Radio

Radio Tuner gives you an easy way to tune into **Internet radio stations** that are either built into iTunes or whose addresses you have entered. These stations play a wide variety of music, news, and talk show programs, and netcast the "streaming MP3" format.

To play the radio in iTunes:

1. Click the Radio Tuner icon in the Source column to see the radio options in the Stream column (the same column that is labeled "Song" when the Source is a CD or your Library).

2. Click the disclosure triangle of a radio category to see the various choices of "streams" (streaming Internet connections).

3. Double-click a stream to begin playing it. iTunes will open the designated URL (web address) and "prebuffer" a stream (see page 437 about buffering). Prebuffering usually takes just a few seconds.

Streaming files download a certain amount of information to your computer before they start playing, then continue to download data as the file plays. If you do not have a full-time Internet connection, iTunes will try to connect to the Internet for you when you double-click your radio selection.

Choose which columns to display in the Radio Tuner window: From the Edit menu, choose "View Options...."

To enter another radio address:

If you know the web address of a streaming MP3 radio station that's not in the iTunes Radio Tuner, you can manually enter it.

1. From the Advanced menu in the upper menu bar, choose "Open Stream...."

2. Enter the URL (web address) in the text field in the "Open Stream" window.

iTunes works with four common **audio file formats:** MP3, CD-DA, AIFF, and WAV. iTunes, using the Import feature, can encode CD-DA files from a CD to MP3, AIFF, or WAV files. It can also encode MP3, AIFF, and WAV files to CD-DA format when burning a CD. Each file format is suited for a specific purpose.

▼ **CD-DA** (Compact Disc Digital Audio) is the file format used on all music CDs. This format is also known as "Red Book" because the specifications were originally published in a book with a red cover, which started a tradition of naming CD specifications by color. When you burn a CD from a Playlist, iTunes automatically encodes the files in the Playlist as CD-DA formatted files so they'll play on CD players.

▼ **MP3** is a highly efficient compression system that reduces music files up to 90 percent, but maintains a very high quality. Because they are so highly compressed, MP3s are ideal for downloading from the Internet or for storing on your computer. The full name of an MP3 is "MPEG-1 audio layer-3" and was developed by the Moving Pictures Experts Group.

When iTunes imports a song from a CD to your computer, it encodes the CD-DA formatted song to an MP3 format. The file size of the Beatles song "I Want To Hold Your Hand" is 24.3 MB as a CD-DA file. The file size changes to 2.7 MB when encoded as an MP3 file. The compression efficiency and high quality of the MP3 format is responsible for the explosion of music file sharing on the Internet and the popularity of digital music. MP3s are also ideal for storing music on your personal computer, requiring 80 to 90 percent less disk space than other formats.

▼ **AIFF** (Audio Interchange File Format) is sometimes referred to as Apple Interchange File Format. It is a music format used by the Macintosh operating system. Web designers use the AIFF format for sound files that can play in web pages on a Macintosh computer. The file size of the Beatles song "I Want To Hold Your Hand" is 24.3 MB as an AIFF file, compared to 2.7 MB as an MP3 file.

▼ **WAV** (Windows waveform format) is a music file format used by the Microsoft Windows operating system. Web designers use the WAV format for sound files that can play in web pages on a Windows computer. The file size of the Beatles song "I Want To Hold Your Hand" is 24.3 MB as a WAV file, compared to 2.7 MB as an MP3 file.

Music File Formats

Page 435 has an explanation of how to select an encoder when importing files.

The iTunes Interface

Most of the controls you need are located directly on the **iTunes interface**. Almost every control is explained in detail elsewhere in this chapter.

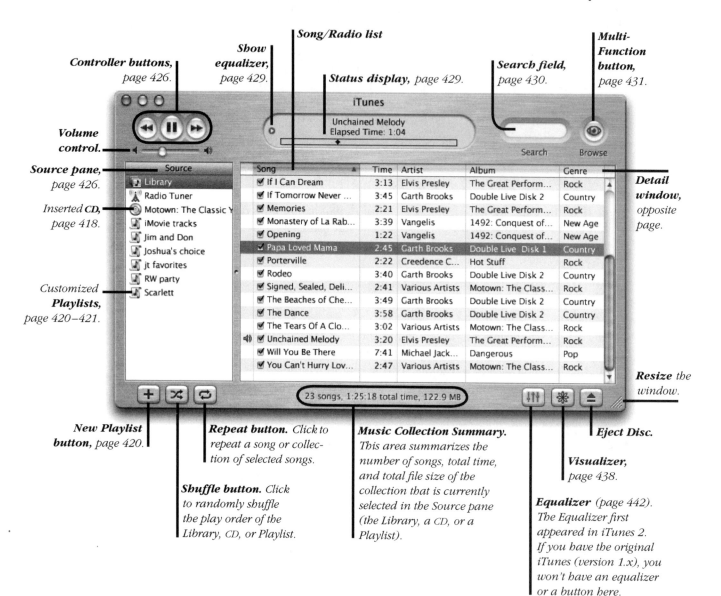

Controller buttons, page 426.

Show equalizer, page 429.

Song/Radio list

Status display, page 429.

Search field, page 430.

Multi-Function button, page 431.

Volume control.

Source pane, page 426.

Inserted CD, page 418.

Customized **Playlists,** page 420–421.

Detail window, opposite page.

Resize the window.

New Playlist button, page 420.

Shuffle button. Click to randomly shuffle the play order of the Library, CD, or Playlist.

Repeat button. Click to repeat a song or collection of selected songs.

Music Collection Summary. This area summarizes the number of songs, total time, and total file size of the collection that is currently selected in the Source pane (the Library, a CD, or a Playlist).

Eject Disc.

Visualizer, page 438.

Equalizer (page 442). The Equalizer first appeared in iTunes 2. If you have the original iTunes (version 1.x), you won't have an equalizer or a button here.

The **Detail window** displays various columns of song information. The visible columns in the Detail window will vary depending on which type of collection you've selected in the Source pane and which options you've chosen in View Options (from the Edit menu). The columns typically include Song, Time, Artist, Album, and Genre.

The Detail Window
of songs and radio stations

Play any selection in the Song column by double-clicking its title. When the selection has finished playing, iTunes plays the next song in the list that has a checkmark next to it.

Selecting and playing songs

When you insert a CD, by default *all* the song titles have a check next to them, which means they will all play in order when you click the Play button. The check mark also determines which songs will be encoded and placed in the iTunes Library when you click the Import button.

▼ **To deselect (uncheck) all the songs at once,** Command-click on any song.

▼ **To select (check) all songs at once,** Command-click on any song.

▼ **To select a group of contiguous songs** in the song list, click on one song, then Shift-click another song. All titles between the two clicks will be automatically added to your selection.

▼ **To select a group of non-contiguous songs** to your group selection, Command-click on the selections.

If song titles are cut off by the narrow width of the Song column, **resize the column.** Place your cursor over the thin, gray, dividing line, then press-and-drag the line to the right as far as necessary to see the song titles.

Resize or rearrange columns

To **rearrange the columns,** click on a column's title to select it, then drag the column left or right to a new position.

The information in the Detail window is always **organized** by the selected column. In the example on the opposite page, the information is organized alphabetically by Song title—you can see that the Song column heading is selected.

Organize the column information

When you select a column heading, a small triangle appears to the right of the column name to indicate that you can **reverse the order** in which the column information is displayed. For instance, if the song titles are sorted in alphabetical order, click the triangle to sort them alphabetically backwards. If they are sorted in order of longest song first (Time), click the triangle to sort them in order of shortest song first.

Controller Buttons

The three big round buttons are the controller buttons.

The **controller buttons** act like the controls on most any CD player.

▾ **To select the Next song,** single-click the Forward button (double arrows pointing to the right).

▾ **To Fast Forward** the current selection, press-and-hold the Forward button.

▾ **To select the Previous song,** single-click the Back button (double arrows pointing to the left).

▾ To **Rapid Reverse** the current selection, press-and-hold the Back button.

▾ The middle button toggles between **Play** and **Pause** when a CD or MP3 file is playing.

The same button toggles between **Play** and **Stop** when the Radio Tuner is active.

The Source Pane

The **Source pane,** on the left side of the iTunes window, displays the iTunes Library, the Radio Tuner, any current CD that is in your CD drive, and any custom Playlist that you've created.

This is the Source pane. You can see the Library icon, the Radio Tuner icon, the icon for the CD that is currently in the Mac, and several customized Playlists.

*To **resize** the Source pane, drag this tiny dot.*

Close, Minimize, and Zoom

As usual for every window in Mac OS X, you see the **three colored buttons** in the upper-left of the window, but they act a little differently.

▾ Click the **red button** (the close button) to hide the iTunes window, even while music is playing. It won't affect the music.

To show the player again, click the iTunes icon in the Dock.

Or use the keyboard shortcut Command 1 (one) to toggle between Hide Player and Show Player while iTunes is active.

▾ Click the **yellow button** to minimize the Player in the Dock.

▾ Click the **green button** (the zoom button) to reduce the size of the Player window to its smallest possible size, as shown to the left. Click the green button again to return to the full window.

Get information about song tracks, add comments to songs, and adjust the volume control in the **Song Information** window.

To open the Song Information window:

1. Select one song track or multiple song tracks.
2. Type Command I to open the window.

If you made a single song selection, the Song Information window contains three tabs: "Info," "Tags," and "Options."

The **Info** pane gives some minimal information about the CD track (or other selected music file in your Library or Favorites).

The **Tags** pane provides additional information, plus a Comments field in which you can add your own comments, such as "Use this track on the Bourbon Street iMovie."

—continued

The settings in the **Options** pane allow you to set the Volume Adjustment for each individual song. This is helpful if you're a serious rocker and cranking up the other volume controls just isn't loud enough (the Sound settings in System Preferences, plus the iTunes window volume control). This Volume Adjustment can put your speakers into *Spinal Tap* mode ("Most speakers just go to 'Ten,' but ours go to 'Eleven.'").

The Options tab also lets you set a "Start/Stop Time" for a song. In the event you want to **play or import just a section** of a long song, enter the "Start playback" and "Stop playback" times in a minutes:seconds format (00:00).

To determine which time settings you need, first play the whole song. Watch the Status display at the top of the iTunes window, and write down the beginning and ending "Elapsed Time" of your desired music segment.

If you selected more than one song, the **Multiple Song Information** window, as shown below, combines all the previous information and options into one window. The Volume Adjustment will affect all selected tracks.

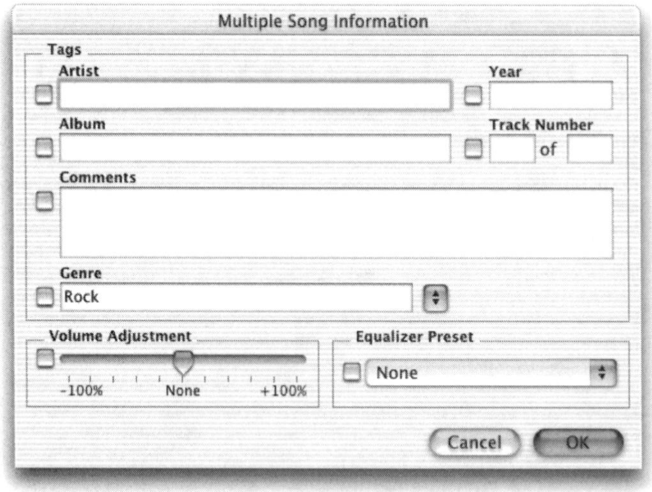

When iTunes is playing a song selection from a CD, the iTunes Library, or from a Playlist, the **Status display** (at the top of the iTunes window) displays three lines of information: music identification, music track time, and an audio track bar.

The **music identification** (top line) in the Status window automatically scrolls through song name, artist name, and album name. Click on the top line to manually cycle through these three bits of song information.

The **time duration** of a song is shown in the middle line. Click on it to cycle between "Remaining Time," "Total Time," and "Elapsed Time."

The **audio track bar** on the bottom line indicates the current location of playback in relation to the entire song. **To move to any point in a song,** drag the black diamond left or right.

When iTunes is playing the **Radio Tuner,** the Status window is similar.

Click the top line to manually toggle between the **URL** (Internet address) of the radio station and its **station name** or call letters.

The middle line shows the **Elapsed Time.**

The bottom line is a **blank audio track** line. A streaming connection can continue indefinitely and you can't drag ahead or back in a streaming file.

No matter what you're listening to, you can turn the Status window into a **graphic equalizer:** click the small round/triangle button on the left side of the window. This feature doesn't offer control of any kind, but it's fun.

iTunes 2 includes a real equalizer; see page 442.

iTunes Search The **Search** field enables you to quickly find songs in the current song list (songs from the Library, a CD, or a custom Playlist).

To search:

▼ In the Search field (circled, below), type one or more key letters or words that are in any part of the artist, song, or album name.

You don't need to hit the Return or Enter key—a list will appear instantly in the Song pane that includes only songs that contain your key words. As you type, the list will change constantly to reflect the matching results.

For instance, in the example below I'm looking for a song by Roy Orbison called "Almost Eighteen." I start typing the word "almost" into the Search field and the Song list instantly shows four songs that match the letters typed ("al" so far). The match can be anywhere in the song title, artist name, or album name; capital letters or lowercase doesn't matter. If I continue to type the word "almost," the list will be narrowed down to a single choice.

Type your search in here.

Multi-Function Button

The button in the upper-right corner of the iTunes player changes appearance and functionality according to the type of source selected in the Source pane and if "Visuals" are turned on. That's why I call it the **Multi-Function button.** Following are its different states.

Browse button: If *Library* is the selected source in the Source pane, the Browse button appears. Click Browse and the top section of the iTunes window displays two new panes for browsing: Artist and Album. Click on any item (or multiple items) in these two panes and the display below will show only songs that match the selections above. When you've located the desired song or album, you can drag the selection straight from the Browse section to a Playlist in the Source pane.

To add a Genre column to the Browse area: from the iTunes menu, choose "Preferences...." Click the checkbox to "Show Genre When Browsing."

Import: Select a *CD* in the Source pane to activate the Import button. Import encodes selected CD audio tracks into the MP3 format and places them in the iTunes Library. See more about importing on page 432.

Refresh: When *Radio Tuner* is selected in the Source pane, the Multi-Function button becomes the Refresh button. Click the Refresh button to check the Internet for the latest radio listings available through iTunes.

Burn CD: The Burn CD button becomes visible when a *Playlist* is selected in the Source pane.

To burn a CD:

1. Select a Playlist you've created in the Source pane.
2. In the Song list, uncheck any songs you do not want recorded on the new CD.
3. Click the Burn CD button and the button cover opens to reveal the Burn icon.
4. The Status window will instruct you to insert a blank CD.
5. After you've inserted a disc, iTunes will begin burning the songs onto the disc.
6. When finished, a new CD icon will appear on the Desktop.

Options: If *Visuals* are turned on, the Multi-Function button becomes the Options button. Click the Options button to present the "Visual Options" window. You can choose to display the animation frame rate, cap the animation frame rate at 30 frames per second, always display the song info, and set a faster display or a better quality display. See pages 438–441 for details about Visuals.

Ripping Music Files to MP3 Format

To **rip** a file is to encode it (convert it) from one format to another. To copy a CD music track **to your computer,** you'll convert it (rip it) from the CD-DA format to MP3.

To rip music files:

1. Insert a music CD and the CD tracks appear in iTunes' Detail window.

   If iTunes does not automatically go to the Internet and get the title names and other track information, go to the Advanced menu and choose "Get CD Track Names." After a few moments, the CD database will fill in the track titles, artist, album, and genre.

2. Select the tracks in the list you want to rip. By default all tracks in the list are checked when you first open a music CD. Uncheck any track that you don't want to rip and save on your computer.

3. Click the "Import" button in the upper-right corner of the iTunes window. The checked tracks will be ripped and added to the iTunes Library in the Source pane.

An orange icon (a circle with an animated wave symbol) appears next to the track that is being ripped.

When the file is finished, the orange icon is replaced by a green icon (a circle with a check mark), indicating that it has already been imported.

Ripping music files to other formats

You may want to **encode a music file to some format other than MP3,** especially if you plan to embed the file in a web page. Encode MP3 files as AIFF or WAV formats by changing the Import settings.

1. From the iTunes menu, choose "Preferences...."

2. Click the Importing tab in the Preferences window.

3. Change the "Import Using..." setting to AIFF or WAV.

The **iTunes** preferences allow you to adjust a number of settings. From the iTunes application menu, choose "Preferences...."

Click the **General** tab to set "Text," "CD Insert," and "Internet" preferences.

▼ **Source Text** and **Song Text:** Choose "Small" or "Large" text to display in the Source pane and in the Song pane. The actual size difference between "Large" and "Small" is not dramatic, so most users will probably choose to leave these settings on the default choice of "Small."

▼ The **Show Genre When Browsing** option can be helpful when using the Browse feature (page 431) to search through a large collection of music files—it adds a "Genre" column to the "Artist" and "Album" columns that become visible when you click the "Browse" button.

The **On CD Insert** pop-up menu offers options for what happens when you insert a CD. You can only choose one of the options:

▼ "Show Songs" displays the music titles, artist, and album information, but will not play music until you double-click a selection. If you haven't retrieved the cd track names from the CDDB, only the CD track numbers and times will display.

▼ "Begin Songs" automatically starts playing a CD when it's inserted.

▼ "Import Songs" automatically begins encoding songs on the CD into MP3 format and placing them in iTunes' Library when a disk is inserted.

▼ "Import Songs and Eject" does the same thing as above, then automatically ejects the CD.

If **Connect to Internet When Needed** is checked, iTunes will connect to the Internet whenever you insert a CD so it can retrieve song titles and other information from CDDB, an Internet database of CD albums. iTunes will also connect to the Internet when you choose certain items in the iTunes Help window. If you have a modem connection instead of a full-time, broadband Internet connection, you may prefer to uncheck this item to avoid having your modem dial up at unwanted times.

As an alternative, you can manually retrieve CD titles whenever you choose: from the "Advanced" menu in the upper menu bar, choose "Get CD Track Names."

Use iTunes for Internet Playback sets iTunes as your default multimedia audio file player when you download an audio file or click an audio file link on the web.

Effects preferences   Click the **Effects** tab to access a couple of extra features.

- ▼ Check the **Crossfade Playback** checkbox to fade music smoothly between songs without a long gap of silence. The slider adjusts the amount of time it takes to fade out of one song and to fade in to the next song. Move the slider all the way to the right for the smoothest transition with the least silence between songs.

- ▼ Check the **Sound Enhancer** box to add depth and liven the quality of the music. The slider increases or decreases the effect, which is subtle, but noticeable.

When you burn a CD, these effects do not carry over to the CD.

Click the **Importing** tab to set encoding and configuration preferences.

Importing preferences

▼ **Import Using** lets you choose which format the music files will be encoded into: MP3, AIFF, or WAV (as explained on page 423). The default setting of MP3 is ideal for listening to and storing music on your computer. If you want to encode music files for use on the Internet, choose AIFF Encoder (a Macintosh format) or WAV Encoder (Microsoft Windows format).

▼ **Configuration** is a quality setting.

For MP3 encoding, choose between "Good Quality," "Better Quality," and "High Quality." Higher quality settings create larger file sizes.

For AIFF or WAV encoding, choose between "Automatic" or "Custom...." (To learn all about customizing the configurations, see *The Little iTunes Book*, by Bob Levitus, available from Peachpit Press.

▼ You can listen to a song as it's being ripped (encoded) by checking the **Play Songs While Importing** option. Encoding is very fast, usually four to ten times faster than the music plays. The encoding (also referred to as importing or ripping) of a song finishes well before the music has finished playing.

CD Burning preferences
Click the **CD Burning** tab to set the speed at which your Mac burns the CD, choose a format for the disc, and determine the amount of time between songs.

▼ **Burn Speed:** From this menu, set the speed at which your CD burner will burn CDs. The default setting of "Maximum" will let iTunes adjust to the speed of your hardware. If you have problems burning a CD, try setting "Burn Speed" to a slower speed (a lower number).

▼ **Disc Format:** Choose "Audio CD" or "MP3 CD" as the format for burning CDs.

"Audio CD" uses the standard CD-DA format common to all commercial CD players. You can store approximately 75 minutes of music on a CD using this format.

You can choose to burn a CD using the MP3 format instead of the CD-DA format. An MP3 CD can store over 12 hours of music, but can only be played on computers and some special consumer CD players.

If you want to store MP3 music files on CDs, choose "MP3 CD" for the most efficient storage solution.

▼ **Gap Between Songs** can be set to your own personal preference. Set the amount of pause you want to hear between songs.

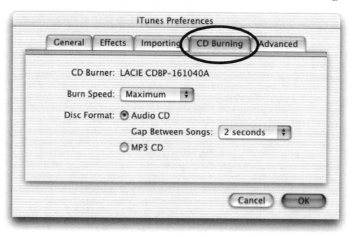

CD-RW or CD-R?
You can burn music CDs using either **CD-RW** discs or **CD-R** discs. CD-RW (CD ReWritable, sometimes called Read-Write) discs will play in your computer, but most stereos and commercial CD players don't recognize them. CD-R (CD Recordable) discs can play on computers and most CD players.

Discs must be blank to record music on them. You can erase a CD-RW disc (see page 499) and then use it to burn a music CD. A CD-R disc cannot be erased or used if it already has files on it. Only a new, blank CD-R disc will work for burning a music CD.

The **Advanced** pane has settings to designate a location for storing your music files, as well as options for burning CDs.

Advanced preferences

▼ **Music Folder Location:** Music files created by iTunes are automatically stored on your startup hard disk. Specifically, they are stored in a folder called "iTunes Music," which is in a folder called iTunes, which is in your Documents folder. This folder contains all of the MP3 files you've encoded. You can change this default location to any location you choose. Click the "Change..." button, then navigate to another folder on your hard disk and choose that other folder.

Every user who uses iTunes will have their own iTunes folder inside their Documents folder.

▼ **Streaming Buffer Size** refers to the Radio Tuner. The buffer size determines how much streaming data is cached (temporarily stored) on your hard disk when you listen to an Internet radio stream. The buffer is like padding that compensates for connection problems that would harm the quality of a direct stream. If you've determined that your connection to the Internet is low-quality, or if your Radio Tuner playback breaks up often, change this setting from the default of "Medium" to the "Large" setting. A large buffer gives iTunes more downloaded streaming data to use for compensation as it deals with slow or faulty connections.

▼ **Battery Saver** does just what it says: it conserves battery power if you're using a laptop and the laptop is not plugged in to an external power source.

iTunes Visualizer

Even on the simplest level, the **iTunes music visualizer** can be mesmerizing. Just double-click a song, then click the Visualizer button at the bottom-right corner of the iTunes window and watch the show. You can also turn Visuals on by pressing Command T, or by selecting "Turn Visuals On" in the Visuals menu.

You can play iTunes' Visuals within the iTunes window in three optional **sizes:** from the Visuals menu, choose Small, Medium or Large.

You can also display iTunes' Visuals in three different sizes while in **Full Screen** mode: From the Visuals menu, choose "Full Screen" to dedicate your entire monitor screen to iTunes' visual effects.

Your previous choice of Small, Medium, or Large will still determine how large the actual visuals appear while in full-screen mode. The Small or Medium option will fill the extra screen space with black.

Toggle between "Full Screen" and iTunes window view of Visuals with the keyboard shortcut, Command F. When in "Full Screen" mode, click the mouse anywhere on the screen to return to a Song list view without interrupting the music.

This is how "Small" visual effects appear in the iTunes window.

Visualizer button

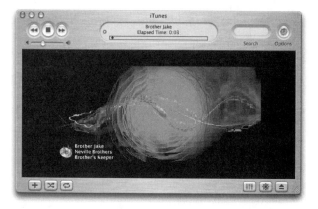

This is how "Medium" visual effects appear in the iTunes window.

This is how "Large" visual effects appear in the iTunes window.

The **iTunes Visualizer** can be even more fun if you know how to interact with it. The Visual Effects Generator uses three different **configurations** to create visuals. You can see these listed at the top-right of the screen if you press the C key while visual effects are playing. The three configurations listed change randomly and morph into one another as music plays. You can change any, or all, of these configurations while music is playing.

The first configuration in the list affects the **foreground** of the visualizer, the primary lines and shapes that modulate and interact with the beat of the music more obviously than the other graphics on the screen. You can cycle through all the built-in effects for this configuration by alternately pressing the Q and W keys (Q for "Previous" selection and W for "Next" selection).

The second configuration in the list affects the **background** graphics, the shapes and patterns that stream from the primary shapes in the top configuration. You can cycle through all the built-in effects for this configuration by alternately pressing the A and S keys (A for "Previous" selection and S for "Next" selection).

The third configuration in the list affects the **color scheme** that is applied to the visuals. You can cycle through all the built-in effects for this configuration by using the Z and X keys (Z for "Previous" selection and X for "Next" selection).

Visualizer configurations

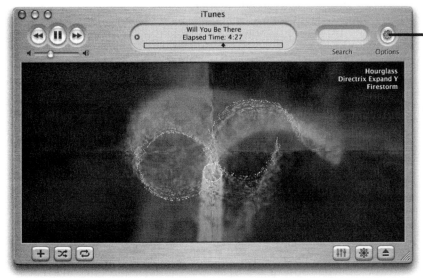

Click this button to set a few options. You can choose to display the animation frame rate, cap the animation frame rate at 30 frames per second, always display the song info, and set a faster display or a better quality display.

Press the C key while visuals are playing to see the current configuation of effects that are generating visuals for iTunes. They're displayed in the upper-right corner of the window, as shown above.

—continued

Visualizer modes Cycle through three different visualizer modes by pressing the M key.

▾ **To play the random visual effects** generated by iTunes, press the M key to cycle to "Random slide show mode."

▾ **To force iTunes to play the current configuration** until instructed otherwise, press the M key to cycle to "Freezing current config."

▾ **To play only the configurations that have been saved as presets** under the numeric keys, as described below, press the M key to cycle to the "User config slideshow mode."

To manually and randomly change configurations at any time, press the R key. Pressing the R key in beat with the music makes you the conductor of an amazing musical light show.

Save a favorite configuration When you change an individual configuration (by using the keys mentioned on the previous page), the new effect fades slowly in as the configuration description in the upper-right corner fades out. If you fall in love with an effect, you can save that particular configuration as a preset that can be activated at any time.

To save a favorite configuration as a preset:

1. Press the M key to cycle through the three different options: "Random slide show mode," "User config slideshow mode," and "Freezing current config."

2. When you get to the "User config slideshow mode," stop. This mode plays configurations that you, the user, have saved as presets.

3. Wait until you see a visual effect you like, then hold the Shift key and tap one of the numeric keys (0 through 9) while the desired effect is playing. You can save up to ten different preset effects.

To play your preset, tap the number key that you assigned to your preset configuration. Try tapping different preset keys to the beat of the music for fantastic visual effects.

A separate **Help** file of keyboard shortcuts is available in the Visualizer feature of iTunes. While Visuals are turned on, press the **?** key (or the H key) to show "Basic Visualizer Help," a list of keyboard shortcuts that appears on the left side of the visual display.

Visualizer Help

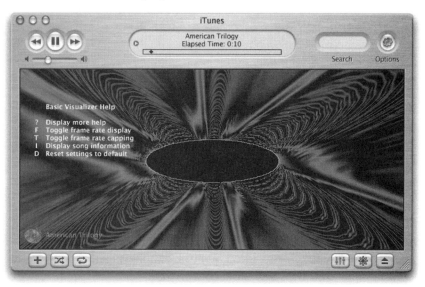

Press the **?** key again to toggle to another list of keyboard shortcuts, "Visualizer Config Help."

iTunes Equalizer

iTunes2 provides an **Equalizer** that enables you to make dramatic adjustments to the sound output of your music files. Make adjustments manually or select from over twenty presets. You can even save custom settings as a preset and add it to the preset pop-up menu, as explained below.

An equalizer represents the various frequencies of the sound spectrum, or more specifically, the spectrum of human hearing. The spectrum is expressed as a measurement known as *hertz* (hz).

The iTunes Equalizer represents the frequencies of the spectrum with vertical sliders, also known as **faders.** The faders are used to increase or decrease the volume of each frequency, expressed as decibles (dB).

> The lowest frequencies (bass) are represented
> by the 32, 64, and 125 hz faders.

> The mid-range frequencies are represented
> by the 250 and 500 hz faders.

> The highest frequencies (treble) are represented
> by the 1K through 16K (kilohertz) faders.

This is the Equalizer button in iTunes2.

To show the Equalizer, click the Equalizer button at the bottom-right corner of the iTunes window. Check the **On** box to activate the Equalizer.

Choose a preset from the pop-up **menu** to automatically adjust the faders.

The **Preamp** slider on the left side of the Equalizer is a secondary volume adjustment. If a music file was originally recorded too quietly or loudly, adjust the volume here. Or if you're looking for the maximum room-booming sound, slide the Preamp up to the top.

To save your custom settings as a preset:

1. Adjust the faders to your satisfaction.

2. From the pop-up menu (where it says "Acoustic" in the example above), choose "Make Preset...."

3. In the "Make Preset" dialog box, enter a name for your preset, then click OK.

   Your new, custom preset now appears in the pop-up menu.

To apply equalizer settings to a song, use one of the following two methods.

▾ **Either** select a song, then click the Equalizer button to open the Equalizer. Select a pre-set from the pop-up menu, or use the faders to create a custom setting.

▾ **Or** add an Equalizer column to the iTunes Detail window: From the Edit menu, choose "View Options...," check the "Equalizer" checkbox, then click OK. An Equalizer column will appear in the Details window, from which you can choose a preset for each song in the list.

Experiment with different sound settings by choosing presets in the Equalizer column.

Transfer songs to an MP3 player

You can use iTunes to **transfer** one or more Playlists **to an MP3 player.**

1. When you connect a supported MP3 player to your computer using a FireWire or USB connection, the player's name appears in the iTunes Source pane.

2. Drag songs from the Library or a Playlist to the MP3 player's name in the Source list.

...or an iPod

If you're using the Apple iPod, you can choose to have iTunes automatically transfer all your MP3 songs or selected Playlists to the iPod, or you can manually drag selections to the iPod in the Playlist. For details, from the iTunes application menu choose "Help," then choose "iPod Help."

Favorite Keyboard Shortcuts

These are the **keyboard commands** that you'll have most fun with:

Command 1	toggles between Show Player and Hide Player
Command T	toggles Visuals on and off
Command F	toggles full-screen mode on and off
Command LeftArrow	turns the volume down
Command RightArrow	turns the volume up
Command UpArrow	selects the previous song
Command DownArrow	selects the next song
Option Command DownArrow	mutes the sound
Spacebar	toggles between Pause and Play
R	instantly changes Visualizer to a new random set of visual effects

Other keyboard shortcuts:

Command N	creates a new Playlist
Shift Command N	creates a new Playlist from the selected songs
Command A	selects all songs in the current song list
Shift Command A	deselects all songs in the current song list
Command R	shows current song file in the Finder
Command E	ejects a CD
Command M	minimizes Player window to the Dock
Command ?	launches iTunes Help
Command Q	quits iTunes
N	toggles between Normal and High Contrast colors
D	resets Visualizer to the default settings
I	displays song information
F	toggles Frame Rate Display on and off
B	displays the Apple logo briefly when Visuals are turned on

iMovie

27

Making movies is incredibly fun and easy with **iMovie.** Connect a digital video camera to your computer with a FireWire cable, launch iMovie, and you're ready to create home movies with sound tracks, transitions between scenes, special effects, and customized titles.

If you didn't get a **FireWire cable** with your camera, check the small box that came with your Mac—often there is a FireWire cable in it (see Chapter 38 for details about FireWire and to make sure your Mac has a FireWire port). If you don't have a cable and need to order one, go to **www.cameraworld.com** and order one.

This is the icon that designates a FireWire port.

Digital video (DV) requires a lot of disk space: One minute of DV footage uses about 220 MB of hard disk space. A four-minute iMovie that contains sound tracks, transitions, and titles may use 4 to 6 *gigabytes* of disk space.

If you're serious about making iMovies, or if you just can't control yourself after making your first iMovie, buy an extra, very large drive to use when working with video. You'll be surprised how fast you can fill a dedicated 80 GB hard drive when you start making movies.

The Basic Steps
Making an iMovie consists of **five basic steps.** This chapter will walk you through each step.

1. Import video clips to the shelf (page 447).
2. Edit the clips (pages 448–450).
3. Place edited clips into the movie Timeline (pages 450–451).
4. Add transitions, titles, effects, and audio (pages 453–457).
5. Export the iMovie (pages 458–459).

As you shoot video, keep in mind that every time you start and stop the camera, iMovie will interpret that as a "scene." Each scene will appear in its own little slot on the "shelf." You can then rearrange the order, edit each scene individually, and much more. Of course, you can always split a scene, cut from one scene and make a separate one, etc., but it's good to keep the scene divisions in mind as you shoot.

Import Clips to the Shelf
Before you can **import,** of course, you must connect the camera to the Mac.

Connect your camera:

1. With the camera off, plug one end of the FireWire cable into the camera and the other end into the Mac's FireWire port.
2. Put the camera into VTR mode (VTR stands for Video Tape Recorder).
3. Open iMovie.
4. Turn on the camera. In a couple of seconds, the monitor area will display the words "Camera Connected," as shown below.

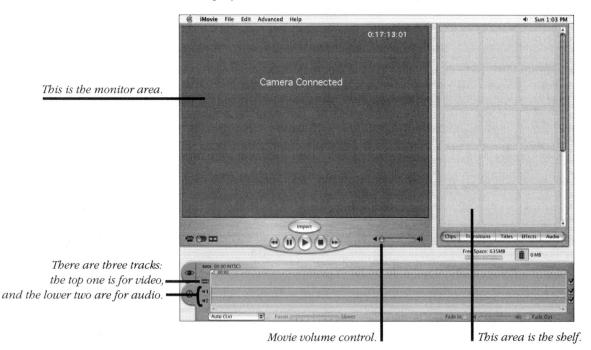

This is the monitor area.

There are three tracks: the top one is for video, and the lower two are for audio.

Movie volume control.

This area is the shelf.

Once the camera is connected, you can preview the raw footage:

1. In the iMovie interface, click the "Camera Mode" button, circled below.

2. Then click the "Play" button to play the video in the iMovie monitor.

   At this point you are just *previewing* the video. iMovie will not digitize and import any video until you click the "Import" button. To economize disk space, preview your footage, then rewind and import just the best footage.

To import video footage into iMovie:

1. Click the Play button to view the raw footage.

2. When you see footage you want to import, click the "Import" button (circled, below). The Import button is blue when it is selected and importing files. You can back up while in Play mode (click the Reverse arrows), but not while Importing.

3. To stop importing, click the "Import" button again. Each time you start and stop importing, iMovie will place that segment (called a "clip") into a separate slot on the "shelf" at the upper-right corner of the iMovie window.

   If you have plenty of disk space, you can let the camera run. iMovie will import all "scenes" (individual segments that were created when you started and stopped the camera, as described on the opposite page) as separate clips and place them on the shelf.

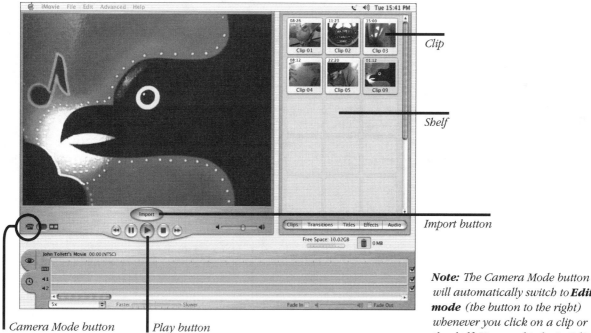

Clip

Shelf

Import button

Camera Mode button   Play button

*Note: The Camera Mode button will automatically switch to **Edit mode** (the button to the right) whenever you click on a clip or the shelf. You need to be in Edit mode to create your movie.*

Edit Clips   Many **clips** are longer than necessary and should be **trimmed** or **cropped**.

▼ Trimming, in iMovie, means to select and delete *unwanted* video frames either at the beginning or the end of a clip.

▼ Cropping means to delete all frames in a clip *other than* the selected frames.

To display and preview a clip:

1. Click a clip on the shelf to select it. The clip is displayed in the monitor. A blue "scrubber bar" appears, as shown below. The scrubber bar represents the time length of the clip.

2. Preview the entire clip by dragging the Playhead (the large white triangle) across the scrubber bar, or click the Play button.

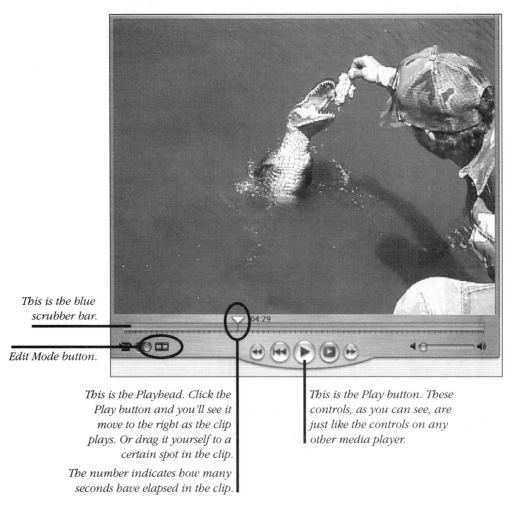

This is the blue scrubber bar.

Edit Mode button.

04:29

This is the Playhead. Click the Play button and you'll see it move to the right as the clip plays. Or drag it yourself to a certain spot in the clip.

The number indicates how many seconds have elapsed in the clip.

This is the Play button. These controls, as you can see, are just like the controls on any other media player.

To trim a clip:

1. Click directly beneath the scrubber bar to show the crop markers, two small triangles. Drag the crop markers to select the frames at the beginning or the end of a clip that you *want to delete*.

2. From the Edit menu, choose "Clear" to delete all of the selected frames.

To crop a clip:

1. Click directly beneath the scrubber bar to show the crop markers, two small triangles. Use the crop markers to select a range of frames in the clip that you *want to keep*.

2. Drag the crop markers individually to select a range of frames. The selected frames are highlighted in yellow.

3. From the Edit menu, choose "Crop" to delete all of the frames that were *not* selected.

The circles point out the crop markers.

This shows a selection of the clip that is going to be cropped. After choosing "Crop" from the Edit menu, this section is all that will remain of the clip.

Tip: When you crop or trim a clip on the shelf, the deleted data goes in the Trash, located just below the shelf. Once a clip is in the Trash, you can't take it out.

Because even a moderate amount of editing results in a huge amount of Trash, you can preserve disk space if you keep an eye on the Trash and empty it occasionally: From the File menu choose "Empty Trash...."

After you've edited a clip, you're going to drag it to the **Timeline** at the bottom of the iMovie window, as explained on the following page, so you can put your movie together.

But when you crop and trim clips as described above, you eliminate the possibility of ever going back later to use segments of clips that you deleted. You might want to keep the original, unedited footage available and accessible. In that case, **copy and paste** a clip segment.

To copy and paste a clip:

1. Use the crop markers to select a range of frames that you want to add to your movie.

2. Press Command C to copy the selection.

3. Click in the Timeline at the bottom of the iMovie window.

—continued

4. Press Command V to paste the selection into the Timeline.

If there are already other clips in the movie track, you can place the copied selection wherever you want: click on an existing clip in the movie track. Type Command V and your selection will be pasted *to the right* of the clip you clicked on.

If later you decide that you need a longer segment from that original clip (to sync with a music track, for instance), the clip in its entirety is still on the shelf instead of forever lost in the Trash.

Place Clips in a Movie

There are two overlapped editing areas at the bottom of the iMovie window: the **Timeline** (indicated by the clock icon) and the **Clip Viewer** (indicated by the eyeball icon). If you put a clip in either the Timeline or the Clip Viewer, it automatically appears in the other area.

Click this to display the Clip Viewer.

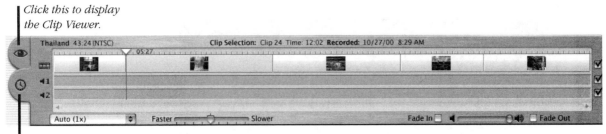

This example is displaying the Timeline.

The Timeline

Use the **Timeline** to arrange the order of clips, add transitions between clips, add effects, create titles, and add audio to your movie.

To add clips to the Timeline:

▼ **Either** drag the clips you created from the shelf to the Timeline.

▼ **Or,** as explained above, copy segments of clips and paste them into the Timeline.

To rearrange clips in the Timeline:

1. Click on a clip in the Timeline to select it.

2. Press Command X to delete it from its current position in the Timeline.

3. Next, select a clip (click on it) in the Timeline immediately to the left of where you want the new clip.

4. Press Command V to paste the clip to the right of the selected clip.

The **Zoom** pop-up menu lets you view the Timeline at different zoom levels. Higher zoom levels show the Timeline in greater detail for precise editing. Lower zoom levels show more clips in the Timeline, to reduce the amount of scrolling necessary.

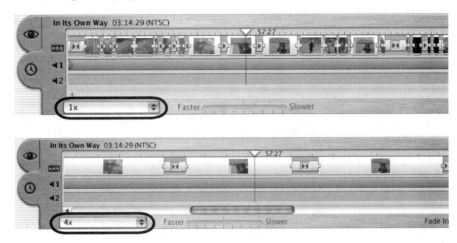

A low zoom level makes more clips visible in the Timeline.

A higher zoom level makes it easier to precisely place the Play-head or to drag a sound track to a certain position. When you use very short clips, you need a higher zoom level to see them clearly.

You can also use the **Clip Viewer,** shown below, to place and rearrange clips, add transitions and effects, and create titles. You cannot work with sound tracks while using the Clip Viewer, but, unlike in the Timeline, you *can* drag clips out of the movie and back to the shelf.

The Clip Viewer

To place clips in a movie using the Clip Viewer, either drag clips from the shelf to the Clip Viewer, or use the copy-and-paste technique explained on pages 449–450.

To rearrange clips in the Clip Viewer, simply drag a clip to a new location.

This is the Clip Viewer.

You can rename these clips. Just click on the clip number to highlight the text, then type the name.

Preview the Assembled Clips

To **preview** your movie, move the Playhead (the white triangle) in the Timeline to the beginning of the movie, or wherever you choose, then click the Play button.

Notice that if you click on a specific *clip* in the Timeline, only that clip shows and plays in the monitor. To load the entire movie into the monitor, click anywhere in the Timeline *except* on a clip (click in the Timeline above the clips or in one of the audio tracks).

Click this button to play your movie in full-screen mode on your Mac.

When the monitor displays the entire movie, the scrubber bar is divided into segments. Each segment is a separate clip in the movie. The small objects that appear between clips in the Timeline are the transitions that were dragged from the Transitions window to the Timeline, as described on the opposite page.

If your movie requires precise synchronization between music tracks and video footage, it's best to assemble all your clips in the Timeline before adding transitions and effects because transitions and effects can alter clip lengths. For some movies, this may not be an issue.

A **transition** is a visual effect that creates a bridge from one scene to the next scene. It might be a cross dissolve, a fade out, a spinning image, or any of a wide variety of other effects.

To add a transition effect between two clips:

1. Click the "Transitions" button beneath the shelf to reveal the Transitions window, as shown below.

2. Click on a transition to see its effect previewed in the small preview window. The "Preview" button plays the effect full-size in the monitor, but the preview may be too slow to be very useful.

3. Use the "Speed" slider to determine the time length of the transition.

4. Drag the selected transition to the Timeline (or Clip Viewer) and drop it between two clips of your choosing.

   To delete a transition at any time: select it in the Timeline and hit the Delete key.

   To change a placed transition: select it in the Timeline, make changes in the Transitions window, then click "Update."

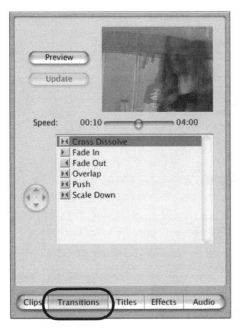

Add Transitions, Titles, Effects, and Audio

Transitions

A limited number of transitions come with iMovie, but you can download others from the Apple web site at **www.apple.com/ imovie,** *or buy collections of transitions and effects from third-party vendors.*

Cross Dissolve vs. Overlap:

The Cross Dissolve transition smoothly dissolves from one scene to another, retaining full motion of the first scene until it dissolves away.

The Overlap effect freezes on the last frame in a scene as it dissolves into the next scene.

Titles   A **title** is text that you place in its own frame or on top of a scene. A title can show credits, act as captions, or add comments. There are many styles of titles to choose from and you can use different typefaces, sizes, and colors.

To add titles to your movie:

1. Select a clip in the Timeline (click once on it).

2. Click the "Titles" button beneath the shelf, then select a title style.

3. Type your title text into the text fields at the bottom of the window.

4. Use the font pop-up menu to select a font.

5. Use the font slider to enlarge or reduce the type.

6. Click the "Color" box to choose a color from a palette.

7. By default, a title is superimposed over a video clip. If you want to superimpose a title over a black background instead of a clip, check the "Over Black" box. This option creates new frames for the title sequence and does not affect other clips. It does, however, add to the length of your movie.

8. If you plan to export the movie as a QuickTime file, check the "QT Margins" box to allow the title to expand within the limitations of the QuickTime margin.

   If you plan to show it on the television, make sure this button is *not* selected or your type may be cut off on the edges, or leave it unchecked all the time to play it safe for any media.

9. Drag your selected title style from the list of styles to the desired position in the Timeline.

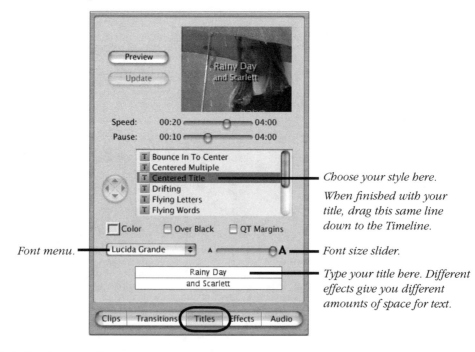

Font menu.

Choose your style here.

When finished with your title, drag this same line down to the Timeline.

Font size slider.

Type your title here. Different effects give you different amounts of space for text.

An **effect** is a visual distortion or alteration that is applied to a clip. The effect may be used for aesthetic reasons, or for visual impact. A limited number of effects come with iMovie, but many more are available from third-party vendors.

To add effects to a clip in your movie:

1. Select a clip in the Timeline (click once on it).

2. Click the "Effects" button beneath the shelf.

3. Select an effect from the effects list.

4. Use the "Effect In" and "Effect Out" sliders to set the amount of time it takes for the effect to fade in and to fade out.

5. If there are other settings sliders below the effects list, set those as well.

6. When you're satisfied with the effect, click the "Apply" button.

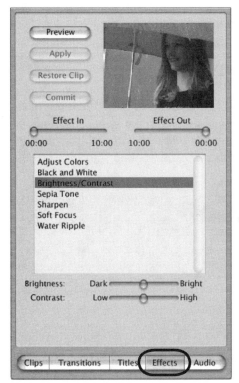

The Preview button plays the effect full-sized in the monitor window of iMovie.

Click the "Restore Clip" button to restore a clip to its original state after applying and previewing an effect.

Once you click the "Commit" button, you cannot restore a clip to its original state (which is a good reason to use the copy and paste technique for clips as explained on page 449).

Audio Place as many **audio clips** in a sound track as you like. Drag audio clips to other positions or to another track, if necessary. Audio clips can overlap in the same track or in separate tracks. When two audio clips overlap, both are audible, although you can adjust the volume of individual sound tracks with the clip volume control slider beneath the Timeline.

*Use these checkmarks to **mute** the sound in a video track or in either of the audio tracks.*

album 02:32:00 (NTSC)   Clip Selection: Clip 17 Time: 06:19

Auto (3x)   Faster ——————— Slower   Fade In □ ◀ ———— ◀) □ Fade Out

*Select an audio clip and check the **Fade In** and **Fade Out** boxes to apply the effects to the clip.*   *Clip volume control.*

To add audio files to your movie:

1. Click the "Audio" button beneath the shelf.

2. Position the Playhead (the white triangle) in the Timeline where you want the recording to start.

3. The top of the audio window contains a Library of sound files that you can drag to either of the audio tracks at the bottom of the Timeline. Select a sound from the library and drag it to a point in one of the sound tracks where you want it to start playing.

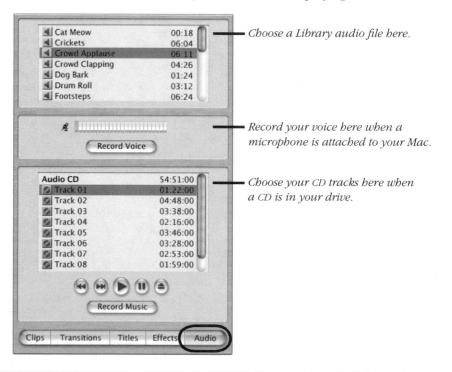

◀ Cat Meow	00:18
◀ Crickets	06:04
◀ Crowd Applause	06:11
◀ Crowd Clapping	04:26
◀ Dog Bark	01:24
◀ Drum Roll	03:12
◀ Footsteps	06:24

Choose a Library audio file here.

Record Voice

Record your voice here when a microphone is attached to your Mac.

Audio CD	54:51:00
Track 01	01:22:00
Track 02	04:48:00
Track 03	03:38:00
Track 04	02:16:00
Track 05	03:46:00
Track 06	03:28:00
Track 07	02:53:00
Track 08	01:59:00

Choose your CD tracks here when a CD is in your drive.

Record Music

Clips Transitions Titles Effects Audio

To import an MP3 or AIFF sound file:

1. From the File menu, choose "Import File...."

2. In the "Import File" window, navigate to an MP3 or AIFF file that is stored on your computer, select it, then click "Import." The entire audio file is placed in one of the audio tracks.

   Some of your MP3 file names may be gray, which means you can't use them in the movie because iMovie can only import MP3s that support the QuickTime format.

Files that can be imported are shown in the Import File window.

To import a CD sound track:

1. Insert a CD into your CD drive.

2. To review CD tracks without importing them, click the Play button.

3. To record the song, select a CD track from the "Audio CD" list.

4. In the Timeline, move the Playhead (the white triangle) to a point where you want to start recording.

5. Click the "Record Music" button. Click "Stop" when you've recorded as much of the CD track as you want.

To record your voice to use for narration:

If you have a microphone for your Mac, plug it into the microphone jack, click the "Record Voice" button, and start speaking.

Adjust the placement of an imported audio file in the Timeline by dragging the file's purple bar left or right. **Edit the start and stop point** of audio clips by moving the audio crop markers at either end of the audio clip's purple bar in the audio track. To fine tune the placement of an audio crop marker, click it, then use the left and right arrows to move it.

Adjust and edit the audio clips

Export iMovie   Once you've finished creating your movie, you can store it on your hard drive, but that uses a lot of disk space, and the only place you can show it is on your computer. Since iMovies are usually large, from several gigabytes on up, you can't pass them around on a Zip disk or even on a CD. So you need to **export the movie.** Fortunately, iMovie is able to export movies in several formats, depending on the final intended use of the movie.

To export your movie:

1. From the File menu, choose "Export Movie...."

2. The "Export Movie" dialog box appears. From the "Export" menu, choose to export "To Camera," "To QuickTime," or "For iDVD."

▼ **Export To Camera:** Put a writable tape in your camera and put it in VTR mode. Make sure it is connected to your computer with a FireWire cable, then click the "Export" button.

Exporting your edited movie back out to your digital camera puts the movie on the digital video tape in your camera. The tape in your camera can store from 30 to 180 minutes of movies, depending on the model of your camera. You can attach your camera to a TV to show your edited movies, or you can transfer movies from your camera to a VHS tape. If your movie contains scenes that are in slow motion or reversed, iMovie will tell you that it needs to render those scenes before it can export the movie.

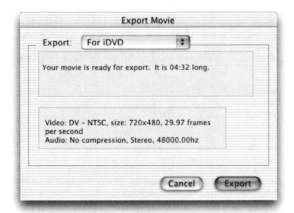

▼ **Export To QuickTime:** QuickTime format is a popular standard for multimedia files. QuickTime compresses movies so that their sizes are manageable for transport and delivery, either on the web or other media.

From the "Formats" pop-up menu, select one of the compression options, then click "Export." In the "Expert…" option, you can customize "Image Settings," "Audio Settings," and "Internet Settings."

▼ **Export For iDVD:** This option creates a QuickTime file that can be used with Apple's iDVD software. iDVD is amazing software for putting a collection of movies onto a DVD disc that will play on your computer (if you have a supported DVD drive) and will also play on most popular commercial DVD players. Exporting for DVD actually saves your movie in a QuickTime format, but with different compression settings from those used for other types of QuickTime files. If some scenes in your movie need to be rendered because they use a motion effect such as slow motion, iMovie alerts you that it needs to render those scenes before you can export the movie.

Extra Tips   If your selected music track plays just a few seconds too long past the end of the video or ends too soon, select a clip or a transition somewhere in the movie and slow it down using the **motion effects slider.** This slider is located beneath the Timeline, next to the Zoom pop-up menu. This is an easy way to help synchronize the length of a movie with an audio track.

> ▾ **Either** select a clip in the Timeline, then drag the slider left (Faster) or right (Slower).

> ▾ **Or** select a transition, then drag the slider left or right.

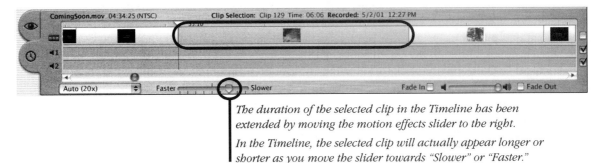

The duration of the selected clip in the Timeline has been extended by moving the motion effects slider to the right.

In the Timeline, the selected clip will actually appear longer or shorter as you move the slider towards "Slower" or "Faster."

Located above the Timeline, next to the Trash, the **Free Space status bar** alerts you to how much free space is left on the disk or partition being used for your movie. The bar indicator is color coded to indicate the amount of free disk space.

> **Green:** More than 400 megabytes available.

> **Yellow:** Less than 400 megabytes available.

> **Red:** Less than 200 megabytes available.

If you have less than 100 megabytes of free disk space, you cannot import more video until you remove clips from the shelf or empty the iMovie Trash.

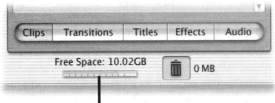

This is the Free Space status bar.

Applications on Your Mac

Mac OS X includes a number of small but useful **applications.** This chapter explains what each of these does and when to use it.

If you're an experienced Mac user, you might notice that an application written specifically for Mac OS X does not come in a folder—it comes in one file called a "package." For instance, you know that iMovie must have hundreds of supporting files, yet you only have one icon for iMovie—no folder full of stuff. These packages have a file name extension of .app. If you get special plug-ins and other files to customize your application, they will be stored in your user's Library folder (or the main Library folder, if everyone on the Mac has access to the customized tools).

Acrobat Reader

Acrobat Reader

The **Acrobat Reader** will open and display PDF files for you. PDF files are all over the place. Often the manual for new software is a PDF file on the CD—double-click the manual and it will open in Acrobat Reader; you can search for terms, read it on the screen, or print it up. Many information files on the web are PDF files that you can download, like your tax forms, requirements for entering the Bodleian Library, job application forms, or syllabi from your instructors.

PDF files are documents that contain all of the information for all of the graphics, fonts, and the layout, compressed into one package that any computer can open and display—even if it doesn't have the application you created the document in, or the fonts, or the graphics. For instance, let's say you use your favorite page layout application to create an eight-page newsletter for your beloved dog shelter, export it as a PDF, then email that PDF to your clients. They get the PDF, double-click it, it opens in the Acrobat Reader, and what your clients see on their computer looks exactly like what you see on your computer, even if they use PCs.

You can create PDFs in any Mac OS X application that uses the OS X Print dialog boxes, even TextEdit:

1. Press Command P to print.

2. Choose "Output Options," as shown below.

3. Click the "Save as File" box, then choose "PDF" from the menu on the right.

4. Notice the "Print" button has turned into a "Save…" button. You need to give this file a name.

   The file will not print at this point—you will be returned to your original document, and your saved PDF will be in the folder. You can send the PDF by email to anyone you like.

Months before this book was published, I created a PDF of the appendix to this book, shown above, and posted it on the Santa Fe Mac User Group web site for anyone to use. I wrote and designed the chapter in Adobe InDesign and used a number of fonts, but anyone can download the file, open it in Acrobat Reader, and print it up. It looks exactly like the chapter in the book. Amazing.

The **Address Book** works with the Mail program. Use it to store your email addresses and other contact information. Full details of how to use it are in Chapter 34.

Address Book

An **AppleScript** is a series of commands written in the AppleScript language that tells your Mac to do something for you. AppleScripts can perform repetitive tasks for you, such as change all of your .tiff file names to .tif, or number all of the items in a folder. Or let's say you get lots of files from PC users who name files with all caps and it makes you crazy—you can write a script that will change all of the file names to lowercase; once you write the script, you can run it anytime.

AppleScript

AppleScript

Actually, all of the scripts described above are already written for you and are in the AppleScript "Example Scripts" folder. To see how a script works, run the "Current Temperature by Zipcode" script, as described below. To run this script, you have to be connected to the Internet.

To open and run the "Current Temperature" script, do this:

1. Press Command Option A to open the Applications folder, or click on the Applications icon in any Finder window.

2. Double-click the "AppleScript" folder.

3. Inside that folder, double-click the "Example Scripts" folder.

4. Inside that folder, double-click the "Internet Services" folder.

5. Inside that folder, double-click on the file named "Current Temperature by Zipcode.scpt," shown to the upper-right.

6. The Script Editor will open, as shown to the right.

7. Click the "Run" button.

8. You will be asked to enter a zip code. Do so, then click the "OK" button. The current temperature will appear.

9. Quit the Script Editor. You will be asked if you want to save changes—you don't need to.

   If you want this script to always open with your zip code, find the line in the code that starts with "set," find the zip code in that line, and change that zip code to the one of your choice. Save the changes.

Current Temperature by Zipcode.scpt

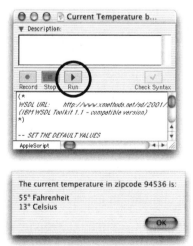

To learn how to write AppleScripts, go to Apple's site and use the tutorial (www.apple.com/applescripts). Also, open the Script Editor and then go to the Help menu to get help specific to AppleScript.

Calculator

Calculator

The **Calculator** isn't very sophisticated, but it comes in handy. You can use your mouse and pointer to enter numbers, or use your numeric keypad. The asterisk (*) is the multiplication symbol, and the slash (/) is division.

You can **copy** a number from any application and paste it into the Calculator: Go to your other application, select the number, copy it, then simply show the Calculator and paste.

Once a result is in the window, copy it with Command C; you can then **paste** it into any application (remember, like anything else, the answer will paste in where the insertion point is flashing or replace selected text, as explained on page 212).

Chess

Chess

Chess is just what it appears to be—an electronic chess game between you and the computer, or you can watch the computer play against itself. From the Window menu in Chess, you can choose to play on a three-dimensional or two-dimensional board, as shown on the opposite page.

Before you begin a game, get the Chess Preferences (from the Chess menu) and determine how difficult you want the game to be, who is playing and what color you each have, and whether to use speech recognition or not. You can't change these settings once you begin a game.

The more difficult the game, the faster the moves.

This is where you can choose to watch the computer play against itself.

Check this box to speak your moves instead of using your mouse, as explained on the opposite page.

This is the three-dimensional board.   *This is the two-dimensional board.*

If you choose to use **Speech Recognition,** a round microphone will appear on your screen; in fact, if you take a break (like go back to work) in another application, this microphone will still be sitting right in front of your face. See pages 337–339 for details about how to work with this particular speech recognition software. (If you don't want to bother reading that, just try this: Hold down the Escape key, and wait one second. Keep holding the key down, then speak your move, as explained below. Have your move ready before you start speaking so you don't have to stumble. Let go of the Escape key when you're finished. If that doesn't work, go read those pages.)

This is the speech recognition microphone.

Use the modern coordinate notation system when speaking to the microphone. For instance, speak "g1 to f3" to move your knight into the position shown above. The computer also understands if you say the name of the chess piece, as in "Bishop f1 to b5," but you don't need to. Tell it to "Take back move" if you don't like what you just did.

This is the Controls window.

Sometimes the computer takes longer than you would expect to make its move. From the File menu, choose "Controls…" to get the window shown to the right. Then you can "watch" the computer as it thinks (the bar turns progressively white). If it takes too long, click the button at the bottom, "Force Computer To Move."

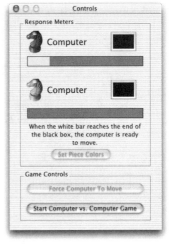

The button on the bottom, "Start Computer vs. Computer Game" is only available if you have chosen to play "Computer vs. Computer" in the Chess Preferences, as shown on the opposite page.

DVD Player

DVD Player

The **DVD Player** plays DVD (digital versatile disc) movies on your computer. It includes the Viewer (a window in which a movie plays) and the Controller (the device that controls the movie playback). Insert a DVD in your computer's DVD drive and the Player will automatically open. You'll see something like the example below.

The DVD Player plays commercial DVDs and home-movie DVDs, such as this one created with Apple's iDVD software.

The Controller

You can use either a horizontal or vertical **Controller.** From the Controls menu, choose "Controller Type," then choose "Horizontal" or "Vertical."

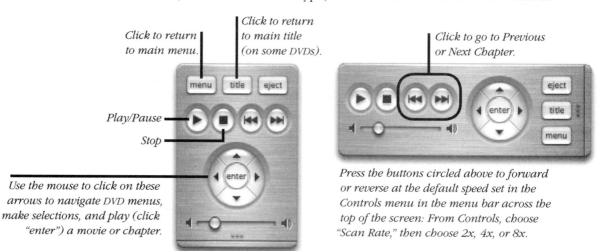

Click to return to main menu.

Click to return to main title (on some DVDs).

Click to go to Previous or Next Chapter.

Play/Pause

Stop

Use the mouse to click on these arrows to navigate DVD menus, make selections, and play (click "enter") a movie or chapter.

Press the buttons circled above to forward or reverse at the default speed set in the Controls menu in the menu bar across the top of the screen: From Controls, choose "Scan Rate," then choose 2x, 4x, or 8x.

Click the small bumps near the edge of the Controller to reveal a number of **additional controls.** as shown below.

Additional controls

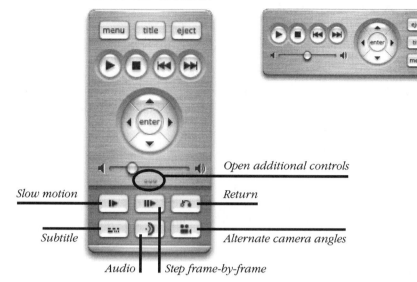

Hover the pointer over a control and a help tag appears to tell you the name of the control.

Open additional controls

Slow motion

Return

Subtitle

Alternate camera angles

Audio

Step frame-by-frame

Slow Motion: Click to cycle through speeds of ½ speed (slow), ¼ speed (slower), and ⅛ speed (slowest).

Click the Play button to resume normal playback speed, or tap the Spacebar.

Step frame-by-frame: Click to advance the playback one frame at a time.

Click the Play button to resume normal playback, or tap the Spacebar.

Return: Click to return to a previous DVD menu. The DVD that you play may have a different function applied to this button, or none at all.

Subtitle: Click to turn subtitles on or off. Language settings for subtitles can usually be set in the DVD movie's menu, or in the Preferences, as explained on the following page.

Audio: Some DVD videos (not all) include additional audio tracks, such as director's comments, that you can select with this button. You can also use this button to switch to alternate languages.

Angle: Some DVDs have alternate scenes that were filmed from different angles. The Angle button lets you select these alternate angles, if they're available.

DVD Player Preferences   You can customize some of the Player and Disc settings. From the DVD Player application menu, choose "Preferences...." The Player pane and the Disc pane show the options available.

The options in the **Full Screen Mode** section of the Player pane are self-explanatory.

In the **Windows** section, check "Display Controller Help Tags" to turn on the feature that makes descriptive text boxes pop-up when you mouse over a button or icon, as shown on the previous page.

Check "Display Status Window" to show commands in the upper-left corner of the Viewer, such as "Stop," "Pause," "Chapter 3," and other messages that serve as visual confirmations of certain commands.

The **Disc** pane is rather self-explanatory.

Under **Default Language Settings,** set your language preferences. If you turn on "Subtitle" and the subtitles don't appear, click the "Subtitle" button, one of the additional controls hidden in the Controller, as shown on the previous page.

In the **Features** section of the Disc pane, check "Enable DVD@ccess Web Links" to activate an advanced feature which enables some DVDs to provide hot spot links that connect to web sites, right in a movie.

The following **keyboard shortcuts** make using the DVD Player easier.

**DVD Player
keyboard shortcuts**

Play/Pause	Spacebar
Stop	Command Period
Scan Backward	Command LeftArrow
Scan Forward	Command RightArrow
Next Chapter	RightArrow
Previous Chapter	LeftArrow
Display DVD menus	Command ~
Highlight menu items	Arrow keys
Activate menu items	Return or Enter
Volume Up	UpArrow
Volume Down	DownArrow
Mute	Command K
Full Screen Viewer	Command 0 (zero)
Half Size Viewer	Command 1
Normal Size Viewer	Command 2
Maximum Size Viewer	Command 3
Close Windows	Command W
Show/Hide Controller	Control C
Show/Hide Viewer Window	Control V
Horizontal Controller	Shift Command H
Vertical Controller	Shift Command V
Show Info Window	Control I
Eject Disc	Command E
Quit	Command Q

Clock

Clock

If the time display in your menu bar is not enough (or if you prefer to turn off the menu bar display altogether), you can choose to have a nice **Clock** sitting right in the middle of your screen.

After you open the Clock, go to the Clock menu and choose "Preferences..." so you can adjust it to suit yourself. You can choose to display an analog or digital clock, as shown below, with some variations in the digital version. If you display the clock in a floating window, you can adjust its transparency. Even if you choose to see the clock as a floating window, it will still appear in your Dock.

If you have trouble making the Clock go away because its menus have disappeared, click on the Clock icon in the Dock, and choose "Quit."

Move the "Transparency" slider to the left to make the clock more transparent, to the right to make it more solid.

These examples show the solid and most transparent states.

Image Capture transfers images from supported digital cameras (with USB connections) to your computer. You can choose to download all photos in the camera, or just selected photos. Image capture can build a web page which you can publish on the World Wide Web, and it can build preview sheets in different size formats so you can print them on your printer. Image Capture can also transfer video clips and MP3 audio files if the camera can create those types of files.

To find information about which cameras are supported by Mac OS X, visit the Apple web site at **www.apple.com,** go to the Support section, select the AppleCare Knowledge Base link, then do a search for "Image Capture."

When you connect your camera with the USB cable and turn it on, Image Capture automatically downloads your images from the camera to the Pictures folder on your Mac. Because Image Capture application settings and Preference settings determine what happens during this process, you should open Image Capture and select your settings *before* you connect to the computer for the first time. After customizing the settings, you won't need to manually open Image Capture the next time you download images.

To open Image Capture and change the settings, click the Applications icon in any Toolbar, then double-click the Image Capture application icon.

Image Capture

Image Capture

Application settings

Download To: From this pop-up menu, select a download location for your camera's files. The option "Pictures, Movies, and Music folders" means that Image Capture will put the pictures from your camera in the Pictures folder; if you have movies on the same camera, those will go in the Movies folder; and any MP3 files on the camera will end up in the Music folder.

Automatic Task: Use this pop-up menu to select an automatic task that occurs after the image files are downloaded to your computer, as described below:

> **Build Web Page:** If you choose this option, Image Capture automatically builds a web site consisting of a home page with thumbnail versions of your photos, and a separate web page for each full-sized photo. All the photos and web pages are put in the Pictures folder,

An "Automatic Task" actually activates an AppleScript, a series of commands that tell an application what to do. The option of "Other…" lets you choose any other script you may have downloaded to your computer or written yourself.

in a folder named "Index." The page design is stark, but it works. If you're familiar with web design or HTML, you can open the files and make changes, or at least change the name beneath the photos.

To avoid building a web page with an image that needs to be rotated, as shown here, see Steps 4a and 4b in the process on pages 476–477.

See Chapter 37 for details on how people can view your web pages from your own Mac!

Format: Choose one of the "Format" options (3x5, 4x6, 5x7, or 8x10) to automatically create image preview pages that are built in HTML code and that open in Internet Explorer for viewing or printing. The size refers to the size the downloaded images will appear in the Internet Explorer preview, as well as the size they will print.

3x5index02.html
3x5index01.html
3x5 tips.html

In this example, Image Capture created three HTML pages (each HTML page is a web page): two pages were created to show the eight downloaded images (four per page) in an orientation that will print on most printers. The third page (3x5 tips.html) is not for printing or viewing on the Internet—it's for you to read because it contains tips for printing the other HTML pages.

The preview pages open automatically in Internet Explorer as soon as Image Capture creates them. To open them again later, double-click the HTML file icons.

Hot Plug Action: Select the application you want to use to open images when a camera is connected. It's best to use the default setting of "Image Capture Application" but if your camera is unsupported, try installing the download software that came with the camera, then select "Other…" from this menu. Navigate to the camera's download application, select it, then click "Open." Some unsupported cameras may supply a plug-in to work with Image Capture. Read the manufacturer's documentation or check their web site for information.

The **Image Capture Preferences** provide Download Options and View Options. These options directly affect how the camera downloads your photos. Go to the Image Capture menu and choose "Preferences…."

Image Capture Preferences

Click the Download Options tab, if the pane isn't already showing.

Delete items from camera after downloading: This erases all items from the camera's storage as soon as they are transferred to your computer. Uncheck this option if you want to keep the current images on the camera.

Create custom icons: Creates an icon for each image that looks like the photo, rather than using a generic JPEG icon. You can see what the images look like without having to open them.

Add item info to Finder file comments: Adds information about an item to the Comments section of the item's Show Info window, such as width/height pixel measurements and image resolution.

Embed ColorSync profile: This will attach color profile information to an image file for color management; choose a color profile from the "Profile" pop-up menu. Color management strives to accurately capture, display, and output color by using standard color protocols. Located in System Preferences, Apple's ColorSync lets you set profiles for Input, Display, Output, and Proof devices.

Automatically download all items: This will download items from the camera without giving you a chance to preview them. If you want to preview items so you can delete or rotate some images before downloading them, uncheck this box. I prefer to uncheck this option so I can see an immediate preview window of the images, then select and download only the images that look good.

Set camera's date & time: Adds the date and time that an image was created to the camera preview window. You'll see this information in the List View if "Date" is selected in the View Options pane, as described on the following pages. You have to set the date and time in your camera, of course, before this feature can work.

Tip: When you download cameras from your photo, keep the camera plugged into its AC adapter so you won't use up all the battery juice.

The **View Options** pane has settings for the Icon View and List View. These settings do not apply to the regular Finder window, but to a special camera preview window, as explained below.

In the Download Options pane (as described on the previous page), you could choose to have the camera "Automatically download all items." If you did *not* choose to do this, then when you plug in your camera to the Mac a window opens that lets you choose to either "Download Some..." or "Download All" of the images in the camera.

If you choose "Download Some...," a camera preview window opens in which you can preview images in the camera before they're downloaded. The window's title bar will show the name of the attached camera.

Click the "Icon View" or "List View" button, circled on the opposite page, located at the upper-left corner of the *preview window* to select a view. This special window is where you'll see the effects of the View Options settings shown below.

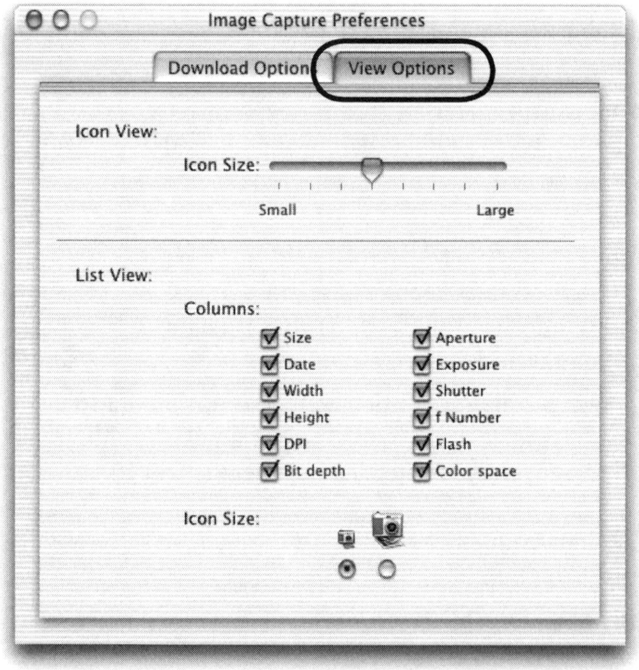

Icon View: Use the "Icon Size" slider to determine the size that an image file's icon will appear in the camera preview window when "Icon View" is active.

List View: From the "Columns" list, choose which columns to show in the camera preview window when "List View" is active. Also choose an "Icon Size" to display.

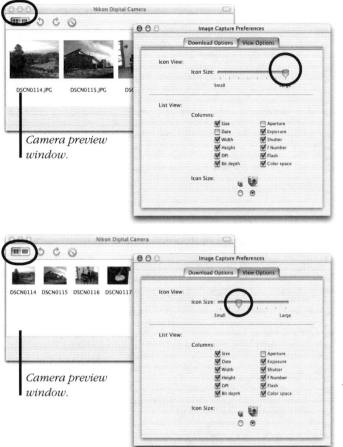

These top two examples show the Icon View with two different icon sizes chosen.

Camera preview window.

Camera preview window.

The date (and time) the image was created will appear in a column if you chose "Set camera's date & time" in the "Download Options" pane, as explained on page 473.

These bottom two examples show the List View with different options selected.

Click once on an image to select it, then use these buttons to rotate the image or delete it.

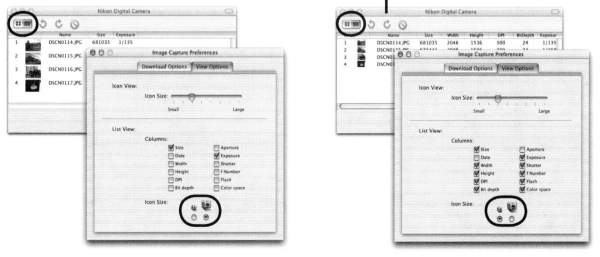

The Image Capture process

After you've customized the settings in the Image Capture application window and in Image Capture Preferences, follow these five steps:

1. With the camera turned off, connect it to your computer using a USB cable that came with the camera.

2. Turn the camera on. Some cameras may require that you press a "Transfer" button—check your camera manual.

3. Check to make sure a generic external drive icon appears on the desktop that indicates the media card in your camera has been mounted (such as a CompactFlash card or a SmartMedia Card).

4a. If you chose the setting "Automatically download all items," as explained on page 473, Image Capture downloads your images according to the choices you made in the settings and preferences (as explained on the previous pages) and places the images in the designated folder. You have no opportunity to select or rotate images before downloading, but if you are running off of battery power and you need to conserve it, this is the fastest way to download.

This shows the process of the images downloading to your Mac.

4b. If you did *not* select "Automatically download all items," as explained on page 473, a window opens in which you choose between "Download Some…" and "Download All."

Click the **Download All** button if you want to download all the images in the camera to your computer.

If you click the "Download All" button, a download progress sheet drops down to show images as they download, as shown below.

Click the **Download Some** option if you want to preview the images that are in the camera. A camera preview window opens, displaying a "thumbnail" image of each photo.

The window has List View and Icon View buttons in the upper-left corner. The appearance of each view is determined by the options you chose in the Preferences' View Options pane, as explained on pages 474–475.

To rotate an image, select it, then click one of the two "Rotate" buttons at the top of the window. If you rotate the photo here in Preview mode, it will download to your Mac in the rotated version.

Select the images you want to download, then click the "Download" button. The "Download" button is gray until you select something.

A "thumbnail" is a small view of a larger object, used for making choices, not for viewing pleasure.

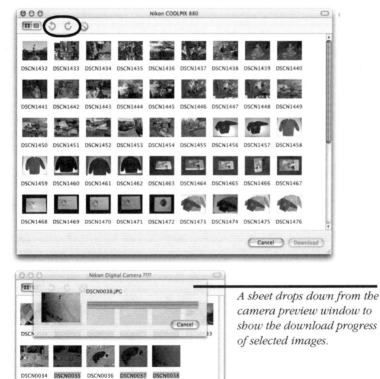

A sheet drops down from the camera preview window to show the download progress of selected images.

5. Unmount the media card: Select the media card icon on the Desktop and press Command E, or drag the icon to the Trash.

Important: It's very important to unmount the camera's media card *before* you disconnect the USB cable or turn off the camera. If you don't, you may lose images and other data from the camera.

Internet Connect

Internet Connect

If you connect to the Internet through a telephone modem, then you'll use **Internet Connect** to tell your modem to dial up your service provider and connect you. This is explained in detail in Chapter 31. If you have an "always on" broadband connection to the Internet, such as cable, DSL, ISDN, satellite, or T1 line, you won't ever need to use Internet Connect.

Internet Explorer

Internet Explorer

Internet Explorer is Microsoft's web browser that is installed on your Mac and has an icon in your Dock. The basics of how to use it are in Chapter 32. If you prefer not to be part of Microsoft's Domination of Society, you can install any other browser of your choice, such as Netscape, OmniWeb, iCab, Opera, or a number of others. I personally choose to keep a Microsoft-free environment.

iTunes

iTunes   iTunes

You might have iTunes (left) or iTunes 2 (right) on your Mac. See Chapter 26 to learn all about iTunes.

With the application **iTunes,** you can play not only music or other audio files on your Mac, you can create a *Playlist* of selected songs from any number of your own music CDs or downloaded MP3 files. iTunes will go to the Internet and find all the information about each song on your CD (like artist, title, length of song, etc.), then add that information to your Playlist. You can use iTunes to manage your music collection, play wild visuals on the screen in time with the music, encode music files from one format to another, burn music CDs of your selected collection of music that you can then use anywhere, and copy MP3 files directly to your MP3 player or iPod. If you don't have iTunes 2, it's a free download from the Apple site at **www.apple.com**.

Mail

Mail

Apple has provided you with an email program (often referred to as an email *client*) called **Mail.** Here you can send and receive email. You don't have to have an iTools account to use it—you can use your existing email account from anywhere (except America Online). The **Address Book** is used in conjunction with Mail.

If you have more than one email account, Mail can check them all at once and send mail back out to each account, even if your accounts are on different servers. You can create "rules" that let you filter messages into different mailboxes; for instance, perhaps you want all email from "John" to go into a mailbox named "My LoverMan" so it doesn't get mixed in with the junk mail. Or maybe you want all email with the word "free," "enlargement," or "mortgage" in its subject to go straight to the trash.

Mail may seem a little confusing at first, but if you take the time to go through Chapter 34, you'll find that it is a good, useful email client.

Preview

Preview

Preview is a little application that looks like it doesn't do much except display your photos and PDF files, but it actually has quite a powerful image-conversion feature built in.

First of all, you've probably already noticed that when you double-click on many photos and other images, they automatically open in Preview, as shown directly below. You can zoom in on an image (enlarge it) and zoom out. You can flip it vertically or horizontally and then save it in that new rotation. You can copy images in Preview and then paste them into an icon's Info window to change the icon image (see page 117 for details on that).

jane.jpg

This is the icon that indicates a file will automatically open in Preview when you double-click on it.

This is an open Preview window.

Robin's Stuff

This is actually a folder whose icon I customized.

But Preview can also **convert** a large number of graphic formats into other formats. If you understand graphic file formats and when you might need one over the other, take advantage of Preview's quick and easy conversion feature. You can change the bit depth, the quality level, the compression method, and a number of other specifications, depending on what type of file you are converting into what other type of file. For instance, if you have a Mac TIFF file you want to send to a PC user, you can export it as a TIFF with the "Little Endian" code attached so the PC user is more likely to be able to see it (Macs use Big Endian). If someone sent you a Photoshop file and you want to put it on your web page, you can convert it to a JPEG, and even control the quality level while you're at it.

To convert a graphic, open the graphic in Preview, go to the File menu, and choose "Export…." Click on the format menu to choose a format, then click the "Options…" button. The options change for the different formats.

Convert graphic file formats

Also see the tip on page 493 about previewing a page you are about to print, and then saving it as a PDF in Preview.

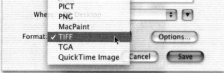

These are the graphic file format options you can export to. Choose one, then click the "Options…" button.

These are a couple of the options available for different formats.

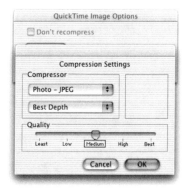

QuickTime Player

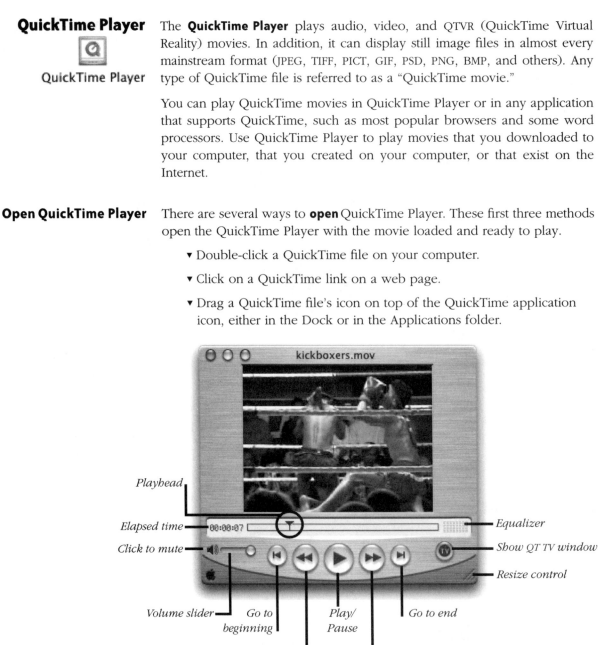

QuickTime Player

The **QuickTime Player** plays audio, video, and QTVR (QuickTime Virtual Reality) movies. In addition, it can display still image files in almost every mainstream format (JPEG, TIFF, PICT, GIF, PSD, PNG, BMP, and others). Any type of QuickTime file is referred to as a "QuickTime movie."

You can play QuickTime movies in QuickTime Player or in any application that supports QuickTime, such as most popular browsers and some word processors. Use QuickTime Player to play movies that you downloaded to your computer, that you created on your computer, or that exist on the Internet.

Open QuickTime Player

There are several ways to **open** QuickTime Player. These first three methods open the QuickTime Player with the movie loaded and ready to play.

▾ Double-click a QuickTime file on your computer.

▾ Click on a QuickTime link on a web page.

▾ Drag a QuickTime file's icon on top of the QuickTime application icon, either in the Dock or in the Applications folder.

If you use either of the next two methods, a version of the Player **opens** that contains QuickTime content links and your personal QuickTime Favorites.

The QuickTime TV pane

▼ Click on the QuickTime Player's icon in the Dock.

▼ Open the Applications folder, then double-click the QuickTime application icon.

Click this button to collapse the player to a small size that shows only the audio track and controller buttons.

Two tabs are visible in this window: a **QuickTime TV** tab and a **Favorites** tab (the heart icon). The QT TV pane contains a collection of preset QuickTime TV channels that offer a variety of content including news, sports, weather, music, and music videos. You can get links to additional entertaining content at **www.apple.com/quicktime**.

Click any icon in the QT TV pane to connect to that site's streaming Quick-Time content. For details about the Favorites pane, see the next page.

The Favorites pane

The **Favorites** pane (the heart tab) is a convenient place to store your favorite QuickTime content links. In Favorites, you can add links to streaming QuickTime movies on the Internet, QuickTime movies that are on your local computer, and almost any image file on your computer.

To add an image file to Favorites, drag its icon to the Favorites pane.

To add streaming QuickTime content from the Internet to Favorites:

1. Click on a streaming QuickTime movie link on a web page to start playing the movie.

2. From the QTV menu, choose Favorites, then choose "Add Movie As Favorite." The movie is not *copied* to your computer. Instead, a *link* to the online movie is created in Favorites.

To add a QuickTime movie that's on your computer to Favorites:

1. Drag the movie's QuickTime file icon to the Favorites pane.

2. Or, double-click the QuickTime movie to open it, then from the QTV menu, choose Favorites, then "Add Movie As Favorite."

The Favorites pane gives you instant access to your favorite QuickTime content located on the Internet and on your computer, plus almost any kind of image file that you want to access easily and quickly.

To remove a Favorite:

▼ **Either** Control-click on a Favorite, then from the pop-up menu, choose "Delete Favorite."

▼ **Or** select a favorite using the arrow keys, then press Delete.

You will see different channels in different **views.** Some of the providers, such as ESPN (shown on the left) play streaming audio in the QuickTime player. Others open in the full multimedia version of the player that includes streaming audio and streaming video.

The views in Favorites

QuickTime Player adjusts its appearance to the type of content it needs to play.

The Player above is connected to a streaming radio station.

The Player on the right is connected to a site that streams audio and video.

The thumbnail image that appears in Favorites is called the **Poster Frame.** A Poster Frame is one frame of a movie that is used as a preview, or thumbnail image. By default, the Poster Frame is usually the first frame in a movie. If the first frame of your selected movie is not visually descriptive enough, you can choose any frame to use as the Poster Frame. (You can only do this to movies that are actually stored on your hard disk, not those that are streaming in from the Internet.)

Change the Poster Frame

To change the Poster Frame:

1. Open the movie in QuickTime Player.

2. Drag the playhead (the black triangle in the video track) to select the frame you want to use as the Poster Frame.

3. From the Movie menu, choose "Set Poster Frame."

4. Press Command S to save your changes, then close the movie.

5. Drag the QuickTime movie's icon to the Favorites window.

Play QuickTime movies

There are several ways to play QuickTime movies.

To play a QuickTime movie that's on your computer, do one of these:

▼ **Either** double-click on the QuickTime movie's file icon.

▼ **Or** from the File menu, choose "Open Movie in New Player...." Navigate to a QuickTime movie, select it, then click "Open."

▼ **Or** locate a movie file, then drag the file icon on top of the QuickTime Player icon.

To play a QuickTime movie located on the Internet:

Most QuickTime movies you encounter on the Internet are links on a web page that you simply click to play. The Louvre Museum web page, shown to

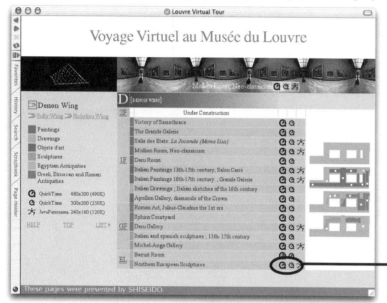

the left, offers a virtual tour with links to many QTVR movies (QuickTime Virtual Reality), which are 360-degree panoramic photos that you can pan and zoom in on. The large and small QuickTime logos on the web page are links that offer a choice of both large and small QuickTime movies for viewers who have fast or slow Internet connections.

The larger of these little icons indicates that a file is large; the smaller icon indicates the file is small.

If you know the specific web address:

If you know the specific web address of a QuickTime movie, from the File menu, choose "Open URL...." Type the address in the text field, then click "OK." The trick is that the address must be a complete path name to the QuickTime *file,* and not just to a web page.

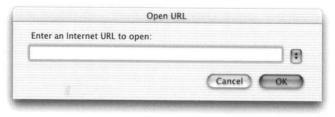

When you play a QuickTime movie, you can adjust the left/right speaker balance and the bass/treble levels of QuickTime movies with **Sound Controls.**

To show or hide Sound Controls:

▾ **Either** go to the Movie menu and choose "Show Sound Controls" to show the controls in the status window.

Choose "Hide Sound Controls" when you don't want them visible.

▾ **Or** click on the small equalizer on the right side of the status window, if an equalizer is visible, to show the Sound Controls.

Click the equalizer again to hide the Sound Controls.

Click the small equalizer to show or hide the Sound Controls.

The small equalizer on the right side of the movie track gives a visual representation of the audio.

If you have **QuickTime Pro,** as discussed on page 487, you can also **adjust the video** in QuickTime Player.

From the Movie menu, choose "Show Video Controls." To adjust the Brightness with the control bar that pops up in the Player window, click anywhere in the bar, drag in the bar with your mouse, or use your left and right arrow keys on your keyboard.

To access the Contrast, Tint, and Color controls, click on the name of the control. You can also cycle through the controls by clicking the small up and down arrows to the right of the control name.

To hide the controls, from the Movie menu choose "Hide Video Controls."

QuickTime Player Preferences

The **QuickTime Player Preferences** give you a few more options for customizing the behavior of the Player.

From the QuickTime Player application menu, choose "Preferences," then choose "Player Preferences…" to open the General Preferences window, as shown below.

Select your choices for the **options** listed for Movies, Sound, Favorites, and Hot Picks. They're self-explanatory.

If you're using QuickTime to listen to **Internet Radio** while you work, select "Play sound when application is in background" to let QuickTime audio continue to play when another window is active and when the Player has been minimized in the Dock.

The **Hot Picks** option connects to the Internet and takes you to QuickTime's currently featured content whenever you open QuickTime Player.

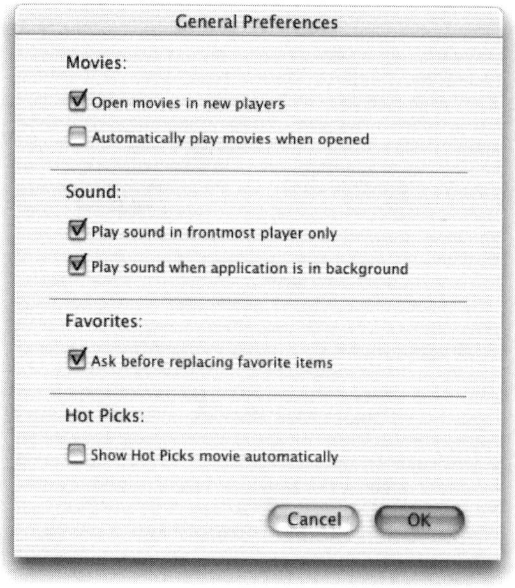

Uncheck the Hot Picks item unless you have a full-time broadband connection or your modem will automatically try to dial and connect to the Internet whenever you double-click on QuickTime Player.

General Preferences

Movies:

☑ Open movies in new players

☐ Automatically play movies when opened

Sound:

☑ Play sound in frontmost player only

☑ Play sound when application is in background

Favorites:

☑ Ask before replacing favorite items

Hot Picks:

☐ Show Hot Picks movie automatically

(Cancel) (OK)

QuickTime Pro

On the Apple web site, for a reasonable fee, you can upgrade to **QuickTime Pro,** a more powerful version of QuickTime that adds multimedia authoring features for audio and video. QuickTime Pro includes capabilities for slide shows, editing, special effects, and the ability to export content to over a dozen standard file formats.

Register online with Apple to receive a registration number that will unlock these features and put new menu options in your copy of QuickTime. Most users don't need QuickTime Pro, so don't bother with it unless you have a real interest in multimedia.

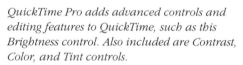

QuickTime Pro adds advanced controls and editing features to QuickTime, such as this Brightness control. Also included are Contrast, Color, and Tint controls.

At the bottom-left of the movie track are crop markers (small triangles) that enable QuickTime Pro users to crop and trim movies.

iMovie

iMovie

iMovie is so much fun and so useful that an entire chapter is devoted to it. It is literally as easy as writing a letter in your word processor to create your own digital movie in iMovie. Check it out in Chapter 27.

Sherlock

Sherlock

With **Sherlock** you can search for files on your hard disk, web pages online, shopping bargains, research items, and more. You can limit the search to certain "search sites" on the Internet, and to certain folders or disks on your Mac. Please see Chapter 24 for details.

Stickies

Stickies

The **Stickies** application can be very useful. Use it to leave notes to yourself or to others who might use your Mac. Create your shopping list, notes on your upcoming presentation, gossip, snippets for poems you will write later, tidbits to add to your research, interesting stuff from web pages, etc. Below are examples of Stickies and the sorts of things you can do with them.

From the File menu, you can **import** text directly into a Sticky note, or **export** text from the active Sticky so you can use it in other applications. You can **print** the active note (the one in front with the title bar visible) or all of the open notes.

From the Edit menu, you can **find** certain words that might appear in any of the open notes. You can run the **spell checker** (the "Spelling…" command) on *all* open notes, or ask to **check the spelling** of just the *active* note, in which case each time you choose the command ("Check Spelling") or press Command Semicolon (;), a misspelled word is underlined with dots.

From the Note menu, you can **change the typeface** of selected text, or **change the style** (bold or italic if one is designed into the font). You can **copy the font,** size, and color of a word (*click* inside the typeface example in the note; *do not* select the word; choose "Copy Font"), then select a word in another note (or the same note) and **"Paste Font."** The selected word will take on the typeface, color, and size of the word you copied from.

If you've created a style of note that you like, with the font, size, and color of note, you can make this note's formatting your **default,** so every new note you create will have this same font, size, and color. Just create a note with the formatting you like (only one style of text will apply), then from the Note menu, choose **"Use as Default."** The color of the text will not apply to the default.

Drag a **graphic** from any folder and drop it into a Sticky note.

You can **change the color of selected text**—select the text (drag over certain words or press Command A to select all), then choose "Text Colors…" from the Note menu. In the Colors panel that appears, drag the little square around until you find a color you like, then drag the slider bar up or down to make the color darker or lighter.

"Note Info" will tell you the date the note was created and modified.

The Color menu **changes the color of the note,** not the text.

Use the Window menu to **close the active note, miniaturize it,** as shown below, or **deminiaturize** it. You can also use the keyboard shortcut Command M or double-click the title bar to miniaturize and deminiaturize a note ("deminiaturize" is not in my dictionary, and the spell checker in Stickies flags the word as a misspelling). You can choose to neatly arrange your notes (choose **"Arrange in Front"**) whether they are miniaturized or not.

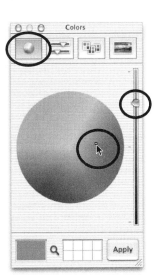

Drag the tiny square around the circle to choose a color, and use the slider bar to make the color darker or lighter.

These four notes are miniaturized and arranged in front. Double-click the title bar of any note to open it.

You can use **Services** to do a number of things with the selected text in a Sticky. For instance, select the text, go to the Stickies menu, and from the Services submenu, choose "Mail" and "Mail Text," as shown below. This will automatically copy the text from the Sticky, open the Mail program, open an email form, and paste this text into the form, ready for you to add the email address and send it.

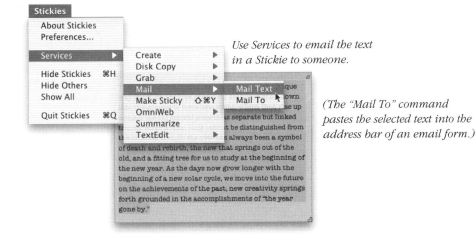

Use Services to email the text in a Stickie to someone.

(The "Mail To" command pastes the selected text into the address bar of an email form.)

And in any other OS X application, even from a browser, you can select text, then go to the application menu and use **Services to make a Sticky** of your selected text.

System Preferences

System Preferences

The **System Preferences** is one "pane" that displays all of the different preferences you can customize. Click one (such as "Date & Time") to select it and its pane will replace the existing one; click the icon "Show All" in the upper-left corner to return to the pane that displays all of the preferences. With System Preferences you can adjust the time that appears in your menu bar, change the picture on your Desktop, choose a language for your menus and dialog boxes to appear in, enter the networking and Internet settings, and much more. See Chapter 21 for details on all of the preferences.

TextEdit

TextEdit

The application **TextEdit** is a small word processor. It can do some surprising things, but is missing enough serious features that you might not want to use it as your only word processor. But here is what it can do:

From the File menu, you can **"Open Recent"** files. This is nice so you don't have to go scrounging around in your hard disk looking for that file you created several days ago.

From the Edit menu, you can do all the basic stuff like **cut, copy, paste, delete** (clear), **undo,** and **select all.** If you don't know how to use those features, please see Chapter 13.

The **Find** command has some fairly robust features. You can *find* words or phrases, and you can *replace* found words or phrases with entirely new words or phrases. For instance, you might have written a novel with a main character named "Peter," then you decide, after 173 pages, that you want his name to be "John." Use the Find panel to "Find: Peter" and "Replace with: John," then click the "Replace All" button. Almost instantly, your hero has a new name.

Position your pointer over a button and wait a second or two—
a Help tag appears to tell you what that button will do.

The **Spelling** command gives you three options. "Spelling…" brings up the spell checker for the active document. "Check Spelling" will point out your misspelled words in the active document one at a time; press Command Semicolon (;) to find the next misspelled word. The option to "Check Spelling As You Type" will underline words with red dots as you misspell them.

Use the **Speech** command to have your text read out loud by the voice chosen in the Speech preferences pane (see page 339). If text is selected, that is what will be read. If nothing is selected, the reader will start at the beginning.

From the **Format** menu, use the **Font** and **Text** submenus to format your text, most of which is explained in Chapter 13. To learn to use the Font Panel, see pages 204–209.

The command to **"Make Plain Text"** will turn your document into a "text-only" or ASCII file, which removes all font choices, styles, underlines, etc., and takes the text down to its most basic form. This file is then safe to send through the Internet to any other computer user, regardless of the kind of computer or applications she has on her machine.

If you choose **"Make Read Only,"** TextEdit will lock the file so it can be read by others, but no one can make changes to it or delete it. Well, they could if they went up to the Format menu and chose "Make Editable," so it's not a very safe way to protect your document. This command is only meant to prevent accidental damage to the file.

"Wrap to Page" will display the printing guidelines in the window. You can't change the margins—they are stuck at one inch all the way around. But in "Wrap to Page" you are guaranteed that what you see on the screen is what will print, as opposed to "Wrap to Window," explained below.

While in **"Wrap to Window,"** the lines of type stretch to fill the space as wide as you drag your window. When you print, the printer will try to match your line endings, but if your window is wide, it may have to reduce the size of the type to fit your sentences on the same lines of the page that you have on the screen. So if your page of text prints too small, reduce the size of your window and print again.

"Allow Hyphenation" does just what it says—it will allow words to be hyphenated at the ends of lines.

Be sure to go to the TextEdit menu and check the **"Preferences…."** They are pretty self-explanatory. The "New Document Font" lets you choose a default font and size so every time you open a new document in TextEdit, you will automatically start to type with your choice of font.

—continued

You can drag **pictures** into your TextEdit documents:

1. On your Desktop, position your open Pictures folder (or whichever folder you store your pictures in) on the right side of your screen.

2. In TextEdit, position your page on the left side of the screen.

3. From the Pictures folder, press-and-drag an image to your TextEdit document—watch carefully to see the insertion point move around the page as you drag the image around! (See page 196 if you're not clear on what the insertion point is and why it is so important.)

4. When the insertion point is flashing in the position you want the image, as shown below, drop it on the page (just let go of the mouse button). The picture will insert itself where the insertion point was flashing.

5. To make more space *above* the picture, position your insertion point to the left of the photo and hit a Return.

   To make more space *after* the picture, position your insertion point to the right of the image and hit a Return.

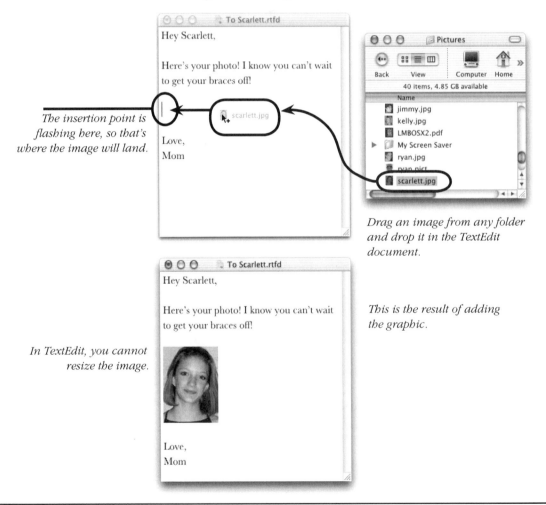

The insertion point is flashing here, so that's where the image will land.

Drag an image from any folder and drop it in the TextEdit document.

In TextEdit, you cannot resize the image.

This is the result of adding the graphic.

When you **save** a text document in TextEdit, it creates what is called a Rich Text Format file with a file name extension of **.rtf**. "Rich Text" means it can include fonts, styles, different point sizes, and other formatting (as opposed to "Plain Text" as described on page 491).

If you insert a photo or other graphic into a TextEdit document, it will become a "Rich Text Format with Attachments" file and must be saved with an extension of **.rtfd** (the "d" stands for "directory" because an .rtfd file is actually a folder, or directory, that bundles the text with the graphics). Don't worry about remembering that—as soon as you try to save a document that has an image in it, the Mac will tell you that you have to change the extension and will actually do it for you. See page 227 for details about file name extensions.

Tip: As discussed in Chapter 15 about printing, you can go to the Print dialog box and click the Preview button. This will make a PDF preview of your document which will open in the application Preview. From there, you can save it as a PDF file so you can email the document to anyone in the world and they can see it just like you created it.

You can also save a file as a PDF by going to the "Output Options" in the Print dialog box and choosing the PDF format to save the file.

You'll get this message when you try to save a TextEdit document with a graphic in it.

TextEdit does not have a feature that automatically creates real **apostrophes** and **quotation marks,** so you have to learn to type them yourself. Don't ever print your work with typewriter apostrophes and quotation marks—it looks stupid. This is what the marks look like and how to type real ones:

Typewriter apostrophe: It's Mary's turn.

Typewriter quotation marks: "Go get 'em, Mary."   *(Oooh, these are so nasty.)*

Typesetter's apostrophe: It's Mary's turn.

Typesetter's quotation marks: "Go get 'em, Mary."

To type true typesetter's apostrophe and quotation marks:

apostrophe   '   Shift Option]

opening quotation mark   "   Option [

closing quotation mark   "   Shift Option [

Name the best Mac OS X application to use to accomplish each of the following tasks:

1. Change a graphic image from one format to another.

2. Find the current temperature of any zip code.

3. Download all of the photos and movies from your digital camera to your Mac.

4. Listen to NPR while you work.

5. Make reminder notes, to-do lists, and snag bits of information and images off the Internet and save them for future reference.

6. Check the email for all of your email accounts with one click.

7. Watch commercial or homemade DVDs.

8. View PDF files that your PC-user friend sent you.

9. Write letters to your mother and finish your thesis, both with photos in the text.

10. Make individual playlists of your favorite songs and record them onto a CD.

Answers on page 752.

Utilities on Your Mac

Mac OS X provides you with a number of **utilities,** which are small applications that perform specific functions, such as help you troubleshoot problems on your computer, manage color, provide security, find special characters in your fonts, and more.

The Utilities folder is stored inside the Applications folder. If you find you get into it often, drag the Utilities folder up to the Finder window Toolbar so you can open it with the click of a button, no matter where you are.

AirPort Setup Assistant

AirPort Setup Assistant

AirPort is Apple's wireless networking technology. You can plug a "base station" into your existing telephone connection to the Internet, to your cable or DSL modem, or even your T1 connection. Then that base station will send out radio waves to connect any other Mac to the Internet, any Mac that has an AirPort card installed. In fact, the one base station can send the signal out to fifty different Macs. This means you can have an entire classroom or small school connected to the Internet from one connection. The Macs don't have to be plugged into any modem. We have an AirPort installed in our office, and we can surf the Internet on the iMac in the painting studio where there is no physical connection. You can take your laptop up to the attic and surf. (You might see ads showing people connecting while they sit by the pool or at an outdoor cafe, but notice you never see the screen in those ads—that's because you can't *see* the screen in broad daylight. I know this.)

The **AirPort Base Station** looks like a small flying saucer about the size of a danish pastry and costs about $300. An **AirPort card** costs about $100 and can be installed in desktop Macs and newer laptops. When you install Mac OS X, whether you have AirPort or not, you get the **AirPort Setup Assistant** and the **AirPort Admin Utility.** If OS X discovers an AirPort card in your Mac, it automatically puts the AirPort status menu in your menu bar, as shown to the left.

The AirPort Setup Assistant will walk you through setting up your AirPort to connect to the Internet and establish the network.

The darkness of the four stripes in the AirPort menu bar icon indicates how good your signal is. If all four bars are gray, it's not working at all yet—perhaps you need to walk through the Setup Assistant. Or perhaps you turned it off.

When all four bars are black, you've got a great signal.

The AirPort Setup Assistant will walk you through establishing your connection and setting up the network.

The **AirPort Admin Utility** lets you change connection settings when necessary. When you installed the AirPort software that came with your AirPort Base Station and card, all of this information was filled in for you.

If you need to make changes, open the AirPort Admin Utility. You will see the first dialog box shown below, which gives you a list of all the base stations that you have access to.

AirPort Admin Utility

AirPort Admin Utility

To actually get to the administrative utility, as shown below, double-click on the name of the base station in the "Select Base Station" dialog box, shown above. You will have to enter the password that you chose when you set up the base station. So you won't have to enter it again, click the box to add the password to your Keychain (see pages 508–516 about Keychain Access). Once you have entered the password, click OK and you'll get the administrative preferences shown below. You'll need a network administrator to take care of most of these items.

Tip: To remove the AirPort status icon in the menu bar, hold down the Command key and drag it off the bar. If you want to put the status icon back in the menu bar, go to the System Preferences and click on the Network icon. In the "Show" pop-up menu, choose "AirPort." Then click on the "AirPort" tab. Check the box to "Show AirPort status in menu bar."

If a microwave or other radio device is near the AirPort, it can cause interference. Check this box to help the AirPort overcome that interference.

Apple System Profiler

Apple System Profiler

The **Apple System Profiler** (in your Utilities folder) is the place to go to find out your Mac's serial number, all the details about your hardware and software, memory chips, every application on your hard disk, and more. You won't need to use it very often, but it's good to check it out so you know what information is available here. If you ever have to call tech support, they will probably ask you to open this.

Apple System Profiler				
System Profile	Devices and Volumes	Frameworks	Extensions	Applications

Serial number: XA0900AZAFS

▼ **Software overview**

Mac OS overview	System:	Mac OS X 10.1 (5L14)
Startup device	Name:	Mac OS X

▼ **Memory overview**

▼ Built-in memory: 1.18 GB

Location	Size	Memory type
DIMM0/J21	128 MB	PC100-222S
DIMM1/J22	64 MB	PC100-222S
DIMM2/J23	512 MB	PC100-322S
DIMM3/J24	512 MB	PC100-322S

Backside L2 cache: 1 MB

▼ **Hardware overview**

Machine ID:	406	Processor info:	PowerPC G4
Model name:	Power Mac G4 (AGP graphics)	Machine	450 MHz
Keyboard type:	Apple Pro Keyboard		

▶ **Network overview**

▼ **Production information**

ROM revision:	
Boot ROM version:	4.18f5
Serial number:	Xffff-3-1 HSF-fff
Software bundle:	Not applicable
Sales order number:	M7628LL/A

The **Disk Utility** provides five different features. Only the Administrator (or someone with the Administrator's name and password) can run Disk Utility.

Disk Utility

Disk Utility

▼ You can get **Information** on any mounted disk, as shown below, such as its size, how much space is available, and how many files and folders are stored on the disk.

▼ You can run **First Aid** to check for problems and to repair many problems on any mounted disk, *except* the disk that has the operating system on it (the startup disk), CD-ROMs, locked disks, and disks that have open files (quit all applications before you try to run First Aid). First Aid is a good place to start when things start acting weird. It automatically verifies and repairs the startup disk when you first turn on your Mac.

▼ You can **Erase** removable disks and any partitions except the startup disk. Erasing, of course, destroys all the data on the disk. You can erase CD-RW disks, but they may deteriorate if you do it too often.

▼ If you have a very large hard disk, use Disk Utility to **Partition** it into several smaller volumes. Step-by-step directions for how to do this are in Chapter 39.

▼ **RAID** stands for "redundant array of independent disks" and is a professional storage solution involving multiple disks that store the same data in different places (that's why it's redundant). The operating system thinks the array is one hard disk. If you don't already know what RAID is, you won't need this panel of Disk Utility.

Disk Utility	

0 Disks and 1 Volume Selected

| Information | First Aid | Erase | Partition | RAID |

▼ 19.12 GB WDC
  Mac OS X
  Robin's Projects
  Robin's Hard

Mount Point: /
Format: HFS+
Capacity: 6.37 GB (6,841,447,424 Bytes)
Available: 4.86 GB (5,223,010,304 Bytes)
Used: 1.51 GB (1,617,866,752 Bytes)
Number of Files: 39,559
Number of Folders: 11,919

Click the lock to prevent further changes.

TROUBLESHOOTING UTILITIES

Mac OS X has quite a slew of **troubleshooting utilities.** To use most of these items, you need to really know what you're doing—these are not tools for messing with lightly. All I'm going to do here is provide a brief description of each utility. If you are a typical user who never (or very rarely) needs to use these tools, you might want to store them inside a new folder inside the Utilities folder so they don't get in your way.

Console

The **Console** shows you technical messages from the system software and Mac OS X applications. If you are a programmer or if you need to do some serious troubleshooting, these messages, as Apple says, "may" be useful.

CPU Monitor

CPU Monitor provides a visual representation of what your Mac's central processing unit (the CPU) is doing. If you know what to look for, it can be interesting (and perhaps helpful) to see what the CPU does during video editing, 3D-rendering, and other graphics-intense processes. To see exactly which processes the CPU is working on, open *ProcessViewer* at the same time (you can open it from the CPU Monitor's Processes menu). This is often used in conjunction with "Top" in the *Terminal,* which you can also open from the Processes menu.

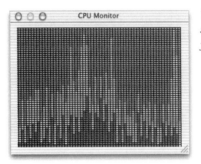

The bars march across the screen constantly, showing you what the CPU is doing.

Directory Setup

Directory Setup is a tool for network administrators on campus or corporate networks to set up search policies, attribute mappings, define LDAP data, and select NetInfo domains and other directories. Home and small business users, even those with local networks, won't need to use this.

NetInfo Manager

Your Mac uses a built-in directory service called **NetInfo** to store information about the computer, the users, and the networks that may be connected to it. It's a tool for network administrators that most of us won't need. The one time you might want to open NetInfo is to **enable the root user** so you can throw away perfectly safe files that the Mac won't let you throw away otherwise. Directions for logging in as the root user are on pages 298–299.

If you understand basic networking, **Network Utility** can be helpful for finding specific information and for troubleshooting.

Network Utility

> **Info:** Check your computer's network interfaces.
>
> **Netstat:** Review network performance statistics.
>
> **Ping:** Test access to specific hosts or IP addresses.
>
> **Lookup:** Convert between IP addresses and host names.
>
> **Traceroute:** Trace the route that packets take from one computer to another (type in a web address and see how many times and where the packet stops to ask directions).
>
> **Whois, Finger:** Find user information (see below for Whois).
>
> **Port Scan:** Scan the active TCP ports.

If you know how to use Terminal, you can find more information about these tools: type "man" followed by the tool's name, such as **man lookup.**

*You can **look up a domain name** to see if it's already been taken by someone. (This does the same thing as going to the Internic web site.) Type in the domain name you want to check, click the "Whois" button, and you can find out if someone already owns the domain. Of course, you must be connected to the Internet to get this information.*

Whois no longer gives you the administrative or other contacts, due to security issues.

A "process" is an application of some sort. It might be an application that *you* open and use, or it might be something the Mac opens and uses internally that you never even know is happening. **ProcessViewer** lets you see exactly which processes are running. This is useful to programmers and system administrators in troubleshooting situations. If you call Apple Tech Support, they might ask you to open this and tell them what it's doing.

ProcessViewer

Mac OS X runs on a non-graphical operating system called **Darwin,** which is based on Unix. If you want to access Darwin directly, use the **Terminal** utility. Here in the Terminal window you can use "command lines" to make your Mac do things that you can't do otherwise, like totally destroy your entire computer. Well, of course if you know what you're doing, you won't destroy it, but if you *don't* know what you're doing, leave the Terminal to the programmers.

Terminal

JAVA UTILITIES

Java is a programming language. Some of the very common things created with Java are applets, or small applications, that can be sent along with a web page. You, as a user, go to the web page and see interactive animations, calculations, live news scrolling across the page, and other tasks. Java also runs more complex actions, such as Internet chats and working with databases.

Applet Launcher

Applet Launcher

Applet Launcher lets you run Java applets that are stored on your Mac or on a web site—without having to open a web browser. (You do have to connect to the Internet.)

To run an applet that's on a web site, type the URL in the edit box shown below, including the **http://**. Then click the "Launch" button.

You can also click the "Open..." button to open an HTML file that contains Java applets. The Applet Launcher will connect to the page and run all of the applets on the page.

When the applet runs, another applet from Sun Microsystems will open and provide you with basic controls for starting and stopping the applets.

Java Web Start

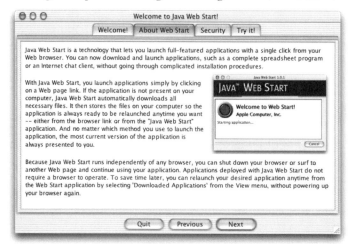

Java Web Start is attractive to large companies that maintain hundreds of thousands of workstations and have to keep up-to-date software on these computers. Java Web Start applications (which are HTML-based) can be launched securely via any browser on any platform from anywhere on the web. You can try it out: open Java Web Start, click the "Start" button, and walk through the process using the dialog box shown below.

COLOR UTILITIES

If you are a professional in the graphics field and rely on precise color reproduction, Apple has provided a suite of **color utilities.** Use these in combination with your graphics applications to help you capture, display, and output accurate color. Color gets very complicated, so I'm only going to give you the highlights of these utilities. To learn all about ColorSync and how to really take advantage of it, Apple has provided a tutorial on their web site at **www.apple.com/colorsync.** At that site you can also find a ColorSync consultant (or become one).

The **Display Calibrator** will adjust your monitor to give you the most accurate color, and these specifications will be made into a color "profile" that you can use in ColorSync. Open the Display Calibrator and walk through the process to adjust your monitor—it's easy.

Display Calibrator

Use the **ColorSync Utility** and the ColorSync preferences (in the System Preferences) to specify color profiles for the capture, display, proofing, and final output devices you use.

ColorSync Utility

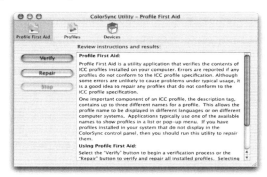

▼ If an ICC profile that you need doesn't appear in the ColorSync pane of System Preferences, it may contain information in a non-standard format. Use **Profile First Aid** to validate and repair the profile.

▼ Click **Profiles** to see which profiles you have installed and to get information about each one, such as what color space it uses, its ICC version, or when it was created. Click the black triangle in the right corner of the list to organize that list by location (which is probably what you see when you open it), by class (which groups them according to input displays, output profiles, etc.), or by color space (such as LAB color, RGB, CMYK, etc.).

▼ Click **Devices** to check the capabilities, contained in its color profile, of a camera, printer, display, or other device you have attached to your Mac. If you don't see a profile for your chosen device, maybe you didn't install the software that came with it. Also check the vendor's web site to see if you can download a profile if you don't have one.

*An **ICC profile** is a standard developed by the International Color Consortium for documenting the color characteristics of input and output devices. These profiles help correct visual data for viewing on different devices.*

*Not all images contain color space information. The World Wide Web Consortium has declared that all colors specified in cascading style sheets and HTML should be in the **sRGB** color space.*

—continued

Once you've got your ColorSync profiles worked out, turn on the color management features of your image capture, editing, and output applications. For example, in Internet Explorer you can more accurately view web images that use profiles: open the Preferences; in the Web Browser list, choose "Web Content"; then click the button to "Use ColorSync™."

DigitalColor Meter

Use the **DigitalColor Meter** to get the hexadecimal colors of any item on your screen, or the actual RGB values, or the percentage values of red, green, and blue. If you have certain Apple monitors, the DigitalColor Meter can translate the RGB values to CIE, LAB, and Tristimulus.

Open the DigitalColor Meter and move your mouse around. The bigger window on the left will display an enlarged view of whatever your mouse is positioned over, and the exact pixel color will appear in the little window to the right. To move the measurement aperture (the tiny square inside the larger window) one pixel at a time, use the arrow keys. To "hold" a particular color in the little window so you can move your mouse somewhere else, get the color you want, then press Command Shift H. Press the keyboard shortcut again to release the hold.

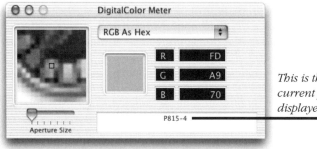

This is the name of the current profile being displayed on your monitor.

Disk Copy

Disk Copy

Disk Copy is a utility that will open itself up and do what it needs to do when it needs to, without you having to go get it. Disk Copy works with "disk images," which are like pretend hard disks that store compressed data. Disk images typically have an extension of .img or .dmg—double-click one and it will open Disk Copy, extract itself, and create an icon of a disk on your Mac, from which you can install files. See pages 302–306 for information on disk images and how to work with them.

Files with the extension of .smi are also disk images, but they are "self-extracting" and don't need to use Disk Copy.

Installer

The **Installer** is another utility that does what it needs to do without you asking it. Whenever you install new software, Installer will take care of the process for you, then quietly disappear.

Installer

Grab is a utility that lets you take pictures of what is visible on your monitor, called screen shots. This book is filled with thousands of screen shots, many of them taken with Grab. If you're a teacher, it's great to include screen shots in your handouts. If you're having trouble with something, you can send a screen shot to your favorite tech support person so they have a clearer idea of the problem. You can even use the Grab service to take a quick screen shot and drop it into an email or a TextEdit document.

Grab

Grab

Note: *Grab is the only screen shot program that let me take screen shots of Classic while running* OS X.

To use Grab:

1. Double-click to open Grab.

2. To capture the **entire screen,** press Command Z.

   To capture a **selected portion** of the screen, press Command Shift A. You'll get a pointer as shown below; press-and-drag to select the area you want to capture.

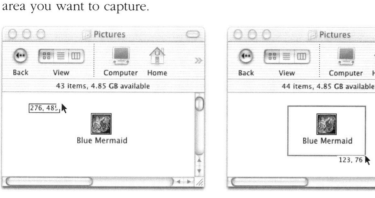

This is what the pointer looks like as you start to grab a portion of the screen.

When you let go, the new file will open instantly in Grab, waiting for you to save it.

With the Command-Shift-A procedure above, you cannot grab the **pointer** nor can you grab **active windows** — the windows are always in the background. You can't get **pop-up menus,** either. So to get one of these items, press Command Shift Z; you'll get the message shown below, the "Timed Screen Grab." Hit Return to activate it, then go to the window, pop-up menu, dialog box, etc., that you want a screen shot of, put everything in position, and hold it until the timer goes off. The screen shot will open instantly in Grab.

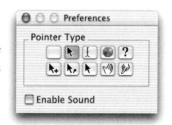

If you need the pointer to show where you've positioned it, or if you want to make sure it doesn't, go to the Grab menu and choose "Preferences..." to get this dialog box. Choose the pointer that you want to appear in the screen shot, then close the box.

Key Caps

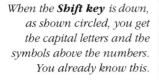

Key Caps

You are probably accustomed to the two main keyboard layouts on your Mac, the regular lowercase letters and numbers, and the capital letters and symbols that appear when you hold down the Shift key. But you actually have two more keyboard layouts that give you lots of extra characters, including dozens of accented letters. To find them, use **Key Caps.**

Double-click Key Caps to open it. Once it's open, you have a Font menu from which you can select any font to see the characters it contains. Choose a font, then follow along with the examples shown below.

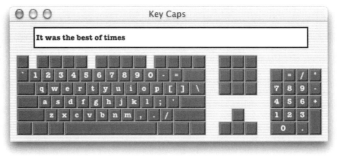

*This is the regular key layout you have when **no keys** are pressed down. You already know this.*

*When the **Shift key** is down, as shown circled, you get the capital letters and the symbols above the numbers. You already know this.*

*When the **Option key** is down, as shown circled, you get access to a hidden keyboard. To type these characters, hold down the Option key and press the character key. It's just like using the Shift key to get capital letters or the symbols above the numbers.*

The white boxes around some characters indicate they contain two-step accent marks. For instance, if you press Option e, let go, then press the letter e, you get é. See the chart in Appendix B.

To type the following symbols:

™	Option 2
£	Option 3 (which is also the pound symbol)
¢	Option 4 (which is also the dollar sign)
©	Option G

Hold down both the Shift and Option keys together and you get still another keyboard layout with more characters to choose from.

See the chart in Appendix B.

For instance, to type the following symbols:

±   Option Shift =

Ø   Option Shift O

Ç   Option Shift C

»   Option Shift \ (« is Option \)

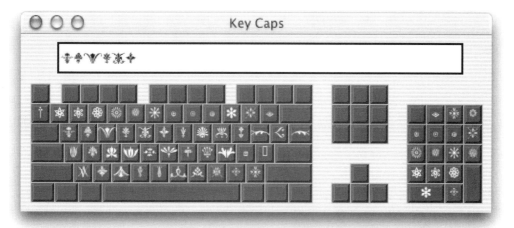

*Key Caps is especially useful for fonts that contain **ornaments, dingbats, and special characters.** Above you see one of the four key layouts for Bodoni Ornaments.*

You can either type the ornaments you want right into Key Caps, then copy and paste them into your document. Or you can use Key Caps to figure out which combinations of keys creates the character you need, then select the font and type that combination directly in your document.

It's really a pity the Key Caps window does not enlarge.

Keychain Access

Keychain Access

Keychain Access provides a secure place to store information that can only be accessed with a user name and password. Use Keychains to safely store passwords for applications, and passwords to access secure servers or web sites. You can also use Keychains for secure storage of credit card numbers, PINs (Personal Information Numbers used by bank cards and phone cards), or other brief information.

Keychain Access has been around for awhile, but many of us ignored it, not realizing how useful it can be. Now that Mac OS X automatically creates a Keychain account for you, this is a good time to learn more about it.

Your Keychain account

When you set up Mac OS X and assigned yourself a user name and password, that same information was used to create a **Keychain account for you.** This assures that your Keychain will unlock automatically when you log in. If you're the only user on your computer, Keychain has been working in the background even though you weren't aware of it.

You (and any other users set up on your computer) can set up as many Keychain accounts as you need. You might want one Keychain for work-related passwords, another for online shopping passwords, and another for personal information.

Keychain gives you a secure place to store small amounts of information, like **credit card numbers.** Keychain is not going to enter your card number for you while you shop, but you can keep a list of your card numbers in a locked Keychain account, which is much safer than keeping a list on a Stickie or in a TextEdit document.

Have you collected quite a few **passwords** over the years? Like one for your online banking, another for your teenagers' credit cards, rare book sites, PayPal, PhotoDisc, Amazon, Barnes&Noble, beta software sites, online catalogs, research sites, your Apple Store account, several different email accounts, etc., etc., etc. Make a Keychain account just to store all of your passwords so they are safe and secure, yet you can find out what they are whenever necessary.

	jtratz			
Keychain: "jtratz" on disk "SmallDisk" 11 items				Lock
Name ▲	Kind	Date Created	Date Modified
iTools	iTools password	10/18/01	10/18/01
iTools	iTools password	10/1/01	10/1/01
mail.cybermesa.com	Internet password	10/29/01	10/29/01
mail.cybermesa.com	Internet password	10/15/01	10/15/01
mail.mac.com	Internet password	10/18/01	10/18/01
mail.ratz.com	Internet password	10/16/01	10/16/01
roadrat	iTools password	10/5/01	10/15/01
smtp.mac.com	Internet password	10/18/01	10/18/01
smtp.mac.com	Internet password	10/5/01	10/5/01

Add... | Get Info | Remove

If an application is "password aware," such as your email client, Keychain can store that information and actually enter your password for you. One **example** of an application that uses a password is Mail, Apple's email client that comes with Mac OS X. In the illustration below, "jtratz" is the default Keychain for my partner John, but it's locked. When John tries to get mail, the "Unlock Keychain" dialog box opens and requests the Keychain password so it can be unlocked.

An example

Once the Keychain is unlocked, all the passwords stored in it are available to the applications that need them, so you won't have to repeat this process over and over. You can, however, set a preference (explained on page 516) that tells Keychain to automatically lock everything again after a certain period of time.

Keychains are **secure** because they're locked. When an application needs the password information that's stored in a locked keychain, as shown above, it asks for your permission and the password. You can either deny permission or you can type in the password and choose to grant permission "one time only" or "always." This gives the application access to the password so it can function normally.

Security

The default Keychain that was automatically created when you set yourself up as a user in Mac OS X uses the same user and password information so that it automatically unlocks when you log in. If you're the only user on your computer, your default Keychain unlocks when you start your computer; if you create other accounts, they are not unlocked automatically. A locked Keychain is, in effect, turned off; an unlocked keychain is turned on.

—continued

Basic Keychain tasks

Keychain Access

Tip: Keychain Access sets up your initial Keychain file, the one based on your user name and password, as the default keychain. This default keychain is automatically opened when you start up your Mac or log on.

To make other Keychains more secure, such as your list of credit card numbers or banking passwords, be sure to make *new* Keychain files for these instead of *adding* them to your default file.

Below are the **basic tasks** to get you started using Keychain. You can create as many Keychain files as you need.

To locate and open the Keychain Access application:

Click the "Applications" icon in the Toolbar (or press Command Option A) to open the Applications window. Then double-click the Utilities icon to open its window, then double-click the Keychain Access icon.

To create a new Keychain file:

1. Open Keychain as described above. Then from the File menu choose "New Keychain…."

   Or from the Edit menu choose "Keychain List…," then click the "New…" button at the bottom of the Keychain List window.

2. In the Save window that opens, enter a descriptive name for the new Keychain, select a location in which to save it, then click "Save."

3. When the "New Keychain Passphrase" dialog box opens, enter a password for the new Keychain, then click OK.

> **New Keychain Passphrase**
>
> Enter a password or phrase for keychain "Client passwords".
>
> Password or phrase: ••••••
>
> Verify: ••••••
>
> ▷ Details
>
> Cancel   OK

4. In the next dialog that appears (named with the new Keychain name) click "Add…" to add password items to the window (start with Step 5 on the opposite page).

> ● ● ●   Client passwords
>
> Keychain: "Client passwords" on disk "SmallDisk"   Lock
> 0 items
>
> | Name | Kind | Date Created |
> |------|------|--------------|
> | | | |
>
> (?)   Add…   Get Info   Remove

To manually add a new password item to a Keychain:

1. Open Keychain (it's in the Utilities folder, which is in the Applications folder).

2. From the File menu, choose "Keychain List...."

3. From the Keychains menu, select a Keychain file.

4. Click the "Add..." button to open the "New Password Item" dialog box.

5. Enter a descriptive name for the new password item in the "Name" field, a name that will remind you what it is.

6. Enter an account name associated with this password, if there is one, in the "Account" field. For instance, at Amazon.com you have an account name, plus a password. Enter that account name here (not the Keychain account name!). This is sometimes called the User ID. If there is no account name associated with the information you're entering (such as your bike lock combination), enter your user name.

7. Enter the password, registration number, or other type of information you want to make secure in the "Password" field.

   The password is displayed as bullets (round dots) unless you check the "Show Typing" checkbox. Check "Show Typing" to see the characters as you type and to proofread the password.

8. Click the "Add" button to add the new password item to the current Keychain file. If the Keychain file to which you're adding an item is locked, enter the password for the associated Keychain in the "Unlock Keychain" dialog box that appears.

Tip: If you make a number of Keychain files, you're going to have more passwords to remember! You can make a Keychain file to store all of your Keychain passwords. Then you must remember that one password.

—continued

To automatically add a new password item to a Keychain:

When you try to access a keychain-aware application, a password-protected server (such as an FTP server, shown below) or a secure web site, see if there is an "Options…" button where you can choose to "Add Password to Keychain." If you do add the account name and password information this one time, then next time you access the same server, or application, Keychain will automatically grant access unless the Keychain is locked at the time (see details of locking and unlocking keychains on the opposite page).

When connecting to a server, type in the account name and password, then click the "Options…" button to get the dialog box shown below. If you add the password to Keychain, the next time you go to this server you'll never even see the password dialog box—you'll just get right in.

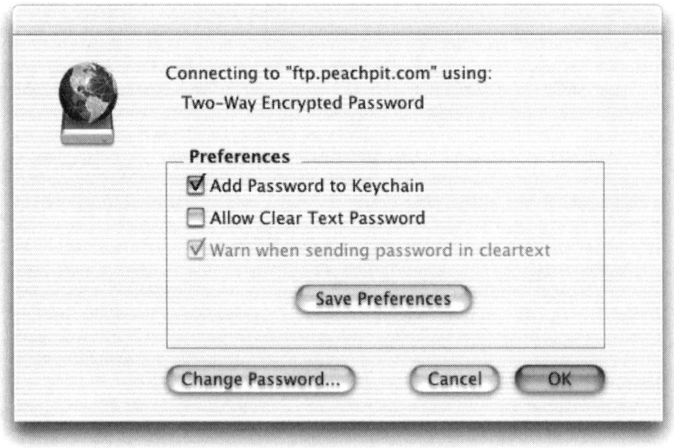

"Allow Clear Text Password" shows the password in less secure (but readable) text rather than encrypted as dots.

"Warn when sending password in cleartext" alerts you that your Clear Text password will be sent in an insecure manner. Make your choices, then click OK.

To see a list of your Keychains, from the Edit menu, choose "Keychain List...."

Name	Kind	Location
credit cards	keychain file	~/Library/Keychains
jt applications	keychain file	~/Library/Keychains
jtratz	keychain file	~/Library/Keychains

Keychain List

New... Add... Remove

To open a specific Keychain file in a Keychain list, double-click on it. Or from the Keychains menu, select one of the Keychain files listed.

To take a Keychain file to another computer, copy it from the Keychains folder, which is in your Library folder, which is in your Home folder.

Client passwords

This is what a Keychain file looks like in the Keychain folder.

To add a Keychain that you brought to your computer from another Mac, open the Keychain List, then click the "Add..." button. You can navigate to the folder where you stored the Keychain file.

To lock a Keychain: Even though your default Keychain opens automatically when you start your computer or when you log in, you can lock it (or any other Keychain) whenever you want extra security. Click the "Lock" button at the top right of any Keychain window to lock it. The window will collapse to show just the top section and an "Unlock" button.

jt applications

Keychain: "jt applications" on disk "SmallDisk"
This keychain is locked.

Unlock

To unlock a Keychain: Click the "Unlock" button on a locked Keychain to open the "Unlock Keychain" window. Type the Keychain's password in the "Password or phrase" field, then click OK.

If a Keychain file is locked when you try to access a password-enabled item, Keychain opens the "Confirm Access to Keychain" window. Choose if you want to "Deny" access, "Allow Once," or "Always Allow." The "Allow Once" option grants access this one time, then presents these same options next time. "Always Allow" grants access every time.

Confirm Access to Keychain

Keychain Access wants permission to decrypt item "iTools" in keychain "jtratz". Do you want to allow this?

▷ Details

Deny   Allow Once   Always Allow

—continued

Get Info See information about a Keychain file, including the encrypted password, by opening the file's **Get Info** window.

1. Open the Keychain Access application, if it isn't already.

2. From the Keychains menu, select the name of the Keychain account that holds the Keychain file you want information about. You'll get a small window with the list of files in this account.

3. Then, to get the Get Info window, *either* double-click the name of any file, *or* single-click a file name and press Command I or click the "Get Info" button at the bottom of the window.

The name of the selected account is shown in the title bar and in the text field at the top of the Get Info window. The "Show" pop-up menu options are "General Information" and "Access Control."

View Password: Click this button and a small box appears with the password for that file.

General Information: The window displays some general information about the Keychain item and a "Comments" field. The "Comments" field lets you add comments or additional information you may want to keep concerning this Keychain item.

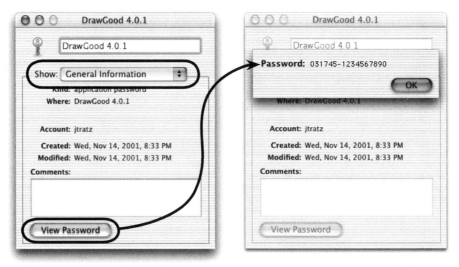

Click "View Password" to get the password for this Keychain file, as shown to the right.

Type pertinent comments in this box. You can see these comments in the Keychain folder window, as explained on pages 89–90.

Access Control: In this area you can set different levels of security.

Allow access to this item without warning: Refers to whether applications will have access to the secure information in the Keychain without showing the "Confirm Access to Keychain" window (page 513). If you uncheck this option, every password-aware application will open a "Confirm Access to Keychain" window to get authorization from you.

Allow access by any application: If you select this, you increase the risk of a computer virus or some other cracker software retrieving your passwords.

Allow access only by these applications: To limit access to certain applications that you know and trust.

To add an application to the trusted list, click the **Add** button. In the "Add Trusted Application" window that opens, navigate to an application, select it, then click "Choose."

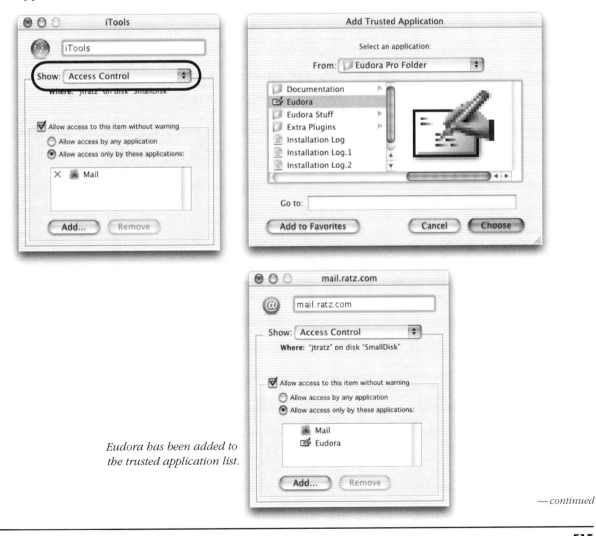

Eudora has been added to the trusted application list.

—continued

Keychain settings   You can change some of the **Keychain settings** in the "Change Settings" dialog. To get to the settings, open a Keychain from the Keychains menu, or select a Keychain in the Keychain List window if it's open. From the Edit menu choose "*'Keychain'* Settings." The actual name of your selected Keychain will appear in place of the word "Keychain."

Change "jtratz" Settings

☐ Lock after 5 ⬍ minutes of inactivity
☐ Lock when the system sleeps

[Change Passphrase...]   (Cancel)   (Save)

Lock after: Check this box to lock the Keychain after a specified time period. This helps to prevent you from accidently leaving privileged information unlocked and available.

Lock when the system sleeps: Check this box for extra security. If you've walked away from your computer long enough for it to sleep, you may want to make sure your Keychains are secure.

Change Passphrase: Click this to change the Keychain's password or passphrase. Don't change the passphrase if this is a Keychain that you want to open automatically when you log in as a user or when you start your computer. If you change the password to one that's different from your Mac OS X password, the Keychain will not open automatically when start your computer.

The **Print Center** manages printing your files. You can add printers to your list, start and stop printing, put files in a queue for printing later, delete files from the queue so they won't print at all, and more. The Print Center is explained at length in Chapter 15.

Print Center

Print Center

StuffIt Expander works all by itself to uncompress (unstuff) .sit files, as well as a number of other compressed file formats. You rarely have to open it yourself—just double-click a compressed file, StuffIt Expander will open and unstuff the file, and then put itself away. Anytime you like, however, you can drag a compressed file onto the StuffIt Expander icon to unstuff it. I keep it in my Dock so I can drag files onto it whenever necessary.

StuffIt Expander

StuffIt Expander

OTHER STUFF There are several other useful features of your Mac that don't fall into the applications or utilities category.

Battery If you're using a laptop, the **battery** icon will appear in the upper-right of your menu to show you either how much time in hours and minutes you have left, or what percentage of your battery is left. If you don't have the battery icon in the menu bar, go to the Energy Saver preferences and check the box to turn it on.

Screen Shots As you might have read on page 505, you can take **screen shots** with Grab. But there are lots of times you just want a quick snapshot, in which case you can use one of the tricks listed below. The pointer will not appear in the shot, though, which might or might not be an issue in a particular shot.

Picture 1

Each time you take a screen shot you'll hear the sound of a camera shutter snapping, and an icon will appear on your Desktop called Picture 1. As you create more shots, the files will be named Picture 2, Picture 3, etc.

Double-click any screen shot to open it in Preview. Drag any screen shot to a Photoshop icon to open it in Photoshop.

▼ **To take a screen shot of the entire screen,** press Command Shift 3.

▼ To get a crosshair cursor to take a screen shot of **just a portion of the screen,** press Command Shift 4. Drag over an area.

▼ To take a screen shot that will go **straight to the Clipboard** (it will not make a Picture file) so you can then just paste it directly into a document or into something like a Photoshop file, hold down the Control key, then (keep holding it down) press Command Shift 4 to get the crosshair. Drag over an area. You'll hear a much smaller snapping sound.

Go to your document. If it's a text document, click the insertion point where you want the graphic to paste in. Then press Command V to paste the screen shot onto the page.

Show Info is a small window that gives you pertinent information about any selected file. The kind of information you get depends on what type of file is selected, as shown below and on the following pages.

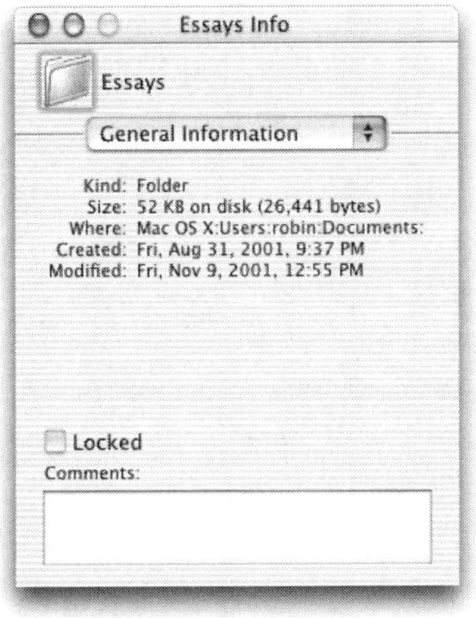

Show Info

Get **general information** about any file. **Lock** a file (if you have the privileges to do so). Locking a file prevents accidental changes. No one can print a locked file.

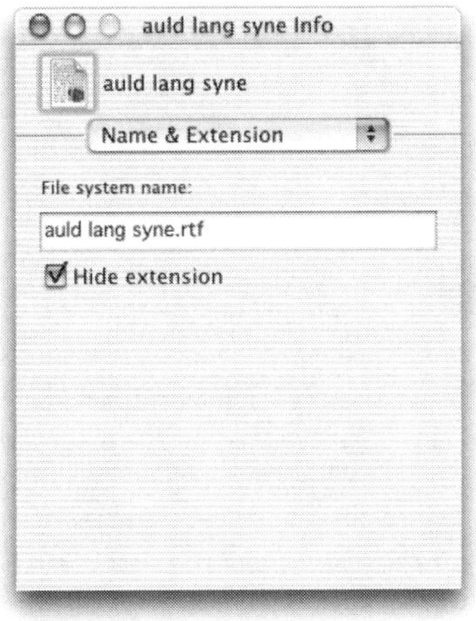

Rename a file. Hide or show the *file name extension* (depends on the setting in Finder preferences). Notice if you hide the extension, it hides it from the name at the top and in your windows, but the "File system name" still holds onto the extension because it is just hidden from public view, not gone.

Select a **new original** for an alias. See Chapter 22 about aliases.

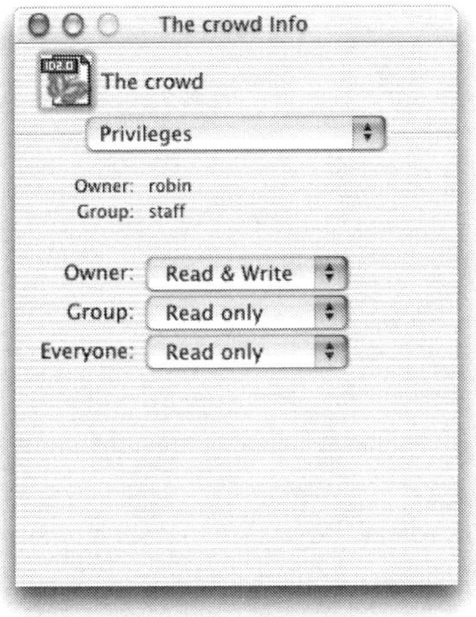

Change the **sharing privileges,** if you have the privileges to do so. See Chapter 35 for details on sharing privileges.

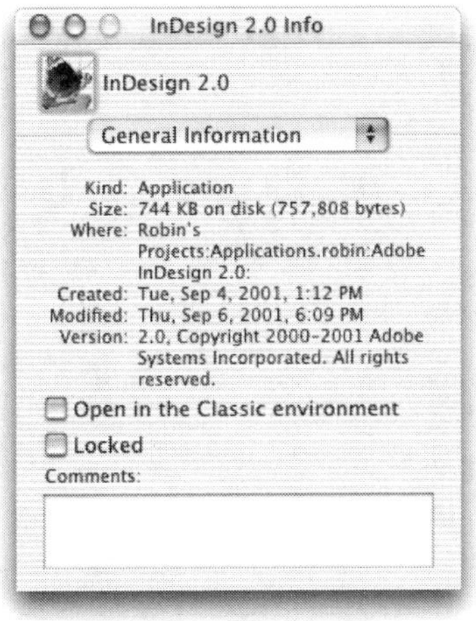

Tell **Carbon applications** to open in the Classic environment. A Carbon application is one that will work in both Mac OS 9 and OS X.

Allocate more memory to a Classic application. See Chapter 40 for more details.

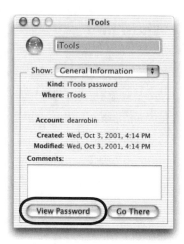

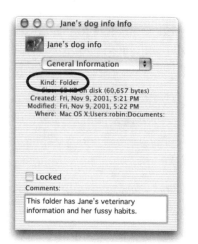

*In the Keychain window, as discussed on page 515, select a Keychain. Then click "View Password" to get your **password** for that particular item.*

*Change the picture of the **icon:** in a Mac OS X graphics application, copy the image you want to use as the icon for this file. Click on the existing icon in this window; paste.*

*Write **comments** in the Comments box. You can choose to display your comments in the Finder windows: use the View Options (see pages 89–90).*

Turn a document into a stationery template. See page 231.

Then click the "Change All…" button, which gives you the message shown above. If you're sure, click the "Continue" button.

You can always override this global specification on a per-document basis.

*One of the most important things you can do with the Info window is **assign an application** to open certain file formats. For instance, let's say you keep a Microsoft-free environment, but people often send you Microsoft Word files, which end in an extension of .doc. Using the Info window, you can choose that every .doc file you get will open in Nisus Writer (your favorite word processor) instead of looking for Microsoft Word. To do that: Show Info on a .doc file. Click the application icon in the middle, and from the menu or dialog box, choose your preferred application.*

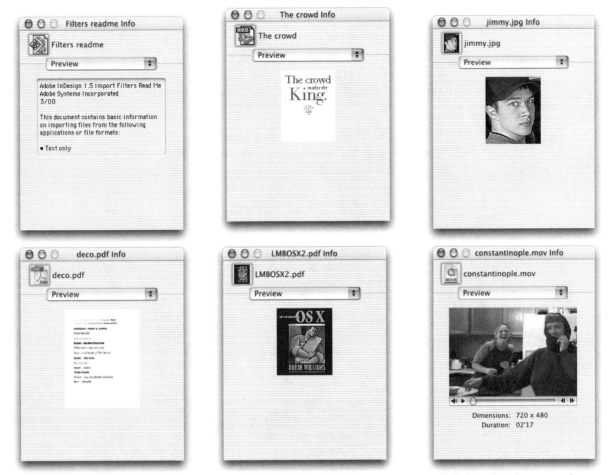

Preview some text documents, PDFs, most images, and most movies right here in the Info window.

Click the "Play" button to play a movie in the Info window.

Spelling Checker

Like the *Colors Palette* and *Find and Replace* (explained on the following pages), you'll find the same **Spelling Checker** in a number of Mac OS X applications, including TextEdit, Stickies, and Mail, as well as other applications that follow the Mac OS X specs, such as the great applications from Stone Design (www.stone.com) and OmniGroup (www.omnigroup.com).

To check the spelling in a document or email message, from the Edit menu, choose "Spelling," then choose "Check Spelling..." to open the Spelling window, as shown below.

Click the **Find Next** button to find misspelled words.

When an application finds a word it doesn't recognize, the word is highlighted in the document and shown in the text field of the Spelling pane, as you see above. Suggested spellings are listed in the **Guess** pane.

If one of the guesses looks correct, double-click the guess to replace the misspelled word. Or, you can select the correct spelling in the "Guess" pane, then click the **Correct** button.

If the application finds a misspelled word but can't guess the correct spelling, **type** the correct spelling. Now, you have to be careful here and be very conscious of whether the Spelling Checker window is active or your document window—whichever one is **active** is the one where the spelling will be corrected. If the word gets corrected in the document itself, that's fine. If it's corrected in the Spelling Checker window, then click the "Correct" button to make the correction. This might not make sense until you actually use the Spelling Checker.

Often, even though words are not misspelled, they're not recognized by an application because they're not included in the Spelling Checker's built-in dictionary. When an application finds such a word, either click the **Ignore** button, or, add the word to the dictionary: Click in the text field that contains the unrecognized word, then click the **Learn** button.

If you've added a misspelled word to the dictionary by mistake, remove it by entering the word in the text field, then click **Forget.**

Like the *Spelling Checker* and the *Colors Palette,* **Find and Replace** is a Mac **Find and Replace**
OS X feature that is accessible through a number of applications. You can
find a word, any occurrence that includes a part of a word, or find a certain
word or phrase and replace it with another. Knowing how to use Find and
Replace can help speed up your work; for instance, if you often have to type
something like "Santa Fe Community College," you can type "sf" instead,
then when you're finished with the report, search for "sf" and replace it with
the longer phrase.

	Find Panel
Find:	the Presidential Suite
Replace with:	the Ambassador's Suite

Replace All Scope: ● Entire File ○ Selection
Find Options: ☑ Ignore Case

[Replace All] [Replace] [Replace & Find] [Previous] [Next]

Find: Search a document or email message for a specific word or phrase.
Leave the "Replace with" field empty if you just want to *find* the phrase.

> **Find Options:** Check "Ignore Case" to search without considering if
> uppercase or lowercase letters are used. This ensures that you find
> all occurrences of a word, whether they're capitalized or not.
>
> If you want to restrict the search to find occurrences that are
> "case sensitive" and match exactly your search term, capital letters
> as typed, uncheck "Ignore Case."

Replace with: Enter text you're searching for in the "Find" text field. In the
"Replace With" field, enter the text which will replace found text.

> **Replace All Scope:** Choose "Entire File" to search the entire document
> or email message. If you selected text *before* you opened the Find
> Panel, you can choose to search just that "Selection."

Buttons: When your fields are filled in and your Scope and Options chosen,
click one of the buttons along the bottom of the Find Panel.

> **Replace All:** This immediately finds all occurrences of your phrase
> in the entire document and replaces each with the replacement text.
>
> If you prefer to make changes more slowly so you can see each
> one and make a decision on it, click the **Next** button to find the
> next occurrence of your text, then click the **Replace** button to
> change only the current selection.
>
> **Replace & Find:** This replaces the found text, then immediately finds
> the next occurrence.
>
> To find the previous unchanged occurrence that you skipped over,
> click the **Previous** button.

Colors Palette

The **Colors Palette** is a simple yet powerful feature. Many applications written specifically for Mac OS X call on this Color Palette whenever you want to change the color of your font, as in TextEdit or Mail, or graphic objects in certain applications (the background of your Finder windows uses a Color Picker which is a little different).

The Colors Palette **toolbar** at the top contains four different color selection tools, which are described below. Click each one to see the various modes of color you can work with.

Along the bottom of the Colors Palette are other tools:

- ▾ At the bottom-left of the picker is a **color box** where the color you created will appear.

- ▾ Drag the **magnifying glass** anywhere on your screen, then click when the crosshairs of the glass are on top of a color you want to select. The color will appear in the color box.

- ▾ To save a color for later use, drag the color from the color box to one of the wells in the small **color swatch collection,** located to the right of the magnifying glass.

- ▾ When you've found a color you like and it's in the color box, click the **Apply** button to apply it to the selected text or object in your document.

Color Wheel: Select a color by clicking or dragging the cursor in the Colors Palette's color wheel. As you move the cursor around the Color Wheel, the color swatch in the bottom-left corner changes.

You can also adjust the value (the lightness or darkness) of the selected color by sliding the vertical slider next to the color wheel.

Image Palettes: You can use the built-in "Spectrum" palette, or select an image from your computer to use as a color palette. Click the "Palette" pop-down menu, then choose "New from File...." Navigate to an image on your computer, then click the "Open" button to display the image. Drag the mouse over any area of the image to select a color from the image. This is a good way to get an exact match of a color for another project.

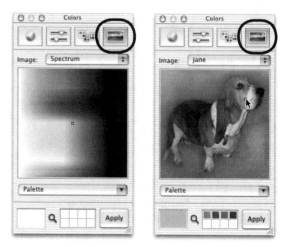

Color Sliders: Choose colors from four different standard color spaces: Grayscale, RGB, CMYK, and HSB. A one-color book like this one uses grayscale. For email, the web, and on the screen, RGB is the preferred color space. For high-quality printing on expensive printing presses, CMYK is the standard. HSB is based on the human perceptions of color, with hue (the color itself), saturation (how deep and true that color is), and brightness (how much white is added to it). It's easier to create a color in HSB than in RGB, so you can create a color in HSB, then click the RGB palette to see how it translated and to actually choose the color (in RGB you're working with colors of light, so red and green make yellow, which can make you crazy). If you know the numeric color values, you can enter those in the boxes of any palette.

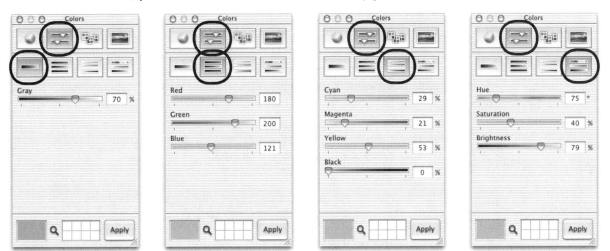

Color Palettes: Choose from a palette of Apple or Developer color swatches, open other palettes you may have, or make your own. **To make your own palette,** click on the "List" pop-up menu and choose "New." Give it a name. Then go to the other color tools, create colors, and put them in the swatch collection. Go back to your new palette and drag each color from the swatch collection into the little window. Then click on a color in your palette list, go down to the Color pop-up menu, and choose "Rename…" to give your color a memorable name.

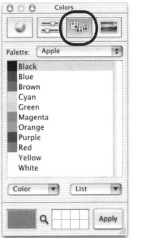

Your custom palette will be available in every application that uses these Mac OS X services.

Name the utility that could accomplish each task listed below.

1. Assign an application to open certain file formats. For instance, assign Photoshop to open all .tif files.

2. Find out who owns an Internet domain name.

3. Log in as the root user.

4. Find the flower ornament in a special font, or the © symbol in any font.

5. Check for and repair problems on a disk.

6. Find out what kind of processor is in your Mac, the speed of your Mac, and the serial number.

7. Take screen shots of what you see on your monitor.

8. Safely store passwords, credit card numbers, bicycle lock numbers, ftp logon account names and passwords, and other important bits of information.

9. Preview a movie file without opening an application.

10. Erase a disk.

Answers on page 752.

What is the Internet?

30

This chapter explains what the **Internet** is and how the **World Wide Web** is *part* of the Internet. It explains the difference between America Online and the World Wide Web and how they are related. This chapter also clears up a lot of the jargon you probably hear all the time, such as modem, browser, newsgroup, dial up, etc.

The Internet   The **Internet** is a system of computers all over the world that are linked together using phone lines or other sorts of wires or satellites. This linking together of computers is called a "network." It was created by the United States government's Advanced Research Projects Agency (ARPA) in response to the Soviet's Sputnik project. The government wanted to encourage scientists in academic, military, and research institutions to work together to catch up to the Soviet's advances in science. The scientists demanded computers, which were enormously expensive at the time, and ARPA realized they would need fewer computers if the machines were connected by means of a network. So Dr. Leonard Kleinrock and his team established the first ARPANET communication link in September of 1969.

This connectivity now lets regular people like you and me send messages all over the world. The messages bounce from one computer to another along the network until they reach their destination. If one of the computers along the route is down, the message just finds another route.

Modems   Your computer receives these messages through some sort of intermediary **modem,** a piece of hardware that translates the signals coming through the wires into information that your Mac can use.

There are different modems depending on how you connect to the Internet. For instance, you might use the internal modem in your Mac, which is designed to plug into a **phone** jack or telephone in your house. Information goes from your computer, through the modem, over the phone lines to the Internet, and comes back in the same way. This kind of connection is called a **dial up** because the modem dials a phone number to *log on,* or connect to the Internet, and when you are finished with your business online, you *log off,* or hang up. One person at a time can connect through a dial-up account.

Or you might have a box sitting outside of your computer that connects your Mac to a **television** cable, or to a **DSL** line (IDSL or ADSL), **ISDN** line, a **T1** or **T3** line, or a **satellite** dish. These connections do not dial up—they are considered *permanent,* or *always on* connections, also known as *broadband.* All of these options are significantly faster than a phone connection, and generally cost from a little more to a lot more. A whole bunch of computers can connect to the Internet at the same time through a broadband connection.

Although the technology is different in each type of modem, they are similar in that **every modem** must translate the information that comes through the cable, say a television signal through a TV cable, into Internet "packets" that your Mac can understand. And the information from your Mac must be translated into a form that the connection cables can understand so they can send it out.

Let's look at a **very simplified version** of how a Mac sends and receives signals through a phone modem, like the one that is built into your Mac. Your computer is *digital,* meaning it can only work with countable, finite information, like ice cubes. The phone lines are *analog,* meaning they can only work with information that is flowing and infinite, like water. So the computer sends the digital info (ice cubes) to the modem, which translates the digital info into analog info (water) so it can be sent over the phone lines. The modem on the other end takes the analog info (water) and turns it back into digital info (ice cubes) so the computer on the other end can understand and use it.

Connection speeds

Different types of **connections** process information through to your computer at different **speeds,** which indicate how much information can be sent at a time. The faster the speed, the more "ice cubes" can be translated into "water" and sent through the lines. Below is a chart of the most common speeds at the moment. This will also change, of course.

The abbreviation **bps** stands for bits per second, and **Mbps** is megabits per second. The **k** stands for kilo, which basically means a thousand. You don't need to worry about exactly how much a bit per second is—just understand that the more, the better.

modem	speed	say it	write it		how is it
phone	2400 bps	twenty-four hundred	2.4	2400	slo-o-o-o-w
	9600	ninety-six hundred	9.6	9600	not much better
	14,400	fourteen-four	14.4		frustratingly slow for the Internet
	28,800	twenty-eight eight	28.8		faster; the Internet is do-able at this speed
	33,600	thirty-three six	33.6		okay for home
	56,000	fifty-six k	56k		very common now for home
IDSL	128,000 bps	one twenty-eight	128k		lower end of DSL, but it's great
ADSL	128,000 to 2,500,000	one twenty-eight k to two point five megabits	128k to 2.5 Mbps		higher end of DSL, really great
cable	1,000,000 bps	one megabit	1 Mbps		cable has a fast download, but uploads are at telephone modem speed
T1	1,540,000 bps	one point fifty-four megabits	1.54 Mbps		generally too expensive for home
T3	45,000,000 bps	45 megabits	45 Mbps		way expensive

Email For over thirty years people have been using the Internet to send **email,** which is a message typed on a computer and sent over the wires to another computer. The "e" in email stands for "electronic." One of the first things most people use the Internet for is to send and receive email. With all the things we can do on computers, it seems to have evolved that our favorite thing to do is to communicate with other human beings. Far from being an isolating medium, the computer and the Internet have helped develop millions of new relationships between people.

Newsgroups Another original feature of the Internet is **newsgroups,** which are sort of like online clubs. Each newsgroup is a collection of people with a common interest, such as golf, the Shakespearean authorship question, llama breeding, Zoroastrianism, cancer, Esperanto, children with brain tumors, Wicca, and over 60,000 other topics. Members of newsgroups "post" ongoing discussions on a public "bulletin board," which is similar in concept to tacking notes on a cork bulletin board in the lounge. Whenever you like, you can pop in to the newsgroup, read the messages, and post your own response, question, or opinion. This is a wonderful resource for information about a topic important to you. These groups often form strong communities, since they are people bonded together with a common interest. Go to **www.google.com** and click "Groups."

Mailing lists **Mailing lists,** or **listservs** (yes, "listserv" is spelled correctly) are another popular feature of the Internet. A listserv is similar to a newsgroup in that it is a collection of people who want to discuss a common interest, but instead of posting messages on a bulletin board, they send email. Piles of email. When anyone sends an email message to the mailing list, it goes to every single person on the list. There are about 49,000 different mailing lists. Go to **www.lsoft.catalist.html**

So why does the Internet seem new? So with all this going on for so many years, why is it that the Internet seems like a fairly new thing? Because all those years the "interface" for the Internet, the way it looked and how you used it, had been pretty ugly and geeky. Only nerds were attracted to it. (Now, don't be offended; "nerd" is not a pejorative term—I'm a nerdette myself. A nerdette in high heels and a hat.) Getting on the Internet was very DOS-like, with command lines and backslashes and codes, and a typical computer monitor displayed yellow text on a black background, monospaced and ugly. No pictures and no music and no color. Then a miraculous event occurred.

The Macintosh was invented.

Now, it's not part of official Internet history, but I do personally believe the World Wide Web would not have happened if the Macintosh computer had not been invented. It was the Mac that changed computing. For the first time, we had a monitor capable of displaying professional type, and it was black type on a white background, so much easier to read. We became accustomed to color, graphics, sound, animation, beautiful text, etc. Microsoft, of course, "borrowed" this technology and soon other computers were able to act (albeit clumsily) like Macintoshes.

As Steve Wozniak, one of the inventors of the Macintosh, says, "Today, essentially every computer is a Macintosh."

This new expectation of computers—graphical and colorful—paved the way for the invention of new software in 1993 that allowed full "pages" to be sent over the Internet and displayed on a computer screen. These pages could have color, graphics, sound, animation, beautiful text, etc. Finally the Internet started to look like something regular people would be interested in. This is the **World Wide Web,** and those pages are called **web pages.** The World Wide Web is a collection of billions of individual web pages displaying text, graphics, sound, and more.

A collection of related web pages about one topic—say, for instance, about your worm farm—is a **web site.** A web site is like a book in that there may be several parts to it, like chapters, and there is a "table of contents" that shows you the organization of the book. On a web site, this table of contents page is called the **home page.** You'll return over and over again to the home page; it's sort of like home base.

So the World Wide Web, then, is one more facet of the Internet. The Internet is sort of like the electrical wiring in your house: the same wiring goes all through your house, but you can use it to do different things, like turn on light bulbs, run a computer, wash your clothes, and power your TV. The Internet network runs all over the world, and you can use it to send email, join newsgroups, discuss matters on a listserv, view web pages, pay your bills, watch video, hear music, and more. Wow.

I don't capitalize the word "web" because in English we don't capitalize any other form of communication, such as television, telephone, or radio.

Web Browsers

Internet Explorer

Netscape Communicator™

OmniWeb

To see web pages, you need special software that can display them. It's just like anything else on your Mac—if you want to crunch a bunch of numbers, you need spreadsheet software; if you want to write a letter, you need a word processor; **if you want to view web pages, you need a browser.** A browser is simply the software that displays web pages.

Along with your Mac operating system software you got browsers—Netscape Communicator and Microsoft Internet Explorer.

Internet Explorer has an icon in the Dock, as shown to the left, and its application is in the "Applications" folder.

Netscape Communicator is in your "Applications (Mac OS 9)" folder because at the time I write this, it's not ready yet for Mac OS X. But you can still use it (I do) in Classic mode.

OmniWeb is a great browser that is not included with your Mac, but directions on how to download and install it are on pages 303–304.

There are other browsers. For instance, when you use America Online (explained on the following pages), you can view web pages through America Online's special browser, which at the moment is a version of Internet Explorer. There are quite a few browsers, each with loyal fans. You can keep as many browsers as you like on your hard disk. You can switch between them as often as you like. They each display web pages a little differently, and they each have their own special features. I'll show you how to actually use them in the next chapter.

This is the OmniWeb browser displaying a web page.

This is the Internet Explorer browser displaying the same web page.

So how do you get to the Internet and the World Wide Web? You need a computer, a modem, a browser, and an **Internet Service Provider.**

You see, there are many thousands of special computers around the world hooked into the Internet 24 hours a day that act as "nodes," or connection points, that redistribute Internet connections to people like you and me. These companies are Internet Service Providers, or ISPs. From your home or business, you need to pay a provider to provide you with a connection to the Internet. You pay them; they give you any necessary software, instructions for connecting, and if necessary (for phone modems) a local phone number. In the case of a phone modem, you'll have your modem dial the phone number; that puts your computer in touch with your provider's computer and its Internet connection; and you can go anywhere in the world from there, on a local phone call. It's truly amazing.

There are probably several Internet Service Providers in your area. There are also a number of national providers that can set you up with a connection. Ask around your town and at your local Mac user group for the names of the favored providers.

There is an alternative to getting a connection through an Internet Service Provider, as described below.

Another way to get to the Internet and the World Wide Web is through **America Online (AOL).** *America Online is **not** the Internet!* This is how it works: America Online is an online *service* that you join for a monthly fee. If you use a phone modem, your modem dials a local number that AOL gave you and you "log on" (connect) to the service; if you have broadband, you still have to open the AOL application and log on to connect to the Internet.

You are not directly on the Internet—you are safely contained in the AOL "village," where there are clubs and organizations, conferences, chat rooms, a "post office" for sending and receiving email, online magazines, news sources, kids' places, teen hangouts, parent support groups, research resources, romance rooms, your own calendar, and much more. There are live guides to help you figure things out; there are "police officers" who make their rounds and kick out people who act inappropriately; there are classes and interviews; there are friends to make and parties to crash. Everything is nicely organized and easy to find. Wherever you go on America Online, you are still within the village—***until*** you click the button that says "Go to the Web," type in a web address, or click a link that takes you to the web. When you head for the web, you're going out the back door of the village, onto the Internet, straight to the web itself. It opens AOL's own special browser and you can surf the world. There are no guides, no police

Internet Service Providers

America Online is not the Internet!

Notice you can also go to "Newsgroups" from this menu. If you are on AOL, check it out!

officers, no maps. You're on your own. You have actually left America Online, even though the AOL menu bar is still there. AOL has integrated the web into its own system so well that it is often difficult to tell when you have left—but don't worry, it's not that important to know when you have left. ***The important thing to know is that AOL acts as your Internet service provider (ISP), so you do not need to get another one.***

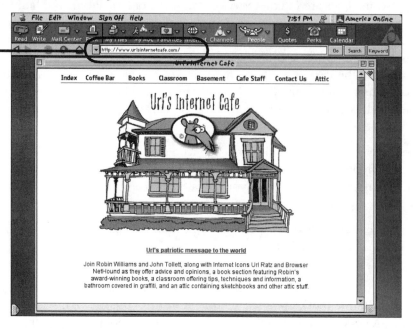

Type in a web address (as explained fully in Chapter 32) in this area, then hit the Return key. The browser will appear and take you to that page.

Notice this is not a Mac OS X version of America Online. As I write this, the OS X version will not be out for a while. But it works just fine in the Classic mode.

America Online and other browsers

Using America Online is actually a great way to get to the Internet and the World Wide Web. You pay a monthly fee, something like $20 a month, which is fairly comparable to what you might pay an Internet Service Provider for a phone connection to the Internet.

If you don't like AOL's browser, you can actually surf the web using Netscape, OmniWeb, or **any other browser** of your choice while connected to AOL. This is how to do it:

1. If you don't already have an alias of your favorite browser sitting on your Desktop, make an alias (page 346) and put it within easy reach.

2. Log on to America Online as usual.

3. Then double-click the browser alias on your Desktop.

Et violà! You're on the Internet using your favorite browser to surf the World Wide Web through your AOL account.

America Online is a wonderful service. There are complaints about it, of course, but when you're trying to make forty million ardent users happy, there are bound to be problems here and there. In general, AOL is the easiest, most fun, and least painful introduction to the online world. If you've never been online before, it's not a bad idea to start with AOL. You can explore the Internet and the World Wide Web very easily from America Online. You can have seven separate email addresses, each with its own password, so your whole family can use it. There are parent-controlled features to help keep your kids out of trouble.

If America Online is not already installed on your Macintosh, you can install it from any of the hundreds of CDs you've probably received in the mail, inside magazines, or on airplanes. Just put in the CD and double-click the file called "Install." After it's installed, double-click the AOL icon and it will walk you through the registration process. You're on. ***You do not need to sign up with an Internet Service Provider to use America Online,*** not even if you want to use a different browser from the one that AOL supplies.

If, however, you have no need for America Online and its services, then you might want to get a "direct" Internet connection from an **Internet Service Provider.** This connection, along with a browser, will get you to the Internet and the World Wide Web, newsgroups, mailing lists, and email.

And it's certainly possible to do **both.** You might have a "broadband" connection (DSL, cable, etc., that is fast and always on), for which you pay a monthly fee, and that broadband connection is your ISP. You can also have AOL at the same time. You will pay *two* monthly fees, but AOL has a separate fee (less per month) for their service if you use a different provider. In my house, for instance, I personally use a direct Internet connection through a service provider, but we also have an America Online account because my kids like to use it.

**Should you choose
America Online
or an
Internet Service Provider?**

1. What are the four major ways people use the Internet?

2. Which is a faster modem speed, 56k or 2.5Mbps?

3. If you wanted to get a lot of email, would you join a newsgroup or a listserv?

4. What is a collection of web pages called?

5. What is the "home page" of a web site?

6. Why do you need a browser on the World Wide Web?

7. Explain the connection between America Online and the Internet.

8. If you use America Online exclusively, do you need to get an Internet connection through an Internet Service Provider?

9. Explain how to use your favorite browser to surf the web if your connection is through America Online.

10. What great invention was a critical factor in the development of the World Wide Web?

Answers on page 752.

Connecting to the Internet
and the Web

31

Your Mac is a machine made for the **Internet.** Not only does it provide you with tools for easy access, Apple fully *expects* that you are connected to the Internet and uses this expectation in many ways—OS X automatically tries to connect to the Internet in Sherlock, iTools, iTunes, QuickTime Player, with Internet Location Files, the Date & Time server, Software Update, a number of icons in the Dock go to the Internet, many Help files get their information from the Internet, and a number of other features depend on the connection.

In this chapter I'll walk you through getting connected, if you aren't already, and help you manage your Internet features. It's easier than you might think. If you got yourself all connected with the Internet setup program that ran as soon as you turned on your Mac for the first time, you won't need this chapter at all unless you want to make changes in settings.

If you decided not to go through the Internet setup when you turned on your Mac, you can't ever go through it again. But you *can* go to the individual dialog boxes and preferences and set things up just the way the Mac would have done it in the first place.

Are ya ratty for the Net?

Step by Step: What To Do

Below are the **steps** you'll follow to get yourself connected to the Internet so you can browse the World Wide Web and do email.

1. Decide on a **provider.** See pages 535–537 and 542–543.
The only way to get to the Internet is to pay someone money to connect you, as explained in Chapter 30 and again on page 543.

2. Get your **modem** hooked up. See the opposite page.

3. Get the **setup information** from your provider. See page 544.

4. *Either* walk through the **setup process** (pages 544–547) if you're turning on your Mac for the first time.

   Or do it yourself. To do it yourself, you'll use the Network preferences (pages 548–553) and the Internet preferences (pages 554–557).

5. After you've set up the preferences, you're **ready to connect.**

   If you have a **broadband account,** just open your browser or email program; see page 558.

   If you have a telephone modem with a **dial-up account,** use Internet Connect; see pages 558–559.

You Need a Modem

Before you can get connected in the first place, you need a **modem** (if you don't know what a modem is, and you care, see pages 530–531). The kind of modem you need depends on how you plan to connect to the Internet.

You have basically two choices. You will connect through:

Either a phone line with the modem that is built into your Mac, as explained below. (If your Mac is older and doesn't have a built-in modem, you'll need to buy one. Go to any office supply store or call MacWarehouse at 800.622.6222 and tell them you need a 56K modem for your Macintosh.)

Or a high-speed, broadband connection such as DSL, ISDN, cable, T1, T3, or satellite. The company that provides your service will sell you a special modem.

If you have a choice, go for the broadband—it's always on, it's fast, and Mac OS X really prefers broadband.

If your Mac is capable of running OS X, it should have a built-in 56K **telephone** modem for connecting through a phone (every iMac has a built-in modem). Look at the back or side of your computer—if you see a phone jack, that's your telephone modem. If you connect through a phone line, you have what's called a **dial-up account** because your modem will dial a phone number to connect to your Internet Service Provider. Only one person at a time can connect through a dial-up account.

This is the modem port on your Mac. It looks just like a phone jack in your house.

If you are going to connect through a high-speed, **broadband,** "always-on" connection such as DSL, ISDN, cable, T1, T3, or satellite, you will still use a modem—but it's not a telephone modem, you don't use the telephone jack in your Mac, and the modem is not built-in to your Mac. The company that provides you with the broadband service will provide you with the modem. You will connect to this modem with an **Ethernet** cable, which you'll plug into the Ethernet port on your Mac. The connectors (the things on the ends) on an Ethernet cable look very similar to a standard phone cable, but a little larger. The Ethernet port looks very similar to the telephone modem port, but a little larger.

This is the Ethernet port on your Mac. If you plug a phone line into this, it won't work.

When you're connected through a broadband modem, you will **not dial** any phone numbers to connect—you will just open your browser and you're on the web. You just open your email application and get your email. More than one computer can connect at the same time with one broadband connection.

Some phone companies that provide DSL (like QWest) might make you go through a little connection process every time you want to get online. That's so cheesy. It defeats half the purpose of having a broadband connection. If possible, don't settle for that. Find a provider who does it right.

*Note: If you have **fax** software so you can fax from your Macintosh, you must plug the telephone cable into the modem port and into a wall jack or telephone, even if you have a broadband connection. Your fax will not go through the broadband connection—it must go through the phone line.*

If You Have an America Online Account

America Online

If you have or plan to have an **America Online** account (AOL), you do not need to do anything to set up your Mac for the Internet—you can skip most of this chapter. You do not need to go through the Internet setup process, find a provider (AOL *is* your provider, as well as an online service, as explained on pages 535–536), or anything. **To sign up for America Online,** just plug the phone line into your Mac, put the AOL CD in your drive, double-click it, and follow the directions to set up a **dial-up** account. If you don't have a CD, call AOL at 1-800-509-7538 and have them send you one.

One issue with Mac OS X and AOL is that Mac OS X loves to go to the Internet. There are dozens of menu commands, icons, buttons, Sherlock searches, even help files, etc., that go to the Internet without asking your permission. This is fine if you're on a broadband connection, but if AOL is your only provider, you cannot connect until you first log on to AOL.

Now, you can have a broadband connection *and* an AOL account. You will have to pay the broadband provider a monthly fee, plus you will pay AOL a monthly fee, but AOL has a significantly lower fee if you use another Internet Service Provider for access (broadband or dial-up).

To log on to AOL, double-click the AOL icon. Drag the icon to the Dock since you'll be using it every day.

If You Don't Have a Provider
and don't want to think about it

EarthLink

If you just brought your Mac home or had it delivered and you want to get connected but you don't want to wait to find out who can get you broadband service in your area or who the local Internet Service Providers are, you can sign up, through your Mac, with the **EarthLink** service over your telephone modem. Later, if you discover a better deal in your area is available, you can cancel EarthLink. Or you might check around and end up deciding that EarthLink dial-up is exactly what you need after all, or you could possibly get a broadband connection through EarthLink, if you live in the right place. The point is that with Apple's set up, you can get started right away without having to make any permanent decisions, and in ten minutes you can be on the web.

To sign up with EarthLink, choose the option for a new connection as you go through the Setup Assistant when you first turn on your Mac. This will walk you through the entire easy process of signing up with EarthLink. You will get an account with a password, as well as an email address.

EarthLink Connect

This icon might be in your Applications folder.

If your Mac was already set up, look in your Applications folder and see if you have the icon named "EarthLink Connect." If so, double-click the icon and it will walk you through the process, complete with lengthy audio explanations, of signing up for an account.

If you don't have the EarthLink Connect icon and your Mac is already set up, call EarthLink and have them send you a CD with connection software: 1-800-395-8425. You can skip the rest of this chapter, up to page 558.

Whether you walk through the connection setup as described on the following pages (which is only available the first time you plug in and turn on your Mac), or if your Mac is already set up and you need to get connected now, first you have to make a **decision** about who is going to be your Internet provider (if you don't already have one). These are your options, summed up from the information on the previous pages:

Dial Up (telephone modem)

America Online: Skip this connection setup and use the AOL CD (credit card in hand). You're all done—go to the web. If you don't have a CD, call AOL at 1-800-509-7538 and have them send you one. Skip this chapter.

EarthLink: If you follow the Apple Setup Assistant when you first turn on your Mac, click the button that says you want a new connection. This will lead you to EarthLink, and EarthLink will take care of all the setup—you don't need to worry about a thing. Be sure to check the fine print on the monthly charges to see what applies in your area.

Local provider or national provider: Ask your friends and neighbors, ask your local Mac user group, ask your phone company. Before you can get set up on your Mac, you must call the provider, set up an account, pay them money, and they will give you certain information, such as your user ID/account name, account password, email address, email password, SMTP server, and some other stuff. Write it all down, labeled, and keep it somewhere—I guarantee you will need that information again. Often the provider will walk you through the process, in which case you had better make sure you write down all the names and numbers they give you.

Broadband (high-speed connection)

You need to call a provider and set up an account. Someone will come to your house with a special modem and get you all put together. They will probably get you connected on your Mac, although some broadband providers don't know how to deal with Macs and so you will have to set it up yourself.

There are local and national broadband companies. Ask around your neighborhood to find out who provides the best service. If you are an EarthLink customer, EarthLink can provide DSL if you live in the right area.

AirPort

Whatever your main connection is, that's what the AirPort connection is. If your connection is a dial-up, AirPort serves that dial-up connection. If your connection is broadband, AirPort serves the broadband. All the AirPort does is transmit the signal that comes in.

So This is the Decision You Must Make

What You Need Before You Start

Whether you walk through the Setup Assistant the first time you turn on your Mac, or you decide to do it later, there is **information you need to have** from your service provider or network administrator (*unless* you plan to use EarthLink at home or in your small office; see page 542). And remember, if you have or plan to have an America Online account as your only connection, you don't need to go through this setup process at all.

If you have a provider other than EarthLink, before you begin make sure you have the information your provider gave you:

▾ User account name and password.

▾ Email address and password (which might or might not be the same as your account name and password—often it is not!)

▾ If the account is a dial-up, you need that phone number, plus they will probably give you several DNS (domain name server) numbers that look something like this: **198.162.34.8.**

▾ If the account is broadband, make sure to ask your provider for the connection type and ask if you'll need a router number.

▾ If you are on a local area network (LAN) in a large corporation or school, ask your system administrator for pertinent information.

Write all of this information down! I guarantee you will need it again some-day! And don't forget to write down every password as well.

To add an existing email account you will need:

▾ Your email address at that account.

▾ **Incoming mail server name.** This will be something like mail.mydomainname.com.

This is not always the same as your provider's name. For instance, I own the domain ratz.com and I get email there so my incoming mail server name is mail.ratz.com. But my provider is actually cybermesa.com.

▾ **Outgoing mail server (SMTP).** SMTP stands for Simple Mail Transfer Protocol. This name will be something like **mail.myprovider.com** or **smtp.myprovider.com.**

This is always the name of your Internet Service Provider because that is where your email gets sent out from.

▾ **Account type: IMAP or POP.** Most email accounts are POP (Post Office Protocol) accounts. Services like America Online and iTools are usually IMAP accounts (Internet Message Access Protocol). Ask your provider to be sure. See pages 606–607 if you want to know the difference.

If you choose not to connect to the Internet when you first turn on your Mac, that's okay! You can always do it later. The beginning of the process is just to get your Mac set up with your personal specifications. You will have a number of screens like the first one shown below, with simple questions.

Welcome

In a few steps, you'll register your Apple products, set up your system to take advantage of iTools, Apple's suite of Internet services, and connect to the Internet.

Begin by personalizing your settings. Click the name of the country or region you're in, then click the Continue button below.

United States
Australia
Canada
United Kingdom

☐ Show All

(Go Back) (Continue)

Walking Through the Connection Setup

If you skipped the setup when you first turned on your Mac, you can't go back to it. Use the Network and Internet preferences on pages 548–557 and just fill in the information yourself.

If you click the "Show All" box, you'll see a list of many more countries in the world.

If you have all of your setup information ready, go ahead and follow the process to connect to the Internet. If you don't know the answer to anything that is required (as opposed to the boxes that say "Optional"), call your provider and ask.

How Do You Connect?

Select how your computer connects to the Internet.

○ Telephone modem
○ Local area network (LAN)
○ Cable modem
● DSL (Digital Subscriber Line)
○ AirPort wireless

(Go Back) (Continue)

If you are connected through an ISDN, T1, or T3 line, your Mac is not directly connected to that incoming box, so you will choose "Local area network."

Your Internet Connection

Enter the information for connecting to the Internet through your local area network (LAN).

If you don't know this information, ask your network administrator.

TCP/IP Connection Type
[Using DHCP ⬍]

IP Address
<will be supplied by server>

DHCP Client ID
[|]

DNS Hosts (optional for DHCP & BootP)

Domain Name (optional)

Proxy Server (optional)

☐ Connect using PPPoE

(Go Back) (Continue)

Even though our connection is a DSL, as chosen above, we have a small local area network in the office to serve the connection to all the Macs (and the PC). The Mac detected this and gave me this dialog box.

PPPoE is Point-to-Point Protocol over Ethernet, generally used in apartment houses or office buildings sharing one DSL so online sessions can be individually monitored for billing purposes.

In the process of getting connected to the Internet, the Mac will ask if you want an **iTools account.** You can read all about iTools in Chapter 33, and/or click the "iTools" button in this screen to get a little tour from Apple. You'll get a free email account with iTools (although you still need an Internet Service Provider), storage space on Apple's server so you can share files across the Internet, and more. It's totally free, so why not?

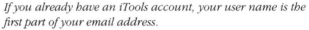

If you already have an iTools account, your user name is the first part of your email address.

If, before you started the setup process, you already had an iTools account that you created in Mac OS 9 or on another computer, the Mac will set that up for you automatically, as you can see here.

In this example, I chose to add an existing email account.

This is an example of an email account that has a completely different **email** name and password from the **provider** account name and password.

The email address is for my partner, John, at the domain ratz.com, and he has a password for that email address. But the provider account ("User Account ID") is under my name with my account name and password because we use one provider for our home office.

Even if you have one email account, you still might have an account name and password for your email and a different account name and password for your provider.

By the time you finish going through the set up, your Mac will be ready to connect to the Internet and Apple will use that connection to send in your registration.

Entering the Setup Information Yourself

Network

Skip this entire section if you already set up your connection with Apple's Setup Assistant, as described on the previous pages.

If you skipped the Internet setup when you first turned on your Mac, it's okay because you can just **enter the information yourself.** You'll use the Network and Internet preferences, as explained below and on the following pages. You will also need to use these preferences when you decide to switch providers, when you upgrade to a broadband connection from a dial-up, when you connect your Macs over Ethernet to share files, when things go wrong, etc.

To open the Network preferences:

1. From the Apple menu, choose "Preferences…," or click on the System Preferences icon in the Dock.

2. Single-click on the "Network" icon. There is probably a Network icon in the toolbar across the top of the System Preferences pane, and there is one in the third row of preferences. They're exactly the same thing.

Many of these settings you don't have to worry about, so don't let all this scare you.

If you have a simple situation with your home or office computer in that you have one Internet Service Provider and you won't be switching between your dial-up connection and an AirPort connection and your office network, then **skip** the following information about making a Location. You will be just fine with the "Automatic" Location that Apple will create for you.

Do you need to make a Location?

If you think you're going to add other connections, like an AirPort connection when you take your laptop to your treehouse or a network connection in your office, it's a good idea to make a new **Location.** A Location is simply a collection of your specifications (a "configuration") for that particular connection. If you have several Locations, you can just switch Locations from the Apple menu and all the rest of the changes are made for you.

Making a Location, if necessary

To make a new Location:

1. In the Network preferences, click on the "Location" pop-up menu and choose "New Location…." Type in a name and click OK.

2. From the "Show" pop-up menu, choose your method of connection. For instance, if this is a dial-up account through your telephone modem, choose "Internal Modem."

   (If you don't see your connection method in that menu, which is unlikely, choose "Active Network Ports" from the Show menu and make sure all of the ports available to your Mac are checked on. To get back to the main Network pane, from the "Show" menu, choose the port through which you want to connect, such as "Internal Modem.")

3. Follow the steps on the next pages to set up the configuration for this Location.

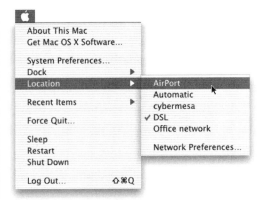

Once you've made a Location, you can go to the Apple menu, choose the "Location" item, then choose the name of your Location. All of your settings will switch immediately and you won't have to go to the Network preferences to change everything.

TCP/IP pane for telephone modem connections

The acronym **TCP/IP** sounds rather intimidating, but it's actually very interesting. If you know basically what it does, it's not so scary:

When we send or receive an email message or request a web page, most of us picture a little letter or a nice, colorful page squeezing itself through the lines, speeding across the country, and landing in someone's computer, unruffling itself just in time.

What actually happens is that the message or web page gets chopped up into little pieces called *packets,* and all these packets go through the lines on different routes, and they're all put back together again at the other end. TCP, or Transmission Control Protocol, is the layer of the TCP/IP program that divides the email file or web page into the individual packets and numbers them. TCP then sends the packets to the IP, or Internet Protocol, layer of the program. The IP sends the packets on their ways, sending each one in a different direction, and the packets stop at all kinds of computers along their paths, asking directions to make sure they're still going the right way. At the computer on the other end, TCP puts all the packets back together again in the right order. Once they are all reassembled correctly, it sends the single file to your mailbox or browser so you can read it. Amazing.

An IP (Internet Protocol) address identifies a computer or device on a TCP/IP network, like the Internet. Networks using TCP/IP route messages based on the IP address of the destination. The format of an IP address is written as four numbers separated by periods, and each number can be from 0 to 255.

Below you see the TCP/IP pane for a **telephone modem connection.** Your service provider will most likely give you an "IP Address" to enter in that edit box, shown below-left.

No one expects you to know whether to use a manual configuration, as shown above, or the option of "Using PPP," as shown to the right. Get this information, plus an IP address if necessary, from your Internet Service Provider (ISP).

Ask your ISP if you should enter the numbers for DNS (Domain Name Servers). They will be in the same format as the IP address; that is, something like 192.254.10.93.

If you are setting up the configuration for a **telephone modem,** click the **PPP** tab. Enter the name of your service provider, the phone number they told you to dial, and an alternate (if they give you one) in case that one is busy.

PPP pane for telephone modem connections

The account name and password, in this case, is your account name and password with your service provider. Often it is different from your email name and password! You can change your email password whenever you like, but your account password for your ISP is given to you by your provider and cannot be changed unless you call them up and arrange it.

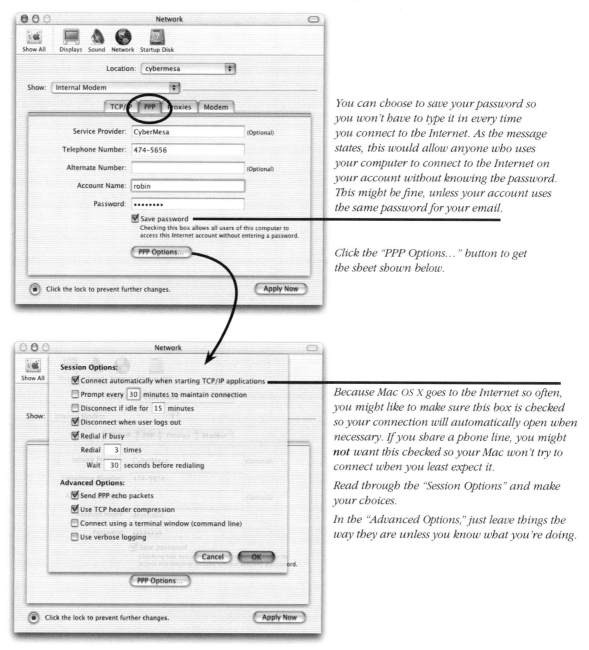

You can choose to save your password so you won't have to type it in every time you connect to the Internet. As the message states, this would allow anyone who uses your computer to connect to the Internet on your account without knowing the password. This might be fine, unless your account uses the same password for your email.

Click the "PPP Options..." button to get the sheet shown below.

*Because Mac OS X goes to the Internet so often, you might like to make sure this box is checked so your connection will automatically open when necessary. If you share a phone line, you might **not** want this checked so your Mac won't try to connect when you least expect it.*

Read through the "Session Options" and make your choices.

In the "Advanced Options," just leave things the way they are unless you know what you're doing.

Modem pane for telephone modem connections

In the **Modem** pane, the Mac has already chosen your internal modem for you. If you have a different modem attached to your Mac, you can choose it from the Modem pop-up menu.

Sound: Annoying as the sound of the modem is, it's a comforting feeling when you hear it connecting. I usually leave it on because then I can instantly tell whether things are working properly or not.

Dialing: If you have a very old telephone that uses a pulse instead of a tone, choose "Pulse." If you actually dial a round wheel to make phone calls, you've got a pulse phone. If you can play little songs with the musical tones when you punch the buttons to make a call, choose "Tone."

This is the modem status in the menu bar.

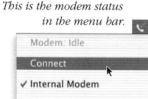

Wait for dial tone before dialing: If you're outside of North America, you might want to uncheck this box because most foreign phone systems use a dial tone that your built-in modem won't recognize.

Show modem status in menu bar: Check this box to put a little phone icon on the right side of the menu bar. Choose this modem status menu to connect, change your port, or open Internet Connect (which is shown and explained on page 559).

If you are a home or small office Mac user, you won't need to bother with the **Proxies** pane. If you work in a large corporation or university, ask the network administrator if you should change any of the Proxies settings. Proxies are designed to work around a *firewall,* which is a system designed to prevent unauthorized access to or from a private network, such as a corporate *intranet* (a private, in-house network). A firewall might be implemented with software or hardware, or a combination of both.

Proxies pane for all connections

If you have a **broadband connection,** you need to choose "Built-in Ethernet" from the "Show" pop-up menu, circled below, because your Mac connects to the special broadband modem with an Ethernet cable.

TCP/IP pane for broadband connections

In the **TCP/IP** pane, the necessary information has probably been filled in by the technician who brought you the modem and set up your connection. If not, you can get the information from your provider (the IP address, the Subnet mask, and the Router number) and fill them in yourself: From the "Configure" pop-up menu, choose "Manually" and fill in the blanks.

If your connection doesn't work, call your provider and go through these settings over the phone to make sure all information is correct and in the right places.

DHCP stands for Dynamic Host Configuration Protocol, which is used for assigning dynamic IP addresses (see page 550 about IP addresses).

PPPoE is Point-to-Point Protocol over Ethernet, generally used in apartment houses or office buildings sharing one DSL so online sessions can be individually monitored for billing purposes. If you use PPPoE, ask your provider what to enter in that pane.

AppleTalk is networking software that allows your Mac to connect with other kinds of networks. You'll use it when you start file sharing.

Internet Preferences

If you went through the Apple setup when you first turned on your Mac, or if you entered all of the information yourself, most of the details in the **Internet preferences** are already filled in for you.

iTools pane

The **iTools pane** gives you another chance to create your iTools account, if you haven't already. Click the "Sign Up" button and your Mac will connect to the Internet and take you to Apple's web site. If you have an account, your member name and password will be filled in for you in this pane.

See Chapter 33 for details about iTools and iDisk and what great things you can do with them.

The **Email pane** is already filled in for you if you went through the initial setup process as shown on pages 545–547. If not, you can fill in the data here in this pane. See page 544 for explanations of incoming and outgoing mail servers, POP vs. IMAP, and your account names.

Email pane

The **Default Email Reader** pop-up menu gives you a choice between Mail and Outlook Express, or you can select any other email client you have installed, such as Eudora Pro. The default you choose here is what will open when you click on an email link while using Internet Explorer to browse the web.

If you check the box to **Use iTools Email account,** *any information that was in this pane will disappear and won't come back* so be sure you write down any of this data that you might not have stored elsewhere. The account shown here is what will be used in your chosen default mail program, and it will appear as your return address. You can override this default in your email program's preferences.

Web pane The **Web pane** lets you set several default settings, as shown and explained below. But except for the "Default Web Browser" setting, your browser will override the browser preferences you set in this pane.

To set these same settings in your browser, open your browser and find the menu called "Preferences." If your browser is made for OS X, "Preferences" will be in the application menu; if you use your browser in the Classic environment, "Preferences" or "Options" can usually be found in the Edit menu. In America Online, click the "My AOL" button in the toolbar to find the Preferences command.

Default Web Browser: Choose a browser that you want to open automatically whenever you choose a Mac OS X command that goes to the web.

Home Page: When you click the "Home" icon in any browser, it will take you to the Home page that you type in here or in your browser preferences.

Search Page: When you click the "Search" icon in any browser, it will take you to the page that you type in here or in your browser preferences.

Download Files To: When you download files from a web page, they will automatically be stored in the folder specified here. If you want them stored somewhere else, click the "Select..." button and navigate to another folder. But remember, your browser will probably override this option and use the folder specified in the browser preferences.

The **News pane** is not as important now as it once was. Not long ago you needed software that was capable of reading and displaying newsgroup messages (as explained on page 532) and you needed to ask your Internet Service Provider to carry the particular newsgroup you needed, if it wasn't included in the select thousands that they had in their news server.

But Google now owns the entire Usenet archive (the collection of all newsgroups) and you can just go to **www.google.com** and click the "Groups" button. You can access every newsgroup from their web site. It is so great.

If your Internet Service Provider has given you a **News Server** address, account ID, and password, you can enter them here. The only software you have as a news reader is one of the Netscape Communicator modules called Newsgroups (from the Communicator menu, choose "Newsgroups"), and Outlook Express, both found in the "Applications (Mac OS 9)" folder.

Connect to the Internet with Your Broadband Account

If you have a **broadband account,** then you are already connected to the Internet. All you have to do is open a browser or your email application and there you are. It's fabulous. You don't need to disconnect—broadband is an "always on" connection.

Some low-class companies will make you go through a little connection process, like a dial-up, which defeats half the purpose of having a broadband connection. Try to find a company that doesn't do that.

Connect to the Internet with Your Dial-up Account

Okay, you're all set up with your new telephone modem **Internet** account and you want to actually **connect** and go to the web. There are several ways to do this.

Connect automatically

If you checked the box to **"Connect automatically when starting TCP/IP applications,"** as explained on page 551, then you can just single-click on the Mail icon or the Internet Explorer browser icon (or any other browser you choose) in your Dock. The Mac will automatically dial up your connection and log on, then open the application.

If you have any trouble doing that, manually log on to the Internet yourself, as explained below, and then open your browser:

Use the modem status icon

If you have the modem status icon in your menu bar, go to it and choose "Connect." You'll hear the modem start squeaking (if you didn't turn off the sound, as shown on page 552) and the icon in the menu bar will send off "sound waves" to indicate that you are connecting and connected.

Once you are connected to the Internet, open your browser or email application and surf or check your mail.

If the modem icon is not in your menu bar, you can add it; see the opposite page.

If you choose "Open Internet Connect...," you'll get the dialog box shown on the opposite page.

If you have the modem icon in the menu bar, the animated sound waves give you a visual clue that you are connected.

To disconnect from the Internet, go to the modem status menu and choose "Disconnect."

If you do NOT have the modem status icon in your menu bar, click on the Applications icon in a Finder window Toolbar to open the Applications window (or press Command Option A). Then find "Internet Connect" and double-click it. You'll get the dialog box shown below.

Click the **Connect** button to connect to the Internet, and then open your browser or email application and surf or check your mail.

Use Internet Connect

Internet Connect

Internal Modem

Configuration: Internal Modem

Service Provider: CyberMesa

Telephone Number: 474-5656

Alternate Number:

Name: dearrobin

Password: ••••••••••

☑ Show modem status in menu bar

These settings can be changed in Network Preferences. Edit...

Status: Idle   Connect

To hide the details, click this disclosure triangle. Click it again to show the details, as shown here.

Check this box if you want the modem status icon to appear in your menu bar.

✓ ☐ **Internal Modem**

Keep In Dock
Show In Finder
Quit

When you open Internet Connect, its icon appears in the Dock. If you want to keep the icon in the Dock so you don't have to open the Application window every time you want to go to the Internet, press on the icon to get the pop-up menu, then choose "Keep in Dock."

Internal Modem

Configuration: Internal Modem

Service Provider: CyberMesa

Telephone Number: 474-5656

Alternate Number:

Name: dearrobin

Password: ••••••••••

☑ Show modem status in menu bar

These settings can be changed in Network Preferences. Edit...

Status: Connected to 198.59.168.5 at 26400 bps

Send: ▨▨▨▨▨▨

Receive: ▨▨

Connect Time: 00:00:12

IP Address: 198.59.168.147   Disconnect

You will see the connection process in the lower part of this dialog box.

Tip: You can close the Internet Connect window while you're online. But then when you make it active again, the dialog box is gone. Choose "New Connection" from the Internet Connect File menu, or press Command N, to get the dialog box back.

To disconnect from the Internet, click the "Disconnect" button.

Here are a few **web addresses** you might find handy. Web addresses have a habit of changing as soon as you print them in a book, so I've tried to give you only well-established sites that won't change. If they have changed and any of these addresses don't work, I apologize!

Macintosh	MacinTouch.com, MacCentral.com, MacMinute.com, MacFixIt.com
Definitions	webopedia.com
Books (retail)	borders.com, amazon.com, bn.com *[Barnes & Noble]*
For writers	bookwire.com *[inside the book world]*
Family	family.com
Movies	film.com, imdb.com *[Internet Movie Database]*
Television	gist.com
Sports	espn.com, cnnsi.com *[CNN and Sports Illustrated]*
Travel	LonelyPlanet.com, MapQuest.com
Weather	accuweather.com, weather.com
Music	listen.com, rollingstone.com, allmusic.com
Science	discovery.com, sciam.com *[Scientific American]*
Games	gamesmania.com, play.games.com
Health	ReutersHealth.com, health.com, vh.org *[The Virtual Hospital]*
Money	money.cnn.com
Genealogy	genealogy.com, ancestry.com, genhomepage.com
Recipes	AllRecipes.com, recipes.alastra.com, epicurious.com
Stain removal	tide.com
Gardening	gardening.com, OrganicGardening.com, KidsGardening.com
Home improvements, recipes, decorating	bhglive.com *[Better Homes & Gardens]*
IRS	www.irs.gov *[download IRS forms]*
Peachpit Press	peachpit.com

Also go to About.com and type in your passion. As indicated above, you don't need to type "www" on any of these particular addresses.

Using the World Wide Web

The **World Wide Web** is addictively fun to use. That's one of the amazing things about this incredible technology—it's so easy. You just need to know a few things about getting around. This chapter contains only a brief introduction, but it's probably more than many people know who are surfing the web already.

If you're not connected yet, the previous chapter will help you get there. Even if you're not, just skim through this chapter to become familiar with the web, what you can expect, how to type in an address to get where you want to go, and what to do once you get there.

I browse. Deal with it.

What are Web Pages?

Hypertext is a term coined in the 1960s by Theodor Nelson. He explained, "By hypertext, I mean nonsequential writing—text that branches and allows choices to the reader, best read at an interactive screen. As popularly conceived, this is a series of text chunks connected by links which offer the reader different pathways [through the information]."

In the Chapter 30 I explained that the World Wide Web is comprised of millions of individual **web pages.** These pages are literally the same as the pages you create in your word processor—in fact, many of them *are* created in word processors, and the code for any web page can be viewed in a word processor.

The big deal about web pages is that they have "hypertext links"—text you click on to make another page appear in front of you. It's like this: Imagine that you could open a book to its table of contents and touch, say, "Chapter 3," and the book instantly flips to Chapter 3. In Chapter 3, there is a reference to Greek mythology. You touch the word "Greek mythology," and a book about Greek mythology instantly appears in front of you, open to the page you want. As you're reading about Greek mythology, you see a reference to goddess worship so you touch that reference and instantly that book appears in front of you, open to the page you want. That's what web pages do, that's what hypertext is. That is incredible.

If you want to connect right now

You don't have to **connect to the Internet** and the web to read this chapter—just skim through and get the gist of how to use your browser and the web. But if you have a full-time broadband connection (something like a cable modem, DSL, ISDN, or T1 line) and want to connect to experiment, all you need to do to get to the Internet is double-click your browser icon. If your connection uses a telephone modem, please see pages 558–559 for details about connecting. If you're not connected at all or if you have no idea *how* you are connected, please see the previous chapter.

This is the icon for the browser that came with your Mac, called Microsoft Internet Explorer. If you have a full-time connection, just single-click this icon to get to the web.

Practice: If you want to practice using the web, first open your connection.

If you have a full-time connection, just single-click the browser icon in your Dock, as shown above.

If you connect through a phone line and you've never done it before, please see page 558.

Every web page has **links** on it. You single-click on a link with your mouse and a new web page appears. A link might be text or it might be a graphic. If it's text, it almost always has an underline; if it's a graphic, it sometimes has a border around it. Even if the **visual clues** of the underline or the border are missing, you can always tell when something is a link because the pointer turns into a hand with a pointing finger, as shown to the right. Just run your mouse over the page (without pressing the button down) and you'll see the pointer turn into the browser hand whenever you run over a link.

Links

This is a typical "browser hand" that you'll see in a browser.

To the left is a typical web page. You can see the browser hand positioned over underlined text, about to click the link.

You also see a row of buttons across the top that look like you should probably click on them.

When you click on a link like the one circled above, "Luddite Lounge," the browser jumps to another page, in this case the page shown to the right. You can see there are more links on this new page. You can click links for the rest of your life and still not have time to read everything. That's the World Wide Web.

Practice: The first web page that opened up for you is probably the Apple/Excite page. Just click any of the hundreds of underlined links on that page that interest you. Poke around for a while!

Web Addresses, also known as URLs

Something you will become intimately familiar with is a **web address.** Just as every home in the country has its own address so you can find it, every web page on the World Wide Web has its own address. The address is also called a **URL** (pronounced *you are ell*), which stands for Uniform Resource Locator (who cares). A typical web address looks like this:

http://www.ratz.com/robin/hats.html

Knowing what a web address represents helps you find your way around on the web. This is what the different parts mean:

http://   These letters stand for hypertext transfer protocol, but who cares. The important thing to know is that the **http** means this address leads to a **web page.** You might also see addresses that start with news:// or ftp://. Those are different from web pages.

www   This stands for World Wide Web, of course, but this is not the definitive clue that tells you (and the browser software) that the address goes to a web page! The "www" is just a convention; many addresses don't even include it. (The "http" means it's a web page.)

Domain names

The domain name gives you a clue to the general type of site:

.com *commercial*

.edu *educational*

.gov *government*

.mil *military*

.org *organization, usually non-profit*

.net *network business*

ratz.com   This is the **domain name.** Typically it is the name of the business or vendor. The **com** stands for **commercial.**

The period is pronounced *dot.* So "ratz.com" is pronounced *ratz dot com.*

You can **buy your own** domain name; it generally costs $70 for two years, renewable every year after that for $35. I bought ratz.com. Ask your service provider to help you buy a domain name.

/robin   The slash tells the browser to go down one more level, to look into the next folder (just like the path names on your Mac). So in this address, the slash tells the browser to go to the domain name "ratz.com" and then look inside the folder named "robin."

/hats.html So here's a slash again, which tells the browser to look inside that *folder* (named "robin") and find the *page* that has been saved with the name "hats.html." The "html" is a clue that this is a web page because all *basic* web pages (just about) end with ".htm" or ".html."

Practice: As you poke around clicking on links and going to web pages, notice the web addresses. Be conscious of what they are telling you.

I'm also known as Url.

The **browser,** as you've learned, is the software that displays web pages on your screen. You enter the address of a web page in the browser, you use search tools through your browser, you watch movies and hear music through your browser, you can print from your browser, and on and on. So it's important to know how to use it. The Help files are usually very good—while you're in your browser, go to the Help menu and choose the command for your application. Right now I'm just going to give you some basic tips that will get you started right away.

Using a Browser

To enter a web address, type it into the "Address," "Location," or "Go To" box (or it might be called something else) at the **top** of the window, in the toolbar. After you type it in, hit Return or Enter to tell the browser to go find that page. Notice carefully in the illustrations below where the Address bar is located!

Entering a web address

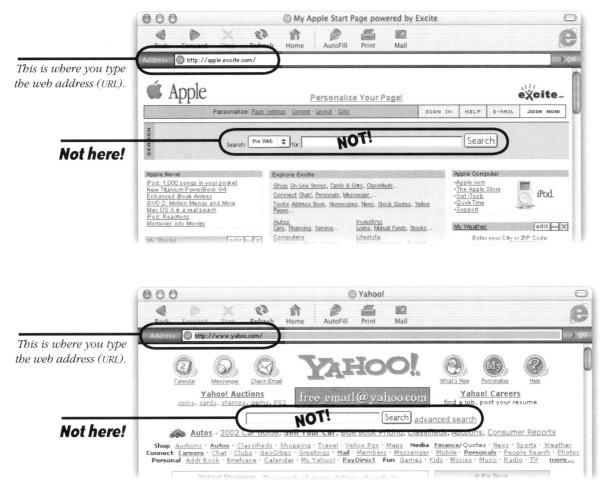

This is where you type the web address (URL).

Not here!

This is where you type the web address (URL).

Not here!

Going back and forth from page to page

You see **buttons** in your **toolbar.** The ones you will use most often are "Back" and "Forward." The Back button, of course, takes you back through pages you have visited. Once you've gone back, then the Forward button appears so you can go forward again.

Use these buttons to go back and forth through pages you have already seen.

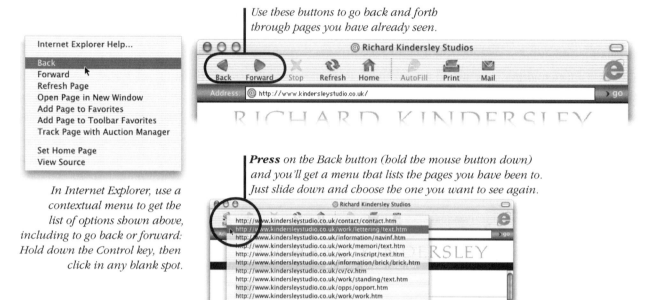

In Internet Explorer, use a contextual menu to get the list of options shown above, including to go back or forward: Hold down the Control key, then click in any blank spot.

__Press__ on the Back button (hold the mouse button down) and you'll get a menu that lists the pages you have been to. Just slide down and choose the one you want to see again.

You can also use the **Go menu** to go back through pages you have visited.

You can have lots and **lots of browser windows open.** This comes in handy when you really like a page, or maybe this page has lots of links you want to follow so when you go to another page you don't want this one to disappear. So instead of *clicking* on the link to get another page, *press* on it (hold the mouse button down). You will get a menu right there in the middle of the page, and one of the options is something like "Open Page in New Window" or "New Window with this Link." Choose that option—a new window with the new page will open, and the previous window will still be open on your screen as well, behind this new one.

The Back button on the new page will be gray because, since this is a new page, it has no where to go back to! Your original page still retains all of the Back pages.

Open a new browser window

Practice: On any link on any page, *press* on a link instead of *clicking* on it. Choose the option to open the link in a new page.

(In Internet Explorer, the menu comes up quicker if you Control-click on the link.)

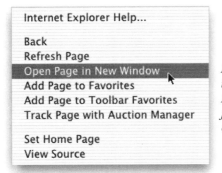

Press—don't click—on a link to get this menu. In Internet Explorer this menu comes up faster if you hold down the Control key and click on the link.

And here's an extra-special shortcut you will love. If you are using Netscape or Internet Explorer (on a Mac), you don't have to type in the entire ugly web address with the http:// and all. For one thing, you never need to type http://. So skip that part altogether. If the rest of the address is in this format, www.**something**.com, all you need to type is **something**. Really. For instance, to get to http://www.**apple**.com, all you need to type is **apple**, then hit Return or Enter. The browser looks for a .com address with the name you entered, and if it finds one, it takes you there. (If the browser cannot find a web site with that domain name, it does a search for that topic and shows you the results of the search.)

If the address uses another top-level domain, such as .org or .net instead of .com, you'll have to type .org or .net, etc. And if the address has other slashes and stuff, you'll have to type everything after the domain name.

Shortcut to enter address

Practice: In your browser, type Command L. This will either open a "Location" box or will highlight the address box where you typically enter an address.

Type "apple."

Hit Return.

Customize your toolbar

You can **customize your toolbar.** One of the first things you might want to do is get rid of the big buttons so you have more room for the web pages. Find your browser's preferences settings—go to the application menu (the one with the name of your browser) and choose "Preferences...." Find the section that controls the toolbar, as shown in the example below. Experiment with different settings to discover what you like best!

In the Preferences dialog box, choose "Show Tool Tips" to display those little clues when you pause the pointer over a button. Or turn them off if they bore you.

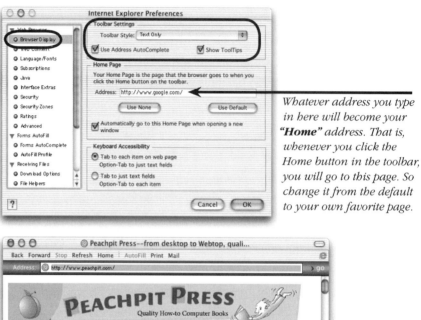

Whatever address you type in here will become your "Home" address. That is, whenever you click the Home button in the toolbar, you will go to this page. So change it from the default to your own favorite page.

Notice how much smaller this toolbar is than the one on page 566. This means you have more room for the web page.

In the OmniWeb browser, which was created specifically for Mac OS X, you can customize the browser toolbar just like you customize a Finder window Toolbar.

In Internet Explorer, go to the View menu and choose "Customize Toolbars..." for something similar (but not nearly as elegant.)

The other most important feature to **customize** is **the typeface** you see on most web pages. The default that has been set for you is usually Times, 12 point. On a Macintosh screen, Times is very difficult to read. New York, however, has been designed specifically for the resolution of a monitor. Change your font to New York 10 or 12 point and see what an incredible difference it makes. And use Geneva instead of Helvetica, or try Verdana, which looks lovely on the screen.

Customize your typeface

THE ENEMY CAMP
Dr. Richard Hallmark examines the Apple/Microsoft deal in his editorial "An alliance reborn?" It's a thought-provoking piece that really makes you wonder if Rick's been hanging around with Puff Daddy.

THE INTERFACE POLICE
Lunetta and Howe, fresh from their stint as Honda's ad agency, say—"Here's an idea, Simplify." And we agree! See any old copies of Windows 95 cluttering up your office? Simplify—toss 'em in the incinerator.

THE ENEMY CAMP
Dr. Richard Hallmark examines the Apple/Microsoft deal in his editorial 'An alliance reborn?' It's a thought-provoking piece that really makes you wonder if Rick's been hanging around with Puff Daddy.

THE INTERFACE POLICE
Lunetta and Howe, fresh from their stint as Honda's ad agency, say-'Here's an idea, Simplify.' And we agree! See any old copies of Windows 95 cluttering up your office? Simplify-toss 'em in the incinerator.

PAINTER TIPS AND TRICKS
David Roberts, (who once posed for a famous statue in Rome), says 'Make mine Monet.' David, I hate to tell you this, but any artist's brain can tell you Monet did not use Painter. He used Photoshop. (kidding, just a joke!)

The **Coffee Bar** is where Url spills his guts about his adventures, his loves, and his pathetic life.

And this is Verdana, which is particularly clean and easy to read on the screen.

On the left is New York 12 point. On the right is Times 12 point. Which is easier to read, especially on a screen?

Change the font in the Preferences dialog box in your browser: go to the application menu (the one with the name of your browser) and choose "Preferences…." Find the button that opens the Fonts panel (circled, below), then select the fonts that are easiest for you to read. Not all web pages will listen to your choice—many designers create pages that override your choice. But this will help on a large number of pages.

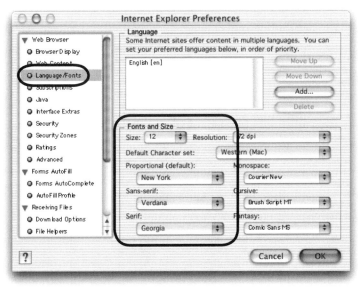

If you don't know your fonts very well, choose the same ones shown in this example. As you become more familiar with your typefaces, feel free to change these preferences whenever you like. Don't forget to choose a size that is easy for you to read on the screen.

Favorites or Bookmarks

The Favorites in Internet Explorer have nothing to do with your Favorites folder or Favorites in general on the Mac.

As you wander around the web, you'll run across web sites you really like and want to come back to. For these sites, make a **Favorite** (Internet Explorer) or **Bookmark** (Netscape and OmniWeb). Once you have a bookmark, the title of the page shows up in your Favorites or Bookmarks menu and you can just choose it from that menu.

As you make lots of bookmarks, you'll need to organize them. Below you see a neatly organized Favorites menu.

Favorites	
Add Page to Favorites	⌘D
Organize Favorites	▶
Update Subscriptions	⌘U
Subscribe...	
☜ Mary Sidney	▶
☜ Shakespeare	▶
☜ Chess	▶
☜ Stonecarving	▶
☜ Woodcarving	▶
☜ Screenwriting	▶
☜ Libraries	▶
☜ Mosaic	▶
☜ Rare book sites	▶
☜ Travel	▶
☜ Typography	▶
☜ Mac OS X stuff	▶
☜ Toolbar Favorites	▶

Stonecarving submenu:
- @ Southwest Stone Carving Symposium
- @ marble sculpting workshops
- @ Learning Stone – Sculpture and Carving
- @ Stone Sculptors Supplies & Studio
- @ Richard Kindersley Studios
- @ Montoya Sculpture & Supply – Workshops

This is a bookmark list. Whenever I want to return to one of these pages, I just choose it from the Favorites menu.

Notice these bookmarks are nicely organized, with hierarchical menus. If you want your bookmarks to act like this, see the tips below.

To make a favorite: Simply view the page you want to save a link to. Press Command D. The title of the page is now in your Favorites or Bookmark menu. If you're using a browser other than Netscape or Internet Explorer, check the menu to see what its keyboard command is.

To organize your favorites: I can't explain how to organize your favorites or bookmarks for every browser, but as I show you how to do it in Internet Explorer, you can use that same information in other browsers.

1. From the Favorites menu, click on the "Organize Favorites" item. I know it looks like you're supposed to go get something from the submenu, but this is a Microsoft product. Don't expect clarity.

*Click right here on the "Organize Favorites" line, **not** in the submenu.*

2. The Favorites window will open, as shown below. This is where you can create new folders in which to store your favorites, delete favorites, rename them, re-order them, add divider spaces, etc.

To make a new folder in this Favorites window, go to the Favorites menu, slide down to "Organize Favorites," and choose "New Folder" from the submenu. A new, untitled folder will appear in the window.

To rename a folder, drag over its name, then type, just as you would change any other folder's name at the Desktop.

To move a folder to another position, drag it.

To add a dividing line (which in the Favorites menu will appear as a blank space), go to the Favorites menu, slide down to "Organize Favorites," and choose "New Divider" from the submenu. Drag it to the position you want.

To move an existing favorite into a folder, drag it.

To add a new favorite into a folder, drag the little icon (shown to the right) from the Address bar and drop it into a folder (or directly into the Favorites window, then drag it into the folder of your choice).

 Drag this icon from the Address bar into a folder.

To delete a bookmark, select it, then press Command Delete.

You can even **save** your favorites or bookmarks list as a **web page** and then open that page in your browser (open the Favorites window, then from the File menu, choose "Save As"). Each folder will appear as a heading, and each bookmark will be a link! The Mac automatically saves your file in the Documents folder. After you save it, drag the file from the Documents folder and drop it in the middle of any web page, or double-click it. You can give this file to your friends.

Favorites.html
Open this in any browser.

Don't Forget the Help Files!

Y'know why I have a job? Because I **read the directions.** You must be a good direction-reader too, if you've gotten this far. Then I suggest you dive into your browser's Help files. I guarantee that if you actually read the Help files and follow the directions, you will know more than 99 percent of the people using a browser.

As in every Macintosh application, go to the Help menu and choose the application-specific help. Below you see one example of the Internet Explorer Help windows.

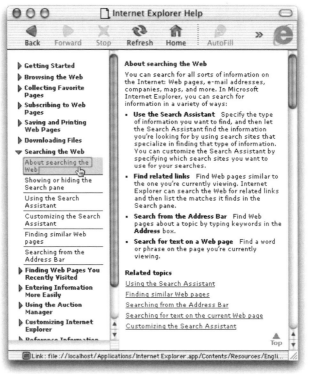

This Help file works like a browser—click links to open new pages of information.

Once you know how to use your browser and start surfing, you'll quickly run up against this problem: There are over a billion web pages out there. How do you find the one you want? You find it with a **search tool,** often referred to as a search engine. You don't have to buy or install search tools—they are just on the web, like any of the other web pages. But they are different from other web pages in that you can type in the names of subjects you want to find, and the search tool will look for it.

Oh, there is so much to tell you about search tools, but that's not the purpose of this book. I can only tell you a couple of important points, and you will have to move on from there.

When you enter a query in a search tool, it does not go running all over the world looking for pages that match your query. **It looks only in its own database** that it has compiled according to its own special criteria. There are many search tools, and they each have their own criteria and their own way of adding sites to their database. So you might ask three different search tools to find "Briards" and come up with three very different lists of web pages about Briards (a dog breed).

Every search tool has different rules for finding information. **Read the Tips or Help section.** It will tell you critical details about how to enter a query so results can be found. As search tools are improved, their rules change a little, so when you see a new look on your favorite search page, check the Tips or Help section again.

Search Tools

Important Point Number One

Important Point Number Two

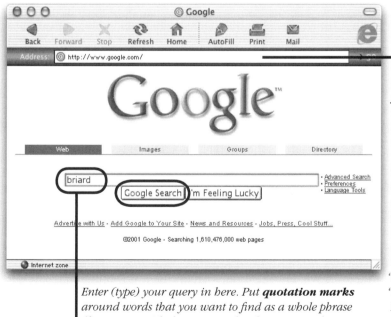

This is for the web address (URL). But most browsers will do a **quick search** for you right here. Try this: Type a question mark, then a space, then the text (in quotes, if a phrase) you want to find. Hit Return.

The **I'm Feeling Lucky** button is great. Use it in this sort of situation: You want to find a college, but you know the college's web address is some long, obscure .edu sort of name. In that case, type in what you can, using quotation marks where appropriate, such as "santa fe community college" "santa fe" "new mexico," then hit the "I'm Feeling Lucky" button. Instead of getting a list of results, Google will bring up the actual web site for the college. Try it.

Enter (type) your query in here. Put **quotation marks** around words that you want to find as a whole phrase (for instance, "shakespeare authorship question").

Then press Return or click the "Google Search" button. See the results on the following page.

These are the results of the simple search shown on the previous page. Click any link to go to that page. Remember, you can press on a link (or Command-click on it) to get a menu option to open this link in a new window. That way you won't lose this page full of results.

If you want to narrow the search, read the Help or Tips page of the web site! Every search tool gives you tips on how to find specifically the item you want.

*There is a great book from Peachpit Press called **Search Engines for the World Wide Web, Visual QuickStart Guide** by Alfred and Emily Glossbrenner.*

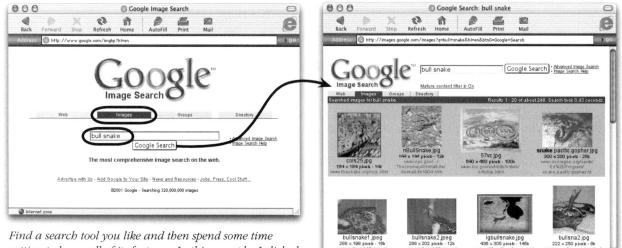

Find a search tool you like and then spend some time getting to know all of its features. In this example, I clicked the button to search for images, typed in "bull snake," and got the results shown to the right.

*In Google, as in most search tools, put a + sign in front of a word to make sure your search **includes** that word, and a – sign to **exclude** words. For instance, to search for images of the bird phoenix, but not the city, enter:*
phoenix +bird –arizona.

Some search tools, called **search engines,** work best by entering words or phrases within quotation marks. The database in search engines is compiled automatically by software "robots." Other search tools, called **directories,** work best by "drilling" down through their selection of web sites. Directories are compiled by human beings who filter out the useless sites.

Use a directory, like the one shown below, to find entire web sites about a topic, such as Sri Lanka or the Wiccan religion. **Use a search engine,** such as the one shown on the previous pages (many search tools include both directories and search engines), when you want to include information that might be contained in web sites about other things, such as people's family vacations or their geneaology research.

You will probably find yourself using the directory called Yahoo, or a similar one called Google Directory, shown below. Instead of typing in a word for the directory to find, try clicking your way down through the list. Click on a category and keep clicking down to narrow your choices.

The Internet itself is the best source of information about how to do things on the Internet. You just have to *find* the stuff. For lots of information, drill down through the Computer category in Google (explained below) until you find the articles on searching the web.

Other Sorts of Search Tools

URLs for several popular search tools:

google.com

yahoo.com

altavista.com

go.com

excite.com

about.com

hotbot.com

search.com

lycos.com

infospace.com

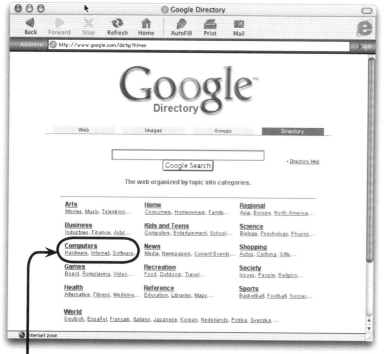

To drill down through a directory, *do something like this:*

Click Internet, then on the page that comes up click Searching, then click Help and Tutorials, then choose any of the many articles about searching the web. Try it.

You might have noticed that Google is my favorite search tool. I love it because it is so clean, the page is not filled with all sorts of junk I don't want, there are no annoying banner ads, it is incredibly fast, and it finds the kinds of things I look for on a daily basis.

*If you're a **New York Times crossword puzzler,** take advantage of Google to fill in just enough letters so you can figure out everything else. You can usually find the answers right in the results page. For instance, let's say you need to find the* Winning coach *of Super Bowl IV. In the Google search engine (not the directory), enter* "winning coach" *in quotes, and* "super bowl IV" *in quotes. Hit Return. Try it: Ta da—Hank Stram. Or you need to find an* ingredient in sealing wax. *Enter* "sealing wax" *in quotes, and the word* ingredient. *Ta da— lac. Amazing.*

1. **The World Wide Web is made up of millions (or billions) of:**
   a. spiders
   b. individual pages, similar to word processing pages
   c. individual corporations
   d. government troops

2. **You can tell an item on a Web page is a link because:**
   a. it is underlined
   b. it has a border around it
   c. the cursor turns into a hand
   d. any of the above

3. **Hypertext refers to:**
   a. text that branches out non-sequentially, and the reader can choose which path to follow
   b. text on drugs
   c. text you can read really fast
   d. any text on a web page

4. **A URL is a:**
   a. rat
   b. search tool
   c. web page address
   d. domain name

5. **The letters "htm" or "html" at the end of a file name indicate:**
   a. any web page
   b. a domain name
   c. a server
   d. only home pages

6. **To view web pages, you need a:**
   a. search tool
   b. domain name
   c. bookmark or favorite
   d. browser

7. **To find the information you need, use a:**
   a. search tool
   b. domain name
   c. bookmark or favorite
   d. browser

8. **If you want the URL of your web site to be the name of your business, you need to buy a:**
   a. search tool
   b. domain name
   c. bookmark or favorite
   d. browser

9. **To save the location of a page that you want to find again, use a:**
   a. search tool
   b. domain name
   c. bookmark or favorite
   d. browser

10. **In most browsers, to get to a web page with the address** http:// www.peachpit.com **what is the minimum you have to type:**
    a. http:// www.peachpit.com
    b. www.peachpit.com
    c. peachpit.com
    d. peachpit

11. **In most browsers, to get to a web page with the address** http://www.newmexico.org **what is the minimum you have to type:**
    a. http:// www.newmexico.org
    b. www.newmexico.org
    c. newmexico.org
    d. newmexico

12. **Which of these fonts will be the easiest to read on the screen?**
    a. Times
    b. Verdana
    c. Helvetica
    d. Palatino

Answers on page 752.

The iTools Collection 33

iTools is a collection of online tools provided by Apple that only Macintosh users can access. iTools includes:

- ▾ **iCards:** Customized electronic postcards which can be created using Apple's high-quality, professional graphics, or by using your own great photos.

- ▾ **Email:** A free IMAP email service and five megabytes of email server space provided by Apple. (But Apple is not an ISP; you need to have your own Internet Service Provider if you want to use Apple's email.)

- ▾ **iDisk:** Twenty megabytes of free, personal storage space on Apple's Internet servers, which can be used to store web pages, photos, and movies; provide a personal FTP site so you can share large files with others; and serve as a current source of Mac OS software, software updates, and music files.

- ▾ **HomePage:** A free, customizable web site you can build using Apple's web page templates.

Although only Macintosh users can have an iTools account, you can send iCards and email to anyone on any computer, and all computer users can access the web site you create and share files from your web site.

Everything in iTools is on the Internet, so you must connect to the Internet before you use any of these features. This is a time when a full-time broadband connection is the best thing to have (actually, it's always best to have a broadband connection, if you're lucky enough).

To Start Using iTools To use **iTools,** you need to register and become a member, but it's free and there are no obligations and you won't get a bunch of junk mail just because you register.

To create your iTools account:

1. Go to **www.apple.com** and click on the iTools tab.

2. On the iTools web page, click one of the iTools icons (iCards, Email, HomePage, or iDisk) to get to the "iTools Login" page, which is shown below.

3. Click the "Sign Up" button to register and assign yourself a **user name** and a **password.**

   The user name will act as your iTools Email address and for your HomePage web site address. For example, if I designate "**roadrat**" as my user name, my email address will be roadrat@mac.com and my iTools HomePage web site address will be http://homepage.mac.com/roadrat.

The iTools login screen lets you sign up for iTools membership if you don't have one yet, or you can log in with your existing membership name and password.

Once you've registered, Apple will send an email to your new iTools email address confirming your registration (your Mail application automatically adds your Mac.com account and checks it for email), then you can start using iTools. The iTools web site (**www.apple.com/itools**) will walk you through each step of using each feature.

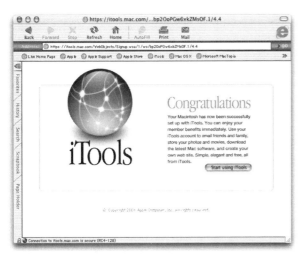

After you've completed the registration process, you can start using any of iTools features.

The iTools tab opens the iTools page. Click any of the iTools icons at the top of the page to open an iTools login screen.

Once you've got your iTools account, check your **Internet preferences** and make sure your member name and password are filled in; if not, enter that information. This will make everything else in this chapter work.

Check Your Internet Preferences

If you signed up for an iTools account when you first turned on your Mac, this information is already filled in for you, and your Mail settings are set up as well.

iCards Anyone can send **iCards** to friends and family, even without an iTools account; to send an iCard using your own photo, you do need an iTools account. An iCard is simply an electronic postcard you can send to anyone on any computer. iCard is better than most e-postcards for two reasons: The quality of the graphics is superior, and iCards are sent straight to the recipient instead of requiring a visit to a web page to "pick up" a card.

To send an iCard:

Note: AOL users will not be able to see iCards! The card and your message turns into crummy ol' text. Dang.

1. Go to **www.apple.com** and click the iTools tab.

2. Click the "iCards" button. You may have to log in with your member name and password if you haven't already.

3. On the iCards web page, choose a category, then click on a specific iCard image to open a full-sized, editable version.

4. On the editable iCard web page that appears, write a message and select a font, then click the "Continue" button.

5. The next page previews your card and lets you address the card to as many recipients as you like.

6. Click the "Send Your Card" button and your customized iCard is sent.

7. A "Thank you" page opens, with the options of sending the same card to someone else or selecting a new card.

The iCards web page offers a variety of card categories.

Click this button to use photos you've put in your iDisk (as explained on pages 584–585) to make your own customized greeting cards.

The editable iCard page lets you type a short message and choose a font. Click the "Continue" button in the upper-right corner to see a preview of your card.

If you want to make changes to your message or change the font, click the "Edit Card" button.

Enter your name and email address in the provided fields. Enter a recipient's email address in the provided field, then click "Add Recipient." Add as many recipients as you like, one at a time, to the Recipient List, then click "Send Your Card."

Of course, you can always send that one card to just one special person. In that case, enter their email address in the first box, then click the "Send Your Card" button.

Email   When you register for an iTools account, a new Mac.com **email** account is automatically set up for you in the Mail application. When you registered for iTools, if you chose the option of announcing your new email address, you will receive a copy of that announcement. You'll also receive a welcome message that confirms your account information.

See the following chapter on Mail for all the details about your Mac.com account and how to use Mail to send and receive your email. It's great.

The first item is a copy of the message that was sent to announce this new email address (see the opposite page).

The second item is an email from Apple with confirmation of your new account.

On the far right, in the Mailbox drawer, is the new Mac.com account.

Extra email features   Although you have the application Mail to do your daily emailing, the iTools **Email web page** provides a few extra features. You can use the links on this page to automatically "Forward your mail," set up an "Auto Reply," and "Spread the word" (send iCard announcements of your new email address), as explained below.

To get to the Email page, go to the Apple web site, then click the iTools tab. On the iTools page click the "Email" link in the navigation bar beneath the iTools tab. Or, click the Email icon on the page.

In the iTools Login page that opens, enter your password, then click the "Enter" button. You see the page shown below.

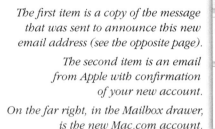

Click the iTools tab, then the "Email" link to get to this page.

Click one of the icons to go to a web page where you can activate that feature.

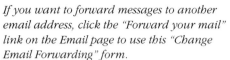

If you want to forward messages to another email address, click the "Forward your mail" link on the Email page to use this "Change Email Forwarding" form.

If you're going away or under a deadline and won't be checking your mail for a period of time, set up an automatic email response—when people send you a message, they will get an automatic reply telling them that you can't answer their email for a while.

Keep in mind that messages automatically disappear from the Apple server after thirty days, so if you're going to be unavailable for longer than that, you might want to also forward your messages to another account.

Send iCard announcements of your new Mac.com address. Click the "Spread the word" link on the Email page to send an elegant notification.

iDisk   When you register and become an iTools member, you automatically get twenty megabytes of free storage space on Apple's Internet servers. This server storage space is called **iDisk.** You can mount your iDisk so that it appears on your Desktop just like any other disk to which you have access, then drag and drop files and folders between iDisk and your computer. You can drag movies, photos, and documents to iDisk so they can be shared by other iTools members or used by HomePage in creating web pages.

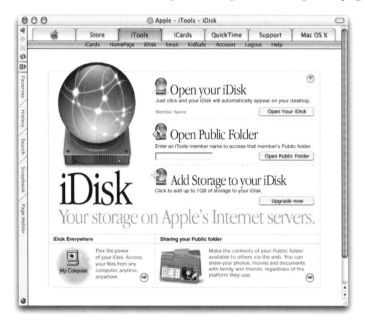

Open your iDisk   If you haven't already connected to the Internet, do so now. Then from the Go menu at your Desktop, choose "iDisk," or press Command Option I.

roadrat

If this icon appears on your Desktop but no window, double-click this to open your iDisk window.

If you've never logged on to your iTools account before, you might have to click the button "Open Your iDisk" on the Apple web page that appears. After a few moments, an iDisk icon will appear on your Desktop, as shown to the left. (If you've used the Finder Preferences to prevent your disk icons from appearing on the Desktop, click the Computer icon in the Toolbar or press Command Option C to open the Computer window, where you'll find the iDisk icon.)

If you've logged in to your iTools account before, then when you choose iDisk from the Go menu, a window opens that displays your iDisk, as shown on the opposite page. Amazing. Don't get confused with these folders that are named exactly the same as the folders in your Home window (why do they do that?!). Keep track of the icon in the title bar—notice it has the magic iDisk crystal ball.

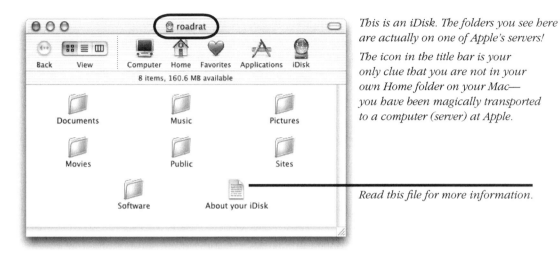

This is an iDisk. The folders you see here are actually on one of Apple's servers!

The icon in the title bar is your only clue that you are not in your own Home folder on your Mac— you have been magically transported to a computer (server) at Apple.

Read this file for more information.

iDisk contents

When you double-click the **iDisk** icon on your Desktop to open its **window,** you're actually looking at files and folders that are on Apple's server, which explains why there may be a delay opening the window. The example above shows an iDisk whose storage space has been upgraded (increased), so the status bar shows more space available (160.6 MB) than your iDisk window may show. When you open iDisk, you see a collection of folders.

Documents: Drag into this folder any kind of document that you want to store and make available to yourself over the Internet. This folder is private and only you have access to it.

Music: Drag music files and playlists to this private iDisk folder so you can have access to it from anywhere over the Internet.

Pictures: Drag photos, or folders of photos, that you plan to use in a HomePage web site into this iDisk Pictures folder so you'll have access to them when you're building the web page.

Movies: Drag movies that you plan to use in a HomePage web site into this iDisk Movies folder so you'll have access to them when you're building the web page.

Public: *Other iTools members can access files that you drag to your iDisk Public folder, if they have your iTools member name.* Or, you can open any other Public folder if you have another person's iTools member name. See Chapter 37 for details.

Sites: The Sites folder contains any web pages or web sites that you've created using iTools HomePage or any other web authoring software.

Software: Check this out. The Software folder contains Apple software, Mac OS X software that you can download by dragging files to your computer, and a folder named "Extras" that contains royalty-free music files that you can use in your iMovies. The contents of this folder do not count against iDisk storage space allotment.

If you don't have a high-speed connection, waiting for these files to load can be painful.

Buy More iDisk Space

You can create multiple sites with HomePage, limited only by the amount of your iDisk storage space on Apple's servers. You can **purchase** up to one gigabyte of **iDisk storage** in addition to the twenty megabytes provided free with your iTools membership. To upgrade your iDisk, go to the iTools web page and click the "Get More Space" link. Or go to the iDisk page and click the "Upgrade now" button.

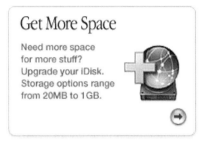

Connection Time Limits

If your iDisk storage space is less than fifty megabytes, your **maximum connect time** is one hour.

If you have more than fifty megabytes of iDisk space, your connect time can be up to twelve hours, although it will be shorter if there is no activity between you and the server.

If you are using Mac OS X version 10.1, there is no timeout if you've connected by clicking the iDisk icon in the Finder Toolbar.

This is the Hide/Show Toolbar button.

To place an iDisk icon in the Toolbar:

1. From the View menu, choose "Customize Toolbar," or Shift-click on the Hide/Show Toolbar button.

2. From the Customize sheet, drag the iDisk icon to the Toolbar.

3. Click the "Done" button.

With **HomePage** you can easily create and publish a single web page, an entire web site, or several sites. Choose from a variety of great looking themes that are designed to display photo albums, QuickTime movies, résumés, newsletters, invitations, and more.

From the iTools web page, click the "HomePage" link to open the page shown below, from which you can build a single web page or a collection of pages.

The "Pages" pane at the top of the window lists web pages you've created using the "Create a page" templates shown at the bottom of the window. To give your site a password, click the arrow button next to "Protect this site."

HomePage

*In this box, you'll see the list of **pages** you've created with HomePage.*

*If you've created more than one web page, designate one to be the **first page** (the home page): drag it to the top of this list.*

HomePage
Help

*Select a page in the list, then click the **Minus** button to remove it.*

*To add a new page, click the **Plus** button.*

*Click the **Edit** button to make changes to a selected page.*

*Click each of these links to explore the **categories** of design themes and web page ideas.*

*With this button you choose a **navigation style** and page for your site. If you use this option to create a navigation page, that page should be the **first page** of the web site.*

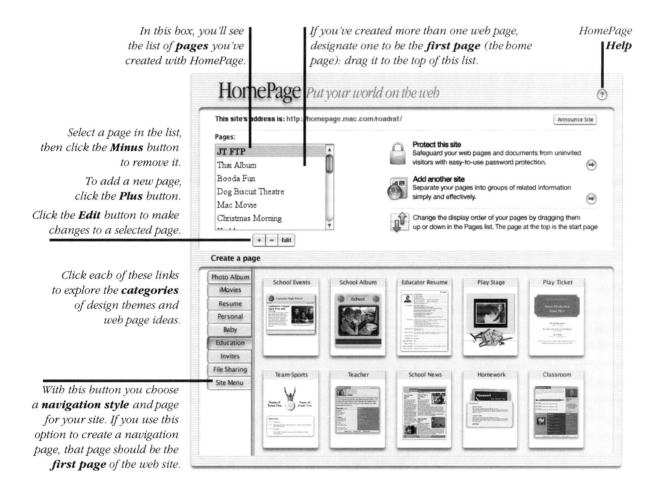

Overview of the page-building process

Click the Help button at the top-right corner of the web page to open the Help files which have extensive instructions for working with HomePage. A brief step-by-step **overview of the process** to build and publish a web page is shown below just to show you how easy it is.

1. On the HomePage web page, choose a page category: click one of the category tabs in the "Create a page" section. Then **choose one of the thumbnail themes** that appears on the right.

This page is showing the Education themes.

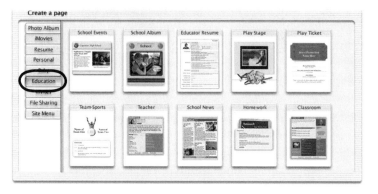

2. When you select a thumbnail, a full-sized version of the page opens in your browser. If you like this theme design, click the "Edit" button in the top-right corner to **open an editable version of this page.**

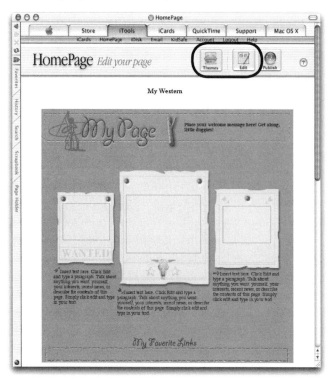

This preview version of the web page gives you a good idea what the final page will look like, minus photos.

If you want to choose another theme, click the "Themes" button.

If this theme is satisfactory, click the "Edit" button.

3. Add images and text.

HomePage accesses all photos and movies from three folders:

> To make images available for use in HomePage, log in to your iDisk (see page 584) and drag individual images or an entire folder of images from your hard disk to the **Pictures** folder on the iDisk.
>
> If you plan to use movies on your HomePage, drag QuickTime movies from your hard disk to the **Movies** folder on your iDisk.
>
> If you don't have pictures of your own, you can select from those that Apple has provided in iDisk's **Library** folder, available from the Library tab. You'll see this tab when you click a "Choose" button to place a photo.

To add **images** in designated areas, click the "Choose" button, then from the window provided, select a photo from your Pictures folder, a movie from your Movies folder, or something from Apple's Library folder.

Type your **text** into the various text fields.

Tip—A file-size reminder:
When you drag photos to the Pictures folder on your iDisk, HomePage can access those photos to use on web pages. But make sure the images you place in the Pictures folder are a reasonable size—the smaller an image is, the faster it will download to a web browser. HomePage automatically creates small thumbnail versions of photos for most pages, but those thumbnails usually link to the original full-sized photo that you put in the Pictures folder. If the original photos in the Pictures folder are unnecessarily large, some of your web pages will be painfully slow to download and you'll fill up your allotted server storage space very quickly.

Ideally, photos destined for a web page should be saved in a JPEG format, have a resolution of 72 ppi, and a maximum size of 640 x 480 pixels.

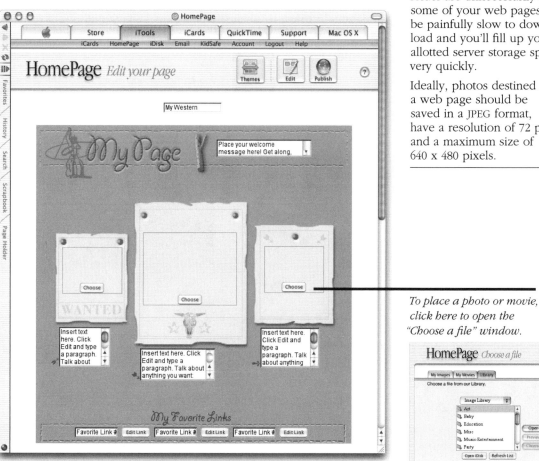

To place a photo or movie, click here to open the "Choose a file" window.

4. Preview and **publish** your page: When you've edited the page to your satisfaction, click the "Preview" button at the top-right of the page to proof the page, then click "Publish" to publish your page on Apple's servers.

When you've finished building your web page and published it, you'll be presented with a "Congratulations" web page that shows your new HomePage web address and a link for sending an iCard announcement to family and friends.

The address that appears here is the address you give people so they can visit your site. It will always be homepage.mac.com/username.

If you use HomePage to create web pages that show QuickTime movies, you'll drag your movies to the iDisk "Movies" folder. QuickTime movies, even short ones, are large. The 33-second QuickTime movie shown below takes 2.3 megabytes of storage space. If you want to have a large QuickTime movie on your HomePage website, or lots of small ones, consider upgrading your allotted iDisk space (see page 586).

This is an example of a web site full of movies and photos created with Apple's HomePage.

When you create multiple sites in HomePage, the HomePage web page shows a "Sites" pane and a "Pages" pane, as shown below. Select one of your sites in the "Sites" pane on the left to show a list of that site's individual pages in the "Pages" pane on the right. Use the buttons below each pane to **add, remove, and edit pages or sites.**

Multiple sites

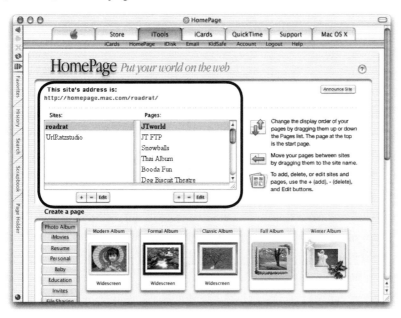

In the main HomePage window you see a "Site Menu" tab in the "Create a page" section, as shown below. With this feature you can create an **optional navigation page** that will provide a *graphic* representation of all the pages in the site.

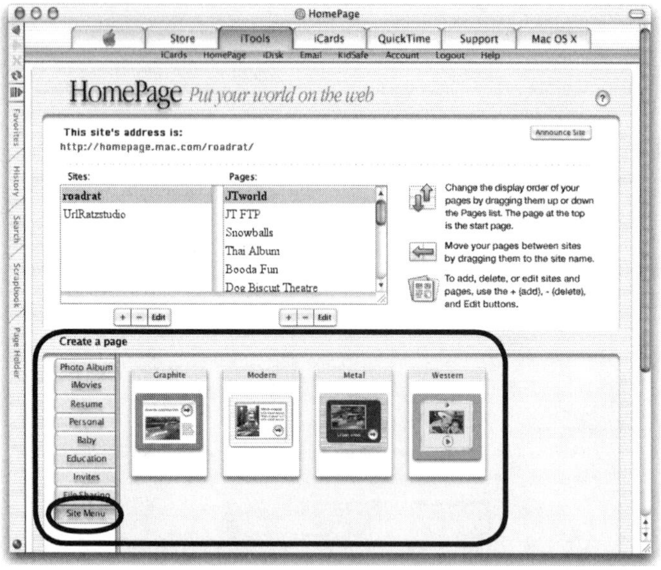

Click the "Site Menu" button to see thumbnails of theme choices.

Then click on a theme thumbnail to open an editable, full-size version of the selected navigation page.

This navigation page uses the "Modern" theme, as shown above.

If you choose not to create a "Site Menu" page, every page of your site will still be accessible via text links at the tops of the pages, just as shown on this Site Menu page.

Another feature of HomePage is that you can create a web page for sharing your photos, movies, and documents over the Internet that anyone, regardless of platform, can access. See Chapter 37 for the details.

Mail and Address Book

The Mac OS X application for handling email is called **Mail.** As you'd expect, Mail enables you to write email messages, send messages, and receive messages. Beyond those basic functions, Mail has many useful tools for organizing, formatting, searching, and filtering email.

The **Address Book** is a separate application that works in conjunction with Mail. You can save your favorite email addresses, make a mailing to send a message to a number of people at once, enter an address in a new message with the click of the mouse, and more.

Mail

Mail

The **basic** things you will be doing in **Mail** are checking messages, replying to messages, and composing new messages. On these next few pages are directions for how to do just that, but there is lots more your Mail program can do for you. You can create folders to organize your mail, create "rules" to filter incoming messages and automatically sort them into special folders, spell-check your compositions, search your mail, and add entries to your Address Book.

But since you probably want to get started right away just using email, jump right in. You must have an Internet connection already set up, as explained in Chapter 31, and you must have **already set up your email account** with Mac.com (or any other provider, as mentioned below). If you haven't set up your Mac.com account yet, and you want one (you don't have to have one), see pages 578–579.

If you have an account with any other provider, you can set it up as an account in Mail so you can use Mail as your email "client"; see pages 608–612. In fact, if you have several email accounts, Mail will check them all for you at the same time, and you can send messages from any account (you cannot get your AOL mail through any other client except AOL).

The Viewer Window

Mail opens up to the **Viewer Window.** It consists of a customizable "favorites" toolbar, a Status Bar, a Message List pane that lists all the messages in a selected mailbox, a Message pane that displays a selected message from the Message List, and the Mailboxes drawer which slides in and out of view from the side of the Viewer Window. Each of these is discussed in detail throughout this chapter.

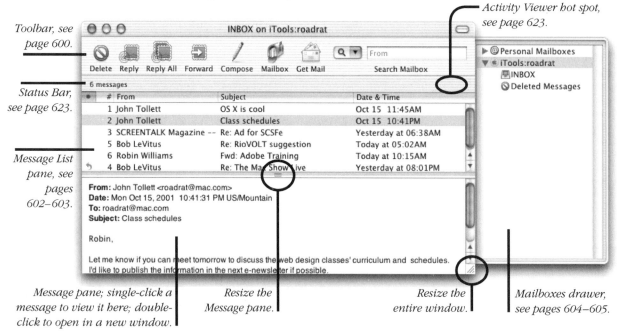

Toolbar, see page 600.

Status Bar, see page 623.

Message List pane, see pages 602–603.

Message pane; single-click a message to view it here; double-click to open in a new window.

Resize the Message pane.

Resize the entire window.

Activity Viewer hot spot, see page 623.

Mailboxes drawer, see pages 604–605.

To check for messages:

1. Connect to the Internet if you're not already connected.

2. Click once on the Mail icon in the Dock to open Mail.

3. Click the "Get Mail" icon in the toolbar.

   Mail checks any "Accounts" that you've set up (pages 608–612). Any account in the Mailboxes drawer that receives new email displays a notice next to the Inbox that indicates how many unread messages are in the Inbox.

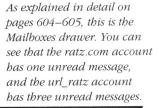

Get Mail

4. Your messages will appear in the Message List pane. Single-click a message to display its contents in the Message pane.

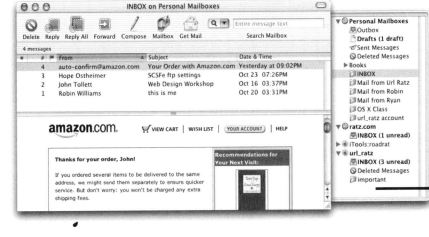

As explained in detail on pages 604–605, this is the Mailboxes drawer. You can see that the ratz.com account has one unread message, and the url_ratz account has three unread messages.

To reply to the sender of a message:

1. If the message is not already open, select the message in the Viewer Window, then click the "Reply" button in the toolbar.

2. A Message window opens which contains the original sender's address in the "To" field, and the original message formatted as a quote. Type your reply above the quote, then click the "Send" button in the toolbar.

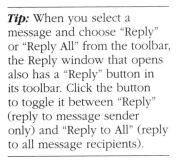

Reply   Reply All

To reply to ALL recipients of a message:

Mail that you receive may have been sent to multiple recipients, either directly as a Carbon copy (Cc) (now called a Courtesy copy since it's no longer a copy on carbon paper), or secretly as a Blind carbon copy (Bcc). You can choose to reply to all recipients with one email (the reply will not include anyone in the Bcc list).

1. If the message is not already open, select the message in the Viewer Window, then click the "Reply All" button in the toolbar.

2. Type your reply above the original quoted message, then click the "Send" button in the toolbar.

Tip: When you select a message and choose "Reply" or "Reply All" from the toolbar, the Reply window that opens also has a "Reply" button in its toolbar. Click the button to toggle it between "Reply" (reply to message sender only) and "Reply to All" (reply to all message recipients).

To forward a message

Forward

1. If the message is not already open, select the message in the Viewer Window, then click the "Forward" button in the toolbar.

2. Type any comments above the original quoted message, then click the "Send" button in the toolbar.

Tip: If you want to forward all of your messages to another email address *for yourself,* go to the iTools email page, as explained on pages 582–583. For instance, maybe you're going to spend three weeks in Europe and you want to pick up all your email at public computers in Internet cafes and libraries while you're there—have your email forwarded to your traveling account, such as excite.com.

To compose and send a message

Compose

1. Click the "Compose" icon in Mail's toolbar to open a "New Message" window.

2. Type an email address in the "To" field.

3. Type an email address in the "CC" field if you want to send a copy to someone.

   To send to more than one person in either the To or the CC fields, separate the email addresses with commas.

4. Type a message description in the "Subject" field.

5. Type a message in the blank message area.

6. Connect to the Internet if you're not already connected.

Send

7. Click the "Send" icon in the "New Message" toolbar.

   Your copy of the sent message will be placed in the Mailboxes drawer, in "Personal Mailboxes," in the "Sent" folder.

Tip: If you won't be able to answer your email for a while, have a message automatically sent to every person who sends you email. This is called an "auto-responder." You can set this up on the iTools web page; see pages 582–583.

When you click the **Compose** button to open a "New Message" window, the buttons in the "New Message" toolbar provide easy access to commands that are also in the menu bar at the top of your screen. The following describes what each button is about.

Send: Click "Send" to deliver a message. The "Send" button remains gray until you enter an email address in the "To" field of a message. See the example of a message ready to send on the previous page.

Attach: To attach a file to your message, click the "Attach" button in the toolbar, or choose "Attach" from the Message menu. A directory window opens for you to navigate to the file you wish to attach. Find the file, select it, then click "Open." (If you don't know how to find files in this directory window, please see Chapter 12.)

Another way to attach a file to a message is to drag the file's icon from its Finder window and drop it in the "New Message" window. This means you need to go to the Desktop and either arrange an open window to the side of your screen, or drag that file out of its folder and let it sit on the Desktop. Then when you are in Mail and writing your message, you can reach the file to drag it into the message window to attach it, as shown below.

More about composing messages

Send

Attach

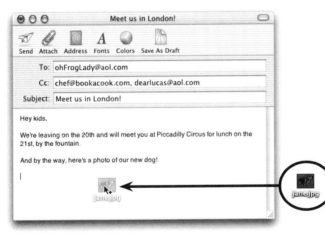

I put the photograph I want to send on the Desktop. Then I opened Mail and wrote my message. Now I can just drag the photo and drop it directly in the message, as shown above.

This is what the attachment looks like once I have dropped it into the message area. The receiver can usually just double-click on the icon to open it. Or drag it to the Desktop first, and then open it.

To remove an attachment from a message, select the attachment in the "New Message" window (drag across it), then press the Delete key.

Fonts: Choose the "Fonts" button in the toolbar to open the Fonts palette. Select text in the "New Message" window, then select a font family, typeface (regular, bold, italic), and size. The text in the "New Message" window will show style changes as you make them.

This is the same Font Panel that TextEdit and other Mac OS X applications use. Read all about it in Chapter 25.

If you can't apply formatting to the selected text, perhaps your mail is set up as "Plain Text." Change it to "Rich Text Format" from the Format menu.

Save As Draft: Some messages may be difficult or time-consuming to write. If you want to finish a message later, click "Save As Draft" in the toolbar, or press Command S. The message will be saved in the Drafts folder within your Mailboxes drawer.

To open the Draft ("restore" it) for editing, select the "Drafts" icon in the Mailboxes drawer, then double-click the desired draft in the message list (or choose "Restore From Draft" from the File menu). The draft will open in a "New Message" window for you to complete.

It's also a good idea to save a draft whenever you're writing a lengthy letter just in case something happens and your computer goes down, you won't lose the entire letter. Just press Command S regularly, as you would in any document.

Address: Click the "Address" button in the toolbar to open the Address Book application. See page 627–640 for full details about it.

Colors: Choose the "Colors" button in the toolbar to open the Colors palette. The "color wheel" button is selected (if not, click once on it).

For details on the Colors Palette, see pages 524–525.

▾ **Select text** in a message (just like anywhere else, you must *select* the text before you can apply any formatting to it), then select a color by clicking or dragging the cursor in the Color palette's color wheel. As you move the cursor around the color wheel, the color swatch in the bottom-left corner changes.

▾ When you've found a hue of color you like, click the "Apply" button to apply the color to the selected text in the message.

▾ You can also adjust the value (the lightness or darkness) of the selected color by sliding the vertical slider next to the color wheel.

▾ To save the color for later use, drag the color from the large swatch to one of the wells in the small color swatch collection, located to the right of the magnifying glass.

▾ Click the magnifying glass to use it as a color picker. Move the magnifying glass anywhere on your screen, then click when the crosshairs of the glass are on top of a color you want to select.

Just press-and-drag around in the color wheel, then click "Apply."

The Favorites Toolbar

The buttons in the **favorites toolbar** are duplicates of some of the commands that are also available in the menu bar at the top of the screen. You can customize this toolbar just like you customize the one in the Finder window.

To add additional tool buttons to the favorites toolbar, go to the View menu and choose "Customize Toolbar...." A pane of buttons appears that represent various functions, as shown below. Drag any of these buttons to the favorites toolbar for easy access.

To remove a button from the toolbar, Command-drag it off the bar.

To rearrange a button, Command-drag it to another position.

Command-click this button at any time to switch the toolbar between icons, icons with text, or just text.

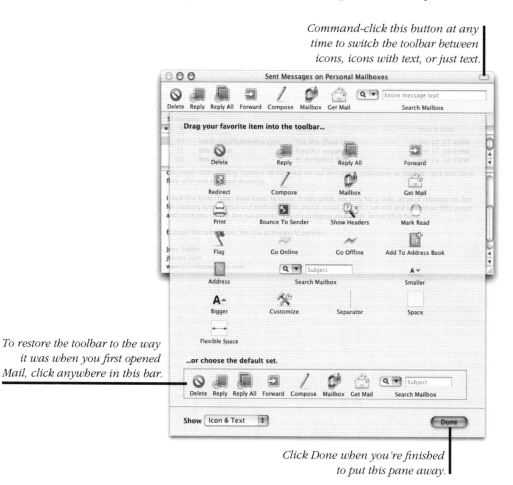

To restore the toolbar to the way it was when you first opened Mail, click anywhere in this bar.

Click Done when you're finished to put this pane away.

Most of the buttons in the favorites toolbar are self-explanatory, except the **Search Mailbox** button. You can search mailboxes based on the content of email headers (To, From, etc.), or based on the content of the body of a message.

1. Select a mailbox to search in the Mailboxes drawer.

2. Click on the magnifying-glass pop-down menu in the toolbar.

3. Choose the type of content on which to base the search:
   ▼ "Entire message text" searches the content of the message body.
   ▼ "To," "From," or "Subject" searches the content of a header.

4. Type one or more words in the text field on the right side of the pop-down menu.

5. As you type, the Message List pane will display only the files that contain the text you're entering. If multiple messages qualify for the search, the "Rank" column displays a relevance control that indicates the relative ranking of search results. A message with a longer bar in the "Rank" column is more relevant to the search criteria.

Other buttons that don't have obvious functions are "Bounce To Sender" and "Redirect."

The **Bounce To Sender** button is meant to discourage unwanted email: Select an unwanted message in the Message List pane, then from the Message menu, choose "Bounce To Sender" (or click the button in your toolbar, if it's there). The sender will receive a reply that says your email address is invalid and that the message was not delivered. The unwanted message is moved to your "Deleted Messages" folder. The recipient cannot tell if the message has been read. Unfortunately, this does not work for most spam (junk email) because spam return addresses are usually invalid (to prevent spammers from being spammed).

Redirect is similar to "Forward," except that redirected mail shows the original sender's name in the "From" column instead of yours, and shows the time the message was originally composed in the "Date & Time" column of Mail's Viewer Window. When you redirect mail, your name remains in the "To" header at the top of the message so the new recipient will know that you received the message and that you redirected it.

Search Mailbox

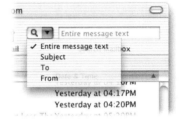

Bounce To Sender

Redirect

Message List Pane

The **Message List pane** displays a list of all messages in the currently selected Mailbox from the Mailboxes drawer. The list is divided into several columns. The Message List pane provides different views of a list, depending on which column is selected.

The columns of information

The **column headings** are all explained on these pages. Besides the default headings that appear, you can choose to show two additional columns.

From the View menu, choose:

- ▾ "Show Contents Column" to show email attachments.
- ▾ "Show Message Sizes" to show email file sizes, including attachments, in a column.

Also from the the View menu, you can choose to **hide** the Number, Contents, Flags, and Sizes columns.

To change the column widths, position the pointer over the gray dividing line in the column headings, then press-and-drag the column left or right.

To rearrange the list according to the column heading, just click the heading at the top of a column. The column heading that is blue is the one that items are currently arranged by.

These are the column headings. Click a heading to sort the messages by that column.

The first column is the Message Status column.

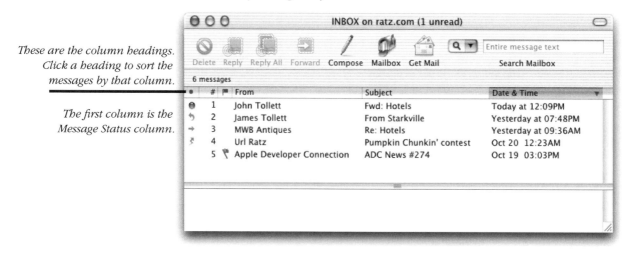

The **Message Status** column (●) uses different icons to indicate if you've read the message, replied to it, forwarded it, or redirected it. These icons are applied automatically when one of those actions takes place. In addition, you can manually mark an email that you've already read as "unread." You can use this as a reminder to go back and read a message more carefully, or to make a message stand out in the list: Select a message or multiple messages, then from the Message menu, select "Mark As Unread."

Click the column heading to group similar Categories, such as unread or returned messages, together in the list. Click again in the column heading to reverse the order of the list.

Message Status **icons** give visual clues to the status of messages.

    Blue orb: message has not been read.

    Curved arrow: message was replied to.

    Right arrow: message was forwarded.

    Segmented arrow: message was redirected.

Number column: In a series of email exchanges, it may be useful to know in what order messages were received. The Number column keeps track of the order for you. Click the **#** symbol in the column heading to arrange messages by order. Click again in the column heading to reverse the order of the list.

Flags column: Mark a message as flagged when you want it to stand out in the list, or if you want to temporarily tag a group of related messages. **To search for flagged files** in a list, click the "Flag" column heading; all flagged messages will move to the top of the list. Click the heading again to reverse the order and put flagged messages at the bottom of the list.

Subject column: The Subject column shows the text that the sender typed into the Subject header of their email message. Click the heading of the column to show the subjects in alphabetical order; click again to reverse the order of the list.

Date & Time column: The Date & Time column shows when you received a message. Click the heading of the column to show messages in the time sequence they were received; click again to reverse the order of the list.

Icons in the Message Status column

Mailboxes Drawer   The **Mailboxes drawer** slides out from the side of the Viewer Window. The drawer might slide out from either side of the Viewer Window, depending on how much screen space is available to the left or right.

To open (or close) the Mailboxes drawer, click the Mailbox button in the toolbar. **Or** drag the edge of the drawer.

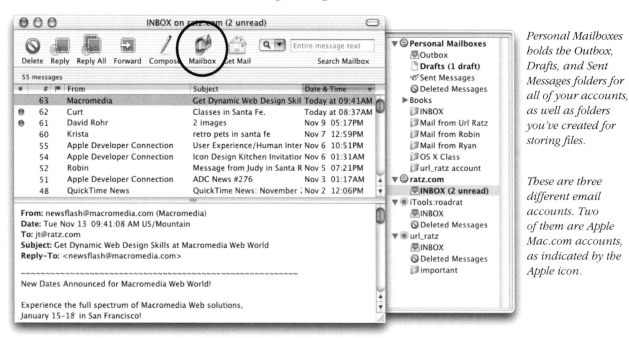

Personal Mailboxes holds the Outbox, Drafts, and Sent Messages folders for all of your accounts, as well as folders you've created for storing files.

These are three different email accounts. Two of them are Apple Mac.com accounts, as indicated by the Apple icon.

What's in the   The Mailboxes drawer contains all the **mailboxes** (which are really folders,
Mailboxes drawer?   even though they don't use folder icons) that hold all your messages.

> **Outbox icon:** those that are waiting to be sent (Outbox).
>
> **Document icon:** the ones you're still writing (Drafts).
>
> **Paper airplane icon:** those that have been sent (Sent Messages).
>
> **Red Delete icon:** the ones you've thrown away (Deleted Messages).

Besides the mailboxes that appear automatically when you create new accounts, you can manually create new mailboxes at any time to customize the storage and management of your email accounts (page 607).

The first account listed in the Mailboxes drawer is the **default account.** In the example on the opposite page, "ratz.com" is the default account. (The Personal Mailboxes area is where you create folders, called "mailboxes," for storing and organizing mail.)

Outgoing messages are automatically sent from the default account. If you only have one account, that of course is your default and you can skip the next couple of paragraphs. But some people, like me and my partner John, get email at several different addresses, each coming from a different server. **Mail can check all of your email accounts at once.** When you answer mail, you can choose to have it answered from any one of your accounts, no matter to which account the original message was mailed.

If you have more than one account in the Mailboxes drawer, the "New Message" window provides a pop-up "Account" menu that contains the names of any accounts you've created. From the pop-up menu, choose the account that you want the message sent from.

To set up your other accounts so Mail can check them all, see pages 608–612.

To change the default account in Mail, drag another account to the top of the list in the Mailboxes drawer (below Personal Mailboxes).

Accounts in the Mailboxes drawer are marked with either a blue **@ icon** or a red **Apple icon.**

This is John's Mail. If he received an email to his ratz.com account, he could answer it with a return address from any of his other accounts.

- Items in an account marked with the blue @ icon are actually being stored on your computer's hard disk.

- Items that are in an account marked with the Apple icon are not on your computer. They are on an Apple IMAP server far away, but you can view them and manipulate them. There's important information about storing your mail on Apple's IMAP server on the following two pages.

Mailbox accounts

Mailboxes for your non-Apple accounts are shown in the Personal Mailboxes Category of the Mailboxes drawer. You can change this, as shown above; see page 612.

What do the little circular icons mean?

IMAP vs. POP

Apple's Mail program can handle two types of incoming mail "protocol": **IMAP** and **POP** (or POP3, to be specific). A protocol is a particular set of standards or rules having to do with communications between computers.

Email from a POP account is stored on your hard disk.

POP3 (Post Office Protocol 3) is a protocol in which the server automatically downloads the mail to your computer when you check mail, then *deletes* the mail from the server. With POP you cannot read mail until it has been downloaded to your computer. POP works best for users who always use one computer on which the email files are stored and managed. Although Mac OS X uses IMAP to handle Mac.com email accounts, you can also setup POP accounts in Mail just as easily (pages 608–612).

You can choose to leave your mail on the POP server after it has been downloaded to your Mac (see page 612), but check with your service provider before you do that—it might make them mad to have all of your email clogging up space on their server.

Email from an IMAP account is stored on a remote server (not your hard disk).

IMAP (Internet Message Access Protocol) is a protocol that receives and *holds* email on a server for you a certain amount of time, typically thirty days. IMAP allows you to view email before deciding whether or not to download it to your computer.

One advantage of IMAP is that you can manage your email from multiple computers because the email files are kept on the IMAP server for storage and manipulation; this means if you check your mail on one computer while you're away from home, say in Glasgow, then when you come home and check your mail, you can get the same messages at home that you read in Glasgow.

Another advantage is that you can choose *not* to download emails that have large attachments, or email from people you don't want to hear from. You can wait until it's convenient, until you know who an attachment is from, or you can just delete unwanted or unsolicited email and attachments before they ever get to your computer.

When you sign up for a free Mac.com email service through iTools, you're assigned a five-megabyte mailbox on Apple's IMAP mail server. All messages within an account, *even deleted messages,* are stored on Apple's server for one month by default, unless you designate a different length of time. If you get more than 5 megabytes of mail and attachments, people will not be able to send you any more email at that account until you clear it out.

America Online uses an IMAP server. That's why you can choose whether or not to download a file, and your email disappears automatically after thirty days whether you like it or not.

To choose how long your *deleted* Mac.com email remains stored on Apple's IMAP server before it's totally erased:

1. From the Mail menu, choose "Preferences...."

2. Click the "Viewing" button in the favorites toolbar.

3. In the pop-up menu "Erase deleted mail when," you have the options of "Never," "One day old," "One week old," "One month old," and "Quitting Mail."

   If you choose to "Never" erase deleted mail, you'll eventually fill up your five megabyte allocation on the server and you won't be able to receive any new mail. To avoid this, you need to copy important mail to your computer.

If you choose any of the other options for erasing deleted mail, plenty of IMAP server space will remain available, *but you won't have a permanent copy of your email unless you create a local mailbox on your computer and copy the email that you want to keep into that local mailbox.*

To create a new mailbox for permanently storing selected email messages:

1. Open the Mailboxes drawer by clicking the Mailbox button in the favorites toolbar.

2. Click the "Personal Mailboxes" folder to select it so your new mailbox will be created within the Personal Mailboxes folder. You want to create the new local mailbox (which is really a folder) inside the Personal Mailboxes folder because messages and folders stored here will be on your Mac's hard drive, not on the Apple server.

3. From the "Mailbox" menu, choose "New Mailbox...."

4. Type a name in the "New Mailbox name" field and click OK.

5. In the Viewer Window, select the emails you want to keep and drag them to the new, local mailbox.

"Local" means it is on your hard disk, as opposed to "remote," which means it is on someone else's hard disk, usually far away.

Notice that the messages you just moved to your new, local mailbox have disappeared from the Inbox they were in; those messages are now in a folder on the Apple IMAP server called "Deleted Messages."

Select the remaining, unwanted messages that remain in the IMAP Inbox and click the "Delete" button in the toolbar. The deleted messages will remain on Apple's server for the length of time you specified in Mail Preferences (above), unless you remove them manually.

Tip: You can also drag an entire mailbox from an IMAP account in the Mailboxes drawer to "Personal Mailboxes." This will make a copy of the mailbox and its contents on your computer.

To permanently delete messages, from the Mailbox menu, choose "Empty Deleted Messages." The Mailbox menu may show "Compact Trash," "Empty Deleted Items," or "Empty Trash," depending on how you set up Mail.

Set Up a New Account

Accounts

Use **Mail Preferences** to create new mail accounts, edit existing accounts, and to customize Mail's behavior.

To open Preferences and get the Accounts pane:

1. From the Mail menu, choose "Preferences...."

2. The "Mail Preferences" toolbar shows six buttons representing different Categories of preferences. Click **Accounts.**

   The **Description** list shows all the email accounts you've created.

   To **create** a new account, see the opposite page.

   To **edit** the preferences of an existing account, select the account in the list, then click "Edit" to show the "Account Preferences" sheet (or double-click the account name). See the following pages for a detailed description of the "Account Preferences" pane.

   To **remove** an account from the list, select it, then click "Remove."

Check accounts for new mail: Set how often you want to check for new mail. This only works if Mail is open (if the triangle is under its icon in the Dock). If you don't have a full-time, always-on connection to the Internet (such as DSL or cable modem), you'll probably want to select the "Manually" option to avoid having your modem dialing and trying to connect when you least expect it.

Play sound when new mail arrives: Choose various sound alerts when mail appears, or "None."

Create Account: You may have more than one email account in your life. For instance, you might have one that is strictly for business, one for friends and family, one for your lover, and one for your research. Mail can manage them all for you—just add new email accounts to the Mailboxes drawer.

1. From the Mail menu, choose "Preferences...."

2. Click "Accounts" in the toolbar, then click "Create Account."

3. You should see the "Account Information" pane; if not, click the tab.

*Mail cannot get your AOL email. Nothing can get AOL email except AOL (although you can use any browser anywhere in the world and go to **www.aol.com** to get your mail).*

4. Choose an **Account Type** from the pop-up menu.

   Choose "Mac.com Account" if you're setting up an email account that you created using the Apple iTools web site.

   If you're setting up an account that comes from some other service provider, they can tell you if they use POP, IMAP, or UNIX (it's most likely POP).

5. In the **Description** field, type a name that will identify the account in the Mailboxes drawer. You can name it anything, such as "Lover Boy" or "Research Mailing List."

6. If you're setting up a Mac.com address, the **Email Address** field will automatically be filled in with your Mac.com email address.

7. **Host name** is the "incoming" email server name. If your account type is "Mac.com Account," the host name will automatically be filled in with "mail.mac.com."

   If you're setting up another account type, the mail service provider can tell you what name to use. Tell them you need the "incoming" mail server name, also known as the "POP address." (It's probably something like "mail.domainname.com," where "domainname" is the name in your email address, such as mail.ratz.com)

—continued

8. If you're setting up a Mac.com account, **User name** and **Password** are the same ones you chose when you signed up for a Mac.com account through Apple's iTools web site. You should have received an email from Apple verifying this information.

   If you're setting up a POP or UNIX account, your user ID and password may have been assigned by your provider, or they may have been chosen by you. *These are not necessarily the same user ID and password that you use to access your email.* If necessary, ask your provider for the User ID and password information.

9. **SMTP Host** refers to the "outgoing" email server address. It will be "smtp.mac.com" for a Mac.com account.

   If you're setting up another account type, ask your provider what name to use for the "outgoing" email server, also known as the SMTP address. No matter where your email account comes from, the SMTP address is almost always your Internet service provider's name, such as "mail.providername.com.

10. The **SMTP User** and **SMTP Password** fields are disabled unless you've checked the option "Use authentication when sending mail." As a deterrent to spam (unsolicited email, usually junk mail), this option instructs the mail server to verify your identity and password as someone who has permission to send outgoing mail through the server. The SMTP User ID and the SMTP Password for a Mac.com account would be the same as the Host User name and Password above. Apple's IMAP email server recognizes SMTP authentication, but not all servers do.

    If you're setting up an account other than Mac.com, ask your service provider if they support this feature. Or just leave it unchecked.

Next, click the **Account Options** tab of the window. The items in the Account Options tab change, depending on whether you're creating an IMAP account (such as a Mac.com account) or a POP account (most others).

If you're creating an IMAP account, the following options are shown in the Accounts Options pane:

See the following page for the POP options.

> **Enable this account:** Check to make the account active, and uncheck it to make the account inactive. This does not delete the account; it just tells Mail to ignore it.
>
> **Include this account when checking for new mail:** Uncheck this box to prevent Mail from checking email at this address. This is useful if you have several email addresses and you choose not to check some accounts as often as others.
>
> **Compact mailboxes when closing:** On an IMAP server, when you select and delete messages, they don't really get deleted—they get placed in a "Deleted" folder on the server. The server stores these deleted files for a user-specified length of time before they are erased. If you check "Compact mailboxes," then the files you deleted will be erased immediately when you close the Mail application. This frees up your space on Apple's server.
>
> **Message caching:** This menu offers options for copying (storing, or caching) email messages from an IMAP server onto your own Mac.

Cache is pronounced "cash," not "cashay."

> > "Cache all messages and attachments locally" will copy all of your email to your hard disk.
> >
> > "Cache messages bodies locally" will cache the body of the message, but not attachments.
> >
> > "Cache messages when read" will only cache messages if you've read them.
> >
> > "Don't cache any messages" will not copy any of your mail to your hard disk. This option provides you with extra security and privacy if other people have access to your computer. If you choose this option, be aware that your IMAP server will eventually erase messages that have been stored for a user-specified length of time (thirty days at the most, generally).
>
> **Connect to server using port:** This field lets you enter a nonstandard port number for connecting to your mail server. If this number needs to be changed, your network administrator or your ISP can provide the appropriate port number.
>
> **Account Directory:** Shows the path on your computer to the folder of the email account currently selected in the "Accounts" preferences window. The path is grayed-out because Mac OS X prefers that this setting remain unchanged.
>
> **Account Path Prefix:** If you need to enter something here, ask your network administrator or your provider to give you that information.

See the previous page for the IMAP options.

If you're creating a POP account, the following options are shown in the Accounts Options tab.

Enable this account: Check this to make the account active, and uncheck it to make the account inactive.

Include this account when checking for new mail: Check or uncheck it to prevent Mail from checking messages at this address.

Delete messages on server after downloading: POP servers can be instructed to keep copies of your mail. This can be useful if you're checking your mail from another computer and you want to leave messages on the server so they'll be available for downloading later to your own computer. Eventually, the POP server will run out of room for storing your messages, so check this option to keep plenty of POP server space available, and uncheck it when you need to temporarily keep a copy of your mail on the server.

Show this account separately in Mailboxes drawer: Click this button and your new account will appear outside the "Personal Mailboxes" folder in the Mailboxes drawer. This will not affect how the account functions, just the visual organization in the Mailbox drawer.

If you don't choose the option above, click the next button, "Download messages from this account into folder," and choose a folder from the pop-up menu (to make a folder that appears in this list, see page 607). The new account *will* appear within the "Personal Mailboxes" folder when you choose this option.

Prompt me to skip messages over __ KB: When checking for mail, you can choose to skip over messages that are larger than you want to receive. This can eliminate unsolicited attachments. Enter the maximum file size that you'll permit Mail to download.

Connect to server using port: In this field you can enter a nonstandard port number for connecting to your mail server. If this number needs to be changed, your network administrator or your ISP can provide the appropriate port number.

Account Directory: Shows the path on your computer to the folder of the email account currently selected in the "Accounts" preferences window. The path is grayed-out because Mac OS X prefers that this setting remain unchanged.

All done? When all the "Accounts" preferences are set, click OK. Your new account will appear in the Mailboxes drawer.

You can select fonts, font sizes, and text colors for various parts of your email messages.

Fonts & Colors

Fonts & Colors

To open Preferences and get the Fonts & Colors pane:

1. From the Mail menu, choose "Preferences…."

2. The "Mail Preferences" toolbar shows six buttons representing different Categories of preferences. Click **Fonts & Colors**.

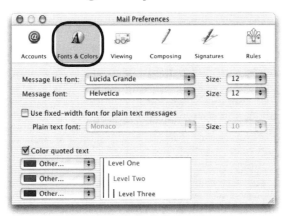

Message list font is the font used in the list of messages.

Message font is the font that you will type your email messages in. If you choose a font that your recipient does not have installed on their computer, it will turn into their default font.

Email replies often contain quotes from previous emails. Color coding and indenting the quotes makes messages easier to read and helps to visually organize the quotes in a hierarchy of responses. To apply color to quotes, check the **Color quoted text** box. Choose colors for up to three levels of quotes from the three color pop-up menus.

Viewing

Viewing

I don't know why they call this preference **Viewing.** Why the eyeglasses?

To open Preferences and get the Viewing pane:

1. From the Mail menu, choose "Preferences...."

2. The "Mail Preferences" toolbar shows six buttons representing different Categories of preferences. Click **Viewing.**

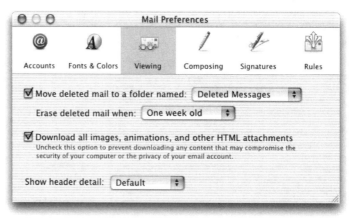

To keep deleted messages in a folder, check **Move deleted mail to a folder named,** then choose "Deleted Messages," "Deleted Items," or "Trash." Mail will make a folder of that name for you. You might not see this folder right away—you might even have to delete a message first before the folder appears.

If you change your mind and decide to use a different folder name, then you'll have two folders for deleted messages with two different names. You can throw away the one you don't need (select it, then from the Mailbox menu, choose "Delete Mailbox...").

If you *don't* put a checkmark in this box, the mail will be deleted and you won't have it in a folder anywhere. You can see the deleted messages in the Message list, in gray, if you choose "Show Deleted Messages" from the View menu.

Erase deleted mail when: Choose how long to store deleted email by choosing an option from this pop-up menu. Remember, if you're setting up a Mac.com account you only have five megabytes of storage space for messages. Choosing the option of "Never" will eventually use a lot of your storage space to store "deleted" mail.

You can choose **not to download attachments** by unchecking "Download all images, animations, and other HTML attachments."

Show header detail: This menu lets you choose how much, if any, header information (all that to/from/date stuff) shows at the top of emails. Choose "Custom..." to customize what information shows in headers. "Default" means the stuff you usually see.

The **Composing** pane applies to email messages as you write them.

To open Preferences and get the Composing pane:

1. From the Mail menu, choose "Preferences...."
2. The "Mail Preferences" toolbar shows six buttons representing different Categories of preferences. Click **Composing**.

Save unsent mail in: By default, mail you have written but not yet sent is saved in a folder named "Drafts." Change this, if you like, by choosing a location from the pop-up menu. Only current mailboxes (folders) in your Mailboxes drawer are available as options. To create a folder so it will appear in this menu, see page 607.

Save sent mail in: This is similar to the option above, but for copies of mail you have already sent.

Default message format: "Rich Text" allows you to stylize messages with fonts and formatting, but not everyone will be able to see these features. "Plain Text" can be seen by everyone, but does not show any color and style formatting. Choose the format you'll use most often as the "Default message format," then change to the other format when necessary by choosing it from the Format menu in the main menu bar.

Check spelling as I type in Compose windows: Check this to catch spelling errors immediately. When Mail doesn't recognize a word, it underlines it with a dotted red line. If you need help with the correct spelling, from the Edit menu choose "Spelling," then choose "Spelling..." from the submenu. For more about checking spelling, see page 522.

List private group members individually: When sending mail to a group that you created in Address Book, check this option to list the members of the group individually in the "To" field. Uncheck this option if you want the "To" field to show only the group name.

Lookup addresses in network directories: If you have access to an LDAP directory (page 636), check this option to search LDAP directories as you type an address in the "To" field of a message.

When replying to messages: Check "Use the same format as original message" to reply using the same format (Rich Text or Plain Text) as the original message. This assures that the recipient will see the message as you intended.

Always CC myself to send a copy of outgoing messages to yourself.

Include the original message to automatically paste the original message in your new message as a quote. This helps to remind the recipient of the previous message's content.

Composing

Tip: If you select some text in an email message and hit the Reply button, only the selected text will appear in the reply as a quoted message.

Signatures A **signature** is a blurb of pre-prepared information about you or your company that can be added to the end of a message, either manually or automatically, as shown on the opposite page. You can create different signatures that include different types of information for various types of messages. For instance, in addition to a signature for personal mail that may include your address and phone number, you may want to create a different business signature that doesn't include personal information.

To open Preferences and get the Signatures pane:

1. From the Mail menu, choose "Preferences...."

2. The "Mail Preferences" toolbar shows six buttons representing different Categories of preferences. Click **Signatures.**

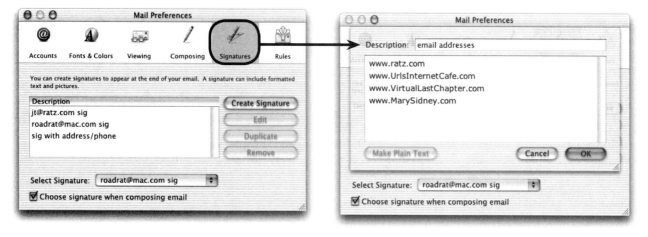

Create Signature: To create a signature, click the "Create Signature" button. In the "Description" field, enter a name for the signature that is descriptive to you. In the big box, enter any information you want to include in the signature. If you want to add a photograph, drag it into the text field. The image format should be JPEG (.jpg) to optimize file size and to minimize translation problems across computing platforms. If your message is going to another Macintosh, other formats will work, such as TIFF, PICT, or PNG, but JPEG is still the recommended format.

To create a new signature that's similar to an existing signature, select the signature you want to use as a model, then click the "Duplicate" button. This duplicate now shows up in the list of signatures; select it, then click the "Edit" button. Make necessary changes to the signature, change its name in the "Description" field, and click OK.

To edit the information in a signature, choose a signature in the Description list, then click the "Edit" button. Make changes in the signature file, then click OK.

To remove a signature from the list, select it, then click the "Remove" button.

To choose a default signature, select its name in the "Select Signature" pop-up menu. This signature will be used in all messages unless you override it by choosing another signature or "None" from the pop-up menu (discussed below) when you're writing a new email.

Choose signature when composing email: Check this to install a pop-up menu in the "New Message" window that contains all of your signatures. Then in any email message, just choose the one you want to include at the end of that message.

This is the pop-up menu that will appear so you can choose a signature.

This is what a signature looks like in the email message.

Rules

Rules

Use **Rules** to manage and organize your messages automatically. Rules act as filters that sift through your messages and put them in their proper mailboxes, delete them, forward them, or follow other actions, according to your directions. You might belong to a mailing list about pack rats, so you can have every email that comes in from that mailing list automatically delivered to the Pack Rat Mailbox. Or you might want to delete every email with a subject that contains the words "mortgage," "enlargement," "babes," "hot," "free," or other obvious junk-mail words.

To open Preferences and get the Rules pane:

1. From the Mail menu, choose "Preferences...."

2. The "Mail Preferences" toolbar shows six buttons representing different Categories of preferences. Click **Rules.**

See the note on page 621 about these blue rules.

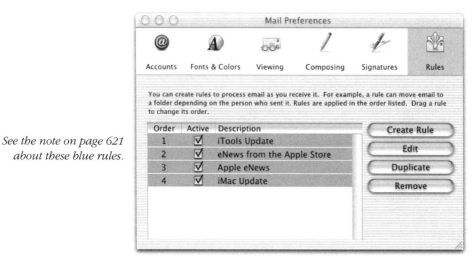

Before you create a new rule: If you want your mail to be automatically organized into different mailboxes, you need to create those mailboxes *before* you make the rule.

To make a new mailbox:

1. If the Mailboxes drawer is not open, open it (click on the Mailbox icon in the toolbar).

2. In the Mailboxes drawer, click on a main heading (such as "Personal Mailboxes") or on a folder, inbox, outbox, or just about any other item to create your new mailbox inside that area.

3. From the Mailbox menu, choose "New Mailbox...."

4. Name the mailbox and click OK. Now you're ready to create a rule that will send mail automatically into that mailbox.

To create a new rule:

1. Click the "Create Rule" button. You'll get the dialog box shown below.

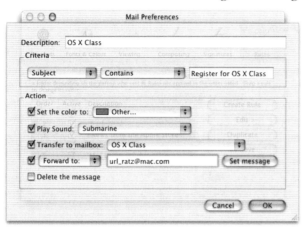

2. The **Description** field contains a default name, such as "Rule #5." Change this name to something that describes your intended Rule. In the example below, I want all the mail from my son Ryan to go into a special mailbox, so I named it "Mail from Ryan."

3. In the **Criteria** section, specify which elements of an email message are to be searched and what the subject of the search will be.

   The first pop-up menu contains types of message **headers** that usually are included with an incoming message, such as To, From, Subject, etc., or you can choose to find text in the body of the message. Choose which area to search.

   Then choose a "modifier" from the second pop-up menu, such as "Contains," "Does not contain," or others.

   Type an appropriate word or words into the text field. The rule shown above will search for messages whose "From" field "Contains" the word "Ryan."

—continued

4. Action determines what actions will be applied to messages that match the criteria you specified. You can check as many or as few of these actions as you like.

Set the color to: Choose a color for highlighting messages that match the criteria. Then you can quickly identify various Categories of filtered email that may appear in a message list.

Play Sound: Choose a sound that will alert you when you receive a message that matches the criteria.

Transfer to mailbox: Select an existing mailbox (that you previously made according to the directions on page 607) to transfer the messages into.

Forward to: To forward targeted incoming mail to another email address, check and enter an email address in the text field that you want the forwarded mail sent to. From the pop-up menu, you can also choose "Redirect to" or "Reply."

There is a difference between "Forward" and "Redirect." Forwarded mail shows your name in the "From" column of Mail's message list plus the date and time you forwarded it in the "Date & Time" column. Redirected mail shows the original sender's name in the "From" column, and shows the time the message was originally composed in the "Date & Time" column of Mail's message list. When you redirect mail, your name will remain in the "To:" header at the top of the message so the new recipient will know that you received the message and redirected it.

Set Message: This opens a text box in which you can type a message that will automatically be included before the original message being forwarded or replied to.

Delete the message: Trash any message that meets the criteria. You can use the header information of mail you suspect to be unwanted email and create a rule that automatically deletes the unwanted mail.

5. OK: Click OK and the rule is made. All incoming mail will now be searched and sorted using the criteria you just created.

Rules are listed in an order and will be applied in that order. **Change the priority order** by dragging a rule to another position in the list.

Make a rule active or inactive with the checkbox in the **Active** column.

To **edit a rule,** select it in the list, then click the "Edit" button, *or* double-click the rule name in the list.

Duplicate a rule if you want to create a new rule that is similar to an existing one. Select an existing rule in the list, click "Duplicate," then select and edit that new rule.

To remove a rule, select it in the Rule list, then click the "Remove" button or press the "Delete" key on your keyboard.

Rules affect new messages that are received *after* a Rule was created. **To apply Rules to older messages,** select the desired messages from the Message List. From the "Message" menu, choose "Apply Rules to Selections."

Blue Apple rules: When you first open the Rules window, there are already four rules in the list. As you can tell from their names, these rules refer specifically to email you may receive about Apple products. These rules don't do anything—they don't have any actions selected yet. If you want to keep these preset rules, edit them and select one or more actions from the "Action" section. If you want to get rid of them, select them and click the "Remove" button.

File Menu
These are some of the items in the **File menu** that aren't explained elsewhere in this chapter.

New Viewer Window: If you've closed the main Viewer Window and realize that you need it back, use this command, or press Command N.

Import Mailboxes: Mail can import the mailboxes of many popular email applications. If you have custom mailboxes already set up in another email application, from the File menu, choose "Import Mailboxes...." Select one of the email clients in the list, then click the right arrow button for instructions. Mail will open a directory window so you can navigate to the appropriate mailbox file and import it.

You can't import AOL mailboxes (not because of Mail's limitations, but because of AOL's prohibitions).

To print an email message: Double-click a message to open it. Click the "Print" icon in the open message's toolbar to open the Print dialog box.

Or select a message in the Message List pane, then go to the File menu and choose "Print...."

Make the appropriate selections in the Print dialog box and click "Print."

To print multiple email messages: From the Message List pane, select multiple messages. From the File menu, choose "Print...." All selected messages, including header information, will print out in continuous fashion—it will not print a separate page for each message.

Edit Menu

These are some of the items in the **Edit menu** that aren't explained elsewhere in this chapter or that are not self-explanatory.

Paste As Quotation: Use this command when you want to paste text from another document into an email message as a quotation. In Mail, a quotation is styled with indentation, a vertical bar, and a user-specified color, as explained on page 613.

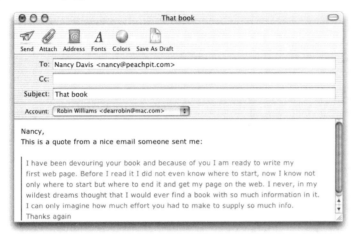

Find and **Spelling:** Mail uses the standard "services" to find text and check spelling. See page 523 for directions on how to use the Find dialog box, and page 522 for spelling. Or just dive in and figure it out—it's pretty easy.

View Menu

Focus on Selected Messages: Select messages (Command-click to select more than one), then choose this option so only those selected messages will be visible in the Message List. To show all of the messages again, go back to the View menu and choose "Show All Messages."

Hide Status Bar or **Show Status Bar:** The Status Bar is located just below the toolbar. The left side of the Status Bar provides information about your Internet connection when checking for mail, and it displays the number of messages in the current Mailbox. The right side of the Status Bar displays rotating arrows when connecting to a remote server to send mail. Click the rotating arrows to open the Activity Viewer, as shown below, and see more information about the current connection.

Click the rotating arrows again to close the Activity Viewer (or click the red close button in the upper-left corner of the Activity Viewer).

Mailbox Menu

Go Offline: If you have a dial-up account that ties up your phone line while you're connected to the Internet, you can choose to "Go Offline." This will disconnect you, but leave Mail open. Before you go offline, transfer any messages you want to read to your Personal Mailboxes Inbox (just drag them over and drop them in). Then go offline, read your mail, compose messages, etc. Messages you compose while offline are stored in the Outbox of Personal Mailboxes in the Mailboxes drawer, where you can open and edit them. When you're ready to send mail, from the Mailbox menu, choose "Go Online."

Rebuild Mailbox: If you have unexplained problems with a mailbox, rebuilding it may help. Select a POP mailbox or folder in the Mailboxes drawer, then from the Mailbox menu choose "Rebuild Mailbox."

POP accounts (blue @ symbol) can rebuild mailboxes because those files are on your computer. IMAP accounts (such as your Mac.com account, marked with the red Apple icon) will not rebuild mailboxes because the files are on a remote server, not on your computer.

Message Menu

The other commands in the **Message menu** are either self-explanatory or have been explained elsewhere in this chapter.

Add Sender To Address Book automatically adds the sender of a selected message to your Address Book. This command is also available as a toolbar button: choose "Customize Toolbar…" from the View menu.

Show offers alternative views of a message, depending on the format of the current message. If you receive email that's hard to read because of its styling or formatting, choose "Plain Text Alternative" to see if it makes the text more readable.

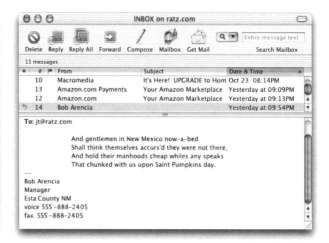

The original message showing styled text.　　　　The original message viewed as "Plain Text Alternative."

Transfer opens a submenu from which you can choose any existing mailbox in which to transfer selected messages.

Append Selected Messages: This command will add entire email messages from others to the end of your current message that you're composing.

To append other messages to your own email message:

1. Compose your letter.

2. Go to the Message List pane and select one or more messages in the list (Command-click to select more than one).

3. Go back to your letter.

4. From the Message menu, choose "Append Selected Messages." The entire email messages you selected, including the header information and the signatures, will be added at the end of your email message.

If you need to append files often, add the "Append" button to the toolbar of the New Message window: From the View menu, choose "Customize Toolbar…," then drag the "Append" button from the Customize dialog box to the toolbar.

Format Menu

In the Format menu, under "Text," there is a command to make the selected text **Bigger.** The menu says the keyboard shortcut is Command +, but that doesn't work—use Shift Command +.

Copy Style copies the style and formatting of selected text, but not the text itself. After you copy a style, select some other text and **Paste Style** to apply the formatting to the newly selected text.

Make Plain Text changes messages from "Rich Text" format to "Plain Text" format, which will strip out all of the formatting, different fonts, colors, etc. If the message is already in Plain Text, this command appears as "Make Rich Text." This will *not* restore any formatting that was removed.

Text Encodings: If you receive email that does not display correctly because it was originally written in a foreign language on a foreign keyboard, it may help to choose "Text Encodings," then select one of the text encoding options from the list.

Increase Quote Level: To format text as a Mail-style quote or to increase the existing quote level, click within a line of text, then choose "Increase Quote Level." Choose the command again to further increase the quote level, as shown below.

The operation is much easier and faster if you learn the keyboard shortcuts: Click within the appropriate text, then type Command ' (that's the typewriter apostrophe, just to the left of the Return key) to "Increase Quote Level," or type Option Command ' to "Decrease Quote Level."

Each of these quoted sections has been increased one more level than the one above it.

The **Address Book** works both independently and with Mail to create Address Cards that store contact information for individuals or groups. When *Mail* is open, you can automatically create an Address Book entry for anyone who sent mail to you. When *Address Book* is open you can automatically address email to an individual or group. You can search the Address Book by name, email address, or by a user-defined Category.

Address Book

If an address can be found in Address Book, the complete address is automatically filled in for you when you start to type it in the "To" field of a message header.

The **Address Book window** consists of the Toolbar, Search bar and Show menu, Address Card pane, and the vCard at the bottom of the window.

The Address Book window

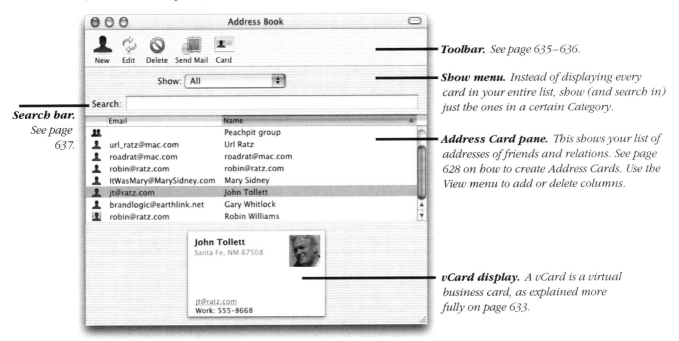

Toolbar. See page 635–636.

Show menu. Instead of displaying every card in your entire list, show (and search in) just the ones in a certain Category.

Search bar. See page 637.

Address Card pane. This shows your list of addresses of friends and relations. See page 628 on how to create Address Cards. Use the View menu to add or delete columns.

vCard display. A vCard is a virtual business card, as explained more fully on page 633.

The **Address Card pane** lists the Address Cards according to the group you've chosen in the "Show" pop-up menu, as well as the "Available Fields" (or columns of information) you've chosen from the View menu in the main menu bar.

The **Show** menu lists different Categories that you can sort your addresses into, such as Home, Work, Buddy, Group. An address can be in more than one Category. A group list is automatically placed in the Group Category.

To sort the Address Cards by the column heading, click on a column heading. To reverse the order, click the small triangle in the heading.

To rearrange the position of columns, drag a column heading left or right to a new position.

Open Address Book

Address Book

Of course, Address Book must be **open** and active before you can add cards to it or work with it in any way.

To open Address Book, do one of the following:

▼ If Mail is open, go to the Window menu and choose "Address Book," or press Command Option A.

▼ If Mail is open and you see a "vCard" in a message, single-click on the blue underlined name of the vCard.

▼ If Mail is not open, go to the Applications window (click on the Applications icon in any Finder window), then double-click on the Address Book icon.

▼ If you use Address Book regularly or want it accessible even when Mail is not open, add its icon to the Dock.

Add an Address Card

An **Address Card** contains the email address of your contact person, plus you can add lots of other information to the card, such as phone and fax numbers, birthdates, names of their children, and more; see page 630–631. To add a card, first open Address Book in any of the ways mentioned above.

Add an Address Card to Address Book in one of the following ways:

▼ To automatically create an Address Card for someone who sent email to you, select their email message in the Mail message window. Then from the Message menu, choose "Add Sender To Address Book," or press Command Y.

▼ **Or** in the Address Book, go to the File menu and choose "New," or click the "New" button in the toolbar to open an "untitled Address Card." Enter the appropriate information and click "Save."

▼ **Or** drag a vCard (virtual business card, explained on page 633) that someone sent you to the Address Book window, as shown below.

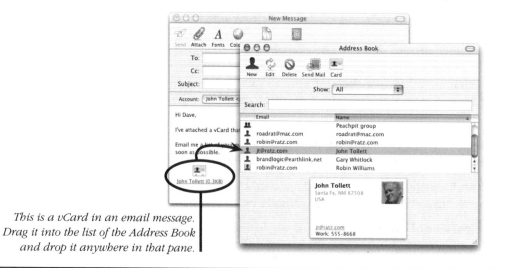

This is a vCard in an email message. Drag it into the list of the Address Book and drop it anywhere in that pane.

A **group,** or private mailing list, in Address Book is a sub-collection of your email addresses so you can send a message to everyone in that group at once. You might have a group for your family, a different group for your fellow office workers, and a group for your rugby team or chess team. The same address can be in more than one group.

Create a Group

To create a new group, do one of the following:

▼ From the File menu choose "New Group."

▼ **Or,** if you've customized the toolbar (as explained on page 636) to include the "New Group" button, click it.

▼ **Or** Command-click to select multiple cards in the Address Card List, then from the File menu, choose "New Group From Selection."

Each method opens an "untitled Address Card" window designed to include a group of email addresses and assign a group name, as shown below.

Enter a group name and description, then click the **Categories…** button and select one or more Categories. A group list is automatically placed in the Group Category as well as any other you select. See page 632 for details about Categories.

To add an email address to the group, type it in the "Address" field, then click the "Plus" button. **Or** drag an Address Book entry from the Address Book window and drop it in the list pane.

To remove an address from the group, select it and click the "Minus" button.

To send email to the entire group: Select a group in the Address Book window (click once on it), then click the "Send Mail" button in the toolbar. Mail opens and a "New Message" window opens, addressed to the group.

Tip: You can choose whether the email will be addressed to the group name or will display each individual email address in the group:

From the Mail menu (not the Address Book menu), choose "Preferences…."

Click the "Composing" button.

Check or uncheck "List private group members individually."

```
⊖ ○ ○            Peachpit group

   Group Name:  Peachpit group
   Description: key contacts for project

  ( Categories… )  New project

            Enter email addresses below, or drag address cards
            from the Address Book or Directory Search window.

   Address: [                    ]  ⊖ ⊕

   👤  John Tollett <jt@ratz.com>
   👤  Url Ratz <roadrat@mac.com>
   👤  rw@vlc.com
   👤  dave@vlc.com

                        ( Cancel )  ( Save )
```

Drag an Address Card from the Address Book window and drop it in here to add it to the group.

Address Card Details   You can add lots of information to **Address Cards** so they become quite useful. Besides contact information, you can keep track of birthdays, meetings, make notes, and more.

Expand the Card   **To expand the Address Card** and store more contact information, click the disclosure triangle above the "Save" button.

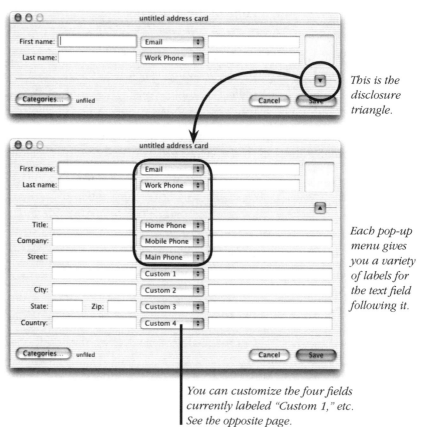

This is the disclosure triangle.

Each pop-up menu gives you a variety of labels for the text field following it.

You can customize the four fields currently labeled "Custom 1," etc. See the opposite page.

From the first five pop-up menus (circled, above), **choose the label** you want to apply to the field.

Customize any of the other four fields as explained on the opposite page.

You can **define your own labels** for the four "Custom" pop-up menus. These four options will apply to every one of your Address Cards. You can change the labels at any time, although the data in the fields won't change to match the new label.

To define the Custom labels:

1. From any one of the four "Custom" pop-up menus, choose "Edit...." A sheet will drop down from the title bar, as shown below.

2. Name the "Custom Fields," then click "Save." You don't have to name all four of them at this point.

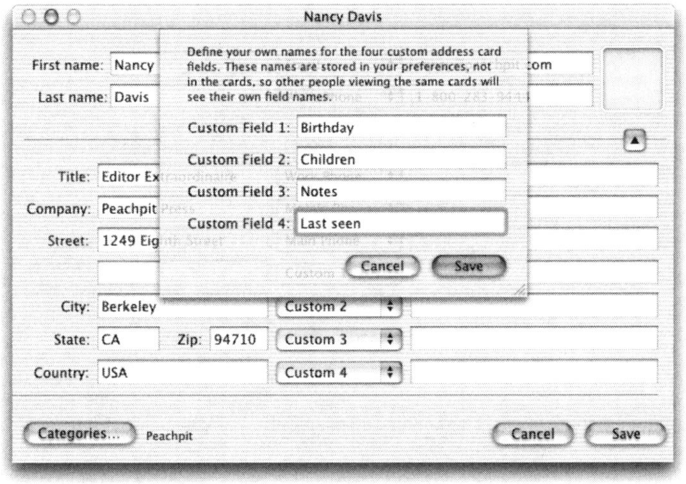

These four Custom Field labels are shown in finished form below.

You can type quite a long message in a field. To show the information in custom fields in the Address Book window, use the View menu and choose from the "Available Fields."

Tip: You can use Services to make a Sticky note out of the text in any field.

Just select the text in a field (press Command A to select all of the text, even if you can't see all of it).

From the Apple menu, choose "Services," then choose "Make Sticky."

Or press Command Shift Y instead of going to the menu at all.

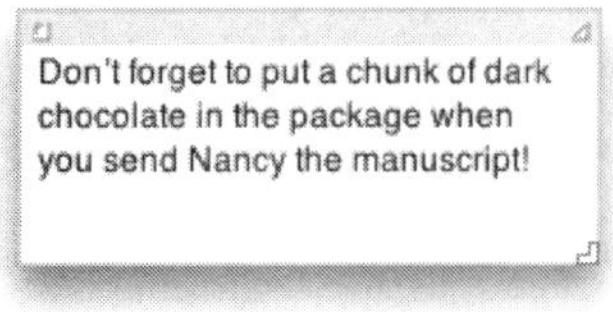

This is a Sticky note made from the Notes field in the Address Card.

Make a new Category

You will eventually have quite a few email addresses in your list. To keep them organized and make it easier to find what you need, you can create separate **Categories** and then file each Address Card into a Category. Then from the "Show" pop-up menu in the Address Book window, you can choose to show just one Category at a time.

One Address Card can be in as many Categories as you like. Categories are also helpful when conducting a search for email addresses because you can limit the search to just certain Categories.

Several Categories have been made for you already. You can add to the existing list, and you can delete any that you make (you can't delete the ones Apple made for you).

The Categories listed in bold are the ones Apple made for you; you cannot delete these.

The Categories you create will not appear in bold type.

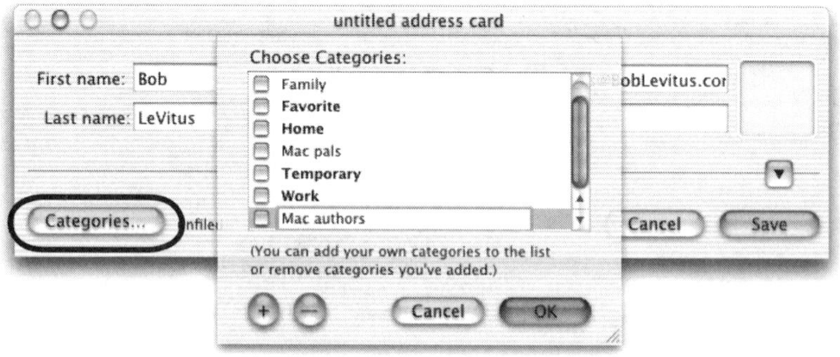

To file a card into a Category, open any Address Card. Click the "Categories…" button in the bottom-left corner to show the "Choose Categories" sheet, as shown above. Select from the existing list.

To make a new Category, open any Address Card. Click the "Categories…" button in the bottom-left corner to show the "Choose Categories" sheet, as shown above. Click the "Plus" button to create and name a new Category.

To make a new Category appear in the "Show" pop-up menu, you have to quit Address Book, then open it again. Hopefully Apple will fix that.

To remove a Category that you created, select it, then click the "Minus" button.

To display the Categories in the Address Book main window, choose a Category from the "Show" pop-up menu (other than "All"). Only cards that have been filed in the chosen Category will appear in the Address Book window.

A **vCard** is a **virtual business card.** When you receive a vCard from someone, it has a .vcf extension (virtual card file) and appears in your email message as an attachment. Address Book automatically makes a vCard for every card in your list.

To create a new Address Card from a vCard that someone sent you, drag the vCard icon from the Mail window to the Address Book window.

To see the vCard for anyone in your Address Book, select that person's entry, then click the "Card" button in the toolbar. The vCard that appears at the bottom of the Address Book window provides a quick view of the essential contact information. **To hide the vCard,** click the "Card" button again.

vCards

Here you see the vCard for the selected entry.

You can **attach your vCard** to email messages. (But keep in mind that some people don't appreciate getting a vCard because it's another file that has to be downloaded, and if it's attached to every email you send someone, they have to download it everytime they hear from you.)

Attach your vCard to outgoing messages

To add your vCard to an email message, open a "New Message" window (open Mail, then click the "Compose" button in the toolbar). From the Address Book, grab the small icon (the head-and-shoulders silhouette) next to your email address and drag it to Mail's "New Message" window.

vCards can **include images** to help identify Address Book entries, as shown on the following page. But support for vCards in Mail is limited at this time. Currently, when you attach a photo to your Address Card, the photo is not automatically sent with the vCard. If you want to include your photo, you have to send it as an attachment. After sending a photo, the recipient can drag your vCard into their Address Card list, as explained on the following page, and *your* photo will appear on *your* vCard in *their* list.

Add a Photo to an Address Card

If you have a photograph of someone who sends you email, you can **add their photo** to their Address Card in your Address Book. Then when you get mail from that person, their little photo will apear in the message. Photos work best if they're sized to 48x48 pixels, at a resolution of 72 dpi, in RGB mode. If you don't know how to do that, try any photo.

To add a photo to an Address Card, double-click the card in the Address Card list pane. Open a Finder window that contains the photo you want to add. Drag the photo icon from the Finder window to the empty photo well in the top-right corner of the Address Card window. Click "Save."

To change photos, select the original image in the photo well, delete it, then click "Save." Next, reopen that Address Card, drag the new image to the photo well, and "Save" again.

This Is Me

You may want to **create an Address Card for yourself** so you'll have a vCard that you can attach to emails (see all about vCards on the previous page). Just create one for yourself as you would for anyone else (press Command N and fill in the information).

To attach your vCard to an email message, drag the icon you see to the left of your Address Card (the head-and-shoulders silhouette) to the message area of a new email message.

If you have a lot of Address Cards showing in the Address Card list, you can highlight *your* card so it will stand out. Select your card in the list, then from the Edit menu, choose "This Is Me."

The card selected as "This Is Me" has a highlighted silhouette.

The **toolbar** has a number of useful buttons that are explained below. You can customize the toolbar in Address Book, or hide it altogether.

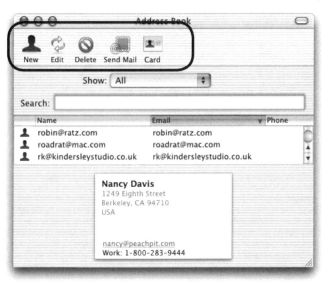

New: Opens an "untitled Address Card" in which you enter an email address and contact information, as shown on the previous pages.

Edit: Opens a *selected* Address Card. Or you can double-click an Address Card to open it for editing.

Delete: Removes a *selected* Address Card. Or select a card, then press the Delete key on your keyboard.

Send Mail: Opens Mail, then automatically opens a "New Message" window addressed to the person *selected* in the Address Book window.

Card: Toggles between hiding and showing the "vCard" at the bottom of the Address Book window, for a *selected* Address Card. The example above shows a vCard being displayed. A vCard is a virtual business card that contains contact information; see page 633 for details.

To hide or show the toolbar, click the clear button at the top-right corner of the window.

If you closed the Address Book window, click the Address Book icon in the Dock to **bring the window back.**

—continued

Customize the toolbar

To customize the toolbar, hold down the Control key and click on the toolbar. From the contextual menu that appears, choose "Customize toolbar...." Drag any button from the customize toolbar sheet up to the toolbar and drop it.

Display the toolbar:
From the "Show" pop-up menu, choose "Icon & Text," "Text Only," or "Icon Only."

Or *cycle through these "Show" choices when the customize toolbar sheet is not visible: Command-click on the clear button at the top-right corner of the Address Book window.*

Or *Control-click on the toolbar, then from the contextual menu, choose one of these three toolbar views.*

The **Separator** is a visual device to help organize items in the toolbar. The only buttons that are not on the toolbar by default are the "New Group" button and the "Directory" button.

New Group: Opens an "untitled Address Card" window so you can create a group of email addresses. See page 629 for details.

Directory: Refers to LDAP (pronounced *el dap*) directories. LDAP (Lightweight Directory Access Protocol), is a scaled-back version of DAP (Directory Access Protocol), a protocol for accessing large, searchable, online directories of information, similar to phone books, over a network or on the Internet. LDAP is referred to as "lightweight" because it's less complicated and easier to implement than DAP.

Mail and Address Book can look up email addresses and contact information in LDAP directories, if you have access to such a directory. Chances are you do not have access to an LDAP directory unless you're on a large network, in which case you should have the network administrator help you set up access, which may require special software. There are public LDAP directories on the Internet, and Mac OS X will enable you to access those in the near future.

Search

A **search** in Address Book is based on information from the *available fields* (columns) that are currently shown in the Address Card pane. For instance, the default fields that are visible are "Email" and "Name." A search conducted while those two fields are visible will search only the information in those fields of the Address Cards. To make more fields visible and searchable, from the View menu choose "Available Fields," then select any field name you want to include. The fields listed in this menu are the same ones that are available in the expanded, editable view of an Address Card (as shown on page 630).

The search will also only apply to the *Category* you choose in the "Show" pop-up menu. If you want to search every Address Card you have, choose "All" from the Show menu. If you want to limit the search to just one Category, choose that one from the Show menu.

To search through your Address Book, make sure you have the fields visible and the Category chosen that you want to search. Then start typing a name, address, or other information in the "Search" text field. As you type, matches will appear in the window. As you continue to type, the list of matching entries becomes more limited.

Most of the choices in the "Available Fields" are self-explanatory except for AIM and Jabber.

AIM, also known as AOL Instant Messenger, is a proprietary messaging service developed by America Online that lets you chat with people whom you've added to a "Buddy List," whether or not either of you are using America Online. AIM lets you check to see if a Buddy is online and send a private "instant message" that appears on your Buddy's screen. The AIM field of an Address Card would contain that person's AIM screen name.

You don't even have to subscribe to AOL to use the instant messenger system, although you do have to download the free software from **www.aol.com/aim,** or go to **www.netscape.com** and click the "Instant Messenger" icon. If you use Netscape 6, AIM is built-in.

Jabber is another instant messaging system for Windows machines that is gaining popularity; it is "Open Source" rather than proprietary, meaning the source code is available to anyone. Jabber *clients* (Jabber chat software on a computer) can communicate with other instant messaging systems, such as AIM, ICQ, MSN, and IRC. The Jabber field of an Address Card would contain that person's Jabber identity. See **www.jabber.com.**

Import Existing Addresses into Address Book

If you want to **import addresses** from an application *other* than Address Book, first open the other email client and export the address information as a "tab-delimited" file. Then open Address Book, and from the File menu, choose "Import." Use the "Open" window to select the tab-delimited file on your computer, then click "Open."

Keep in mind that if you had information in the other address list that was in a different order from your list in Address Book, data might appear in odd places. It's a good idea to **save a copy** of your original Address Book file in case you need to replace the new one; see the last paragraph.

At the moment, unfortunately, you cannot *export* your list of addresses from Address Book to *add* them to someone else's list. You can give someone else a *copy* of your Address Book file, as explained below, but that will *replace* their existing Address Book list. If that's okay, then copy the file described below and replace an existing file with yours (or vice versa, of course).

If you plan to reformat your hard disk, **save a copy of your Address Book** file so you can place it in the same location after you reinstall Mac OS X. To find the Address Book file, open your Home folder, then open the "Library" folder, then the "Addresses" folder. The address book file is located here, named **Address Book.addressbook.**

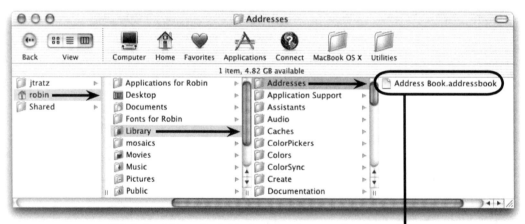

This is the Address Book file that contains your list of email address and contact information. Before you do anything that might change it, drag a copy of this original file into another folder, like your Documents folder: Hold down the Option key and drag it to another folder.

Many people use email everyday without being aware of **email etiquette** **Email Etiquette**
and without realizing that they're **1)** annoying co-workers, friends, and
relatives; **2)** making themselves look naive and amateurish in the email
world; and **3)** turning themselves into junk mailers, albeit well-intentioned.

If no one has complained about your email etiquette, you're probably in
good shape. Or it could be that family members and friends do not want to
risk embarrassing you. To be safe, consider the following suggestions and
see if your email manners are up to date.

1. Get permission before you add someone to a mailing list.

You may be well-intentioned, but most people get so much spam and
junk mail that they'd rather not receive the inspirational messages that
someone sent you—especially since they probably received five other
copies already. Not everyone is a curmudgeon about getting email like
this, but it's polite, professional, and considerate to ask for permission
before putting someone on your mailing list. And please, don't take it
personally if they decline. Privacy on the Internet is hard to come by,
and many people try to keep their email address off as many mailing
lists as possible. When you add someone's address to your mailing
list without their permission, you're publishing private information
without permission.

2. Clean up the email headers.

Even if someone wants to be on your mailing list, it's extremely
annoying to get email that has dozens (or hundreds) of lines of header
information before the message. This happens when you receive an
email message that was sent to a list, then someone sent it to their
list, then someone else sent it to their list. This kind of email makes
the sender look like the clueless amateur they are. Before you send
a forwarded message like this, delete all that header stuff so the
recipient can see the message at a glance with having to scroll through
pages of junk. (To delete the header information, click the Forward
button to forward the message, then select all those email addresses
and other stuff, and hit the Delete button.)

3. Hide the mailing list addresses.

When you send a message to your mailing list (called a "group"
in Mail), you are essentially providing every reader of the message
with the email addresses of all your friends and relations. Then if
those people forward your message, all of their recipients have the
email addresses of all your friends and relations. Not many people
appreciate that. Use the tip on page 629 to hide the list of addresses
when you send a message. Not only is it neater, it is more polite to
everyone involved. *—continued*

Tip: If you want to send photographs as email attachments to a wide variety of computer users on all different sorts of computers, follow these guidelines:

Make sure the file is in the *JPEG format.* If you're not sure, open it in Preview and change the format, as explained on page 479.

Name the file with a short name with no special characters such as ! ? / or : .

The file must have the *extension .jpg* at the end; see page 227 for details on extensions, their importance, and how to make sure you don't end up with double extensions.

4. Take the time to personalize your email.

If you send well-intentioned junk email to an aquaintance, friend, or relative, it will be appreciated if you take the time to add a personal note to the forwarded message, such as "Hi Jay, I thought you might enjoy this." To receive an unsolicited, unsigned, almost-anonymous, forwarded email makes me wonder when I can expect to start receiving the rest of the sender's postal service junk mail and Sunday supplements.

5. Identify your email attachments.

When you attach a file to an email message, don't make the recipient guess what kind of file it is or what program might open it. Include a description of the attachment and the file type, or what program is needed to open it. Say something like, "Barbara, the attached file is a photograph that I saved as a .tif in Photoshop 6 on a Mac." Dealing with attachments can be confusing, and any helpful information is usually appreciated.

6. Don't fall for the urban legends and hoaxes that travel around the Internet.

When you get a panic-stricken email from a friend warning you of an apocalyptic virus and to "Please forward this email to everyone you know," do not forward it to anyone you know. This email message usually contains the words "THIS IS NOT A HOAX!" That means that this is a hoax. These messages float around the Internet constantly and some of them are many years old. If there's a deadly virus about to destroy the world as we know it, you're more likely to hear about it from the national news services and online news sites than from your cousin who's been using email for three months.

Also, do not forward the email messages that tell you Microsoft is paying one dollar every time you use HotMail or visit the Microsoft web site. And don't forward the warning that the postal service is going to start charging us for every email, or that the phone company is going to tax every message, and please stop sending the Neiman Marcus cookie recipe around, and that little boy in the hospital who is waiting for your postcard went home years ago.

And make darn sure your email recipient has *begged* you to send all those messages that say "Send this to at least ten other people. Do not break this chain!"

Multiple Users
Sharing Files on One Mac

35

Sharing files between multiple users on one Macintosh is useful in homes, schools, and many offices. In homes, for instance, each member of the family can have their own Home area, but parents can leave notes and photos for kids in a special folder, or kids can leave school papers for parents to proofread, and no one gets in anyone's way. In schools, instructors can leave files accessible for all students, and students can drop off files for the instructor and no one else. In offices, people can leave important memos, reports, or photos for any other user to access. And it's really easy.

Privileges

First of all, before you start sharing files on your Mac you should understand what **privileges** are. Every file and folder has an owner (the person who created the file), a group (automatically set for you), and a set of privileges (permissions). These privileges are displayed and can be changed in the Info window, as shown below. (Directions are on pages 646–647.)

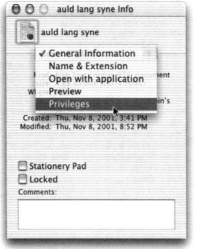

Select a file or folder, then press Command I to get the Info window.

From the pop-up menu in the window, choose "Privileges."

This is the Privileges pane of the Info window.

Privilege options

The owner of each file or folder can determine whether other people can use the file or folder, and in which ways. These are the **privilege options:**

- ▾ **Read & Write:** A user with Read & Write privileges has full access to the file or folder. She can open it, make changes, copy it, read the document, print the document, put files into the folder, etc.

- ▾ **Read Only:** A user with Read Only privileges can open the document, read it, print it, copy it, or open the folder and see what's inside. He cannot make changes to the document, or add or delete anything in a folder.

  If a user copies a Read Only file to his own Home folder, then that user becomes the "owner" and the original owner's privileges automatically switch to the new owner.

Robin's Stuff

A folder will display a red "Do not enter" sign to any user who has privileges of "None."

- ▾ **None:** A user cannot open a file, copy it, move it, or print it. She cannot open a folder, put things inside of it, copy it, or move it.

- ▾ **Write Only (Drop Box):** This is for folders only, not documents. If a folder is Write Only, users can put files inside, but they can't open the folder to see what's in it, take things from it, copy it, or move it. The Drop Box in the Public folder is Write Only.

Location privileges

In addition to the privileges assigned to a file or folder, users must have appropriate privileges for the **locations** where they want to copy or move a file to, such as the disk or folder. So if you get confusing messages about not being able to copy or move files around, check the privileges for the file itself, *plus* the folder you are moving it into, *plus* the disk on which the folder is stored.

Access files with privileges

Although these privileges sound secure, they're really not. Here are several examples of ways to **get around the privileges** that have been set for a file. I tell you this for two reasons: One is so you understand that files are not totally safe if they are sitting on your Mac, no matter what privileges (or lack of) you apply. And two is because you might need to remove someone's files, like a student's files after the student has left class, or files of an usavory nature that you've found on the Mac.

To access files that have limited privileges:

- Restart in Mac OS 9. None of the privileges set in Mac OS X will apply in OS 9. (Don't be tempted to set privileges in Mac OS 9 because it can cause problems for OS X users using Classic.)
- If you are an Administrator and access another Mac across the network, you will bypass most privileges.
- Log in as the root user, as explained on pages 298–299.
- Also, other Administrators on the Mac can change many privileges.

Setting Privileges Don't go randomly **setting privileges** for files and folders until you really have a good reason and know what you're doing. When you're ready, here are the simple directions.

To set or change privileges for a file:

1. Click once on a file to select it.

2. Press Command I to show the Info box for the file (or you can go to the file menu and choose "Show Info").

3. In the Info box, choose "Privileges" from the menu.

4. Press each little pop-up menu to change the privileges for yourself, the "group," and every user on the Mac.

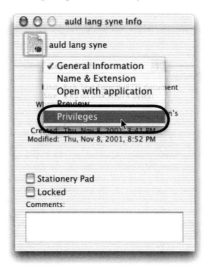

Different files show different items in the pop-up menu.

In the open menu shown above, you can see the privilege options. If the selected file is a folder, there is an additional option called "Write only (Drop Box)," as shown on page 651.

A "Group" cannot have fewer privileges than "Everyone." So if you discover that you can't change the privileges for "Group," check the settings for "Everyone." For instance, if "Everyone" has "Read & Write" privileges, then "Group" cannot have "Read Only" privileges.

These are typical privileges for a **document.** *The owner has full privileges, and other users can read, copy, and print the file.*

A **disk** *offers the option of "Ignore all privileges on this volume," which means it will let anyone do anything on the whole disk. Use this only in an emergency—if users are having access troubles and nothing else works.*

Folders and disks *have an "Apply" button. If you choose to "Apply to all enclosed folders," you will override any privileges that the subfolders had.*

A new folder automatically picks up the privileges of the folder it was created within.

Most **applications** *that came with your Mac are owned by the "system" and you cannot change the privileges.*

An **application** *that you installed in your own Home folder area belongs to you and you can change the privileges to allow other users to use it or not.*

Post a File for All Users to Access

In the Users folder, which is on your main hard disk (if you have more than one partition), you see a folder called **Shared.** Every user on the Mac will see the same Shared folder. So any file that you want everyone to be able to open, copy, or print (depending on the privileges you set), put it in the Shared folder.

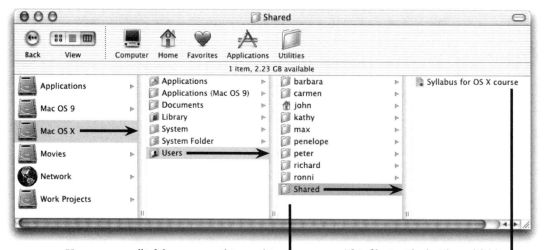

Here you see all of the users on this machine. You will always see the Shared folder in this list. At the moment, "john" is using the Mac. He can put items into the Shared folder, and he can take items out.

This file, inside the Shared folder, is accessible to anyone who uses this Mac. You can also make new folders inside the Shared folder.

Only the user who put a file *into* the Shared folder can remove that original file. When any other user drags the file out of the folder, the Mac automatically creates a *copy* of the file. Not even the Administrator can remove a file that another user put in the Shared folder (log in as root, if you must remove a file; see pages 298–299).

Only the user who put the file in this folder can remove that original file. When anyone else drags that file out of the Shared folder, the Mac automatically creates a copy.

When any user drags a file out of the Shared folder, the Mac automatically makes a **copy;** the only user who can remove a file from the Shared folder is the **original owner.**

Original owners vs. new owners

When a user makes this copy, she becomes the "owner" and picks up the "Read & Write" privileges of the owner, no matter what privileges the original owner had set for the group and everyone else. So if you don't want other users to be able to make changes to a document, set the "owner" privileges to "Read only." **New owners** will not be able to save changes, as shown below, but the **original owner** is still able to make and save changes, even though the privileges are "Read only."

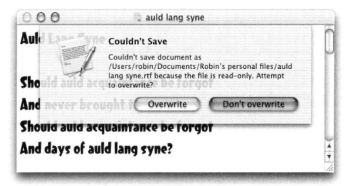

*If you are the **original owner** of this file, you will be allowed to overwrite the file so your changes are saved, even though the owner privileges are set for "Read only."*

*If you are **not** the original owner of this file, you will **not** be allowed to overwrite this file.*

The Shared folder is owned by the system so no one is allowed to make changes.

Post a File for Others to Copy

If you put a file in your **Public** folder, everyone else on the Mac has access to it, just like in the Shared folder, but other users have to open your Home folder to get to it. Files in the Public folder are also accessible over a network, as explained in the following chapter, whereas files in the Shared folder are only available to users on the local Mac.

If you threw away your Public folder because you thought you'd never need it, follow the steps below to create a new one. If you still have yours, skip to page 652.

Do You Need to Make a New Public Folder?

I do hope you heeded the warnings early in the book not to throw away or rename any of the folders in your Home area, particularly the one named **Public.** If you did, it's really okay—you can create a new one, plus the Drop Box inside of it, and the new folder will work just like the original. It will even have the fancy little icon on it.

To make a new Public folder (if you previously threw yours away):

1. Open your Home window (click on the Home icon in the window Toolbar, or press Command Option H).

2. To make the new folder, press Command Shift N. A new, untitled folder will appear in your Home window.

3. Rename the folder **Public.** Click anywhere to set the name (or hit Return or Enter).

4. Now you need to create a Drop Box folder inside the Public folder. So double-click on the new Public folder to open its window.

5. To make the new folder, press Command Shift N. A new, untitled folder will appear in your Public window.

6. Rename the folder **Drop Box.** Be sure to use a capital D and B, and put a space between the words. Click anywhere to set the name (or hit Return or Enter).

7. Now you have to change the privileges for Drop Box so other users can put files into this folder, but not open it: Click once on the folder, then press Command I to Show Info. You'll get the Info window as shown on the opposite page, the illustration on the left.

Tip: You can recreate any of the folders you might have thrown away that you now realize you need, such as Pictures or Sites.

8. From the menu at the top of the Info window, choose "Privileges." The Drop Box folder you just made probably has the privileges shown below, left, so the owner can "Read & Write," but others can "Read only." That's not what you want.

9. Press on the "Everyone" menu (not "Group" yet) and choose "Write only (Drop Box)."

10. Now press on the Group menu and choose "Write only (Drop Box)."

11. Close the Info box and you're all set.

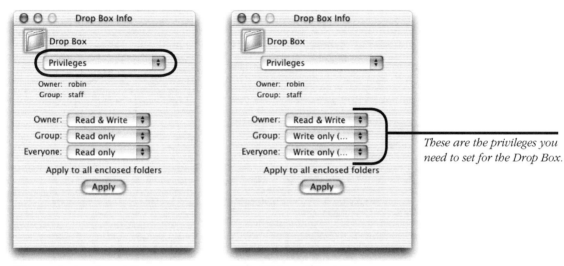

These are the privileges you need to set for the Drop Box.

When reducing the privileges, as when going from "Read only" to "Write only," you have to apply the lower privilege to "Everyone" first because a "Group" cannot have fewer privileges than "Everyone."

With "Write only" privileges, your Public folder and Drop Box are back to their original state.

Using the Public Folder

As I mentioned on the previous page, you can put files in your **Public folder** to share with other users on the same Mac. File Sharing does not need to be turned on to do this (to share files in your Public folder over a network, File Sharing does need to be turned on, as discussed in the following chapter).

Just drop files into your Public folder and all other users on the Mac can copy them to their Home folder.

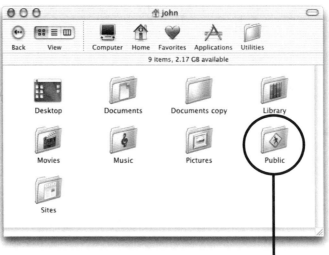

Drop the files you want to share in here.

To pick up a file in a Public folder, click once on that user's Home folder, then click on their Public folder. Just drag a file out—it will be automatically copied for you. Notice most of the other folders in every other user's Home have the "Do not enter" symbol, as shown on page 644.

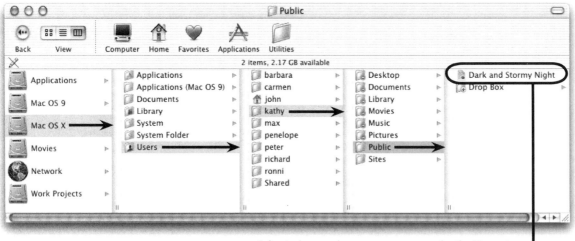

John is the user here, as you can see by the Home icon.
He opened Kathy's Home folder to get to her Public folder, where
she stored a file he needs called "Dark and Stormy Night."

Inside each Public folder is a **Drop Box.** This is a place where you can leave a file *for that one particular user whose Home it is.* No one but that one user can see the file—no one else can even look inside the folder.

Using the Drop Box

To put a file in someone's Drop Box, open their Home folder, then open their Public folder, then drag your file into their Drop Box. You'll get the message shown below every time you drop in a file.

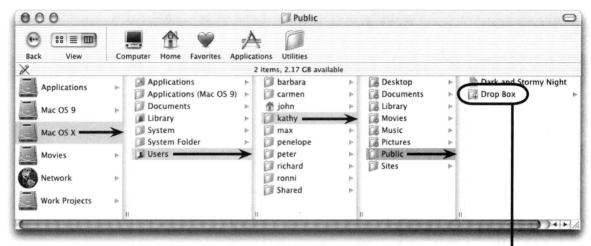

John is the user here, as you can see by the Home icon. He opened Kathy's Home folder to get to her Public folder, where he found her Drop Box, where he can drop in a file for her.

Drop Box

The Drop Box has an icon that indicates you can "write" to it, or put things inside of it. But that's all you can do—you can't open it.

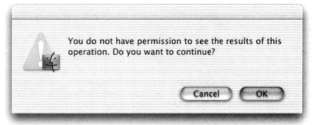

You'll get this message when you drop a file in someone's Drop Box because you will not be allowed to open the Drop Box folder to make sure the file transferred properly. You have to simply trust that it's there.

Change Privileges on Home Folders

You can **change the privileges** on any of your own Home folders, if you want others to have access to them. For instance, perhaps you used your digital camera and Image Capture to "offload" a whole bunch of family photos into your Pictures folder. Rather than copy the photos into your Public folder or the Shared folder, or drop them into individual family member folders, you can make your Pictures folder accessible and everyone else can go into the folder and view the photos.

To change the privileges, just follow the directions on pages 646–647.

The user John is logged in at the moment. You can see that the user named Ronni has changed the privileges of her Pictures folder so all other users can access it.

Sharing Files
in a Small Office or Home Office

This chapter is only for you if you have more than one Mac in the same house or small office. If you do have more than one Mac, it is incredibly easy—in fact, it's so easy it's spooky—to **share files between Macs.** You can just drag a file onto the other computer's window, right there on your own Desktop. Or you can set it up so each person can get to the other person's entire hard disk. This works even if the other Macs are not using Mac OS X.

Simple Networking

The Macs you want to share files between must be **networked** together—you must have some sort of cable connecting them to each other or both to the same printer, or AirPort cards installed so they can connect to each other wirelessly. Networking a couple of Macs is a simple procedure.

There are entire books written on networking, and it *can* get very complex, so complex that people make a living being network specialists and in a large office there is usually a full-time *network administrator*. I am only going to explain the simplest method to get a couple of Macs talking to each other. We've got five Macs and a PC in this office, plus an iMac in the studio and a laptop in the library, plus three printers, all networked together, using a combination of DSL, Ethernet cables, and wireless AirPort. It is the coolest, most efficient way to get work done.

If you have a number of machines in your home office or small office, you will need something called a *switch* or *Ethernet hub* that can connect all of your machines together, including your networkable printers. The hub/switch will have a number of Ethernet ports; you connect each Mac and printer to that box with straight Ethernet cables. See the opposite page for specific details.

If you have several computers in your office and a broadband connection, you probably have a *router* and all your Macs are connected into it—this means they're all set up for networking. Plug any network-capable printers into this router and you've got a fully networked small office.

Peer-to-peer network

This simple network in a small office is called a **peer-to-peer network,** where every computer on the network is considered a *server,* or a computer that can "serve" files to others. This is different from a client-server situation in a large corporation, where lots of computers connect to one huge, main server and everyone gets files from that main server, rather than from each other's computers.

You will probably have to buy **Ethernet cables.**

> ▾ If the cables are going to directly connect two computers (or any two Ethernet devices, like a Mac directly to a printer), you need **crossover cables.**

> ▾ If the cables are going from the computer into a hub, router, or switcher, you need **straight cables**—not crossover.

To tell if an Ethernet cable is crossover or not, hold both ends up, facing the same direction, with the locking clip facing up. Look at the colored wires coming through the end.

> A straight cable has the colored wires in *exactly the same order.*

> A crossover cable does *not* have the colored wires in the same order.

The first thing you must do before you can actually share files is **connect the computers together with cables.**

A. Connect two computers directly to each other using a **crossover Ethernet cable** for the fastest connection (for instance, G3 to G4 or iMac to G4). Just plug each end of the crossover cable into the Ethernet ports on each Mac.

B. Connect any number of computers together with **straight Ethernet cables** that go from each computer into an Ethernet hub, router, or switch. If you have a high-speed connection, you already have a router that you can plug the Ethernet cables into. If the router doesn't have enough ports for the Macs and printers in your office, you can buy a small hub or switch and connect the router to the hub/switch with a crossover Ethernet cable.

C. Connect two computers directly to the same PostScript printer (either through Ethernet ports, if the printer has them, with crossover Ethernet cables; or through the regular serial port on older printers with something like a Farallon EtherMac iPrint adapter). Once both computers are connected to a printer, they are also connected to each other, whether the printer is turned on or not.

D. Connect two computers to a non-PostScript printer with Ethernet cables or a third-party solution. Once both computers are connected to a printer, they are also connected to each other, whether the printer is turned on or not. There are devices available that will connect anything to anything. For instance, Milan Technology has an adapter that will plug into the parallel port on your color inket (the parallel port is the long one) that you can then plug two Ethernet cables into. Other vendors have other great solutions. The best source for solutions from a variety of vendors is DrBott.com.

Ethernet Cables

Step 1:
Connect your Macs with Ethernet Cables

*At **www.DrBott.com** you can find hubs, switches, crossover Ethernet cables, straight Ethernet cables, network printing solutions, transceivers for older Macs that don't have RJ45 Ethernet ports, and much more.*

Step 2:
Turn on File Sharing

Okay, so you have your two Macs either directly connected to each other with a crossover Ethernet cable, or you have several Macs all connected into a router, hub, or switcher with straight Ethernet cables. Now you need to turn on **File Sharing.**

Sharing preferences

Sharing

Turn on File sharing on every Mac that you want to share files between.

To turn on File Sharing:

1. Open the System Preferences: click on the icon in the Dock, or from the Apple menu, choose "System Preferences...."

2. Single-click on the Sharing icon. You'll get the pane shown below.

3. In the section labeled "File Sharing Off," click the Start button.

4. If necessary, change the **Computer Name** to something that will tell you which Mac this is. For instance, you might name it "G4 by the West Window" or "Cliff's Business Mac." You want a distinctive name that will tell you exactly which Mac this is when looking at a list; names like Mac1, Mac2, and Mac3 are not going to help much unless you paste big name tags on each Mac in your office.

5. Write down the **IP Address** on a piece of paper, and label it as the IP Address that shows up in the Sharing preferences pane for that particular computer. The IP Address might change now and then, so don't be surprised if that happens.

If you have a DSL, cable, or other **broadband** connection, your Macs are all connected with Ethernet cables through the hub or router. This means your Network settings are probably right where you need them. Skip to page 661.

If you have a telephone **dial-up** connection, but your Macs are connected through Ethernet, you need to make a few adjustments in your Network preferences pane. If you are connected through AirPort, walk through the Network preferences and make sure things are set up correctly for you.

To open the Network preferences pane:

1. Open the System Preferences: click on the icon in the Dock, or from the Apple menu, choose "System Preferences...."

2. Single-click on the Network icon (there's probably a Network icon right in the toolbar). You'll get the pane shown below.

Step 3:
Check your Network Pane

Network preferences

Note: The Network icon in the Computer window is not the one you want—that one is a completely different thing (even though it looks exactly the same; I wish they wouldn't do that). You must go to the System Preferences to get the Network preferences for sharing files.

```
┌─────────────────────────────────────────────────────────┐
│ ⦿⦿⦿                    Network                        ▭ │
│  [Show All] [Sound] (Network) [Startup Disk] [Displays]   │
│                                                           │
│            Location: ( Office network        ▾ )          │
│    Show: ( Built-in Ethernet              ▾ )             │
│                                                           │
│          ╱ TCP/IP ╲ PPPoE  AppleTalk  Proxies             │
│                                                           │
│     Configure: ( Manually              ▾ )                │
│                         Domain Name Servers (Optional)    │
│    IP Address: [ 192.168.244.4   ]  ┌──────────────────┐  │
│                                     │                  │  │
│   Subnet Mask: [ 255.255.255.0   ]  └──────────────────┘  │
│                                                           │
│        Router: [ 192.168.244.244 ]  Search Domains        │
│                                     (Optional)            │
│                                     ┌──────────────────┐  │
│                                     │                  │  │
│                                     └──────────────────┘  │
│                                     Example: apple.com, earthlink.net │
│  Ethernet Address: 00:30:65:56:7d:2c                      │
│                                                           │
│  🔒  Click the lock to prevent further changes.  (Apply Now) │
└─────────────────────────────────────────────────────────┘
```

3. If you have a **dial-up** connection, or if you have a mixture of connections (for instance, in the office we use DSL, but the iMac in the studio and the laptop in the library use the DSL through an AirPort connection), you should make a new *Location* so you can switch networking preferences back and forth without having to redo all the settings (a Location is a collection of settings).

First you need to **save the current Location:** From the Location pop-up menu, choose "New Location...."

Give it a name you will remember, such as "Santa Fe Dial-up." Click the "Apply Now" button in the bottom-right corner.

Make a new Location, if necessary

—continued

4. Now you need to make a *new* Location for the file sharing setup. This way you can switch back and forth between Locations depending on whether you need to share files over Ethernet or AirPort or connect to the Internet through your phone line.

To make a new Location, from the Location pop-up menu, choose "New Location…."

Name the Location something you will recognize, such as "AirPort to Studio iMac" or "Office Network" or "Connect to Sweetheart." Click OK. Now you will make your settings for this Location.

Choose the connection method

5. If you have a **dial-up** connection, your Network preferences probably has the "Show" option selected as "Internal Modem" because that's how you connect to the Internet. You need to **change this to** "Built-in Ethernet" so you can connect to the other computers in your office.

If you want to connect through **AirPort,** choose "AirPort" in the "Show" pop-up menu. The AirPort Base Station itself might be connected to DSL or other broadband, or to a telephone connection, but if you want to connect to another Mac through an AirPort connection, you need to select "AirPort" in the "Show" menu.

This pop-up menu should display the name of your new Location.

Choose "Built-in Ethernet" here, unless you want to connect to a Mac using AirPort, then choose "AirPort."

6. Adjust the **settings** in the TCP/IP pane according to the information in Chapter 31. Most of the settings will be automatic and you can just leave them as they are.

Note: Depending on your connection, your IP Address may change now and then. If you have a dial-up connection, it will change every time you log on to the Internet.

7. An important setting to notice is the **IP Address** that was assigned to your Mac. For instance, in the Sharing preferences example on page 658, using Built-in Ethernet, my computer's IP Address is 192.168.244.4 because that's my IP Address for my DSL connection (today) and the office network. But when I switch to "Show" AirPort so I can send files to the studio, my IP Address changes to 10.0.1.3 because that's my computer's address on the AirPort network.

Write down the IP Address! And make a note for which network the address applies, which computer, and the date.

8. Click the **AppleTalk** pane and check the box to "Make AppleTalk Active."

9. When you have adjusted the settings for the new Location, click the "Apply Now" button in the bottom-right corner.

Mac OS X provides you with several ways to actually make the connection. Let's start with the Go menu, and then I'll tell you some shortcuts.

Step 4: Connect

To connect to another Mac on your network:

1. Click on any blank area of the Desktop to make the Finder active. Once the Finder is active, you should see the Go menu.

2. From the Go menu, choose "Connect to Server…," or press Command K. You'll get the dialog box shown below.

Depending on how your computers are networked, you will see their names listed under the AppleTalk option or the Local Network option.

If you see the same computer listed more than once, don't worry—at some point that computer had another IP address. That's why you want to know which one it has today.

3. Choose the name of the computer you want to share files with, then click the "Connect" button. Or you can type in the IP address in the "Address" field. Type **afp://** and then the IP address. Then click "Connect."

AFP stands for Apple File Protocol.

4. You'll get the dialog box shown below.

*See page 665 about adding the user name and password to your **keychain** so you can connect without having to even see this dialog box.*

Registered user: You must know the user name and password of the computer you are connecting to. If you enter the Administrator's user name and password, you have access to the entire computer. You can even get into the Home folders of every user on that Mac.

If you enter any regular user's name and password, it is the same as entering as a guest, as described on the following page.

—continued

If you don't understand about Public folders and Drop Boxes, please see pagest 296 and Chapter 35.

Guest: You will only be allowed to see and copy the Public folders on the other Mac. The only folders you can put files into are the Drop Box folders inside users' Public folders.

5. When this dialog box appears, it shows up with your name in it, as shown on the left, below (actually, it shows up with the name of the current user of this computer, which might or might not be you). That's kind of confusing because it makes you think it wants *your* password. It doesn't—you need to enter the user name (either the long name or the short name) and password of the user whose files you want to share.

As explained on the previous page, if you enter the Administrator name and password, you will have access to every file on the entire computer.

Connect to the file server "TheBigG4" as:	**Connect to the file server "TheBigG4" as:**
○ Guest	○ Guest
● Registered User	● Registered User
Name: Robin Williams	Name: john
Password:	Password: ••••••
Options... Cancel **Connect**	Options... Cancel **Connect**

Unless you are a user on the other computer you are trying to connect to, entering your name and password won't get you anywhere.

*Entering the name and password of any user **on the other computer** will get you access to every user's Public folder and Drop Box.*

Connect as Registered User and Administrator

See page 664 for an example of what happens when you connect as a guest or regular user.

6. Let's say you connected to the other Mac as a **Registered User** and you entered the name and password of an **Administrator** on that Mac. You will see the dialog box shown below. In this example, the other Mac has five partitions and one Administrator (john). Double-click on any partition you want to mount on your Mac, or hold down the Command key and select several volumes (partitions), then click OK.

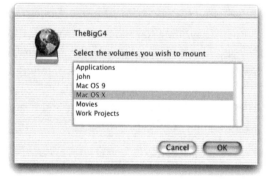

TheBigG4

Select the volumes you wish to mount

Applications
john
Mac OS 9
Mac OS X
Movies
Work Projects

Cancel OK

To connect to more than one volume at once, Command-click on each one you want to connect to, then click OK.

7. After you click the OK button in Step 6, you will see a server icon on your Desktop and/or in your Computer folder, as shown below.

This icon indicates you are successfully connected to the other Macintosh.

8. Double-click the server icon circled above. This will open a window that displays the contents of the other Macintosh. It might *look* like it's one of your own windows, but it's really displaying the files on the other computer. Anything you delete from this window will be immediately deleted from the other Mac.

Ta da! You're sharing files

To make it easier to share files, *press Command N to open a new window. Now you can have this window from the other Mac open, plus a window from your own Mac, and you can drag files back and forth from one to the other. Any files you drag back and forth will be automatically **copied** from one place to the other—not **moved**.*

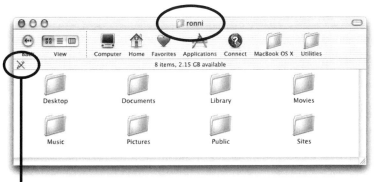

I can't add or delete any files, but I can copy, read, and print anything.

This shows an example of how accessible all files are if you log in to the other Mac as an Administrator. I opened the folder named Users, above, then opened the folder of one of the users, left. I have access to all folders. This can be very handy if you are the Administrator for a school lab or large office, or discouraging if you are a user who thinks your files are safe.

Connect as Guest or Regular User   When you connect as a **guest** or as a **regular user,** you do not have access to the entire computer—you will have access to any or all users on the other Mac, but all you'll be able to see are their Public folders and Drop Boxes.

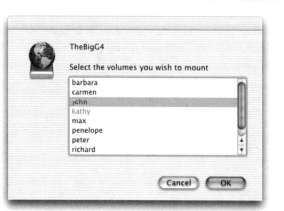

Connect as a guest, or as a registered user with the name and password of a regular user.

You have access to every user on that Mac. Double-click a user name, or Command-click on several users and then click the OK *button.*

You will be able to copy files from any user's Public folder, as shown here. Or you can drop files into any user's Drop Box.

You cannot open the Drop Box (or any other folder on the entire Mac).

Do you **connect** to another Mac **regularly**? You can easily add the password for a Mac into your Keychain so you don't have to type the password each time you want to connect. Then add that server icon to your Favorites folder. Next time you want to connect to that computer, open your Favorites window, double-click the server icon, and you are instantly connected.

Connect with a Double-Click

To add the password to a keychain:

1. Go through the connection process as explained on the previous pages, until you come to the dialog box shown below.

Note: Please see pages 508–516 about Keychain.

Connect to the file server "TheBigG4" as:

○ Guest
● Registered User

Name: | john

Password: | ••••••

(Options...)   (Cancel)   (Connect)

2. Enter the correct user name and password, then click the Options…" button. You'll get the dialog box shown below. Check the box to "Add Password to Keychain." Click OK.

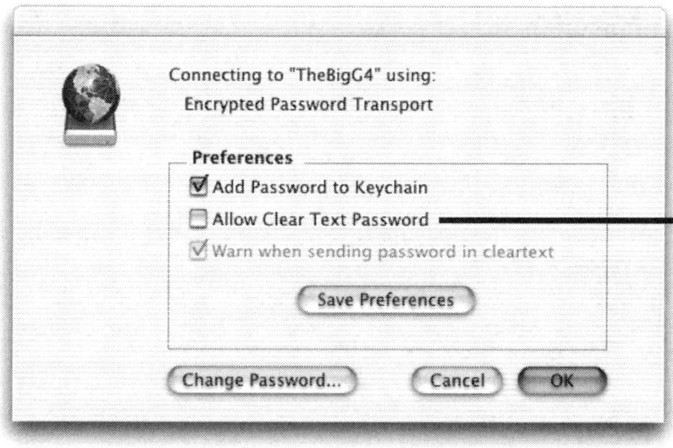

Connecting to "TheBigG4" using:
Encrypted Password Transport

Preferences
☑ Add Password to Keychain
☐ Allow Clear Text Password
☑ Warn when sending password in cleartext

(Save Preferences)

(Change Password...)   (Cancel)   (OK)

Some remote servers cannot accept encrypted passwords. The Mac AFP servers you're working with have no problem with it, so you can uncheck this box for greater secutiry.

—continued

3. After you are connected, drag the server icon up to the Favorites icon in the Toolbar and drop it on the heart. This will make an alias in the Favorites folder, as shown below.

Here you see aliases to three different Macs.

4. Now whenever you want to connect to that Mac, open the Favorites folder and double-click on the alias. The other Mac will be instantly mounted in your hard disk, and its window will open.

You can even do this with remote servers. The icon shown above, "Kate at Production," is the FTP site at Peachpit Press in Berkeley, California. I double-click that icon here in Santa Fe, New Mexico, and I am instantly connected with Kate's computer in Berkeley. Then I just drag my files into her folder and she's got 'em. Amazing.

Delete the Keychain Access password

Keychain Access

You can **delete the Keychain Access** password, if you like, to prevent easy access to the other Mac.

1. Click on the Applications icon in the Toolbar to open the Applications folder.

2. Double-click the Utilities folder.

3. Double-click the Keychain Access icon to get the window shown below.

4. Select the keychain for the connection you want to delete, then click the Remove button. You must restart your Mac before this takes effect.

Name	Kind	Date Created	Date Modified
AirPort studio connection	application password	11/20/01	11/20/01
ftp.peachpit.com	AppleShare password	11/20/01	11/20/01
iTools	iTools password	10/3/01	10/3/01
John's Big One	AppleShare password	11/20/01	11/20/01
LANB password	application password	11/9/01	11/9/01
mail.marysidney.com	Internet password	11/13/01	11/13/01
smtp.mac.com	Internet password	10/9/01	10/9/01
TheBigG4	AppleShare password	11/28/01	11/28/01

Keychain: "robin" on disk "Mac OS X"
8 items
Lock

Add...   Get Info   Remove

Actually, you can share files with Macs running System 8.x, as well as up through Mac OS 9.2. Do the following four steps on the Mac running OS 9 (or earlier), then connect as usual from your Mac OS X machine. This is a great way to transfer files from your older Mac to your new one.

Share Mac OS 9 Files with Mac OS X

1. Set up File Sharing in Mac OS 9:

a. Go to the Apple menu, slide down to "Control Panels," and choose "File Sharing."

b. Follow each of the callouts below to set up File Sharing properly.

Make sure the Start/Stop pane is visible: Click on this tab.

Enter your name, password, and a computer name so you'll recognize this Mac. If the password is already filled in and you don't know what it is, replace it by typing a new one (very secure, huh?).

If this button says "Start," click it to start file sharing. (If it says "Stop," leave it alone because that means file sharing is already turned on.)

File Sharing

Start/Stop / Activity Monitor / Users & Groups

Network Identity

Owner Name: Scarlett Williams
Owner Password: ••••••••
Computer Name: Scarlett's Computer
IP Address: 192.168.254.82

File Sharing on

Stop — Status
Click Stop to turn off file sharing. This prevents other users from accessing shared folders.

☑ Enable File Sharing clients to connect over TCP/IP

Program Linking off

Start — Status
Click Start to turn on program linking. This allows other users to link to shared programs.

☐ Enable Program Linking clients to connect over TCP/IP

Check this box to enable file sharing over TCP/IP.

Make note of this IP Address (write it down).

—continued

2. Set up File Sharing User in Mac OS 9:

   a. If the File Sharing control panel is not already open, go to the Apple menu, slide down to "Control Panels," and choose "File Sharing."

   b. Click the "Users & Groups" tab.

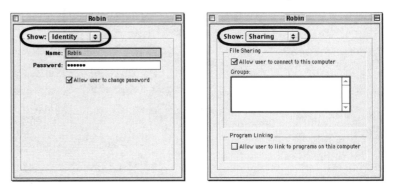

Click here to close.

   c. Click the button, "New User."

   d. In the "Identity" pane, shown below, type in a name and password. Write down this name and password on a piece of paper!

   e. From the "Show" menu, choose "Sharing," and make sure the box is checked to "Allow user to connect to this computer."

   f. Click the close box to put this little dialog box away.

   g. Click the close box to put the File Sharing control panel away.

3. Set up File Sharing Info in Mac OS 9:

a. Click once on the hard disk icon that you want to share files from.

b. Press Command I, or go to the File menu, choose "Get Info," then choose "Sharing."

c. If you do not see "Sharing" in the "Show" pop-up menu in the Get Info box, as circled below, choose "Sharing" from that menu.

Click here to close.

d. Check the box to "Share this item and its contents."

e. In the "User/Group" pop-up menu, choose the name of the user you created in Step 2.

f. In the "Privilege" column, choose the "Read & Write" icon (the eyeglasses and pencil).

g. Close the Get Info box.

4. Set up AppleTalk Ethernet in Mac OS 9:

a. Go to the Apple menu, slide down to "Control Panels," and choose "AppleTalk."

b. In the "Connect via" pop-up menu, choose "Ethernet."

c. Close the AppleTalk control panel. If you are asked to save changes, click "Yes."

Connect and share files Okay, now that the OS 9 Mac is ready, go to the OS X machine, connect to the other Mac, and share files.

To connect to the Mac OS 9 machine and share files:

1. In the OS X Mac Finder, go to the Go menu and choose "Connect to Server…." (If you don't see the Go menu, click on the Desktop.)

2. In the "Connect to Server" dialog box, in the left pane, click either "AppleTalk" or "Local Network." Depending on how your computers are networked, the other Mac will be in one of these lists.

3. In the pane on the right side, the name of the OS 9 Mac will appear. Single-click the name, then click the "Connect" button, or double-click the computer name.

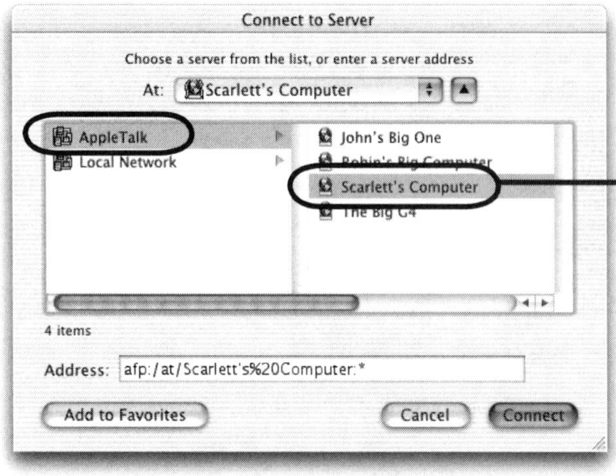

When you choose the computer name here, that name automatically appears in the "At" pop-up menu above, and its address appears in the "Address" field below.

When the Address field shows the name of a computer, it puts "%20" in place of every empty space. Don't let that worry you in this case.

4. You'll get the dialog box shown below. Enter the name and password that you set up as a User on the OS 9 machine, in Step 2 on page 668. The click the Connect button.

—continued

5. You'll get the dialog box shown below. Select a hard disk, then click the OK button. If there is more than one partition on the other Mac and you previously set up sharing privileges in the Get Info box for the others, you'll see those listed here as well.

6. On your Desktop and/or in your Computer window, you'll see a network icon for the disk you selected above. Double-click that icon to open the hard disk on the other computer.

7. The window that opens displays the files on the Mac OS 9 computer. To make it easier to copy these files from this computer to your OS X machine, press Command N to open another window. Now you can drag files from one window to the other, between computers.

It's no easy task to keep track of which windows are on which machine!

Don't open any applications from the window of the other Mac because you will actually be working on the other machine at that point, which might affect the person using it.

Disconnect

This is the contextual menu to eject a selected server.

Disconnect from any connected servers in the same ways you disconnect from any other hard disk.

- ▼ **Either** drag the server icon to the Trash basket.
- ▼ **Or** select the server icon. Go to the File menu and choose "Eject."
- ▼ **Or** select the server icon and press Command E for Eject.
- ▼ **Or** Control-click on a server icon to get the contextual menu; choose "Eject."

Other Tips

Here are a couple of **extra tips** to make networking easier.

- ▼ Put a "Connect" icon in your Toolbar; see pages 80–81 about customizing the Toolbar. Drag the Connect icon up to the Toolbar.

- ▼ Once you are connected, drag the server icon up to the Finder window Toolbar and drop it on the Favorites icon. Now that server is in the Favorites menu (which is in the Go menu), in your Open and Save As dialog boxes, and in the Favorites window. Just double-click it to connect. If you added the user name and password to your Keychain, as explained on page 665, you'll go straight to the server with just that double-click.

- ▼ Remember that Location you created on pages 659–660? Well, you can use the Location menu under the Apple to switch locations, as shown below.

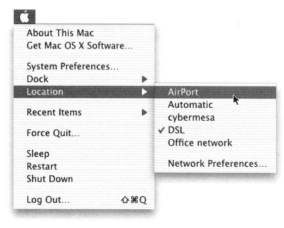

*Well, this is **supposed** to switch your locations, but I have found that it often neglects to switch the actual connection from, say, the built-in modem to the built-in Ethernet. So if you can't connect after changing Locations, choose "Network Preferences..." to check the "Show" menu setting.*

Sharing Files over the Internet

Built into your Mac are a number of ways to **share files with anyone in the world,** or with yourself when you are away from your own Mac. You can put up to twenty megabytes of stuff in your iDisk that other iTools members can pick up, or that you can access from a remote location. Or you can set up a web page with the HomePage feature in iTools that lets anyone, even Windows users, access certain files in your iDisk. You can even turn on FTP access on your Mac and people can download files from your Mac using a web browser, and they can download or upload files to you with an FTP program, such as Fetch.

You can also turn on "Web Sharing" on your Mac so your friends, family, and coworkers can view web pages that you store in your Sites folder. Oh, it's all so amazing.

Get an iDisk

With a free **iTools** account, you get twenty megabytes of free disk space, called **iDisk,** on Apple's server. In this space you can store files for your own safekeeping, or upload files so others can download them. You might want to put vacation photos in your iDisk so your family, friends, and coworkers can download them and you don't have to email them as attachments. Or post your annual holiday letter as a PDF file so if someone actually wants to read it, they can go get it (now, I'm teasing—I personally find holiday letters delightful).

iDisk is a great tool for getting files back and forth across the Internet without the inconvenience of waiting for a large attachment to download along with the rest of your email. (I have set my email program to refuse any file over 50K to avoid getting strange, unwanted files—and having to wait for the pleasure.)

If you have a dial-up Internet account, be sure to connect to the Internet before you open your iDisk.

If you signed up for iTools when you first turned on your new Mac or when you installed Mac OS X, then **you already have an iDisk.** Just go to the Go menu and choose "iDisk" to open your iDisk window.

If you don't have an iTools account yet, it's easy to create one, as explained below. This chapter will explain just how to share files using your iDisk, not all the other interesting stuff you can do with iTools—for all of the other details about iDisk and iTools, please see Chapter 33.

To create your iTools account and get your iDisk space:

1. Go to **www.apple.com** and click on the iTools tab.

2. On the iTools web page, click the iDisk icon to get to the "iTools Login" page, shown below.

3. Click the "Sign Up" button to register and assign yourself a **user name** and a **password.**

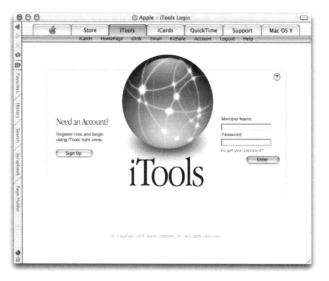

When you **connect to your iDisk** (choose "iDisk" from the Go menu when you're in the Finder, or press Command Option I), you will see a new window on your Desktop, as explained in Chapter 33. This is your iDisk; this window is actually displaying your personal files on Apple's server (that's why everything is a little slow to happen). Although *you* can see all of these folders, the only folder any other iTools member can get into is your Public folder.

Share Files with Your iDisk

To put files into your iDisk Public folder:

Just drag files from your hard disk into the iDisk Public folder (*not* the Public folder that is in your own Home folder!). Make sure the window you are dragging into has an iDisk icon in the title bar.

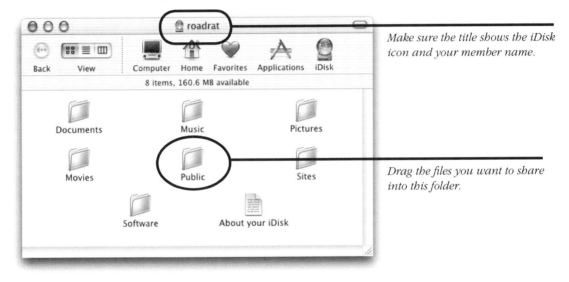

Make sure the title shows the iDisk icon and your member name.

Drag the files you want to share into this folder.

Other iTools members can access files that you put in your iDisk Public folder, *if* they have your iTools member name (they don't need to know your password). Or you can open anyone else's Public folder if you have *their* iTools member name.

To take files out of someone else's iDisk Public folder:

1. Go to www.apple.com and click on the iTools tab.

2. Click on the iDisk icon.

3. Log in with *your* member name and password, not the member name of the person whose Public folder you want to access.

—continued

4. You'll get the web page shown below. Enter the account name of an iTools member in the "Open Public Folder" text field, then click the "Open Public Folder" button.

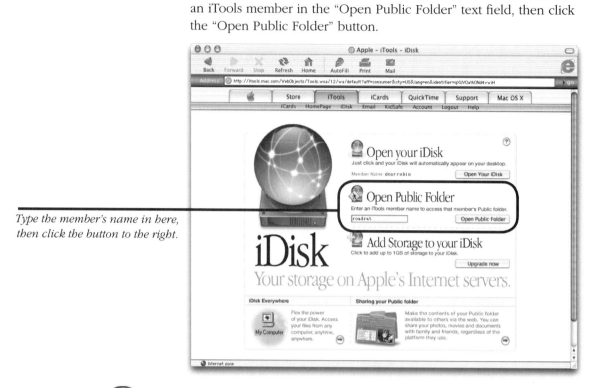

Type the member's name in here, then click the button to the right.

Public

5. After a minute or two (longer on a telephone modem connection), an icon, shown to the left, will appear on your Desktop and/or in your Computer window. Double-click the icon to open the Public folder as a window on your Desktop, as shown below.

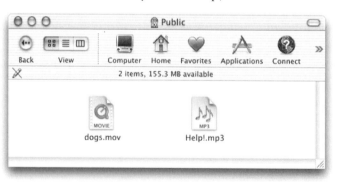

6. When the member's Public folder opens, drag a file from their Public folder to your Desktop. Wow.

If you need to grab files from another iTools member's iDisk regularly, there **iDisk tips**
are several things you can do to make it fast and convenient

To set up a direct connection:

1. From the Go menu choose "Connect to Server…"

2. Enter the address of the iDisk you want to access. A Public
   folder address on iDisk is always http://idisk.mac.com/username/Public
   where "username" is the iTools member's user name. Be sure to use
   caps and lowercase as shown here, and make sure there are no extra
   spaces at the end of the address.

3. Click the "Connect" button. The Public iDisk folder icon will appear
   on your Desktop and/or in your Computer window.

To make a Favorite of a Public folder:

1. Connect to the Public folder of the other member as usual.

2. When the iDisk Public folder icon appears on your Mac,
   drag it to the Toolbar in any Finder window and drop it
   on the Favorites icon.

3. Open the Favorites window (click on the Favorites icon in the
   Toolbar, or press Command Option F).

4. Rename the iDisk alias so you can easily identify the iTools member
   to whom it belongs, as shown to the right.

roadrat

Now in the Go menu this connection will appear under "Favorites," where
you can select it. It's also in your Favorites folder, as shown below, where
you can double-click it. Open the Public folder with this Favorite and you
won't even need to open a browser at all.

*If you want to provide access
to anyone (not just Mac iTools
members), use HomePage to
set up a file sharing page that
allows anyone on the Internet
to download files that are in
your iDisk Public folder. See
the following pages.*

File Sharing with HomePage

You can create a **web page for sharing** your photos, movies, and documents over the Internet that everyone, regardless of platform, can access. They don't even need to be iTools members. Use the HomePage feature of iTools; step-by-step directions are on pages 587–592.

To create a file-sharing web page:

1. Put the files you want to share in your iDisk Public folder, as explained on page 675. You can put other folders inside of the Public folder, and visitors can open each one separately and download individual files.

2. Log in to your iTools page and click the HomePage icon. You'll see a page similar to the one shown below.

3. Click the File Sharing tab in the section labeled "Start by selecing a theme below" on the HomePage web page.

4. Select a theme for the design of the file sharing page.

5. After the "My iDisk" page opens for review, click the "Edit" button to open an editable version of the page. Enter appropriate text into the available text fields.

6. Any files and folders that you've dragged to the Public folder of your
iDisk will show in the list on the graphical folder, shown below.

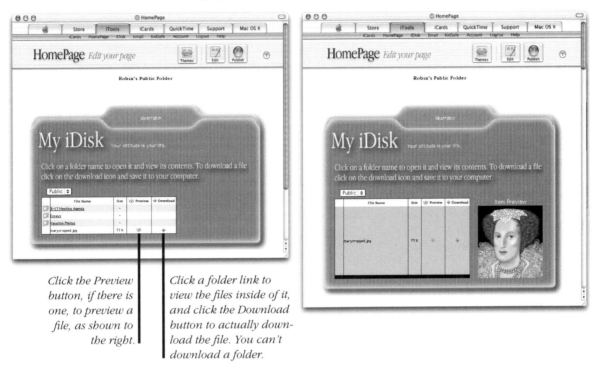

*Click the Preview
button, if there is
one, to preview a
file, as shown to
the right.*

*Click a folder link to
view the files inside of it,
and click the Download
button to actually down-
load the file. You can't
download a folder.*

7. See the information in Chapter 33 (pages 590–592) about publishing
this web page. If you created a site with other pages, this file
sharing page will be a link in the main navigation. You can edit
the name of that link.

Visitors to your web site can navigate to the page you've set up as
your file sharing page, select a file from the list of downloadable
files, then click the "Download" arrow to download the file.

The address to your web site created and published with iTools HomePage
is http://homepage.mac.com/username (insert your user name).

Web Sharing

Another way you can share files is through the Web Sharing feature on your Mac: In a shared folder on your hard disk you can place web pages, web sites, files, and folders. From any computer, someone can use a web browser to access these special shared folders on your Mac. Depending on the quality and speed of your Internet connection, Web Sharing can function as a local area network or as an easy way to share files across the Internet or within a corporate intranet.

Web Sharing does *not* provide you with the ability to remotely upload files to a shared folder. To upload files to your computer from somewhere else, use FTP access, as explained on pages 684–685, or iDisk, as explained on pages 675–677.

First, get this information

There are **two pieces of information** you need to have before you can share this way: your short user name and your computer's IP address.

▼ Your **short user name** is not your iTools member name. It is the name that you chose when you first set up your Mac, or when you established yourself as a new user.

If you don't remember what your short name is, go to System Preferences and click the User icon. Select your name in the User list, then click the "Edit User…" button. You'll see your short name.

▼ Your **computer's IP address** is shown in the Sharing preferences: Go to System Preferences and click the Sharing icon. In the "File & Web" pane, as shown below, you see the IP address.*

*If you have a **broadband connection,** this number is usually the same.*

But if you have a **dial-up telephone modem connection, **this number will change everytime you connect to the Internet!** This means if you want to do Web Sharing, you must first connect to the Internet, then look here and find out what the IP address is while you are connected, and tell the person you want to share with what that number is. That IP address will only be good for that Web Sharing session until you disconnect.*

There are **two separate folders** on your hard drive that are available for Web Sharing. One is available to all users, the **Sites folder;** every user can Web Share their own files. The other folder can only be modified (files added or deleted) by an Administrator of that particular computer, the **Documents** folder deep inside the main Library folder. You can put documents, movies, photos, or entire folders full of stuff that you want to share in either of these folders.

Then put files in your Web Sharing folder

▼ **Sites folder:** This is the one every user will see in their own Home folder. Every user on the machine can put files into their own Sites folder for sharing with others.

When Web Sharing is on, you (or anyone) can access files in the Sites folder with a web browser. You just type in:

http://your.computer.address/~yourusername/

Use your short user name, the IP address of your Mac, and be sure to include the ending slash (/).

▼ **WebServer Documents folder:** Only Administrators can modify the contents of this folder for Web Sharing.

To find this folder, open your Home folder, then open your Library folder, then open the WebServer folder, then open the Documents folder (see the illustration below). This folder is full of files, but you can throw them all away (or copy them somewhere, if that makes you feel better), then replace them with your own.

When Web Sharing is on, you (or anyone) can access files in the WebServer Documents folder with a web browser. You just type in:

http://your.computer.address/

Your computer address, of course, is the IP address of your Mac.

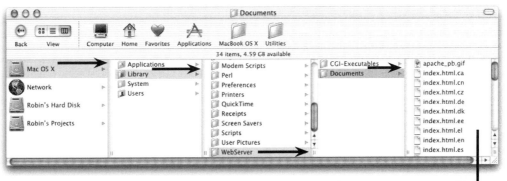

As an Administrator, you can safely delete everything in this folder and replace it with your own files.

Then turn on Web Sharing
Only an Administrator can turn Web Sharing on or off, so if you want regular users to be able to Web Share, you must turn it on before they log in.

To turn on Web Sharing, open System Preferences and click "Sharing." In the "File & Web" pane (as shown on page 680) click the "Start" button to turn Web Sharing on.

Access the shared folder
To access the shared folder from another computer, open the current version of Internet Explorer. In the Address field, type **http://** followed by the IP address of the computer you want to access, plus the user name, as explained on the previous page and as shown below.

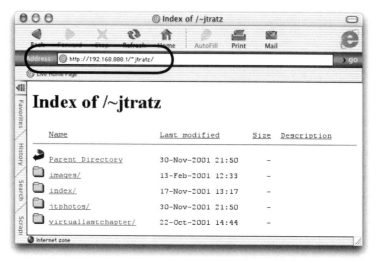

When you access another computer's folder through Web Sharing, a web page opens with a list view of the contents of the Sites folder (in this case), as shown above. **Click on a folder to see a list of its contents.** If you click on a file name that is a link to a web page or web site, you can view it in the browser just as you would any web site.

To open a file or to download it, click on the file name link. If the computer you're using knows which application to use, the file will usually open automatically. If the file you click on is an MP3 music file or a QuickTime movie, your Mac will probably recognize it and open the file with QuickTime or iTunes.

You can also Control-click on the link, then from the contextual menu that appears, as shown to the left, choose "Download Link to Disk." This will prevent the Mac from automatically trying to open the file.

If the file on the web page does not open automatically when you click on its link, an "Unhandled File Type" window opens with several options, as shown below. You can probably find an application to open the file later, so click "Save File As…" to open the standard Save As dialog box where you can give the file a name and store it on your hard disk.

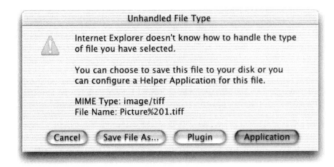

If you clicked the "Application" button in the window shown above, you'll get the standard Open dialog box from which to choose an application to open the file with. If there's not an appropriate application available, click "Cancel" and go back to the "Save File As…" button to download the file to your computer.

Your Mac as an FTP Server

FTP (File Transfer Protocol) is a method of allowing access to a computer for either uploading or downloading files. Mac OS X includes FTP server software so you can do this from home or any small office.

Over the Internet, you can access files stored in a user's Home folder, no matter where in the world you are. To *download* files, a web browser is sufficient. To *upload* files to an FTP-enabled Mac, use an FTP "client," such as the popular shareware Fetch. Fetch can also download files, as explained on the following pages.

Turn on FTP access

To enable FTP file sharing, you need to **turn on FTP access.** The person logging in to your Mac needs to know your current **IP address,** as well as the **user name and password** of the person who owns the files they want to access.

On the Mac that you want to make accessible, open System Preferences and choose "Sharing," as shown below. In the "File & Web" pane, check the box to "Allow FTP access."

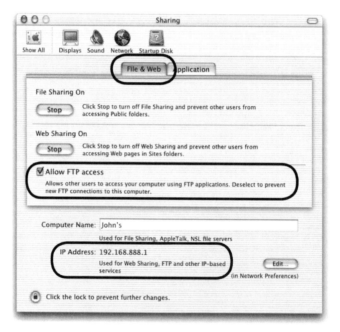

Tip: You don't have to be across town or out of the country to take advantage of FTP sharing. If you have multiple Macs in your office that are not networked, you can use FTP sharing to transfer files between computers in the office. Make sure you trust anyone to whom you give FTP access—they'll have access to your entire computer when "Allow FTP access" is turned on.

Note the "IP Address" at the bottom of the pane. That is the Internet Protocol address for this computer. The IP number is necessary to access a computer from the Internet.

▼ If you have a full-time **broadband** connection to the Internet, this number stays fairly constant. You can take the number with you to another computer or give it to someone else so files can be shared.

▼ If you have a **telephone dial-up** connection, this number will change every time you connect. So connect first, then make note of the IP address. The FTP session will only last until you disconnect.

With an **FTP client** such as Fetch, not only can you download files from an FTP-enabled Mac, you can also upload files over the Internet from another computer. You can download Fetch from **www.FetchSoftworks.com**. It's inexpensive ($25 at the moment) and indispensable.

To access an FTP-enabled Mac using Fetch:

1. Double-click the Fetch icon to open the application.

2. Enter the IP address into the "Host" field.

3. In the "User ID" field, type the user name for the account whose Home folder you want to access.

4. In the "Password" field, enter that User's account password.

5. Click OK.

Fetch 4.0.1

This is the Fetch application icon.

This is the IP address, user name, and password of the Mac that has FTP access turned on.

If you choose to add this to your Keychain, the next time you connect you won't see this dialog box at all—you'll get straight in (assuming the IP address hasn't changed).

Fetch opens a window that shows the folders and files on the other computer, as shown below.

Click the little triangles to hide or show this status bar on the right.

To open a folder, double-click its icon. If you navigate deep into the folder structure and want to return, click the pop-down menu at the top of the window to access the folder hierarchy.

To download a file, find the file in the Fetch window, then drag it to your Desktop. Or select a file with a single-click and use the "Get…" button.

To upload a file or folder, in the Fetch window navigate to the folder in which you want to put a file, then drag the file from your Desktop into the Fetch window. Or click the "Put Files…" button to find a file on your Mac that you want to upload.

Use a web browser for FTP access

With a current web browser, you can go to the FTP site and download files; you cannot upload files through the browser.

Read the information on page 684 and make sure you have those three pieces of data: the current IP address, the user name, and the password (not *your* user name and password, but the user name and password of the person whose Home folder you are going to access with FTP).

To access an FTP-enabled Mac using a web browser:

1. On another computer, open a web browser.
2. In the Address field, type **ftp://** and then the IP address, as shown below.
3. Hit the Return key or Enter key, or click the browser's Go button.

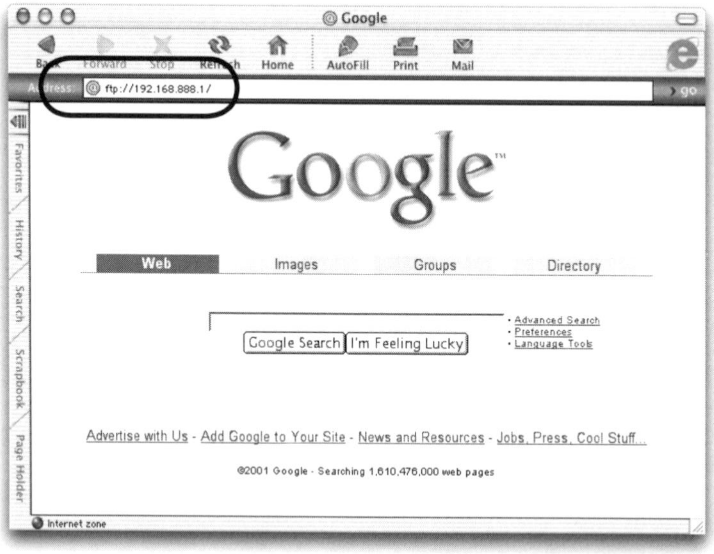

Only the most current web browsers will do this. If you use a browser and it doesn't work, try another browser.

4. In the login dialog box that appears, as shown below, enter the User ID (short name) and password of the person whose Home folder you want to access. You can only access and share files in accounts for which you know the user name and password.

You don't need to enter anything in the "Account" field.

If you check "Remember Password," you won't have to enter it next time.

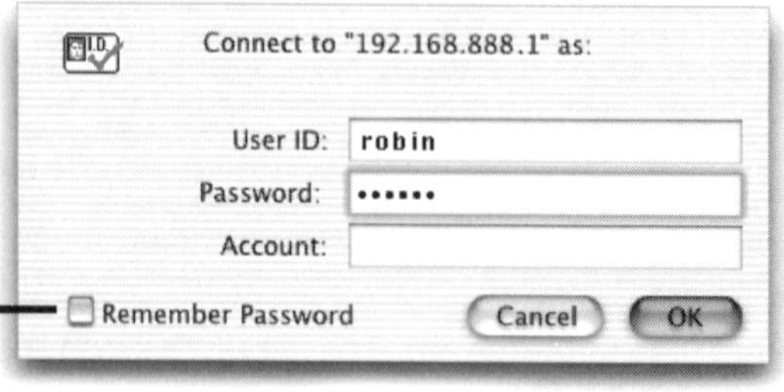

5. A web page containing the folders and files that belong to the targeted user opens in the browser, as shown below. Click on a folder (identified in the "Kind" column) to open another web page that lists the Folder contents.

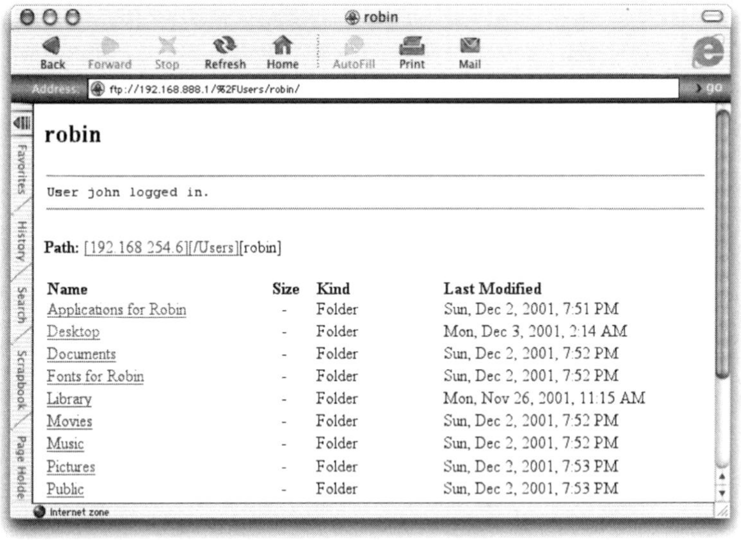

To download a file, click on it.

If an "Unhandled File Type" dialog opens, click "Save File As…" to open the standard Save As dialog box in which to enter a file name and choose a location, then click "Save."

Or Control-click on a file to download it: From the contextual menu that appears, choose "Download Link to Disk." In the "Save" dialog that opens, enter a file name and choose a location in which to save the file.

Security When you enable file sharing over the Internet with a broadband connection, you are opening your Mac up to **potential security risks.** To help
protect yourself, follow these simple guidelines.

▼ If you have multiple users, don't assign Administrator status
unnecessarily. In fact, if you want one extra step of protection,
create yourself a non-Admin user account and use it regularly,
even if you are the only user. Only log on as the Administrator
when you need to install software or change system-wide settings.

▼ Sharing files through your iDisk and HomePage is quite safe since
no one gets anywhere near your Mac—the files are all on the Apple
server.

▼ General file sharing as explained in Chapters 35 and 36 is relatively
safe. Just be sure to assign the privileges appropriately.

▼ Web sharing is fairly safe as well because there are no passwords
that can be taken, and you're only exposing one folder on your Mac.
Just make sure you don't put any files into the Sites folder or Web
Sharing Documents folder that you don't want to share. You can
assign few or no privileges (explained in Chapter 35) to the Sites
folders to even further limit access to them.

▼ Enabling FTP access is also rather risky because passwords are not
encrypted as they go through the network. Make sure every user has
a safe and different password, and uncheck the "Allow FTP access"
box except when you need it.

▼ The Remote Login feature is the riskiest form of file sharing because
it allows users to connect to your Mac through a terminal emulator
(which years ago I dubbed the "terminator emulator"). I didn't even
explain how to do it in this chapter.

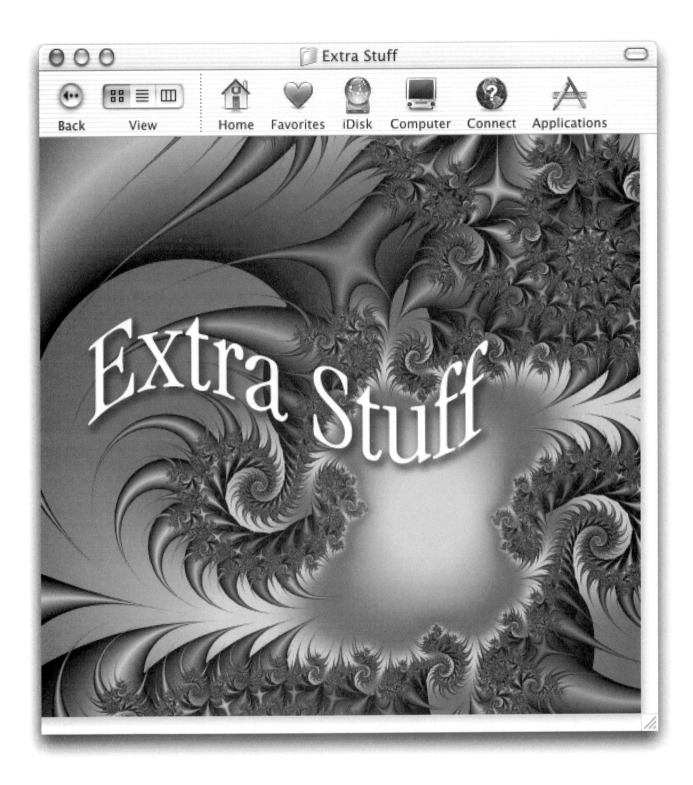

Ports and Peripherals

38

This chapter describes those places on the back or side of your computer where you plug things in **(ports)** and the things you plug into them **(peripherals).** You can spend years on your Mac without knowing the information in this chapter because one of the greatest things about the Mac is that if a cable fits into a port, it's the right match. It's not possible to plug something into the wrong place. So you don't really have to know anything about the back of your computer—it it fits, plug it in and move on. But when you get to the point where you want to know the difference between a FireWire port and a USB port and a serial port, then dive into this short chapter.

What is a Peripheral?

A **peripheral** is any item (or "device") that is outside of the main computer box, but attached to it. Your monitor (except for iMacs) is actually a peripheral device, and so are your mouse, keyboard, and printer. Scanners, many CD writers, and external hard disks are peripherals. Devices that are internal (built in) on some machines might be external devices, or peripherals, on another. For instance, I have a little, lightweight PowerBook that has no built-in Zip drive, but it has an external Zip drive that I can attach when I need it, so that Zip drive is a peripheral. Many computers have built-in modems, others use modems as peripheral devices.

The main computer box is often called a CPU, although the CPU itself is actually a tiny chip in the middle of the main board (the motherboard) inside the box. So a CPU is not a peripheral. You might install a *card* (plastic board with circuitry on it) inside of your computer to expand its capabilities, such as a video card or a modem card. Some people consider that the devices on those cards are also peripherals because they are added on, even though they are in the computer box. (But isn't "internal peripheral" an oxymoron?)

What is a Port?

A **port** is a socket, a kind of receptacle, on the back (or side, as on the iMac) of a computer or on the backs of peripheral devices. The port is where you connect the peripheral device. A port is very different from a regular socket like electrical sockets in the wall, in that information goes both ways through a port. A wall socket sends power in only one direction—to a device. A port sends information back and forth between the computer and the device.

There are lots of different kinds of ports, and peripherals are made to match a certain port type. For instance, you might have *USB* ports, to which you can only connect USB devices, such as *USB* printers. If you have *serial* ports, you'll connect *serial* printers.

The cables that connect peripherals to the CPU (or to another peripheral) have **connectors** on the ends. The connectors match the ports. On a Mac, if the connector matches the port, it works. You can't plug a connector into the wrong port.

On pages 694–697 are pictures of all these ports so you'll know exactly what you have (or don't have).

What is a Connector?

Connectors are the parts on the ends of the cables that actually make the connection to the other device. The connector is the part that tells you what kind of cable it is—an Ethernet cable has a very different connector from a serial cable, which is very different from a USB cable (as illustrated on the following pages).

Every connector is either **male or female;** take one look and you can guess why. The male or female shape is a very important identifying feature. When you start connecting lots of things together (like to project a presentation from the computer to a large wall screen), you will find yourself looking for either a male or female connector.

Another identifying feature of connectors are the **pins,** or slender metal prongs on the male versions (not all connectors have pins). The number of pins is particularly useful in describing what you need. For instance, I once needed a cable for a video card that I installed in my computer. I didn't know exactly what kind of cable I needed, so I counted the little pin holes and told the guy I needed a 15-pin connector and he thought I knew what I was talking about.

The **shape** is important. Some connectors are long and skinny, short and fat, rectangular or round, etc. Many connectors have identifying symbols that match the symbol on the port. On the next few pages are illustrations of the most common symbols that identify both the connectors and the ports.

What is a Slot?

On the back of your computer (not an iMac or laptop) you might see some larger, rectangular pieces that look like metal covers to openings. They are. Those are your **expansion slots;** the more slots you have, the more "expand-ability" your computer has.

You might buy an add-on like a video card for a second monitor. The card (also called a *board* or an *adapter*) is a flat, plastic piece with circuitry all over it and a port on one end. You open your computer box, and there are slots in the motherboard (the main board that runs the computer; of course it's a mother) where you stick this card in, usually perpendicular to the motherboard. You pop that rectangular metal piece out of the opening in the back of the Mac, and the port sticks out that end. Thus when you close the computer box, you have another port to which you can attach another peripheral.

You might get a game card, a modem card, a video card with extra VRAM (video RAM) just for your monitor, or other sorts of boards to expand the capability of your Mac.

Ethernet Ports

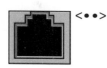

This is what an RJ45 Ethernet port looks like, and the symbol that identifies it.

This is the port for an internal modem, and the symbol that identifies it. Don't get the modem port confused with the larger Ethernet port.

Ethernet (pronounced *eether-net*) is the most common *networking* system for local area networks (LANs), which means the computers that are connected together are close enough to be connected with cables (as opposed to a wide area network, a WAN). All newer Macs, including all iMacs, have Ethernet ports, which look like large phone jacks. You can use Ethernet even in your home or small office to connect several computers so you can send files back and forth (see Chapter 36).

Your printer might have an Ethernet port, in which case you can send data to the printer much faster than through the serial port. Even if it doesn't have an actual Ethernet port, you can get adapters for some printers so you can add the printer to your Ethernet network. In my office we use EtherMac iPrint Adapters from Farallon to network our good ol' workhorses—seven-year-old Apple LaserWriters.

You might also have a **modem port** for your *internal* modem, which looks exactly like an RJ11 phone jack (because it is), so don't get it confused with the Ethernet port. The Ethernet port is larger than the internal modem port.

If your modem is an external box, you'll plug its cable into the serial modem port, which is illustrated on page 697.

AAUI Ports

This is what an AAUI port looks like, and the symbol that identifies it.

The **AAUI port** (which stands for Apple Adapter Unit Interface) takes a variety of adapters for different networking systems, but the symbol for its port is the same as the symbol for an Ethernet port because Ethernet has become the most commonly used local area network. As explained in Chapter 36, you can get an Ethernet adapter for this port, called a transceiver, so you can connect this computer to one that has an actual Ethernet port.

The **USB ports** are on Macs built since late 1998. USB stands for Universal Serial Bus, which replaces both the Apple Desktop Bus and the serial ports, as described on page 697. With USB, input devices (like mice and keyboards) as well as scanners, printers, Zip drives, and other devices can all connect into the same ports.

You can't daisy chain USB devices, like you can the SCSI devices mentioned on page 698, but you can buy a **hub** (shown to the right). The hub connects into one of the USB ports on the Mac, and several devices can plug into the hub. You can connect another hub to the first one, and so on, so you can supposedly connect up to 127 USB devices to one Macintosh. I don't know why you would, but you could.

Also check the base of your monitor—you might find USB ports there, which is a great convenience.

One of the greatest things about USB devices is that you can **hot swap** them; that is, you can connect and disconnect devices such as keyboards, mice, Zip drives, printers, or scanners without having to shut down the computer like you do with SCSI, serial, and even ADB devices. Just don't swap devices while they're doing something, like copying to a Zip or scanning a photo or printing.

USB Ports

This drawing shows two USB ports and the symbol that identifies USB.

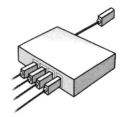

This is a USB hub. The one connector goes into the computer's port, and the other connectors lead to extra devices.

FireWire is Apple's trademarked version of the standard called IEEE 1394. It's a high-performance serial bus (see the description of a bus in the ADB explanation on page 697) for connecting up to 63 devices through one port on your Mac. FireWire is only built into the newer Macs, like the 1999 blue-and-white G3s and up. Many iMacs and laptops have FireWire ports.

The big deal about FireWire is this: It's extremely fast; you can connect 63 devices in any which way you like, such as in a star or tree pattern, and up to 16 in a single chain; you can hot swap them in and out without having to turn off the computer; they connect with a simple snap-in cable; and there's no termination necessary (see the SCSI explanation for termination, if you care). FireWire replaces the serial connection.

You can connect a vast array of consumer electronics to FireWire, such as digital cameras, video tapes, and camcorders, as well as DVD (digital video disk), plus hard disks, optical disks, and printers.

You might hear the FireWire ports called IEEE, but IEEE actually stands for the professional society, Institute of Electrical and Electronics Engineers, and the IEEE is a standard they developed. For instance, the Ethernet standard is IEEE 802.3.

FireWire Ports

This symbol identifies a FireWire port.

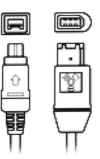

These are the two ends of a FireWire cable.

PCI Bus and Slots

PCI (Peripheral Component Interconnect) is yet another **bus** system. A bus is a system of hardware, software, and wiring that lets different parts of your computer communicate with each other. There are different kinds of buses, and PCI is focused on the expansion slots, which are described on page 693. PCI is now installed on most desktop computers, so if your computer was built in 1998 or later, it has PCI (except if it's an iMac—there is no PCI in an iMac). If your machine doesn't have PCI, it has what's called NuBus, Apple's prior technology.

When you read the specifications for a computer, it often brags about how many PCI slots it has. The more, the better if you plan to expand.

PC Slots and PC Cards

Most laptop computers, as well as other devices like digital cameras, have **PC slots** into which you slip **PC cards.** You might have heard these slots and cards referred to as PCMCIA, but that term is now limited to the association itself (the Personal Computer Memory Card International Association) and the cards and slots are simply called PC cards and slots.

PC cards are really little, as small as credit cards or half a stick of gum. There are a variety of PC cards for a variety of purposes. You can get cards for a cellular phone interface, Ethernet, global positioning system, hard drive, joystick, memory, modem, sound input and output, video capture, and much more. Cards that contain TV tuners, video teleconferencing, AM/FM radio tuners, and even CPUs (the CPU is the powerful chip that runs the entire computer) are available or in the works.

Unlike expansion slots, as explained on page 693, PC slots are accessible from the outside of the computer; like expansion slots, the purpose is to allow expanded capabilities. The slot, or socket, typically has a little flapping door covering the empty space where you slip in the card. Peek inside—you might actually have two sockets that you can use for two different cards.

None of the iMacs, iBooks, blue-and-white G3s, G4s, or newer machines have ADB ports or serial ports—Apple switched over to a new system, the Universal Serial Bus, which replaces both ADB and serial (below). Also, there are no SCSI connections on newer Macs. So unless you have an older Mac, **skip these two pages.**

Read this note before you take time to read this page

ADB Ports

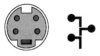

This is what an ADB port looks like, and the symbol that identifies it.

ADB stands for Apple Desktop Bus. A *bus* is a system of hardware, software, and wiring that lets all the different parts of your computer communicate with each other. There are different kinds of buses, and the ADB is specifically for *input devices.* An input device includes those items you input information into the computer with, such as a keyboard, mouse, trackball, joystick, or drawing tablet.

So most commonly, the ADB ports are where you connect your keyboard and mouse. Many Macs have only one ADB port on the back of the machine, plus one or two ADB ports on the keyboard, so you plug the keyboard into the port on the back of the computer box and then plug the mouse into the keyboard.

Serial Ports
Printer and external modem ports

This is what a serial port looks like (above), and the symbols that identify the two on your Mac (below).

A **serial port** is the little round one that looks similar to the ADB port, but it has more holes (to match the pins on the connector). There are two data wires in a serial cable, so the port can send and receive information at the same time.

There are usually two serial ports on the back of older Macs—one labeled with a little picture of a printer, and the other with a picture of a telephone. Although you can use either port for either a printer or an external modem cable, the printer port is actually slightly different in that it is the Mac's LocalTalk network port. This just means it's faster and more complex than the modem port, and if possible you should plug your serial printer cable into that one and the serial modem into the other one, although either one will work.

Until recently, almost all printers for the Mac were "serial printers," which means they connected to the serial port. As mentioned above, newer Macs don't have serial ports; they've been replaced with USB (see page 695).

SCSI Ports

This is what a SCSI port on the back of your Mac looks like (above). There are actually several different shapes of SCSI ports, but they are all identified with the symbol below.

SCSI (pronounced scuzzy, not sexy) stands for Small Computer Systems Interface, which is a standard for connecting personal computers to peripheral devices and having them send information to each other.

There is only one SCSI port on a Mac, but there are two on the back of every SCSI device, which are things like scanners, extra hard disks, external CD drives, or CD writers. The ones on the device itself might look different, much larger, from the one on the back of your computer.

You can *daisy chain* up to seven SCSI devices together; that is, you plug one SCSI device directly into the port on the computer, then hook the others to each other. To daisy chain SCSI devices, you need a cable that has two connectors that match the two ports you are plugging into. For instance, a SCSI Zip drive uses the same connector as the Mac on both ends of its cable, but an older scanner might have two larger SCSI ports that are different from the SCSI port on the back of the Mac. So even if the ports on the two connecting devices are different, you can get cables with different connectors on each end.

Each device on the chain has to be pre-set to a different SCSI address. Look on any SCSI device and you'll see a tiny set of changeable numbers—that's the **SCSI address.** And SCSI devices have to be **terminated;** that is, the last device in the chain has to have a little stopper in the second port because the data goes in one port and out the other and gets confused if it finds an empty port. Some manufacturers use *internal termination,* which is great except it can limit the way devices are connected, and you have to *know* that device is internally terminated, which means you have to read the manual and Mac users are famous for not reading manuals (I'm surprised you're even reading this).

SCSI devices are infamous for being unpredictable—sometimes they don't work in one configuration of connections and termination, but they work if you just plug things in differently or if you turn them on in a different order. SCSI devices often refuse to *mount* (when a drive's icon appears on the Desktop, it is mounted), so often that there is a special little utility that most Mac users have called SCSIProbe to force them to mount. If you have SCSI devices, get SCSIProbe from the Internet at **www.download.com** or **www.shareware.com.** You can keep it anywhere on your hard disk—it doesn't have to be in any special folder to work.

Parallel Ports

You Mac doesn't have a **parallel port,** but your printer might. It's a big, horsey-looking port that looks like it came from a PC, which it did; it looks much like the old SCSI port shown above. Parallel ports transfer data through eight wires, so all eight bits in a byte can go through the line at once (in parallel). Sounds like it should be fast, but most parallel ports are not capable of sending and receiving data at the same, which slows them down.

Reformatting & Partitions

Hard disks are usually so huge these days that it is often a good idea to separate one large hard disk into several **partitions.** Each partition then acts like a separate hard disk, or volume—each partition has a separate icon, a separate window, and an individual name.

Using different partitions might also improve the speed of your Mac because it won't have to search the entire hard disk to find your data—it will just search the one partition that your work is stored on.

To create partitions, you have to **reformat** your hard disk. This will entirely destroy every piece of data on your disk, so make sure you back up everything you need before you reformat!

Why Partition? If you have a large hard disk, like over 8 gigabytes, you should think about **partitioning** it (separating it) into several smaller **volumes** (individual hard disks). This makes it easier for your computer to find what it needs, helps prevent files from becoming too fragmented, and can help your computer work faster. If you ever need to recover the data from a bad disk, it can sometimes be less expensive to recover an individual partition than to recover the entire hard disk. Or perhaps you need to install a different operating system such as Virtual PC so you can run Windows applications on your Mac—make a partition specifically for Windows stuff.

Dividing one disk into partitions can also help you keep things organized; you might have one small partition that is just for the operating system and its components, another partition for your applications, and another partition for your projects. Everything will still work together as if it was one big hard disk.

On the Mac I'm using at the moment, I separated the 20 gigabyte drive into three volumes: one for the Mac OS X operating system and applications, one for Mac OS 9 and applications that only work in Classic mode, and one for all my books and other projects.

This is one hard disk partitioned into three separate volumes. Each volume looks and acts like a separate hard disk.

If you open up your Mac and look inside, you'll see a case like this icon inside your Mac—that's your hard disk. It fits in your hand. Amazing.

To partition your disk, you must **reformat** it. To *format* a disk means to prepare it for use; to *reformat* a disk means to wipe everything off the disk and prepare it for a fresh new use. There's no way to partition a disk without reformatting it first.

Once you have partitions, you can erase individual partitions without affecting the data on other volumes. For instance, while I was in the process of working with beta versions of Mac OS X and upgrading them constantly, it worked best to reformat just the one partition I had set aside for Mac OS X.

Sometimes you might need to reformat a disk because things get so screwy on your computer that, as a last resort, you totally reformat and start over from scratch. For instance, on a new iMac DV last year, all sorts of little things were going wrong—I couldn't receive faxes, eventually I couldn't even send faxes, my Zip drive wouldn't always work, sometimes I couldn't shut down, etc. So I backed up everything I had installed (as explained below) and reformatted and reinitialized the entire hard disk. Now everything works beautifully, as it should.

Very important: Reformatting your hard disk will absolutely positively without a doubt destroy every single thing on your entire hard disk and it will be impossible to recover any of it!!! If you have installed any new software or fonts at all or if you have created any new documents, before you reformat you must back them up (make copies of them) onto something like Zip or Jaz disks or onto CDs. If you don't feel comfortable doing that (see pages 170–177), have your power user friend help you. **Do not proceed without first backing up everything.**

Except: All of the software that came on your Mac will be restored at the end of this process, so don't worry about that. But even though the software applications themselves will be restored, any address lists you created in your email program, bookmarks in your browser, etc., will be gone.

You *don't* need to back up any software for which you have the original CD. You *do* need to back up software that you downloaded, especially if you didn't make a backup copy at the time you installed it. It's best, when downloading files, to always save the installer file, rather than the file that appears *after* you install it (as explained on page 306).

If you're not perfectly clear on how to back up your necessary files, please have a friend over to help you, a friend who knows what she's doing!

If you've only had your computer a couple of days and haven't created anything of your own, go ahead and reformat and partition.

Why Reformat?

Tip: If reformatting doesn't fix squirrely problems like these, check your memory chips. Bad memory can make all sorts of weird things happen.

Back up everything you installed or created!!!

Reformat and Partition Your Hard Disk

Disk Utility

This is the Disk Utility that will format and partition disks for you. You can use it to erase a Zip disk or a partition (Disk Utility is in the Utilities folder).

Back up everything before you begin. I cannot be held responsible for any files you lose if you insist on not backing up everything you need! **Proceed at your own risk.**

You cannot reformat the disk that is running the computer, so you have to insert a system CD and let the system on the CD run the computer. What you are about to do is this: You're going to insert a system CD and start up from that CD, reformat the drive (destroying every iota of data on the entire hard disk), then reinstall everything like it was when it came from the factory. Follow these directions:

1. You have a CD called "Mac OS X" or "Mac OS X Install." Put this CD in your Mac.

   You might also have one or more "Software Restore" disks for Mac OS X. Do *not* put the Restore disk in the Mac at this time— make sure you use the Install disk.

2. Wait for the CD to mount (its icon will appear on your Desktop and/or in your Computer window).

3. Go to the Apple menu, choose "Restart," and then *immediately* hold down the letter **C** on the keyboard and keep it down until the Mac starts up from the CD, which is what you want.

4. The Mac thinks you want to install OS X, so it automatically prepares the hard disk for installation and opens the Installer window. That's okay—just ignore it.

5. When you see the first installation window, ignore it and go up to the menu at the top of the screen. From the Installer menu, choose "Open Disk Utility…."

6. The Disk Utility window opens, as shown on the opposite page.

7. Click the "Partition" tab.

8. In the upper-left corner you'll see names that represent two disks, your big hard disk and the CD that started up your Mac. Click once on your hard disk (that would be the larger-sized one, as shown on the opposite page).

9. In the Partition pane, under "Volume Scheme," there is a pop-up menu that says "Current." Click on this menu and choose the number of partitions you want to make. The "Volume Scheme" panel below

the menu will divide itself into equal parts according to the number of partitions you choose.

If you decide later (like in a minute or two) that you want to make **more** partitions, click inside one of these partitions, then click the "Split" button.

If you decide you want **fewer** partitions, click on a partition you want to delete, then click the "Delete" button.

10. Name each partition: Click in a partition box, then in the edit box below "Volume Information," type a name.

The "Format" choice is probably already selected as "Mac OS Extended." That's correct.

Don't worry about the "Size" for now. Just click on each individual partition and name it.

11. Resize the partitions: Press on the dividing line between each partition and drag it up or down. You'll see the actual size reflected in the "Size" box. If you plan to do something like make a lot of movies, you probably want one extra-large partition.

These "names" indicate the hard disk and the CD. They actually indicate the disk sizes, not the names of the disks.

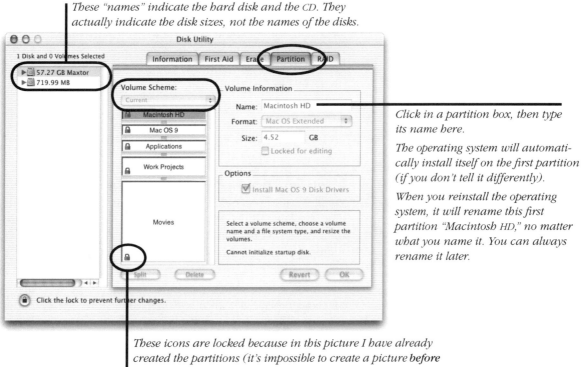

Click in a partition box, then type its name here.

The operating system will automatically install itself on the first partition (if you don't tell it differently).

When you reinstall the operating system, it will rename this first partition "Macintosh HD," no matter what you name it. You can always rename it later.

These icons are locked because in this picture I have already created the partitions (it's impossible to create a picture before I partition the disk because the picture gets destroyed along with all the other data on the disk).

*When **you** do this, the lock will be open. **Do not** click the lock to close it or you won't be able to copy files onto the disk!*

—continued

12. Okay, you've named and resized your partitions. This is your last chance to back out. *If you really want to destroy every single piece of data on your Mac and start all over again with a perfectly clean slate,* click "OK."

13. It doesn't take long. In a couple of seconds you can see the names of your new partitions in the panel on the left, as shown below.

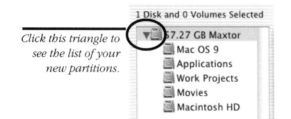

Click this triangle to see the list of your new partitions.

14. Now you're ready to quit the Disk Utility and re-install the operating system and software. There is no operating system on your Mac anymore because you just destroyed it, so you have to start up with a CD again.

> *If the only install disk you have* for Mac OS X is the one that's already in the machine, then quit Disk Utility (go to the Disk Utility menu and choose "Quit Disk Utility"). You will be taken back to the Installer window and the disk will walk through the process of re-installing Mac OS X and all the software it had originally.
>
> You might need to re-install Mac OS 9 as well, depending on the CD you use. Many people like to install Mac OS 9 on a separate volume from OS X.
>
> *If you have a number* of Mac OS X "Software Restore" disks, you'll want to use those. But you have to swap CDs. So do this: Quit the Disk Utility, then quit the Installer. Choose "Restart" (you have no other choice). Instantly after clicking the "Restart" button, press the mouse button down *and hold it down*—this will force the CD tray to open or the CD to pop out of the slot (depending on the Mac you have). Take out the CD that's in the Mac and replace it with the "Software Restore" CD. It will walk you through the process of restoring all the software as if the Mac just came out of the factory.

15. Whew. When you restart after all is said and done, you'll see a separate hard disk icon for each volume you created. Good job.

If you prefer not to have the partition icons cluttering up your Desktop, since they all appear in your Computer window anyway, see page 131.

This is an example of a newly partitioned Mac. You can see the five different partitions that I named in the Disk Utility. Each one is an individual volume.

1. Can you reformat the hard disk that contains the operating system that is running the Mac?

2. What happens to all the data on a disk that you reformat?

3. What should you do very carefully before you divide your hard disk into partitions?

4. If you create four partitions, how many hard disk icons will appear on your Mac?

5. If you reformat your hard disk because it's acting a little weird and it still doesn't get better, what else should you check?

Answers on page 752.

Using the Classic Environment 40

Mac OS X is a fabulous operating system. But at the moment, there are many applications that can't run in OS X because every application has to be rewritten from scratch for the new system. So the Mac opens and runs the OS 9 operating system in what is called the **Classic environment.** Applications that can't run in Mac OS X will automatically open in Mac OS 9. These applications are considered "Classic applications."

I wrote this entire book in Adobe InDesign 1.5 and used Photoshop 6 to clean up screenshots. Both of these are Classic applications that ran in the Classic environment, while I made screen shots and worked in OS X. It was easy and fluid. Except for the old-fashioned look of Mac OS 9, I hardly noticed when the Mac switched between operating systems.

If you have Mac OS X on your machine but you start up your Mac with OS 9 most of the time, you'll need to know more about OS 9 than is in this chapter. If so, please read *The Little Mac Book, seventh edition,* from Peachpit Press.

Opening Classic

The **Classic environment** does not open automatically when you start up in Mac OS X. If you double-click on a Classic application, it will open OS 9 for you, but I found there are fewer problems if I open Classic first, and then open the Classic application.

To open the Classic environment:

System Preferences icon

Classic icon

1. Open System Preferences: either click on the icon in the Dock, or go to the Apple menu and choose "Preferences...."

2. In System Preferences, click on the Classic icon, or choose "Classic" from the View menu.

3. In the Classic preferences pane, click the "Start" button. It takes a minute or two for Classic to get up and running.

The volume that holds Mac OS X will be selected here.

After you start Classic, this preferences pane changes, as shown on page 710.

4. While Classic is starting, you'll see the window shown below, with the status bar telling you how much time is left, relatively.

   If you want to see the whole "Desktop" and the extensions that are loading into Mac OS 9, click the disclosure triangle in the bottom-left corner of this small window.

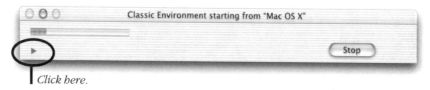

Click here.

5. Click the triangle, as mentioned in Step 4, to display the OS 9 Desktop as it loads.

One thing you cannot do in Classic is get to the Mac OS 9 Desktop—this is the closest you will ever come. See page 726 for information about accessing any files you might have left on the Desktop last time you started up your Mac with OS 9.

First-Time Trouble?

If the first time you open Classic it says it **can't find a system,** try this:

1. Open System Preferences: either click on the icon in the Dock, or go to the Apple menu and choose "Preferences...."

2. In System Preferences, click the Startup Disk icon.

3. Select the Mac OS 9 System Folder or partition.

4. Click the "Show All" icon in the upper-left of the preferences pane.

5. Open the Classic preferences pane again and choose the OS 9 system as your startup volume.

6. Start Classic.

7. Go back to the Startup Disk (its icon is probably in the toolbar across the top of the pane) and reset your Mac OS X System Folder as the one to start up with.

Classic Options

Once **Classic is up and running,** as explained on the previous two pages, you can make it automatically start up whenever you turn on your Mac, make it quit, restart, force quit, rebuild the Desktop, put it to sleep, and a few other things, as explained below.

Open the System Preferences, then click on the Classic icon to get the Classic preferences pane, as shown below.

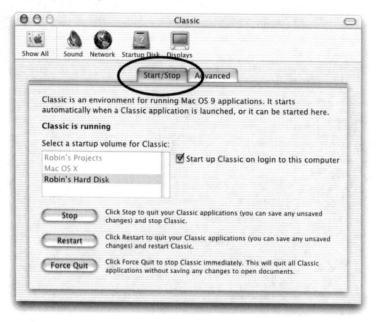

- ▼ If you use Classic applications everyday, **have Classic open automatically when you start up:** In the Classic pane above, check "Start up Classic on login to this computer."

- ▼ **Stop Classic from running:** Click the "Stop" button. You will be asked to save any changes to documents, and all Classic applications will quit.

- ▼ **Restart Classic:** Click the "Restart" button. Sometimes this can fix things that are acting weirdly. You will be asked to save any changes to documents, and all Classic applications will quit.

- ▼ **Force quit Classic:** Click the "Force Quit" button in the Classic pane. Use this as a last resort when you can't stop or restart Classic and you're having problems with it (try rebuilding the Desktop first, as explained on the opposite page). All applications will quit instantly, and you'll lose any changes you made to documents that you hadn't already saved. Force quitting Classic will not affect Mac OS X.

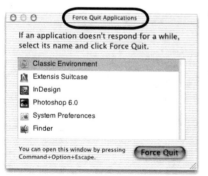

Or you can press Command Option Escape to get the "Force Quit Applications" window. Choose Classic, then click "Force Quit."

Click the **Advanced** tab to find these two options, plus more information on the following page.

▾ **Put Classic to sleep** when you're not using it to save on processing power: Drag the slider bar to the number of minutes before Classic will sleep.

▾ **Rebuild Desktop:** If things act a little squirrely, like you double-click a file created with a Classic application and it doesn't open with that application, or if files don't have the correct icon in the Finder, try rebuilding the Desktop. The process does not affect your open applications or documents, and you do not have to restart to rebuild. Click the "Rebuild Desktop" button in the Advanced pane.

Also in the **Advanced** pane are several **Startup Options.** Two of these deal with "extensions," small files that add functionality to the operating system and to individual applications. (Mac OS X doesn't use extensions.)

Managing extensions

If you are an experienced Mac user and are accustomed to dealing with extensions, you'll be overjoyed to know you can turn them all off when starting Classic: choose **Turn Off Extensions** in the Advanced pane. This does not turn them off every time Classic starts up—it only works if you come to this Advanced pane and choose this option, and then click the "Start" or "Restart" button in this pane.

—continued

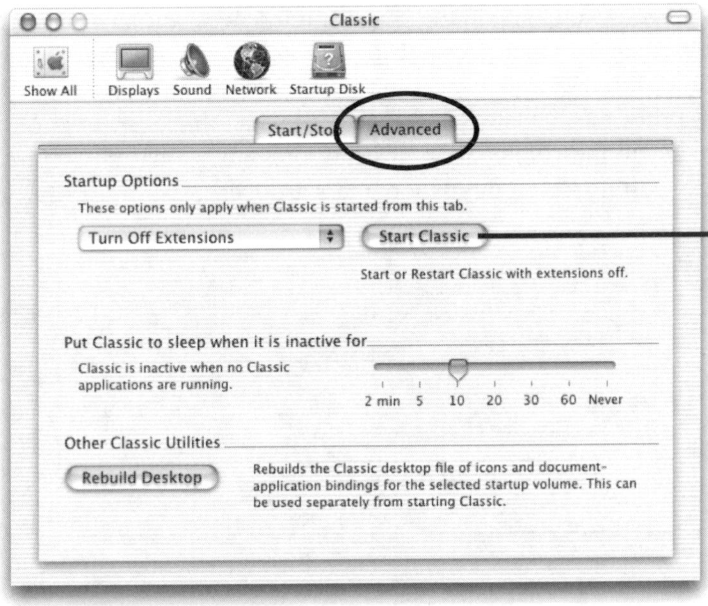

If Classic is already running, this button says "Restart Classic."

Or you can choose to **Open Extensions Manager** as Classic starts up so you can turn on or off extensions and control panels that you need or that you think might be causing trouble. Classic only opens certain extensions, so if you've installed a Classic application that needs extensions or control panels that Classic doesn't open, you can use this feature to turn them on. Otherwise that application might not work properly.

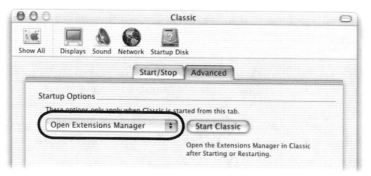

Start up Classic with certain keys held down

Another troubleshooting feature involves holding down certain keys when you start Mac OS 9. You can force Classic to act as if these keys are held down when you restart from the Advanced pane (not when you restart Classic in general or automatically on startup).

Click on the Advanced pane in the Classic preferences, and then choose **Use Key Combination.** You can press up to five keyboard characters in a row, one at a time, and they will appear in the edit box. You can't use the Delete key to get rid of these characters because the Mac thinks you want to add the Delete key to the combination; instead, press the "Clear Keys" button to remove the existing key combination and start over.

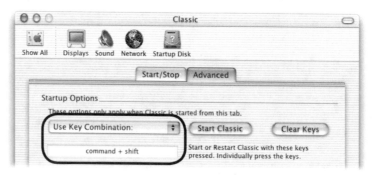

Unfortunately, there is no visual clue that tells you whether Classic is open or has quit on you. I wish there was at least a little dot in the menu bar that would let me know that Classic is open because sometimes it up and quits altogether and I don't even know until I see that the triangles under my Classic applications in the Dock have suddenly disappeared. A great consolation when Classic crashes is that it doesn't affect Mac OS X—OS X just keeps running happily along.

Classic will quit automatically and safely when you Shut Down, Restart, or Log Out.

You can quit Classic yourself:

1. Open System Preferences: either click on the icon in the Dock, or go to the Apple menu and choose "Preferences...."

2. In System Preferences, click on the Classic icon, or choose "Classic" from the View menu.

3. In the Classic preferences pane, click the "Start/Stop" tab.

4. Click the "Stop" button.

There is also a **keyboard shortcut** that will quit Classic. Be careful because if you use this shortcut, Classic and every application open in Classic will quit in less than one second and you will not be asked if you want to save any documents, you won't get any warning, just zap—everything is gone.

To use the keyboard shortcut, Classic must be active; that is, you need to have a Classic application open in front of you on the screen. Then press Command Option Shift Q.

If you have **trouble when quitting,** if Classic just won't quit or Mac OS X has trouble shutting down, you might have set up something in Mac OS 9 that is causing a problem. For instance, I've had a sound in my Shut Down Items folder in the System Folder for years in previous operating systems—when I shut down, I hear myself say, "Oooh, baby baby, goodbye." In OS X, this sound would try to play on Shut Down by opening iTunes, so iTunes would start up as I'm shutting down and that just couldn't be done.

So if you have trouble, check your Shut Down Items folder, check your control panels, and check anything else you might have set up in Mac OS 9 to happen on Shut Down.

Quit Classic

Keyboard shortcut to quit

Trouble at quitting time

Allocate Memory to Classic Applications

Mac OS X manages memory very well. In the Classic environment, Mac OS 9 is not so good at it. If a particular Classic application crashes on you regularly, it might be because it needs more RAM (random access memory) to accomplish what you're trying to do. If you don't have a lot of RAM (like 256 megabytes or less), don't try to open more than one or two applications in Classic. If you have plenty of RAM (or at least plenty for your most-used applications), you can **allocate more memory** to your Classic applications. (It's not possible, nor is it necessary, to allocate more memory to OS X applications.)

If you don't know what RAM is, or if you want to know how much you have in your Mac, see pages 219–221 or page 258.

To allocate more memory to a Classic application:

1. Make sure the application is not open—it must be quit. If it has an icon in the menu bar, there should be no triangle under it. If there is a triangle, press on the icon in the Dock and choose "Quit."

2. Find the original icon for the application in its folder. Not the folder icon—you must find the *application icon* itself.

   If an icon for this application is in the Dock, press on it and choose "Show in Finder." The application's folder will open and the application icon will be selected.

Check the "Kind" column to make sure you have selected the application icon.

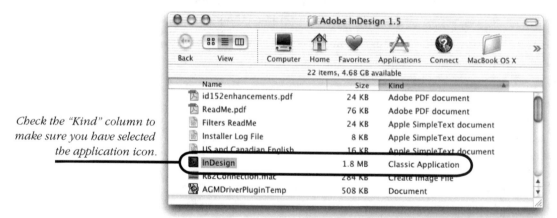

3. Single-click on the application icon to select it.

4. Press Command I to get the Info window (*or* go to the File menu and choose "Show Info," *or* Command-click on the icon and choose "Show Info"). You'll get the Info window, as shown on the opposite page.

5. From the pop-up menu inside the Info window, choose "Memory." Only Classic applications have this option; if you don't see this option in the menu, either you did not select the actual application icon, or the application you selected is not a Classic application.

6. You see two boxes for memory allocation.

   If you have enough built-in memory to handle it, raise the **Preferred Size** by at least 50 percent (if you don't have much memory, raise it by 25 percent).

   Then raise the **Minimum Size** to match. This ensures the application will never open with less than what it needs.

Of course, you cannot allocate more memory than you have! And about 128 megabytes of your memory is needed to run Mac OS X and Classic. Adding more memory to your Mac is the cheapest and most effective way to add working power.

I allocated a lot of memory to InDesign because I open large chapters with lots of graphics. And because I can.

Installing and Opening Classic Applications

Here are a few tips and recommendations for **installing and opening Classic applications** in Mac OS X.

▼ The Administrator is the one who will have the fewest restrictions installing software. Make sure to log in as the Administrator (the name and password you used when you first turned on your Mac).

▼ If you partitioned your disk, it's best to install Classic applications (and store your documents) on a separate partition from the Mac OS X disk. This is primarily to avoid having access privilege problems (access privileges are discussed in Chapter 35).

Information about partitioning your disk is in Chapter 39.

▼ The next best place for installing Classic applications is in the folder called "Applications (Mac OS 9)."

(If you partitioned your disk and installed Mac OS 9 on another partition, then this folder is on that other partition.)

▼ If you can't install a Classic application while running in Mac OS X, you'll have to restart your Mac in OS 9: use the Startup Disk preferences in the System Preferences.

On some Macs, you can hold down the Option key when you restart to get the option to start up with either operating system, *if* the two operating systems are on two different partitions.

▼ If a Classic application installs an old version of QuickTime, make sure you reinstall the newest version. You can find it on the Mac OS 9 CD or download it from the Apple site.

▼ Time and technology move on—you can't hang onto the same software package you've owned for ten years and expect it to work with Classic. I'm afraid you'll have to upgrade if you've got really old stuff that won't work in Classic.

▼ As mentioned on page 712, Classic opens with a certain set of extensions, which might not include any special extensions that your application needs to run properly. Manage your extensions with the features mentioned on pages 711–712. If you don't know what extensions are or have any idea how to manage them, please call your local guru to come help you. Extension conflicts can be tricky and frustrating.

▼ Some applications are what's called "Carbon," which means they can open in both Mac OS 9 and OS X. Sometimes an application is capable of opening in OS X, but some of its features depend on extensions installed in Mac OS 9. In this case, you need to open the application in Classic (Mac OS 9) to get full functionality. **To force an application to open in Classic,** use the Info window.

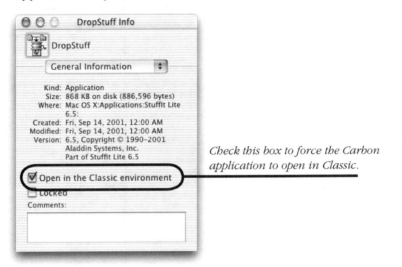

Check this box to force the Carbon application to open in Classic.

(Please don't think this great little utility, DropStuff, needs to open in Classic—this is just an example of the Info window.)

Working in Classic

If you've never worked in Mac OS 9, you'll find a number of minor things to be different from OS X. Let's start with the differences between the **windows,** since you will be using windows whenever you open a Classic application.

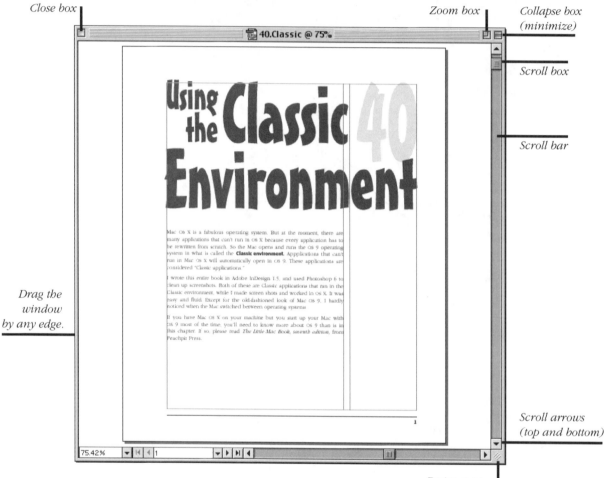

Close box

Zoom box

Collapse box
(minimize)

Scroll box

Scroll bar

Drag the
window
by any edge.

Scroll arrows
(top and bottom)

Resize corner

Classic windows

Moving the window: In Classic, you can drag a window by any edge, as well as by the title bar. This is a feature I miss in OS X.

Red close button: The Classic *close box* to close a window is in the same position as the red close button in Mac OS X, but it's a boring gray box instead. It does the same thing.

Green zoom button: The Classic *zoom box* is in the right corner of the window. It does pretty much the same thing as the zoom button in OS X.

Yellow minimize button: You can't minimize a Classic window to the Dock. You can, however, click in the *collapse box* in the right corner (or double-click the title bar) to "roll up the windowshade," or "collapse" it, which leaves just the title bar on the screen.

If double-clicking the title bar does not roll up the window and you want it to, do this:

1. In the Classic environment, go to the Apple menu, down to Control Panels, and choose "Appearance."

2. Click the "Options" tab.

3. Click in the checkbox to "Double-click title bar to collapse windows."

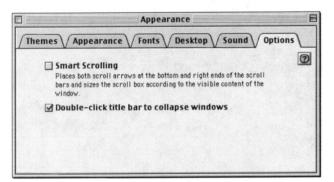

4. Notice in this control panel you can also turn on "Smart Scrolling," which puts both scroll arrows at the bottom of the scroll bar, which you probably have in Mac OS X. If you want this in OS 9, check the box.

5. Click in the close box to put away this control panel.

The **Hide Others** command is not under the Apple menu in OS 9. You'll find it in the **Application menu,** which is over in the far-right corner.

Also in this menu you'll see a list of all **open applications.** You can switch applications from here, which can be handy if you choose to hide your Dock.

The keyboard shortcut to **switch applications** works in Classic and Mac OS X seamlessly. Watch the Dock as you press Command Tab (hold down the Command key and tap the Tab key several times); you see that each time you hit the Tab key, the next *open* application in order is selected. When the icon of the application you want to be active is selected, let go of both the Tab and Command keys and the selected application will come forward.

Press Shift Command Tab to select applications in the reverse order.

The Application menu

In the Classic environment, this is the Application menu, over in the far-right of the menu bar.

Saving Documents

The **Save As dialog box** is different in Mac OS 9. Similar, but different. You won't have the column view to navigate in, and you won't have your OS X Favorites (see Chapter 23 about Favorites). You can make Favorites, though, here in the Save As dialog box to make it easier to find your folder to save into; these Favorites won't appear in the OS X Favorites folder or Save As dialog box.

Shortcuts button to access the files on your OS 9 Desktop, all volumes, servers, and even your iDisk.

Favorites button. In Save As, you see your Favorite folders. In Open, you'll also see your Favorite documents.

Recents button shows the folders and volumes you have used recently.

The **contents** listed in the window are the contents of the folder whose name appears here.

Click on this menu to open it and choose another folder.

If you're accustomed to the column view, this menu is like going to the left in the columns.

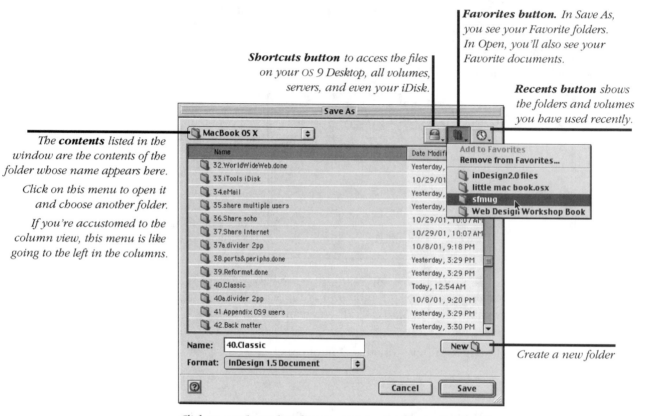

Create a new folder

Click on a **column heading** to organize the files by that heading.

Click on the **Sort Order triangle** (at the top of the scroll bar, as shown on the opposite page) to organize in the opposite direction.

To add or remove a Favorite, select a folder, then use the Favorites button, as shown above.

The **Open dialog box** is just like the Save As dialog box shown on the opposite page, with the extra feature of showing a preview of many types of documents.

Opening Documents

Favorites button. In Open, you'll see your Favorite documents as well as folders.

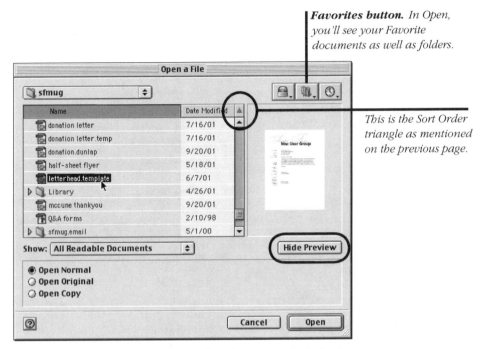

This is the Sort Order triangle as mentioned on the previous page.

*Click once on a file to see a **preview** of it, if one is available for that file type. If you don't see the preview area, click on the "Show Preview" button that will be where "Hide Preview" is in the example above.*

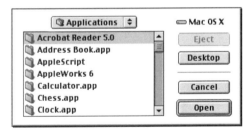

Some Classic applications will display this Open or Save As dialog box. It works the same as the other examples on these pages, but with fewer features for finding your folders and volumes.

Click on the menu at the top of the list to see the hierarchy of folders that the current folder is stored within.

Click the Desktop button to get to the Mac OS X Desktop, where you can open your hard disk and the other folders on it.

Printing Documents

When you **print** in the Classic environment, you won't get the Print Center application. Instead, Mac OS 9 will use the Print Monitor, which you'll probably never actually see. The dialog box for printing will look different, but it's basically the same sort of thing: choose the pages you want to print, the quality, etc. Many applications will provide their own print dialog boxes that won't look anything like the one shown below, but they all have the same purpose and the same general features.

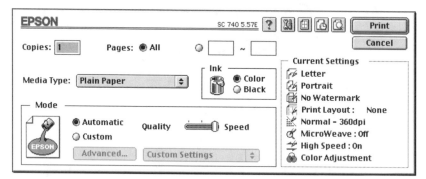

This is a typical sort of print dialog box for a small color printer.
For details, see the manual for your printer.

Before you print

Before you print for the first time in Classic, you will need to go to the Chooser, as explained on the following pages. If you have a color inkjet printer, you will probably need to install the software that came with it, if you haven't already, and you might need to restart in Mac OS 9 to install that software. If you have a PostScript printer, the LaserWriter 8 driver that is installed will work just fine.

Is your printer PostScript? Here's a good way to tell:

▼ If it prints black and white and cost around $1,000, it's probably PostScript.

▼ If it prints color and cost around $4,000, it's probably PostScript.

▼ If it prints color and cost from $50 to $800, it's definitely *not* PostScript.

Read more about PostScript and non-PostScript printers in Chapter 15.

To set up printing in Classic if you have a PostScript printer:

1. Turn on the printer and let it warm up.

2. Open a Classic application.

3. From the Apple menu, select "Chooser." You'll get the window shown below.

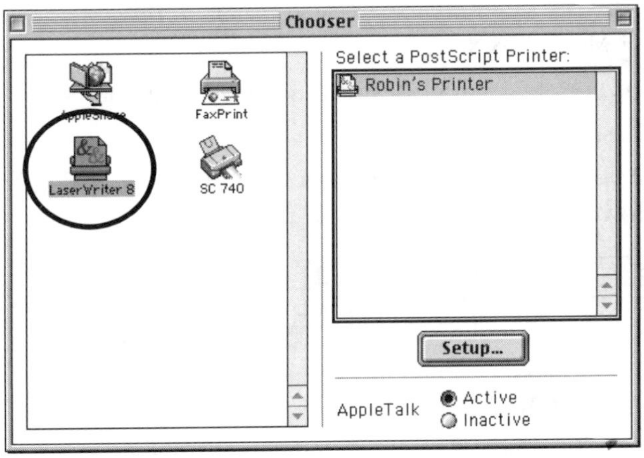

Set up your PostScript printer

4. On the left side of the window, click once on the icon named "LaserWriter 8."

5. On the right side of the window, the name of your PostScript printer should appear. If it doesn't, these are the likely causes:

   ▾ The printer is not a PostScript printer.

   ▾ The printer is not turned on or is not quite warmed up enough.

   ▾ The cable attached to the printer is not plugged in snugly enough on both ends (you really shouldn't reattach it while the computer is on).

   ▾ The cable attached to the printer is a bad cable; try another one.

   ▾ If you're on a small network (a "peer-to-peer" network like you would most likely have at home or in a small office), the computer between you and the PostScript printer is turned off.

   ▾ If you've tried everything and the printer name still won't appear, rebuild the Desktop in Classic (see page 711) and start over.

6. When you get the name of your printer to appear on the right side, click once on it.

7. If the printer name does not have a little icon directly to the left of its name, like the one shown in the example, click the "Setup…" button. After the Mac runs the setup, the tiny icon will appear.

8. You're all set. Close the Chooser (click in its close box) and print your document.

Set up your
non-PostScript printer

To set up printing in Classic if you have a non-PostScript printer:

1. If you *haven't* already installed your software, restart your computer in Mac OS 9 (see page 709 if you're not sure how to do that).

   If you *have* already installed your printer software, skip to step 4.

2. Use the CD that came with your printer and follow the instructions to install it.

3. Restart your Mac in OS X.

4. Turn on your printer and let it warm up (wait 'til all the noises stop).

5. Open a Classic application.

6. From the Apple menu, select "Chooser." You'll get the dialog box shown below.

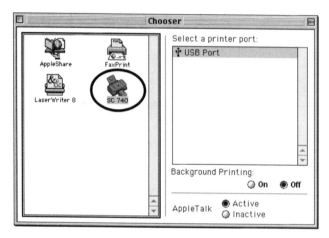

7. On the left side, click once on the type of printer you have. Above, I've selected an Epson 740. (I wish they'd name these printer drivers with names that match the printer, or at least the brand.) If you didn't install the software, you probably won't see the printer driver at all. Install the software as described in Steps 1 and 2.

8. On the right side, the name of your printer should appear. If it doesn't, these are the likely causes:

   ▾ The printer is not turned on or is not quite warmed up enough.

   ▾ The printer driver you selected on the left side is not the right one; try another one.

   ▾ The cable attached to the printer is not plugged in snugly enough on both ends.

   ▾ If you've tried everything and the printer name still won't appear, rebuild the Desktop in Classic (see page 711) and start over.

   ▾ The cable attached to the printer is a bad cable; try another one.

When you open a **Classic** application, the Dock will keep you linked to **Mac OS X,** as you can see in the example below. Even if you choose to hide the Dock, when you move your mouse into that area the Dock will appear, even while you work in the Classic environment. It's great. You can jump back and forth all day long with the click of a button.

Classic and Mac OS X Together

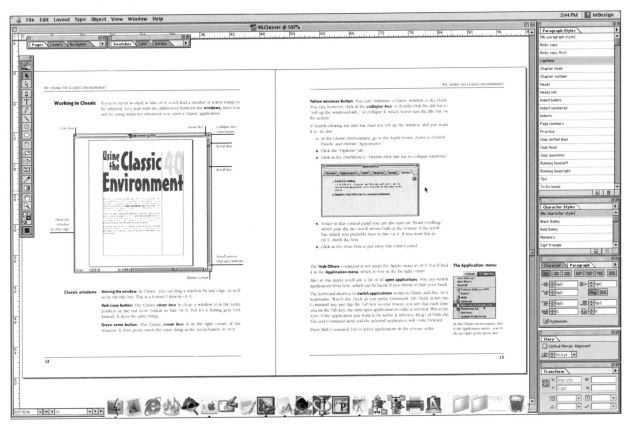

Here on my monitor you can see the Dock from Mac OS X, with my pages open in InDesign in the Classic environment. I hold down the Option key and click on the Finder icon in the Dock, and instantly I'm back in OS X and InDesign is hidden (it's hidden because I held down the Option key when I clicked on the Finder icon).

Where's the OS 9 Desktop?

Maybe you used Mac OS 9 for a while and added Mac OS X to your Mac, or perhaps you switch back and forth between the operating systems. If so, you might feel nervous at first because you cannot get back to the **OS 9 Desktop** while running OS X. You can't get to the Desktop itself, but Mac OS X made a folder for you that contains all of the items you left on the other Desktop.

In fact, if you have more than one partition, OS X made a "Desktop Folder" for each partition. Just open the partition, and on the top level you'll see the folder.

Desktop (Mac OS 9)

If your hard disk is not separated into individual partitions, then Mac OS X made a folder for you on the OS X Desktop called "Desktop (Mac OS 9)." This folder is actually an alias, but it will open a window that will show you everything you had left on the Desktop.

You can also **open items** that you had left on the Desktop in any Classic Open dialog box, as shown on page 721. You can **save into** any folder you had on the Desktop through the Classic Save As dialog box, as shown on page 720. In both dialog boxes, use the Shortcuts button to choose the partition, then in the list you'll see the "Desktop Folder."

Where Did it Go?

For Experienced Mac OS 9 Users

If you have grown fondly familiar with previous Macintosh operating systems, it will be confusing at first to use Mac OS X because all your favorite tools and tricks have changed. Here is an overview of where you can find your old favorite features in brand new dress.

Desktop and Finder Features

The **Desktop** and the **Finder** in Mac OS 9 look like the same thing. Actually, the Finder is the software that runs the Desktop, but when we would say, "Go to the Finder" or "Go to the Desktop," we meant the same place.

In Mac OS X, the Desktop and the Finder are more clearly separated. The Desktop is the background, and you can still place things on it and save to it. The Finder is a defined application with its own special windows. The menu across the top of the Desktop is the Finder menu, and all windows that display documents and application files are "Finder windows." Apple calls the Finder "the gateway to your computer and network."

Keep an eye on the menu bar and you will eventually become accustomed to recognizing when you are in the Finder and when you are working with some other feature of the system. See Chapter 9 for details.

This is the Application menu. At the moment, the Finder is the active application.

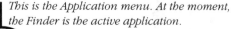

The name of this menu changes depending on which application is active.

*Although this might look like a Finder window, it's not. If the menu bar does not say "Finder" on the left side, then the window is an active application. You must **quit**, not just **close** the window, to put the application away.*

The Dock

You can't miss the Dock across the bottom of the screen. The Dock takes the place of Mac OS 9's application switcher, Apple menu, and Control Strip. Applications are to the left of the dividing line; all other files are stored on the right. The Trash basket cannot be moved, nor can you make an alias of it. You can move the Dock to either side: hold down the Control key, click on the dividing line, and choose a position from the menu. For a brief overview of the Dock, see Chapter 1; for all the details, see Chapter 8.

There are three different **window views** available for every Finder window. It can be confusing at first because although they look similar to what you are accustomed to, they act a little weird. You'll get used to it. For all the details and tips for working with these windows and views, see Chapter 6.

Window Views

*Depending on which view you are in, you can click the **Back button** to go back to the previous window.*

*The **View button** gives you the same choices as the View menu: as Icon, List, or Column.*

*This is the **Icon View.** Double-click a folder to open that folder's contents in this same window (the contents of the new folder **replace** the current contents).*

*This is the **List View,** which acts very much like what you're used to.*

*This is the **Column View,** a brand new concept for the Mac. As you click each folder, its contents appear in a new column to the right. You can see that this window shows you (in the third column) what is in the Documents folder (selected in the second column) that belongs to the user named "robin" (selected in the first column).*

Finder Windows

Windows for folders and disks are called **Finder windows.** See Chapter 6 for details about navigating through them without getting confused, and how to color the backgrounds of windows or add photographs as backgrounds, change the icon sizes, set global preferences and individual preferences, and even more (from the View menu, choose "Show View Options").

▼ Use the little colorful buttons in the top-left of the active window.

Red: Close the window. If it is an *application* window, this does not *quit* the application.

Yellow: Minimize the window, which sends an icon of the window to the Dock. Single-click that icon in the Dock to open the window again. Shift-click for slow motion (try it).

Green: Enlarge or reduce the size of the window.

Tip: When you open a window, you'll probably change the view and adjust the size, etc., to suit your purpose at the moment. If you click the **red** button and **close** the window, it **removes** all the customizing you did and when you reopen the window, you'll have to reset everything in the way you want it.

But if you click the **yellow** button and **minimize** the window, it **retains** all of your customizing, and when you reopen the window (click on its icon in the Dock), it will reappear exactly as you left it. Until you turn off your computer.

▼ **Customize the Toolbar:** From the View menu, choose "Customize Toolbar...." Drag items from the panel into the Toolbar; drag them off the edge and drop them onto the Desktop to remove them. See Chapter 6.

▼ **If the Toolbar is showing** when you double-click a disk or folder icon, the contents of that folder **replace** the contents that were previously in that window space. That is, you don't get a brand-new window each time you open a folder. This can be nice as it reduces the clutter of lots of windows overlapping each other. Click the Back button to go back to the previously open window.

But sometimes you *want* a new, **separate** window. If so, either **hide the Toolbar** (click the Hide/Show Toolbar button in the upper-right of the window) *or* hold down the **Command key** when you double-click to open the folder or disk. You will get a new window in Icon view and the previous window will still be visible on your Desktop.

If you hold down the Option key instead of the Command key, you will get a new window *and* the previous window will disappear.

▼ **Same ol' tricks:** Hold down the Command key and click on the title of the window to see the hierarchy of the active window, as shown to the right.

Hold down the Command key to move an **un**active window without making it active.

Option–double-click a folder to open the window and make the previous window disappear.

Press Command Option W to close all open windows.

One window or several?

*Click this button to **hide or show** the Toolbar.*

Command-click the title.

Selecting Files

There has been a serious change in the way we **select multiple files** in some window views. Try these actions:

In a window that is in a **List** or **Column View,** click on an icon at the top of the list. Hold down the Shift key and click on an icon in the middle of the list. *Every file between the two clicks is selected.*

To select individual files that are not next to each other, hold down the Command key.

In a window that is in an **Icon View,** use the Command key *or* the Shift key to select more than one file.

Naming Files

A **file name** can have 255 characters, which is rarely useful. In Mac OS X, file name extensions are often very important! For instance, if you take the .rtf off of the name of a document you created in TextEdit, then TextEdit can't open it. If you name a folder with an extension of .dock, it's no longer a folder. See page 227 for details.

Apple Menu

The **Apple menu** is not at all what it used to be. Below is a list of where you can find the comparable features in Mac OS X that you used to find in the Apple menu (some of the following items were also eliminated from the Apple menu in Mac OS 9).

To open the Applications folder directly, click once on this icon, found in the Finder window Toolbar.

Or use the Go menu, or press Command Option A.

About This Computer: This item is still the first item in the Apple menu, but it's called "About This Mac."

Apple System Profiler: Open the Applications folder, then open the Utilities folder. It's still called "Apple System Profiler."

AppleCD Audio Player: When you insert a music CD, iTunes automatically opens so you can play the CD.

Automated Tasks: Gone. But you can write and use scripts. See page 463 for some information, and check **www.apple.com/applescript/ macosx/script_menu** for lots of information.

Calculator: This is now in the Applications folder. Unfortunately, it has not been improved.

Chooser: Gone. When you are in an application and choose to print, you will automatically get the Print Center where you can set up and choose any printer on the network. To open the Print Center directly, go to the Applications folder, open the Utilities folder, and you'll find it in there. See Chapter 15.

Control Panels: Gone. These are now System Preferences; see the following page.

Favorites: These are all stored in the Favorites window; click on the red heart in any Finder window. You can also access a submenu of Favorites from the Go menu, and you'll also find them in the Open and Save As dialog boxes. See Chapter 23.

Graphing Calculator: Gone.

Internet Access: The Control Panel is gone, but the Internet preferences pane is very similar. See the list of Internet features on page 739. See Chapters 31, and 3 for all the details.

Jigsaw Puzzle: Gone.

Key Caps: Open the Applications folder, then open the Utilities folder. Don't forget to *quit* Key Caps when you're done; don't just *close* its window. It's still too small to be very useful.

Network Browser: At the Desktop, click the Go menu, then choose "Connect to Server...."

Note Pad: Gone. You can still use Stickies, though, and Stickies have more features.

Recent Applications, Recent Documents, Recent Servers: There are two different places to find your recently opened files.

▼ To open recent applications, utilities, and documents, use the Apple menu.

▼ To open recent folders, favorites, and servers, use the Go menu.

You will also find Recent items in the Save As and Open dialog boxes. Use the General preferences to determine how many items appear in the Recent menu (open System Preferences, then click on General).

Scrapbook: Gone.

Sherlock: Click its icon in the Dock. It still works just the same. You can also find Sherlock in the Applications folder, or press Command Option F. See Chapter 24.

Stickies: Stickies are in the Applications folder, and they now have more features. You can add graphics, check spelling, search all notes, print all notes at once, and more. See pages 488–489.

Other:

▼ To store your most-used applications and other items for easy accessibility, use the Dock; see Chapter 8. (To add items to the Dock, just drag and drop the icons onto the Dock; drag them out of the Dock to remove them. The Mac automatically creates aliases for you.)

▼ For details about the new Apple Menu, see Chapter 9.

Control Panels

This is the System Preferences icon you'll find in the Dock.

Control panels are now called System Preferences. Access them by first opening the System Preferences window, located in the Dock: click once on the icon in the Dock. Then click once on the various icons to get their individual preferences panes. See Chapter 21 for details. Below is a list of the most standard control panels in Mac OS 9 and where you can find comparable features.

AirPort: If you have an AirPort card installed, you'll see the AirPort icon in the menu bar, as circled below. If not, open the Applications folder, then open the Utilities folder. You'll find the "Airport Setup Assistant" and the "Airport Admin Utility." See pages 496–497.

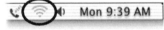

Appearance: There are no sound effects, and you can't choose a font for the system. You can't set up a theme for your Desktop, but individual users can customize their own Desktops (see the User preferences pane or Chapter 20).

> **Desktop picture:** In the System Preferences pane, click on "Desktop." See pages 127–128.
>
> **Highlight colors:** Use the General preferences pane. See page 136.
>
> **Size of icons on the Desktop:** Click on the Desktop. From the View menu, choose "Show View Options," then drag the "Icon Size" slider bar. See page 129 for details.

Apple Menu Options: Gone.

AppleTalk: Open the Network preferences pane. In the "Show" menu (the menu above the row of tabs, not the one in the menu bar), choose "Built-In Ethernet." Then click the "AppleTalk" tab.

Battery: If you have a laptop and you don't see the battery icon in the menu bar, go to the Energy Saver preferences, click the "Options" tab, and check the box to show the icon in the menu bar.

ColorSync: Use the ColorSync preferences pane. Also check out the ColorSync Utility, DigitalColor Meter, and Display Calibrator in the Utilities folder (which is in the Applications folder). See pages 503–504.

Control Strip: Use the Dock. See Chapter 8.

Date & Time: Use the Date & Time preferences pane. You can also use the Clock application in the Applications folder to make either an analog (with hands) or digital (with numbers) clock appear in the Dock or float around on your screen.

Energy Saver: Use the Energy Saver preferences pane. There is no automatic startup feature. Dang.

Extensions Manager: To access the Extensions Manager in Classic after starting or restarting OS 9, open the Classic preferences pane. Click the "Advanced" tab. From the menu in the "Startup Options" section, choose "Open Extensions Manager." See Chapter 40. There is no Extensions Manager for Mac OS X.

This is the Classic preferences icon.

File Exchange: Use the Show Info window (Command I, similar to the Get Info window in Mac OS 9) to choose an application for the selected document, or to choose an application for all documents of a particular file type. See pages 520.

File Sharing: Use the Sharing preferences pane. You can set certain sharing privileges in the Show Info window: select a file, press Command I, then choose "Privileges" from the Show menu. See Chapters 35–37.

File Synchronization: Gone.

General Controls: The General preferences pane is different from the General Controls control panel you are used to. Here you can change the overall color and highlight color, make several changes to the function of the scroll bars, choose the number of Recent items,, and adjust the point size of font smoothing. See page 136.

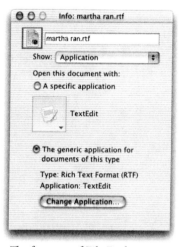

The features of File Exchange are built into the Show Info window.

Internet: For the "Web," "Email," and "News" settings that used to be in this control panel, use the Internet preferences pane. See Chapter 31.

Keychain Access: Use the Keychain Access utility: open the Applications folder, then open the Utilities folder. See pages 508–516.

Launcher: Use the Dock. You can add applications, utilities, documents, photographs, folders, etc., to the Dock. See Chapter 8.

Location Manager: To *make* a new location, open the Network preferences pane and use the "Location" menu to choose "New Location...." To *use* any location, go to the Apple menu and use the "Location" submenu. See Chapter 31.

Memory: Gone. Mac OS X takes care of managing the memory for you and it does a much better job than OS 9. It is still possible to allocate memory for Classic applications, however, in the Show Info window (Command I), per usual.

Modem: Open the Network preferences pane. Make sure the "Show" menu (the menu above the row of tabs, not in the menu bar) has "Internal Modem" selected. Click the "Modem" tab.

Internet Connect

Monitors: Use the Displays preferences pane. You'll notice you can't choose 640 x 480 resolution, nor 256 color mode—Mac OS X doesn't like them. If you use a Classic application that switches to 256 colors or the lower resolution, be sure to check the monitor settings and reset them if necessary as soon as you quit the application.

You can put a Displays icon in the menu bar, as shown to the left, so you can change your monitor resolution easily. Open System Preferences, then single-click on the Displays icon. Check the box, "Show displays in menu bar."

Mouse: Use the Mouse preferences pane.

Multiple Users: Use the Users preference pane to set up new users, and use the Login preferences pane to customize what each user can do. Each user has his or her own Desktop, Home folders, Trash basket, and most of the preferences. See Chapter 20.

Numbers: Use the International preferences pane.

QuickTime Settings: Use the QuickTime preferences pane.

Remote Access: To *set up* your dial-up connection, use the Network preferences pane. To *log on,* open the Applications folder and double-click "Internet Connect." Click the "Connect" button. See Chapter 31.

Remember when you are finished to click the "Disconnect" button and to *quit* the Internet Connect window. If you happen to *close* the window and later you want to connect again, first click the Internet Connect icon in the Dock to make it active, then go to the File menu and choose "New Connection" to get the window back.

Make an alias of the Internet Connect application and leave it on your Desktop for easy access to it, or drag the application icon right into the Dock.

Software Update: Use the Software Update preferences pane. Also see pages 138 and 336 about the command in the Apple menu to "Get Mac OS X Software...."

Sound: Use the Sound preferences pane. You cannot add your own alert sounds.

Speech: Use the Speech preferences pane.

Startup Disk: Use the Startup Disk preferences pane.

TCP/IP: Use the Network preferences pane.

Text: Use the International preferences pane.

Trackpad: Use the Mouse preferences pane.

Web Sharing: Use the Sharing preferences pane.

All of the **Internet functionality** you have grown accustomed to is still here, just in different places.

Internet Features

This is the AirPort icon and menu in the menu bar.

> **AirPort:** If you have an AirPort card installed, you'll see the AirPort icon in the menu bar, as shown to the right. If not, open the Applications folder, then open the Utilities folder. You'll find the "Airport Setup Assistant" and the "Airport Admin Utility." See pages 496–497.

> **Browsers:** Microsoft Internet Explorer is the only browser included with Mac OS X, but you can of course install your own copy of Netscape or America Online. You'll have to use them in Classic mode until they are OS X–savvy. Try the OmniWeb browser—download it from www.OmniGroup.com.

> **Connect automatically:** If you use a dial-up connection and want to make your Mac connect to the Internet automatically when you open an email program, a browser, Sherlock, etc., do this:
> 1. Open the Network preferences pane.
> 2. In the "Show" menu, choose "Internal Modem."
> 3. Click the PPP tab.
> 4. Click "PPP Options…."
> 5. Check the box to "Connect automatically when starting TCP/IP applications." Then click OK.

Internet: Use the Internet preferences pane to set web, email, and news settings, similar to the Internet control panel in OS 9.

Modem: Open the Network preferences pane and click the "Modem" tab. If you don't see the "Modem" tab, make sure the "Show" menu (the menu above the row of tabs, not in the menu bar) has "Internal Modem" selected.

TCP/IP: Use the Network preferences pane.

Remote Access: To *set up* your dial-up connection, use the Network preferences pane. To *log on,* open the Applications folder and double-click "Internet Connect." Click the "Connect" button. See the notes about Internet Connect (under "Remote Access") on the opposite page. See Chapter 31 for details.

Web Sharing: Use the Sharing preferences pane. See Chapter 37.

▼ **New Stuff:** Check out Chapter 33 for an overview of iTools, iDisk, and a special email account for you at **Mac.com.** See Chapter 34 for details on how to use the Mail program, and Chapter 37 about sharing files across the Internet. Learn to use iTunes in Chapter 26 and iMovie in Chapter 27. Use QuickTime Player to watch television or listen to radio from around the world; see pages 480–487. Use Image Capture to offload your digitial photos directly into your Pictures folder and make a web site for you, all with one click of a button; see pages 471–477.

Miscellaneous Features

This is a list of common features or actions you were familiar with in Mac OS 9 or previous versions and where they have gone to in OS X.

Application menu: The Application menu as we knew it in previous operating systems is gone, but the Dock takes its place. See Chapter 8.

▼ Use the Dock to switch between applications (fondly called "apps")—just click once on the icon for any open app.

▼ **Or** press Command Tab to switch between open apps; when you let go of both keys, the selected application (as shown in the Dock) will come forward. This even works when you are using an application in the Classic environment. Press Shift Command Tab to return to the previous application.

Hide or Show other applications: Just to the *right* of the Apple menu is the name of the currently active application. In that menu you'll find the commands to "Hide Others" and "Show All."

Empty Trash: Press and hold the mouse button on the Trash basket and you'll get a little pop-up menu to "Empty Trash." If you empty the trash this way, you won't get the warning message. If you use the "Empty Trash" command in the Finder menu or press Command Shift Delete to empty the trash, you *will* get a warning message. ***To turn off the warning,*** go to the Finder menu and choose "Preferences...."

Shut Down: From the Apple Menu, choose "Shut Down." On some keyboards, you can press Control Eject (the Eject key is the one in the top-right on some keyboards; it has a triangle over a bar).

Restart: From the Apple Menu, choose "Restart."

Sleep: From the Apple Menu, choose "Sleep." To set the sleep conditions, use the Energy Saver preferences pane.

Force quit in OS X: There are several ways to force quit, and they won't even make your entire computer crash.

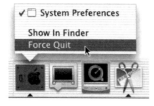

▼ Press Command Option Escape. From the little menu that appears, choose the application name and click "Force Quit."

▼ **Or** hold down the Option key, click the app icon in the Dock, then choose "Force Quit" from the pop-up menu that appears.

▼ **Or** if possible, go to the Apple Menu and choose "Force Quit...." From the little menu that appears, choose the app and click "Force Quit."

Force quit Classic: Open the System Preferences window (click its icon in the Dock). Click the "Classic" icon, then the "Force Quit" button.

Rebuild the Desktop: In the Classic preferences pane, click the "Advanced" tab, then click the "Rebuild Desktop" button. The Mac will rebuild the Desktop immediately—you don't have to restart. You cannot rebuild the Desktop in OS X.

Aliases: Aliases work pretty much the same. Use the same keyboard shortcuts you are familiar with (except to make an alias in the same window is Command L, not Command M). You can still Command-Option-drag to create an alias in a new folder or on the Desktop, and find an original with Command R. See Chapter 22.

The name of an alias is no longer in italic. You see a tiny (very tiny) arrow in the bottom-left corner.

Favorites: These are all stored in the Favorites window; click on the red heart in any Finder window Toolbar to open the Favorites window, or press Command Option F. You can also access a submenu of Favorites from the Go menu, and you'll find them in the Save As and Open dialog boxes. See Chapter 23.

Startup Disk: There is a Startup Disk preferences pane where you can choose to start up your Mac with OS 9 or OS X. On some machines (G4s, iBooks, slot-loading iMacs, and PowerBooks with FireWire) you can hold down the Option key when you turn on the Mac and you'll get a choice of which operating system to boot with *if* you installed OS X and OS 9 on two separate partitions.

Startup Items: There is a "StartupItems" folder, but don't touch it. Use the Login preferences pane to choose which applications or documents will open on login. See Chapter 20.

Control Strip: Use the Dock. To access your most-used preference panes more easily, drag their icons to the Toolbar in the System Preferences window (you can't drag them to a Finder window or to the Desktop. Dang.)

Print the window: Take a screen shot with the tricks explained on page 518 or use the Grab utility, then print the screen shot. To find Grab, open the Applications folder, then open the Utilities folder. See page 505 on how to work with Grab.

Get Info windows: Select the icon, then from the File menu, choose "Show Info," *or* use the Command I shortcut. Depending on the file you select, there are more options now in the Info window—you can even see a preview of a graphic file or watch a movie! You can specify which applications open which sorts of documents, change the sharing privileges, and more. See page 519–521.

You can no longer open two different Show Info windows simultaneously so as to compare files.

Memory allocation and virtual memory: Mac OS X uses completely different memory management than previous operating systems. There is no Memory control panel; you cannot allocate memory to individual OS X applications; you cannot turn off virtual memory; you cannot set up a RAM disk. You can, however, still change the memory allocation of Classic (OS 9) applications as usual, using Show Info.

Spring-loaded folders: Gone, apparently never to return. Dang.

Tabbed windows: Gone. But you can put folders in the Dock.

Labels: Gone (you can still search for labels applied under OS 9).

Utilities and Small Applications

A number of your favorite **utilities and small applications** have changed their name or location.

Calculator: The same ol' Calculator is in the Utilities folder, which is in the Applications folder. See page 464.

Disk First Aid: Use the Disk Utility: Open the Applications folder, then open the Utilities folder, where you'll find the icon shown to the left. See page 499.

Disk Utility

Drive Setup: Use the Disk Utility: Open the Applications folder, then open the Utilities folder. Double-click "Disk Utility." Click the large button on the left side, called "Drive Setup." See Chapter 39.

Erase Disk: Use the Disk Utility as noted above.

Extensions Manager: To access the Extensions Manager in Classic after starting or restarting OS 9, open the Classic preferences pane. Click the "Advanced" tab. From the menu in the "Startup Options" section, choose "Open Extensions Manager." See Chapter 40. There is no Extensions Manager for OS X. See pages 711–712.

Key Caps: Open the Applications folder, then open the Utilities folder. Don't forget to *quit* Key Caps when done; don't just *close* its window.

Scrapbook: The Scrapbook is gone. Stickies can now contain images, sounds, etc., and even has a spell checker.

Screen Saver: Use the Screen Saver preferences pane. Apple has provided a number of photographs and images for you to use, or you can use your own. See pages 316–319.

Screen shots: As usual, Command Shift 3 takes a screen shot of the entire screen. Command Shift 4 gives you a crosshair with which you can select a portion of the screen. See page 518 for other tricks.

Or use Grab: Open the Applications folder, then open the Utilities folder, then double-click the Grab utility. Unfortunately, Grab doesn't work nearly as efficiently as the screen capture keyboard shortcuts in previous versions of the OS. To capture just an active window, for instance, you must take a picture of the entire screen with the Grab timer, then open that screen shot in Grab and make another screenshot of just the window you want, then throw away the first one. See page 505.

Sherlock: Still there, works the same. Click once on the Sherlock hat in the Dock or double-click the Sherlock application in the Applications folder. Or press Command F while you're at the Desktop.

SimpleText: SimpleText is gone; use TextEdit, found in the Applications folder. TextEdit has a spelling checker and many other more advanced features. Also, it is capable of using "UniCode," which lets you type with over 65,000 characters in a font instead of the 256 we have been limited to all these years. See Chapter 13.

Fonts

Kind: Font suitcase
Size: 496 KB
Created: 2/22/01
Modified: 3/27/01
Version: 1.15

Not only can you use your existing TrueType and PostScript **fonts** in Mac OS X, you can also use some Microsoft Windows fonts, which means using cross-platform files can be less of a problem. You do not need Adobe Type Manager to display PostScript fonts clearly on the screen nor to rasterize fonts sent to your PostScript printer.

Fonts are not stored in the System Folder, but in the various Fonts folders which are located in the various Library folders. In the multi-user environment of Mac OS X, there is a *root* Fonts folder, plus individual users of that Macintosh have their own *user* Fonts folders. Applications can also open their own fonts. This means different users can have different font collections. See Chapter 25 for more information. (There is also a System Fonts folder that you are not allowed to change.)

Apple also created a new font format called "data fork suitcase format"; fonts of this sort have a suffix of .dfont (and a file type of dfon). But most people don't need to worry about that.

If you know what QuickDraw is, Apple has replaced it with what is called Quartz.

▼ **To install new fonts:** Drag font files into the *appropriate* Fonts folder.

That is, to install the fonts so **only you** have access to them, click the Home button in a Finder window to see *your* user folder. Open *your* user folder icon, then open *your* Library folder icon, then you'll see *your* Fonts folder. Drag the fonts into this folder so *you* have access to them.

If you have administrative access to this computer and you want **every user** to have access to the new fonts, drag them into the *root* Fonts folder, as shown below: click the Computer icon in the Finder window Toolbar, then open the hard disk that has Mac OS X on it, then open the Library folder icon, then you'll see the Fonts folder that is accessible to all users. Drag the fonts into this folder so every user has access to them.

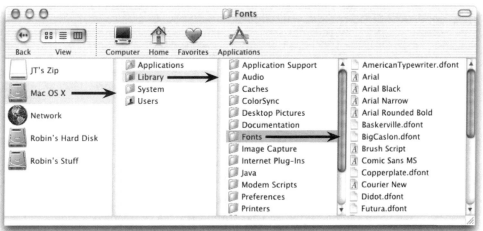

*Here you can see the path to the Fonts folder that stores fonts for all users (follow the selected items from left to right): Mac OS X hard disk, to the Library folder, to the Fonts folder. Because the Fonts folder is selected, you see the list of files in that folder. Drag files into the **selected Fonts folder icon,** or click once on an empty space in the last column and then drag items into the last column.*

Networking and File Sharing

Mac OS X is very involved with networking and file sharing. Below is a list of where you will find your old features. Also see Chapters 35–37.

Network Browser: Instead, at the Desktop, click on the Go menu. Then click "Connect to Server."

Chooser: Instead, to share from servers, see the tip above.

File Sharing: Instead, use the Sharing preferences pane.

Web Sharing: Instead, use the Sharing preferences pane.

Disconnect from server: Select the server icon on the Desktop, then from the File menu, choose "Eject," *or* drag the server icon to the Trash.

Printing

You don't need to go to the **Chooser** to select or change a printer. When you choose to print from any application, the **Print Center** will automatically appear and you can select any printer that is connected and turned on. If you need to go to the Print Center directly, open the Applications folder, then open the Utilities folder. See Chapter 15 about printing.

Desktop printers: Gone.

Print Window, Print Desktop: Gone. Make screen shots as explained on page 742 and print them.

Using Classic (Mac OS 9)

While running your Mac under OS X, there are times you will need to run in the "Classic" environment, Mac OS 9. You can just open any Mac OS 9 application and the Mac will automatically open Classic, but I find there are fewer problems if I open Classic first, then open my OS 9 application. See Chapter 40 for details.

Open Classic: Open the System Preferences window and click on the Classic icon. Click the button "Start."

Automatically open Classic on startup: Open the Classic preference, as explained above. Click the checkbox, "Start up Classic on login to this computer."

Force quit a Classic application: From the Apple menu, choose "Force Quit...." You'll get a dialog box with all of the open applications listed. Click once on the app you want to force quit, then click the "Force Quit" button.

Force quit Classic while in OS X: Open the System Preferences and click on the Classic icon. Click the button "Force Quit."

Restart Classic: Open the System Preferences and click the Classic icon. Click "Restart." You will be asked to save any unsaved documents.

There are a number of things you can do that will make the **transition** to working in Mac OS X a little easier.

Have Classic open on startup. You will undoubtedly be using applications in the Classic environment, so go ahead and have it open on startup so when you double-click an application, Classic is ready and waiting.

Fix your windows. It might make you crazy that every time you open a folder window, the previous folder's contents disappear, plus the view of the window is generally a surprise. You can do several things to make your windows behave as you are accustomed to.

To always open folders into their own, separate window:

Either click once in the Hide/Show Toolbar button in the upper-right of any Finder window. As long as the Toolbar is hidden, folders will always open in new windows. (Click the button again to revert to opening folders in the same window.)

Or go to the Finder menu and choose "Preferences...." Check the box to "Always open folders in a new window."

This is the Hide/Show Toolbar button.

Also in that Preferences window, check the box to "**Keep a window's view the same** when opening other folders in the window." This will prevent window views from switching to Column View or List View when you least expect it.

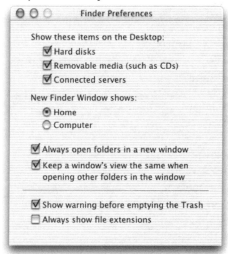

Setting your Finder Preferences to these settings will help you through the transition to Mac OS X by making your Mac behave more like you are used to.

Show the status bar. If you choose to view your windows without the Toolbar, you might want to see the status bar: Open any Finder window. Go to the View menu and choose "Show Status Bar."

Open new windows to Home. The default is set so that every time you ask for a new window, it automatically opens the Computer level window. If you keep your disk icons on the Desktop, then this Computer window is just a repeat of what you see on your Desktop. So change the default to open new Finder windows to your Home window, which is much more useful. In the Finder Preferences window, as shown above, click the radio button so "New Finder Window shows" Home.

Make a folder of aliases. If you store a lot of application icons in the Dock, the Dock gets very full and the icons become very tiny and difficult to select. Instead of putting every application's icon in the Dock, only store the ones you use the most. For the rest, put aliases of all your apps into one folder, then put that one folder into the Dock. Press on the folder icon to pop up a list where you can select the app, as shown to the left.

It takes a split second for the folder menu to pop up, unless you hold down the Control key as you click—then it pops up instantly. If you *click* on the folder icon in the Dock, its window appears on the Desktop.

This is the pop-up menu from a folder of aliases in the Dock.

Take advantage of Favorites. You might not have used Favorites much in Mac OS 9, but they are a lifesaver in OS X. Put aliases of the folders and documents you use most often into the Favorites window—just drag their original icons and drop them onto the Favorites icon in the Toolbar (if your Toolbar is still showing; if not, select the document or folder and press Command T). Now you don't have to go digging through disappearing windows to find the things you need the most. Just click the Favorites icon in the Toolbar or press Command Option F to open the Favorites window.

Favorites are also important when you use the **Open** or **Save As** dialog boxes. To prevent yourself from having to hunt down your folder to open or save into, make it a Favorite. Then in the Open or Save As dialog box, click to open the menu and your folders are right in that list—you won't have to navigate through the columns to find them.

Your Favorite folders will appear in the Open or Save As menu.

Put folders in the Toolbar. Sometimes you have to really wiggle around to move a file from one folder to another. If you have folders that you get into and store files into regularly, put them in the Toolbar (just drop the folder on the Toolbar). Even if your folder is on a different partition, you can put it in the Toolbar. That way you can open it with one click.

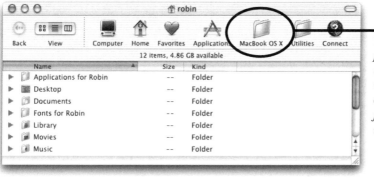

This folder is stored on another partition so it's always a pain in the boompah to get files into and out of it. As an icon in the Toolbar, I can open it with a click, and I can drop files directly into it from anywhere in the Finder.

Keep your most-used folder or two in the Dock. It's crazy-making to have to search for the folder you need the most. Once your folder is in the Dock, click once on it to open it as a window, or press on it to open the folder to a pop-up menu.

Now, once you've done this, that window will stay in the View you prefer and won't be taken over by any other folder window **unless** you click the Finder icon in the Dock to open a new window *while* your work folder is open. See, when you click the Finder icon, it activates your open work folder and all new folders will replace that one. So you need to get in the habit of using Command N to open a new window rather than clicking on the Finder icon to get a new window. I guarantee this won't make much sense until you have the problem. Once you have the problem, come back here, walk yourself through this process, and you'll see what a great tip it is.

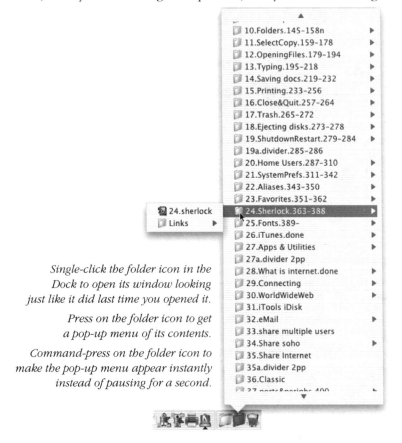

Single-click the folder icon in the Dock to open its window looking just like it did last time you opened it.

Press on the folder icon to get a pop-up menu of its contents.

Command-press on the folder icon to make the pop-up menu appear instantly instead of pausing for a second.

Do you miss the windowshade feature, where you could double-click a title bar and it rolled up the window, but stayed right there on the Desktop? If so, then download WindowShade X at **www.unsanity.com/haxies.php**. It's great. When you install it, its preferences will start a new row in the System Preferences main pane.

Accent Marks

People always seem surprised to discover that you can type just about any accented character on the Mac. In fact, you've been able to do this since about 1984.

Tilde	Press	Let go, then press
˜	Option n	Spacebar
ã	Option n	a
Ã	Option n	Shift a
ñ	Option n	n
Ñ	Option n	Shift n
õ	Option n	o
Õ	Option n	Shift o

Diaeresis	Press	Let go, then press
¨	Option u	Spacebar
ä	Option u	a
Ä	Option u	Shift a
ë	Option u	e
Ë	Option u	Shift e
ï	Option u	i
Ï	Option Shift f	
ö	Option u	o
Ö	Option u	Shift o
ü	Option u	u
Ü	Option u	Shift u
ÿ	Option u	y
`	Option Shift ` (` is next to 1, or next to Spacebar; the same key as the regular ˜key)	

Circumflex	Press	Let go, then press
^	Option i	Spacebar
â	Option i	a
Â	Option Shift m	
ê	Option i	e
Ê	Option i	Shift e
î	Option i	i
Î	Option Shift d	
ô	Option i	o
Ô	Option Shift j	
û	Option i	u
Û	Option i	Shift u

Acute	Press	Let go, then press
´	Option e	Spacebar
á	Option e	a
Á	Option e or Option Shift y	Shift a
é	Option e	e
É	Option e	Shift e
í	Option e	i
Í	Option e or Option Shift s	Shift i
ó	Option e	o
Ó	Option e or Option Shift h	Shift o
ú	Option e	u
Ú	Option e or Option Shift ;	Shift u

Grave	Press	Let go, then press
`	Option ` (` is next to 1, or next to Spacebar; the same key as the regular ˜key)	Spacebar
à	Option `	a
À	Option `	Shift a
è	Option `	e
È	Option `	Shift e
ì	Option `	i
Ì	Option `	Shift i
ò	Option `	o
Ò	Option ` or Option Shift l (letter el)	Shift o
ù	Option `	u
Ù	Option `	Shift u

Miscellaneous	Press:
å	Option a
Å	Option Shift a
ç	Option c
Ç	Option Shift c

Quiz Answers

3. The Mouse
1. Single-click.
2. Double-click.
3. Single-click.
4. Double-click.
5. Double-click.
6. Single-click.
7. Single-click.
8. Control-click.
9. Shift-click or Command-click
10. Command-click.

4. Keys and the Keyboard
1. Tab.
2. Return or Enter.
3. *Hide menu bar:*   F9
   Open Bookmarks folder: F5
   Close all open windows: Option Command W
   Tile windows vertically: Shift Command L
   Go to first page: Shift Command PageUp
   Go to previous view: Command LeftArrow
4. Escape key: c
   Option key: l
   Control key: q
   Command key: f
   Tilde key: d
   Asterisk: t
   Shift key: m
   Forward slash: p
   Backslash: j
   Tab key: e
   Delete key: i
   PageUp key: a
   PageDown key: h
   LeftArrow key: u
   RightArrow key: s
   UpArrow key: b
   DownArrow key: o
   Home key: g
   End key: r
   Forward Delete: n
   Enter key: k
   Spacebar key: v

5. Menus
1. "Close."
2. Three (New, Macros, and Open Recent).
3. Seven (Open, Save As, Properties, Insert, Mail Merge, Page Setup, Print).
4. Two.
5. Seven.
6. Command W.
7. You'll get a dialog box with Print options.
8. Seven menus.
9. Five edit boxes.
10. Command Period.

6. Windows
1. See page 65.
2. Click in the yellow button, double-click the title bar, or press Command M.
3. By the size of the scrollers.
4. Hold down the Command key and drag the title bar.
5. The red button has a dot in it.
6. Single click.
7. List View with a Size column, then click the Size column heading.
8. Command–double-click on a folder, or hide the Toolbar and then open the folder.
9. Click on any column heading.
10. Hold down the Option key as you drag the thumb.
11. From the View menu, choose "Arrange by Name."
12. Press Command Option W.
13. Hold down the Command key and click on the name in the title bar.
14. Use the General preferences.
15. From the View menu, choose "Show Status Bar."

7. Icons
application:	TextEdit
hard disk:	Mac OS X
CD:	FontDisc
folder:	Ryan's Writings
document:	sonnets.idd
Zip disk:	Little Mac Book
unknown document:	PkgInfo
selected icon:	Favorites
locked icon:	Holiday Letter
Trash can:	wastebasket icon
DVD:	CASABLANCA
ready to rename:	great words
stationery/template:	To Do List

8. Dock
1. Hold down the Control key, click on the dividing line of the Dock, choose "Position on screen," then choose Left, Right, or Bottom. Or go to the Dock preferences (see answer 9).
2. Drag the item out of the Dock and drop it on the Desktop.
3. Drag items anywhere else in the Dock (apps to the left, everything else to the right).
4. The Finder window and the Trash basket.
5. Web sites, folders, documents, applications, or any icon at all on your entire hard disk.
6. It opens the folder in a window.
7. It opens a menu from which you can select any item in the folder.
8. Press on the dividing line and drag it larger or smaller.
9. a) Control-click on the dividing line and choose "Dock Preferences…."
   b) Go to the Apple menu and choose "Dock…," then choose "Dock Preferences…."
   c) Open the System Preferences, then click on the Dock icon.
10. Go to the Dock preferences (see #9), and choose "Automatically hide and show the Dock," or hold down the Control key, click on the dividing line of the Dock, and choose "Turn Hiding On."

9. Desktop and Finder
1. Computer window.
2. Desktop folder in your Home.
3. From the Finder menu, open Preferences; check the "Home" box.
4. Yes.
5. Use "View Options" from the View menu ("Show View Options").
6. Use the Desktop preferences in the System Preferences pane.
7. Use "View Options" from the View menu ("Show View Options").
8. From the application menu, choose "Hide Others."
9. Option-click on the Desktop.
10. Shared folder in Users folder.

10. Folders

1. To organize and contain your files.
2. It appears in the active window.
3. Command N.
4. Select the folder, wait until you see the border (visual clue) around the name, then type.
5. Double-click on it.
6. Folder opens to a window and you see the files that are stored inside.
7. *To expand:* select folder(s), press Command RightArrow.
   To compress: select folder(s), press Command LeftArrow.
8. Press Command A to select all; press Command LeftArrow.
9. You don't have folders all over the screen, and you can select items from more than one folder simultaneously.
10. Put a folder in the Toolbar; put a folder in the Dock; make an alias of a folder on the Desktop; put a folder in the Favorites window; Command–doube-click to open the folder in a new window; Command Shift N to open another window.

11. Selecting and Copying Files

1. a
2. c
3. b
4. c
5. c
6. False; always check to make sure you're not copying unnecessary or duplicate files.
7. False; it's the Shift key or Command key.
8. True (assuming they are in the same window).
9. True of course.
10. False; Tab will select files alphabetically.

12. Opening Documents and Applications

1. Document.
2. The application will open and display this document.
3. Application.
4. The application will open.
5. Make sure the window is in List View, then click on the "Kind" column header.
6. New opens a brand-new, blank document. Open opens a document you or someone else has already created and named.
7. a. The two lists.
   b. "typos.rtf" or "sherlock tips."
   c. Documents
   d. "From" menu at top

13. Word Processing

1. Select first, then do it to it.
2. I-beam: ⌶
   Insertion point: |
   Pointer: ▶
3. I-beam.
4. Insertion point.
5. Either the character to its left, or the specifications you choose from the menu while the insertion point is flashing.

---

6. Usually Command B for Bold, Command I for Italic, Command U for Underline. Some applications also use a Shift key in combination (for instance, Command Shift B to change to Bold).
7. Press Command B (or whatever the command is), type the bold word(s), then press Command B again to toggle off the command.
8. 1) Select the paragraph (press-and-drag over it with the text tool, or try triple-clicking on it).
   2) Cut the paragraph (from the Edit menu, choose "Cut," or press Command X).
   3) Position the I-beam where you want to insert the paragraph, then click to set the insertion point at that spot.
   4) Paste (from the Edit menu, choose "Paste," or press Command V).
9. *Cut:* Command X.
   Copy: Command C.
   Paste: Command V.
10. "Cut" removes the item and places it on the Clipboard. "Clear" removes the item and does *not* place it on the Clipboard—it's just gone.

14. Saving Documents

1. A.
2. B.
3. You would select the Pictures folder.
4. That column would move over to the left and the contents of the Hogmanay folder would appear in the right-hand column.
5. Tab key.
6. The "Where" menu.
7. Your Home folders would appear in the left-hand column.
8. Close the document or revert.
9. In RAM.
10. Save As from the File menu.

15. Printing Documents

1. See page 234.
2. See page 234.
3. In the Printer List, click once to select the printer that you want to be the default. From the Printers menu, choose "Make Default."
4. Use Page Setup. Some applications have this option in their own print dialog box.
5. In the Print dialog box, choose the "Layout" pane.
6. Click on the Print Center icon in the Dock, then choose "Show Queues."
7. If there is only one job running, there is no difference. If more than one job: "Hold" stops one job from printing. "Stop Queue" stops all jobs from printing.
8. In the Print dialog box, choose "Collate" in the "Copies & Pages" pane.
9. Drag the Print Center icon from the Utilities folder down to the Dock. Or, while a job is printing and the Print Center icon is already in the Dock, click once on the icon to get the pop-up menu and choose "Keep in Dock."
10. "Output Options."

---

16. Closing and Quitting

1. Close.
2. Quit.
3. Close.
4. Quit.
5. Close.
6. Quit.
7. Six applications are open.
8. Press on the Sherlock icon in the Dock and choose "Quit" from the pop-up menu.
9. Log Out or Shut Down (Restart will also work).
10. Apple menu, choose Force Quit; or Option-click an application icon in the Dock and choose Force Quit; or press Command Option Escape and choose Force Quit.

17. Using the Trash

1. It has something in it.
2. When you choose "Empty Trash" from the Finder menu.
3. Drag the file to the Trash; Select the file, from the File menu choose "Move to Trash"; Select item, press Command Delete; Hold down Control key and click on item, then select "Move to Trash."
4. It opens to a window, displaying its contents.
5. Click the Trash basket, then drag the item out of the window.
6. Press Command Z.
7. No.
8. Temporarily: Hold down the Option key when you choose "Empty Trash" from the Finder menu, or use the Trash pop-up menu in the Dock.
   Permanently: Uncheck the warning box in the Finder Preferences.
9. Unlock it.
10. Drag the file down toward the Dock and the Trash will pop up. Or use the keyboard shortcut Command Delete.

18. Ejecting Disks

1. Drag the disk to the Trash; Select the disk and choose "Eject" from the File menu (or press Command E); Hold down the Control key and click on the disk, then choose "Eject" from the contextual menu; Press F12; Press the Media Eject key.
2. Check the Dock to see if "TextEdit" or other word processing program is open; it might have opened the ReadMe file. Then quit that program.
3. The computer cannot "read" the disk; its icon does not show up on the Desktop.
4. Hold down the mouse or the Media Eject key on restart, or use the paperclip.

19. Restart, Shut Down, or Log Out

1. Shut Down.
2. Log Out.
3. Solid triangle.
4. All applications will automatically quit.
5. Command Option W.

20. Multiple Users and their Homes
1. Yes, any regular user can be given Administrative privileges.
2. No, only Admins can create more users.
3. The only way to change the short name is to delete the user and create another.
4. The original Admin is the first one in the list.
5. It has a space in it, and it can be found in the dictionary.
6. No. The user passwords are case sensitive.
7. Login preferences, the Login Window pane.
8. No, the files are reassigned to an Admin of your choice.
9. In the main Applications folder on the main hard disk.
10. In the user's Home folder (make a new folder for applications, if you like).

21. System Preferences
1. Mouse preferences; set to fastest speed.
2. Desktop.
3. File Sharing; set File Sharing to Start.
4. Keyboard preferences.
5. Displays; change the "Resolution."
6. Date & Time; set to correct time.
7. Users.
8. Internet.
9. Network.
10. Universal Access.

22. Aliases
1. A representation of the real file. An alias goes and gets the real file.
2. 2 to 3 K.
3. Select a file, then from the File menu choose "Make Alias." Or select a file, then press Command L. Or hold down the Control key, click on the file, choose "Make Alias." Or hold down Command and Option, drag the file to another window or to the Desktop.
4. Drop the file on the Favorites icon in the Toolbar.
5. Nothing.
6. Nothing; they stay, now useless, right where you left them.
7. Click once on the alias. From the File menu, choose "Show Original" (or press Command R).
8. On the Desktop.
9. The file is actually put into the **real** folder.
10. Nothing. The alias can still find it.

23. Favorites
1. No.
2. Documents, applications, disks, servers, web pages, folders, photographs, partitions.
3. No. It would be better to make a folder full of aliases and put that folder in the Dock.
4. Yes.
5. It *moves* the file into the Favorites window without making an alias.
6. An alias is made and placed in the Favorites folder.
7. Save the document, then drag the title bar icon to the Desktop.

8. Folders and disks.
9. Yes you can. It can come in handy if you save files directly onto it.
10. No, not every item in the Favorites window is necessarily an alias.

24. Sherlock
1. No. The more characters you give the computer, however, the faster it can find your file.
2. No. It is not "case specific," meaning it does not check for caps and lowercase letters.
3. Yes. A space is a character to the computer.
4. a) Press Command F *or* click the hard disk channel ("Files"); make sure the "File Names" button is checked. b) First index the hard disk, then click the "Contents" button. c) Click one of the Internet channels.
5. Click the "Edit…" button. Search for "name contains budget." Also search for "date created is within 2 weeks of 3/15/02."
6. Double-click on the site name right there in the list of results.
7. From the search results panel, drag the file to the Desktop to make a Web Internet Location.
8. Select the file in the top portion of the window, then press Command E.
9. Drag its icon right out of the top portion of the results list and into the Trash.
10. Click on the header name (Name, Size, Kind, Date) of the view you want them sorted (organized) by. Or choose a view from the View menu while the Sherlock results window is active.

25. Fonts
1. Serif faces.
2. In very large type only.
3. OS stands for oldstyle and indicates the font includes lovely oldstyle numerals and perhaps some other special characters.
4. In your Fonts folder, which is in your Library folder, which is in your Home folder.
5. In the Fonts folder in the Library folder on the main hard disk (not in the System's Library folder!).
6. A font where every character is designed to take up the same amount of space as every other character.
7. Proportional.
8. No because there is no designed style for either of those fonts.
9. Yes, Windows .ttf and .otf.
10. I hope so!

28. Applications on the Mac
1. Preview
2. AppleScript
3. Image Capture
4. QuickTime Player
5. Stickies
6. Mail
7. DVD Player
8. Acrobat Reader or Preview
9. TextEdit
10. iTunes

29. Utilities on Your Mac
1. Show Info.
2. Network Utility.
3. NetInfo Manager
4. Key Caps
5. Disk Utility.
6. Apple System Profiler
7. Grab, as well as the keyboard shortcuts.
8. Keychain Access.
9. Show Info.
10. Disk Utility.

30. What is the Internet?
1. Email, newsgroups, mailing lists, World Wide Web.
2. 2.5Mbps.
3. Listserv.
4. A web site.
5. The "table of contents" page, often the first page you come to.
6. So you can see the web pages.
7. You can access the Internet by going through America Online.
8. No.
9. Log on to AOL, the double-click your browser icon.
10. The Macintosh!

32. Using the World Wide Web
1. b
2. d
3. a
4. c
5. a
6. d
7. a
8. b
9. c
10. d
11. c
12. b

39. Reformatting and Partitions
1. No.
2. It is erased off the disk, removed forever.
3. Back up.
4. Four.
5. Check your memory chips.

Index

*This index is dedicated to one of my favorite people, **Phil Russell** of the Corvallis Mac User Group, who always appreciates a good index. I thought of you in every entry, Phil!*

with love,
Robin

Symbols

A

J

K

Q

U

Icon View
    overview of, 4, 66, 148
    how to use it, 83–84
    add color or photo to background, 87
    alphabetize the files, 84
    clean up the window, 84
    icons snap into an arrangement, 86
    opening files, 107, 109
    resize icons, 86
    selecting files in, 83, 107
    status bar indicates arrangement, 86
    View Options for Icon View, 85–88
List View
    overview of, 4, 66, 148–149
    advantages of, 148
    alphabetize the columns, 88
    comments in List View, 90
    open a folder in the same window, 91
    open a folder to a new window, 91
    opening files, 107, 109
    rearrange the columns, 89
    resize the columns, 89
    resize the icons, 89
    selecting files, 107, 160
    selecting files from different folders, 163
    selecting multiple files, 162
    sort the columns, 88
    view comments in, 90
    View Options for List View, 89–90
    which columns will appear, 89
minimize windows
    all at once, 69
    double-click in title bar, 100
    Genie or Scale effect, 122
    slow motion, 69, 123
    with yellow button, 69
move around in window without scroll bars, 167
move windows
    around the screen, 67
    without making them active, 67
odd little icons under the Toolbar, 73
open a new window in the same view, 91
open folders in the same or a new window, 91
path of folders is in title bar, 68, 100, 147
red button in, 5, 69
    has dot in the middle, 102
red, yellow, and green buttons, 5
resize a window
    using the green button, 69
    with the resize corner, 68
scroll bars and sliders, 65, 70, 71
    if you see none at all, 70
    move around in window without them, 167
    value of in document windows, 99
show all windows, 141
status bar in windows, 73, 86
    indicates arrangement of icons, 86
    indicates available space on hard disk, 73
    indicates privileges, 73

tabbed windows are gone, 741
tips for working with windows in OS X, 745–748
title bars in. *See* title bar.
Toolbar. *See* Toolbar.
Trash window, 268
triangles in
    List View, 149
    right-pointing in Column View, 6
View buttons and views, 66
view of, change it or keep it the same, 96
View Options
    for Icon View, 85–87
    for List view, 89–90
Window menu to find all open windows, 95
windowshade feature, 748
yellow button, 5, 69

Windows, Microsoft. *See* **Microsoft Windows.**

windowshade feature, 748

wireless networking
    AirPort, 496–497
    do you have a wireless card? 498

word processing
    what is it? 195
    accent marks
        complete list of, 749
        how to type them, 215
        short list of, 215
    alignment of text, 206–207
    Backspace key, 197
    blank spaces in text, 208
    centering text, 209
    changing the alignment, 206–207
        centering text, 209
    changing type size, 205
    changing type style (bold, italic, etc.), 203
    changing typefaces (fonts), 202
    character-specific formatting, 206
    Clipboard
        what is it? 210
        cut, copy, and the Clipboard, 210
    contiguous text, 199, 207
    copy
        copying graphics, 213
        copying text, 210
        how to do it, 211
        keyboard shortcut for, 214
    correct typos as you go, 197
    cut
        cutting graphics, 213
        cutting text, 210
        how to do it, 211
        keyboard shortcut for, 214
    Delete key, 197
        vs. cut, 214
    delete text to the right, 197
    deselect text, 198
    discontiguous text, 199, 207
    double-space entire document, 201

Colophon

I wrote and produced this entire
book in InDesign 1.5 in the Classic
environment while running under Mac
OS X. I used Grab, Snapz Pro X, and
keyboard shortcuts to make thousands
of screen shots. I cleaned up the screen
shots in Photoshop 6. The fonts used
are ITC Garamond for the body copy,
Bailey Bold for the heads and subheads,
and Mister Earl for the chapter heads.